Metaphysics and Epistemology

BLACKWELL PHILOSOPHY ANTHOLOGIES

Each volume in this outstanding series provides an authoritative and comprehensive collection of the essential primary readings from philosophy's main fields of study. Designed to complement the *Blackwell Companions to Philosophy* series, each volume represents an unparalleled resource in its own right, and will provide the ideal platform for course use.

Metaphysics and Epistemology

A Guided Anthology

Edited by

Stephen Hetherington

WILEY Blackwell

Contents

Source Acknowledgments

The editor and publisher gratefully acknowledge the permission granted to reproduce the copyright material in this book:

1. Plato, *Republic*, 475b–480, 514a–520d (excerpts). From *The Republic of Plato*, trans. Allan Bloom (New York: Basic Books, 1968). Copyright © 1991 Allan Bloom. Reprinted by permission of Basic Books, a member of the Perseus Books Group.

2. Bertrand Russell, *The Problems of Philosophy* (London: Oxford University Press, 1959 [1912]), ch. 15 (excerpts). Reprinted with permission of Oxford University Press.

3. W.F. Sellars, "Philosophy and the Scientific Image of Man," in *Science, Perception and Reality* (London: Routledge & Kegan Paul, 1963), ch. 1 (excerpts). Reprinted with permission of University of Pittsburgh Press.

4. P.F. Strawson, *Analysis and Metaphysics: An Introduction to Philosophy* (Oxford: Oxford University Press, 1992), ch. 1 (excerpts). Reprinted with permission of Oxford University Press.

5. Robert Nozick, *Philosophical Explanations* (Cambridge, MA: The Belknap Press of Harvard University Press, 1981), "Introduction" (excerpts). Copyright © 1981 by Robert Nozick. Reprinted with permission of Harvard University Press.

6. Bertrand Russell, *The Problems of Philosophy* (London: Oxford University Press, 1959 [1912]), ch. 1 (excerpt). Reprinted with permission of Oxford University Press.

7. John Locke, *An Essay Concerning Human Understanding* (1690), Book II, ch. VIII, sects. 8–17, 22–25. Reprinted with permission of Oxford University Press.

8. George Berkeley, *The Principles of Human Knowledge* (1710), sects. 1–3, 5–10, 15–20 (excerpts).

9. D.M. Armstrong, "The Causal Theory of the Mind" (excerpts), in *The Nature of Mind and Other Essays* (St. Lucia, Queensland: University of Queensland Press, 1980). Reprinted with permission of the publisher.

10. Frank Jackson, "Epiphenomenal Qualia," *The Philosophical Quarterly* 32 (1982), 127–136 (excerpts). Cuts made with approval. Reprinted with permission of John Wiley & Sons Ltd.

11. David Hume, *An Enquiry Concerning Human Understanding* (1748), sect. VII (excerpts).

12. G.E.M. Anscombe, *Causation and Determination* (excerpts), in *The Collected Philosophical Papers of G.E.M. Anscombe*, vol. 2: *Metaphysics and the Philosophy of Mind* (Minneapolis: University of Minnesota Press, 1981).

13. Plato, *Parmenides* 130b–135b (excerpts), trans. F.M. Cornford. From *The Collected Dialogues of Plato*, ed. E. Hamilton and H. Cairns (Princeton: Princeton University Press, 1961). © 1961 by Princeton University Press. Reprinted with permission of Princeton University Press.

14. D.M. Armstrong, *Nominalism and Realism*, vol. 1 of *Universals and Scientific Realism* (Cambridge: Cambridge University Press, 1978), ch. 2 (excerpts). © Cambridge University Press 1978. Reprinted with permission.

15. Bertrand Russell, "The Philosophy of Logical Atomism" [1918], lectures I, II (excerpts). From his *Logic and Knowledge: Essays 1901–1950*, ed. R.C. Marsh (London: George Allen & Unwin, 1956). Reprinted with permission of the Bertrand Russell Peace Foundation.

16. John Searle, *Mind, Language and Society* (London: Phoenix, 1999), ch. 5 (excerpts). W&N copyright © 1999 John R. Searle. Reprinted with permission of Basic Books, a member of the Perseus Books Group.

17. Plato, *Theaetetus* 152a–c, 161b–e, 169d–172c, 177c–179c (excerpts), trans. F.M. Cornford. From *The Collected Dialogues of Plato*, ed. E. Hamilton and H. Cairns (Princeton: Princeton University Press, 1961). © 1961 by Princeton University Press. Reprinted with permission of Princeton University Press.

18. David Hume, *Dialogues Concerning Natural Religion* (1779), parts II–VII (excerpts).

19. St. Anselm, *Proslogion*, chs. I–V (excerpts) and *The Author's Reply to Gaunilo* (excerpts), plus Gaunilo's *A Reply on Behalf of the Fool* (excerpts). In *St. Anselm's "Proslogion,"* trans. M.J. Charlesworth (Oxford: Clarendon Press, 1965). Reprinted with permission of Oxford University Press.

20. G.W. Leibniz, *Monadology* [1714], paragraphs 31–46, 52–56, 58–59. In *Philosophical Papers and Letters: Gottfried Wilhelm Leibniz*, 2nd edn., ed. L.E. Loemker (Dordrecht: D. Reidel, 1969).

21. Nicholas Rescher, *Nature and Understanding: The Metaphysics and Method of Science* (Oxford: Clarendon Press, 2000), ch. 8 (excerpts). Reprinted with permission of Oxford University Press.

22. Plato, *Euthyphro* 9e–11b, trans. L. Cooper. From *The Collected Dialogues of Plato*, ed. E. Hamilton and H. Cairns (Princeton: Princeton University Press, 1961). © 1961 by Princeton University Press. Reprinted with permission of Princeton University Press.

23. René Descartes, "Meditation VI" (excerpts), in *Meditations on First Philosophy* [1641]. From *The Philosophical Works of Descartes*, vol. 1, trans. E.S. Haldane and G.R.T. Ross (Cambridge: Cambridge University Press, 1911). Reprinted with permission of Cambridge University Press.

24. John Locke, *An Essay Concerning Human Understanding* (1690), Book II, ch. XXVII, sects. 4–26 (excerpts). Reprinted with permission of Oxford University Press.

25. Roderick M. Chisholm, "Identity through Time" (excerpts), in H.E. Kiefer and M.K. Munitz (eds.), *Language, Belief, and Metaphysics* (Albany: State University of New York Press, 1970). © 1970, State University of New York. All rights reserved.

26. Derek Parfit, *Reasons and Persons* (Oxford: Clarendon Press, 1984), pp. 199–201, 245–247, 253, 254–257, 258, 261–262 (excerpts). Reprinted with permission of Oxford University Press.

27. Eric T. Olson, "An Argument for Animalism" (excerpts), in R. Martin and J. Barresi (eds.), *Personal Identity* (Malden, MA: Blackwell, 2003). © Eric T. Olson. Reprinted with kind permission of the author.

28. Aristotle, *De Interpretatione*, ch. 9 (excerpts), trans. E.M. Edghill, in *The Basic Works of Aristotle*, ed. R. McKeon (New York: Random House, 1941). From *The Oxford Translation of Aristotle*, ed. W.D. Ross, vol. 1 (Oxford University Press, 1928). Reprinted with permission of Oxford University Press.

29. David Hume, *An Enquiry Concerning Human Understanding* (1748), sect. VIII (excerpts).

30. P.F. Strawson, "Freedom and Resentment" [1962] (excerpts), in P.F. Strawson (ed.), *Studies in the Philosophy of Thought and Action* (London: Oxford University Press, 1968). Reprinted with permission of the British Academy.

31. Harry G. Frankfurt, "Alternate Possibilities and Moral Responsibility" [1969] (excerpts), in *The Importance of What We Care About* (Cambridge: Cambridge University Press, 1988).

32. Susan Wolf, "Asymmetrical Freedom" (excerpts), *The Journal of Philosophy* 77 (1980), 151–166. Reprinted with permission of the Journal and the author.

33. Epicurus, "Letter to Menoeceus" (excerpt), in *Hellenistic Philosophy: Introductory Readings*, 2nd edn., trans. B. Inwood and L.P. Gerson (Indianapolis: Hackett, 1997). Reprinted with permission of Hackett Publishing Company Inc.

34. Lucretius, *De Rerum Natura*, Loeb Classical Library vol. 181, trans. W.H.D. Rouse (1924), revised Martin F. Smith (Cambridge, MA: Harvard University Press, 1975), Book III (excerpts). Copyright © 1975 by the President and Fellows of Harvard College. Loeb Classical Library (R) is a registered trademark of the President and Fellows of Harvard College. Reprinted by permission of the publishers and the Trustees of the Loeb Classical Library.

35. Bernard Williams, "The Makropulos Case: Reflections on the Tedium of Immortality" (excerpts), in *Problems of the Self: Philosophical Papers 1956–1972* (Cambridge: Cambridge University Press, 1973). © Cambridge University Press 1973. Reproduced with permission.

36. Fred Feldman, *Confrontations With the Reaper: A Philosophical Study of the Nature and Value of Death* (New York: Oxford University Press, 1992), ch. 8 (excerpts). Reprinted with permission of Oxford University Press.

37. Plato, *Meno* 97a–99d, trans. W.K.C. Guthrie. From *The Collected Dialogues of Plato*, ed. E. Hamilton and H. Cairns (Princeton: Princeton University Press, 1961). © 1961 by Princeton University Press. Reprinted with permission of Princeton University Press.

38. W.K. Clifford, "The Ethics of Belief" (excerpts), in *Lectures and Essays*, vol. 2 (London: Macmillan, 1879).

39. A.J. Ayer, *The Problem of Knowledge* (London: Macmillan, 1956), pp. 28–32. Reprinted with permission of Palgrave Macmillan.

40. Edmund L. Gettier, "Is Justified True Belief Knowledge?" *Analysis* 23 (1963), 121–123. Reprinted with permission of Oxford University Press Journals.

41. Alvin I. Goldman, "A Causal Theory of Knowing" [1967] (excerpts) (revised), in M.D. Roth and L. Galis (eds.), *Knowing: Essays in the Analysis of Knowledge* (New York: Random House, 1970). First published in *Journal of Philosophy* 64/12 (June 22 1967), pp. 357–373. Reprinted with permission.

42. Alvin I. Goldman, "Discrimination and Perceptual Knowledge" (excerpts), *The Journal of Philosophy* 73 (1976), 771–791. Reprinted with permission.

43. Catherine Z. Elgin, "The Epistemic Efficacy of Stupidity" (excerpts), in N. Goodman and C.Z. Elgin, *Reconceptions in Philosophy and Other Arts and Sciences* (Indianapolis: Hackett, 1988). Reprinted with permission of Hackett Publishing Company Inc. All rights reserved.

44. Linda Trinkaus Zagzebski, *Virtues of the Mind: An Investigation into the Nature of Virtue and the Ethical Foundations of Knowledge* (Cambridge: Cambridge University Press, 1996), pp. 268–271, 273–275, 277–280, 294–298 (excerpts). © Cambridge University Press 1996. Reproduced with permission.

45. David Hume, *An Enquiry Concerning Human Understanding* (1748), sect. II (excerpts).

46. René Descartes, 'Meditation I' (excerpt), in *Meditations on First Philosophy* [1641]. From *The Philosophical Works of Descartes*, vol. 1, trans. E.S. Haldane and G.R.T. Ross (Cambridge: Cambridge University Press, 1911). Reprinted with permission of Cambridge University Press.

47. David Lewis, "Veridical Hallucination and Prosthetic Vision," *Australasian Journal of Philosophy* 58 (1980), 239–249. Reprinted with permission of Taylor & Francis Journals.

48. Hilary Putnam, *Reason, Truth and History* (Cambridge: Cambridge University Press, 1981), ch. 1 (excerpts). © Cambridge University Press 1981. Reproduced with permission.

49. John McDowell, "The Disjunctive Conception of Experience as Material for a Transcendental Argument" (excerpts), in A. Haddock and F. Macpherson (eds.), *Disjunctivism: Perception, Action, Knowledge* (Oxford: Oxford University Press, 2008). Reprinted with permission of Oxford University Press.

50. Plato, *Meno* 80c–86c (excerpts), trans. W.K.C. Guthrie. From *The Collected Dialogues of Plato*, ed. E. Hamilton and H. Cairns (Princeton: Princeton University Press, 1961). © 1961 by Princeton University Press. Reprinted with permission of Princeton University Press.

51. John Locke, *An Essay Concerning Human Understanding* (1690), Book I, chs. II–IV (excerpts), Book II, ch. I (excerpts). Reprinted with permission of Oxford University Press.

52. René Descartes, *Discourse on Method* [1637], part II (excerpts). From *The Philosophical Works of Descartes*, vol. 1, trans. E.S. Haldane and G.R.T. Ross (Cambridge: Cambridge University Press, 1911). Reprinted with permission of Cambridge University Press.

53. Immanuel Kant, *Critique of Pure Reason* [1781], "Introduction" (excerpts), trans. N. Kemp Smith (London: Macmillan, 1929). Reprinted with permission of Palgrave Macmillan.

54. John Stuart Mill, *A System of Logic* [1841], 8th edn. (1882), Book II, chs. V, VI (excerpts).

55. C.S. Peirce, "Some Consequences of Four Incapacities" [1868] and "How To Make Our Ideas Clear" [1878] (excerpts). In N. Houser and C. Kloesel (eds.), *The Essential Peirce: Selected Philosophical Writings*, vol. 1 (1867–93) (Bloomington and Indianapolis: Indiana University Press, 1992).

56. Saul A. Kripke, *Naming and Necessity* (excerpts) (Cambridge, MA: Harvard University Press, 1980), lecture III (excerpts). Reprinted with permission of John Wiley & Sons Ltd.

57. Gilbert Ryle, "Knowing How and Knowing That" [1946] (excerpts), in his *Collected Papers*, vol. 2 (London: Hutchinson, 1971). Reprinted with permission of Hertford College.

58. G.E.M. Anscombe, *Intention* [1957], 2nd edn. (Cambridge, MA: Harvard University Press, 2000), pp. 56–57, 82–83, 84–89 (excerpts). Copyright © 1957, 1963 by G.E.M. Anscombe. Reprinted with permission of Harvard University Press.

59. Jennifer Lackey, "Knowing from Testimony" (excerpts), *Philosophy Compass* 1 (2006), 432–448. Cuts made with approval. Reprinted with permission of John Wiley & Sons Ltd.

60. Bertrand Russell, *The Analysis of Mind* (London: George Allen & Unwin, 1921), lecture IX (excerpts). Reprinted with kind permission of the Bertrand Russell Peace Foundation.

61. Sextus Empiricus, *Outlines of Pyrrhonism*, Loeb Classical Library vol. 273, trans. R.G. Bury (Cambridge, MA: Harvard University Press, 1933), Book I (excerpts). Copyright © 1933 by the President and Fellows of Harvard College. Loeb Classical Library (R) is a registered trademark of the President and Fellows of Harvard College. Reprinted by permission of the publishers and the Trustees of the Loeb Classical Library.

62. René Descartes, "Meditation I" (excerpt), in *Meditations on First Philosophy* [1641]. From *The Philosophical Works of Descartes*, vol. 1, trans. E.S. Haldane and G.R.T. Ross (Cambridge: Cambridge University Press, 1911). Reprinted with permission of Cambridge University Press.

63. David Hume, *An Enquiry Concerning Human Understanding* (1748), sect. IV (excerpts).

64. René Descartes, "Meditation II" (excerpt), in *Meditations on First Philosophy* [1641]. From *The Philosophical Works of Descartes*, vol. 1, trans. E.S. Haldane and G.R.T. Ross (Cambridge: Cambridge University Press, 1911). Reprinted with permission of Cambridge University Press.

65. Thomas Reid, *Essays on the Intellectual Powers of Man* [1785], Essay I, ch. II, and Essay VI, chs. 2, 4, 5 (excerpts), ed. D.R. Brookes (University Park, PA: Pennsylvania State University Press, 2002).

66. Karl R. Popper, "On the Sources of Knowledge and of Ignorance" (excerpts), in his *Conjectures and Refutations: The Growth of Scientific Knowledge* (London: Routledge & Kegan Paul, 1963). Reprinted with permission of the Karl Popper Library.

67. Robert Nozick, *Philosophical Explanations* (Cambridge, MA: The Belknap Press of Harvard University Press, 1981), ch. 3, "Knowledge and Skepticism" (excerpts). Copyright © 1981 by Robert Nozick. Reprinted with permission of Harvard University Press.

Every effort has been made to trace copyright holders and to obtain their permission for the use of copyright material. The publisher apologizes for any errors or omissions in the above list, and would be grateful to be notified of any corrections that should be incorporated in future reprints or editions of this book.

Preface and Acknowledgments

What is real?

(a) Everything.
(b) Nothing.
(c) Some – but only some – stuff.
(d) Hmm. What does that question *mean*?

Who really has knowledge?

(a) Everyone.
(b) No one.
(c) Some – but only some – people.
(d) Hmm. What does that question *mean*?

… and so to this book. Welcome.

Prepare to immerse yourself in provocative and powerful philosophical thoughts about reality and knowledge. Your thinking will take you back and forth, up and down, hither and thither. You will contemplate lots of ideas – competing ones; complementary ones. The book is designed to be used in some university and college courses – beginning philosophy courses on reality and knowledge, on metaphysics and epistemology. Within these pages, you will encounter thematically focused instances of philosophical writing on those topics, from some of philosophy's most justly famous thinkers.

Prepare also for manifest struggle and potential triumph. I have introduced each reading (usually an excerpt) with remarks explaining its historical setting and/or philosophical point. Nevertheless, at times you will be puzzled, even exasperated, by the challenges in these readings – challenges to your senses of yourself, others, and the world at large. Much will seem new: "I hadn't thought of *that*." Your mission will then be to question and to evaluate: "Should I *accept* that? Why? Why not?" But such challenges are also precious *opportunities*. Intellects and characters – mine; yours – do not improve without effort and focus. So, here is a book intended precisely to assist you in that respect. I hope you will come to appreciate some of the vitality and depth that philosophy can bring to your life.

The idea for this book was suggested to me in 2009 by Nick Bellorini, who was then the philosophy editor at Blackwell in the UK. His proposal was for an introductory metaphysics-and-epistemology anthology, blending classic with contemporary writings, offering editorial guidance for each of the book's many readings. Nick's model for some of this was John Cottingham's more general – and terrific – anthology, *Western Philosophy* (2nd edn. Blackwell, 2008). A little later, Nick moved to a new position with another publisher. But Jeff Dean (at Wiley-Blackwell in the USA) continued to be extremely supportive of this project. He gathered many excellent referees' suggestions for me when I was mulling over the book's possible contents and organization. ("Thank you," after all this time, to those referees.) I have appreciated Jeff's clear-headed and friendly editorial guidance. Jennifer Bray and Janet Moth at Wiley-Blackwell have been very helpful with the production process. Brent Madison provided good feedback on the contents (as did Michaelis Michael and Markos Valaris), as well as on my own writing for the book. Lindsay Yeates was an invaluable proofreader.

Introduction

You know – excitedly, I hope – that this is a book of philosophy. Yet how well do you know this? After all, do you know what philosophy really is? Remarkably, even experienced philosophers can disagree as to philosophy's identity or nature. So it would be rash for me to insist at the outset on what could be a needlessly limited characterization of philosophy. Instead of picking out one or two possible proposals as to what philosophy is, I will allow this book's first few readings – those in Part I – to begin telling the story.

From among philosophy's many specific areas or topics, the book introduces you, in Parts II and III, to two of the historically central ones – respectively, metaphysics and epistemology. Metaphysics is the philosophical study of being, of reality, of existence. Fundamentally, what is real? Fundamentally, what is it to *be* real? And epistemology is philosophy's focus upon knowing, upon inquiry, upon rational belief. Fundamentally, what is knowledge, and in what ways do we attain it? Fundamentally, *do* we ever attain it?

Here is a cautionary note: It is very possible to reflect *non*-philosophically upon those two topics – upon reality and upon knowing. There can be something quite artless and simple about philosophical questions; there can also be an art and sophistication to them. How does some thinking become philosophical, about these or any other topics? At any time, philosophy *is* what has been *done* in its name – and so its history remains part of it – along with what is *still* being done in its name and possibly what *could* then be done in its name. We tend to identify philosophy, too, by its *best* exemplars – what has been, plus what is being, done *well* in its name. All of that leads us into this book, which gives you an opportunity to examine exemplary exemplars – both historical and contemporary – of philosophical thinking about being and about knowing.

In calling those exemplars exemplary, I do not mean to presume that either you or I will accept all of them as *correct* in what they conclude. Presumably, it is possible for some philosophy to be good yet mistaken. In fact, there are many ways in which, it seems, that is possible. Sometimes, a piece of philosophy is good because it raises good questions. Sometimes, a piece of philosophy is good because it develops an imaginative answer to someone else's good question. Sometimes, a piece of philosophy is good because it finds surprising and instructive flaws in an otherwise tempting answer to a good question. Sometimes, a piece of philosophy is good in one respect, yet not so good in another respect. And on it goes, for the many possible respects in which a piece of philosophy may *deserve* respect.

Please be alert, then, when reading this book's extracts from some excellent instances of philosophy, each of which is good in at least one notable respect. Look for each reading's insight, and/or its unusual question, and/or its bold idea, and/or the clever reasoning, and/or etc. *Then* start forming your potential morals about what philosophy can, or what it cannot, accomplish. Once you reach the end of the book, hopefully you will have witnessed for yourself a representative sample of what philosophy can achieve. You could even have taken a step or two yourself, maybe three or four, toward that achievement.

Part I

The Philosophical Image

1

Life and the Search for Philosophical Knowledge

Plato, *Republic*

Systematic Western philosophy began in Greece, most influentially with the engagingly profound dialogues written by Plato (c.428–c.348 BC). They are centered upon his teacher Socrates (469–399 BC) being constructively puzzled by ... well, almost anything about which others within his hearing claim *not* to be puzzled. When Socrates wanders around Athens, he meets many people who are eager to share with him their confidently held views as to what is ethically right, what is religiously proper, what is natural, what is socially just, what is beauty, what is knowledge, what is real, etc. Socrates listens – before asking for more details, requesting help in understanding, suggesting alternative formulations and ideas. Time and again, he enters into other people's thoughts, earnestly wondering, seeking clarity on one point after another as he professes slowness of wit and paucity of comprehension. (He was inquiring with what philosophers now call the *Socratic method* of inquiry used by many teachers: questions guiding gently and adaptively, sometimes professing a lack of understanding even when the questioner understands better than the audience does.)

What happens as a result of Socrates' questioning? Subtle thinking occurs; new possibilities emerge; and Socrates' companions tend to acquire feelings of uncertainty and frustration. Thanks to Plato's writing, we are privileged to be able to immerse ourselves in this fascinating process, this way of improving our powers of reflection. That Socratic form of thinking has contributed powerfully to the subsequent centuries of philosophy.

Plato, *Republic*, 475b–480, 514a–520d (excerpts). From *The Republic of Plato*, trans. Allan Bloom (New York: Basic Books, 1968). Copyright © 1991 Allan Bloom. Reprinted by permission of Basic Books, a member of the Perseus Books Group.

Metaphysics and Epistemology: A Guided Anthology, First Edition. Edited by Stephen Hetherington.
© 2014 John Wiley & Sons, Inc. Published 2014 by John Wiley & Sons, Inc.

But philosophy has also been influenced by some of Socrates' *themes*. We see this in our extract from the *Republic*, one of Plato's most famous dialogues. Two themes are especially important in this reading. (1) Philosophy seeks *knowledge*. (2) Not just any knowledge, though; it should be knowledge of a reality worth knowing, indeed a reality deeply worth knowing. With philosophy spurring on our hearts and minds, we should strive to know the true nature of *goodness* ("the Good," Socrates names it). We should settle for nothing less than that ultimate prize. And we should hold in mind that what *seems* good and ultimately valuable might not be. We must learn the difference between settling for an appearance of something ultimately good (e.g. something really only transiently or superficially valuable) and finding something that really is fundamentally good.

Plato brings alive that human mission with what has become one of philosophy's lasting images – a picture of how we are if we do *not* succeed in knowing true goodness. This is Plato's celebrated image of *the cave*. It is a metaphor for how too many of us do, yet how none of us should, live our lives – by being trapped within a cave of shadows and human lighting, settling for mere appearances of ultimate value. Even when not held back by poverty and oppression, people might be trapped in the way envisioned by Socrates – constricted by their lack of philosophical imagination about, and genuine insight into, their real underlying natures and achievements. Can we escape this? Suitable knowledge is needed. Philosophy is the means.

Book V

[…]

[Socrates:] "Then affirm this or deny it: when we say a man is a desirer of something, will we assert that he desires all of that form, or one part of it and not another?"

"All," he [Glaucon] said.

"Won't we also then assert that the philosopher is a desirer of wisdom, not of one part and not another, but of all of it?"

"True."

"We'll deny, therefore, that the one who's finicky about his learning, especially when he's young and doesn't yet have an account of what's useful and not, is a lover of learning or a philosopher, just as we say that the man who's finicky about his food isn't hungry, doesn't desire food, and isn't a lover of food but a bad eater."

"And we'll be right in denying it."

"But the one who is willing to taste every kind of learning with gusto, and who approaches learning with delight, and is insatiable, we shall justly assert to be a philosopher, won't we?"

And Glaucon said, "Then you'll have many strange ones. For all the lovers of sights are in my opinion what they are because they enjoy learning; and the lovers of hearing would be some of the strangest to include among philosophers, those who would never be willing to go voluntarily to a discussion and such occupations but who – just as though they had hired out their ears for hearing – run around to every chorus at the Dionysia, missing none in the cities or the villages. Will we say that all these men and other learners of such things and the petty arts are philosophers?"

"Not at all," I said, "but they are like philosophers."

"Who do you say are the true ones?" he said.

"The lovers of the sight of the truth," I said.

"And that's right," he said. "But how do you mean it?"

[...]

"Well, now," I said, "this is how I separate them out. On one side I put those of whom you were just speaking, the lovers of sights, the lovers of arts, and the practical men; on the other, those whom the argument concerns, whom alone one could rightly call philosophers."

"How do you mean?" he said.

"The lovers of hearing and the lovers of sights, on the one hand," I said, "surely delight in fair sounds and colors and shapes and all that craft makes from such things, but their thought is unable to see and delight in the nature of the fair itself."

"That," he said, "is certainly so."

"Wouldn't, on the other hand, those who are able to approach the fair itself and see it by itself be rare?"

"Indeed they would."

"Is the man who holds that there are fair things but doesn't hold that there is beauty itself and who, if someone leads him to the knowledge of it, isn't able to follow – is he, in your opinion, living in a dream or is he awake? Consider it. Doesn't dreaming, whether one is asleep or awake, consist in believing a likeness of something to be not a likeness, but rather the thing itself to which it is like?"

"I, at least," he said, "would say that a man who does that dreams."

"And what about the man who, contrary to this, believes that there is something fair itself and is able to catch sight both of it and of what participates in it, and doesn't believe that what participates is it itself, nor that it itself is what participates – is he, in your opinion, living in a dream or is he awake?"

"He's quite awake," he said.

"Wouldn't we be right in saying that this man's thought, because he knows, is knowledge, while the other's is opinion because he opines?"

"Most certainly."

[...]

"Since knowledge depended on what *is* and ignorance necessarily on what *is not*, mustn't we also seek something between ignorance and knowledge that depends on that which is in between, if there is in fact any such thing?"

"Most certainly."

"Do we say opinion is something?"

"Of course."

"A power different from knowledge or the same?"

"Different."

"Then opinion is dependent on one thing and knowledge on another, each according to its own power."

"That's so."

"Doesn't knowledge naturally depend on what *is*, to know of what *is* that it is and how it is? However, in my opinion, it's necessary to make this distinction first."

"What distinction?"

"We will assert that powers are a certain class of beings by means of which we are capable of what we are capable, and also everything else is capable of whatever it is capable. For example, I say sight and hearing are powers, if perchance you understand the form of which I wish to speak."

"I do understand," he said.

"Now listen to how they look to me. In a power I see no color or shape or anything of the sort such as I see in many other things to which I look when I distinguish one thing from another for myself. With a power I look only to this – on what it depends and what it accomplishes; and it is on this basis that I come to call each of the powers a power; and that which depends on the same thing and accomplishes the same thing, I call the same power, and that which depends on something else and accomplishes something else, I call a different power. What about you? What do you do?"

"The same," he said.

"Now, you best of men, come back here to knowledge again. Do you say it's some kind of power, or in what class do you put it?"

"In this one," he said, "as the most vigorous of all powers."

"And what about opinion? Is it among the powers, or shall we refer it to some other form?"

"Not at all," he said. "For that by which we are capable of opining is nothing other than opinion."

"But just a little while ago you agreed that knowledge and opinion are not the same."

"How," he said, "could any intelligent man count that which doesn't make mistakes the same as that which does?"

"Fine," I said, "and we plainly agree that opinion is different from knowledge."

"Yes, it is different."

"Since each is capable of something different, are they, therefore, naturally dependent on different things?"

"Necessarily."

"Knowledge is presumably dependent on what *is*, to know of what is that it *is* and how it is?"

"Yes."

"While opinion, we say, opines."

"Yes."

"The same thing that knowledge knows? And will the knowable and the opinable be the same? Or is that impossible?"

"On the basis of what's been agreed to, it's impossible," he said. "If different powers are naturally dependent on different things and both are powers – opinion and knowledge – and each is, as we say, different, then on this basis it's not admissible that the knowable and the opinable be the same."

"If what *is*, is knowable, then wouldn't something other than that which *is* be opinable?"

"Yes, it would be something other."

"Then does it opine what *is not*? Or is it also impossible to opine what *is not*? Think about it. Doesn't the man who opines refer his opinion to something? Or is it possible to opine, but to opine nothing?"

"No, it's impossible."

"The man who opines, opines some one thing?"

"Yes."

"But further, that which *is not* could not with any correctness be addressed as some one thing but rather nothing at all."

"Certainly."

"To that which *is not*, we were compelled to assign ignorance, and to that which *is*, knowledge."

"Right," he said.

"Opinion, therefore, opines neither that which *is* nor that which *is not*."

"No, it doesn't."

"Opinion, therefore, would be neither ignorance nor knowledge?"

"It doesn't seem so."

"Is it, then, beyond these, surpassing either knowledge in clarity or ignorance in obscurity?"

"No, it is neither."

"Does opinion," I said, "look darker than knowledge to you and brighter than ignorance?"

"Very much so," he said.

"And does it lie within the limits set by these two?"

"Yes."

"Opinion, therefore, would be between the two."

"That's entirely certain."

"Weren't we saying before that if something should come to light as what *is* and what *is not* at the same time, it lies between that which purely and simply *is* and that which in every way *is not*, and that neither knowledge nor ignorance will depend on it, but that which in its turn comes to light between ignorance and knowledge?"

"Right."

"And now it is just that which we call opinion that has come to light between them."

"Yes, that is what has come to light."

"Hence, as it seems, it would remain for us to find what participates in both – in *to be* and *not to be* – and could not correctly be addressed as either purely and simply, so that, if it comes to light, we can justly address it as the opinable, thus assigning the extremes to the extremes and that which is in between to that which is in between. Isn't that so?"

"Yes, it is."

"Now, with this taken for granted, let him tell me, I shall say, and let him answer – that good man who doesn't believe that there is anything fair in itself and an *idea* of the beautiful itself, which always stays the same in all respects, but does hold that there are many fair things, this lover of sights who can in no way endure it if anyone asserts the fair is one and the just is one and so on with the rest. 'Now, of these many fair things, you best of men,' we'll say, 'is there any that won't also look ugly? And of the just, any that won't look unjust? And of the holy, any that won't look unholy?' "

"No," he said, "but it's necessary that they look somehow both fair and ugly, and so it is with all the others you ask about."

"And what about the many doubles? Do they look any less half than double?"

"No."

"And, then, the things that we would assert to be big and little, light and heavy – will they be addressed by these names any more than by the opposites of these names?"

"No," he said, "each will always have something of both."

"Then is each of the several manys what one asserts it to be any more than it is not what one asserts it to be?"

"They are like the ambiguous jokes at feasts," he said, "and the children's riddle about the eunuch, about his hitting the bat – with what and on what he struck it. For the manys are also ambiguous, and it's not possible to think of them fixedly as either being or not being, or as both or neither."

"Can you do anything with them?" I said. "Or could you find a finer place to put them than between being and not to be? For presumably nothing darker than not-being will come to light so that something could *not be* more than it; and nothing brighter than being will come to light so that something could *be* more than it."

"Very true," he said.

"Then we have found, as it seems, that the many beliefs of the many about what's fair and about the other things roll around somewhere between not-being and being purely and simply."

"Yes, we have found that."

"And we agreed beforehand that, if any such thing should come to light, it must be called opinable but not knowable, the wanderer between, seized by the power between."

"Yes, we did agree."

"And, as for those who look at many fair things but don't see the fair itself and aren't even able to follow another who leads them to it, and many just things but not justice itself, and so on with all the rest, we'll assert that they opine all these things but know nothing of what they opine."

"Necessarily," he said.

"And what about those who look at each thing itself – at the things that are always the same in all respects? Won't we say that they know and don't opine?"

"That too is necessary."

"Won't we assert that these men delight in and love that on which knowledge depends, and the others that on which opinion depends? Or don't we remember that we were saying that they love and look at fair sounds and colors and such things but can't even endure the fact that the fair itself is something?"

"Yes, we do remember."

"So, will we strike a false note in calling them lovers of opinion rather than lovers of wisdom? And will they be very angry with us if we speak this way?"

"No," he said, "that is, if they are persuaded by me. For it's not lawful to be harsh with what's true."

"Must we, therefore, call philosophers rather than lovers of opinion those who delight in each thing that is itself?"

"That's entirely certain."

Book VII

"Next, then," I [Socrates] said, "make an image of our nature in its education and want of education, likening it to a condition of the following kind. See human beings as though they were in an underground cave-like dwelling with its entrance, a long one, open to the light across the whole width of the cave. They are in it from childhood with their legs and necks in bonds so that they are fixed, seeing only in front of them, unable because of the bond to turn their heads all the way around. Their light is from a fire burning far above and behind them. Between the fire and the prisoners there is a road above, along which see a wall, built like the partitions puppet-handlers set in front of the human beings and over which they show the puppets."

"I see," he [Glaucon] said.

"Then also see along this wall human beings carrying all sorts of artifacts, which project above the wall, and statues of men and other animals wrought from stone, wood, and every kind of material; as is to be expected, some of the carriers utter sounds while others are silent."

"It's a strange image," he said, "and strange prisoners you're telling of."

"They're like us," I said. "For in the first place, do you suppose such men would have seen anything of themselves and one another other than the shadows cast by the fire on the side of the cave facing them?"

"How could they," he said, "if they had been compelled to keep their heads motionless throughout life?"

"And what about the things that are carried by? Isn't it the same with them?"

"Of course."

"If they were able to discuss things with one another, don't you believe they would hold that they are naming these things going by before them that they see?"

"Necessarily."

"And what if the prison also had an echo from the side facing them? Whenever one of the men passing by happens to utter a sound, do you suppose they would believe that anything other than the passing shadow was uttering the sound?"

"No, by Zeus," he said. "I don't."

"Then most certainly," I said, "such men would hold that the truth is nothing other than the shadows of artificial things."

"Most necessarily," he said.

"Now consider," I said, "what their release and healing from bonds and folly would be like if something of this sort were by nature to happen to them. Take a man who is released and suddenly compelled to stand up, to turn his neck around, to walk and look up toward the light; and who, moreover, in doing all this is in pain and, because he is dazzled, is unable to make out those things whose shadows he saw before. What do you suppose he'd say if someone were to tell him that before he saw silly nothings, while now, because he is somewhat nearer to what *is* and more turned toward beings, he sees more correctly; and, in particular, showing him each of the things that pass by, were to compel the man to answer his questions about what they are? Don't you suppose he'd be at a loss and believe that what was seen before is truer than what is now shown?"

"Yes," he said, "by far."

"And, if he compelled him to look at the light itself, would his eyes hurt and would he flee, turning away to those things that he is able to make out and hold them to be really clearer than what is being shown?"

"So he would," he said.

"And if," I said, "someone dragged him away from there by force along the rough, steep, upward way and didn't let him go before he had dragged him out into the light of the sun, wouldn't he be distressed and annoyed at being so dragged? And when he came to the light, wouldn't he have his eyes full of its beam and be unable to see even one of the things now said to be true?"

"No, he wouldn't," he said, "at least not right away."

"Then I suppose he'd have to get accustomed, if he were going to see what's up above. At first he'd most easily make out the shadows; and after that the phantoms of the human beings and the other things in water; and, later, the things themselves. And from there he could turn to beholding the things in heaven and heaven itself, more easily at night – looking at the light of the stars and the moon – than by day – looking at the sun and sunlight."

"Of course."

"Then finally I suppose he would be able to make out the sun – not its appearances in water or some alien place, but the sun itself by itself in its own region – and see what it's like."

"Necessarily," he said.

"And after that he would already be in a position to conclude about it that this is the source of the seasons and the years, and is the steward of all things in the visible place, and is in a certain way the cause of all those things he and his companions had been seeing."

"It's plain," he said, "that this would be his next step."

"What then? When he recalled his first home and the wisdom there, and his fellow prisoners in that time, don't you suppose he would consider himself happy for the change and pity the others?"

"Quite so."

"And if in that time there were among them any honors, praises, and prizes for the man who is sharpest at making out the things that go by, and most remembers which of them are accustomed to pass before, which after, and which at the same time as others, and who is thereby most able to divine what is going to come, in your opinion would he be desirous of them and envy those who are honored and hold power among these men? Or, rather, would he be affected as Homer says and want very much 'to be on the soil, a serf to another man, to a portionless man,' and to undergo anything whatsoever rather than to opine those things and live that way?"

"Yes," he said, "I suppose he would prefer to undergo everything rather than live that way."

"Now reflect on this too," I said. "If such a man were to come down again and sit in the same seat, on coming suddenly from the sun wouldn't his eyes get infected with darkness?"

"Very much so," he said.

"And if he once more had to compete with those perpetual prisoners in forming judgments about those shadows while his vision was still dim, before his eyes had recovered, and if the time needed for getting accustomed were not at all short, wouldn't he be the source of laughter, and wouldn't it be said of him that he went up and came back with his eyes corrupted, and that it's not even worth trying to go up? And if they were somehow able to get their hands on and kill the man who attempts to release and lead up, wouldn't they kill him?"

"No doubt about it," he said.

"Well, then, my dear Glaucon," I said, "this image as a whole must be connected with what was said before. Liken the domain revealed through sight to the prison home, and the light of the fire in it to the sun's power; and, in applying the going up and the seeing of what's above to the soul's journey up to the intelligible place, you'll not mistake my expectation, since you desire to hear it. A god doubtless knows if it happens to be true. At all events, this is the way the phenomena look to me: in the knowable the last thing to be seen, and that with considerable effort, is the *idea* of the good; but once seen, it must be concluded that this is in fact the cause of all that is right and fair in everything – in the visible it gave birth to light and its sovereign; in the intelligible, itself sovereign, it provided truth and intelligence – and that the man who is going to act prudently in private or in public must see it."

"I, too, join you in supposing that," he said, "at least in the way I can."

"Come, then," I said, "and join me in supposing this, too, and don't be surprised that the men who get to that point aren't willing to mind the business of human beings, but rather that their souls are always eager to spend their time above. Surely that's likely, if indeed this, too, follows the image of which I told before."

"Of course it's likely," he said.

"And what about this? Do you suppose it is anything surprising," I said, "if a man, come from acts of divine contemplation to the human things, is graceless and looks quite ridiculous when – with his sight still dim and before he has gotten sufficiently accustomed to the surrounding darkness – he is compelled in courts or elsewhere to contest about the shadows of the just or the representations of which they are the shadows, and to dispute about the way these things are understood by men who have never seen justice itself?"

"It's not at all surprising," he said.

"But if a man were intelligent," I said, "he would remember that there are two kinds of disturbances of the eyes, stemming from two sources – when they have been transferred from light to darkness and when they have been transferred from darkness to light. And if he held that these same things happen to a soul too, whenever he saw one that is confused and unable to make anything out, he wouldn't laugh without reasoning but would go on to consider whether, come from a brighter life, it is in darkness for want of being accustomed, or whether, going from greater lack of learning to greater brightness, it is dazzled by the greater brilliance. And then he would deem the first soul happy for its condition and its life, while he would pity the second. And, if he wanted to laugh at the second soul, his laughing in this case would make him less ridiculous himself than would his laughing at the soul which has come from above out of the light."

"What you say is quite sensible," he said.

"Then, if this is true," I said, "we must hold the following about these things: education is not what the professions of certain men assert it to be. They presumably assert that they put into the soul knowledge that isn't in it, as though they were putting sight into blind eyes."

"Yes," he said, "they do indeed assert that."

"But the present argument, on the other hand," I said, "indicates that this power is in the soul of each, and that the instrument with which each learns – just as an eye is not able to turn toward the light from the dark without the whole body – must be turned around from that which *is coming into being* together with the whole soul until it is able to endure looking at that which *is* and the brightest part of that which *is*. And we affirm that this is the good, don't we?"

"Yes."

"There would, therefore," I said, "be an art of this turning around, concerned with the way in which this power can most easily and efficiently be turned around, not an art of producing sight in it. Rather, this art takes as given that sight is there, but not rightly turned nor looking at what it ought to look at, and accomplishes this object."

"So it seems," he said.

"Therefore, the other virtues of a soul, as they are called, are probably somewhat close to those of the body. For they are really not there beforehand and are later produced by habits and exercises, while the virtue of exercising prudence is more than anything somehow more divine, it seems; it never loses its power, but according to the way it is turned, it becomes useful and helpful or, again, useless and harmful. Or haven't you yet reflected about the men who are said to be vicious but wise, how shrewdly their petty soul sees and how sharply it distinguishes those things toward which it is turned, showing that it doesn't have poor vision although it is compelled to serve vice; so that the sharper it sees, the more evil it accomplishes?"

"Most certainly," he said.

"However," I said, "if this part of such a nature were trimmed in earliest childhood and its ties of kinship with becoming were cut off – like leaden weights, which eating and such pleasures as well as their refinements naturally attach to the soul and turn its vision downward – if, I say, it were rid of them and turned around toward the true things, this same part of the same human beings would also see them most sharply, just as it does those things toward which it now is turned."

"It's likely," he said.

"And what about this? Isn't it likely," I said, "and necessary, as a consequence of what was said before, that those who are without education and experience of truth would never be adequate stewards of a city, nor would those who have been allowed to spend their time in education continuously to the end – the former because they don't have any single goal in life at which they must aim in doing everything they do in private or in public, the latter because they won't be willing to act, believing they have emigrated to a colony on the Isles of the Blessed while they are still alive?"

"True," he said.

"Then our job as founders," I said, "is to compel the best natures to go to the study which we were saying before is the greatest, to see the good and to go up that ascent; and, when they have gone up and seen sufficiently, not to permit them what is now permitted."

"What's that?"

"To remain there," I said, "and not be willing to go down again among those prisoners or share their labors and honors, whether they be slighter or more serious."

"What?" he said. "Are we to do them an injustice, and make them live a worse life when a better is possible for them?"

"My friend, you have again forgotten," I said, "that it's not the concern of law that any one class in the city fare exceptionally well, but it contrives to bring this about for the whole city, harmonizing the citizens by persuasion and compulsion, making them share with one another the benefit that each class is able to bring to the commonwealth. And it produces such men in the city not in order to let them turn whichever way each wants, but in order that it may use them in binding the city together."

"That's true," he said. "I did forget."

"Well, then, Glaucon," I said, "consider that we won't be doing injustice to the philosophers who come to be among us, but rather that we will say just things to them while compelling them besides to care for and guard the others. We'll say that when such men come to be in the other cities it is fitting for them not to participate in the labors of those cities. For they grow up spontaneously against the will of the regime in each; and a nature that grows by itself and doesn't owe its rearing to anyone has justice on its side when it is not eager to pay off the price of rearing to anyone. 'But you we have begotten for yourselves and for the rest of the city like leaders and kings in hives; you have been better and more perfectly educated and are more able to participate in both lives. So you must go down, each in his turn, into the common dwelling of the others and get habituated along with them to seeing the dark things. And, in getting habituated to it, you will see ten thousand times better than the men there, and you'll know what each of the phantoms is, and of what it is a phantom, because you have seen the truth about fair, just, and good things. And thus, the city will be governed by us and by you in a state of waking, not in a dream as the many cities nowadays are governed by men who fight over shadows with one another and form factions for the sake of ruling, as though it were some great good. But the truth is surely this: that city in which those who are going to rule are least eager to rule is necessarily governed in the way that is best and freest from faction, while the one that gets the opposite kind of rulers is governed in the opposite way.' "

"Most certainly," he said.

2

Philosophical Questioning

Bertrand Russell, *The Problems of Philosophy*

Plato was encouraging us to expand our intellectual horizons: an escape from the cave would be an enlarging of one's sense – even one's knowledge – of what really matters. That underlying image has stayed with many philosophers, particularly because Plato took it to convey why *philosophy* is important. A variation on Plato's picture is found in this reading, from Bertrand Russell's *The Problems of Philosophy* (1912). Russell (1872–1970) was an English philosopher, from an aristocratic and politically prominent family. He won the Nobel Prize in Literature in 1950, having written widely and influentially on philosophy and far beyond – discussing abstract ideas but also practical social controversies. *The Problems of Philosophy* is probably the most widely read book of introductory philosophy from the twentieth century. What makes this more remarkable is that the book is not merely introductory. It includes some challenging ideas from an outstanding thinker. Even when the idea being presented is not original with Russell, his exposition is exceptionally succinct and sharp.

Russell's variation on Plato's picture highlights the role of *questioning*, within philosophy and within the possible development of a self. Philosophy is nothing if not a home for questions. It cannot be questioning always, in each sentence and with every breath. Nor should it be questioning mindlessly, asking "Why?" merely for the sake of questioning. But questions – good questions, thoughtful ones, imaginative ones – are vital to philosophy's progress. This is not only so that philosophical answers to them can be proffered, thereby laying before us a range of philosophical truths. It is because the questions themselves – when insightful and

Bertrand Russell, *The Problems of Philosophy* (London: Oxford University Press, 1959 [1912]), ch. 15 (excerpts). Reprinted with permission of Oxford University Press.

Metaphysics and Epistemology: A Guided Anthology, First Edition. Edited by Stephen Hetherington.
© 2014 John Wiley & Sons, Inc. Published 2014 by John Wiley & Sons, Inc.

apt – are essential to philosophy's value. They *are* part of its value. Without them, it is less than it should be. So much that, without them, it disappears. What remains is not really philosophical.

Does this imply that philosophy – always at least somewhat questioning – is never final and definitive in its suggestions, its claims? Maybe so. Does it tell us that philosophical certainty will never properly be ours? Maybe again so. And is that a worry? Far from it, argues Russell: without philosophical questioning, we will live mentally smaller lives. We would be living as lesser selves, too: we would not have allowed our selves to grow accordingly. We – our selves – would not have met and pondered possibilities that were always present, always inherent within our lives and the rest of the world, but that would be revealed only by philosophical questioning.

To shun such questioning would be like never exposing a child to words he or she has not yet heard. How else will the child gain expanded linguistic skills? "Ah, but we must not cause the child the stress of a puzzling and unknown new word." Why not? Again, how else will the child develop really new thoughts, encompassing fresh possibilities? Philosophy helps us in a similar way. It sparks new questions, exposing new possibilities. Puzzlement, even stress, is thereby present. But we should find that exhilarating, not a threat.

The Value of Philosophy

Having now come to the end of our brief and very incomplete review of the problems of philosophy, it will be well to consider, in conclusion, what is the value of philosophy and why it ought to be studied. It is the more necessary to consider this question, in view of the fact that many men, under the influence of science or of practical affairs, are inclined to doubt whether philosophy is anything better than innocent but useless trifling, hair-splitting distinctions, and controversies on matters concerning which knowledge is impossible.

This view of philosophy appears to result, partly from a wrong conception of the ends of life, partly from a wrong conception of the kind of goods which philosophy strives to achieve. Physical science, through the medium of inventions, is useful to innumerable people who are wholly ignorant of it; thus the study of physical science is to be recommended, not only, or primarily, because of the effect on the student, but rather because of the effect on mankind in general. Thus utility does not belong to philosophy. If the study of philosophy has any value at all for others than students of philosophy, it must be only indirectly, through its effects upon the lives of those who study it. It is in these effects, therefore, if anywhere, that the value of philosophy must be primarily sought.

But further, if we are not to fail in our endeavour to determine the value of philosophy, we must first free our minds from the prejudices of what are wrongly called 'practical' men. The 'practical' man, as this word is often used, is one who recognizes only material needs, who realizes that men must have food for the body, but is oblivious of the necessity of providing food for the mind. If all men were well off, if poverty and disease had been reduced to their lowest possible point, there would still remain much to be done to produce a valuable society; and even in the existing world the goods of the mind are at least as important as the goods of the body. It is exclusively among the goods of the mind that the value of philosophy is to be found; and only those who are not indifferent to these goods can be persuaded that the study of philosophy is not a waste of time.

Philosophy, like all other studies, aims primarily at knowledge. The knowledge it aims at is the kind of knowledge which gives unity and system to the body of the sciences, and the kind which results from a critical examination of the grounds of our convictions, prejudices, and beliefs. But it cannot be maintained that philosophy has had any very great measure of success in its attempts to provide definite answers to its questions. If you ask a mathematician, a mineralogist, a historian, or any other man of learning, what definite body of truths has been ascertained by his science, his answer will last as long as you are willing to listen. But if you put the same question to a philosopher, he will, if he is candid, have to confess that his study has not achieved positive results such as have been achieved by other sciences. It is true that this is partly accounted for by the fact that, as soon as definite knowledge concerning any subject becomes possible, this subject ceases to be called philosophy, and becomes a separate science. The whole study of the heavens, which now belongs to astronomy, was once included in philosophy; Newton's great work was called 'the mathematical principles of natural philosophy'. Similarly, the study of the human mind, which was a part of philosophy, has now been separated from philosophy and has become the science of psychology. Thus, to a great extent, the uncertainty of philosophy is more apparent than real: those questions which are already capable of definite answers are placed in the sciences, while those only to which, at present, no definite answer can be given, remain to form the residue which is called philosophy.

This is, however, only a part of the truth concerning the uncertainty of philosophy. There are many questions – and among them those that are of the profoundest interest to our spiritual life – which, so far as we can see, must remain insoluble to the human intellect unless its powers become of quite a different order from what they are now. Has the universe any unity of plan or purpose, or is it a fortuitous concourse of atoms? Is consciousness a permanent part of the universe, giving hope of indefinite growth in wisdom, or is it a transitory accident on a small planet on which life must ultimately become impossible? Are good and evil of importance to the universe or only to man? Such questions are asked by philosophy, and variously answered by various philosophers. But it would seem that, whether answers be otherwise discoverable or not, the answers suggested by philosophy are none of them demonstrably true. Yet, however slight may be the hope of discovering an answer, it is part of the business of philosophy to continue the consideration of such questions, to make us aware of their importance, to examine all the approaches to them, and to keep alive that speculative interest in the universe which is apt to be killed by confining ourselves to definitely ascertainable knowledge.

Many philosophers, it is true, have held that philosophy could establish the truth of certain answers to such fundamental questions. They have supposed that what is of most importance in religious beliefs could be proved by strict demonstration to be true. In order to judge of such attempts, it is necessary to take a survey of human knowledge, and to form an opinion as to its methods and its limitations. On such a subject it would be unwise to pronounce dogmatically; but if the investigations of our previous chapters have not led us astray, we shall be compelled to renounce the hope of finding philosophical proofs of religious beliefs. We cannot, therefore, include as part of the value of philosophy any definite set of answers to such questions. Hence, once more, the value of philosophy must not depend upon any supposed body of definitely ascertainable knowledge to be acquired by those who study it.

The value of philosophy is, in fact, to be sought largely in its very uncertainty. The man who has no tincture of philosophy goes through life imprisoned in the prejudices derived from common sense, from the habitual beliefs of his age or his nation, and from convictions which have grown up in his mind without the co-operation or consent of his deliberate reason. To such a man the world tends to become definite, finite, obvious; common objects rouse no questions, and unfamiliar possibilities are contemptuously rejected. As soon as we begin to philosophize, on the contrary, we find, as we saw in our opening chapters, that even the most everyday things lead to problems to which only very incomplete answers can be given. Philosophy, though unable to tell us with certainty what is the true answer to the doubts which it raises, is able to suggest many possibilities which enlarge our thoughts and free them from the tyranny of custom. Thus, while diminishing our feeling of certainty as to what things are, it greatly increases our knowledge as to what they may be; it removes the somewhat arrogant dogmatism of those who have never travelled into the region of liberating doubt, and it keeps alive our sense of wonder by showing familiar things in an unfamiliar aspect.

Apart from its utility in showing unsuspected possibilities, philosophy has a value – perhaps its chief value – through the greatness of the objects which it contemplates, and the freedom from narrow and personal aims resulting from this contemplation. The life of the instinctive man is shut up within the circle of his private interests: family and friends may be included, but the outer world is not regarded except as it may help or hinder what comes within the circle of instinctive wishes. In such a life there is something feverish and confined, in comparison with which the philosophic life is calm and free. The private world of instinctive interests is a small one, set in the midst of a great and powerful world which must, sooner or later, lay our private world in ruins. Unless we can so enlarge our interests as to include the whole outer world, we remain like a garrison in a beleagured fortress, knowing that the enemy prevents escape and that ultimate surrender is inevitable. In such a life there is no peace, but a constant strife between the insistence of desire and the powerlessness of will. In one way or another, if our life is to be great and free, we must escape this prison and this strife.

One way of escape is by philosophic contemplation. Philosophic contemplation does not, in its widest survey, divide the universe into two hostile camps – friends and foes, helpful and hostile, good and bad – it views the whole impartially. Philosophic contemplation, when it is unalloyed, does not aim at proving that the rest of the universe is akin to man. All acquisition of knowledge is an enlargement of the Self, but this enlargement is best attained when it is not directly sought. It is obtained when the desire for knowledge is alone operative, by a study which does not wish in advance that its objects should have this or that character, but adapts the Self to the characters which it finds in its objects. This enlargement of Self is not obtained when, taking the Self as it is, we try to show that the world is so similar to this Self that knowledge of it is possible without any admission of what seems alien. The desire to prove this is a form of self-assertion and, like all self-assertion, it is an obstacle to the growth of Self which it desires, and of which the Self knows that it is capable. Self-assertion, in philosophic speculation as elsewhere, views the world as a means to its own ends; thus it makes the world of less account than Self, and the Self sets bounds to the greatness of its goods. In contemplation, on the contrary, we start from the not-Self, and through its greatness the boundaries of Self are enlarged; through the infinity of the universe the mind which contemplates it achieves some share in infinity.

For this reason greatness of soul is not fostered by those philosophies which assimilate the universe to Man. Knowledge is a form of union of Self and not-Self; like all union, it is impaired by dominion, and therefore by any attempt to force the universe into conformity with what we find in ourselves. There is a widespread philosophical tendency towards the view which tells us that Man is the measure of all things, that truth is man-made, that space and time and the world of universals are properties of the mind, and that, if there be anything not created by the mind, it is unknowable and of no account for us. This view, if our previous discussions were correct, is untrue; but in addition to being untrue, it has the effect of robbing philosophic contemplation of all that gives it value, since it fetters contemplation to Self. What it calls knowledge is not a union with the not-Self, but a set of prejudices, habits, and desires, making an impenetrable veil between us and the world beyond. The man who finds pleasure in such a theory of knowledge is like the man who never leaves the domestic circle for fear his word might not be law.

The true philosophic contemplation, on the contrary, finds its satisfaction in every enlargement of the not-Self, in everything that magnifies the objects contemplated, and thereby the subject contemplating. Everything, in contemplation, that is personal or private, everything that depends upon habit, self-interest, or desire, distorts the object, and hence impairs the union which the intellect seeks. By thus making a barrier between subject and object, such personal and private things become a prison to the intellect. The free intellect will see as God might see, without a *here* and *now*, without hopes and fears, without the trammels of customary beliefs and traditional prejudices, calmly, dispassionately, in the sole and exclusive desire of knowledge – knowledge as impersonal, as purely contemplative, as it is possible for man to attain. Hence also the free intellect will value more the abstract and universal knowledge into which the accidents of private history do not enter, than the knowledge brought by the senses, and dependent, as such knowledge must be, upon an exclusive and personal point of view and a body whose sense-organs distort as much as they reveal.

The mind which has become accustomed to the freedom and impartiality of philosophic contemplation will preserve something of the same freedom and impartiality in the world of action and emotion. It will view its purposes and desires as parts of the whole, with the absence of insistence that results from seeing them as infinitesimal fragments in a world of which all the rest is unaffected by any one man's deeds. The impartiality which, in contemplation, is the unalloyed desire for truth, is the very same quality of mind which, in action, is justice, and in emotion is that universal love which can be given to all, and not only to those who are judged useful or admirable. Thus contemplation enlarges not only the objects of our thoughts, but also the objects of our actions and our affections: it makes us citizens of the universe, not only of one walled city at war with all the rest. In this citizenship of the universe consists man's true freedom, and his liberation from the thraldom of narrow hopes and fears.

Thus, to sum up our discussion of the value of philosophy; Philosophy is to be studied, not for the sake of any definite answers to its questions, since no definite answers can, as a rule, be known to be true, but rather for the sake of the questions themselves; because these questions enlarge our conception of what is possible, enrich our intellectual imagination and diminish the dogmatic assurance which closes the mind against speculation; but above all because, through the greatness of the universe which philosophy contemplates, the mind also is rendered great, and becomes capable of that union with the universe which constitutes its highest good.

3

Philosophy and Fundamental Images

Wilfrid Sellars, "Philosophy and the Scientific Image of Man"

Plato's image of the cave exhorted us to use philosophy to gain some deeply important knowledge – the knowledge of true goodness. How might philosophy help us to accomplish that? This depends on what it is to be philosophical. We have received Bertrand Russell's general advice: In being philosophical, be open to questioning, even while seeking only knowledge – and do not strive for needless certainty. Still, *how* should we achieve all of that? Is philosophy somehow special and unique in its ways of inquiring and investigating? Or can science, most notably, answer all philosophical questions?

Wilfrid Sellars (1912–89) was an eminent American philosopher whose career was mainly at the University of Pittsburgh. He begins this reading with an influential characterization of philosophy: basically, philosophy is a search for an exhaustive understanding of how whatever is real combines into the whole of whatever is real. Is that science's goal, too? Sellars does not quite believe so. He distinguishes between what he calls the *manifest* image and the *scientific* image. Each is a guiding vision, even while still being developed, of people and of how we fit into how the world is. The manifest image is of *observable* aspects of all that. The scientific image reaches also *beyond* what is observable. The manifest image can be scientific, by charting observable patterns, for instance. The scientific image is more deeply scientific, thinking its way beyond what is merely manifest. Yet even that scientific image need not include all philosophy. Can philosophy somehow link the manifest and the scientific? This book includes many proposed elements in what we may hope will be a completed *philosophical* image. Sometimes we will be asked to reflect upon parts of the manifest image, at other times parts of the scientific image. But maybe,

W. F. Sellars, "Philosophy and the Scientific Image of Man," in *Science, Perception and Reality* (London: Routledge & Kegan Paul, 1963), ch. 1 (excerpts). Reprinted with permission of University of Pittsburgh Press.

courtesy of philosophy, there will also be more than these. Maybe there is the manifest image, the scientific image, and the philosophical image. In short, is philosophy a *further* manifestation of humanity's powers of creative inquiry? That is a question to remember when reading this book's varied pieces of the overall puzzle that is philosophy in progress.

I. The Philosophical Quest

The aim of philosophy, abstractly formulated, is to understand how things in the broadest possible sense of the term hang together in the broadest possible sense of the term. Under 'things in the broadest possible sense' I include such radically different items as not only 'cabbages and kings', but numbers and duties, possibilities and finger snaps, aesthetic experience and death. To achieve success in philosophy would be, to use a contemporary turn of phrase, to 'know one's way around' with respect to all these things, not in that unreflective way in which the centipede of the story knew its way around before it faced the question, 'how do I walk?', but in that reflective way which means that no intellectual holds are barred.

Knowing one's way around is, to use a current distinction, a form of 'knowing *how*' as contrasted with 'knowing *that*'. There is all the difference in the world between knowing *how* to ride a bicycle and knowing *that* a steady pressure by the legs of a balanced person on the pedals would result in forward motion. Again, to use an example somewhat closer to our subject, there is all the difference in the world between knowing *that* each step of a given proof in mathematics follows from the preceding steps, and knowing *how* to find a proof. Sometimes being able to find a proof is a matter of being able to follow a set procedure; more often it is not. It can be argued that anything which can be properly called 'knowing how to do something' presupposes a body of knowledge *that*; or, to put it differently, knowledge of truth or facts. If this were so, then the statement that 'ducks know *how* to swim' would be as metaphorical as the statement that they know *that* water supports them. However this may be, knowing how to do something at the level of characteristically human activity presupposes a great deal of knowledge *that*, and it is obvious that the reflective knowing one's way around in the scheme of things, which is the aim of philosophy, presupposes a great deal of reflective knowledge of truths.

Now the subject-matter of this knowledge of truths which is presupposed by philosophical 'know-how', falls, in a sense, completely within the scope of the special disciplines. Philosophy in an important sense has no special subject-matter which stands to it as other subject-matters stand to other special disciplines. If philosophers did have such a special subject-matter, they could turn it over to a new group of specialists as they have turned other special subject-matters to non-philosophers over the past 2500 years, first with mathematics, more recently psychology and sociology, and, currently, certain aspects of theoretical linguistics. What is characteristic of philosophy is not a special subject-matter, but the aim of knowing one's way around with respect to the subject-matters of all the special disciplines.

Now the special disciplines know their way around in their subject-matters, and each learns to do so in the process of discovering truths about its own subject-matter. But each special discipline must also have a sense of how its bailiwick fits into the countryside as a whole. This sense in many cases amounts to a little more than the unreflective 'knowing one's way around' which is a common possession of us all. Again, the specialist must have a sense of how not only his subject-matter, but also the methods and principles of his thinking about it fit into the intellectual landscape. Thus, the historian reflects not only on historical events themselves, but on what it is to think historically. It is part of his business to reflect on his own thinking – its aims, its criteria, its pitfalls. In dealing with historical questions, he must face and answer questions which are not, themselves, in a primary sense historical questions. But he deals with these questions as they arise in the attempt to answer specifically historical questions.

Reflection on any special discipline can soon lead one to the conclusion that the *ideal* practitioner of that discipline would see his special subject-matter and his thinking about it in the light of a reflective insight into the intellectual landscape as a whole. There is much truth in the Platonic conception that the special disciplines are perfected by philosophy, but the companion conception that the philosopher must know his way around in each discipline as does the specialist, has been an ever more elusive ideal since the scientific revolution began. Yet if the philosopher cannot hope to know his way around in each discipline as does the specialist, there is a sense in which he can know his way around with respect to the subject-matter of that discipline, and must do so if he is to approximate to the philosophic aim.

The multiplication of sciences and disciplines is a familiar feature of the intellectual scene. Scarcely less familiar is the unification of this manifold which is taking place by the building of scientific bridges between them. I shall have something to say about this unification later in this chapter. What is not so obvious to the layman is that the task of 'seeing all things together' has itself been (paradoxically) broken down into specialities. And there *is* a place for specialization in philosophy. For just as one cannot come to know one's way around in the highway system as a whole without knowing one's way around in the parts, so one can't hope to know one's way around in 'things in general', without knowing one's way around in the major groupings of things.

It is therefore, the 'eye on the whole' which distinguishes the philosophical enterprise. Otherwise, there is little to distinguish the philosopher from the persistently reflective specialist; the philosopher of history from the persistently reflective historian. To the extent that a specialist is more concerned to reflect on how his work as a specialist joins up with other intellectual pursuits, than in asking and answering questions within his speciality, he is said, properly, to be philosophically-minded. And, indeed, one can 'have one's eye on the whole' without staring at it all the time. The latter would be a fruitless enterprise. Furthermore, like other specialists, the philosopher who specializes may derive much of his sense of the whole from the pre-reflective orientation which is our common heritage. On the other hand, a philosopher could scarcely be said to have his eye on the whole in the relevant sense, unless he has reflected on the nature of philosophical thinking. It is this reflection on the place of philosophy itself, in the scheme of things which is the distinctive trait of the philosopher as contrasted with the reflective specialist; and in the absence of this critical reflection on the philosophical enterprise, one is at best but a potential philosopher.

[...]

[...] [T]he philosopher is confronted not by one complex many-dimensional picture, the unity of which, such as it is, he must come to appreciate; but by *two* pictures of essentially the same order of complexity, each of which purports to be a complete picture of man-in-the-world, and which, after separate scrutiny, he must fuse into one vision. Let me refer to these two perspectives, respectively, as the *manifest* and the *scientific* images of man-in-the-world.

[...]

II. The Manifest Image

The 'manifest' image of man-in-the-world can be characterized in two ways, which are supplementary rather than alternative. It is, first, the framework in terms of which man came to be aware of himself as man-in-the-world. It is the framework in terms of which, to use an existentialist turn of phrase, man first encountered himself – which is, of course, when he came to be man. For it is no merely incidental feature of man that he has a conception of himself as man-in-the-world, just as it is obvious, on reflection, that 'if man had a radically different conception of himself he would be a radically different kind of man'.

[...]

[...] For what I mean by the manifest image is a refinement or sophistication of what might be called the 'original' image; a refinement to a degree which makes it relevant to the contemporary intellectual scene. This refinement or sophistication can be construed under two headings; (*a*) empirical; (*b*) categorial.

By empirical refinement, I mean the sort of refinement which operates within the broad framework of the image and which, by approaching the world in terms of something like the canons of inductive inference defined by John Stuart Mill, supplemented by canons of statistical inference, adds to and subtracts from the contents of the world as experienced in terms of this framework and from the correlations which are believed to obtain between them. Thus, the conceptual framework which I am calling the manifest image is, in an appropriate sense, itself a scientific image. It is not only disciplined and critical; it also makes use of those aspects of scientific method which might be lumped together under the heading 'correlational induction'. There is, however, one type of scientific reasoning which it, by stipulation, does *not* include, namely that which involves the postulation of imperceptible entities, and principles pertaining to them, to explain the behaviour of perceptible things.

[...] [I]t will enable us to define a way of looking at the world which, though disciplined and, in a limited sense, scientific, contrasts sharply with an image of man-in-the-world which is implicit in and can be constructed from the postulational aspects of contemporary scientific theory. And, indeed, what I have referred to as the 'scientific' image of man-in-the-world and contrasted with the 'manifest' image, might better be called the 'postulational' or 'theoretical' image. But, I believe, it will not be too misleading if I continue, for the most part, to use the former term.

Now the manifest image is important for our purpose, because it defines one of the poles to which philosophical reflection has been drawn. It is not only the great speculative systems of ancient and medieval philosophy which are built around the manifest image, but also many systems and quasi-systems in recent and contemporary thought, some of which seem at first sight to have little if anything in common with the great classical systems.

[...]

The first point I wish to make is that there is an important sense in which the primary objects of the manifest image are *persons*. And to understand how this is so, is to understand central and, indeed, crucial themes in the history of philosophy. Perhaps the best way to make the point is to refer back to the construct which we called the 'original' image of man-in-the-world, and characterize it as a framework in which *all* the 'objects' are persons. From this point of view, the refinement of the 'original' image into the manifest image, is the gradual 'de-personalization' of objects other than persons. That something like this has occurred with the advance of civilization is a familiar fact. Even persons, it is said (mistakenly, I believe), are being 'depersonalized' by the advance of the scientific point of view.

[…]

I am now in a position to explain what I mean when I say that the primary objects of the manifest image are persons. I mean that it is the modification of an image in which *all* the objects are capable of *the full range* of personal activity, the modification consisting of a gradual pruning of the implications of saying with respect to what *we* would call an inanimate object, that it *did* something. Thus, in the original image to say of the wind that it blew down one's house would imply that the wind *either* decided to do so with an end in view, and might, perhaps, have been persuaded not to do it, *or* that it acted thoughtlessly (either from habit or impulse), or, perhaps, inadvertently, in which case other appropriate action on one's part might have awakened it to the enormity of what it was about to do.

In the early stages of the development of the manifest image, the wind was no longer conceived as acting deliberately, with an end in view; but rather from habit or impulse. Nature became the locus of 'truncated persons'; that which things could be expected to do, its habits; that which exhibits no order, its impulses. Inanimate things no longer 'did' things in the sense in which persons do them – not, however, because a *new* category of impersonal things and impersonal processes has been achieved, but because the category of *person* is now applied to these things in a pruned or truncated form. It is a striking exaggeration to say of a person, that he is a 'mere creature of habit and impulse', but in the early stages of the development of manifest image, the world includes truncated persons which *are* mere creatures of habit, acting out routines, broken by impulses, in a life which never rises above what ours is like in our most unreflective moments. Finally, the sense in which the wind 'did' things was pruned, save for poetic and expressive purposes – and, one is tempted to add, for philosophical purposes – of implications pertaining to 'knowing what one is doing' and 'knowing what the circumstances are'.

[…]

III.   Classical Philosophy and the Manifest Image

[…]

[…] [M]uch of academic philosophy can be interpreted as an attempt by individual thinkers to delineate the manifest image (not recognized, needless to say, as such) an image which is both immanent in and transcendent of their thinking. In this respect, a philosophy can be evaluated as perceptive or imperceptive, mistaken or correct, even though one is prepared to say that the image they delineate is but one way in which reality appears to the human mind. And it is, indeed, a task of the first importance to delineate this image, particularly in so far as it concerns man himself, for, as was pointed out before, man is what he is because he thinks of himself in terms of this image, and the latter must be understood before it is proper to ask, 'to what extent does manifest man survive in the synoptic view which does equal justice to the scientific image which now confronts us?'

I think it correct to say that the so-called 'analytic' tradition in recent British and American philosophy, particularly under the influence of the later Wittgenstein, has done increasing justice to the manifest image, and has increasingly succeeded in isolating it in something like its pure form, and has made clear the folly of attempting to replace it *piecemeal* by fragments of the scientific image. By doing so, it is made apparent, and has come to realize, its continuity with the perennial tradition.

[...]

It is in the *scientific* image of man in the world that we begin to see the main outlines of the way in which man came to have an image of himself-in-the-world. For we begin to see this as a matter of evolutionary development as a group phenomenon, a process which is illustrated at a simpler level by the evolutionary development which explains the correspondence between the dancing of a worker bee and the location, relative to the sun, of the flower from which he comes. This correspondence, like the relation between man's 'original' image and the world, is incapable of explanation in terms of a direct conditioning impact of the environment on the individual as such.

[...]

IV.   The Scientific Image

I devoted my attention in the previous sections to defining what I called the 'manifest' image of man-in-the-world. I argued that this image is to be construed as a sophistication and refinement of the image in terms of which man first came to be aware of himself as man-in-the-world; in short, came to be man.

[...]

The scientific image of man-in-the-world is, of course, as much an idealization as the manifest image – even more so, as it is still in the process of coming to be. It will be remembered that the contrast I have in mind is not that between an *unscientific* conception of man-in-the-world and a *scientific* one, but between that conception which limits itself to what correlational techniques can tell us about perceptible and introspectible events and that which postulates imperceptible objects and events for the purpose of explaining correlations among perceptibles. [...] Our contrast then, is between two ideal constructs: (*a*) the correlational and categorial refinement of the 'original image', which refinement I am calling the manifest image; (*b*) the image derived from the fruits of postulational theory construction which I am calling the scientific image.

It may be objected at this point that there is no such thing as *the* image of man built from postulated entities and processes, but rather as many images as there are sciences which touch on aspects of human behaviour. And, of course, in a sense this is true. There *are* as many scientific images of man as there are sciences which have something to say about man. Thus, there is man as he appears to the theoretical physicist – a swirl of physical particles, forces, and fields. There is man as he appears to the biochemist, to the physiologist, to the behaviourist, to the social scientist; and all of these images are to be contrasted with man as he appears to himself in sophisticated common sense, the manifest image which even today contains most of what he knows about himself at the properly human level. Thus the conception of *the* scientific or postulational image is an idealization in the sense that it is a conception of an integration of a manifold of images, each of which is the application to man of a framework of concepts which have a certain autonomy. For each scientific theory is, from the standpoint of methodology, a structure which is built at a different 'place' and by different procedures within the intersubjectively accessible world of perceptible things. Thus 'the' scientific image is a construct from a number of images, each of which is *supported by* the manifest world.

[…] [A]lthough methodologically a development *within* the manifest image, the scientific image presents itself as a *rival* image. From its point of view the manifest image on which it rests is an 'inadequate' but pragmatically useful likeness of a reality which first finds its adequate (in principle) likeness in the scientific image. I say, 'in principle', because the scientific image is still in the process of coming into being […]

V.   The Clash of the Images

How, then, are we to evaluate the conflicting claims of the manifest image and the scientific image thus provisionally interpreted to constitute *the* true and, in principle, *complete* account of man-in-the-world?

[…]

VII.   Putting Man into the Scientific Image

Even if the constructive suggestion of the preceding section were capable of being elaborated into an adequate account of the way in which the scientific image could recreate in its own terms the sensations, images, and feelings of the manifest image, the thesis of the primacy of the scientific image would scarcely be off the ground. There would remain the task of showing that categories pertaining to man as a *person* who finds himself confronted by standards (ethical, logical, etc.) which often conflict with his desires and impulses, and to which he may or may not conform, can be reconciled with the idea that man is what science says he is.

[…]

4

Philosophy as the Analyzing of Key Concepts

P.F. Strawson, *Analysis and Metaphysics*

In the previous reading Wilfrid Sellars, by distinguishing the manifest image from the scientific one, laid a foundation that might prompt us to think of philosophy as a quest for the *philosophical* image of ourselves and the wider world. How will that quest proceed? In the past fifty or so years, perhaps the most common answer to that question has been this: Philosophy tries to understand our most humanly central *concepts*, of ourselves and of the world more generally; and the sort of understanding being sought reflects our attempts to *analyze* those concepts. This reading from a somewhat introductory book by P.F. Strawson (1919–2006), an esteemed Oxford philosopher, offers a clear statement of that way of doing philosophy. It is one way of pursuing what is often called *analytic* philosophy.

Such an approach will encourage us to begin by highlighting the key concepts with which people claim to describe themselves and the world. Can we then analyze those concepts, in the sense of "dividing" them into further concepts? You might be asked, "What is it to be an X?" (for some important X). After pondering that, you could reply with an instance of this: "To be an X is to be a P-plus-Q-plus-R." You would be claiming to understand being X, in terms of being P, being Q, and being R. This could have been quite difficult, requiring a lot of thought on your part. You might even take yourself to have described the essence, the core, of what it is to be an X: 'Being a person amounts to this: ….' And that would be welcomely insightful, if you really can do it. (You could become known as someone who really understands what it is to be a person, say.)

So, think of our most pressing concepts, those we would use in developing the details of what we would believe to be the ultimate manifest or scientific images.

P.F. Strawson, *Analysis and Metaphysics: An Introduction to Philosophy* (Oxford: Oxford University Press, 1992), ch. 1 (excerpts). Reprinted with permission of Oxford University Press.

Metaphysics and Epistemology: A Guided Anthology, First Edition. Edited by Stephen Hetherington.

(These concepts would capture what we believe are the most fundamental parts of reality, either observable or unobservable parts of it.) Then, as carefully and precisely as is possible and apt, try to analyze those concepts. If you do this well, would you have reached a state of philosophical knowledge? Is this *all* that we should want from philosophy? It does sound potentially valuable; is it enough?

You might have gained an accurate and revelatory philosophical image of what most matters to us, about ourselves and the wider world. And maybe our achieving an ultimate philosophical image would enable us to *use* our most important concepts more judiciously and profitably. We could now avoid misclassifications of the world and ourselves, mistakes of which we might otherwise never have been aware. We could know better how to describe the world and ourselves, by understanding and using more accurately our key concepts.

Analytical Philosophy

Two Analogies

[...]

What is it, then, his [the analytic philosopher's] aim? What is he concerned with? Well, with ideas or concepts, surely. So his self-awarded title of 'analytical philosopher' suggests 'conceptual analysis' as the favoured description of his favoured activity. [...] An analysis, I suppose, may be thought of as a kind of breaking down or decomposing of something. So we have the picture of a kind of intellectual taking to pieces of ideas or concepts; the discovering of what elements a concept or idea is composed and how they are related. Is this the right picture or the wrong one – or is it partly right and partly wrong? [...] We are offered other pictures from time to time, some of them overtly analogies or metaphors. Professor Ryle, for example, used to speak of conceptual geography or conceptual mapping or charting. This picture has merits. A map or chart gives us a representation of an area, a representation which is in some measure abstract and such as we do not ordinarily get through normal perceptual encounters. Maps can vary in scale, show more or less detail, reflect different particular interests. They can help us to get about. With an accurate chart we are less likely to suffer shipwreck; and intellectual or conceptual shipwreck is surely a possibility.

All the same, the picture remains uncomfortably metaphorical. If we discard the metaphorical elements, we are left simply with the notion of an abstract representation of certain relations between certain concepts made for a certain purpose. But what concepts, what relations, what purpose? All this is, so far, unspecified.

Another, quite different image, which has been familiar for some time, yet may still seem surprising, is that of the analytical philosopher as a kind of therapist, who undertakes to cure certain characteristic kinds of intellectual disorder. He offers no doctrine, no theory; rather, he brings to bear a technique. When we try to think at a philosophical level, we are apt, according to this view, to fall into certain obsessive muddles or confusions; to see ourselves as led by reason to conclusions which we can neither accept nor escape from; to ask questions which seem to have no answers or only absurd answers; to become unable to see how what we know very well to be the case can possibly be the case; and so on. The role of the analytical philosopher is then to straighten us out or to help us to straighten ourselves out; to free us from the obsessive confusions, the false models which dominate our thinking, and to enable us to see clearly what is in front of us. Thus Wittgenstein says: 'The philosopher's treatment of a question is like the treatment of an illness.'[1] We are to go to him, it seems, somewhat as a neurotic goes to an analyst.

[...]

Let us leave this question, and this analogy of therapy, on one side for a while, and consider, instead, another analogy. [...]

When the first Spanish or, strictly, Castilian grammar was presented to Queen Isabella of Castile, her response was to ask what use it was. The reply made on behalf of the grammarian was of a world-historical character, referring to language as an instrument of empire – and that need no longer concern us. What does concern us is the point of her question. For of course the grammar was in a certain sense of no use at all to fluent speakers of Castilian. In a sense they knew it all already. They spoke grammatically correct Castilian because grammatically correct Castilian simply *was* what they spoke. The grammar did not set the standard of correctness for the sentences they spoke; on the contrary, it was the sentences they spoke that set the standard of correctness for the grammar. However, though in a sense they knew the grammar of their language, there was another sense in which they did not know it.

If Isabella had been asked to state, in a maximally systematic way, a system of rules or principles in the light of which one could decide, with respect to any sequence of Castilian words, whether or not it constituted a grammatically complete and correct sentence, she would have been quite at a loss. Her practice and that of her courtiers, in constructing Castilian sentences, showed that she and they in a sense observed such a set or system of rules or principles. Her and their practice was in a sense governed by such rules or principles. But from the fact that she and they effortlessly observed the rules it by no means follows that they could, effortlessly or with an effort, state the rules, say what they were.

We can draw the general moral that being able to do something – in this case speak grammatically – is very different from being able to say how it's done; and that it by no means implies the latter. Mastery of a practice does not involve an explicit mastery (though it may sometimes be allowed to involve an implicit mastery) of the theory of that practice. Grammars were implicitly mastered long before grammars were ever explicitly written; and implicit grammars are necessary to speech and therefore necessary to any but the most rudimentary thinking. But of course rational human beings, capable of developed thinking, must have an implicit mastery of more than grammars; or, rather, their implicit mastery of their grammars is intertwined with an implicit mastery of all the concepts, all the general ideas which find expression in their speech, which they operate with in their thought. In our transactions with each other and the world we operate with an enormously rich, complicated, and refined conceptual equipment; but we are not, and indeed could not be, taught the mastery of the items of this formidable equipment by being taught the *theory* of their employment.

Thus, for example, we know, in a sense, what knowing is perfectly well long before we hear (if we ever do hear) of the Theory of Knowledge. We know, in one sense, what it is to speak the truth without perhaps suspecting that there are such things as Theories of Truth.

We learn to handle the words 'the same', 'real', 'exists', and to handle them correctly, without being aware of the philosophical problems of Identity, Reality, and Existence. In the same way, we learn to operate with a vast and heterogeneous range of notions: ethical notions: good, bad, right, wrong, punishment; temporal and spatial concepts; the ideas of causality and explanation; ideas of emotions: sadness, anger, fear, joy; of mental operations of various kinds: thinking, believing, wondering, remembering, expecting, imagining; of perception and sense experience: seeing, hearing, touching, having sensations; whole ranges of classificatory concepts for types of people, animals, plants, natural objects, processes, or events, human artefacts, institutions, and roles; and the properties, qualities, doings, and undergoings of all these. Of course we learn the words which express these concepts in a variety of ways; but we learn them largely without benefit of anything which could properly be called general theoretical instruction. We are not introduced to them by being told their place in a general theory of concepts. Such instruction as we do receive is severely practical and largely by example. We learn largely by copying and by occasional correction; as children learn to speak grammatically before they hear of grammars.

To press on, then, with the analogy. Just as we may have a working mastery of the grammar of our native language, so we have a working mastery of this conceptual equipment. We know how to handle it, how to use it in thought and speech. But just as the practical mastery of the grammar in no way entails the ability to state systematically what the rules are which we effortlessly observe, so the practical mastery of our conceptual equipment in no way entails the possession of a clear, explicit understanding of the principles which govern our handling of it, of the theory of our practice. So – to conclude the analogy – just as the grammarian, and especially the model modern grammarian, labours to produce a systematic account of the structure of rules which we effortlessly observe in speaking grammatically, so the philosopher labours to produce a systematic account of the general *conceptual structure* of which our daily practice shows us to have a tacit and unconscious mastery.

[...] We have mastered a practice, but can't state the theory of our practice. We know the rules because we observe them and yet we don't know them because we can't say what they are. In contrast with the ease and accuracy of our use are the stuttering and blundering which characterize our first attempts to describe and explain our use.

[...]

[...] [W]e must certainly acknowledge that there is indeed a distinction between the theoretical concepts of, say, nuclear physics or economics and non-technical concepts like those of knowledge and identity; and we must acknowledge, too, that we learn to master the former, if we do, by a route of explicit theoretical instruction such as we do not follow, are not led along, in the case of the latter, the ordinary non-theoretical concepts. But we must ask what is the point and purpose of this route of explicit theoretical instruction. And the answer is that it is precisely to enable us to operate effectively *inside* the discipline concerned, *within* that discipline. The purpose is achieved if we become good economists, physicists, or whatnot; or, more modestly, if we are able to follow, with understanding, the reasonings and conclusions of good economists, physicists, etc. But there is no guarantee that theoretical instruction which achieves this purpose automatically confers on the instructed the ability to form an undistorted picture of the relation of the specialized discipline concerned to other human and intellectual concerns. But one of the principal philosophical drives is precisely to relate and connect our various intellectual and human concerns in some intelligible way.

The critic might well concede this point; but then add that it merely mentions another philosophical task which has no obvious connection with the general picture of philosophy presented by the grammatical analogy. That there is such a connection can be shown, however – as follows. The scientific specialist, let us suppose, is perfectly capable of explaining what he is doing with the special terms of his specialism. He has an explicit mastery, within the terms of his theory, of the special concepts of his theory. But he is also bound to use certain concepts which have a wider application than that of his specialism, concepts which are not really specialist concepts at all: for example, the concepts of explanation, demonstration, proof, conclusion, cause, event, fact, property, hypothesis, evidence, and theory itself – to mention only a few. Now in relation to these general concepts, as they figure in his discipline, the specialist may be in much the same position as we all are in relation to the pre-theoretical or non-technical concepts which we handle so easily in our ordinary intercourse with each other and the world. That is to say, the specialist may know perfectly well how to handle these concepts inside his discipline, i.e. be able to use them perfectly correctly there, without being able to say, in general, how he does it. Just as we, in our ordinary relations with things, have mastered a pre-theoretical practice without being necessarily able to state the principles of that practice, so he, the scientific specialist, may have mastered what we may call a theoretical practice without being able to state the principles of employment, within that practice, of terms which are not peculiar to it, terms which have a more general employment. Thus, for example, a historian may produce brilliant historical explanations without being able to say, in general, what counts as a historical explanation. A natural scientist may be fertile of brilliantly confirmed hypotheses but at a loss to give a general account of the confirmation of a scientific hypothesis, or even of the general nature of scientific hypotheses themselves. Again, a mathematician may discover and prove new mathematical truths without being able to say what are the distinctive characteristics of mathematical truth or of mathematical proof. So we have, besides history, the philosophy of history; besides natural science, the philosophy of science; besides mathematics, the philosophy of mathematics.

[…]

We see, then, how the question of the special sciences can, after all, be fitted into the framework of that positive conception of analysis presented by the grammatical analogy. But now, to balance the picture a little, let me note how a philosopher who favoured the negative, therapeutic conception of his role could present the considerations I have just been advancing in a very different fashion. All goes well, he might say – or well enough, aside from the ordinary difficulties of life and theory – so long as we are content simply to employ our ordinary concepts in their ordinary roles; to employ our technical concepts in their technical roles; and to employ the concepts which are common to different disciplines or to different disciplines and to daily life in the particular roles which they have in these different departments of their employment. Philosophical problems arise only because we are not satisfied to follow, or simply take note of, these employments; because we seek to unify, to theorize, to establish connections, in order to arrive at a comprehensive and unified conception of the world and our relation to it. Then our minds drift away from attention to our actual practice, from the role our concepts actually play in our lives; and we allow ourselves to be seduced by inappropriate models or pictures and to weave out of them bizarre and ultimately senseless theories, which are (to repeat the phrase of Wittgenstein's) 'nothing but houses of cards'.

What is needed, then, is not a general explanatory theory, but a curative discipline which will remind us of the facts of use (remember, 'assemble reminders for a particular purpose') and perhaps also diagnose the sources of the philosophical illusions to which we are subject when our minds drift away from those facts.

[...]

Note

1. Wittgenstein, *Philosophical Investigations*, § 255.

5

Philosophy as Explaining
Underlying Possibilities

Robert Nozick, *Philosophical Explanations*

Whether or not philosophy proceeds in quite the way Strawson describes – namely, by analyzing concepts – it does seek understanding. This could involve knowing, and it might (as Plato advocated) involve knowing ultimately important truths. Even so, something *more* might be involved in philosophical understanding. Somehow, it could be what we need if we are to understand *whatever possibilities underlie all else*. There can be a philosophical art in understanding underlying possibilities as such. We saw how Bertrand Russell regards philosophy's value as residing partly in its *questioning* sense of further possibilities. The emphasis in this reading from Robert Nozick (1938–2002), a provocative Harvard philosopher, is on underlying possibilities and on explaining them.

Here is a distinction that clarifies this suggestion. It is one thing to know *that you are* a person. It is something more to know *what it is for you to be* a person. It might be something more again to know how it is *even possible at all* for the world to include such a being. In this excerpt from his much-discussed book *Philosophical Explanations*, Nozick offers a clear statement of the need for philosophy not to forget to seek such explanations of possibilities as such. These could be a necessary element in the final philosophical image.

Nozick also has some apt advice for readers of philosophy. As you travel through this book, you will encounter arguments. Most philosophers proceed most of the time by creating lines of thought in support of favored conclusions. Most philosophers most of the time regard good arguments as essential to good

Metaphysics and Epistemology: A Guided Anthology, First Edition. Edited by Stephen Hetherington.
© 2014 John Wiley & Sons, Inc. Published 2014 by John Wiley & Sons, Inc.

philosophy. Still, when you read someone's philosophical argument, is there a best way of reacting to it, of experiencing it? Nozick urges us not to feel *coerced* by philosophical arguments. Even while retaining the image of truth as an essential part of what is being sought within philosophy, we can treat the arguments along the way as also hoping to illuminate, even to enlighten. So, feel free to test out that idea as you read this book. You are encouraged also to spark this spirit within your own philosophical thinking as, even if slowly, your thinking takes shape and flight.

I, too, seek an unreadable book: urgent thoughts to grapple with in agitation and excitement, revelations to be transformed by or to transform, a book incapable of being read straight through, a book, even, to bring reading to *stop*. I have not found that book, or attempted it. Still, I wrote and thought in awareness of it, in the hope this book would bask in its light. That hope would be arrogant if it weren't self-fulfilling – to face toward the light, even from a great distance, is to be warmed. (Is it sufficient, though, when light is absent, to face in the direction it would emanate from?)

Familiar questions impel this essay: Does life have meaning? Are there objective ethical truths? Do we have free will? What is the nature of our identity as selves? Must our knowledge and understanding stay within fixed limits? These questions moved me, and others, to enter the study of philosophy. I care what their answers are. While such other philosophical intricacies as whether sets or numbers exist can be fun for a time, they do not make us tremble.

[...]

No philosophical inquiry can restrict itself to the central questions; in pursuing these, we are led to others as well. Common themes unite our consideration of the diverse questions but, rather than begin with these as first principles, I prefer to let linkages emerge. Philosophers often seek to deduce their total view from a few basic principles, showing how all follows from their intuitively based axioms. The rest of the philosophy then strikes readers as depending upon these principles. One brick is piled upon another to produce a tall philosophical tower, one brick wide. When the bottom brick crumbles or is removed, all topples, burying even those insights that were independent of the starting point.

Instead of the tottering tower, I suggest that our model be the Parthenon. First we emplace our separate philosophical insights, column by column; afterwards, we unite and unify them under an overarching roof of general principles or themes. When the philosophical structure crumbles somewhat, as we should expect on inductive grounds, something of interest and beauty remains standing. Still preserved are some insights, the separate columns, some balanced relations, and the wistful look of a grander unity eroded by misfortunes or natural processes. We need not go so far as to hope that the philosophical ruin, like some others, will be even more beautiful than the original. Yet, unlike the philosophical tower, this structure will remain as more than a heap of stones.

Coercive Philosophy

It was not arbitrary of philosophers to start with apparently necessary first principles, given their desire to prove their views. If the tower-like structure is abandoned, we must forsake its purpose as well. But can philosophy have an aim other than proof? Philosophical training molds arguers: it trains people to produce arguments and (this is part of the arguing) to criticize and evaluate them. A philosopher's seriousness is judged by the quality of his arguments.

Children think an argument involves raised voices, anger, negative emotion. To argue with someone is to attempt to push him around verbally. But a philosophical argument isn't like that – is it?

The terminology of philosophical art is coercive: arguments are *powerful* and best when they are *knockdown*, arguments *force* you to a conclusion, if you believe the premises you *have to* or *must* believe the conclusion, some arguments do not carry much *punch*, and so forth. A philosophical argument is an attempt to get someone to believe something, whether he wants to believe it or not. A successful philosophical argument, a strong argument, *forces* someone to a belief.

Though philosophy is carried on as a coercive activity, the penalty philosophers wield is, after all, rather weak. If the other person is willing to bear the label of "irrational" or "having the worse arguments", he can skip away happily maintaining his previous belief. He will be trailed, of course, by the philosopher furiously hurling philosophical imprecations: "What do you mean, you're willing to be irrational? You shouldn't be irrational because ..." And although the philosopher is embarrassed by his inability to complete this sentence in a non-circular fashion – he can only produce reasons for accepting reasons – still, he is unwilling to let his adversary go.

Wouldn't it be better if philosophical arguments left the person no possible answer at all, reducing him to impotent silence? Even then, he might sit there silently, smiling, Buddhalike. Perhaps philosophers need arguments so powerful they set up reverberations in the brain: if the person refuses to accept the conclusion, he *dies*. How's that for a powerful argument? Yet, as with other physical threats ("your money or your life"), he can choose defiance. A "perfect" philosophical argument would leave no choice.

What useful purpose do philosophical arguments serve? Do we, trained in finding flaws in history's great arguers, really believe arguments a promising route to the truth? Does either the likelihood of arriving at a true view (as opposed to a consistent and coherent one) or a view's closeness to the truth vary directly with the strength of the philosophical arguments? Philosophical arguments can serve to elaborate a view, to delineate its content. Considering objections, hypothetical situations, and so on, does help to sharpen a view. But need all this be done in an attempt to prove, or in arguing?

Why are philosophers intent on forcing others to believe things? Is that a nice way to behave toward someone? I think we cannot improve people that way – the means frustrate the end. Just as dependence is not eliminated by treating a person dependently, and someone cannot be forced to be free, a person is not most improved by being forced to believe something against his will, whether he wants to or not. The valuable person cannot be fashioned by committing philosophy upon him.

So don't look here for a knockdown argument that there is something wrong with knockdown arguments, for the knockdown argument to end all knockdown arguing. It will not do to argue you into the conclusion, even in order to reduce the total amount of presentation of argument. Nor may I hint that I possess the knockdown argument yet will not present it.

Mightn't there be a legitimate use of argument, in self-defense against argumentative bludgeoning by others? Could one wield arguments to attack the other person's position, but only after he has attacked your own – intellectual karate in response to his initiating argument? Alternatively, arguments might be used solely to disarm an attacker. Deftly, the force of the assault could be diverted or even turned against the attacker – intellectual judo or aikido. Perhaps others could thus be defended from the onslaught of third parties, though it would be difficult to bring our argumentative defense to their attention without thereby subjecting them to coercion from *our* arguments. For one's own protection it should not be necessary to argue at all, merely to note publicly what bludgeoning the others are attempting – intellectual satyagraha, to use Gandhi's term for non-violent resistance.

[…]

Philosophy without arguments, in one mode, would guide someone to a view. The first chapter presents thoughts the reader has had (or is ready to have), only more deeply. Reading this chapter stimulates new thoughts which, pleased with, he tentatively adopts as his own. The second chapter deepens and extends these very thoughts; the reader willingly accepts them in this form. They are almost exactly what he was thinking already; he does not have to be argued into them. This second chapter also stimulates further new thoughts, which please the reader, and he tentatively adopts these thoughts as his own; in the third chapter, he finds these thoughts deepened and extended, and so on.

At no point is the person forced to accept anything. He moves along gently, exploring his own and the author's thoughts. He explores together with the author, moving only where he is ready to; then he stops. Perhaps, at a later time mulling it over or in a second reading, he will move further.

With this manner of writing, an author might circle back more than once to the same topic. Not everything can be said at once or twice; a reader may not be ready yet to think it all himself. Within the structure of each chapter, the thought might go further out as it goes along, reaching finally ideas so speculative that even the author is not willing (yet?) to assert them, barely willing even to entertain them.

Such a book could not convince everybody of what it says – it wouldn't try. (Should it then be judged by goals not its own?) I have said such a book would guide without forcing, but won't it be manipulating its readers? Not every way a teacher can help someone to see something himself, more deeply, counts as manipulation, especially when the activity is acknowledged mutually.

[…]

Philosophical Explanations

There is a second mode of philosophy, not directed to arguments and proofs: it seeks explanations. Various philosophical things need to be explained; a philosophical theory is introduced to explain them, to render them coherent and better understood.

Many philosophical problems are ones of understanding how something is or can be possible. How is it possible for us to have free will, supposing that all actions are causally determined? Randomness, also, seems no more congenial; so, how is free will (even) possible? How is it possible that we know anything, given the facts the skeptic enumerates, for example, that it is logically possible we are dreaming or floating in a tank with our brain being stimulated to give us exactly our current experiences and even all our past ones? How is it possible that motion occurs, given Zeno's arguments? How is it possible for something to be the same thing from one time to another, through change? How is it possible for subjective experiences to fit into an objective physical world? How can there be stable meanings (Plato asked), given that everything in the world is changing? How is it possible for us to have synthetic necessary knowledge? [...] The theological problem of evil also takes this form: how is evil possible, supposing the existence of an omnipotent omniscient good God? One central question of twentieth century philosophy has been: how is language possible? And let us not omit from our list: how is philosophy possible?

The form of these questions is: how is one thing possible, given (or supposing) certain other things? Some statements $r_1, ..., r_n$ are assumed or accepted or taken for granted, and there is a tension between these statements and another statement p; they appear to exclude p's holding true.

[...]

To rebut an argument for not-p from specific apparent excluders removes a reason for thinking p cannot hold, and so counts as a kind of explanation of how p can be possible. This task is unending, for as knowledge advances, or seems to, new apparent excluders come to the fore, and hence new questions arise about the possibility of p. "If we know that whenever a new apparent excluder comes along, we will try to show that p remains standing, wouldn't it be more economical simply to prove p once and for all?" This proposal misconstrues the need. A proof of p will give us the conviction that p is true, but it need not give us understanding of how p *can* be true (given the apparent excluder). Even when the argument from an apparent excluder does not lead us to deny p or to doubt its truth, it still may leave us puzzled as to how p can be true. [...] A proof that p is true, however, need not show how p is compatible with the apparent excluders, or show which apparent excluder is false – it need not mention them at all. So the task of showing how p is possible cannot be done once and for all by a proof that p. What a proof can do – show us that p is true – is not what we need, for we already believe this. Why isn't it enough to know that p is true, why do we also need to understand how it can be true? To see how p can be true (given these apparent excluders) is to see how things fit together. This philosophical understanding, finding harmony in apparent tension and incompatibility, is, I think, intrinsically valuable. Yet I would not try to bludgeon anyone into needing or wanting it.

The task of explaining how p is possible is not exhausted by the rearguard action of meeting arguments from its apparent excluders. There remains the question of what facts or principles might give rise to p. Here the philosopher searches for deeper explanatory principles, preferably with some independent plausibility, not excluded by current knowledge. To show that these principles, if true, would explain p involves deducing p from them – at least so holds the deductive-nomological view according to which each explanation deduces the fact to be explained from general laws and initial conditions. Yet still, this is no attempt to prove p; and the explanatory hypotheses used in the explanation need not be known to be true, or be believed on grounds independent of p itself.

To produce this possible explanation of p is, by seeing one way p is given rise to, to see how p can be true. "How is it possible that p? This way: such and such facts are possible and they constitute an explanatory route to p." The more true-like these explanatory hypotheses, the more we understand how p can be true. The (possible) explanation of p from them is put forward tentatively, subject to withdrawal in the face of difficulties or alternative, better explanations, perhaps using deeper principles that also would explain other things.

[...]

Does the philosopher who explains how p is possible, by putting forth potential explanations of p, differ from the scientist who puts forth and tests potential explanations of p in order to explain why p is true? I would not want to claim that philosophical explanation must be discontinuous with scientific activity. Yet typically, the philosopher's hypothesis is not testable or disconfirmable, because he puts forth only an existentially quantified statement; he says there is something or other, some process or other, that satisfies certain general structural conditions and so yields p. That there is or might be a process of that sort shows how p is possible. To specify the particular details of a process of that sort would be to engage in empirical science: differing scientific specifications each would fit the philosopher's existential statement, which holds merely that there is some or another true specification.

The epistemologist may need for his purposes only the fact that our perceptions somehow respond to presented facts so as to satisfy certain general conditions of responsiveness; to show how knowledge is possible he need only speculate on a linkage of that sort existing. To explain why our perceptions thus respond to the facts, however, is a task for the perceptual and physiological psychologists, who must specify the details of the particular mechanism whereby responsiveness is achieved, and for the evolutionary psychologist who must explain how that mechanism arose and was selected for. Still, although the philosophical and scientific activities typically differ, the philosopher's existential hypothesis may suggest detailed investigations to the scientist; conceivably the philosopher might specify the sort so completely that its existence is immediately open to empirical test.

Explanation versus Proof

Philosophical argument, trying to get someone to believe something whether he wants to believe it or not, is not, I have held, a nice way to behave toward someone; also, it does not fit the original motivation for studying or entering philosophy. That motivation is puzzlement, curiosity, a desire to understand, not a desire to produce uniformity of belief. Most people do not want to become thought-police. The philosophical goal of explanation rather than proof not only is morally better, it is more in accord with one's philosophical motivation. Also it changes how one proceeds philosophically; at the macro-level (as we already have noted), it leads away from constructing the philosophical tower; at the micro-level, it alters which philosophical "moves" are legitimate at various points.

[...]

Philosophical Pluralism

Can a philosophy begin by seeking philosophical explanation? Doesn't the desire for explanation rather than something else already presuppose philosophical views about what is intellectually desirable? And, even given the goal of explanation, won't philosophies differ in their conception of an acceptable or adequate explanation, in the conditions that they hold an explanation must meet?

[...]

I do not see how to satisfy the desire to start philosophy in a neutral way, making no philosophical assumptions, remaining neutral among all possible philosophical views. We cannot reasonably hope to settle on one philosophical view by showing it uniquely satisfies all of the apparently neutral desirable general conditions on a philosophy; many different philosophies will equally well satisfy those. Anyway, why think the goal of neutrality itself is neutral? Would every philosophy accept *it*? And when neutrality ends eventually, as we want, what selective factor will point to one philosophy rather than others, and what status − neutral or not − will *this* factor have? If a neutral beginning is chimerical, the alternative of starting just where we are seems parochial and dogmatic, especially if there are some theoretical places we can't get to from here.

We can build modes of change into a view, hoping parochialism is avoided when any theory can be reached, in principle, given suitable input. Nevertheless, some places will not be reached with specified inputs, starting from here; philosophical views will differ in what gets reached when. [...]

The treatment for philosophical parochialism, as for parochialism of other sorts, is to come to know alternatives. We can keep track of the different philosophical views that have been put forth and elaborated; we can pay attention to foreign traditions and their diverse viewpoints, to the special slant of these traditions on our questions, both the different ways they pose their most nearly equivalent question, and the different answers they offer. There even may be ways of catapulting oneself, at least temporarily, into different philosophical perspectives.

[...]

This fits my experience in studying philosophy: I confess I have found (and not only in sequence) many different philosophies alluring and appealing, cogent and impressive, tempting and wonderful. I think this says something about the subject, not about me − I am not noticeably wishy-washier than most. Treating philosophy as a black box, we might view its "output" not as a single theory, not even as one set of theories, but as a set of questions, each with its own set of associated theories as possible answers. Should we view the highest products of philosophy as the philosophical questions themselves, the theories and systems being commentary to exhibit the value of the questions? On this view, philosophy's wonders are the ones in which it begins; as important as new answers are its new questions.

I feel discomfort, though, with the aesthetic view of philosophy, the uncommitted praise of the diverse philosophical "visions". The goal is finding out the truth, after all. (Yet is that goal, or its specification, neutral among philosophies?) Recall the distinction made earlier between explaining and understanding. Embedding the world in the network of alternative philosophical theories and visions, seeing how each of these different philosophical possibilities gets a grip on the world, does produce understanding. The major philosophical theories of continuing interest are readings of possible worlds accessible from here, that is, possible readings of the actual world. We understand the world by seeing it in its matrix of possibilities, in its possibility neighborhood.

Still, this book does not aim at understanding; by and large, it aims more narrowly – at explanation, at truth. [...]

I see the situation as follows. There are various philosophical views, mutually incompatible, which cannot be dismissed or simply rejected. Philosophy's output is the basketful of these admissible views, all together. One delimiting strategy would be to modify and shave these views, capturing what is true in each, to make them compatible parts of one new view. While I know of no reason in principle why this cannot be done, neither has anyone yet done it satisfactorily. Perhaps, as knowing a subject (such as logic or physics) involves seeing the different ways it can be organized and viewed, the different ways around it, so too (only this time the views are incompatible so the analogy is imperfect) knowing the world involves seeing the different ways it can be viewed.

Are we reduced to relativism then, the doctrine that all views are equally good? No, some views can be rejected, and the admissible ones remaining will differ in merits and adequacy, though none is completely lacking. Even when one view is clearly best, though, we do not keep only this first ranked view, rejecting all the others. Our total view is the basket of philosophical views, containing all the admissible views. This total view notices which component is best, and perhaps will order the others. Yet the first ranked view is not completely adequate all by itself; what it omits or distorts or puts out of focus cannot be added compatibly, but must be brought out and highlighted by another incompatible view, itself (even more) inadequate alone.

The position is not relativism, for the views are ranked, but neither is just one view settled upon.

[...]

The view of philosophy as philosophical explanation is put forth here as a tentative hypothesis, designed to encompass much of the actual historical activity of philosophers while demarcating a legitimate and important task. Moreover, the view applies to and fits itself. In explaining how philosophy is possible, given the formidable obstacles to it as a useful mode of knowledge, the view itself is an instance of what it says philosophy should be: the explanation of how something is possible. In contrast, the view that philosophy is the theory of self-evident fundamental principles and their consequences, for example, seems neither to be self-evident nor derivable from such. No doubt, not everything in this book (and certainly not everything of value in the history of philosophy) fits the mold sketched here. Still, this view has the virtue of delineating one important direction philosophy can pursue, a direction whose nature is reasonably well understood and which does not appear beyond our capacity.

[...]

Part II

Metaphysics
Philosophical Images of Being

How Is the World at all Physical?

6

How Real Are Physical Objects?

Bertrand Russell, *The Problems of Philosophy*

In the book's first reading, from Plato's *Republic*, we met the theme of people needing not to confuse appearances of something with how it really is: a life is quite different when it includes knowledge of what is truly good, as against only what is apparently good. Of course, something's appearing to be a particular way is itself part of reality: there would *really* be an instance of its-appearing-to-you-that- …. Even so, the immediate point is that we must be careful not to confuse how something appears to be with how it really is – *if* these could be different in some particular case. We should therefore be sensitive to when this sort of confusion might realistically arise in our lives. This issue will recur – it will matter – in a few places throughout the book. Appearance versus reality: this is one of *the grand philosophical themes*.

Perhaps that theme's most famous application has long been to the question of what, exactly, it is for something to be physical. A classic statement of that

Bertrand Russell, *The Problems of Philosophy* (London: Oxford University Press, 1959 [1912]), ch. 1 (excerpt). Reprinted with permission of Oxford University Press.

question is developed in this reading from Bertrand Russell. We saw earlier how he ended his classic book *The Problems of Philosophy*, imparting his image of philosophy's nature and value: philosophy welcomes questioning and possibilities; it should eschew demands for certainty. What we now have is the way in which Russell began that book's journey. Consider whatever appears commonsensical. Then begin questioning, opening our minds to possibilities which might otherwise remain unnoticed. This excerpt from Russell's book highlights how readily, by reflecting initially upon the ways in which we apparently interact with physical objects, we may well question whether these objects *are* really what we are interacting with directly. Might our direct interactions only be with how an object *appears* to our senses? If these are our direct interactions, could it be that we are never really interacting at all with any object *itself* beyond these appearances we are experiencing – how it is seen, heard, etc.? Might it even be that the object *is* nothing beyond those appearances? They would not be appearances "of" it – in the sense of being appearances of a genuine "it" existing beyond them.

Russell was presenting that question early in the twentieth century. Our next two readings – from John Locke and from George Berkeley – will show us some of the philosophical history that had earlier posed and sharpened Russell's question. It is a fundamental question about the nature of the physical world, the nature of matter. It is a question that has been asked in different centuries. It is still with us.

Appearance and Reality

Is there any knowledge in the world which is so certain that no reasonable man could doubt it? This question, which at first sight might not seem difficult, is really one of the most difficult that can be asked. When we have realized the obstacles in the way of a straightforward and confident answer, we shall be well launched on the study of philosophy – for philosophy is merely the attempt to answer such ultimate questions, not carelessly and dogmatically, as we do in ordinary life and even in the sciences, but critically, after exploring all that makes such questions puzzling, and after realizing all the vagueness and confusion that underlie our ordinary ideas.

In daily life, we assume as certain many things which, on a closer scrutiny, are found to be so full of apparent contradictions that only a great amount of thought enables us to know what it is that we really may believe. In the search for certainty, it is natural to begin with our present experiences, and in some sense, no doubt, knowledge is to be derived from them. But any statement as to what it is that our immediate experiences make us know is very likely to be wrong. It seems to me that I am now sitting in a chair, at a table of a certain shape, on which I see sheets of paper with writing or print. By turning my head I see out of the window buildings and clouds and the sun. I believe that the sun is about ninety-three million miles from the earth; that it is a hot globe many times bigger than the earth; that, owing to the earth's rotation, it rises every morning, and will continue to do so for an indefinite time in the future. I believe that, if any other normal person comes into my room, he will see the same chairs and tables and books and papers as I see, and that the table which I see is the same as the table which I feel pressing against my arm. All this seems to be so evident as to be hardly worth stating, except in answer to a man who doubts whether I know anything. Yet all this may be reasonably doubted, and all of it requires much careful discussion before we can be sure that we have stated it in a form that is wholly true.

To make our difficulties plain, let us concentrate attention on the table. To the eye it is oblong, brown and shiny, to the touch it is smooth and cool and hard; when I tap it, it gives out a wooden sound. Any one else who sees and feels and hears the table will agree with this description, so that it might seem as if no difficulty would arise; but as soon as we try to be more precise our troubles begin. Although I believe that the table is 'really' of the same colour all over, the parts that reflect the light look much brighter than the other parts, and some parts look white because of reflected light. I know that, if I move, the parts that reflect the light will be different, so that the apparent distribution of colours on the table will change. It follows that if several people are looking at the table at the same moment, no two of them will see exactly the same distribution of colours, because no two can see it from exactly the same point of view, and any change in the point of view makes some change in the way the light is reflected.

For most practical purposes these differences are unimportant, but to the painter they are all-important: the painter has to unlearn the habit of thinking that things seem to have the colour which common sense says they 'really' have, and to learn the habit of seeing things as they appear. Here we have already the beginning of one of the distinctions that cause most trouble in philosophy – the distinction between 'appearance' and 'reality', between what things seem to be and what they are. The painter wants to know what things seem to be, the practical man and the philosopher want to know what they are; but the philosopher's wish to know this is stronger than the practical man's, and is more troubled by knowledge as to the difficulties of answering the question.

To return to the table. It is evident from what we have found, that there is no colour which preeminently appears to be *the* colour of the table, or even of any one particular part of the table – it appears to be of different colours from different points of view, and there is no reason for regarding some of these as more really its colour than others. And we know that even from a given point of view the colour will seem different by artificial light, or to a colour-blind man, or to a man wearing blue spectacles, while in the dark there will be no colour at all, though to touch and hearing the table will be unchanged. This colour is not something which is inherent in the table, but something depending upon the table and the spectator and the way the light falls on the table. When, in ordinary life, we speak of *the* colour of the table, we only mean the sort of colour which it will seem to have to a normal spectator from an ordinary point of view under usual conditions of light. But the other colours which appear under other conditions have just as good a right to be considered real; and therefore, to avoid favouritism, we are compelled to deny that, in itself, the table has any one particular colour.

The same thing applies to the texture. With the naked eye one can see the grain, but otherwise the table looks smooth and even. If we looked at it through a microscope, we should see roughnesses and hills and valleys, and all sorts of differences that are imperceptible to the naked eye. Which of these is the 'real' table? We are naturally tempted to say that what we see through the microscope is more real, but that in turn would be changed by a still more powerful microscope. If, then, we cannot trust what we see with the naked eye, why should we trust what we see through a microscope? Thus, again, the confidence in our senses with which we began deserts us.

The *shape* of the table is no better. We are all in the habit of judging as to the 'real' shapes of things, and we do this so unreflectingly that we come to think we actually see the real shapes. But, in fact, as we all have to learn if we try to draw, a given thing looks different in shape from every different point of view. If our table is 'really' rectangular, it will look, from almost all points of view, as if it had two acute angles and two obtuse angles. If opposite sides are parallel, they will look as if they converged to a point away from the spectator; if they are of equal length, they will look as if the nearer side were longer. All these things are not commonly noticed in looking at a table, because experience has taught us to construct the 'real' shape from the apparent shape, and the 'real' shape is what interests us as practical men. But the 'real' shape is not what we see; it is something inferred from what we see. And what we see is constantly changing in shape as we move about the room; so that here again the senses seem not to give us the truth about the table itself, but only about the appearance of the table.

Similar difficulties arise when we consider the sense of touch. It is true that the table always gives us a sensation of hardness, and we feel that it resists pressure. But the sensation we obtain depends upon how hard we press the table and also upon what part of the body we press with; thus the various sensations due to various pressures or various parts of the body cannot be supposed to reveal *directly* any definite property of the table, but at most to be *signs* of some property which perhaps *causes* all the sensations, but is not actually apparent in any of them. And the same applies still more obviously to the sounds which can be elicited by rapping the table.

Thus it becomes evident that the real table, if there is one, is not the same as what we immediately experience by sight or touch or hearing. The real table, if there is one, is not *immediately* known to us at all, but must be an inference from what is immediately known. Hence, two very difficult questions at once arise; namely, (1) Is there a real table at all? (2) If so, what sort of object can it be?

It will help us in considering these questions to have a few simple terms of which the meaning is definite and clear. Let us give the name of 'sense-data' to the things that are immediately known in sensation: such things as colours, sounds, smells, hardnesses, roughnesses, and so on. We shall give the name 'sensation' to the experience of being immediately aware of these things. Thus, whenever we see a colour, we have a sensation *of* the colour, but the colour itself is a sense-datum, not a sensation. The colour is that *of* which we are immediately aware, and the awareness itself is the sensation. It is plain that if we are to know anything about the table, it must be by means of the sense-data − brown colour, oblong shape, smoothness, etc. − which we associate with the table; but, for the reasons which have been given, we cannot say that the table *is* the sense-data, or even that the sense-data are directly properties of the table. Thus a problem arises as to the relation of the sense-data to the real table, supposing there is such a thing.

The real table, if it exists, we will call a 'physical object'. Thus we have to consider the relation of sense-data to physical objects. The collection of all physical objects is called 'matter'. Thus our two questions may be re-stated as follows: (1) Is there any such thing as matter? (2) If so, what is its nature?

7

Are Physical Objects Never Quite as They Appear To Be?

John Locke, *An Essay Concerning Human Understanding*

Part I's reading from Wilfrid Sellars distinguished the manifest image from the scientific image. We then asked whether the *philosophical* image, while remaining distinct, could profit from building upon these – particularly upon the scientific image. This seems to have occurred in the philosophical use, made by the English philosopher John Locke's (1632–1704) *Essay Concerning Human Understanding* (1690), of the distinction between *primary* qualities and *secondary* qualities.

Those terms were his, although others before him (including Galileo, Robert Boyle, and perhaps even the ancient Greek philosophers Democritus and Epicurus) had described what amounted to the same distinction. The distinction was part of the physics of the day. But Locke's use of it was philosophical, as he possibly was arguing for it in a conceptual way. He was reflecting – in a way not unlike that described in Part I's reading from Strawson – upon what is, and what is not, *conceivable* about physical objects. The result was a metaphysical image, portraying part of *what it is* to be a physical object. Roughly (argued Locke), there is a metaphysical core or essence to the nature of any physical object. That core is a complex of the object's primary qualities. These are such properties as solidity, shape, spatial dimensionality, and movement. Maybe the object as a whole has these; at least its smallest constitutive elements do so. And *by* having them (however it does), the object thereby has various powers. These are powers to cause us and other perceivers to see, hear, feel, taste, and smell the object – to have sensory impressions of it. Those powers are the object's secondary qualities.

John Locke, *An Essay Concerning Human Understanding* (1690), Book II, ch. VIII, sects. 8–17, 22–25. Reprinted with permission of Oxford University Press.

Metaphysics and Epistemology: A Guided Anthology, First Edition. Edited by Stephen Hetherington.
© 2014 John Wiley & Sons, Inc. Published 2014 by John Wiley & Sons, Inc.

Potentially, all of that is extremely significant for our philosophical image of the world. After all, it leads to the idea that these impressions are not showing us directly how the object is in itself. A ball is not red in itself, say, by having a quality precisely *resembling* the redness we are experiencing when looking at it. The ball's redness is a *power* to cause us to see it as red in the way we do; and the power is not *itself* what we see, in seeing the ball's redness in the way we do. Thus, any object is partly – but systematically – *not* in itself as it *appears* to us to be. No matter how red the ball looks to be, in itself it is not red in that way, the way in which it looks red to us. That is so, even though the ball's being red *looks* in that way to be as much a real part of the world "out there" – as much a part of the ball in itself – as does the ball's shape, for example.

This would be a striking conclusion about the physical world. For that is the world with which we most manifestly interact. Yet it is also (we now find) a world from which science – as interpreted philosophically – threatens to detach or even to divorce us. The result would be that we live our sensory lives in the grip of an inescapable form of illusion. This could be disturbing.

§ 8.   Whatsoever the Mind perceives in it self, or is the immediate object of Perception, Thought, or Understanding, that I call *Idea*; and the Power to produce any *Idea* in our mind, I call *Quality* of the Subject wherein that power is. Thus a Snow-ball having the power to produce in us the *Ideas* of *White*, *Cold*, and *Round*, the Powers to produce those *Ideas* in us, as they are in the Snow-ball, I call *Qualities*; and as they are Sensations, or Perceptions, in our Understandings, I call them *Ideas*: which *Ideas*, if I speak of sometimes, as in the things them-selves, I would be understood to mean those Qualities in the Objects which produce them in us.

§ 9.   Qualities thus considered in Bodies are, First such as are utterly inseparable from the Body, in what estate soever it be; such as in all the alterations and changes it suffers, all the force can be used upon it, it constantly keeps; and such as Sense constantly finds in every particle of Matter, which has bulk enough to be perceived, and the Mind finds inseparable from every particle of Matter, though less than to make it self singly be perceived by our Senses. *v.g.* Take a grain of Wheat, divide it into two parts, each part has still *Solidity*, *Extension*, *Figure*, and *Mobility*; divide it again, and it retains still the same qualities; and so divide it on, till the parts become insensible, they must retain still each of them all those qualities. For division (which is all that a Mill, or Pestel, or any other Body, does upon another, in reducing it to insensible parts) can never take away either Solidity, Extension, Figure, or Mobility from any Body, but only makes two, or more distinct separate masses of Matter, of that which was but one before, all which distinct masses, reckon'd as so many distinct Bodies, after division make a certain Number. These I call *original* or *primary Qualities* of Body, which I think we may observe to produce simple *Ideas* in us, *viz*. Solidity, Extension, Figure, Motion, or Rest, and Number.

§ 10.   2*dly*, Such *Qualities*, which in truth are nothing in the Objects themselves, but Powers to produce various Sensations in us by their *primary Qualities*, *i.e.* by the Bulk, Figure,

Texture, and Motion of their insensible parts, as Colours, Sounds, Tasts, *etc.* These I call *secondary Qualities*. To these might be added a third sort which are allowed to be barely Powers though they are as much real Qualities in the Subject, as those which I to comply with the common way of speaking call *Qualities*, but for distinction *secondary Qualities*. For the power in Fire to produce a new Colour, or consistency in Wax or Clay by its primary Qualities, is as much a quality in Fire, as the power it has to produce in me a new *Idea* or Sensation of warmth or burning, which I felt not before, by the same primary Qualities, *viz.* The Bulk, Texture, and Motion of its insensible parts.

§ 11.   The next thing to be consider'd, is how *Bodies* produce *Ideas* in us, and that is manifestly *by impulse*, the only way which we can conceive Bodies operate in.

§ 12.   If then external Objects be not united to our Minds, when they produce *Ideas* in it; and yet we perceive *these original Qualities* in such of them as singly fall under our Senses, 'tis evident, that some motion must be thence continued by our Nerves, or animal Spirits, by some parts of our Bodies, to the Brains or the seat of Sensation, there to *produce in our Minds the particular* Ideas *we have of them*. And since the Extension, Figure, Number, and Motion of Bodies of an observable bigness, may be perceived at a distance *by* the sight, 'tis evident some singly imperceptible Bodies must come from them to the Eyes, and thereby convey to the Brain some *Motion*, which produces these *Ideas*, which we have of them in us.

§ 13.   After the same manner, that the *Ideas* of these original Qualities are produced in us, we may conceive, that the *Ideas of secondary Qualities* are also *produced*, viz. *by the operation of insensible particles on our Senses*. For it being manifest, that there are Bodies, and good store of Bodies, each whereof is so small, that we cannot, by any of our Senses, discover either their bulk, figure, or motion, as is evident in the Particles of the Air and Water, and other extremely smaller than those, perhaps, as much smaller than the Particles of Air, or Water, as the Particles of Air or Water, are smaller than Pease or Hail-stones. Let us suppose at present, that the different Motions and Figures, Bulk, and Number of such Particles, affecting the several Organs of our Senses, produce in us those different Sensations, which we have from the Colours and Smells of Bodies, *v.g.* that a Violet, by the impulse of such insensible particles of matter of peculiar figures, and bulks, and in different degrees and modifications of their Motions, causes the *Ideas* of the blue Colour, and sweet Scent of that Flower to be produced in our Minds. It being no more impossible, to conceive, that God should annex such *Ideas* to such Motions, with which they have no similitude; than that he should annex the *Idea* of Pain to the motion of a piece of Steel dividing our Flesh, with which that *Idea* hath no resemblance.

§ 14.   What I have said concerning *Colours* and *Smells*, may be understood also of *Tastes* and *Sounds, and other the like sensible Qualities*; which, whatever reality we, by mistake, attribute to them, are in truth nothing in the Objects themselves, but Powers to produce various Sensations in us, and *depend on those primary Qualities, viz.* Bulk, Figure, Texture, and Motion of parts; as I have said.

§ 15.   From whence I think it is easie to draw this Observation, That the *Ideas of primary Qualities* of Bodies, *are Resemblances* of them, and their Patterns do really exist in the Bodies themselves; but the *Ideas, produced* in us *by* these *Secondary Qualities, have no resemblance* of them at all. There is nothing like our *Ideas*, existing in the Bodies themselves. They are in the

Bodies, we denominate from them, only a Power to produce those Sensations in us: And what is Sweet, Blue, or Warm in *Idea*, is but the certain Bulk, Figure, and Motion of the insensible Parts in the Bodies themselves, which we call so.

§ 16.   *Flame* is denominated *Hot* and *Light*; *Snow White* and *Cold*; and *Manna White* and *Sweet*, from the *Ideas* they produce in us. Which Qualities are commonly thought to be the same in those Bodies, that those *Ideas* are in us, the one the perfect resemblance of the other, as they are in a Mirror; and it would by most Men be judged very extravagant, if one should say otherwise. And yet he, that will consider, that *the same Fire*, that at one distance *produces* in us the Sensation of *Warmth*, does at a nearer approach, produce in us the far different Sensation of *Pain*, ought to bethink himself, what Reason he has to say, That his *Idea* of *Warmth*, which was produced in him by the Fire, is actually *in the Fire*; and his *Idea* of *Pain*, which the same Fire produced in him the same way, is *not* in the *Fire*. Why is Whiteness and Coldness in Snow, and Pain not, when it produces the one and the other *Idea* in us; and can do neither, but by the Bulk, Figure, Number, and Motion of its solid Parts?

§ 17.   The particular *Bulk, Number, Figure, and Motion of the parts of Fire, or Snow, are really in them*, whether any ones Senses perceive them or no: and therefore they may be called *real Qualities*, because they really exist in those Bodies. But *Light, Heat, Whiteness*, or *Coldness, are no more really in them, than Sickness or Pain is in* Manna. Take away the Sensation of them; let not the Eyes see Light, or Colours, nor the Ears hear Sounds; let the Palate not Taste, nor the Nose Smell, and all Colours, Tastes, Odors, and Sounds, as they are such particular *Ideas*, vanish and cease, and are reduced to their Causes, *i.e.* Bulk, Figure, and Motion of Parts.

[...]

§ 22.   I have in what just goes before, been engaged in Physical Enquiries a little farther than, perhaps, I intended. But it being necessary, to make the Nature of Sensation a little understood, and to make the *difference between the Qualities in Bodies, and the* Ideas *produced by them in the Mind*, to be distinctly conceived, without which it were impossible to discourse intelligibly of them; I hope, I shall be pardoned this little Excursion into Natural Philosophy, it being necessary in our present Enquiry, to distinguish the *primary*, and *real* Qualities of Bodies, which are always in them, (*viz.* Solidity, Extension, Figure, Number, and Motion, or Rest; and are sometimes perceived by us, *viz.* when the Bodies they are in, are big enough singly to be discerned) from those *secondary* and *imputed* Qualities, which are but the Powers of several Combinations of those primary ones, when they operate, without being distinctly discerned; whereby we also may come to know what *Ideas* are, and what are not Resemblances of something really existing in the Bodies, we denominate from them.

§ 23.   The *Qualities* then that are in *Bodies* rightly considered, are of *Three sorts*.

First, The *Bulk, Figure, Number, Situation*, and *Motion, or Rest* of their solid Parts; those are in them, whether we perceive them or no; and when they are of that size, that we can discover them, we have by these an *Idea* of the thing, as it is in it self, as is plain in artificial things. These I call *primary Qualities*.

Secondly, The *Power* that is in any Body, *by* Reason of *its* insensible *primary Qualities*, to operate after a peculiar manner on any of our Senses, and thereby *produce in us* the *different Ideas* of several Colours, Sounds, Smells, Tasts, *etc.* These are usually called sensible Qualities.

Thirdly, The *Power* that is in any Body, *by* Reason of the particular Constitution of *its primary Qualities, to* make such a *change* in the *Bulk, Figure, Texture, and Motion of another Body*, as to make it operate on our Senses, differently from what it did before. Thus the Sun has a Power to make Wax white, and Fire to make Lead fluid. These are usually called Powers.

The First of these, as has been said, I think, may be properly called *real Original*, or *primary Qualities*, because they are in the things themselves, whether they are perceived or no: and upon their different Modifications it is, that the secondary Qualities depend.

The other two, are only Powers to act differently upon other things, which Powers result from the different Modifications of those primary Qualities.

§ 24.   But though *these two later sorts of Qualities are Powers barely*, and nothing but Powers, relating to several other Bodies, and resulting from the different Modifications of the Original Qualities; yet they are generally otherwise thought of. For *the Second sort, viz.* The Powers to produce several *Ideas* in us by our Senses, *are looked upon as real Qualities, in the things* thus affecting us: But *the Third sort are call'd, and esteemed barely Powers. v.g.* the Idea of Heat, or Light, which we receive by our Eyes, or touch from the Sun, are commonly thought *real Qualities*, existing in the Sun, and something more than mere Powers in it. But when we consider the Sun, in reference to Wax, which it melts or blanches, we look upon the Whiteness and Softness produced in the Wax, not as Qualities in the Sun, but Effects produced by *Powers* in it: Whereas, if rightly considered, these Qualities of Light and Warmth, which are Perceptions in me when I am warmed, or enlightned by the Sun, are no other-wise in the Sun, than the changes made in the Wax, when it is blanched or melted, are in the Sun. They are all of them equally Powers in the Sun, depending on its primary Qualities; whereby it is able in the one case, so to alter the Bulk, Figure, Texture, or Motion of some of the insensible parts of my Eyes, or Hands, as thereby to produce in me the *Idea* of Light or Heat; and in the other, it is able so to alter the Bulk, Figure, Texture, or Motion of the insensible Parts of the Wax, as to make them fit to produce in me the distinct *Ideas* of White and Fluid.

§ 25.   The Reason, *Why the one are ordinarily taken for real Qualities, and the other only for bare Powers*, seems to be, because the *Ideas* we have of distinct Colours, Sounds, *etc.* containing nothing at all in them, of Bulk, Figure, or Motion, we are not apt to think them the Effects of these primary Qualities, which appear not to our Senses to operate in their Production; and with which, they have not any apparent Congruity, or conceivable Connexion. Hence it is, that we are so forward to imagine, that those *Ideas* are the resemblances of something really existing in the Objects themselves: Since Sensation discovers nothing of Bulk, Figure, or Motion of parts in their Production; nor can Reason shew, how Bodies by their Bulk, Figure, and Motion, should produce in the Mind the *Ideas* of Blue, or Yellow, *etc.* But in the other Case, in the Operations of Bodies, changing the Qualities one of another, we plainly discover, that the Quality produced, hath commonly no resemblance with any thing in the thing producing it; wherefore we look on it as a bare Effect of Power. For though receiving the *Idea* of Heat, or Light, from the Sun, we are apt to think, 'tis a Perception and Resemblance of such a Quality in the Sun: yet when we see Wax, or a fair Face, receive change of Colour from the Sun, we cannot imagine, that to be the Reception or Resemblance of any thing in the Sun, because we find not those different Colours in the Sun it self. For our Senses, being able to observe a likeness, or unlikeness of sensible Qualities in two different external Objects, we forwardly enough conclude the Production of any sensible Quality in any Subject, to be an Effect of bare Power, and not the Communication of any Quality, which was really in the efficient, when we find no such sensible Quality in the thing that produced it. But our Senses, not being able to discover any unlikeness between the *Idea* produced in us, and the Quality of the Object producing it, we are apt to imagine, that our *Ideas* are resemblances of something in the Objects, and not the Effects of certain Powers, placed in the Modification of their primary Qualities, with which primary Qualities the *Ideas* produced in us have no resemblance.

8

Are Physical Objects Really Only Objects of Thought?

George Berkeley, *The Principles of Human Knowledge*

Let us remind ourselves why we could find disconcerting the image of physical reality that John Locke described in the previous reading. A ball's redness *seems* as much a part of a solid and independently constituted physical object – a world "out there," separate from our subjective sensing – as does the ball's solidity. Yet Locke, we saw, distinguishes fundamentally in that respect between those two qualities of the ball: the solidity in the ball resembles the solidity we feel when handling the ball; the redness in the ball does not resemble what we see when we look at it. Can this be avoided by our interpreting differently the nature of the physical object?

The Irish philosopher George Berkeley (1685–1753) certainly believed so. Consider the ball's solidity and its redness. Neither of these (argued Berkeley) is – in its own nature as the quality it is – genuinely independent of how it is sensed. Locke thought of an object's primary qualities as able to be part of the object even if never sensed or perceived; and he regarded secondary qualities in the same way, as powers able to be dormant when no one is sensing the object. In contrast, Berkeley treated all of those qualities – primary ones, secondary ones – as existing only *as* sensed. For Locke, there is a nature to all physical reality, a nature *beyond* how that reality appears qualitatively; for Berkeley, there is not. Even a primary quality, on Berkeley's interpretation, is only a *sensed* quality. And a secondary quality is not a somewhat hidden power; it is also only a sensed quality. In other words, for Berkeley there is *nothing* to the ball beyond various qualities being perceived. That is what the ball *is*. This is what a physical object is – always, for any physical object.

George Berkeley, *The Principles of Human Knowledge* (1710), sects. 1–3, 5–10, 15–20 (excerpts).

Metaphysics and Epistemology: A Guided Anthology, First Edition. Edited by Stephen Hetherington.
© 2014 John Wiley & Sons, Inc. Published 2014 by John Wiley & Sons, Inc.

Now *that* is a bold metaphysical image: in a rough sense, all *is* image, it implies. Yet Berkeley took this view – an *idealism* (as in: 'idea-lism', not 'ideal-ism') – about the physical world not to be odd or merely academic. It is a *commonsense* view, he believed: when a person thinks of an object, of course she thinks of its qualities; and of course these are thereby conceived of as at least *able* to be sensed. Locke had talked of each object as including an underlying *substance* unobservably supporting the qualities. Berkeley dismissed such talk as senseless.

Also intriguing is the fact that, for Berkeley, this idealist philosophical image was part of his *theism* – his belief in God's existence. (He was a bishop, not only a philosopher.) How is a physical object still existing when no one is sensing it? It does so, courtesy of *God's* having it in mind: He is observing it. This is an elegantly philosophical image of God's literally sustaining the world's existence. It is also a way of including increased *objectivity* within this image: the world's nature is a matter, ultimately, of how God perceives it. (Very soon, we will discuss questions of truth and facts – this form of objectivity.)

1. It is evident to anyone who takes a survey of the objects of human knowledge, that they are either *ideas* actually imprinted on the senses; or else such as are perceived by attending to the passions and operations of the mind; or lastly, *ideas* formed by help of memory and imagination – either compounding, dividing, or barely representing those originally perceived in the aforesaid ways. – By sight I have the ideas of light and colours, with their several degrees and variations. By touch I perceive hard and soft, heat and cold, motion and resistance, and of all these more and less either as to quantity or degree. Smelling furnishes me with odours; the palate with tastes; and hearing conveys sounds to the mind in all their variety of tone and composition. – And as several of these are observed to accompany each other, they come to be marked by one name, and so to be reputed as one THING. Thus, for example, a certain colour, taste, smell, figure and consistence having been observed to go together, are accounted one distinct thing, signified by the name *apple*; other collections of ideas constitute a stone, a tree, a book, and the like sensible things – which as they are pleasing or disagreeable excite the passions of love, hatred, joy, grief, and so forth.

2. But, besides all that endless variety of ideas or objects of knowledge, there is likewise something which knows or perceives them; and exercises divers operations, as willing, imagining, remembering, about them. This perceiving, active being is what I call MIND, SPIRIT, SOUL, or MYSELF. By which words I do not denote any one of my ideas, but a thing entirely distinct from them, wherein they exist, or, which is the same thing, whereby they are perceived – for the existence of an idea consists in being perceived.

3. That neither our thoughts, nor passions, nor ideas formed by the imagination, exist without the mind, is what everybody will allow. – And to me it is no less evident that the various SENSATIONS, or *ideas imprinted on the sense*, however blended or combined together (that is, whatever *objects* they compose), cannot exist otherwise than in a mind perceiving

them – I think an intuitive knowledge may be obtained of this by anyone that shall attend to *what is meant by the term exist when applied to sensible things.* The table I write on I say exists, that is, I see and feel it; and if I were out of my study I should say it existed – meaning thereby that if I was in my study I might perceive it, or that some other spirit actually does perceive it. There was an odour, that is, it was smelt; there was a sound, that is, it was heard; a colour or figure, and it was perceived by sight or touch. This is all that I can understand by these and the like expressions. – For as to what is said of the absolute existence of unthinking things without any relation to their being perceived, that is to me perfectly unintelligible. Their *esse* is *percipi*, nor is it possible they should have any existence out of the minds or thinking things which perceive them.

[…]

5. […] [C]an there be a nicer strain of abstraction than to distinguish the *existence* of sensible objects from their *being perceived*, so as to conceive them existing unperceived? Light and colours, heat and cold, extension and figures – in a word the things we see and feel – what are they but so many sensations, notions, ideas, or impressions on the sense? and is it possible to separate, even in thought, any of these from perception? For my part, I might as easily divide a thing from itself. […] [M]y conceiving or imagining power does not extend beyond the possibility of real existence or perception. Hence, as it is impossible for me to see or feel anything without an actual sensation of that thing, so is it impossible for me to conceive in my thoughts any sensible thing or object distinct from the sensation or perception of it.

6. Some truths there are so near and obvious to the mind that a man need only open his eyes to see them. Such I take this important one to be, viz. that all the choir of heaven and furniture of the earth, in a word all those bodies which compose the mighty frame of the world, have not any subsistence without a mind – that their *being* is *to be perceived or known*; that consequently so long as they are not actually perceived by me, or do not exist in my mind or that of any other created spirit, they must either have no existence at all, or else subsist in the mind of some Eternal Spirit – it being perfectly unintelligible, and involving all the absurdity of abstraction, to attribute to any single part of them an existence independent of a spirit. To be convinced of which, the reader need only reflect, and try to separate in his own thoughts the *being* of a sensible thing from its *being perceived*.

7. From what has been said it is evident there is not any other Substance than SPIRIT, or *that which perceives*. But, for the fuller demonstration of this point, let it be considered the sensible qualities are colour, figure, motion, smell, taste, &c. *i.e.* the ideas perceived by sense. Now, for an idea to exist in an unperceiving thing is a manifest contradiction; for to have an idea is all one as to perceive; that therefore wherein colour, figure, &c. exist must perceive them; hence it is clear there can be no unthinking substance or *substratum* of those ideas.

8. But, say you, though the ideas themselves do not exist without the mind, yet there may be things like them, whereof they are copies or resemblances, which things exist without the mind in an unthinking substance. I answer, an idea can be like nothing but an idea; a colour or figure can be like nothing but another colour or figure. If we look but never so little into our own thoughts, we shall find it impossible for us to conceive a likeness except only between our ideas. Again, I ask whether those supposed originals or external things, of which our ideas are the pictures or representations, be themselves perceivable or no? If they are, then they are ideas and we have gained our point; but if you say they are not, I appeal to

anyone whether it be sense to assert a colour is like something which is invisible; hard or soft, like something which is intangible; and so of the rest.

9. Some there are who make a distinction betwixt *primary* and *secondary* qualities.[1] By the former they mean extension, figure, motion, rest, solidity, impenetrability, and number; by the latter they denote all other sensible qualities, as colours, sounds, tastes, and so forth. The ideas we have of these last they acknowledge not to be the resemblances of anything existing without the mind, or unperceived, but they will have our ideas of the primary qualities to be patterns or images of things which exist without the mind, in an unthinking substance which they call Matter. – By Matter, therefore, we are to understand *an inert, senseless substance, in which extension, figure and motion do actually subsist*. But it is evident, from what we have already shewn, that extension, figure, and motion are only ideas existing in the mind, and that an idea can be like nothing but another idea, and that consequently neither they nor their archetypes can exist in an unperceiving substance. Hence, it is plain that the very notion of what is called *Matter* or *corporeal substance* involves a contradiction in it.

10. They who assert that figure, motion, and the rest of the primary or original qualities do exist without the mind, in unthinking substances, do at the same time acknowledge that colours, sounds, heat, cold, and suchlike secondary qualities, do not – which they tell us are sensations existing in the mind alone, that depend on and are occasioned by the different size texture, and motion of the minute particles of matter. This they take for an undoubted truth, which they can demonstrate beyond all exception. Now, if it be certain that those original qualities are inseparably united with the other sensible qualities, and not, even in thought, capable of being abstracted from them, it plainly follows that they exist only in the mind. But I desire any one to reflect and try whether he can, by any abstraction of thought, conceive the extension and motion of a body without all other sensible qualities. For my own part, I see evidently that it is not in my power to frame an idea of a body extended and moving, but I must withal give it some colour or other sensible quality which is acknowledged to exist only in the mind. In short, extension, figure, and motion, abstracted from all other qualities, are inconceivable. Where therefore the other sensible qualities are, there must these be also, to wit, in the mind and no where else.

[...]

15. In short, let anyone consider those arguments which are thought manifestly to prove that colours and tastes exist *only* in the mind, and he shall find they may with equal force be brought to prove the same thing of extension, figure, and motion. – Though it must be con fessed this method or arguing does not so much prove that there is no extension of colour in an outward object, as that *we* do not know by *sense* which is the *true* extension or colour of the object. But the arguments foregoing plainly shew it to be impossible that any colour or extension at all, or other sensible quality whatsoever, should exist in an unthinking subject without the mind, or in truth, that there should be any such thing as an outward object.

16. But let us examine a little the received opinion. – It is said extension is a mode or accident of Matter, and that Matter is the *substratum* that supports it. Now I desire that you would explain to me what is meant by Matter's *supporting* extension. Say you, I have no idea of Matter and therefore cannot explain it. I answer, though you have no positive, yet, if you have any meaning at all, you must at least have a relative idea of Matter; though you know not what it is, yet you must be supposed to know what relation it bears to accidents, and

what is meant by its supporting them. It is evident "support" cannot here be taken in its usual or literal sense – as when we say that pillars support a building; in what sense therefore must it be taken?

17. If we inquire into what the most accurate philosophers declare themselves to mean by *material substance*, we shall find them acknowledge they have no other meaning annexed to those sounds but the idea of *being in general*, together with the relative notion of its *supporting accidents*. The general idea of Being appeareth to me the most abstract and incomprehensible of all other; and as for its supporting accidents, this, as we have just now observed, cannot be understood in the common sense of those words; it must therefore be taken in some other sense, but what that is they do not explain. [...]

18. But, though it were possible that solid, figured, moveable *substances* may exist without the mind, corresponding to the ideas we have of bodies, yet how is it possible for us to know this? Either we must know it by Sense or by Reason. – As for our senses, by them we have the knowledge only of our sensations, ideas, or those things that are immediately perceived by sense, call them what you will : but they do not inform us that things exist without the mind, or unperceived, like to those which are perceived. This the Materialists themselves acknowledge. – It remains therefore that if we have any knowledge at all of external things, it must be by Reason inferring their existence from what is immediately perceived by sense. But what reason can induce us to believe the existence of bodies without the mind, from what we perceive, since the very patrons of Matter themselves do not pretend there is any *necessary* connexion betwixt them and our ideas? I say it is granted on all hands – and what happens in dreams, frenzies, and the like, puts it beyond dispute – that it is possible we might be affected with all the ideas we have now, though there were no bodies existing without resembling them. Hence, it is evident the supposition of external bodies is not necessary for the producing our ideas; since it is granted they are produced sometimes, and might possibly be produced always in the same order we see them in at present, without their concurrence.

19. But, though we might possibly have all our sensations without them, yet perhaps it may be thought easier to conceive and explain the manner of their production, by supposing external bodies in their likeness rather than otherwise; and so it might be at least probable there are such things as bodies that excite their ideas in our minds. But neither can this be said; for, though we give the materialists their external bodies, they by their own confession are never the nearer knowing *how* our ideas are produced; since they own themselves unable to comprehend in what manner body can act upon spirit, or how it is possible it should imprint any idea in the mind. Hence it is evident the production of ideas or sensations in our minds can be no reason why we should suppose Matter or corporeal substances, since *that* is acknowledged to remain equally inexplicable with or without this supposition. If therefore it were possible for bodies to exist without the mind, yet to hold they do so must needs be a very precarious opinion; since it is to suppose, without any reason at all, that God has created innumerable beings that are entirely useless, and serve to no manner of purpose.

20. In short, if there were external bodies, it is impossible we should ever come to know it; and if there were not, we might have the very same reasons to think there were that we have now. Suppose – what no one can deny possible – an intelligence *without the help of external bodies*, to be affected with the same train of sensations or ideas that you are, imprinted

in the same order and with like vividness in his mind. I ask whether that intelligence hath not all the reason to believe the existence of corporeal substances, represented by his ideas, and exciting them in his mind, that you can possibly have for believing the same thing? Of this there can be no question – which one consideration were enough to make any reasonable person suspect the strength of whatever arguments he may think himself to have, for the existence of bodies without the mind.

Note

1. Locke: See *Essay*, b. II, ch. 8.

9

Is Even the Mind Physical?

D.M. Armstrong, "The Causal Theory of the Mind"

Berkeley issued a challenge, in effect, to any would-be philosophical *materialist* – someone who regards all of reality as physical, as composed entirely of physical matter. D.M. Armstrong – an Australian philosopher (b. 1926) whose prominent career was mainly at the University of Sydney – is one such philosopher. First known for his writings on perception and Berkeley, in the 1960s he developed an influential materialist conception of the nature of mind – of what mentality *is*. In this reading, Armstrong sketches his materialist strategy for conceiving of mental states. It is not claimed to be a complete theory; it is intended to be supplemented by science. But the aim is to do enough philosophy to allow the finished image to be scientific where it should be – and thus to be correct.

How does this relate to Berkeley's approach? If Armstrong's strategy succeeds, it would not automatically show that Berkeley was mistaken in thinking of physical objects as objects only of perception (as against objects able to exist independently of being perceived). Still, Armstrong would have shown that even *if* that Berkeleian image was true of physical objects, the world would not thereby be composed fundamentally of something *non*-physical – non-physical mental experiences and states, and accompanying non-physical minds. His goal is a scientifically informed *physicalism* about the world's nature – a materialist metaphysics.

Armstrong explains how we could achieve this, by applying the concept of *causality*: can we understand mental states in causal terms? Beliefs, purposes, perceptions, etc.: each of these significant manifestations of mind would be causal in its essential nature. Each would be something that tends to arise as an effect, and/

D.M. Armstrong, "The Causal Theory of the Mind" (excerpts), in *The Nature of Mind and Other Essays* (St. Lucia, Queensland: University of Queensland Press, 1980). Reprinted with permission of the publisher.

or something that tends to cause other effects. For example, a purpose will tend to cause appropriate behavior ("He is running because he wants to be fit"); and a purpose will tend to be present because of aspects of one's circumstances and/or one's further beliefs and desires ("He wants to be fit because he believes this will make him happier"). Notice how the same story will be told by Armstrong regarding those other beliefs and desires; then for any further ones; as for any further further ones; and so on.

In the end, a causal analysis offers us a fundamental philosophical image of anyone's mind as *just part* of a larger physical environment – a neighborhood, near and not, of activity and causal influence. So even the existence *of* minds and their states is not a reason for us to doubt the world's being wholly physical. That is Armstrong's position, at any rate.

The Concept of a Mental State

If we consider the mind-body problem today, then it seems that we ought to take account of the following consideration. The present state of scientific knowledge makes it probable that we can give a purely physico-chemical account of man's body. It seems increasingly likely that the body and the brain of man are constituted and work according to exactly the same principles as those physical principles that govern other, non-organic, matter. The differences between a stone and a human body appear to lie solely in the extremely complex material set-up that is to be found in the living body and which is absent in the stone. Furthermore, there is rather strong evidence that it is the state of our brain that completely determines the state of our consciousness and our mental state generally.

All this is not beyond the realm of controversy, and it is easy to imagine evidence that would upset the picture. In particular, I think that it is just possible that evidence from psychical research might be forthcoming that a physico-chemical view of man's brain could not accommodate. But suppose that the physico-chemical view of the working of the brain is correct, as I take it to be. It will be very natural to conclude that mental states are not simply *determined* by corresponding states of the brain, but that they are actually *identical* with these brain-states, brain-states that involve nothing but physical properties.

[...]

Here, it seems to me, is a question to which philosophers can expect to make a useful contribution. It is a question about mental concepts. Is our concept of a mental state such that it is an intelligible hypothesis that mental states are physical states of the brain? If the philosopher can show that it is an *intelligible* proposition (that is, a non-self-contradictory proposition) that mental states are physical states of the brain, then the scientific argument just given above can be taken at its face value as a strong reason for accepting the truth of the proposition.

My view is that the identification of mental states with physical states of the brain is a perfectly intelligible one, and that this becomes clear once we achieve a correct view of the analysis of the mental concepts. [...]

The problem of the identification may be put in a Kantian way: "How is it possible that mental states should be physical states of the brain?" The solution will take the form of proposing an *independently plausible* analysis of the concept of a mental state that will permit this identification. In this way, the philosopher makes the way smooth for a [...] purely physicalist view of man.

The analysis proposed may be called the Causal analysis of the mental concepts. According to this view, the concept of a mental state essentially involves, and is exhausted by, the concept of a state that is *apt to be the cause of certain effects or apt to be the effect of certain causes*.

An example of a causal concept is the concept of poison. The concept of poison is the concept of something that when introduced into an organism causes that organism to sicken and/or die.[1] [...]

The essential point about the concept of poison is that it is the concept of *that, whatever it is, which produces certain effects*. This leaves open the possibility of the *scientific identification* of poisons, of discovering that a certain sort of substance, such as cyanide, is a poison, and discovering further what it is about the substance that makes it poisonous.

Poisons are accounted poisons in virtue of their active powers, but many sorts of thing are accounted the sorts of thing they are by virtue of their *passive* powers. Thus brittle objects are accounted brittle because of the disposition they have to break and shatter when sharply struck. This leaves open the possibility of discovering empirically what sorts of thing are brittle and what it is about them that makes them brittle.

Now *if* the concepts of the various sorts of mental state are concepts of that which is, in various sorts of way, apt for causing certain effects and apt for being the effect of certain causes, then it would be a quite unpuzzling thing if mental states should turn out to be physical states of the brain.

The concept of a mental state is the concept of something that is, characteristically, the cause of certain effects and the effect of certain causes. What sort of effects and what sort of causes? The effects caused by the mental state will be certain patterns of behaviour of the person in that state. For instance, the desire for food is a state of a person or animal that characteristically brings about food-seeking and food-consuming behaviour by that person or animal. The causes of mental states will be objects and events in the person's environment. For instance, a sensation of green is the characteristic effect in a person of the action upon his eyes of a nearby green surface.

The general pattern of analysis is at its most obvious and plausible in the case of *purposes*. If a man's purpose is to go to the kitchen to get something to eat, it is completely natural to conceive of this purpose as a cause within him that brings about, or tends to bring about, that particular line of conduct. It is, furthermore, notorious that we are unable to characterize purposes *except* in terms of that which they tend to bring about. How can we distinguish the purpose to go to the kitchen to get something to eat from another purpose to go to the bedroom to lie down? Only by the different outcomes that the two purposes tend to bring about. This fact was an encouragement to Behaviourism. It is still more plausibly explained by saying that the concept of purpose is a causal concept. The further hypothesis that the two purposes are, in their own nature, different physical patterns in, or physical states of, the central nervous system is then a natural (although, of course, not logically inevitable) supplement to the causal analysis.

[...]

[...][I]f we are to give a purely causal analysis even of the concept of a purpose we also will have to give a purely causal analysis of perceptions and beliefs. We may think of man's behaviour as brought about by the joint operation of two sets of causes: first, his purposes and, second, his perceptions of and/or his beliefs about the world. But since perceptions and beliefs are quite different sorts of thing from purposes, a Causal analysis must assign quite different causal *roles* to these different things in the bringing about of behaviour.

I believe that this can be done by giving an account of perceptions and beliefs as *mappings* of the world. They are structures within us that model the world beyond the structure. This model is created in us by the world. Purposes may then be thought of as driving causes that utilize such mappings.

[...]

[...][I]t has often been remarked by philosophers and others that the realm of mind is a shadowy one, and that the nature of mental states is singularly elusive and hard to grasp. This has given aid and comfort to Dualist or Cartesian theories of mind, according to which minds are quite different sorts of thing from material objects. But if the Causal analysis is correct, the facts admit of another explanation. What Dualist philosophers have grasped in a confused way is that our direct acquaintance with mind, which occurs in introspective awareness, is an acquaintance with something that we are aware of only as something that is causally linked, directly or indirectly, with behaviour. In the case of our purposes and desires, for instance, we are often (though not invariably) introspectively aware of them. What we are aware of is the presence of factors within us that drive in a certain direction. We are not aware of the intrinsic nature of the factors. This emptiness or gap in our awareness is then interpreted by Dualists as immateriality. In fact, however, if the Causal analysis is correct, there is no warrant for this interpretation and, if the Physicalist identification of the nature of the causes is correct, the interpretation is actually false.

[...]

The Problem of the Secondary Qualities

No discussion of the Causal theory of the mental concepts is complete that does not say something about the *secondary qualities*. If we consider such mental states as purposes and intentions, their "transparency" is a rather conspicuous feature. It is notorious that introspection cannot differentiate such states except in terms of their different objects. It is not so immediately obvious, however, that *perception* has this transparent character. Perception involves the experience of colour and of visual extension, touch of the whole obscure range of tactual properties, including tactual extension, hearing, taste and smell the experience of sounds, tastes and smells. These phenomenal qualities, it may be argued, endow different perceptions with different qualities. The lack of transparency is even more obvious in the case of bodily sensations. Pains, itches, tickles and tingles are mental states, even if mental states of no very high-grade sort, and they each seem to involve their own peculiar qualities. Again, associated with different emotions it is quite plausible to claim to discern special emotion qualities. If perception, bodily sensation and emotions involve qualities, then this seems to falsify a purely Causal analysis of these mental states. They are not mere "that whiches" known only by their causal role.

[...]

[...][I]t is not certain whether the phenomenal qualities pose any threat to the Causal analysis of the mental concepts. But what a subset of these qualities quite certainly does pose a threat to, is the doctrine that the Causal analysis of the mental concepts is a step towards: Materialism or Physicalism.

The qualities of colour, sound, heat and cold, taste and smell together with the qualities that appear to be involved in bodily sensations and those that may be involved in the case of the emotions, are an embarrassment to the modern Materialist. He seeks to give an account of the world and of man purely in terms of *physical* properties, that is to say in terms of the properties that the physicist appeals to in his explanations of phenomena. The Materialist is not committed to the *current* set of properties to which the physicist appeals, but he is committed to whatever set of properties the physicist in the end will appeal to. It is clear that such properties as colour, sound, taste and smell – the so-called "secondary qualities" – will never be properties to which the physicist will appeal.

It is, however, a plausible thesis that associated with different secondary qualities are properties that are respectable from a physicist's point of view. Physical surfaces *appear* to have colour. They not merely appear to, but undoubtedly do, emit light-waves, and the different mixtures of lengths of wave emitted are linked with differences in colour. In the same way, different sorts of sound are linked with different sorts of sound-wave and differences in heat with differences in the mean kinetic energy of the molecules composing the hot things. The Materialist's problem therefore would be very simply solved if the secondary qualities could be identified with these physically respectable properties. (The qualities associated with bodily sensations would be identified with different sorts of stimulation of bodily receptors. If there are unique qualities associated with the emotions, they would presumably be identified with some of the physical states of the brain linked with particular emotions.)

But now the Materialist philosopher faces a problem. Previously he asked: "How is it possible that mental states could be physical states of the brain?" This question was answered by the Causal theory of the mental concepts. Now he must ask: "How is it possible that secondary qualities could be purely physical properties of the objects they are qualities of?" A Causal analysis does not seem to be of any avail. To try to give an analysis of, say, the quality of being red in Causal terms would lead us to produce such analyses as "those properties of a physical surface, whatever they are, that characteristically produce *red sensations* in us." But this analysis simply shifts the problem unhelpfully from property of surface to property of sensation. Either the red sensations involve nothing but physically respectable properties or they involve something more. If they involve something more, Materialism fails. But if they are simply physical states of the brain, having nothing but physical properties, then the Materialist faces the problem: "How is it possible that red sensations should be physical states of the brain?" This question is no easier to answer than the original question about the redness of physical surfaces. (To give a Causal analysis of red sensations as the characteristic effects of the action of red surfaces is, of course, to move round in a circle.)

[...]

[...] I think it can be maintained that although the secondary qualities *appear* to be simple, they are not in fact simple. Perhaps their simplicity is [...] a matter of our awareness of them rather than the way they are. The best model I can given for the situation is the sort of phenomena made familiar to us by the *Gestalt* psychologists. It is possible to grasp that certain things or situations have a certain special property, but be unable to analyse that property. For instance, it may be possible to perceive that certain people are all alike in some way without being able to make it clear to oneself what the likeness is. We are aware that all these people have a certain likeness to each other, but are unable to define or specify that likeness. Later psychological research may achieve a specification of the likeness, a specification that may come as a complete surprise to us. Perhaps, therefore, the secondary qualities are in fact complex, and perhaps they are complex characteristics of a sort demanded by Materialism, but we are unable to grasp their complexity in perception.

[...]

[...][A]lthough the model suggested and the case of the secondary qualities undoubtedly exhibit [...] differences, I do not think that they show that the secondary qualities cannot be identified with respectable physical characteristics of objects. Why should not a complex property appear to be simple? There would seem to be no contradiction in adding such a condition to the model. It has the consequence that perception of the secondary qualities involves an element of illusion, but the consequence involves no contradiction. It is true also that in the case of the secondary qualities the illusion cannot be overcome within perception: it is impossible to see a coloured surface as a surface emitting certain light-waves. (Though one sometimes seems to *hear* a sound as a vibration of the air.) But while this means that the identification of colour and light-waves is a purely *theoretical* one, it still seems to be a possible one. And if the identification is a possible one, we have general scientific reasons to think it a *plausible* one.

Note

1. "Any substance which, when introduced into or absorbed by a living organism, destroys life or injures health." (*Shorter Oxford Dictionary*, 3rd edn., rev., 1978.)

10

Is the Physical World All There Is?

Frank Jackson, "Epiphenomenal Qualia"

Physicalism tells us that the world – all of it – is physical. We might welcome this metaphysical image as accommodating especially well the manifest growth of modern science. For we might regard a physical world – and only a physical world – as an apt object of scientific investigation. We might also think that science is in principle our best means of uncovering whatever is real. Would a completed science (assuming, for the present argument, that such a landmark is possible) therefore constitute an exhaustive portrayal of all there is? A physicalist such as D.M. Armstrong, in the previous reading, could well believe so.

Not all philosophers would agree with him, though. This reading famously disputes that picture of physicalism's promise. The reading is from Frank Jackson (b. 1943), an eminent Australian philosopher most recently at Princeton University, known particularly for his writings on metaphysics and the philosophy of language. This excerpt's emphasis is on some aspects of mental reality, as part of Jackson's testing whether physicalism could indeed encompass all there is. Because physicalism claims that all reality is physical, it implies that what we generally call mental reality is likewise actually physical. It can be difficult to appreciate this, given how readily and ordinarily people presume that their beliefs, feelings, purposes, and so on – *simply* by being mental – are not physical. This argument of Jackson's – called the Knowledge Argument – could be thought to provide some support for that popular presumption, by challenging physicalism and thereby drawing an image of the world as including mental-but-not-physical properties. Still, Jackson is not arguing directly for beliefs, feelings, purposes, and so on simply never being physical. He is arguing that there can be non-physical *properties* of at

Frank Jackson, "Epiphenomenal Qualia," *The Philosophical Quarterly* 32 (1982), 127–136 (excerpts). Cuts made with approval. Reprinted with permission of John Wiley & Sons Ltd.

Metaphysics and Epistemology: A Guided Anthology, First Edition. Edited by Stephen Hetherington.
© 2014 John Wiley & Sons, Inc. Published 2014 by John Wiley & Sons, Inc.

least some of our mental aspects. Nevertheless, if he is right about this, then not every component of reality is physical.

In fact, Jackson goes further – and in terms that conflict substantially with those we noticed in the reading from Armstrong. Jackson argues that these non-physical properties – these *qualia* – of our inner experiences have no *causal* powers. (They are *epiphenomenal* – present but causally inert or isolated.) In contrast, we saw that Armstrong's conception of minds regards descriptions of pertinent causal connections as able to be describing *all* that is mental. Armstrong did acknowledge the difficulty of accounting for qualia within a full metaphysical account. (He called these the *phenomenal* properties of our experiences.) Even so, Armstrong did not infer, from the existence of such qualities, that not all is physical. But Jackson does make that inference.

And how does Jackson's reasoning proceed? Pay particular attention to his tale of Mary; for much subsequent metaphysics has done so. Hers is a colorful story.

It is undeniable that the physical, chemical and biological sciences have provided a great deal of information about the world we live in and about ourselves. I will use the label 'physical information' for this kind of information, and also for information that automatically comes along with it. For example, if a medical scientist tells me enough about the processes that go on in my nervous system, and about how they relate to happenings in the world around me, to what has happened in the past and is likely to happen in the future, to what happens to other similar and dissimilar organisms, and the like, he or she tells me – if I am clever enough to fit it together appropriately – about what is often called the functional role of those states in me (and in organisms in general in similar cases). This information, and its kin, I also label 'physical'.

[…]

I am what is sometimes known as a "qualia freak". I think that there are certain features of the bodily sensations especially, but also of certain perceptual experiences, which no amount of purely physical information includes. Tell me everything physical there is to tell about what is going on in a living brain, the kind of states, their functional role, their relation to what goes on at other times and in other brains, and so on and so forth, and be I as clever as can be in fitting it all together, you won't have told me about the hurtfulness of pains, the itchiness of itches, pangs of jealousy, or about the characteristic experience of tasting a lemon, smelling a rose, hearing a loud noise or seeing the sky.

There are many qualia freaks, and some of them say that their rejection of Physicalism is an unargued intuition.[1] I think that they are being unfair to themselves. They have the following argument. Nothing you could tell of a physical sort captures the smell of a rose, for instance. Therefore, Physicalism is false. By our lights this is a perfectly good argument. It is obviously not to the point to question its validity, and the premise is intuitively obviously true both to them and to me.

I must, however, admit that it is weak from a polemical point of view. There are, unfortunately for us, many who do not find the premise intuitively obvious. The task then is to present an argument whose premises are obvious to all, or at least to as many as possible. This I try to do with what I will call "the Knowledge argument".

[...]

I. The Knowledge Argument for Qualia

People vary considerably in their ability to discriminate colours. Suppose that in an experiment to catalogue this variation Fred is discovered. Fred has better colour vision than anyone else on record; he makes every discrimination that anyone has ever made, and moreover he makes one that we cannot even begin to make. Show him a batch of ripe tomatoes and he sorts them into two roughly equal groups and does so with complete consistency. That is, if you blindfold him, shuffle the tomatoes up, and then remove the blindfold and ask him to sort them out again, he sorts them into exactly the same two groups.

We ask Fred how he does it. He explains that all ripe tomatoes do not look the same colour to him, and in fact that this is true of a great many objects that we classify together as red. He sees two colours where we see one, and he has in consequence developed for his own use two words 'red$_1$' and 'red$_2$' to mark the difference. Perhaps he tells us that he has often tried to teach the difference between red$_1$ and red$_2$ to his friends but has got nowhere and has concluded that the rest of the world is red$_1$-red$_2$ colour-blind – or perhaps he has had partial success with his children, it doesn't matter. In any case he explains to us that it would be quite wrong to think that because 'red' appears in both 'red$_1$' and 'red$_2$' that the two colours are shades of the one colour. He only uses the common term 'red' to fit more easily into our restricted usage. To him red$_1$ and red$_2$ are as different from each other and all the other colours as yellow is from blue. And his discriminatory behaviour bears this out: he sorts red$_1$ from red$_2$ tomatoes with the greatest of ease in a wide variety of viewing circumstances. Moreover, an investigation of the physiological basis of Fred's exceptional ability reveals that Fred's optical system is able to separate out two groups of wave-lengths in the red spectrum as sharply as we are able to sort out yellow from blue.[2]

I think that we should admit that Fred can see, really see, at least one more colour than we can; red$_1$ is a different colour from red$_2$. [...]

What kind of experience does Fred have when he sees red$_1$ and red$_2$? What is the new colour or colours like? We would dearly like to know but do not; and it seems that no amount of physical information about Fred's brain and optical system tells us. We find out perhaps that Fred's cones respond differentially to certain light waves in the red section of the spectrum that make no difference to ours (or perhaps he has an extra cone) and that this leads in Fred to a wider range of those brain states responsible for visual discriminatory behaviour. But none of this tells us what we really want to know about his colour experience. There is something about it we don't know. But we know, we may suppose, everything about Fred's body, his behaviour and dispositions to behaviour and about his internal physiology, and everything about his history and relation to others that can be given in physical accounts of persons. We have all the physical information. Therefore, knowing all this is *not* knowing everything about Fred. It follows that Physicalism leaves something out.

[...]

Fred and the new colour(s) are of course essentially rhetorical devices. The same point can be made with normal people and familiar colours. Mary is a brilliant scientist who is, for whatever reason, forced to investigate the world from a black and white room *via* a black and white television monitor. She specialises in the neurophysiology of vision and acquires, let us suppose, all the physical information there is to obtain about what goes on when we see ripe tomatoes, or the sky, and use terms like 'red', 'blue', and so on. She discovers, for example, just which wave-length combinations from the sky stimulate the retina, and exactly how this produces *via* the central nervous system the contraction of the vocal chords and expulsion of air from the lungs that results in the uttering of the sentence 'The sky is blue'. [...]

What will happen when Mary is released from her black and white room or is given a colour television monitor? Will she *learn* anything or not? It seems just obvious that she will learn something about the world and our visual experience of it. But then it is inescapable that her previous knowledge was incomplete. But she had *all* the physical information. *Ergo* there is more to have than that, and Physicalism is false.

Clearly the same style of Knowledge argument could be deployed for taste, hearing, the bodily sensations and generally speaking for the various mental states which are said to have (as it is variously put) raw feels, phenomenal features or qualia. The conclusion in each case is that the qualia are left out of the physicalist story. And the polemical strength of the Knowledge argument is that it is so hard to deny the central claim that one can have all the physical information without having all the information there is to have.

II.   The Modal Argument

By the Modal Argument I mean an argument of the following style.[3] Sceptics about other minds are not making a mistake in deductive logic, whatever else may be wrong with their position. No amount of physical information about another *logically entails* that he or she is conscious or feels anything at all. Consequently there is a possible world with organisms exactly like us in every physical respect (and remember that includes functional states, physical history, *et al.*) but which differ from us profoundly in that they have no conscious mental life at all. But then what is it that we have and they lack? Not anything physical *ex hypothesi*. In all physical regards we and they are exactly alike. Consequently there is more to us than the purely physical. Thus Physicalism is false.[4]

It is sometimes objected that the Modal argument misconceives Physicalism on the ground that that doctrine is advanced as a *contingent* truth.[5] But to say this is only to say that physicalists restrict their claim to *some* possible worlds, including especially ours; and the Modal argument is only directed against this lesser claim. If we in *our* world, let alone beings in any others, have features additional to those of our physical replicas in other possible worlds, then we have non-physical features or qualia.

The trouble rather with the Modal argument is that it rests on a disputable modal intuition. Disputable because it is disputed. Some sincerely deny that there can be physical replicas of us in other possible worlds which nevertheless lack consciousness. Moreover, at least one person who once had the intuition now has doubts.[6]

Head-counting may seem a poor approach to a discussion of the Modal argument. But frequently we can do no better when modal intuitions are in question, and remember our initial goal was to find the argument with the greatest polemical utility.

Of course, *qua* protagonists of the Knowledge argument we may well accept the modal intuition in question; but this will be a *consequence* of our already having an argument to the conclusion that qualia are left out of the physicalist story, not our ground for that conclusion. Moreover, the matter is complicated by the possibility that the connection between matters physical and qualia is like that sometimes held to obtain between aesthetic qualities and natural ones. Two possible worlds which agree in all "natural" respects (including the experiences of sentient creatures) must agree in all aesthetic qualities also, but it is plausibly held that the aesthetic qualities cannot be reduced to the natural.

III.   The "What is it like to be" Argument

In "What is it like to be a bat?" Thomas Nagel argues that no amount of physical information can tell us what it is like to be a bat, and indeed that we, human beings, cannot imagine what it is like to be a bat.[7] His reason is that what this is like can only be understood from a bat's point of view, which is not our point of view and is not something capturable in physical terms which are essentially terms understandable equally from many points of view.

It is important to distinguish this argument from the Knowledge argument. When I complained that all the physical knowledge about Fred was not enough to tell us what his special colour experience was like, I was not complaining that we weren't finding out what it is like to *be* Fred. I was complaining that there is something *about* his experience, a property of it, of which we were left ignorant. And if and when we come to know what this property is we still will not know what it is like to *be* Fred, but we will know more *about* him. No amount of knowledge about Fred, be it physical or not, amounts to knowledge "from the inside" concerning Fred. We are not Fred. There is thus a whole set of items of knowledge expressed by forms of words like 'that it is *I myself* who is …' which Fred has and we simply cannot have because we are not him.[8]

When Fred sees the colour he alone can see, one thing he knows is the way his experience of it differs from his experience of seeing red and so on, *another* is that he himself is seeing it. Physicalist and qualia freaks alike should acknowledge that no amount of information of whatever kind that *others* have *about* Fred amounts to knowledge of the second. My complaint though concerned the first and was that the special quality of his experience is certainly a fact about it, and one which Physicalism leaves out because no amount of physical information told us what it is.

[…]

IV.   The Bogey of Epiphenomenalism

Is there any really *good* reason for refusing to countenance the idea that qualia are causally impotent with respect to the physical world? I will argue for the answer no, but in doing this I will say nothing about two views associated with the classical epiphenomenalist position. The first is that mental *states* are inefficacious with respect to the physical world. All I will be concerned to defend is that it is possible to hold that certain *properties* of certain mental states, namely those I've called qualia, are such that their possession or absence makes no difference to the physical world. The second is that the mental is *totally* causally inefficacious. For all I will say it may be that you have to hold that the instantiation of *qualia* makes a difference to *other mental states* though not to anything physical. Indeed general considerations to do with how you could come to be aware of the instantiation of qualia suggest such a position.[9]

Three reasons are standardly given for holding that a quale like the hurtfulness of a pain must be causally efficacious in the physical world, and so, for instance, that its instantiation must sometimes make a difference to what happens in the brain. None, I will argue, has any real force. [...]

(i) It is supposed to be just obvious that the hurtfulness of pain is partly responsible for the subject seeking to avoid pain, saying 'It hurts' and so on. But, to reverse Hume, anything can fail to cause anything. No matter how often *B* follows *A*, and no matter how initially obvious the causality of the connection seems, the hypothesis that *A* causes *B* can be overturned by an over-arching theory which shows the two as distinct effects of a common underlying causal process.

To the untutored the image on the screen of Lee Marvin's fist moving from left to right immediately followed by the image of John Wayne's head moving in the same general direction looks as causal as anything.[10] And of course throughout countless Westerns images similar to the first are followed by images similar to the second. All this counts for precisely nothing when we know the over-arching theory concerning how the relevant images are both effects of an underlying causal process involving the projector and the film. The epiphenomenalist can say exactly the same about the connection between, for example, hurtfulness and behaviour. It is simply a consequence of the fact that certain happenings in the brain cause both.

(ii) The second objection relates to Darwin's Theory of Evolution. According to natural selection the traits that evolve over time are those conducive to physical survival. We may assume that qualia evolved over time – we have them, the earliest forms of life do not – and so we should expect qualia to be conducive to survival. The objection is that they could hardly help us to survive if they do nothing to the physical world.

The appeal of this argument is undeniable, but there is a good reply to it. Polar bears have particularly thick, warm coats. The Theory of Evolution explains this (we suppose) by pointing out that having a thick, warm coat is conducive to survival in the Arctic. But having a thick coat goes along with having a heavy coat, and having a heavy coat is *not* conducive to survival. It slows the animal down.

Does this mean that we have refuted Darwin because we have found an evolved trait – having a heavy coat – which is not conducive to survival? Clearly not. Having a heavy coat is an unavoidable concomitant of having a warm coat (in the context, modern insulation was not available), and the advantages for survival of having a warm coat outweighed the disadvantages of having a heavy one. The point is that all we can extract from Darwin's theory is that we should expect any evolved characteristic to be *either* conducive to survival *or* a by-product of one that is so conducive. The epiphenomenalist holds that qualia fall into the latter category. They are a by-product of certain brain processes that are highly conducive to survival.

(iii) The third objection is based on a point about how we come to know about other minds. We know about other minds by knowing about other behaviour, at least in part. The nature of the inference is a matter of some controversy, but it is not a matter of controversy that it proceeds from behaviour. That is why we think that stones do not feel and dogs do feel. But, runs the objection, how can a person's behaviour provide any reason for believing he has qualia like mine, or indeed any qualia at all, unless this behaviour can be regarded as the *outcome* of the qualia. Man Friday's footprint was evidence of Man Friday because footprints are causal outcomes of feet attached to people. And an epiphenomenalist cannot regard behaviour, or indeed anything physical, as an outcome of qualia.

But consider my reading in *The Times* that Spurs won. This provides excellent evidence that *The Telegraph* has also reported that Spurs won, despite the fact that (I trust) *The Telegraph* does not get the results from *The Times*. They each send their own reporters to the game. *The Telegraph's* report is in no sense an outcome of *The Times'*, but the latter provides good evidence for the former nevertheless.

The reasoning involved can be reconstructed thus. I read in *The Times* that Spurs won. This gives me reason to think that Spurs won because I know that Spurs' winning is the most likely candidate to be what caused the report in *The Times*. But I also know that Spurs' winning would have had many effects, including almost certainly a report in *The Telegraph*.

I am arguing from one effect back to its cause and out again to another effect. The fact that neither effect causes the other is irrelevant. Now the epiphenomenalist allows that qualia are effects of what goes on in the brain. Qualia cause nothing physical but are caused by something physical. Hence the epiphenomenalist can argue from the behaviour of others to the qualia of others by arguing from the behaviour of others back to its causes in the brains of others and out again to their qualia.

You may well feel for one reason or another that this is a more dubious chain of reasoning than its model in the case of newspaper reports. You are right. The problem of other minds is a major philosophical problem, the problem of other newspaper reports is not. But there is no special problem of Epiphenomenalism as opposed to, say, Interactionism here.

There is a very understandable response to the three replies I have just made. "All right, there is no knockdown refutation of the existence of epi-phenomenal qualia. But the fact remains that they are an excrescence. They *do* nothing, they *explain* nothing, they serve merely to soothe the intuitions of dualists, and it is left a total mystery how they fit into the world view of science. In short we do not and cannot understand the how and why of them."

This is perfectly true; but is no objection to qualia, for it rests on an overly optimistic view of the human animal, and its powers. We are the products of Evolution. We understand and sense what we need to understand and sense in order to survive. Epiphenomenal qualia are totally irrelevant to survival. At no stage of our evolution did natural selection favour those who could make sense of how they are caused and the laws governing them, or in fact why they exist at all. And that is why we can't.

Notes

1. Particularly in discussion, but see, e.g., Keith Campbell, *Metaphysics* (Belmont, 1976), p. 67.
2. Put this, and similar simplifications below, in terms of Land's theory if you prefer. See, e.g., Edwin H. Land, "Experiments in Color Vision", *Scientific American*, 200 (5 May 1959), 84–99.
3. See, e.g., Keith Campbell, *Body and Mind* (New York, 1970); and Robert Kirk, "Sentience and Behaviour", *Mind*, 83 (1974), 43–60.

4. I have presented the argument in an inter-world rather than the more usual intra-world fashion to avoid inessential complications to do with supervenience, causal anomalies and the like.

5. See, e.g., W. G. Lycan, "A New Lilliputian Argument Against Machine Functionalism", *Philosophical Studies*, 35 (1979), 279–87, p. 280; and Don Locke, "Zombies, Schizophrenics and Purely Physical Objects", *Mind*, 85 (1976), 97–9.

6. See R. Kirk, "From Physical Explicability to Full-Blooded Materialism", *The Philosophical Quarterly*, 29 (1979), 229–37. See also the arguments against the modal intuition in, e.g., Sydney Shoemaker, "Functionalism and Qualia", *Philosophical Studies*, 27 (1975), 291–315.

7. *The Philosophical Review*, 83 (1974), 435–50. Two things need to be said about this article. One is that, despite my dissociations to come, I am much indebted to it. The other is that the emphasis changes through the article, and by the end Nagel is objecting not so much to Physicalism as to all extant theories of mind for ignoring points of view, including those that admit (irreducible) qualia.

8. Knowledge *de se* in the terms of David Lewis, "Attitudes De Dicto and De Se", *The Philosophical Review*, 88 (1979), 513–43.

9. See my review of K. Campbell, *Body and Mind*, in *Australasian Journal of Philosophy*, 50 (1972), 77–80.

10. Cf. Jean Piaget, "The Child's Conception of Physical Causality", reprinted in *The Essential Piaget* (London, 1977).

How Does the World Function?

11

Is Causation Only a Kind of Regularity?

David Hume, *An Enquiry Concerning Human Understanding*

D.M. Armstrong, we saw, seeks to understand our mental lives in terms of causality. Frank Jackson, we saw next, denies that we can do this. Armstrong and Jackson share a belief in the significance, for understanding the world, of deciding *when* causality is present. An aspect of John Locke's image of physical objects, we saw earlier, also shared that belief. He argued that we understand the world partly by understanding that a secondary quality is a power to cause perceivers, all else being equal, to have various apt experiences. Thus (for Locke), an object is not only sitting there in front of you; it includes *causality* in its being. Equally (for Armstrong), so do you, in your being aware of the object. In such ways, causation is treated as integral to how the world is, by being integral to how the world functions. With

David Hume, *An Enquiry Concerning Human Understanding* (1748), sect. VII (excerpts).

Metaphysics and Epistemology: A Guided Anthology, First Edition. Edited by Stephen Hetherington.
© 2014 John Wiley & Sons, Inc. Published 2014 by John Wiley & Sons, Inc.

causal relations being present, things *happen*. Some *this* gives rise to some *that*. It is pivotal to understanding the world, then, that we understand causation. What *is* it?

This was a question with which the Scottish philosopher David Hume (1711–76) famously engaged. Like Locke and Berkeley before him, Hume is generally called an *empiricist*: each claimed that all knowledge is observational, ultimately being generated and justified by sensory interactions with the world. (Later in the book we will examine the nature of empirical knowledge – that is, observational knowledge. The word "empirical" is used to reflect the use of observations in establishing or testing a view.) So, here is what Hume, as an empiricist, thought is required if we are to understand the idea of causation: for a start, we need to understand how we gain observationally the idea of a causal interaction.

He asked how we could gain the idea of a *necessary connection*; for that was the usual phrase with which people at the time (like many since) thought they could explain what is most fundamentally involved in causation. When a punch inflicts injury, is there a necessary connection between the punch's impact and the injury? We might claim so, feeling that anything less would lead us into the realm of the accidental, away from that of the causal. Is this feeling well-grounded? Does *the world* give us the idea of a necessary connection when we observe the punch and then the injury, so that to have such an idea in this circumstance is to *mirror* the world? Not according to Hume. He would allow that we can observe the punch and the injury – but not the punch's *making* the bone break. We observe one event, then another; not, however, a necessary connection between them. (*Where* is the connection? Literally where? Does it have a shape, a sound, etc.?)

For Hume, accordingly, the best that we can do towards having a properly grounded idea of causation, while lacking any properly grounded idea of necessary connection, is to lower our ambitions. Hume proposes that we should settle for causation being a kind of uniform and sustained *regularity*. For this specific punch to cause this specific injury is for punches like this regularly to be followed by injuries like this. Not *all* regularities will be causal. But all specific causal interactions – *this* causing *that* – will be instantiations of regularities – this *kind* of event always being followed by that *kind* of event. This has become known as the Humean regularity conception of causation. It is a standard starting-point for philosophical discussions of the nature of causation.

Of the Idea of Necessary Connexion

Part I

[...]

There are no ideas, which occur in metaphysics, more obscure and uncertain, than those of *power, force, energy* or *necessary connexion*, of which it is every moment necessary for us to treat in all our disquisitions. We shall, therefore, endeavour, in this section, to fix, if possible, the precise meaning of these terms, and thereby remove some part of that obscurity, which is so much complained of in this species of philosophy.

It seems a proposition, which will not admit of much dispute, that all our ideas are nothing but copies of our impressions, or, in other words, that it is impossible for us to *think* of any thing, which we have not antecedently *felt*, either by our external or internal senses. [...] Complex ideas may, perhaps, be well known by definition, which is nothing but an enumeration of those parts or simple ideas, that compose them. But when we have pushed up definitions to the most simple ideas, and find still some ambiguity and obscurity; what resource are we then possessed of? [...] Produce the impressions or original sentiments, from which the ideas are copied. These impressions are all strong and sensible. They admit not of ambiguity. They are not only placed in a full light themselves, but may throw light on their correspondent ideas, which lie in obscurity.

[...]

To be fully acquainted, therefore, with the idea of power or necessary connexion, let us examine its impression; and in order to find the impression with greater certainty, let us search for it in all the sources, from which it may possibly be derived.

When we look about us towards external objects, and consider the operation of causes, we are never able, in a single instance, to discover any power or necessary connexion; any quality, which binds the effect to the cause, and renders the one an infallible consequence of the other. We only find, that the one does actually, in fact, follow the other. The impulse of one billiard-ball is attended with motion in the second. This is the whole that appears to the *outward* senses. The mind feels no sentiment or *inward* impression from this succession of objects: Consequently, there is not, in any single, particular instance of cause and effect, any thing which can suggest the idea of power or necessary connexion.

From the first appearance of an object, we never can conjecture what effect will result from it. But were the power or energy of any cause discoverable by the mind, we could foresee the effect, even without experience; and might, at first, pronounce with certainty concerning it, by the mere dint of thought and reasoning.

In reality, there is no part of matter, that does ever, by its sensible qualities, discover any power or energy, or give us ground to imagine, that it could produce any thing, or be followed by any other object, which we could denominate its effect. Solidity, extension, motion; these qualities are all complete in themselves, and never point out any other event which may result from them. The scenes of the universe are continually shifting, and one object follows another in an uninterrupted succession; but the power or force, which actuates the whole machine, is entirely concealed from us, and never discovers itself in any of the sensible qualities of body. We know, that, in fact, heat is a constant attendant of flame; but what is the connexion between them, we have no room so much as to conjecture or imagine. It is impossible, therefore, that the idea of power can be derived from the contemplation of bodies, in single instances of their operation; because no bodies ever discover any power, which can be the original of this idea.[1]

Since, therefore, external objects as they appear to the senses, give us no idea of power or necessary connexion, by their operation in particular instances, let us see, whether this idea be derived from reflection on the operations of our own minds, and be copied from any internal impression. It may be said, that we are every moment conscious of internal power; while we feel, that, by the simple command of our will, we can move the organs of our body, or direct the faculties of our mind. An act of volition produces motion in our limbs, or raises a new idea in our imagination. This influence of the will we know by consciousness. Hence we acquire the idea of power or energy; and are certain, that we ourselves and all other intelligent beings are possessed of power. This idea, then, is an idea of reflection, since it arises from reflecting on the operations of our own mind, and on the command which is exercised by will, both over the organs of the body and faculties of the soul.

We shall proceed to examine this pretension; and first with regard to the influence of volition over the organs of the body. This influence, we may observe, is a fact, which, like all other natural events, can be known only by experience, and can never beforeseen from any apparent energy or power in the cause, which connects it with the effect, and renders the one an infallible consequence of the other. The motion of our body follows upon the command of our will. Of this we are every moment conscious. But the means, by which this is effected; the energy, by which the will performs so extraordinary an operation; of this we are so far from being immediately conscious, that it must for ever escape our most diligent enquiry.

For *first*, is there any principle in all nature more mysterious than the union of soul with body; by which a supposed spiritual substance acquires such an influence over a material one, that the most refined thought is able to actuate the grossest matter? [...]

Secondly, We are not able to move all the organs of the body with a like authority; though we cannot assign any reason besides experience, for so remarkable a difference between one and the other. Why has the will an influence over the tongue and fingers, not over the heart or liver ?

[...]

Thirdly, We learn from anatomy, that the immediate object of power in voluntary motion, is not the member itself which is moved, but certain muscles, and nerves, and animal spirits, and, perhaps, something still more minute and more unknown, through which the motion is successively propagated, ere it reach the member itself whose motion is the immediate object of volition. Can there be a more certain proof, that the power, by which this whole operation is performed, so far from being directly and fully known by an inward sentiment or consciousness, is, to the last degree, mysterious and unintelligible? [...]

We may, therefore, conclude from the whole, that our idea of power is not copied from any sentiment or consciousness of power within ourselves, when we give rise to animal motion, or apply our limbs to their proper use and office. That their motion follows the command of the will is a matter of common experience, like other natural events: But the power or energy by which this is effected, like that in other natural events, is unknown and inconceivable.

Shall we then assert, that we are conscious of a power or energy in our own minds, when, by an act or command of our will, we raise up a new idea, fix the mind to the contemplation of it, turn it on all sides, and at last dismiss it for some other idea, when we think that we have surveyed it with sufficient accuracy? I believe the same arguments will prove, that even this command of the will gives us no real idea of force or energy.

[...]

Volition is surely an act of the mind, with which we are sufficiently acquainted. Reflect upon it. Consider it on all sides. Do you find anything in it like this creative power, by which it raises from nothing a new idea, and with a kind of *Fiat*, imitates the omnipotence of its Maker, if I may be allowed so to speak, who called forth into existence all the various scenes of nature? So far from being conscious of this energy in the will, it requires as certain experience as that of which we are possessed, to convince us that such extraordinary effects do ever result from a simple act of volition.

[…] [W]e only learn experience the frequent *Conjunction* of objects, without being ever able to comprehend anything like *Connexion* between them.

[…]

Part II

[…] We have sought in vain for an idea of power or necessary connexion in all the sources from which we could suppose it to be derived. It appears that, in single instances of the operation of bodies, we never can, by our utmost scrutiny, discover any thing but one event following another; without being able to comprehend any force or power by which the cause operates, or any connexion between it and its supposed effect. The same difficulty occurs in contemplating the operations of mind on body – where we observe the motion of the latter to follow upon the volition of the former, but are not able to observe or conceive the tie which binds together the motion and volition, or the energy by which the mind produces this effect. The authority of the will over its own faculties and ideas is not a whit more comprehensible: So that, upon the whole, there appears not, throughout all nature, any one instance of connexion which is conceivable by us. All events seem entirely loose and separate. One event follows another; but we never can observe any tie between them. They seem *conjoined*, but never *connected*. And as we can have no idea of any thing which never appeared to our outward sense or inward sentiment, the necessary conclusion *seems* to be that we have no idea of connexion or power at all, and that these words are absolutely without any meaning, when employed either in philosophical reasonings or common life.

But there still remains one method of avoiding this conclusion, and one source which we have not yet examined. When any natural object or event is presented, it is impossible for us, by any sagacity or penetration, to discover, or even conjecture, without experience, what event will result from it, or to carry our foresight beyond that object which is imme-diately present to the memory and senses. Even after one instance or experiment, where we have observed a particular event to follow upon another, we are not entitled to form a general rule, or foretell what will happen in like cases; it being justly esteemed an unpar-donable temerity to judge of the whole course of nature from one single experiment, however accurate or certain. But when one particular species of event has always, in all instances, been conjoined with another, we make no longer any scruple of foretelling one upon the appearance of the other, and of employing that reasoning, which can alone assure us of any matter of fact or existence. We then call the one object, *Cause*; the other, *Effect*. We suppose that there is some connexion between them; some power in the one, by which it infallibly produces the other, and operates with the greatest certainty and strongest necessity.

It appears, then, that this idea of a necessary connexion among events arises from a number of similar instances which occur of the constant conjunction of these events; nor can that idea ever be suggested by any one of these instances, surveyed in all possible lights and positions. But there is nothing in a number of instances, different from every single instance, which is supposed to be exactly similar; except only, that after a repetition of similar instances, the mind is carried by habit, upon the appearance of one event, to expect its usual attendant, and to believe that it will exist. This connexion, therefore, which we *feel* in the mind, this customary transition of the imagination from one object to its usual attendant, is the sentiment or impression from which we form the idea of power or necessary connexion. Nothing farther is in the case. Contemplate the subject on all sides; you will never find any other origin of that idea. This is the sole difference between one instance, from which we can never receive the idea of connexion, and a number of similar instances, by which it is suggested. The first time a man saw the communication of motion by impulse, as by the shock of two billiard balls, he could not pronounce that the one event was *connected*: but only that it was *conjoined* with the other. After he has observed several instances of this nature, he then pronounces them to be *connected*. What alteration has happened to give rise to this new idea of *connexion*? Nothing but that he now *feels* these events to be *connected* in his imagination, and can readily foretell the existence of one from the appearance of the other. When we say, therefore, that one object is connected with another, we mean only that they have acquired a connexion in our thought, and give rise to this inference, by which they become proofs of each other's existence.

[…]

Our thoughts and enquiries are, therefore, every moment, employed about this relation: Yet so imperfect are the ideas which we form concerning it, that it is impossible to give any just definition of cause, except what is drawn from something extraneous and foreign to it. Similar objects are always conjoined with similar. Of this we have experience. Suitably to this experience, therefore, we may define a cause to be *an object, followed by another, and where all the objects similar to the first are followed by objects similar to the second*. Or in other words *where, if the first object had not been, the second never had existed*. The appearance of a cause always conveys the mind, by a customary transition, to the idea of the effect. Of this also we have experience. We may, therefore, suitably to this experience, form another definition of cause, and call it, *an object followed by another, and whose appearance always conveys the thought to that other*. But though both these definitions be drawn from circumstances foreign to the cause, we cannot remedy this inconvenience, or attain any more perfect definition, which may point out that circumstance in the cause, which gives it a connexion with its effect. We have no idea of this connexion, nor even any distinct notion what it is we desire to know, when we endeavour at a conception of it. We say, for instance, that the vibration of this string is the cause of this particular sound. But what do we mean by that affirmation ? We either mean *that this vibration is followed by this sound, and that all similar vibrations have been followed by similar sounds*: Or, *that this vibration is followed by this sound, and that upon the appearance of one the mind anticipates the senses, and forms immediately an idea of the other*. We may consider the relation of cause and effect in either of these two lights; but beyond these, we have no idea of it.

Note

1. Mr. Locke, in his chapter of power, says that, finding from experience, that there are several new productions in matter, and concluding that there must somewhere be a power capable of producing them, we arrive at last by this reasoning at the idea of power. But no reasoning can ever give us a new, original, simple idea; as this philosopher himself confesses. This, therefore, can never be the origin of that idea.

12

Is Causation Something Singular and Unanalyzable?

G.E.M. Anscombe, "Causation and Determination"

One much-cited response to Hume's argument in the previous reading was by the British philosopher Elizabeth Anscombe (1919–2001), in her 1971 inaugural lecture as Professor of Philosophy at Cambridge University. She highlighted two central presumptions animating so many accounts of causation, including both Hume's opponents and his own proposal. First, must causation be a kind of necessitation (as was thought by those against whom Hume argued)? Second, must causation be an application or instantiation of a generality or regularity (as Hume proposed), such as a law with that form?

We saw that Hume asked about necessary connections: do people really observe these? And when he could not accept that we do ever observe a necessary connection, his response was not to discard the concept of causation, but rather to conceive of causality as a regularity, something that in principle *can* be observed. (Some regularities will be difficult to observe. Certainly we need not always observe every possible instance of a regularity. In principle, though, the regularity *could* be observed, at least collectively by a lot of people over time in different places.) On Hume's account, a particular interaction – *this* punch causing *that* injury – would be a case of causation only *by* instantiating the applicable regularity.

This view of Hume's is what Anscombe denies. Causation, she argues, is specific and local. It is a singular occurrence or transaction, not needing to be describable in general law-like terms as reflecting one kind of event's always sufficing for another kind of event. Causation can be present, therefore, even if not because of some regularity's obtaining. And you can *know* that the punch caused the injury,

G.E.M. Anscombe, "Causation and Determination" (excerpts), in *The Collected Philosophical Papers of G.E.M. Anscombe*, vol. 2: *Metaphysics and the Philosophy of Mind* (Minneapolis: University of Minnesota Press, 1981).

even if you cannot know a general and exceptionless regularity from which that causation arrives.

Is causation even philosophically *unanalyzable* (such as in Strawson's sense of "analysis," from the reading of his in Part I)? Anscombe believes so. But she is also unworried by this inescapable limitation upon us. We learn to talk of particular cases of causation, understanding them as such, no matter that we are – and will remain – unable to analyze such talk. Again, we do not need to be able to embed our specific causal claims within a precise and general account of the nature of causation. Even as philosophers (concludes Anscombe), we have no such need.

It is often declared or evidently assumed that causality is some kind of necessary connection, or alternatively, that being caused is – non-trivially – instancing some exceptionless generalization saying that such an event always follows such antecedents. Or the two conceptions are combined.

Obviously there can be, and are, a lot of divergent views covered by this account. Any view that it covers nevertheless manifests one particular doctrine or assumption. Namely:

> If an effect occurs in one case and a similar effect does not occur in an apparently similar case, there must be a relevant further difference.

Any radically different account of causation, then, by contrast with which all those diverse views will be as one, will deny this assumption. Such a radically opposing view can grant that often – though it is difficult to say generally when – the assumption of relevant difference is a sound principle of investigation. It may grant that there are necessitating causes, but will refuse to identify causation as such with necessitation. It can grant that there are situations in which, given the initial conditions and no interference, only one result will accord with the laws of nature; but it will not see general reason, in advance of discovery, to suppose that any given course of things has been so determined. So it may grant that in many cases difference of issue can rightly convince us of a relevant difference of circumstances; but it will deny that, quite generally, this *must* be so.

The first view is common to many philosophers of the past. It is also, usually but not always in a neo-Humeian form, the prevailing received opinion throughout the currently busy and productive philosophical schools of the English-speaking world, and also in some of the European and Latin American schools where philosophy is pursued in at all the same sort of way; nor is it confined to these schools. So firmly rooted is it that for many even outside pure philosophy, it routinely determines the meaning of "cause", when consciously used as a theoretical term: witness the terminology of the contrast between 'causal' and 'statistical' laws, which is drawn by writers on physics – writers, note, who would not conceive themselves to be addicts of any philosophic school when they use this language to express that contrast.

The truth of this conception is hardly debated. It is, indeed, a bit of *Weltanschauung*: it helps to form a cast of mind which is characteristic of our whole culture.

The association between causation and necessity is old; it occurs for example in Aristotle's *Metaphysics*: "When the agent and patient meet suitably to their powers, the one acts and the other is acted on OF NECESSITY." Only with 'rational powers' an extra feature is needed to determine the result: "What has a rational power [e.g. medical knowledge, which can kill *or* cure] OF NECESSITY does what it has the power to do and as it has the power, when it has the desire" (Book IX, Chapter V).

Overleaping the centuries, we find it an axiom in Spinoza, "Given a determinate cause, the effect follows OF NECESSITY, and without its cause, no effect follows" (*Ethics*, Book I, Axiom III). And in the English philsopher Hobbes:

> A cause simply, or an entire cause, is the aggregate of all the accidents both of the agents how many soever they be, and of the patients, put together; which when they are supposed to be present, IT CANNOT BE UNDERSTOOD BUT THAT THE EFFECT IS PRODUCED at the same instant; and if any of them be wanting, IT CANNOT BE UNDERSTOOD BUT THAT THE EFFECT IS NOT PRODUCED. (*Elements of Philosophy Concerning Body*, Chapter IX)

It was this last view, where the connection between cause and effect is evidently seen as *logical* connection of some sort, that was overthrown by Hume, the most influential of all philosophers on this subject in the English-speaking and allied schools. For he made us see that, given any particular cause – or 'total causal situation' for that matter – and its effect, there is not in general any contradiction in supposing the one to occur and the other not to occur. That is to say, we'd know what was being described – what it would be like for it to be true – if it were reported for example that a kettle of water was put, and kept, directly on a hot fire, but the water did not heat up.

Were it not for the preceding philosophers who had made causality out as some species of logical connection, one would wonder at this being called a discovery on Hume's part: for vulgar humanity has always been over-willing to believe in miracles and marvels and *lusus naturae*. Mankind at large saw no contradiction, where Hume worked so hard to show the philosophic world – the Republic of Letters – that there was none.

The discovery was thought to be great. But as touching the equation of causality with necessitation, Hume's thinking did nothing against this but curiously reinforced it. For he himself assumed that NECESSARY CONNECTION is an essential part of the idea of the relation of cause and effect (*Treatise of Human Nature*, Book I, Part III, Sections II and VI), and he sought for its nature. He thought this could not be found in the situations, objects or events called "causes" and "effects", but was to be found in the human mind's being determined, by experience of CONSTANT CONJUNCTION, to pass from the sensible impression or memory of one term of the relation to the convinced idea of the other. Thus to say that an event was caused was to say that its occurrence was an instance of some exceptionless generalization connecting such an event with such antecedents as it occurred in. The twist that Hume gave to the topic thus suggested a connection of the notion of causality with that of deterministic laws – i.e. laws such that always, given initial conditions and the laws, a unique result is determined.

The well-known philosophers who have lived after Hume may have aimed at following him and developing at least some of his ideas, or they may have put up a resistance; but in no case, so far as I know,[1] has the resistance called in question the equation of causality with necessitation.

Kant, roused by learning of Hume's discovery, laboured to establish causality as an *a priori* conception and argued that the objective time order consists "in that order of the manifold of appearance according to which, IN CONFORMITY WITH A RULE, the apprehension of that which happens follows upon the apprehension of that which precedes ... In conformity with such a rule there must be in that which precedes an event the condition of a rule according to which this event INVARIABLY and NECESSARILY follows" (*Critique of Pure Reason*, Book II, Chapter II, Section III, Second Analogy). Thus Kant tried to give back to causality the character of a *justified* concept which Hume's considerations had taken away from it. Once again the connection between causation and necessity was reinforced. And this has been the general characteristic of those who have sought to oppose Hume's conception of causality. They have always tried to establish the necessitation that they saw in causality: either *a priori*, or somehow out of experience.

Since Mill it has been fairly common to explain causation one way or another in terms of 'necessary' and 'sufficient' conditions. Now "sufficient condition" is a term of art whose users may therefore lay down its meaning as they please. So they are in their rights to rule out the query: "May not the sufficient conditions of an event be present, and the event yet not take place?" For "sufficient condition" is so used that if the sufficient conditions for X are there, X occurs. But at the same time, the phrase cozens the understanding into not noticing an assumption. For "sufficient condition" sounds like: "enough". And one certainly *can* ask: "May there not be *enough* to have made something happen – and yet it not have happened?"

Russell wrote of the notion of cause, or at any rate of the 'law of causation' (and he seemed to feel the same way about 'cause' itself), that, like the British monarchy, it had been allowed to survive because it had been erroneously thought to do no harm. In a destructive essay of great brilliance he cast doubt on the notion of necessity involved, unless it is explained in terms of universality, and he argued that upon examination the concepts of determination and of invariable succession of like objects upon like turn out to be empty: they do not differentiate between any conceivable course of things and any other. Thus Russell too assumes that necessity or universality is what is in question, and it never occurs to him that there may be any other conception of causality ('The Notion of Cause', in *Mysticism and Logic*).

Now it's not difficult to show it prima facie wrong to associate the notion of cause with necessity or universality in this way. For, it being much easier to trace effects back to causes with certainty than to predict effects from causes, we often know a cause without knowing whether there is an exceptionless generalization of the kind envisaged, or whether there is a necessity.

For example, we have found certain diseases to be contagious. If, then, I have had one and only one contact with someone suffering from such a disease, and I get it myself, we suppose I got it from him. But what if, having had the contact, I ask a doctor whether I will get the disease? He will usually only be able to say, "I don't know – maybe you will, maybe not."

But, it is said, knowledge of causes here is partial; doctors seldom even know any of the conditions under which one invariably gets a disease, let alone all the sets of conditions. This comment betrays the assumption that there is such a thing to know. Suppose there is: still, the question whether there is does not have to be settled before we can know what we mean by speaking of the contact as cause of my getting the disease.

All the same, might it not be like this: knowledge of causes is possible without any satisfactory grasp of what is involved in causation? Compare the possibility of wanting clarification of 'valency' or 'long-run frequency', which yet have been handled by chemists and statisticians without such clarification; and valencies and long-run frequencies, whatever the right way of explaining them, have been known. Thus one of the familiar philosophic analyses of causality, or a new one in the same line, may be correct, though knowledge of it is not necessary for knowledge of causes.

There is something to observe here, that lies under our noses. It is little attended to, and yet still so obvious as to seem trite. It is this: causality consists in the derivativeness of an effect from its causes. This is the core, the common feature, of causality in its various kinds. Effects derive from, arise out of, come of, their causes. For example, everyone will grant that physical parenthood is a causal relation. Here the derivation is material, by fission. Now analysis in terms of necessity or universality does not tell us of this derivedness of the effect; rather it forgets about that. For the necessity will be that of laws of nature; through it *we* shall be able to derive knowledge of the effect from knowledge of the cause, or vice versa, but that does not show us the cause as source of the effect. Causation, then, is not to be identified with necessitation.

If *A* comes from *B*, this does not imply that every *A*-like thing comes from some *B*-like thing or set-up or that every *B*-like thing or set-up has an *A*-like thing coming from it; or that given *B*, *A* had to come from it, or that given *A*, there had to be *B* for it to come from. Any of these may be true, but if any is, that will be an additional fact, not comprised in *A*'s coming from *B*. If we take "coming from" in the sense of travel, this is perfectly evident.

"But that's because we can observe travel!" The influential Humeian argument at this point is that we can't similarly observe causality in the individual case (Ibid. Bk I, Pt III, Section II). So the reason why we connect what we call the cause and what we call the effect as we do must lie elsewhere. It must lie in the fact that the succession of the latter upon the former is of a kind regularly observed.

There are two things for me to say about this. First, as to the statement that we can never observe causality in the individual case. Someone who says this is just not going to count anything as 'observation of causality'. This often happens in philosophy; it is argued that 'all we find' is such-and-such, and it turns out that the arguer has excluded from his idea of 'finding' the sort of thing he says we don't 'find'. And when we consider what we are allowed to say we do 'find', we have the right to turn the tables on Hume, and say that neither do we perceive bodies, such as billiard balls, approaching one another. When we 'consider the matter with the utmost attention', we find only an impression of travel made by the successive positions of a round white patch in our visual fields … etc. Now a 'Humeian' account of causality has to be given in terms of constant conjunction of physical things, events, etc., not of experiences of them. If, then, it must be allowed that we 'find' bodies in motion, for example, then what theory of perception can justly disallow the perception of a lot of causality? The truthful – though unhelpful – answer to the question: "How did we come by our primary knowledge of causality?" is that in learning to speak we learned the linguistic representation and application of a host of causal concepts. Very many of them were represented by transitive and other verbs of action used in reporting what is observed. Others – a good example is "infect" – form, not observation statements, but rather expressions of causal hypotheses. The word "cause" itself is highly general. How does someone show that he has the concept *cause?* We may wish to say: only by having such a word in his vocabulary. If so, then the manifest possession of the concept presupposes the mastery of much else in language. I mean: the word "cause" can be *added* to a language in which are already represented many causal concepts. A small selection: *scrape, push, wet, carry, eat, burn, knock over, keep off, squash, make* (e.g. noises, paper boats), *hurt.* But if we care to imagine languages in which no special causal concepts are represented, then no description of the use of a word in such languages will be able to present it as meaning *cause.* Nor will it even contain words for natural kinds of stuff, nor yet words equivalent to "body", "wind", or "fire". For learning to use special causal verbs is part and parcel of learning to apply the concepts answering to these and many other substantives. As surely as we learned to call people by name or to report from seeing it that the cat was on the table, we also learned to report from having observed it that someone drank up the milk or that the dog made a funny noise or that things were cut or broken by whatever we saw cut or break them.

   [...]

   [...][A]s to that instancing of a universal generalization, which was supposed to supply what could not be observed in the individual case, the causal relation, the needed examples are none too common. "Motion in one body in all past instances that have fallen under our observation, is follow'd upon impulse by motion in another": so Hume (Ibid. Bk II, Pt III, Section I). But, as is always a danger in making large generalizations, he was thinking only of the cases where we do observe this – billiard balls against free-standing billiard balls in an ordinary situation; not billiard balls against stone walls. Neo-Humeians are more cautious. They realize that if you take a case of cause and effect, and relevantly describe the cause *A* and the effect *B*, and then construct a universal proposition, "Always, given an *A*, a *B* follows" you usually won't get anything true. You have got to describe the absence of circumstances in which an *A* would not cause a *B*. But the task of excluding all such circumstances can't be carried out. There is, I suppose, a vague association in people's minds between the universal propositions which would be examples of the required type of generalizations, and scientific laws. But there is no similarity.

   Suppose we were to call propositions giving the properties of substances "laws of nature". Then there will be a law of nature running "The flash-point of such a substance is ...", and this will be important in explaining why striking matches usually causes them to light. This law of nature has not the form of a generalization running "Always, if a sample of such a substance is raised to such a temperature, it ignites"; nor is it equivalent to such a generalization, but rather to: "If a sample of such a substance is raised to such a temperature and doesn't ignite, there must be a cause of its not doing so." Leaving aside questions connected with the idea of a pure sample, the point here is that 'normal conditions' is quite properly a vague notion. That fact makes generalizations running "Always ..." merely fraudulent in such cases; it will always be necessary for them to be hedged about with clauses referring to normal conditions; and we may not know in advance whether conditions are normal or not, or what to count as an abnormal condition. In exemplar analytical practice, I suspect, it will simply be a relevant condition in which the generalization, "Always if such and such, such and such happens ...", supplemented with a few obvious conditions that have occurred to the author, turns out to be untrue. Thus the conditional "If it doesn't ignite then there must be some cause" is the better gloss upon the original proposition, for it does not pretend to say specifically, or even disjunctively specifically, what *always* happens. It is probably these facts which make one hesitate to call propositions about the action of substances "laws of nature". The law of inertia, for example, would hardly be glossed: "If a body accelerates without any force acting on it, there must be some cause of its doing so." [...] On the other hand just such 'laws' as that about a substance's flash-point are connected with the match's igniting because struck.

[...]

[...] [I]n non-experimental philosophy it is clear enough what are the dogmatic slumbers of the day. It is over and over again assumed that any singular causal proposition implies a universal statement running "Always when this, then that"; often assumed that true singular causal statements are derived from such 'inductively believed' universalities. Examples indeed are recalcitrant, but that does not seem to disturb. Even a philosopher acute enough to be conscious of this, such as Davidson, will say, without offering any reason at all for saying it, that a singular causal statement implies *that there is* such a true universal proposition[2] – though perhaps we can never have knowledge of it. Such a thesis needs some reason for believing it! 'Regularities in nature': that is not a reason. The most neglected of the key topics in this subject are: interference and prevention.

Notes

1. My colleague Ian Hacking has pointed out C. S. Peirce to me as an exception to this generalization.
2. 'Causal Relations', *Journal of Philosophy*, 64 (November 1967).

How Do Things Ever Have Qualities?

13

How Can Individual Things Have Repeatable Qualities?

Plato, *Parmenides*

Our first reading was from Plato, as is this one. Back then, we noted that in Plato's dialogues it is usually Socrates who leaves his conversational partners frustrated, as he quietly dominates the shared inquiry. But in the present reading it is the young Socrates, being quizzed by the senior philosopher Parmenides (c.515–c.449/440 BC), who is left genuinely perplexed. What is at stake this time is a kind of metaphysical image with which Plato, especially, has been famously identified. It is a way of thinking about how the world's constituents – you, your hair, your ears, your skin, cats, dogs, pens, mountains, mosquitoes, atoms, and so on – are whatever they are. What *makes* a cat a cat? Yes, it is born from a cat; but what makes *that* cat a cat? The question recurs. What made the first cat a cat? And we can ask similar

Plato, *Parmenides* 130b–135b (excerpts), trans. F.M. Cornford. From *The Collected Dialogues of Plato*, ed. E. Hamilton and H. Cairns (Princeton: Princeton University Press, 1961). © 1961 by Princeton University Press. Reprinted with permission of Princeton University Press.

Metaphysics and Epistemology: A Guided Anthology, First Edition. Edited by Stephen Hetherington.
© 2014 John Wiley & Sons, Inc. Published 2014 by John Wiley & Sons, Inc.

questions about everything, about all of the world's constituents – not only cats; everything. Seemingly, each thing has qualities or properties that coalesce in its being whatever it is. We talked earlier of primary qualities and of secondary qualities. Now we are asking about all qualities, all properties.

Philosophers trace that question back to some of Plato's dialogues. Speedily, it leads to these questions. What *is* a property? How does an individual thing *have* a property? How do distinct individual things have the *same* property? Are there *repeatable* properties (*universals*, as they are often termed)? For instance, probably you have individual hairs on your individual head; as do other people. But is there also a general and repeatable property of having hair on one's head, a property somehow shared in by you and by others? We might talk casually of there being such a property. Does it literally exist, though? If it does, *where* is it within the world? There are individual hairs on your head; is the property – the entire property of having hairs on one's head – also there on your head? If not, where is it? Can it be wholly in different places at the same time – on your head and on the heads of others?

Alternatively, is that property *nowhere* in particular (because it is abstract)? If so, how does it manage to be instantiated or exemplified by the hairs on your head – hairs that *are* in particular locations and that are not abstract?

Does the property, in spite of being abstract, *cause* you to have hairs on your head? Or does no abstract property have causal influence on the non-abstract world, even when the world has part of its complex character by exemplifying a given abstract property? Would the relationship instead be one of *resemblance*? That is, are non-abstract instances like the abstract property, so that individual cases of hair-on-a-head resemble the property of having hair on a head? How similar will all of these be, though? And would this require there to be a further property, shared by those instances and that first property? (How can such a need for further properties *end*, if even a single property is to be exemplified?)

Philosophically puzzling questions thus arise. This reading exemplifies that pattern for the classic Platonic view that there are *abstract universal* properties. These are what Plato influentially called *Forms*. How can these abstract entities have individual, flesh-and-blood, here-and-now, instances or exemplifications (such as you and parts of you)?

Socrates, he [Parmenides] said, your eagerness for discussion is admirable. And now tell me. Have you yourself drawn this distinction you speak of and separated apart on the one side forms themselves and on the other the things that share in them? Do you believe that there is such a thing as likeness itself apart from the likeness that we possess, and so on with unity and plurality and all the terms in Zeno's argument that you have just been listening to?

Certainly I do, said Socrates.

And also in cases like these, asked Parmenides, is there, for example, a form of rightness or of beauty or of goodness, and of all such things?

Yes.

And again, a form of man, apart from ourselves and all other men like us – a form of man as something by itself? Or a form of fire or of water?

I have often been puzzled about those things, Parmenides, whether one should say that the same thing is true in their case or not.

Are you also puzzled, Socrates, about cases that might be thought absurd, such as hair or mud or dirt or any other trivial and undignified objects? Are you doubtful whether or not to assert that each of these has a separate form distinct from things like those we handle?

Not at all, said Socrates. In these cases, the things are just the things we see; it would surely be too absurd to suppose that they have a form. All the same, I have sometimes been troubled by a doubt whether what is true in one case may not be true in all. Then, when I have reached that point, I am driven to retreat, for fear of tumbling into a bottomless pit of nonsense. Anyhow, I get back to the things which we were just now speaking of as having forms, and occupy my time with thinking about them.

That, replied Parmenides, is because you are still young, Socrates, and philosophy has not yet taken hold of you so firmly as I believe it will someday. You will not despise any of these objects then, but at present your youth makes you still pay attention to what the world will think. However that may be, tell me this. You say you hold that there exist certain forms, of which these other things come to partake and so to be called after their names; by coming to partake of likeness or largeness or beauty or justice, they become like or large or beautiful or just?

Certainly, said Socrates.

Then each thing that partakes receives as its share either the form as a whole or a part of it? Or can there be any other way of partaking besides this?

No, how could there be?

Do you hold, then, that the form as a whole, a single thing, is in each of the many, or how?

Why should it not be in each, Parmenides?

If so, a form which is one and the same will be at the same time, as a whole, in a number of things which are separate, and consequently will be separate from itself.

No, it would not, replied Socrates, if it were like one and the same day, which is in many places at the same time and nevertheless is not separate from itself. Suppose any given form is in them all at the same time as one and the same thing in that way.

I like the way you make out that one and the same thing is in many places at once, Socrates. You might as well spread a sail over a number of people and then say that the one sail as a whole was over them all. Don't you think that is a fair analogy?

Perhaps it is.

Then would the sail as a whole be over each man, or only a part over one, another part over another?

Only a part.

In that case, Socrates, the forms themselves must be divisible into parts, and the things which have a share in them will have a part for their share. Only a part of any given form, and no longer the whole of it, will be in each thing.

Evidently, on that showing.

Are you, then, prepared to assert that we shall find the single form actually being divided? Will it still be one?

Certainly not.

No, for consider this. Suppose it is largeness itself that you are going to divide into parts, and that each of the many large things is to be large by virtue of a part of largeness which is smaller than largeness itself. Will not that seem unreasonable?

It will indeed.

And again, if it is equality that a thing receives some small part of, will that part, which is less than equality itself, make its possessor equal to something else?

No, that is impossible.

Well, take smallness. Is one of us to have a portion of smallness, and is smallness to be larger than that portion, which is a part of it? On this supposition again smallness itself will be larger, and anything to which the portion taken is added will be smaller, and not larger, than it was before.

That cannot be so.

Well then, Socrates, how are the other things going to partake of your forms, if they can partake of them neither in part nor as wholes?

Really, said Socrates, it seems no easy matter to determine in any way.

Again, there is another question.

What is that?

How do you feel about this? I imagine your ground for believing in a single form in each case is this. When it seems to you that a number of things are large, there seems, I suppose, to be a certain single character which is the same when you look at them all; hence you think that largeness is a single thing.

True, he replied.

But now take largeness itself and the other things which are large. Suppose you look at all these in the same way in your mind's eye, will not yet another unity make its appearance – a largeness by virtue of which they all appear large?

So it would seem.

If so, a second form of largeness will present itself, over and above largeness itself and the things that share in it, and again, covering all these, yet another, which will make all of them large. So each of your forms will no longer be one, but an indefinite number.

But, Parmenides, said Socrates, may it not be that each of these forms is a thought, which cannot properly exist anywhere but in a mind. In that way each of them can be one and the statements that have just been made would no longer be true of it.

Then, is each form one of these thoughts and yet a thought of nothing?

No, that is impossible.

So it is a thought of something?

Yes.

Of something that is, or of something that is not?

Of something that is.

In fact, of some *one* thing which that thought observes to cover all the cases, as being a certain single character?

Yes.

Then will not this thing that is thought of as being one and always the same in all cases be a form?

That again seems to follow.

And besides, said Parmenides, according to the way in which you assert that the other things have a share in the forms, must you not hold either that each of those things consists of thoughts, so that all things think, or else that they are thoughts which nevertheless do not think?

That too is unreasonable, replied Socrates. But, Parmenides, the best I can make of the matter is this – that these forms are as it were patterns fixed in the nature of things. The other things are made in their image and are likenesses, and this participation they come to have in the forms is nothing but their being made in their image.

Well, if a thing is made in the image of the form, can that form fail to be like the image of it, in so far as the image was made in its likeness? If a thing is like, must it not be like something that is like it?

It must.

And must not the thing which is like share with the thing that is like it in one and the same thing [character]?

Yes.

And will not that in which the like things share, so as to be alike, be just the form itself that you spoke of?

Certainly.

If so, nothing can be like the form, nor can the form be like anything. Otherwise a second form will always make its appearance over and above the first form, and if that second form is like anything, yet a third. And there will be no end to this emergence of fresh forms, if the form is to be like the thing that partakes of it.

Quite true.

It follows that the other things do not partake of forms by being like them; we must look for some other means by which they partake.

So it seems.

You see then, Socrates, said Parmenides, what great difficulties there are in asserting their existence as forms just by themselves?

I do indeed.

I assure you, then, you have as yet hardly a notion of how great they will be, if you are going to set up a single form for every distinction you make among things.

How so?

The worst difficulty will be this, though there are plenty more. Suppose someone should say that the forms, if they are such as we are saying they must be, cannot even be known. One could not convince him that he was mistaken in that objection, unless he chanced to be a man of wide experience and natural ability, and were willing to follow one through a long and remote train of argument. Otherwise there would be no way of convincing a man who maintained that the forms were unknowable.

Why so, Parmenides?

Because, Socrates, I imagine that you or anyone else who asserts that each of them has a real being 'just by itself,' would admit, to begin with, that no such real being exists in our world.

True, for how could it then be just by itself?

Very good, said Parmenides. And further, those forms which are what they are with reference to one another have their being in such references among themselves, not with reference to those likenesses, or whatever we are to call them, in our world, which we possess and so come to be called by their several names. And, on the other hand, these things in our world which bear the same names as the forms are related among themselves, not to the forms, and all the names of that sort that they bear have reference to one another, not to the forms.

How do you mean? asked Socrates.

Suppose, for instance, one of us is master or slave of another: he is not, of course, the slave of master itself, the essential master, nor, if he is a master, is he master of slave itself, the essential slave, but, being a man, is master or slave of another man, whereas mastership itself is what it is [mastership] of slavery itself, and slavery itself is slavery to mastership itself. The significance of things in our world is not with reference to things in that other world, nor have these their significance with reference to us, but, as I say, the things in that world are what they are with reference to one another and toward one another, and so likewise are the things in our world. You see what I mean?

Certainly I do.

And similarly knowledge itself, the essence of knowledge, will be knowledge of that reality itself, the essentially real.

Certainly.

And again, any given branch of knowledge in itself will be knowledge of some department of real things as it is in itself, will it not?

Yes.

Whereas the knowledge in our world will be knowledge of the reality in our world, and it will follow again that each branch of knowledge in our world must be knowledge of some department of things that exist in our world.

Necessarily.

But, as you admit, we do not possess the forms themselves, nor can they exist in our world.

No.

And presumably the forms, just as they are in themselves, are known by the form of knowledge itself?

Yes.

The form which we do not possess.

True.

Then, none of the forms is known by us, since we have no part in knowledge itself.

Apparently not.

So beauty itself or goodness itself and all the things we take as forms in themselves are unknowable to us.

I am afraid that is so.

Then here is a still more formidable consequence for you to consider.

What is that?

You will grant, I suppose, that if there is such a thing as a form, knowledge itself, it is much more perfect than the knowledge in our world, and so with beauty and all the rest.

Yes.

And if anything has part in this knowledge itself, you would agree that a god has a better title than anyone else to possess the most perfect knowledge?

Undoubtedly.

Then will the god, who possesses knowledge itself, be able to know the things in our world?

Why not?

Because we have agreed that those forms have no significance with reference to things in our world, nor have things in our world any significance with reference to them. Each set has it only among themselves.

Yes, we did.

Then if this most perfect mastership and most perfect knowledge are in the god's world, the gods' mastership can never be exercised over us, nor their knowledge know us of anything in our world. Just as we do not rule over them by virtue of rule as it exists in our world and we know nothing that is divine by our knowledge, so they, on the same principle, being gods, are not our masters nor do they know anything of human concerns.

But surely, said Socrates, an argument which would deprive the gods of knowledge would be too strange.

And yet, Socrates, Parmenides went on, these difficulties and many more besides are inevitably involved in the forms, if these characters of things really exist and one is going to distinguish each form as a thing just by itself. The result is that the hearer is perplexed and inclined either to question their existence, or to contend that, if they do exist, they must certainly be unknowable by our human nature. Moreover, there seems to be some weight in these objections, and, as we were saying, it is extraordinarily difficult to convert the objector. Only a man of exceptional gifts will be able to see that a form, or essence just by itself, does exist in each case, and it will require someone still more remarkable to discover it and to instruct another who has thoroughly examined all these difficulties.

14

How Can Individual Things Not Have Repeatable Qualities?

D.M. Armstrong, *Nominalism and Realism*

The previous reading, from Plato, ends with perplexity: How *can* there really be abstract repeatable qualities, applying to individuals so that these – you, me, this, that – have characteristics and features? Yes, individual things have and share characteristics. But is it too confusing to picture this literally as involving the existence of abstract universals – an abstract property of *being a person*, an abstract property of *having hair*, an abstract property of *having two ears*, etc.? Is the philosophical image of the world as containing such abstract entities overly difficult to understand? If so, perhaps we should try to explain how individuals have shared properties *without* our reaching for a Platonic realism (as it is called) about there being such universals. Well and good; except that, as explained in this reading from D.M. Armstrong (whom we also read earlier) the metaphysical alternatives to Platonic realism are no easier to develop in a coherent way.

The main alternative is called *nominalism* (from the Latin word "nomen," for "name"). Nothing that exists (according to this alternative philosophical image of reality) is repeatable, in the sense of really being able to be wholly in more than one place at one time. You cannot simultaneously and entirely be both here and in the next city; nor can any other person. *But nor either* can the property of being a person (says nominalism). Any contrary way of talking is just that: a way of talking, a conventional convenience (continues nominalism). Contrast that nominalist view with Platonic realism, according to which the following is true: although you and I are particular people, only ever in one place at one time as an entire person, the *property* of being a person can be completely present (being wholly exemplified by you and by me) in more than one place at one time. Platonism says that there really are repeatable properties, existing regardless of whether we know of them or have names for

D.M. Armstrong, *Nominalism and Realism*, vol. 1 of *Universals and Scientific Realism* (Cambridge: Cambridge University Press, 1978), ch. 2 (excerpts). © Cambridge University Press 1978. Reprinted with permission.

Metaphysics and Epistemology: A Guided Anthology, First Edition. Edited by Stephen Hetherington.
© 2014 John Wiley & Sons, Inc. Published 2014 by John Wiley & Sons, Inc.

them. Nominalism replies that it *is* merely a matter of how we name or describe or otherwise organize the world's particularities. For example, a nominalist might regard our being people equally as nothing beyond the equal applicability, to each of us, of a particular conventional term or predicate (e.g. "person" in English).

This reading focuses upon versions of that nominalist proposal. D.M. Armstrong presents a few associated conceptual puzzles. (Notice that one of them builds upon our two earlier readings on causation. When the world functions causally, is this because repeatable universals are involved, with *kinds* of individual things having a *kind* of power to have a *kind* of effect? Armstrong describes potential roles in this debate for the Humean view of causation and for Anscombe's competing view.) The central choice here – between a Platonic realism accepting that there are repeatable abstract qualities and a nominalist denial of there being repeatable qualities – is one of philosophy's oldest and most challenging problems.

I.   Nominalism versus Realism

There is one sense in which everybody agrees that particulars have properties and stand in relations to other particulars. The piece of paper before me is a particular. It is white, so it has a property. It rests upon a table, so it is related to another particular. Such gross facts are not, or should not be, in dispute between Nominalists and Realists.

G. E. Moore never tired of emphasizing that in the case of many of the great metaphysical disputes the gross facts are not in dispute. What is in dispute, he contended, is the account or analysis to be given of the gross facts. This appears to be the situation in the dispute between Nominalism and Realism. Both can agree that the paper is white and rests upon a table. It is an adequacy-condition of their analyses that such statements come out true. But the analyses themselves are utterly different.

We start with a basic agreement, then: that in some minimal or pre-analytic sense there are things having certain properties and standing in certain relations. But, as Plato was the first to point out, this situation is a profoundly puzzling one, at least for philosophers. The same property can belong to different things. The same relation can relate different things. Apparently, there can be something identical in things which are not identical. Things are one at the same time as they are many. How is this possible? Nominalists and Realists react to the puzzle in different ways. Nominalists deny that there is any genuine or objective identity in things which are not identical. Realists, on the other hand, hold that the apparent situation is the real situation. There genuinely is, or can be, something identical in things which are not identical. Besides particulars, there are universals.

The fundamental contention of Nominalism is that *all things that exist are only particulars*. The Realist need not deny that all things that exist are particulars, but he must at least deny that there are *only* particulars. [...]

For the present, however, we are concerned with the problems of the Nominalist. How is he to account for the apparent (if usually partial) identity of numerically different particulars? How can two different things both be white or both be on a table? It is natural for the

Nominalist to pose his problem in linguistic terms. Locke summed the matter up with admirable and quite unusual succinctness when he said:

> since all things that exist are only particulars how come we by general terms ...?
>
> (*Essay*, Bk. III, ch. 3 §10)

However, although all Nominalists agree that all things that exist are only particulars, they by no means agree about the way that the problem of apparent identity of nature is to be solved. I classify their attempted solutions under five heads which I call Predicate Nominalism, Concept Nominalism, Class Nominalism, Mereological Nominalism and Resemblance Nominalism. In the next section I explain these five positions (the latter four, only briefly). The rest of the chapter will then be devoted to criticizing Predicate Nominalism.

II. Varieties of Nominalism

Predicate Nominalism. Some predicates, such as 'identical with the planet Venus' or, perhaps, 'the wisest of men' apply to one and only one thing. But other predicates, such as 'circular' and 'man' apply to indefinitely, perhaps infinitely, many things. These latter are Locke's "general terms". The question arises "In virtue of what do these general terms apply to the things which they apply to?" The answer of Predicate Nominalism is "In virtue of nothing". The fundamental fact in this situation, which cannot be further explained, is that the predicates do apply.

Restricting ourselves for simplicity to one-place predicates, we can say that Predicate Nominalists give the following analysis:

> a has the property, F, if and only if
> a falls under the predicate 'F'.

Falling under, of course, is simply the converse of *applying to*.[1]

[...]

Are there any Predicate Nominalists? Is the doctrine really just a straw man or ideal case, approached, but never reached, by actual Nominalists? Even if this were true, criticism of Predicate Nominalism would have its value. But I do not think it is true. We may, for instance, cite John Searle (1969):

> Insofar as the nominalist is claiming that the existence of particulars depends on facts in the world and the existence of universals merely on the meaning of words, he is quite correct. But he lapses into confusion and needless error if his discovery leads him to deny such trivially true things as that there is such a property as the property of being red and that centaurhood exists. For to assert these need commit one to no more than that certain predicates have a meaning, (p. 105)

Again:

> to put it briefly, universals are parasitic upon predicate expressions ... (p. 120)

Concept Nominalism. The Concept Nominalist calls upon concepts, conceived as mental entities, to do the job for which the Predicate Nominalist employs predicates. For him:

> a has the property, F, if and only if
> a falls under the concept F.

[...]

Class Nominalism. For the Class Nominalist:

> a has the property, F, if and only if
> a is a member of the class of Fs.

I have not found an author who explicitly expounds and defends Class Nominalism. Rather, Class Nominalism is a pervasive tendency or occasional assumption among those philosophers who are Nominalist in sympathy, particularly if they are logicians.
[...]

Mereological Nominalism. For this variant of Class Nominalism:

> a has the property, F, if and only if
> a is a part of the aggregate
> (heap) of the Fs.

[...]

Resemblance Nominalism. Resemblance Nominalism is the most carefully articulated form of Nominalism, and both Carnap (1967) and Price (1953) have presented fully worked-out Resemblance Nominalisms. According to this view:

> a has the property, F, if and only if
> a suitably resembles a paradigm case
> (or paradigm cases) of an F.

'Suitable resemblance' here is simply a brief dummy for the much more elaborate account, somewhat different in different versions, which is given by Resemblance Nominalists.
[...]

III.   Can Predicates Determine Properties?

Beginning with this section, I consider various objections to Predicate Nominalism, I believe that they are all conclusive. [Section V (below)] considers and rejects a reformulation of Predicate Nominalism in terms of the applicability of *possible* predicates.

According to Predicate Nominalism, an object's possession of (say) the property, *being white*, is completely determined by the fact that the predicate 'white' applies to this object. But now let us make a thought-experiment. Let us imagine that the predicate 'white' does not exist. Is it not obvious that the object might still be white ? If so, its whiteness is *not* constituted by the object's relation to the predicate 'white'.

[...]

It is very important not to overestimate how much this argument establishes, even if it is sound. It does not establish that the predicate 'white' applies to the object in virtue of the objective property of *whiteness*. [...]

[...] All that the argument shows is that there must be something about the particular, besides the fact that it is a particular, to explain why the predicate 'white' applies to it.

[...]

IV. Predicate Nominalism and Two Infinite Regresses

[...] [I]t will be helpful to recall what was said at the beginning of this chapter. What was pointed out there in effect was that, in the dispute between Realism and Nominalism, the onus of proof lies with the latter. Ordinary thought and discourse recognizes identity both of particulars and of property, sort or kind. Indeed, without the distinction between sameness of thing and sameness of property or kind, thought and discourse would be impossible. The terms "token" and "type" are terms of art, but the distinction which they mark is admitted by everybody. All that the Nominalist can hope to do is to give a reductive analysis or account of what it is for something to have a property or to be of a certain kind or sort: a reductive analysis or account of types.

If, then, in the course of an attempted Nominalist analysis it should happen that covert appeal is made to the notion of property, kind or type, the analysis has failed to achieve its purpose. The failure does not prove the truth of Realism, but it does show that that particular Nominalist analysis has failed in its purpose.

Various of the following arguments, in particular the infinite regress arguments against the varieties of Nominalism, depend upon this point. They aim to show that the Nominalist gives a reductive account of certain types only at the cost of reinstating further types, which is no advance. I now attempt to show this for the case of *Predicate Nominalism*.

Given a class, such as the class of white things, the Predicate Nominalist seeks to give an account of its unity by saying that each member of this class has the same relation (the relation of *falling under*) to the same predicate: the predicate 'white'. But the two samenesses involved here are not samenesses of a particular, rather they are samenesses of sort, kind or type. Each white thing has the same sort of relation to the predicate 'white'. Nor do they have this type of relation to just one token of the predicate. They have this type of relation to any token of the predicate-type 'white'.

Types, however, are the very phenomenon to be reduced. So the Predicate Nominalist has covertly appealed to types in the course of developing a theory which claims to give a reductive analysis of all types. It is clear that, if he is to be consistent, those types which appear on the right-hand side of his analyses must themselves be analysed in Predicate Nominalist style. But such analysis requires appeal to types, and so *ad infinitum*. The theory is involved in an infinite regress.

[...]

V.   Predicates and Possible Predicates

In putting forward the infinite regress argument against Predicate Nominalism, it was tacitly conceded to the Nominalist that he had available to him an infinite stock of predicates. Only so could he provide higher-order predicates in terms of which he could analyse what it is for predicates to be tokens of the same predicate-type.

But at some point in the regress, the Predicate Nominalist will run out of actual predicates. For a Nominalist, a predicate of a certain type can exist only if tokens of that type exist. [...] But [...] [t]okens may be lacking at the very first step. It is clearly possible, and we believe it to be the case, that particulars have certain properties and relations which never fall under human notice. Even where actual predicate-tokens exist for properties and relations, there will not in general be higher-order tokens under which these tokens fall. And even where there are such higher-order tokens, a very few steps up the ladder will ensure that we reach predicate-tokens which are of a certain type but do not fall under any actual predicates.

What is the Predicate Nominalist to do ? At this point it is worth remembering our first criticism of Predicate Nominalism. A simple thought-experiment showed that a particular would still be white even if the predicate 'white' did not exist. The Predicate Nominalist could meet both that difficulty and the present one if he modified his analysis to:

a has the property, F, if and only if
a falls under a *possible* predicate 'F'.

This gets the Predicate Nominalist out of two frying-pans but lands him in a very hot fire. How is the new formula to be understood ? Is the Predicate Nominalist committing himself to *entities* called 'possible predicates'? This may not contradict the letter of Nominalism but certainly contradicts its spirit. [...] If the Predicate Nominalist is not willing to postulate *possibilia*, then his analysis amounts to saying that a exists and that a certain hypothetical proposition is true of a, *viz*. if there were a predicate 'F', then a would fall under it. But what is it in the world which makes the hypothetical proposition true? [...] What other answer can be given except that the object a has a certain *nature* which would serve as ground for applying the predicate 'F' if there were such a predicate ? Yet to give this answer is to abandon Predicate Nominalism. We should then require an account of this nature which a has, and the account cannot be given in terms of possibility.

VI.   Predicate Nominalism and Causality

The next argument depends upon three premises. First, there are causes in nature. Second, the causal order is independent of the classifications which we make. Third, what causes what depends solely upon the properties (including relational properties) of the cause and the effect. From this it follows that properties are independent of the classifications which we make, and thus that the Predicate Nominalist's account of properties is false.

The connection between causation and properties is probably the most controversial premise of this argument. But even this premise is generally acknowledged. If a stone hits a piece of glass and the glass shatters, then what occurs is thought to depend wholly upon what sort of thing the stone is, what sort of state it is in (for instance, its state of motion), what sort of thing and what state the glass is in, and what sort of circumstances surround the encounter of stone and glass. If stone, glass and environment had had certain other properties, then the outcome would have been a different sort of outcome from what in fact it was.

This link between a cause and its effect, on the one hand, and the nature of that cause and its effect, on the other, is made explicit in one theory of causation: the Humean or Regularity view. On this analysis it makes no sense to speak of one thing or event causing another unless this sequence is such that, on other occasions, the same *sort* of antecedent, in the same *sort* of circumstances, is always succeeded by the same *sort* of consequent. A Regularity view is not committed to any particular philosophy of properties, but it is committed to the view that one thing causes another by virtue of its properties. But if it is also granted that causal sequences exist as causal sequences independently of our classifications of them, then the Humean must reject Predicate Nominalism.

A Humean about causation *must* link causality with properties, though he need not give a Realist account of properties. But even if we reject a Humean view of causality (as I believe we should) it is utterly natural to think that what causes what is determined by the properties of the things (events) involved.

There is one analysis of causation which rejects this connection: it is the Singularist view developed by Elizabeth Anscombe (1971) [see reading 12]. According to this view, in a causal sequence it is a particular event *qua* particular which brings about a further particular event. Hume held that it is logically possible that anything should be the cause of anything, but he did stipulate that to be accounted "cause" and "effect" the particulars involved must be instances of a regular sequence. But on the Singularist view even the demand for regularity is dropped from the concept of causation. Unlike the Humean view, there is then no logical connection between the notion of cause and the notion of a law of nature.

I do not know how, if at all, a Singularist theory of causation is to be refuted, although I find it quite unbelievable. I have mentioned it here because it is the only account of causation of which I am aware which denies the connection between causation and properties. But once a Singularist theory of causation is rejected we are committed to saying that whatever is a cause acts causally in virtue of its properties. If it is accepted further that causal relations are objective and do not depend upon our classifications, then Predicate Nominalism must be an unsatisfactory account of what it is for a thing to have a property.

Note

1.   When I wish to refer to a putative property or relation I will italicize the corresponding expression.

References

Carnap, R. (1967) *The Logical Structure of the World*, trans. R.A. George. London; Routledge & Kegan Paul.

Price, H.H. (1953) *Thinking and Experience*. London: Hutchinson.

Searle, J.R. (1969) *Speech Acts: An Essay in the Philosophy of Language*. Cambridge: Cambridge University Press.

How Are There Any Truths?

15

Do Facts Make True Whatever Is True?

Bertrand Russell, "The Philosophy of Logical Atomism"

To understand what it is for an individual to have a quality or property (as the previous two readings sought to do) might be to understand part of what it is for the world to contain *facts*. For possibly some facts *are* simply an individual's having a property – this thing having that feature. At any rate, that could be so *if* there are facts. In this reading, Bertrand Russell (whom we read earlier on appearance versus reality in the physical world) begins developing a metaphysical image of the world that includes at its core the concept of a fact. This reading comes from a series of lectures by Russell that were influential in the development of

Bertrand Russell, "The Philosophy of Logical Atomism" [1918], lectures I, II (excerpts). From his *Logic and Knowledge: Essays 1901–1950*, ed. R.C. Marsh (London: George Allen & Unwin, 1956). Reprinted with permission of the Bertrand Russell Peace Foundation.

twentieth-century philosophy. His first goal in these lectures was to show how to talk of facts with literal and deliberative philosophical intent.

Why so? Russell argued that facts are genuinely what would make *true* or make *false* our beliefs or claims. Not just anything could do this; only facts could. For example, when you believe that your best friend is a person (rather than a disguised robot), what is making your belief true? The belief has a content: "My best friend is a person (not a disguised robot)." That content is true in virtue of something. Of *what*, though? Russell would say that there is an individual (your best friend); there is a repeatable property or quality of being a person; *and* there is a fact – literally a further component of reality – of your best friend being a person. This fact *is* your best friend having or instantiating that repeatable property of being a person. So the fact is composed of, or constituted by, the individual and the property. But the fact is something beyond these components: it is the friend's *having* the property. And this fact, with its inner complexity involving your friend and the property, is what renders your belief true. Your friend – the individual as such – does not render your belief true. Only the *fact* does so – the fact of his or her existing with the property of being a person. He or she is a part – but only a part – of that fact.

What *kinds* of fact would there be in the world? Your best friend's being a person is a *particular* fact – a fact only about a particular individual. But Russell also argued that the world has to include at least one *general* fact, not only particular ones. He reasons in the following way. Even if every particular fact about every particular individual was to be listed, that could not describe all there is. We would have to add this: "and that is *all* of the particular facts." So the world contains at least these two basic *kinds* of fact – particular and general – literally and every bit as much as it includes you as a particular individual, say.

There might be other kinds of fact, too. Russell proceeds to discuss whether, for instance, there are more logically complex kinds of fact, such as negative facts and disjunctive facts (ones with the form "__ or ..."). But thinking about these would take us too far afield for now. We may begin just with simpler facts. Do *these* exist?

The first truism to which I wish to draw your attention [...] is that the world contains *facts*, which are what they are whatever we may choose to think about them, and that there are also *beliefs*, which have reference to facts, and by reference to facts are either true or false. I will try first of all to give you a preliminary explanation of what I mean by a 'fact'. When I speak of a fact [...] I mean the kind of thing that makes a proposition true or false. If I say 'It is raining', what I say is true in a certain condition of weather and is false in other conditions of weather. The condition of weather that makes my statement true (or false as the case may be), is what I should call a 'fact'. If I say 'Socrates is dead', my statement will be true owing to a certain physiological occurrence which happened in Athens long ago. If I say, 'Gravitation varies inversely as the square of the distance', my statement is rendered true by astronomical fact. If I say, 'Two and two are four', it is arithmetical fact that makes my statement true. On the other hand, if I say 'Socrates is alive', or 'Gravitation varies directly as the distance', or

'Two and two are five', the very same facts which made my previous statements true show that these new statements are false.

I want you to realize that when I speak of a fact I do not mean a particular existing thing, such as Socrates or the rain or the sun. Socrates himself does not render any statement true or false. You might be inclined to suppose that all by himself he would give truth to the statement 'Socrates existed', but as a matter of fact that is a mistake. It is due to a confusion which I shall try to explain in [a later] lecture of this course, when I come to deal with the notion of existence. Socrates himself, or any particular thing just by itself, does not make any proposition true or false. 'Socrates is dead' and 'Socrates is alive' are both of them statements about Socrates. One is true and the other false. What I call a fact is the sort of thing that is expressed by a whole sentence, not by a single name like 'Socrates'. When a single word does come to express a fact, like 'fire' or 'wolf', it is always due to an unexpressed context, and the full expression of a fact will always involve a sentence. We express a fact, for example, when we say that a certain thing has a certain property, or that it has a certain relation to another thing; but the thing which has the property or the relation is not what I call a 'fact'.

It is important to observe that facts belong to the objective world. They are not created by our thoughts or beliefs except in special cases. [...] The first thing I want to emphasize is that the outer world – the world, so to speak, which knowledge is aiming at knowing – is not completely described by a lot of 'particulars', but that you must also take account of these things that I call facts, which are the sort of things that you express by a sentence, and that these, just as much as particular chairs and tables, are part of the real world. Except in psychology, most of our statements are not intended merely to express our condition of mind, though that is often all that they succeed in doing. They are intended to express facts, which (except when they are psychological facts) will be about the outer world. There are such facts involved, equally when we speak truly and when we speak falsely. When we speak falsely it is an objective fact that makes what we say false, and it is an objective fact which makes what we say true when we speak truly.

There are a great many different kinds of facts. [...] I will just point out a few kinds of facts to begin with, so that you may not imagine that facts are all very much alike. There are *particular facts*, such as 'This is white'; then there are *general facts*, such as 'All men are mortal'. Of course, the distinction between particular and general facts is one of the most important. There again it would be a very great mistake to suppose that you could describe the world completely by means of particular facts alone. Suppose that you had succeeded in chronicling every single particular fact throughout the universe, and that there did not exist a single particular fact of any sort anywhere that you had not chronicled, you still would not have got a complete description of the universe unless you also added: 'These that I have chronicled are all the particular facts there are'. So you cannot hope to describe the world completely without having general facts as well as particular facts. Another distinction, which is perhaps a little more difficult to make, is between positive facts and negative facts, such as 'Socrates was alive' – a positive fact – and 'Socrates is not alive' – you might say a negative fact. But the distinction is difficult to make precise. Then there are facts concerning particular things or particular qualities or relations, and, apart from them, the completely general facts of the sort that you have in logic, where there is no mention of any constituent whatever of the actual world, no mention of any particular thing or particular quality or particular relation, indeed strictly you may say no mention of anything. That is one of the characteristics of logical propositions, that they mention nothing. [...] Then there are facts about the properties of single things; and facts about the relations between two things, three things, and so on; and any number of different classifications of some of the facts in the world, which are important for different purposes.

It is obvious that there is not a dualism of true and false facts; there are only just facts. It would be a mistake, of course, to say that all facts are true. That would be a mistake because true and false are correlatives, and you would only say of a thing that it was true if it was the sort of thing that *might* be false. A fact cannot be either true or false. That brings us on to the question of statements or propositions or judgments, all those things that do have the duality of truth and falsehood. [...] A proposition, one may say, is a sentence in the indicative, a sentence asserting something, not questioning or commanding or wishing. It may also be a sentence of that sort preceded by the word 'that'. For example, 'That Socrates is alive', 'That two and two are four', 'That two and two are five', anything of that sort will be a proposition.

A proposition is just a symbol. It is a complex symbol in the sense that it has parts which are also symbols: a symbol may be defined as complex when it has parts that are symbols. In a sentence containing several words, the several words are each symbols, and the sentence composing them is therefore a complex symbol in that sense.

[...]

There are two different relations that a proposition may have to a fact: the one the relation that you may call being true to the fact, and the other being false to the fact. Both are equally essentially logical relations which may subsist between the two, whereas in the case of a name, there is only one relation that it can have to what it names. A name can just name a particular, or, if it does not, it is not a name at all, it is a noise. It cannot be a name without having just that one particular relation of naming a certain thing, whereas a proposition does not cease to be a proposition if it is false. It has these two ways, of being true and being false, which together correspond to the property of being a name. Just as a word may be a name or be not a name but just a meaningless noise, so a phrase which is apparently a proposition may be either true or false, or may be meaningless, but the true and false belong together as against the meaningless. That shows, of course, that the formal logical characteristics of propositions are quite different from those of names, and that the relations they have to facts are quite different, and therefore propositions are not names for facts. You must not run away with the idea that you can name facts in any other way; you cannot. You cannot name them at all. You cannot properly name a fact. The only thing you can do is to assert it, or deny it, or desire it, or will it, or wish it, or question it, but all those are things involving the whole proposition. You can never put the sort of thing that makes a proposition to be true or false in the position of a logical subject. You can only have it there as something to be asserted or denied or something of that sort, but not something to be named.

[...]

I explained last time what I meant by a fact, namely, that sort of thing that makes a proposition true or false, the sort of thing which is the case when your statement is true and is not the case when your statement is false. Facts are, as I said last time, plainly something you have to take account of if you are going to give a complete account of the world. You cannot do that by merely enumerating the particular things that are in it: you must also mention the relations of these things, and their properties, and so forth, all of which are facts, so that facts certainly belong to an account of the objective world, and facts do seem much more clearly complex and much more not capable of being explained away than things like Socrates and

Rumania. However you may explain away the meaning of the word 'Socrates', you will still be left with the truth that the proposition 'Socrates is mortal' expresses a fact. You may not know exactly what Socrates means, but it is quite clear that 'Socrates is mortal' does express a fact. There is clearly some valid meaning in saying that the fact expressed by 'Socrates is mortal' is *complex*. The things in the world have various properties, and stand in various relations to each other. That they have these properties and relations are *facts*, and the things and their qualities or relations are quite clearly in some sense or other components of the facts that have those qualities or relations. The analysis of apparently complex *things* such as we started with can be reduced by various means, to the analysis of facts which are apparently about those things. Therefore it is with the analysis of *facts* that one's consideration of the problem of complexity must begin, not by the analysis of apparently complex things.

The complexity of a fact is evidenced, to begin with, by the circumstance that the proposition which asserts a fact consists of several words, each of which may occur in other contexts. Of course, sometimes you get a proposition expressed by a single word but if it is expressed fully it is bound to contain several words. The proposition 'Socrates is mortal' may be replaced by 'Plato is mortal' or by 'Socrates is human'; in the first case we alter the subject, in the second the predicate. It is clear that all the propositions in which the word 'Socrates' occurs have something in common, and again all the propositions in which the word 'mortal' occurs have something in common, something which they do not have in common with all propositions, but only with those which are about Socrates or mortality. It is clear, I think, that the facts corresponding to propositions in which the word 'Socrates' occurs have something in common corresponding to the common word 'Socrates' which occurs in the propositions, so that you have that sense of complexity to begin with, that in a fact you can get something which it may have in common with other facts, just as you may have 'Socrates is human' and 'Socrates is mortal', both of them facts, and both having to do with Socrates, although Socrates does not constitute the whole of either of these facts. It is quite clear that in that sense there is a possibility of cutting up a fact into component parts, of which one component may be altered without altering the others, and one component may occur in certain other facts though not in all other facts.

16

Are There Social Facts?

John Searle, *Mind, Language and Society*

The previous reading, from Bertrand Russell, was arguing that in order to understand the world philosophically we need to reach for the concept of a fact. We might not always know what facts there are. But we should accept that there *are* facts. Once we do so, we will wonder what *kinds* of facts there are. Russell did that to some extent. In this present reading, John Searle (b. 1932), an eminent philosopher from the University of California, Berkeley, continues along that path. Best known for his writings on mind and language, since the mid-1990s he has applied and extended some of those ideas, so as to analyze the concepts of *social* reality and of *social* facts.

Think of the social fluidity, the variety and mutability of societies and how they organize the world around them. Think of your own life. It is crammed with social facts, seemingly – not only because you interact with other people, but because you interact with aspects of reality that are whatever they are partly because of what other people would say they are. Searle recognizes the existence of *brute* facts – those directly about what is physical, for example. On the basis of these, along with how we respond to and use them, Searle then describes how we can conceptually construct what he calls *institutional* reality. This is not a loose or merely suggestive phrase on his part. There can be a genuine (institutional) fact about, say, a piece of paper's being money. This is as much a fact in the world as is the fact of the object's being a piece of paper in the first place, or even its being simply an object. It is a distinctive kind of fact, though. For Searle, social facts are indeed constituted partly by people *agreeing*, at least tacitly, on relevant details. That is particularly significant if you would otherwise be tempted to think that nothing could be a fact if its being

John Searle, *Mind, Language and Society* (London: Phoenix, 1999), ch. 5 (excerpts). W&N copyright © 1999 John R. Searle. Reprinted with permission of Basic Books, a member of the Perseus Books Group.

so would rely on what people would say or believe. If Searle is right, it is not merely everyone's opinion that pieces of paper with various specifiable characteristics are instances of money. It is a *fact* that these are instances of money. Moreover, it is a fact constituted ultimately *by* that shared opinion. (Incidentally, Searle talks of ontology. An ontology is a listing of fundamental types or categories of being or reality. Ontology is part of metaphysics.)

Social and Institutional Reality

Think, for example, about the piece of paper that I have in my wallet. If I take it out of my wallet to inspect it, I see that its physical properties are rather uninteresting. It consists, chemically speaking, of cellulose fibers stained with certain dyes. However, in spite of its trivial physics and chemistry, all of us regard it as of some importance. The reason for this is that it is money. If we ask, "What facts about it make it money?" we find that the chemistry and the physics are insufficient to answer the question. If I try to produce something that looks exactly like this piece of paper, even if I duplicate it exactly down to the last molecule, it would not be money. On the contrary, it would be counterfeit, and I would be subject to arrest and prosecution. So, once again, what facts about it make it money? The beginnings of an answer can be given by saying that a type of phenomenon is money only if we think it is money. Being thought to be money is a necessary but not a sufficient condition. For something to be money there has to be more than just a set of attitudes, even though the attitudes are partly constitutive, and essentially constitutive, of a type of phenomenon being money. I have to say "type" because particular token instances might be counterfeit. A particular bill might be thought to be money, when in fact it is counterfeit. The general point remains: a type of thing is money over the long haul only if it is accepted as money. And what goes for money, goes for social and institutional reality generally. So, money, language, property, marriage, government, universities, cocktail parties, lawyers, presidents of the United States are all partly – but not entirely – constituted under these descriptions by the fact that we regard them as such. An object fits one of these descriptions in part because we think that it does, or we accept or recognize it as such. Furthermore, important consequences follow from the fact that we regard these phenomena as fitting a certain description: from the fact that I and others think that the piece of paper in my pocket is money, I have certain powers that I would not otherwise have. And what is true of money is true of institutional reality generally. From the facts that I am a citizen, or a convicted criminal, or the host at a cocktail party, or the owner of a car, certain powers – including negative powers such as responsibilities and penalties and positive powers such as rights and entitlements – accrue to me. These phenomena ought to puzzle us as philosophers, and the question I want to address in this chapter is: How do such social and institutional phenomena fit into the overall ontology described in the preceding chapters? What is the ontology of the social and the institutional? How can there be an objective reality that is what it is only because we think it is what it is? When I go into a store and present these bits of paper to the clerk, he does not say, "Well, perhaps *you* think it is money, but why should we care what you think?"

[...]

Observer-Dependency and the Building Blocks of Social Reality

[...]

The Distinction Between Observer-Independent and Observer-Dependent

Some of the features of the world exist entirely independently of us humans and of our attitudes and activities; others depend on us. Consider, for example, an object that has both of these sorts of features, the thing I am now sitting on. This object has a certain mass and a certain molecular configuration, and these exist independently of us. Mass and molecular structure are observer-independent features of the world. But this object also has the feature that it is a chair. The fact that it is a chair is a result of its having been designed, manufactured, sold, bought, and used as a chair. Such features as being a chair are observer-relative or observer-dependent, where "observer" is short for "maker, user, designer, and intentionality possessor generally." Such features as mass, force, gravitational attraction, and voltage level are observer-independent; such features as being money, property, a knife, a chair, a football game, or a nice day for a picnic are observer-dependent or observer-relative. In general, the natural sciences deal with features that are observer-independent, such as force, mass, and photosynthesis; the social sciences deal with features that are observer-relative, such as elections, balance-of-payments problems, and social organizations.

[...]

A Simple Model of the Construction of Institutional Reality

[...] I am making a very strong claim: all of institutional reality can be explained using exactly these three notions, collective intentionality, the assignment of function, and constitutive rules. [...] Imagine a group of primitive creatures more or less like ourselves. It is easy to imagine that they individually assign functions to natural objects. For example, an individual might use this stump as a seat and that stick as a lever. And if an individual can assign functions using individual intentionality, it is not hard to imagine that several individuals can assign functions collectively. A group can use this log as a bench and that big stick as a lever to be manipulated by all of them. Now imagine that, acting as a group, they build a barrier, a wall around the place where they live. [...] The wall is designed to keep intruders out and keep members of the group in.

The wall has an assigned function in virtue of its physical features. We suppose that the wall is too big to climb over easily and that the inhabitants of the shelters can easily stop such climbing. [...] A function has been assigned to the wall – the function of acting as a boundary barrier – by the inhabitants acting collectively. [...] Let us suppose that the wall gradually decays. It slowly deteriorates until all that is left is a line of stones. But let us suppose that the inhabitants continue to treat the line of stones as if it could perform the function of the wall. Let us suppose that, as a matter of fact, they treat the line of stones just as if they understood that it was not to be crossed. [...]

[...] [A] very important shift has taken place with this addition. This shift is the decisive move in the creation of institutional reality. It is nothing less than the decisive move in the creation of what we think of as distinctive in human, as opposed to animal, societies. Here is why, Initially the wall performed its assigned function in virtue of its physical structure. But [...] the wall now performs its function not in virtue of its physical structure but in virtue of the collective acceptance or recognition by the individuals acting collectively that the wall has a certain status and with that status goes a certain function [...] I call these functions "status functions."

I believe this move, the move from physics to the collective acceptance of a status function, forms the basic conceptual structure behind human institutional reality. It is generally the case with institutional structures that the structure cannot perform its function in virtue of its physics alone but requires collective acceptance. Where human institutions are concerned, the functions, in short, are status functions.

The Example of Money

Perhaps the clearest case of this phenomenon is money. Money cannot perform its functions in virtue of physics alone. No matter how much by way of function we try to assign to the physics, the physics of money alone – unlike the physics of a knife or a bathtub – does not enable the performance of the function. For functions that are not status functions, such as the functions of a bathtub or a knife, the physics is essential to the performance of the function. The physical structure enables me to use my bathtub as a bathtub but not as a knife, and it enables me to use my knife as a knife but not as a bathtub. With status functions, however, there is a break between the physics of the system, on the one hand, and the status and the functions that go along with that status, on the other.

We can illustrate these points by considering some features of the evolution of paper currency in Western Europe. It is standard in economics textbooks to say that there are three types of money. The first type is "commodity money," which is the use of a commodity that is regarded as valuable as a kind of money. A system of commodity money is essentially a system of barter. The second sort of money is "contract money." Such money consists of contracts to pay the bearer with something valuable on demand. The third sort of money is "fiat money." Fiat money is money only in virtue of the fact that it has been declared to be money, by fiat, by some powerful agency. The puzzle is, what is it that all these have in common that makes them all money, and how does each work?

In the evolution of currency, the first stage was to have valuable commodities, typically gold and silver, which could be used as a medium of exchange and as a store of value. The gold and silver are not intrinsically valuable. The possession of "value" is an imposed function, but in this case, the function is imposed in virtue of the physical features of the object in question. And indeed, in the early days of gold and silver coinage, the value of the coin was exactly equal to the amount of the gold and silver in it. Governments sometimes cheated, but in principle, that was the idea. If you melted down the coin, it did not lose any of its value. The printing on the coin was just a way of identifying how much it was worth by indicating the amount of gold or silver in it.

However, carrying gold and silver around is a rather inefficient way to conduct business, and it is also rather dangerous. So, in Europe in the Middle Ages, possessors of gold and silver found it was safer to keep the gold and silver with a "banker." The banker would give them bits of paper or other sorts of documents on which it was written that the documents could be redeemed in gold or silver on demand. We thus have a move from commodity money to contract money. A piece of paper that substitutes for the gold is now a contract to pay the bearer. At some point, some genius discovered that you could increase the supply of money in the economy by issuing more contracts than you actually have gold or silver, and as long as not everybody runs to the banker at once, demanding their gold or silver, the system continues to work just as well as before the change from commodity money to contract money. The bits of paper, as they say, are as good as gold, or, for that matter, silver.

Finally, and this development took a long time, some later genius discovered that you could forget all about the gold and silver and just have the bits of paper. That is our present situation in the economically advanced nations. Many simple-minded people have the illusion that American currency is "backed by the gold in Fort Knox," but the notion of backing is quite illusory. What one has when one has a twenty-dollar bill, for example, is a bit of paper that functions in virtue of an imposed status function. The bill has no value as a commodity, and it has no value as a contract; it is a pure case of status function.

For a long time the Treasury allowed the illusion to persist that the piece of paper was still a contract. Thus, for instance, it said on the twenty-dollar Federal Reserve note that the Treasury would pay the bearer on demand the sum of twenty dollars. But if one had actually insisted on payment, the only thing that could have been forthcoming was equivalent currency, such as another twenty-dollar Federal Reserve note. The U.S. Treasury has now abandoned this hypocrisy, but the pretense still exists in Britain, where the twenty-pound note contains a promise by the governor of the Bank of England to pay the bearer on demand twenty pounds.

The main point I want to make with this discussion of the evolution of currency is that the move from commodity money to fiat money is a move from the assignment of a function in virtue of physical structure to a pure case of status function. The assignment of status function has the form "X counts as Y in C." Such-and-such patterned bits of paper, issued by the Bureau of Engraving and Printing, under the authority of the Treasury, simply *count as* money, that is, "Legal Tender for All Debts Public and Private," in the United States.

How Institutional Reality Can Be So Powerful

So far, I have described a rather simple mechanism by which we have imposed status functions on entities in virtue of collective intentionality, following the general form "X counts as Y in C." Now, this must seem a very simple and fragile mechanism for the creation of institutional structures such as governments, armies, universities, banks, and so on, and even more fragile if we consider such general human institutions as private property, marriage, and political power. How can such a simple mechanism generate such a vast apparatus? I think the general form of the answer to that can be stated fairly simply. It involves two mechanisms. First, the structure "X counts as Y in C" can be *iterated*. You can pile one status function on top of another. The X term at one level may have been a Y term at an earlier level, and you can keep repeatedly turning Y terms into X terms that count as yet another Y on top of each other. Furthermore, in complex societies, the C term (context) is typically a Y term from an earlier stage. Let me give you some examples of how that works.

I make noises through my mouth. So far, that is a brute fact: there is nothing institutional about noises as such. But, as I am a speaker of English addressing other English speakers, those noises *count as* the utterance of an English sentence; they are an instance of the formula "X counts as Y in C." But now, in an utterance of that English sentence, the Y term from the previous level now functions as an X term at the next level. The utterance of that English sentence with those intentions and in that context counts as, for example, making a promise. But now that Y term, the promise, is the X term at the next level up. Making that sort of promise in those sorts of circumstances counts as undertaking a contract. Notice what I have done. I have taken the brute X term – I made the noises – and piled on further Y terms by the repeated application of the formula. Y_1 becomes X_2, which counts as Y_2, which becomes X_3, and so on, up until we reach the point where I made a contract. Furthermore, we can suppose that that sort of contract, in those sorts of circumstances, counts as getting married. And then, getting married in turn counts as qualifying for all sorts of benefits, obligations, rights, duties, and so on. This is one mechanism for using the apparatus to create complex social structures. You simply repeat, or iterate, the mechanism over and over. Furthermore, in many cases the C term – the context – is itself the product of some prior imposition of status function. So, for example, in the state of California you can get married only if you are in the presence of a qualified official. But being a qualified official, though it is a context C in the application of the rules for getting married, is itself the result of the imposition of a status function. The C term at one level is a Y term from another level. Some individual X was, under circumstance C, certified as the qualified official Y. To summarize this point, one mechanism for producing complex structures out of such a simple device is the repeated application of the device.

A second feature that is crucial in the real-life functioning of institutional structures is that institutional facts do not exist in isolation but in complex interrelations with each other. So, for example, I don't just have money. I have *money* earned as an *employee* of the *state of California*, and I have it in my *bank account*, which I use to pay my *state and federal taxes* as well as the *bills* owing to the *gas and electric companies* and to the *contractor of my credit cards*. Notice that in the previous sentence, all of the italicized expressions are institutional terms. They make reference to assorted interconnected, diverse forms of institutional reality. Thus, we are able to use this simple mechanism to create a fantastically rich social structure by interlocking operations of the mechanism and complex iterations of the mechanism, piling one on top of the other.

But it may all still seem very fragile. How is it possible that we can do so much with so little? […] The answer is that we do not have separate and mutually exclusive classes of brute and institutional facts. The whole point, or at least much of the point, of having institutional facts is to gain social control of the brute facts. Thus, in a recent exchange that I had, it is true that I gave the other people only bits of paper or showed them a piece of plastic, and they only made noises at me through their mouths and gave me other bits of paper, but the result is that, having exchanged the noises and the bits of paper, I could then get on an airplane and fly a long distance away – a brute change of my geographical location. Similarly, as a result of such status functions, I live in a house that I would not otherwise live in. More generally, because of the assignment of status functions, people are thrown in jail, or executed, or go to war. So, it would be a misunderstanding to suppose that there are separate, isolated classes of brute facts and institutional facts. On the contrary, we have complex interpenetrations of brute and institutional facts. Indeed, typically the purpose or the function of the institutional structure is to create and control brute facts.

17

Is There Only Personally Decided Truth?

Plato, *Theaetetus*

Bertrand Russell and John Searle, in our previous two readings, began developing more or less complex philosophical images of the world as literally containing *facts*. In spite of being a social construction, money is real. As Searle explained, once money has been created (partly by our regarding it as money), there are facts involving it – ones about which people can proceed to make factual *mistakes*. That point is more general, of course. The traditional philosophical motivation for talking of facts has included that sort of image of them, as making our beliefs or claims either true or false. Not only that; a fact can accomplish this, even when we do not know which of "true" and "false" applies accurately to something we are thinking or saying.

Still, philosophers have often been puzzled by the idea of a fact. One of the alternatives they have contemplated is a *relativism* about truth. And this reading, from Plato's dialogue *Theaetetus*, offers us an ancient and famous relativist picture of truth and falsity. This picture is attributed by Socrates to Protagoras (c.485–c.415 BC). "Man is the measure" (with "man" meaning "mankind" – all of us): that was Protagoras' doctrine. In contemporary terms, this amounts to the idea that truth is only ever truth-for-an-individual. There is only ever truth-for-you, truth-for-me, truth-for-him, truth-for-her, etc. Truth-for-you on a particular occasion is however reality appears to you to be on that occasion. You are not mistaken, for example, because someone else regards reality as being X, when you view it as being Y-and-not-X. Nor are you mistaken in virtue of the world – courtesy of a fact within it – *making* you mistaken. Whatever appears to you to be true – and not further facts that

Plato, *Theaetetus* 152a–c, 161b–e, 169d–172c, 177c–179c (excerpts), trans. F.M. Cornford. From *The Collected Dialogues of Plato*, ed. E. Hamilton and H. Cairns (Princeton: Princeton University Press, 1961). © 1961 by Princeton University Press. Reprinted with permission of Princeton University Press.

Metaphysics and Epistemology: A Guided Anthology, First Edition. Edited by Stephen Hetherington.
© 2014 John Wiley & Sons, Inc. Published 2014 by John Wiley & Sons, Inc.

obtain even if they are never revealed to you – is what makes your beliefs or claims true, when they are.

But is that enough of an analysis, at any rate of when your beliefs or claims are *not* true? In thinking about truth, we need also to think about falsity – what it is, how it is present. Yet it is not clear that falsity is accorded its due weight by relativism; for it is not clear that (for relativism), unless *you* decide that you have been mistaken, there is anything that can be making your belief or claim false. In this reading, we meet Socrates attempting to describe potential problems for relativism. (Some of the issues here also reflect vitally upon the status of evidence and knowledge. We will return to these in Part III of the book, when discussing skepticism.)

SOCRATES: The account you give of the nature of knowledge is not, by any means, to be despised. It is the same that was given by Protagoras [...] He says, you will remember, that 'man is the measure of all things – alike of the being of things that are and of the not-being of things that are not.' No doubt you have read that.

THEAETETUS: Yes, often.

SOCRATES: He puts it in this sort of way, doesn't he, that any given thing 'is to me such as it appears to me, and is to you such as it appears to you,' you and I being men?

THEAETETUS: Yes, that is how he puts it.

SOCRATES: Well, what a wise man says is not likely to be nonsense. So let us follow up his meaning. Sometimes, when the same wind is blowing, one of us feels chilly, the other does not, or one may feel slightly chilly, the other quite cold.

THEAETETUS: Certainly.

SOCRATES: Well, in that case are we to say that the wind in itself is cold or not cold? Or shall we agree with Protagoras that it is cold to the one who feels chilly, and not to the other?

THEAETETUS : That seems reasonable.

SOCRATES: And further that it so 'appears' to each of us?

THEAETETUS: Yes.

SOCRATES: And 'appears' means that the 'perceives' it so?

THEAETETUS: True.

SOCRATES: 'Appearing,' then, is the same thing as 'perceiving,' in the case of what is hot or anything of that kind. They *are* to each man such as he *perceives* them.

THEAETETUS: So it seems.

SOCRATES: Perception, then, is always of something that *is* [.]
[. . .]

SOCRATES: [...] Theodorus, shall I tell you a thing that surprises me in your friend Protagoras?

THEODORUS: What is that?

SOCRATES: The opening words of his treatise. In general, I am delighted with his statement that what seems to anyone also is, but I am surprised that he did not begin his *Truth* with the words, The measure of all things is the pig, or the baboon, or some sentient creature still more uncouth. There would have been something magnificent in so disdainful an opening, telling us that all the time, while we were admiring him for a wisdom more than mortal, he was in fact no wiser than a tadpole, to say nothing of any other human being. What else can we say. Theodorus? If what every man believes as a result of perception is indeed to be true for him;

if, just as no one is to be a better judge of what another experiences, so no one is better entitled to consider whether what another thinks is true or false, and, as we have said more than once, every man is to have his own beliefs for himself alone and they are all right and true – then, my friend, where is the wisdom of Protagoras, to justify his setting up to teach others and to be handsomely paid for it, and where is our comparative ignorance or the need for us to go and sit at his feet, when each of us is himself the measure of his own wisdom? Must we not suppose that Protagoras speaks in this way to flatter the ears of the public?

    [...]

SOCRATES: Let us see whether or not our discontent was justified, when we criticized it as making every individual self-sufficient in wisdom. Protagoras then conceded that some people were superior in the matter of what is better or worse, and these, he said, were wise. Didn't he?

THEODORUS: Yes.

    [...]

SOCRATES: He says, doesn't he, that what seems true to anyone is true for him to whom it seems so?

THEODORUS: He does.

SOCRATES: Well now, Protagoras, we are expressing what seems true to a man, or rather to all men, when we say that everyone without exception holds that in some respects he is wiser than his neighbors and in others they are wiser than he. For instance, in moments of great danger and distress, whether in war or in sickness or at sea, men regard as a god anyone who can take control of the situation and look to him as a savior, when his only point of superiority is his knowledge. Indeed, the world is full of people looking for those who can instruct and govern men and animals and direct their doings, and on the other hand of people who think themselves quite competent to undertake the teaching and governing. In all these cases what can we say. If not that men do hold that wisdom and ignorance exist among them?

THEODORUS: We must say that.

SOCRATES: And they hold that wisdom lies in thinking truly, and ignorance in false belief?

THEODORUS: Of course.

SOCRATES: In that case [...] [a]re we to say that what men think is always true, or that it is sometimes true and sometimes false? From either supposition it results that their thoughts are not always true, but both true and false. For consider, Theodorus [...] is any Protagorean [...] prepared to maintain that no one regards anyone else as ignorant or as making false judgments?

THEODORUS: That is incredible, Socrates.

SOCRATES: That, however, is the inevitable consequence of the doctrine which makes man the measure of all things.

THEODORUS: How so?

SOCRATES: When you have formed a judgment on some matter in your own mind and express an opinion about it to me, let us grant that, as Protagoras' theory says, it is true for you, but are we to understand that it is impossible for us, the rest of the company, to pronounce any judgment upon your judgment, or, if we can, that we always pronounce your opinion to be true? Do you not rather find thousands of opponents who set their opinion against yours on every occasion and hold that your judgment and belief are false?

THEODORUS: I should just think so, Socrates – thousands and tens of thousands, as Homer says, and they give me all the trouble in the world.

SOCRATES: And what then? Would you have us say that in such a case the opinion you hold is true for yourself and false for these tens of thousands?

THEODORUS: The doctrine certainly seems to imply that.

SOCRATES: And what is the consequence for Protagoras himself? Is it not this? Supposing that not even be believed in man being the measure and the world in general did not believe it either – as in fact is doesn't – then this *Truth* which he wrote would not be true for anyone. If, on the other hand, he did believe it, but the mass of mankind does not agree with him, then, you see, it is more false than true by just so much as the unbelievers outnumber the believers.

THEODORUS: That follows, if its truth of falsity varies with each individual opinion.

SOCRATES: Yes, and besides that it involves a really exquisite conclusion. Protagoras, for his part, admitting as he does that everybody's opinion is true, must acknowledge the truth of his opponents' belief about his own belief, where they think he wrong.

THEODORUS: Certainly.

SOCRATES: That is to say, he would acknowledge his own belief to be false, if he admits that the belief of those who think him wrong is true?

THEODORUS: Necessarily.

SOCRATES: But the others, on their side, do not admit to themselves that they are wrong.

THEODORUS: No.

SOCRATES: Whereas Protagoras, once more, according to what he has written, admits that this opinion of theirs is as true as any other.

THEODORUS: Evidently.

SOCRATES: On all hands, then, Protagoras included, his opinion will be disputed, or rather Protagoras will join in the general consent – when he admits to an opponent the truth of his contrary opinion, from that moment Protagoras himself will be admitting that a dog or the man in the street is not a measure of anything whatever that he does not understand. Isn't that so?

THEODORUS: Yes.

SOCRATES: Then, since it is disputed by everyone, the *Truth* of Protagoras is true to nobody – to himself no more than to anyone else.

THEODORUS: We are running my old friend too hard, Socrates.

SOCRATES: But it is not clear that we are outrunning the truth, my friend. [...] Now, for instance, must we not say that everyone would agree at least to this, that one man can be wiser or more ignorant than another?

THEODORUS: I certainly think so.

SOCRATES: And further, shall we say that the doctrine would find its firmest footing in the position we traced out in our defense of Protagoras, that most things – hot, dry, sweet, everything of that sort – are to each person as they appear to him? Whereas, If there is any case in which the theory would concede that one man is superior to another, it might consent to admit that, in the matter of good or bad health, not any woman or child – or animal, for that matter – knows what is wholesome for it and is capable of curing itself, but that here, if anywhere, one person is superior to another.

THEODORUS: I should certainly say so.

SOCRATES: And again in social matters, the theory will say that, so far as good and bad customs or rights and wrongs or matters of religion are concerned, whatever any state makes up its mind to enact as lawful for itself, really is lawful for it, and in this field no individual or state is wiser than another. But where it is a question of laying down what is for its advantage or disadvantage, once more there, if anywhere, the theory will admit a difference between two advisers or between the decisions of two different states in respect of truth, and would hardly venture to assert that any enactment which a state supposes to be for its advantage will quite certainly be so.

But, in that field I am speaking of – in right and wrong and matters of religion – people are ready to affirm that none of these things is natural, with a reality of its own, but rather that the public decision becomes true at the moment when it is made and remains true so long as the decision stands, and those who do not argue altogether as Protagoras does carry on their philosophy on these lines.

[...]

SOCRATES: Very well. I think the point we had reached was this. We were saying that the believers in a perpetually changing reality and in the doctrine that what seems to an individual at any
time also is for him would, in most matters, strongly insist upon their principle, and not least in
the case of what is right they would maintain that any enactments a state may decide on certainly
are right for that state so long as they remain in force. But when it comes to what is good, we
said that the boldest would not go to the length of contending that whatever a state may believe
and declare to be advantageous for itself is in fact advantageous for so long as it is declared to be
so — unless he meant that the name 'advantageous' would continue to be so applied, but that
would be turning our subject into a joke.

THEODORUS: Certainly.

SOCRATES: We will suppose, then, that he does not mean the name, but has in view the thing that
bears it.

THEODORUS: We will.

SOCRATES: Whatever name the state may give it, advantage is surely the aim of its legislation, and
all its laws to the full extent of its belief and power, are laid down as being for its own best profit.
Or has it any other subject in view when it makes laws?

THEODORUS: None.

SOCRATES: Then does it also hit the mark every time? Or does every state often miss its aim
completely?

THEODORUS: I should say that mistakes are often made.

SOCRATES: We may have a still better chance of getting everyone to assent to that, if we start
from a question covering the whole class of things which includes the advantageous. It is, I suggest, a thing that has to do with future time. When we legislate, we make our laws with the idea
that they *will* be advantageous in time to come. We may call this class 'what is going to be.'

THEODORUS: Certainly.

SOCRATES: Here, then, is a question for Protagoras or anyone else who agrees with him.
According to you and your friends. Protagoras, man is the measure of all things — of white and
heavy and light and everything of that sort. He possesses in himself the test of these things, and
believing them to be such as he experiences them, he believes what is true and real for him. Is
that right?

THEODORUS: Yes.

SOCRATES: Is it also true, Protagoras, we shall continue, that he possesses within himself the test
of what is going to be in the future, and that whatever a man believes will be, actually comes to
pass for him who believes it? Take heat, for example. When some layman believes that he is going
to catch a fever and that this hotness is going to exist, and another, who is physician, believes the
contrary, are we to suppose that the future event will turn out in accordance with one of the two
opinions, or in accordance with both opinions, so that to the physician the patient will not be
hot or in a fever, while he will be both these things to himself?

THEODORUS: That would be absurd.

SOCRATES: And on the question whether a wine is going to be sweet or dry, I imagine the vine-
grower's judgment is authoritative, not a flute player's.

THEODORUS: Of course.

SOCRATES: Or again, on the question whether a piece of music is going to be in tune or not, a
gymnastic trainer would not have a better opinion than a musician as to what the trainer himself
will later judge to be in good tune.

THEODORUS: By no means.

SOCRATES: And when a feast is being prepared, the guest who is to be invited, supposing him not
to be an expert in cookers, will have a less authoritative opinion than the confectioner upon the
pleasure that will result. We will not dispute yet about what already is or has been pleasant to any

individual, but about what will in the future seem and be to anyone, is every man the best judge for himself, or would you, Protagoras – at least in the matter of the arguments that any one of us would find convincing for a court of law – have a better opinion beforehand than any untrained person?

THEODORUS: Certainly, Socrates, in that matter he did emphatically profess to be superior to everybody.

SOCRATES: Bless your soul, I should think he did. No one would have paid huge sums to talk with him, if he had not convinced the people who came to him that no one whatever, not even a prophet, could judge better than he what was going to be and appear in the future.

THEODORUS: Quite true.

SOCRATES: And legislation, too, and the question of advantageousness are matters concerned with the future, and everyone would agree that a state, when it makes its laws, must often fail to hit upon its own greatest advantage?

THEODORUS: Assuredly.

SOCRATES: Then we may quite reasonably put it to your master that he must admit that one man is wiser than another and that the wiser man is the measure, whereas an ignorant person like myself is not in any way bound to be a measure, as our defense of Protagoras tried to make me, whether I liked it or not.

THEODORUS: I think that is the weakest point in the theory, Socrates, though it is also assailable in that it makes others people's opinions valid when, as it turns out, they hold Protagoras's assertions to be quite untrue.

SOCRATES: There are may other ways, Theodorus, of assailing such a position and proving that not every opinion of every person is true. But with regard to what the individual experiences at the moment – the source of his sensations and the judgments in accordance with them – it is harder to assail the truth of these. Perhaps it is wrong to say 'harder'; maybe they are unassailable, and those who assert that they are transparently clear and are instances of knowledge may be in the right [.]

How Is There a World At All?

18

Has the World Been Designed by God?

David Hume, *Dialogues Concerning Natural Religion*

This book will introduce you to some intriguing new-for-you ideas and questions. Occasionally, it will encourage you to revisit an idea with which you do have some previous familiarity. This reading could well be one of those moments. Here is philosophy's most famous engagement with the *argument from design* – an argument still reached for by many theologians. It makes a venerable case for God's having designed nature, for His having created this world in accordance with a *plan* of His own for it. Indeed, the reasoning runs *from* the observed evidence of so much order in all around us, *to* there being a God who has designed that order.

Philosophy and theology overlap at times in some of their possible motivations and ideas. But sometimes there are potential clashes. Within a philosophical culture,

David Hume, *Dialogues Concerning Natural Religion* (1779), parts II–VII (excerpts).

Metaphysics and Epistemology: A Guided Anthology, First Edition. Edited by Stephen Hetherington.
© 2014 John Wiley & Sons, Inc. Published 2014 by John Wiley & Sons, Inc.

the argument from design should receive vigilant scrutiny. Is it a *good* argument? Are its premises or data – the observed instances of order, it seems – likely to reveal its conclusion as true? If we accept them, is the argument's conclusion – that a God has designed all of that order – the most rational one for us to believe? This reading, another from David Hume, gives us a taste of what are often regarded as some philosophically classic criticisms of the argument from design. (They were also socially controversial criticisms when Hume wrote them. So much so that the book from which they come – *Dialogues Concerning Natural Religion* – was first published in 1779, after Hume's death. This delay was at his request.) What we have here is a dialogue between characters thinking about this issue in different ways. Hume himself is best represented by the character Philo. It is Philo's criticisms of the design argument that have been most noted by subsequent philosophers reading these *Dialogues* of Hume's.

For example, even if there is design behind the world's existence, what would indicate this having been due to a *single* designer, let alone to a single and mature and perfectly accomplished designer? What would show that the kind of design involved is not more akin to a naturally produced piece of vegetation or an animal than to an artificially and personally created house, say? How can we properly infer *any* specific image of the world's origins (that is, any specific *cosmogony*) on the basis simply of what we may believe to be the order and regularity in what we observe around us? Hume raises probing questions about how, even if we agree on there being such order and regularity in the world, we can best explain all of that.

[CLEANTHES:] Look round the world, contemplate the whole and every part of it: you will find it to be nothing but one great machine, subdivided into an infinite number of lesser machines, which again admit of subdivisions to a degree beyond what human senses and faculties can trace and explain. All these various machines, and even their most minute parts, are adjusted to each other with an accuracy which ravishes into admiration all men who have ever contemplated them. The curious adapting of means to ends, throughout all nature, resembles exactly, though it much exceeds, the productions of human contrivance – of human design, thought, wisdom, and intelligence. Since therefore the effects resemble each other, we are led to infer, by all the rules of analogy, that the causes also resemble, and that the Author of nature is somewhat similar to the mind of man, though possessed of much larger faculties, proportioned to the grandeur of the work which he has executed. By this argument *a posteriori*, and by this argument alone, do we prove at once the existence of a Deity and his similarity to human mind and intelligence. [...]

[PHILO:] If we see a house, Cleanthes, we conclude, with the greatest certainty, that it had an architect or builder because this is precisely that species of effect which we have experienced to proceed from that species of cause. But surely you will not affirm that the universe bears such a resemblance to a house that we can with the same certainty infer a similar cause, or that the analogy is here entire and perfect. The dissimilitude is so striking that the utmost you can here pretend to is a guess, a conjecture, a presumption concerning a similar cause; and how that pretension will be received in the world, I leave you to consider.

It would surely be very ill received, replied Cleanthes; and I should be deservedly blamed and detested did I allow that the proofs of a Deity amounted to no more than a guess or conjecture. But is the whole adjustment of means to ends in a house and in the universe so slight a resemblance? the economy of final causes? the order, proportion, and arrangement of every part? Steps of a stair are plainly contrived that human legs may use them in mounting; and this inference is certain and infallible. Human legs are also contrived for walking and mounting; and this inference, I allow, is not altogether so certain because of the dissimilarity which you remark; but does it, therefore, deserve the name only of presumption or conjecture?

[...]

[PHILO:] But can you think, Cleanthes, that your usual phlegm and philosophy have been preserved in so wide a step as you have taken when you compared to the universe houses, ships, furniture, machines, and, from their similarity in some circumstances, inferred a similarity in their causes? Thought, design, intelligence, such as we discover in men and other animals, is no more than one of the springs and principles of the universe, as well as heat or cold, attraction or repulsion, and a hundred others which fall under daily observation. It is an active cause by which some particular parts of nature, we find, produce alterations on other parts. But can a conclusion, with any propriety, be transferred from parts to the whole? Does not the great disproportion bar all comparison and inference? From observing the growth of a   hair, can we learn anything concerning the generation of a man? Would the manner of a leaf's blowing, even though perfectly known, afford us any instruction concerning the vegetation of a tree?

But allowing that we were to take the *operations* of one part of nature upon another for the foundation of our judgment concerning the *origin* of the whole (which never can be admitted), yet why select so minute, so weak, so bounded a principle as the reason and design of animals is found to be upon this planet? What peculiar privilege has this little agitation of the brain which we call *thought*, that we must thus make it the model of the whole universe? Our partiality in our own favour does indeed present it on all occasions, but sound philosophy ought carefully to guard against so natural an illusion.

So far from admitting, continued, Philo, that the operations of a part can afford us any just conclusion concerning the origin of the whole, I will not allow any one part to form a rule for another part if the latter by very remote from the former. Is there any reasonable ground to conclude that the inhabitants of other planets possess thought, intelligence, reason, or anything similar to these faculties in men? When nature has so extremely diversified her manner of operation in this small globe, can we imagine that she incessantly copies herself throughout so immense a universe? And if thought, as we may well suppose, be confined merely to this narrow corner and has even there so limited a sphere of action, with what propriety can we assign it for the original cause of all things? The narrow views of a peasant who makes his domestic economy the rule for the government of kingdoms is in comparison a pardonable sophism.

But were we ever so much assured that a thought and reason resembling the human were to be found throughout the whole universe, and were its activity elsewhere vastly greater and more commanding than it appears in this globe, yet I cannot see why the operations of a world constituted, arranged, adjusted, can with any propriety be extended to a world which is in its embryo state, and is advancing towards that constitution and arrangement. By observation we know somewhat of the economy, action, and nourishment of a finished animal, but we must transfer with great caution that observation to the growth of a fœtus in the womb, and still more to the formation of an animalcule in the loins of its male parent. Nature, we find, even from our limited experience, possesses an infinite number of springs and principles which incessantly discover themselves on every change of her position and situation. And what new and unknown principles would actuate her in so new and unknown a situation as that of the formation of a universe, we cannot, without the utmost temerity, pretend to determine.

A very small part of this great system, during a very short time, is very imperfectly discovered to us; and do we thence pronounce decisively concerning the origin of the whole?

Admirable conclusion! Stone, wood, brick, iron, brass, have not, at this time, in this minute globe of earth, an order or arrangement without human art and contrivance; therefore, the universe could not originally attain its order and arrangement without something similar to human art. But is a part of nature a rule for another part very wide of the former? Is it a rule for the whole? Is a very small part a rule for the universe? Is nature in one situation a certain rule for nature in another situation vastly different from the former?

[…] And will any man tell me with a serious countenance that an orderly universe must arise from some thought and art like the human because we have experience of it? To ascertain this reasoning it were requisite that we had experience of the origin of worlds; and it is not sufficient, surely, that we have seen ships and cities arise from human art and contrivance.

[…] [T]he subject in which you are engaged exceeds all human reason and inquiry. Can you pretend to show any such similarity between the fabric of a house and the generation of a universe? Have you ever seen nature in any such situation as resembles the first arrangement of the elements? Have worlds ever been formed under your eye, and have you had leisure to observe the whole progress of the phenomenon, from the first appearance of order to its final consummation? If you have, then cite your experience and deliver your theory.

[CLEANTHES:] But […] [s]uppose that there is a natural, universal, invariable language, common to every individual of human race, and that books are natural productions which perpetuate themselves in the same manner with animals and vegetables, by descent and propagation. Several expressions of our passions contain a universal language: all brute animals have a natural speech, which, however limited, is very intelligible to their own species. And as there are infinitely fewer parts and less contrivance in the finest composition of eloquence than in the coarsest organized body, the propagation of an *Iliad* or *Æneid* is an easier supposition than that of any plant or animal.

Suppose, therefore, that you enter into your library thus peopled by natural volumes containing the most refined reason and most exquisite beauty; could you possibly open one of them and doubt that its original cause bore the strongest analogy to mind and intelligence? When it reasons and discourses; when it expostulates, argues, and enforces its views and topics; when it applies sometimes to the pure intellect, sometimes to the affections; when it collects, disposes, and adorns every considerations suited to the subject; could you persist in asserting that all this, at the bottom, had really no meaning, and that the first formation of this volume in the loins of its original parent proceeded not from thought and design? Your obstinacy, I know, reaches not that degree of firmness; even your sceptical play and wantonness would be abashed at so glaring at absurdity.

But if there be any difference, Philo, between this supposed case and the real one of the universe; it is all to the advantage of the latter. The anatomy of an animal affords many stronger instances of design than the perusal of Livy or Tacitus; and any objection which you start in the former case, by carrying me back to so unusual and extraordinary a scene as the first formation of worlds, the same objection has place on the supposition of our vegetating library. Choose, then, your party, Philo, without ambiguity or evasion; assert either that a rational volume is no proof of a rational cause or admit of a similar cause to all the works of nature.

[...] Consider, anatomize the eye, survey its structure and contrivance, and tell me, from your own feeling, if the idea of a contriver does not immediately flow in upon you with a force like that of sensation. The most obvious conclusion, surely, is in favour of design; and it requires time, reflection, and study, to summon up those frivolous though abstruse objections which can support infidelity. Who can behold the male and female of each species, the correspondence of their parts and instincts, their passions and whole course of life before and after generation, but must be sensible that the propagation of the species is intended by nature? Millions and millions of such instances present themselves through every part of the universe, and no language can convey a more intelligible irresistible meaning than the curious adjustment of final causes. To what degree, therefore, of blind dogmatism must one have attained to reject such natural and such convincing arguments?

[...]

[DEMEA:] Your instance, Cleanthes, said he, drawn from books and language, being familiar, has, I confess, so much more force on that account; but is there not some danger, too, in this very circumstance, and may it not render us presumptuous, by making us imagine we comprehend the Deity and have some adequate idea of his nature and attributes? When I read a volume, I enter into the mind and intention of the author; I become him, in a manner, for the instant, and have an immediate feeling and conception of those ideas which revolved in his imagination while employed in that composition. But so near an approach we never surely can make to the Deity. His ways are not our ways. His attributes are perfect but incomprehensible. And this volume of nature contains a great and inexplicable riddle, more than any intelligible discourse or reasoning.

The ancient Platonists you know, were the most religious and devout of all the pagan philosophers, yet many of them, particularly Plotinus, expressly declare that intellect or understanding is not to be ascribed to the Deity, and that our most perfect worship of him consist, not in acts of veneration, reverence, gratitude, or love, but in a certain mysterious self-annihilation or total extinction of all our faculties. These ideas are, perhaps, too far stretched, but still it must be acknowledged that, by representing the Deity as so intelligible and comprehensible, and so similar to a human mind, we are guilty of the grossest and most narrow partiality, and make ourselves the model of the whole universe.

[...]

It seems strange to me, said Cleanthes, that you, Demea, who are so sincere in the cause of religion, should still maintain the mysterious, incomprehensible nature of the Deity, and should insist so strenuously that he has no manner of likeness or resemblance to human creatures. The Deity, I can readily allow, possesses many powers and attributes of which we can have no comprehension; but, if our ideas, so far as they go, be not just and adequate and correspondent to his real nature, I know not what there is in this subject worth insisting on. Is the name, without any meaning, of such mighty importance? Or how do you mystics, who maintain the absolute incomprehensibility of the Deity, differ from sceptics or atheists, who assert that the first cause of all is unknown and unintelligible? Their temerity must be very great if, after rejecting the production by a mind — I mean a mind resembling the human (for I know of no other) — they pretend to assign, with certainty, any other specific intelligible cause; and their conscience must be very scrupulous, indeed, if they refuse to call the universal unknown cause a God or Deity, and to bestow on him as many sublime eulogies, and unmeaning epithets as you shall please to require of them.

[...]

I can readily allow, said Cleanthes, that those who maintain the perfect simplicity of the Supreme Being, to the extent in which you have explained it, are complete mystics, and chargeable with all the consequences which I have drawn from their opinion. They are, in a word, atheists, without knowing it. For though it be allowed that the Deity possesses attributes of which we have no comprehension, yet ought we never to ascribe to him any attributes which are absolutely incompatible with that intelligent nature essential to him. A mind whose acts and sentiments and ideas are not distinct and successive, one that is wholly simple and totally immutable, is a mind which has not thought, no reason, no will, no sentiment, no love, no hatred; or, in a word, is no mind at all. It is an abuse of terms to give it that appellation, and we may as well speak of limited extension without figure, or of number without composition.

[...]

[PHILO:] But, because I know you are not much swayed by names and authorities, I shall endeavour to show you, a little more distinctly, the inconveniences of that anthropomorphism which you have embraced, and shall prove that there is no ground to suppose a plan of the world to be formed in the Divine mind, consisting of distinct ideas, differently arranged, in the same manner as an architect forms in his head the plan of a house which he intends to execute.

It is not easy, I own, to see what is gained by this supposition, whether we judge of the matter by *reason* or by *experience*. We are still obliged to mount higher in order to find the cause of this cause which you had assigned as satisfactory and conclusive.

If *reason* (I mean abstract reason derived from inquiries *a priori*) be not alike mute with regard to all questions concerning cause and effect, this sentence at least it will venture to pronounce: that a mental world or universe of ideas requires a cause as much as does a material world or universe of objects, and, if similar in its arrangement, must require a similar cause. For what is there in this subject which should occasion a different conclusion or inference? In an abstract view, they are entirely alike; and no difficulty attends the one supposition which is not common to both of them.

How [...] shall we satisfy ourselves concerning the cause of that Being whom you suppose the Author of nature, or, according to your system of anthropomorphism, the ideal world into which you trace the material? Have we not the same reason to trace that ideal world into another ideal world or new intelligent principle? But if we stop and go no farther, why go so far? why not stop at the material world? How can we satisfy ourselves without going on *in infinitum*? And, after all, what satisfaction is there in that infinite progression? Let us remember the story of the Indian philosopher and his elephant. It was never more applicable than to the present subject. If the material world rests upon a similar ideal world, this ideal world must rest upon some other, and so on without end. It were better, therefore, never to look beyond the present material world. By supposing it to contain the principle of its order within itself, we really assert it to be God; and the sooner we arrive at that Divine Being, so much the better. When you go one step beyond the mundane system, you only excite an inquisitive humour which it is impossible ever to satisfy.

To say that the different ideas which compose the reason of the Supreme Being fall into order of themselves and by their own nature is really to talk without any precise meaning. If it has a meaning, I would fain know why it is not as good sense to say that the parts of the material world fall into order of themselves and by their own nature. Can the one opinion be intelligible, while the other is not so?

When it is asked, what cause produces order in the ideas of the Supreme Being, can any other reason be assigned by you, anthropomorphites, than that it is a *rational* faculty, and that such is the nature of the Deity? But why a similar answer will not be equally satisfactory in accounting for the order of the world, without having recourse to any such intelligent creator as you insist on, may be difficult to determine.

[...]

[PHILO:] All the new discoveries in astronomy which prove the immense grandeur and magnificence of the works of nature are so many additional arguments for a Deity, according to the true system of theism; but, according to your hypothesis of experimental theism, they become so many objections, by removing the effect still farther from all resemblance to the effects of human art and contrivance.

[...]

It is still more unreasonable to form our idea of so unlimited a cause from our experience of the narrow productions of human design and invention.

The discoveries by microscopes, as they open a new universe in miniature, are still objections, according to you, arguments, according to me. The further we push our researches of this kind, we are still led to infer the universal cause of all to be vastly different from mankind, or from any object of human experience and observation.

And what say you to the discoveries in anatomy, chemistry, botany? ... These surely are no objections, replied Cleanthes; they only discover new instances of art and contrivance. It is still the image of mind reflected on us from innumerable objects. Add a mind *like the human*, said Philo. I know of no other, replied Cleanthes. And the liker, the better, insisted Philo. To be sure, said Cleanthes.

Now, Cleanthes, said Philo, with an air of alacrity and triumph, mark the consequences. *First*, by this method of reasoning you renounce all claim to infinity in any of the attributes of the Deity. For, as the cause ought only to be proportioned to the effect, and the effect, so far as it falls under our cognizance, is not infinite, what pretensions have we, upon your suppositions, to ascribe that attribute to the Divine Being? You will still insist that, by removing him so much from all similarity to human creatures, we give in to the most arbitrary hypothesis, and at the same time weaken all proofs of his existence.

Secondly, you have no reason, on your theory, for ascribing perfection to the Deity, even in his finite capacity, or for supposing him free from every error, mistake, or incoherence, in his undertakings. There are many inexplicable difficulties in the works of nature which, if we allow a perfect author to be proved *a prior*, are easily solved, and become only seeming difficulties from the narrow capacity of man, who cannot trace infinite relations. But according to your method of reasoning, these difficulties become all real, and, perhaps, will be insisted on as new instances of likeness to human art and contrivance. At least, you must acknowledge that it is impossible for us to tell, from our limited views, whether this system contains any great faults or deserves any considerable praise if compared to other possible and even real systems. Could a peasant, if the *Æneid* were read to him, pronounce that poem to be absolutely faultless, or even assign to it its proper rank among the productions of human wit, he who had never seen any other production?

But were this world ever so perfect a production, it must still remain uncertain whether all the excellences of the work can justly be ascribed to the workman. If we survey a ship, what an exalted idea must we form of the ingenuity of the carpenter who framed so complicated, useful, and beautiful a machine? And what surprise must we feel when we find him a stupid mechanic who imitated others, and copied an art which, through a long succession of ages, after multiplied trials, mistakes, corrections, deliberations, and controversies, had been gradually improving? Many worlds might have been botched and bungled, throughout an eternity, ere this system was struck out; much labour lost, many fruitless trials, made, and a slow but continued improvement carried on during infinite ages in the art of world-making. In such subjects, who can determine where the truth, nay, who can conjecture where the probability lies, amidst a great number of hypotheses which may be proposed, and a still greater which may be imagined?

And what shadow of an argument, continued Philo, can you produce from your hypothesis to prove the unity of the Deity? A great number of men join in building a house or ship, in rearing a city, in framing a commonwealth; why may not several deities combine in contriving and framing a world? This is only so much greater similarity to human affairs. By sharing the work among several, we may so much further limit the attributes of each, and get rid of that extensive power and knowledge which must be supposed in one deity, and which, according to you, can only serve to weaken the proof of his existence. And if such foolish, such vicious creatures as man can yet often unite in framing and executing one plan, how much more those deities or demons, whom we may suppose several degrees more perfect!

[...]

But further, Cleanthes: Men are mortal, and renew their species by generation; and this is common to all living creatures. The two great sexes of male and female, says Milton, animate the world. Why must this circumstance, so universal, so essential, be excluded from those numerous and limited deities? Behold, then, the theogeny of ancient times brought back upon us.

And why not become a perfect anthropomorphite? Why not assert the deity or deities to be corporeal, and to have eyes, a nose, mouth, ears, etc.? Epicurus maintained that no man had ever seen reason but in a human figure; therefore, the gods must have a human figure. And this argument, which is deservedly so much ridiculed by Cicero, becomes, according to you, solid and philosophical.

In a word, Cleanthes, a man who follows your hypothesis is able, perhaps, to assert or conjecture that the universe sometime arose from something like design; but beyond that position he cannot ascertain one single circumstance, and is left afterwards to fix every point of his theology by the utmost license of fancy and hypothesis. This world, for aught he knows, is very faulty and imperfect, compared to a superior standard, and was only the first rude essay of some infant deity who afterwards abandoned it, ashamed of his lame performance; it is the work only of some dependent, inferior deity, and is the object of derision to his superiors; it is the production of old age and dotage in some superannuated deity, and ever since his death has run on at adventures, from the first impulse and active force which it received from him. [...] From the moment the attributes of the Deity are supposed finite, all these have place. And I cannot, for my part, think that so wild and unsettled a system of theology is, in any respect, preferable to none at all.

These suppositions I absolutely disown, cried Cleanthes: they strike me, however, with no horror, especially when proposed in that rambling way in which they drop from you. On the contrary, they give me pleasure when I see that, by the utmost indulgence of your imagination, you never get rid of the hypothesis of design in the universe, but are obliged at every turn to have recourse to it. To this concession I adhere steadily; and this I regard as a sufficient foundation for religion.

[...]

It must be a slight fabric, indeed, said Demea, which can be erected on so tottering a foundation. While we are uncertain whether there is one deity or many, whether the deity or deities, to whom we owe our existence, be perfect or imperfect, subordinate or supreme, dead or alive, what trust or confidence can we repose in them? What devotion or worship address to them? What veneration or obedience pay them? To all the purposes of life the theory of religion becomes altogether useless; and even with regard to speculative consequences its uncertainty, according to you, must render it totally precarious and unsatisfactory.

[...]

But here, continued Philo, in examining the ancient system of the soul of the world there strikes me, all on a sudden, a new idea which, if just, must go near to subvert all you reasoning, and destroy even your first inferences on which you repose such confidence. If the universe bears a greater likeness to animal bodies and to vegetables than to the works of human art, it is more probable that its cause resembles the cause of the former than that of the latter, and its origin ought rather to be ascribed to generation or vegetation than to reason or design. Your conclusion, even according to your own principles, is therefore lame and defective.

[...]

Our friend Cleanthes [...] asserts that, since no question of fact can be proved otherwise than by experience, the existence of a Deity admits not of proof from any other medium. The world, says he, resembles the works of human contrivance; therefore its cause must also resemble that of the other. Here we may remark that the operation of one very small part of nature, to wit, man, upon another very small part, to wit, that inanimate matter lying within his reach, is the rule by which Cleanthes judges of the origin of the whole; and he measures objects, so widely disproportioned, by the same individual standard. But to waive all objections drawn from this topic, I affirm that there are other parts of the universe (besides the machines of human invention) which bear still a greater resemblance to the fabric of the world, and which, therefore, afford a better conjecture concerning the universal origin of this system. These parts are animals and vegetables. The world plainly resembles more an animal or a vegetable than it does a watch or a knitting-loom. Its cause, therefore, it is more probable, resembles the cause of the former. The cause of the former is generation or vegetation. The cause, therefore, of the world we may infer to be something similar or analogous to generation or vegetation.

But how is it conceivable, said Demea, that the world can arise from anything similar to vegetation or generation?

Very easily, replied Philo. In like manner as a tree sheds its seed into the neighbouring fields and produces other trees, so the great vegetable, the world, or this planetary system, produces within itself certain seeds which, being scattered into the surrounding chaos, vegetate into new worlds. A comet, for instance, is the seed of a world; and after it has been fully ripened, by passing from sun to sun, and star to star, it is, at last, tossed into the unformed elements which everywhere surround this universe, and immediately sprouts up into a new system.

Or if, for the sake of variety (for I see no other advantage), we should suppose this world to be an animal: a comet is the egg of this animal; and in like manner as an ostrich lays its egg in the sand, which, without any further care, hatches the egg and produces a new animal, so. ... I understand you, says Demea. But what wild, arbitrary suppositions are these! What *data* have you for such extraordinary conclusion? And is the slight, imaginary resemblance of the world to a vegetable or an animal sufficient to establish the same inference with regard to both? Objects which are in general so widely different ought they to be a standard for each other?

Right, cries Philo: This is the topic on which I have all along insisted. I have still asserted that we have no *data* to establish any system of cosmogony. Our experience, so imperfect in itself and so limited both in extent and duration, can afford us no probable conjecture concerning the whole of things. But if we must needs fix on some hypothesis, by what rule, pray, ought we to determine our choice? Is there any other rule than the greater similarity of the objects compared? And does not a plant or an animal, which springs from vegetation or generation, bear a stronger resemblance to the world than does any artificial machine, which arises from reason and design?

[…]

But methinks, said Demea, if the world had a vegetative quality and could sow the seeds of new worlds into the infinite chaos, this power would be still an additional argument for design in its author. For whence could arise so wonderful a faculty but from design? Or how can order spring from anything which perceives not that order which it bestows?

You need only look around you, replied Philo, to satisfy yourself with regard to this question. A tree bestows order and organization on that tree which springs from it, without knowing the order; an animal in the same manner on its offspring; a bind on its nest; and instances of this kind are even more frequent in the world than those of order which arise from reason and contrivance. To say that all this order in animals and vegetables proceeds ultimately from design is begging the question; nor can that great point be ascertained otherwise than by proving, *a priori*, both that order is, from its nature, inseparably attached to thought and that it can never of itself or from original unknown principles belong to matter.

But further, Demea, this objection which you urge can never be made use of by Cleanthes, without renouncing a defence which he has already made against one of my objections. When I inquired concerning the cause of that supreme reason and intelligence into which he resolves everything, he told me that the impossibility of satisfying such inquiries could never by admitted as an objection in any species of philosophy. *We must stop somewhere*, says

he; *nor is it ever within the reach of human capacity to explain ultimate causes or show the last connec-*
tions of any objects. It is sufficient if any steps, so far as we go, are supported by experience and observa-
tion. Now that vegetation and generation, as well as reason, are experienced to be principles
of order in nature is undeniable. If I rest my system of cosmogony on the former, preferably
to the latter, it is at my choice. The matter seems entirely arbitrary. And when Cleanthes asks
me what is the cause of my great vegetative or generative faculty, I am equally entitled to ask
him the cause of his great reasoning principle. These questions we have agreed to forbear on
both sides; and it is chiefly his interest on the present occasion to stick to this agreement.
Judging by our limited and imperfect experience, generation has some privileges above reason; for we see every day the latter arise from the former, never the former from the latter.

Compare, I beseech you, the consequences on both side. The world, say I, resembles an
animal; therefore it is an animal, therefore it arose from generation. The steps, I confess, are
wide, yet there is some small appearance of analogy in each step. The world, says Cleanthes,
resembles a machine; therefore it is a machine therefore it arose from design. The steps are
here equally wide, and the analogy less striking. And if he pretends to carry on *my* hypothesis
a step further, and to infer design or reason from the great principle of generation on which
I insist, I may, with better authority, use the same freedom to push further *his* hypothesis, and
infer a divine generation or theogony from his principle of reason. I have at least some faint
shadow of experience, which is the utmost that can ever be attained in the present subject.
Reason, in innumerable instances, is observed to arise from the principle of generation, and
never to arise from any other principle.

Hesiod and all the ancient mythologists were so struck with this analogy that they universally explained the origin of nature from an animal birth, and copulation. Plato, too, so far as
he is intelligible, seems to have adopted some such notion in his *Timæus.*

The Brahmins assert that the world arose from an infinite spider, who spun this whole
complicated mass from his bowels, and annihilates afterwards the whole or any part of it, by
absorbing it again and resolving it into his own essence. Here is a species of cosmogony
which appears to us ridiculous because a spider is a little contemptible animal whose operations we are never likely to take for a model of the whole universe. But still here is a new
species of analogy, even in our globe. And were there a planet wholly inhabited by spiders
(which is very possible), this inference would there appear as natural and irrefragable as that
which in our planet ascribes the origin of all things to design and intelligence, as explained
by Cleanthes. Why an orderly system may not be spun from the belly as well as from the
brain, it will be difficult for him to give a satisfactory reason.

19

Is God's Existence Knowable
Purely Conceptually?

St. Anselm, *Proslogion*

In the previous reading, we read David Hume's reflections upon a famous form of argument designed to convince people of there being a God. That argument asked people to notice the world's order and regularity – and to infer from this that God exists, as a supreme metaphysical force responsible for having created such order and regularity. But Hume, we saw, argued against the claim that such observations could establish God's existence. Are we therefore left with no way of establishing His existence? Perhaps not, if observation is not our only possible means of at least attempting to understand how there is a God. So this reading presents us with a further style of reasoning. It comes from the *Proslogion* (1077–8) by St. Anselm (1033–1109), an Italian who became Archbishop of Canterbury in England. (Also included are some famous objections to Anselm's initial formulation of his argument, and part of Anselm's speedy reply. The objections were by Gaunilo, a monk in France. The objections and Anselm's reply are routinely published together with the *Proslogion*.)

What we meet here is called the *ontological* argument. It is *not* an argument based on observation of our surroundings. It involves only reasoning, applied to a supposedly special concept. Seek within yourself the concept of God. Now examine that concept. (And remember, incidentally, how Strawson, in Part I's reading, described philosophy as the analyzing of key concepts.) What does that inner examination reveal? You will find a richly descriptive concept, listing God's excellences. And Anselm thought (as follows) that one of these will be existential. In

St. Anselm, *Proslogion*, chs. I–V (excerpts) and *The Author's Reply to Gaunilo* (excerpts), plus Gaunilo's *A Reply on Behalf of the Fool* (excerpts). In *St. Anselm's "Proslogion,"* trans. M.J. Charlesworth (Oxford: Clarendon Press, 1965). Reprinted with permission of Oxford University Press.

Metaphysics and Epistemology: A Guided Anthology, First Edition. Edited by Stephen Hetherington.
© 2014 John Wiley & Sons, Inc. Published 2014 by John Wiley & Sons, Inc.

conceiving of God, you are conceiving of a being with all and only possible perfections. It would not be possible to conceive of a perfection that is lacking in God. Yet (continued Anselm) this must include God's existing. It is an imperfection not to exist. It is even an imperfection to exist while having the possibility of not existing. So, if your concept really is of God, it is of an existing being – one that genuinely exists, even one that exists as a matter of *necessity*.

Of course, what then makes your concept actually one of God? This is a state of affairs stronger than your simply saying or feeling that the concept is of God. To have this concept could even be an achievement, on Anselm's way of thinking. And maybe this question returns us to the questions raised in the earlier readings (from Russell, Searle, and Plato) about facts and truth. Can a concept really be *of* God only if God exists – that is, only if it is a fact that God exists? Can it be *true* that one's concept is of God, only if God exists?

Anselm did not use his ontological argument to show that there is a God. But some have wanted to do so. Part of the appeal for us right now in a strategy like this argument's is the following: *If* the argument – when applied to someone's concept, apparently of God – reveals God's existing, the argument allows us to understand God as existing without our having either to presuppose or observe there being a world at all, let alone an orderly and regular one. We might think that this enables us, in turn, to use that independently gained understanding of God's existing, so as to understand how there is a world at all, even an orderly and regular one. (Note that the translator's numbering of the Psalms has been adjusted to match the modern convention.)

I do not try, Lord, to attain Your lofty heights, because my understanding is in no way equal to it. But I do desire to understand Your truth a little, that truth that my heart believes and loves. For I do not seek to understand so that I may believe; but I believe so that I may understand. For I believe this also, that 'unless I believe, I shall not understand' [Is. vii. 9].

Chapter II

That God truly exists

Well then, Lord [God], You who give understanding to faith, grant me that I may understand, as much as You see fit, that You exist as we believe You to exist, and that You are what we believe You to be. Now we believe that You are something than which nothing greater can be thought. Or can it be that a thing of such a nature does not exist, since 'the Fool has said in his heart, there is no God' [Ps. xiv.1, liii. 1]? But surely, when this same Fool hears what I am speaking about, namely, 'something-than-which-nothing-greater-can-be-thought', he understands what he hears, and what he understands is in his mind, even if he does not understand that it actually exists. For it is one thing for an object to exist in the mind, and another thing to understand that an object actually exists. Thus, when a painter plans beforehand what he is going to execute, he has [the picture] in his mind, but he does not yet think that it actually exists because he has not yet executed it. However, when he has actually painted it, then he both has it in his mind and understands that it exists because he has now made it. Even the Fool, then, is forced to agree that something-than-which-nothing-greater-can-be-thought exists in the mind, since he understands this when he hears it, and whatever is understood is in the mind. And surely that-than-which-a-greater-cannot-be-thought cannot exist in the mind alone. For if it exists solely in the mind even, it can be thought to exist in reality also, which is greater. If then that-than-which-a-greater-cannot[-]be-thought exists in the mind alone, this same that-than-which-a-greater-*cannot*-be-thought is that-than-which-a-greater-*can*-be-thought. But this is obviously impossible. Therefore there is absolutely no doubt that something-than-which-a-greater-cannot-be-thought exists both in the mind and in reality.

Chapter III

That God cannot be thought not to exist

AND certainly this being so truly exists that it cannot be even thought not to exist. For something can be thought to exist that cannot be thought not to exist, and this is greater than that which can be thought not to exist. Hence, if that-than-which-a-greater-cannot-be-thought can be thought not to exist, then that-than-which-a-greater-cannot-be-thought is not the same as that-than-which-a-greater-cannot-be-thought, which is absurd. Something-than-which-a-greater-cannot-be-thought exists so truly then, that it cannot be even thought not to exist.

And You, Lord our God, are this being. You exist so truly, Lord, my God, that You cannot even be thought not to exist. And this is as it should be, for if some intelligence could think of something better than You, the creature would be above its creator and would judge its creator – and that is completely absurd. In fact, everything else there is, except You alone, can be thought of as not existing. You alone, then, of all things most truly exist and therefore of all things possess existence to the highest degree; for anything else does not exist as truly, and so possesses existence to a lesser degree. Why then did 'the Fool say in his heart, there is no God' [Ps. xiv.1, liii.1] when it is so evident to any rational mind that You of all things exist to the highest degree? Why indeed, unless because he was stupid and a fool?

Chapter IV

How 'the fool said in his heart' what cannot be thought

How indeed has he 'said in his heart' what he could not think; or how could he not think what he 'said in his heart', since to 'say in one's heart' and to 'think' are the same? But if he really (indeed, since he really) both thought because he 'said in his heart' and did not 'say in his heart' because he could not think, there is not only one sense in which something is 'said in one's heart' or thought. For in one sense a thing is thought when the word signifying it is thought; in another sense when the very object which the thing is is understood. In the first sense, then, God can be thought not to exist, but not at all in the second sense. No one, indeed, understanding what God is can think that God does not exist, even though he may say these words in his heart either without any [objective] signification or with some peculiar signification. For God is that-than-which-nothing-greater-can-be-thought. Whoever really understands this understands clearly that this same being so exists that not even in thought can it not exist. Thus whoever understands that God exists in such a way cannot think of Him as not existing.

I give thanks, good Lord, I give thanks to You, since what I believed before through Your free gift I now so understand through Your illumination, that if I did not want to *believe* that You existed, I should nevertheless be unable not to *understand* it.

Chapter V

That God is whatever it is better to be than not to be and that, existing through Himself alone, He Makes all other beings from nothing

WHAT then are You, Lord God, You than whom nothing greater can be thought? But what are You save that supreme being, existing through Yourself alone, who made everything else from nothing? For whatever is not this is less than that which can be thought of; but this cannot be thought about You. What goodness, then, could be wanting to the supreme good, through which every good exists? Thus You are just, truthful, happy, and whatever it is better to be than not to be – for it is better to be just rather than unjust, and happy rather than unhappy.

[...]

Chapter XV

How He is greater than can be thought

Therefore, Lord, not only are You that than which a greater cannot be thought, but You are also something greater than can be thought. For since it is possible to think that there is such a one, then, if You are not this same being something greater than You could be thought – which cannot be.

[...]

Chapter XX

That He is before and beyond even all eternal things

You therefore permeate and embrace all things; You are before and beyond all things. You are before all things of course since, before they came to be, You already *are*. But how are You beyond all things? For in what way are You beyond those things that will never have an end?

Is it because these things can in no way exist without You, though You do not exist any the less even if they return to nothingness? For in this way, in a sense, You are beyond them.

Or is it also that they can be thought to have an end while You cannot in any way? For in this way, in a sense, they do indeed have an end, but You do not in any sense. And assuredly that which does not have an end in any way at all is beyond that which does come to an end in some way. Is it also in this way that You surpass even all eternal things, since Your eternity and theirs is wholly present to You, though they do not have the part of their eternity which is yet to come just as they do not now have what is past? In this way, indeed, are You always beyond those things, because You are always present at that point (or because it is always present: to You) which they have not yet reached.

[...]

Chapter XXII

That He alone is what He is and who He is

You alone then, Lord, are what You are and You are who You are. For what is one thing as a whole and another as to its parts, and has in it something mutable, is not altogether what it is. And what began [to exist] from non-existence, and can be thought not to exist, and returns to non-existence unless it subsists through some other; and what has had a past existence but does not now exist, and a future existence but does not yet exist – such a thing does not exist in a strict and absolute sense. But You are what You are, for whatever You are at any time or in any way this You are wholly and forever.

And You are the being who exists in a strict and absolute sense because You have neither past nor future existence but only present existence; nor can You be thought not to exist at any time. And You are life and light and wisdom and blessedness and eternity and. many such-like good things; and yet You are nothing save the one and supreme good, You who are completely sufficient unto Yourself, needing nothing, but rather He whom all things need in order that they may have being and well-being.

[...]

A Reply to the Foregoing by a Certain Writer On Behalf of the Fool

[By Gaunilo]

1. To one doubting whether there is, or denying that there is, something of such a nature than which nothing greater can be thought, it is said here [in the *Proslogion*] that its exist-ence is proved, first because the very one who denies or doubts it already has it in his mind, since when he hears it spoken of he understands what is said; and further, because what he understands is necessarily such that it exists not only in the mind but also in real-ity. And this is proved by the fact that it is greater to exist both in the mind and in reality than in the mind alone. For if this same being exists in the mind alone, anything that existed also in reality would be greater than this being, and thus that which is greater than

everything would be less than some thing and would not be greater than everything, which is obviously contradictory. Therefore, it is necessarily the case that that which is greater than everything, being already proved to exist in the mind, should exist not only in the mind but also in reality, since otherwise it would not be greater than everything.

2. But he [the Fool] can perhaps reply that this thing is said already to exist in the mind only in the sense that I understand what is said. For could I not say that all kinds of unreal things, not existing in themselves in any way at all, are equally in the mind since if anyone speaks about them I understand whatever he says? Unless perhaps it is manifest that this being is such that it can be entertained in the mind in a different way from unreal or doubtfully real things, so that I am not said to think of or have in thought what is heard, but to understand and have it in mind, in that I cannot really think of this being in any other way save by understanding it, that is to say, by grasping by certain knowledge that the thing itself actually exists. But if this is the case, first, there will be no difference between having an object in mind (taken as preceding in time), and understanding that the object actually exists (taken as following in time), as in the case of the picture which exists first in the mind of the painter and then in the completed work. And thus it would be scarcely conceivable that, when this object had been spoken of and heard, it could not be thought not to exist in the same way in which God can [be thought] not to exist. For if He cannot, why put forward this whole argument against anyone denying or doubting that there is something of this kind? Finally, that it is such a thing that, as soon as it is thought of, it cannot but be certainly perceived by the mind as indubitably existing, must be proved to me by some indisputable argument and not by that proposed, namely, that it must already be in my mind when I understand what I hear. For this is in my view like [arguing that] any things doubtfully real or even unreal are capable of existing if these things are mentioned by someone whose spoken words I might understand, and, even more, that [they exist] if, though deceived about them as often happens, I should believe them [to exist] – which argument I still do not believe!

3. Hence, the example of the painter having the picture he is about to make already in his mind cannot support this argument. For this picture, before it is actually made, is contained in the very art of the painter and such a thing in the art of any artist is nothing but a certain part of his very understanding, since as St. Augustine says [*In Iohannem*, tract, 1, n. 16], 'when the artisan is about actually to make a box he has it beforehand in his art. The box which is actually made is not a living thing, but the box which is in his art is a living thing since the soul of the artist, in which these things exist before their actual realization, is a living thing'. Now how are these things living in the living soul of the artist unless they are identical with the knowledge or understanding of the soul itself? But, apart from those things which are known to belong to the very nature of the mind itself, in the case of any truth perceived by the mind by being either heard or understood, then it cannot be doubted that, this truth is one thing and that the understanding which grasps it is another. Therefore even if it were true that there was something than which nothing greater could be thought, this thing, heard and understood, would not, however, be the same as the not-yet-made picture is in the mind of the painter.

4. To this we may add something that has already been mentioned, namely, that upon hearing it spoken of I can so little think of or entertain in my mind this being (that which is

greater than all those others that are able to be thought of, and which it is said can be none other than God Himself) in terms of an object known to me either by species or genus, as I can think of God Himself, whom indeed for this very reason I can even think does not exist. For neither do I know the reality itself, nor can I form an idea from some other things like it since, as you say yourself, it is such that nothing could be like it. For if I heard something said about a man who was completely unknown to me so that I did not even know whether he existed, I could nevertheless think about him in his very reality as a man by means of that specific or generic notion by which I know what a man is or men are. However, it could happen that, because of a falsehood on the part of the speaker, the man I thought of did not actually exist, although I thought of him nevertheless as a truly exist-ing object – not this particular man but any man in general. It is not, then, in the way that I have this unreal thing in thought or in mind that I can have that object in my mind when I hear 'God' or 'something greater than everything' spoken of. For while I was able to think of the former in terms of a truly existing thing which was known to me, I know nothing at all of the latter save for the verbal formula, and on the basis of this alone one can scarcely or never think of any truth. For when one thinks in this way, one thinks not so much of the word itself, which is indeed a real thing (that is to say, the sound of the letters or syl-lables), as of the meaning of the word which is heard. However, it [that which is greater than everything] is not thought of in the way of one who knows what is meant by that expression – thought of, that is, in terms of the thing [signified] or as true in thought alone. It is rather in the way of one who does not really know this object but thinks of it in terms of an affection of his mind produced by hearing the spoken words, and who tries to imag-ine what the words he has heard might mean. However, it would be astonishing if he could ever [attain to] the truth of the thing. Therefore, when I hear and understand someone saying that there is something greater than everything that can be thought of, it is agreed that it is in this latter sense that it is in my mind and not in any other sense. So much for the claim that that supreme nature exists already in my mind.

5. That, however, [this nature] necessarily exists in reality is demonstrated to me from the fact that, unless it existed, whatever exists in reality would be greater than it and consequently it would not be that which is greater than everything that undoubtedly had already been proved to exist in the mind. To this I reply as follows: if something that cannot even be thought in the true and real sense must be said to exist in the mind, then I do not deny that this also exists in my mind in the same way. But since from this one cannot in any way conclude that it exists also in reality, I certainly do not yet concede that it actually exists, until this is proved to me by an indubitable argument. For he who claims that it actually exists because otherwise it would not be that which is greater than everything does not consider carefully enough whom he is addressing. For I certainly do not yet admit this greater [than everything] to be any truly existing thing; indeed I doubt or even deny it. And I do not concede that it exists in a different way from that – if one ought to speak of 'existence' here – when the mind tries to imagine a completely unknown thing on the basis of the spoken words alone. How then can it be proved to me on that basis that that which is greater than everything truly exists in reality (because it is evident that it is greater than all others) if I keep on denying and also doubting that this is evident and do not admit that this greater [than everything] is either in my mind or thought, not even in the

sense in which many doubtfully real and unreal things are? It must first of all be proved to me then that this same greater than everything truly exists in reality some-where, and then only will the fact that it is greater than everything make it clear that it also subsists in itself.

6. For example: they say that there is in the ocean somewhere an island which, because of the difficulty (or rather the impossibility) of finding that which does not exist, some have called the 'Lost Island'. And the story goes that it is blessed with all manner of priceless riches and delights in abundance, much more even than the Happy Isles, and, having no owner or inhabitant, it is superior everywhere in abundance of riches to all those other lands that men inhabit. Now, if anyone tell me that it is like this, I shall easily understand what is said, since nothing is difficult about it. But if he should then go on to say, as though it were a logical consequence of this: You cannot any more doubt that this island that is more excellent than all other lands truly exists somewhere in reality than you can doubt that it is in your mind; and since it is more excellent to exist not only in the mind alone but also in reality, therefore it must needs be that it exists. For if it did not exist, any other land existing in reality would be more excellent than it, and so this island, already conceived by you to be more excellent than others, will not be more excellent. If, I say, someone wishes thus to persuade me that this island really exists beyond all doubt, I should either think that he was joking, or I should find it hard to decide which of us I ought to judge the bigger fool – I, if I agreed with him, or he, if he thought that he had proved the existence of this island with any certainty, unless he had first convinced me that its very excellence exists in my mind precisely as a thing existing truly and indubi-tably and not just as something unreal or doubtfully real.

7. Thus first of all might the Fool reply to objections. And if then someone should assert that this greater [than everything] is such that it cannot be thought not to exist (again without any other proof than that otherwise it would not be greater than everything), then he could make this same reply and say: When have I said that there truly existed some being that is 'greater than everything', such that from this it could be proved to me that this same being really existed to such a degree that it could not be thought not to exist? That is why it must first be conclusively proved by argument that there is some higher nature, namely that which is greater and better than all the things that are, so that from this we can also infer everything else which necessarily cannot be wanting to what is greater and better than everything. When, however, it is said that this supreme being cannot be *thought* not to exist, it would perhaps be better to say that it cannot be *under-stood* not to exist nor even to be able not to exist. For, strictly speaking, unreal things cannot be *understood*, though certainly they can be *thought* of in the same way as the Fool *thought* that God does not exist, I know with complete certainty that I exist, but I also know at the same time nevertheless that I can not-exist. And I *understand* without any doubt that that which exists to the highest degree, namely God, both exists and cannot exist. I do not know, however, whether I can *think* of myself as not existing while I know with absolute certainty that I do exist; but if I can, why cannot [I do the same] with regard to anything else I know with the same certainty? If however I cannot, this will not be the distinguishing characteristic of God [namely, to be such that He cannot be thought not to exist],

[...]

A Reply to the Foregoing by the Author of the Book in Question

Since it is not the Fool, against whom I spoke in my tract, who takes me up, but one who, though speaking on the Fool's behalf, is an orthodox Christian and no fool, it will suffice if I reply to the Christian.

[I.] You say then – you, whoever you are, who claim that the Fool can say these things – that the being than-which-a-greater-cannot-be-thought is not in the mind except as what cannot be thought of, in the true sense, at all. And [you claim], moreover, that what I say does not follow, namely, that 'that-than-which-a-greater-cannot-be-thought' exists in reality from the fact that it exists in the mind, any more than that the Lost Island most certainly exists from, the fact that, when it is described in words, he who hears it described has no doubt that it exists in his mind. I reply as follows: If 'that-than-which-a-greater-cannot-be-thought' is neither understood nor thought of, and is neither in the mind nor in thought, then it is evident that *either* God is not that-than-which-a-greater-cannot-be-thought *or* is not understood nor thought of, and is not in the mind nor in thought. Now my strongest argument that this is false is to appeal to your faith and to your conscience. Therefore 'that-than-which-a-greater-cannot-be-thought' is truly understood and thought and is in the mind and in thought. For this reason, [the arguments] by which you attempt to prove the contrary are either not true, or what you believe follows from them does not in fact follow.

Moreover, you maintain, that, from the fact that that-than-which-a-greater-cannot-be-thought is understood, it does not follow that it is in the mind, nor that, if it is in the mind, it therefore exists in reality. I insist, however, that simply if it can be thought it is necessary that it exists. For 'that-than-which-a-greater-cannot-be-thought' cannot be thought save as being without a beginning. But whatever can be thought as existing and does not actually exist can be thought as having a beginning of its existence. Consequently, 'that-than-which-a-greater-cannot-be-thought' cannot be thought as existing and yet not actually exist. If, therefore, it can be thought as existing, it exists of necessity.

Further: even if it can be thought of, then certainly it necessarily exists. For no one who denies or doubts that there is something-than-which-a-greater-cannot-be-thought, denies or doubts that, if this being were to exist, it would not be capable of not-existing either actually or in the mind – otherwise it would not be that-than-which-a-greater-cannot-be-thought. But, whatever can be thought as existing and does not actually exist, could, if it were to exist, possibly not exist either actually or in the mind. For this reason, if it can merely be thought, 'that-than-which-a-greater-cannot-be-thought' cannot not exist. However, let us suppose that it does not exist even though it can be thought. Now, whatever can be thought and does not actually exist would not be, if it should exist, 'that-than-which-a-greater-cannot-be-thought'. If, therefore, it were 'that-than-which-a-greater-cannot-be-thought' it would not be that-than[-]which-a-greater-cannot-be-thought, which is completely absurd. It is, then, false that something-than-which-a-greater-cannot-be-thought does not exist if it can merely be thought; and it is all the more false if it can be understood and be in the mind.

I will go further: It cannot be doubted that whatever does not exist in any one place or at any one time, even though it does exist in some place or at some time, can however be thought to exist at no place and at no time, just as it does not exist in some place or at some time. For what did not exist yesterday and today exists can thus, as it is understood not to have existed yesterday, be supposed not to exist at any time. And that which does not exist here in this place, and does exist elsewhere can, in the same way as it does not exist here, be thought not to exist anywhere. Similarly with a thing some of whose particular parts do not exist in the place and at the time its other parts exist – all of its parts, and therefore the whole thing itself, can be thought to exist at no time and in no place. For even if it be said that time always exists and that the world is everywhere, the former does not, however, always exist as a whole, nor is the other as a whole everywhere; and as certain particular parts of time do not exist when other parts do exist, therefore they can be even thought not to exist at any time. Again, as certain particular parts of the world do not exist in the same place where other parts do exist, they can thus be supposed not to exist anywhere. Moreover, what is made up of parts can be broken up in thought and can possibly not exist. Thus it is that whatever does not exist as a whole at a certain place and time can be thought not to exist, even if it does actually exist. But 'that-than-which-a-greater-cannot-be-thought' cannot be thought not to exist if it does actually exist; otherwise, if it exists it is not that-than-which-a-greater-cannot-be-thought, which is absurd. In no way, then, does this being not exist as a whole in any particular place or at any particular time; but it exists as a whole at every time and in every place.

Do you not consider then that that about which we understand these things can to some extent be thought or understood, or can exist in thought or in the mind? For if it cannot, we could not understand these things about it. And if you say that, because it is not completely understood, it cannot be understood at all and cannot be in the mind, then you must say [equally] that one who cannot see the purest light of the sun directly does not see daylight, which is the same thing as the light of the sun. Surely then 'that-than-which-a-greater-cannot-be-thought' is understood and is in the mind to the extent that we understand these things about it.

[...]

[III.] You claim, however, that this is as though someone asserted that it cannot be doubted that a certain island in the ocean (which is more fertile than all other lands and which, because of the difficulty or even the impossibility of discovering what does not exist, is called the 'Lost Island') truly exists in reality since anyone easily understands it when it is described in words. Now, I truly promise that if anyone should discover for me something existing either in reality or in the mind alone – except 'that-than-which-a-greater-cannot-be-thought' – to which the logic of my argument would apply, then I shall find that Lost Island and give it, never more to be lost, to that person. It has already been clearly seen, however, that 'that-than-which-a-greater-cannot-be-thought' cannot be thought not to exist, because it exists as a matter of such certain truth. Otherwise it would not exist at all. In short, if anyone says that he thinks that this being does not exist, I reply that, when he thinks of this, either he thinks of something than which a greater cannot be thought, or he does not think of it. If he does not think of it, then he does not think that what he does not think of does not exist. If, however, he does think of it, then indeed he thinks of something which cannot be even thought not to exist. For if it could be thought not to exist, it could be thought to have a beginning and an end – but this cannot be. Thus, he who thinks of it thinks of something that cannot be thought not to exist: indeed, he who thinks of this does not think of it as not existing, otherwise he would think what cannot be thought. Therefore 'that-than-which-a-greater-cannot-be-thought' cannot be thought not to exist.

[IV.] You say, moreover, that when it is said that this supreme reality cannot be *thought* not to exist, it would perhaps be better to say that it cannot be *understood* not to exist or even to be able not to exist. However, it must rather be said that it cannot be *thought*. For if I had said that the thing in question could not be *understood* not to exist, perhaps you yourself (who claim that we cannot understand – if this word is to be taken strictly – things that are unreal) would object that nothing that exists can be understood not to exist. For it is false [to say that] what exists does not exist, so that it is not the distinguishing characteristic of God not to be able to be understood not to exist. But, if any of those things which exist with absolute certainty can be understood not to exist, in the same way other things that certainly exist can be understood not to exist. But, if the matter is carefully considered, this objection cannot be made apropos [the term] 'thought'. For even if none of those things that exist can be *understood* not to exist, all however can be *thought* as not existing, save that which exists to a supreme degree. For in fact all those things (and they alone) that have a beginning or end or are made up of parts and, as I have already said, all those things that do not exist as a whole in a particular place or at a particular time can be thought as not existing. Only that being in which there is neither beginning nor end nor conjunction of parts, and that thought does not discern save as a whole in every place and at every time, cannot be thought as not existing.

[...]

[V.] [...] [Y]ou often reiterate that I say that that which is greater than everything exists in the mind, and that if it is in the mind, it exists also in reality, for otherwise that which is greater than everything would not be that which is greater than everything. However, nowhere in all that I have said will you find such an argument. For 'that which is greater than everything' and 'that-than-which-a-greater-cannot-be-thought' are not equivalent for the purpose of proving the real existence of the thing spoken of. Thus, if anyone should say that 'that-than-which-a-greater-cannot-be-thought' is not something that actually exists, or that it can possibly not exist, or even can be thought of as not existing, he can easily be refuted. For what does not exist can possibly not exist, and what can not exist can be thought of as not existing. However, whatever can be thought of as not existing, if it actually exists, is not that-than-which-a-greater-cannot-be-thought. But if it does not exist, indeed even if it should exist, it would not be that-than-which-a-greater-cannot-be-thought. But it cannot be asserted that 'that-than-which-a-greater-cannot-be-thought' is not, if it exists, that-than-which-a-greater-cannot-be-thought, or that, if it should exist, it would not be that-than-which-a-greater-cannot-be-thought. It is evident, then, that it neither does not exist nor can not exist or be thought of as not existing. For if it does exist in another way it is not what it is said to be, and if it should exist [in another way] it would not be [what it was said to be].

However it seems that it is not as easy to prove this in respect of what is said to be greater than everything. For it is not as evident that that which can be thought of as not existing is not that which is greater than everything, as that it is not that-than-which-a-greater-cannot-be-thought. And, in the same way, neither is it indubitable that, if there is something which is 'greater than everything', it is identical with 'that-than-which-a-greater-cannot-be-thought"; nor, if there were [such a being], that no other like it might exist – as this is certain in respect of what is said to be 'that-than-which-a-greater-cannot-be-thought'. For what if someone should say that something that is greater than everything actually exists, and yet that this same being can be thought of as not existing, and that something greater than it can be thought, even if this does not exist? In this case can it be inferred as evidently that [this being] is therefore not that which is greater than everything, as it would quite evidently be said in the other case that it is therefore not that-than-which-a-greater-cannot-be-thought? The former [inference] needs, in fact, a premiss in addition to this which is said to be 'greater than everything'; but the latter needs nothing save this utterance itself, namely, 'that-than-which-a-greater-cannot-be-thought'. Therefore, if what 'that-than-which-a-greater-cannot-be-thought' of itself proves concerning itself cannot be proved in the same way in respect of what is said to be 'greater than everything', you criticize me unjustly for having said what I did not say, since it differs so much from what I did say.

[...]

[VI.] You object, moreover, that any unreal or doubtfully real things at all can equally be understood and exist in the mind in the same way as the being I was speaking of. I am astonished that you urge this [objection] against me, for I was concerned to prove something which was in doubt, and for me it was sufficient that I should first show that it was understood and existed in the mind *in some way or other*, leaving it to be determined subsequently whether it was in the mind alone as unreal things are, or in reality also as true things are. For, if unreal or doubtfully real things are understood and exist in the mind in the sense that, when they are spoken of, he who hears them understands what the speaker means, nothing prevents what I have spoken of being understood and existing in the mind. But how are these [assertions] consistent, that is, when you assert that if someone speaks of unreal things you would understand whatever he says, and that, in the case of a thing which is not entertained in thought in the same way as even unreal things are, you do not say that you think of it or have it in thought upon hearing it spoken of, but rather that you understand it and have it in mind since, precisely, you cannot think of it save by understanding it, that is, knowing certainly that the thing exists in reality itself? How, I say, are both [assertions] consistent, namely that unreal things are understood, and that 'to understand' means knowing with certainty that something actually exists? You should have seen that nothing [of this applies] to me. But if unreal things are, in a sense, understood (this definition applying not to every kind of understanding but to a certain kind) then I ought not to be criticized for having said that 'that-than-which-a-greater-cannot-be-thought' is understood and is in the mind, even before it was certain that it existed in reality itself.

[VII.] Next, you say that it can hardly be believed that when this [that-than-which-a-greater-cannot-be-thought] has been spoken of and heard, it cannot be thought not to exist, as even it can be thought that God does not exist. Now those who have attained even a little expertise in disputation and argument could reply to that on my behalf. For is it reasonable that someone should therefore deny what he understands because it is said to be [the same as] that which he denies since he does not understand it? Or if that is denied [to exist] which is understood only to some extent and is the same as what is not understood at all, is not what is in doubt more easily proved from the fact that it is in some mind than from the fact that it is in no mind at all? For this reason it cannot be believed that anyone should deny 'that-than-which-a-greater-cannot-be-thought' (which, being heard, he understands to some extent), on the ground that he denies God whose meaning he does not think of in any way at all. On the other hand, if it is denied on the ground that it is not understood completely, even so is not that which is understood in some way easier to prove than that which is not understood in any way? It was therefore not wholly without reason that, to prove against the Fool that God exists, I proposed 'that-than-which-a-greater-cannot-be-thought', since he would understand this in some way, [whereas] he would understand the former [God] in no way at all.

[VIII.] In fact, your painstaking argument that 'that-than-which-a-greater-cannot-be-thought' is not like the not-yet-realized painting in the mind of the painter is beside the point. For I did not propose [the example] of the foreknown picture because I wanted to assert that what was at issue was in the same case, but rather that so I could show that something not understood as existing exists in the mind.

Again, you say that upon hearing of 'that-than-which-a-greater-cannot-be-thought' you cannot think of it as a real object known either generically or specifically or have it in your mind, on the grounds that you neither know the thing itself nor can you form an idea of it from other things similar to it. But obviously this is not so. For since everything that is less good is similar in so far as it is good to that which is more good, it is evident to every rational mind that, mounting from the less good to the more good we can from those things than which something greater can be thought conjecture a great deal about that-than-which-a-greater-cannot-be-thought. Who, for example, cannot think of this (even if he does not believe that what he thinks of actually exists) namely, that if something that has a beginning and end is good, that which, although it has had a beginning, does not, however, have an end, is much better? And just as this latter is better than the former, so also that which has neither beginning nor end is better again than this, even, if it passes always from the past through the present to the future. Again, whether something of this kind actually exists or not, that which does not lack anything at all, nor is forced to change or move, is very much better still. Cannot this be thought? Or can we think of something greater than this? Or is not this precisely to form an idea of that-than-which-a-greater-cannot-be-thought from those things than which a greater can be thought? There is, then, a way by which one can form an idea of 'that-than-which-a-greater-cannot-be-thought'. In this way, therefore, the Fool who does not accept the sacred authority [of Revelation] can easily be refuted if he denies that he can form an idea from other things of 'that-than-which-a-greater-cannot-be-thought'. But if any orthodox Christian should deny this let him remember that 'the invisible things of God from the creation of the world are clearly seen, through the things that have been made, even his eternal power and Godhead' [Rom. i. 20].

[IX.] But even if it were true that [the object] that-than-which-a-greater-cannot-be-thought cannot be thought of nor understood, it would not, however, be false that [the formula] 'that-than-which-a-greater-cannot-be-thought' could be thought of and understood. For just as nothing prevents one from saying 'ineffable' although one cannot specify what is said to be ineffable; and just as one can think of the inconceivable – although one cannot think of what 'inconceivable' applies to – so also, when 'that-than-which-a-greater-cannot-be-thought' is spoken of, there is no doubt at all that what is heard can be thought of and understood even if the thing itself cannot be thought of and understood. For if someone is so witless as to say that there is not something than-which-a-greater-cannot-be-thought, yet he will not be so shame-less as to say that he is not able to understand and think of what he was speaking about. Or if such a one is to be found, not only should his assertion be condemned, but he himself con-temned. Whoever, then, denies that there is something than-which-a-greater-cannot-be-thought, at any rate understands and thinks of the denial he makes, and this denial cannot be understood and thought about apart from its elements. Now, one element [of the denial] is 'that-than-which-a-greater-cannot-be-thought'. Whoever, therefore, denies this understands and thinks of 'that-than-which-a-greater-cannot-be-thought'. It is evident, moreover, that in the same way one can think of and understand that which cannot not exist. And one who thinks of this thinks of something greater than one who thinks of what can not exist. When, therefore, one thinks of that-than-which-a-greater-cannot-be-thought, if one thinks of what can not exist, one does not think of that-than-which-a-greater-cannot-be-thought. Now the same thing cannot at the same time be thought of and not thought of. For this reason he who thinks of that-than-which-a-greater-cannot-be-thought does not think of something that can not exist but something that cannot not exist. Therefore what he thinks of exists necessarily, since whatever can not exist is not what he thinks of.

[X.] I think now that I have shown that I have proved in the above tract, not by a weak argumentation but by a sufficiently necessary one, that something-than-which-a-greater-cannot-be-thought exists in reality itself, and that this proof has not been weakened by the force of any objection. For the import of this proof is in itself of such force that what is spoken of is proved (as a necessary consequence of the fact that it is understood or thought of) both to exist in actual reality and to be itself whatever must be believed about the Divine Being. For we believe of the Divine Being whatever it can, absolutely speaking, be thought better to be than not to be. For example, it is better to be eternal than not eternal, good than not good, indeed goodness-itself than not goodness-itself. However, nothing of this kind cannot but be that-than-which-a-greater-cannot-be-thought. It is, then, necessary that 'that-than-which-a-greater-cannot-be-thought' should be whatever must be believed about the Divine Nature.

Has This World Been Actualized by God from Among All Possible Worlds?

G.W. Leibniz, *Monadology*

Part of the metaphysical interest in Anselm's ontological argument (the previous reading) was its image of God as being knowable – and thereby knowable as existing – purely by *reflection*. There is no need to observe; simply *think* – and thus know God. And if we can do that, maybe we can know even more by reflection. How much more, though? For example, could we know, purely by reflection, something of how this world exists as it does? Are our minds that powerful?

In this reading from Gottfried Wilhelm Leibniz (1646–1716) we meet a famous argument for our having that capability. It is a version of what is often called the *cosmological* argument. Leibniz was a German philosopher and mathematician, a commanding intellect. Here we find him reasoning to a striking conclusion, using some terms that have since been very influential among philosophers. Leibniz's conclusion is that this world exists as it does, with all of its detailed contingencies, due to the independent existence of something *non*-contingent. In other words, there are contingencies only because there is something non-contingent – something *necessary*. That necessary something is a being. Indeed it is God, with all of His powerful perfections. Whatever happens to happen, therefore, does so only by resting ultimately upon the perfect stability that is God.

There are two keys to Leibniz's reaching that view – his principle of sufficient reason and his image of possible worlds. According to that principle, nothing exists without there being a sufficient cause of, or explanation for, its existing. *This* exists because of *that*; which exists because of *something else*; which derives from *something further*; and so on – until there is a first cause or explanation, underlying all else. *It* exists without depending upon something further existing independently

G.W. Leibniz, *Monadology* [1714], paragraphs 31–46, 52–56, 58–59. In *Philosophical Papers and Letters: Gottfried Wilhelm Leibniz*, 2nd edn., ed. L.E. Loemker (Dordrecht: D. Reidel, 1969).

Metaphysics and Epistemology: A Guided Anthology, First Edition. Edited by Stephen Hetherington.
© 2014 John Wiley & Sons, Inc. Published 2014 by John Wiley & Sons, Inc.

of it. That first cause can exist wholly "in and due to itself." And what could this ultimate cause or explanation be? Nothing other than God: only He could exist necessarily, not needing to be helped into existence by something else.

Now, suppose for the sake of argument that Leibniz is right about this. How does he then use this image to explain the world's existing as it does? It is not merely that there is a necessary being – God. It is also that God (argued Leibniz) comprehends all possible ways for a world to be – all possible worlds – and that God, with His power and understanding, *actualized* one of these. Which one? The best one, of course; only that world would provide God with a sufficient reason for actualizing it in particular, while leaving all other possible worlds as merely possible. So *this* world is the best possible one.

That image of there being an infinitude of possible worlds is highly picturesque, and it has been philosophically fertile. It encompasses alternative possible worlds populated by alternative possible people, eagles, cats, atoms, etc. It is a metaphysical image that has been increasingly prevalent within philosophy, especially over the past fifty or so years.

[...]

31. Our reasonings are based upon two great principles: the first the *principle of contradiction*, by virtue of which we judge that false which involves a contradiction, and that *true* which is opposed or contradictory to the false (*Theodicy* Secs. 44 and 196);

32. and the second the *principle of sufficient reason*, by virtue of which we observe that there can be found no fact that is true or existent, or any true proposition, without there being a sufficient reason for its being so and not otherwise, although we cannot know these reasons in most cases (*Ibid.*, Secs. 44 and 196).

33. There are also two kinds of truths, truths of *reasoning* and truths of *fact*. Truths of reasoning are necessary, and their opposite is impossible. Truths of fact are contingent, and their opposite is possible. When a truth is necessary, the reason for it can be found by analysis, resolving it into more simple ideas and truths until we reach the primitive (*Ibid.*, Secs. 170, 174, 189, 280–82, and 367; Abr. obj. 3).

34. It is thus that speculative *theorems* and *rules* of practice in mathematics are reduced by analysis to *definitions, axioms*, and *postulates*.

35. There are, finally, *simple ideas* which cannot be defined, and there are also axioms and postulates, or in brief, *primitive principles*, which cannot be proved and need no proof. And these are *identical propositions* whose opposites contain an explicit contradiction.

36. But a *sufficient reason* must also be found in *contingent truths* or *truths of fact*, that is to say, in the sequence of things distributed through the universe of creatures, whose analysis into particular reasons could proceed into unlimited detail because of the immense variety of things in nature and the division of bodies into the infinite. There is an infinity of shapes and motions, present and past, which enter into the efficient cause of my present writing, and there is an infinity of small inclination and dispositions of my soul, present and past, which enter into its final cause. (*Ibid., Secs.* 36, 37, 44, 45, 49, 52, 121, 122, 337, 340, and 344.)

37. As all this *detail* includes other earlier or more detailed contingent factors, each of which in turn needs a similar analysis to give its reason, one makes no progress, and the sufficient or final reason will have to be outside the sequence or *series* of these detailed contingent factors however infinite they may be.

38. Thus the final reason of things must be in a necessary substance in which the detail of the changes can be contained only eminently, as in their source. It is this substance that we call God. (*Ibid.*, Sec. 7.)

39. Now since this substance is a sufficient reason for all this detail, and the detail is interconnected throughout, *there is only one God, and this God is enough.*

40. We may conclude, too that this supreme substance, being unique, universal, and necessary, and having nothing outside of it which is independent of it, and being a simple consequence of possible being, must be incapable of limits and must contain as much reality as is possible.

41. It follows from this that God is absolutely perfect; *perfection* being nothing but the quantity of positive reality taken strictly, when we put aside the limits or bounds in the things which are limited. But where there are no bounds, that is, in God, perfection is absolutely infinite. (*Ibid.*, Sec. 22; Preface, 4*a*.)

42. It also follows that creatures receive their perfections from the influence of God but that their imperfections are due to their own nature, which is incapable of being limitless. For it is in this that they differ from God. (*Ibid.*, Secs. 20, 27–31, 153, 167, and 377ff.) This *original imperfection* of creatures is noticeable in the *natural inertia* of the body. (*Ibid.*, Secs. 30 and 380; Abr. obj. 5.)

43. It is also true that the source not only of existences but also of essences is in God, insofar as these essences are real or insofar as there is something real in possibility. This is because the understanding of God is the region of eternal truths or of the ideas upon which they depend and because without him there would be no reality in possibilities – not only nothing existent but also nothing possible. (*Ibid.*, Sec. 20.)

44. For if there is a reality in the essences or possibilities, or in the eternal truths as well, this reality must be founded on something existent and actual, and therefore in the existence of a necessary being, in whom essence includes existence or in whom it is enough to be possible in order to be actual. (*Ibid.*, Secs. 184, 189, and 335.)

45. Thus God alone, or the necessary being, has the privilege of necessarily existing if he is possible. And since nothing can prevent the possibility of that which is without any limits, without any negation, and consequently without any contradiction, this fact alone suffices to know the existence of God a priori. So we have proved it through the reality of eternal truths. But we have also proved it a posteriori, since contingent beings exist, and their final or sufficient reason can be discovered only in a necessary being which has its reason for its existence in itself.

46. We must not imagine as do some, however, that since the eternal truths are dependent upon God, they are arbitrary and dependent on his will, as Descartes and later Mr. Poiret seem to have held. This is true only of contingent truths, whose principle is *fitness* or the choice of the *best*; necessary truths, however, depend solely on his understanding and are its internal object. (*Ibid.*, Secs. 180, 184, 185, 335, 351, and 380.)

[...]

52. It is in this way that actions and passions are mutual among creatures. For God, comparing two simple substances, finds the reasons in each which oblige him to adapt the other to it, with the result that whatever is active in certain respects is passive considered

from another point – *active* insofar as what we distinctly know in it serves as a reason for what happens in another, but *passive* insofar as the reason for what happens in it is found in what we know distinctly in another. (*Ibid.*, Sec. 66.)

53. Now since there is an infinity of possible universes in the ideas of God, but only one can exist, there must be a sufficient reason for God's choice which determines him to one rather than another. (*Ibid.*, Secs. 8, 10, 44, 173, 196–97, 225, and 414–16.)

54. This reason can be found only in the *fitness* or in the degrees of perfection which these worlds contain, each possible one having a right to claim existence in the measure of the perfection which it enfolds. (*Ibid.*, 74, 167, 350, 201, 130, 352, 345–46, and 354.)

55. And this is the cause for the existence of the best, which his wisdom causes God to know, his goodness makes him choose, and his power makes him produce. (*Ibid.*, Secs. 8, 78, 80, 84, 119, 204, 206, and 208; Abr. obj. 1, 8.)

56. Now this mutual connection or accommodation of all created things to each other and of each to all the rest causes each simple substance to have relations which express all the others and consequently to be a perpetual living mirror or the universe. (*Ibid.*, Secs. 130 and 360.)

[...]

58. This is the means of obtaining the greatest variety possible, but with the greatest possible order; that is to say, this is the means of attaining as much perfection as possible. (*Ibid.*, Secs. 120, 124, 241–42, 215, 243, and 275.)

59. It is only this hypothesis, moreover, which I dare say is demonstrated, that exalts the greatness of God as one ought. Mr. Bayle recognized this when he raised objections to it in his *Dictionary* (article Rorarius), where he was even inclined to believe that I ascribed too much to God, more than is possible. Yet he was unable to set forth any reason why this universal harmony, which results in every substance expressing exactly all the others by means of the relations which it has with them, should be impossible.

21

Does This World Exist Because It Has Value Independently of God?

Nicholas Rescher, *Nature and Understanding*

It is difficult to imagine there being a more fundamental question than that of how there is something rather than nothing. It is the question of how there is a world at all – not merely the Earth, but whatever is actual. How does any of this exist? How did it ever exist in the first place? Why was there not simply nothing? Leibniz asked this question; and the previous reading showed us how he answered it: *God* is the reason for all there is. God is a *necessarily* existing entity. His existing could never have depended upon anything contingent. What we are asking about now – independently of a focus upon God – is the existence of the *contingencies* constituting the world. The present reading from Nicholas Rescher (b. 1928) offers an answer inspired by Leibniz's – an answer, nonetheless, that does not rely on positing God's existence and does not need to accord God a special role in the world's existing.

Rescher, from the University of Pittsburgh, is one of the most published of all contemporary philosophers, having written on an astonishing range of topics. One of these is existence. Here, he develops the idea that the world exists as it does because of its *value*. Leibniz also thought this. For him, though, this was a matter of there being a God *who actually valued* this world's existing: He valued it above the other possible worlds that He could otherwise have chosen to actualize. Rescher regards Leibniz's approach as needlessly complex. The underlying idea of the world's having value and thereby existing (argues Rescher) need not be understood in terms of God's purposes and preferences. Rather, God would have valued this world only because it *deserved* to be valued: because of how it is in itself, it has value; and it would do so, regardless of whether or not God had ever given it any attention that could have resulted in His valuing it.

Nicholas Rescher, *Nature and Understanding: The Metaphysics and Method of Science* (Oxford: Clarendon Press, 2000), ch. 8 (excerpts). Reprinted with permission of Oxford University Press.

What form does the world's value take? Rescher thinks of this as involving such things as "stability, symmetry, continuity, complexity, order, and even a dynamic impetus to the development of 'higher' forms possessed of more sophisticated capabilities." These are valuable for a world, insofar as it is "competing" with other possible worlds to be actual.

That proposal allows, but it does not require, there to be a God. Compare Rescher's proposal with the design argument. The latter infers, from the world's observed patterns of order and regularity, that there is a God. Rescher's world's-value argument infers, from the world's existence at all, that it has such order, regularity, and even more. This would be why it exists.

The Riddle of Existence

What is perhaps the biggest metaphysical question of them all was put on the agenda of philosophy by G.W. Leibniz: 'Why is there anything at all?' This question is not only difficult to answer but poses difficulties in its very conception. After all, it is – or should be – clear that such questions as 'Why is there anything at all?', 'Why are things-in-general as they actually are?', and 'Why are the laws of nature as they are?' cannot be answered within the standard causal framework. For causal explanations need inputs: they are essentially *transformational* rather than *formational* pure and simple. And so, if we persist in posing the sorts of global questions at issue, we cannot hope to resolve them in orthodox causal terms. For when we ask about *everything* there are no issue-external materials at our disposal for giving a non-circular explanation. Does this mean that such questions are improper and should not be raised at all – that even to inquire into the existence of the entire universe is somehow illegitimate? Not necessarily. For it could be replied that the question does have a perfectly good answer, but one that is not given in the orthodox causal terms that apply to other issues of smaller scale.

A more radical strategy is thus called for if rejectionism is to be avoided. And such a strategy exists.

[…]

Optimalism and Evaluative Metaphysics

From its earliest days, metaphysics has been understood also to include 'axiology', the evaluative and normative assessment of the things that exist. As early as Aristotle the aim of the enterprise was not just to describe or characterize, but to grade (appraise, rank) matters in point of their inherent value. […] The very possibility of this axiological enterprise accordingly rests on the acceptance of distinctly metaphysical values – as opposed to ethical (right/wrong), aesthetic (beautiful/ugly), or practical (useful/useless) ones.

[…]

[T]he present deliberations will accordingly focus on exploring the role of value in the explanation of existence. The governing idea is to consider the prospect of giving a Leibnizian answer to that Leibnizian question, contemplating the prospect that things exist – and exist as they do – because that is for the best. Can such an optimalism be developed in a way that is at all plausible?

Axiological Explanation: How Optimalism Works

[…]

The approach rests on adopting what might be called an *axiogenetic optimality principle* to the effect that value represents a decisive advantage in regard to realization in that in the virtual competition for existence among alternatives it is the comparatively best that is bound to prevail.[1] Accordingly, whenever there is a plurality of alternative possibilities competing for realization in point of truth or of existence the (or an) optimal possibility wins out. (An alternative is *optimal* when no better one exists, although it can have equals.) The result is that things exist, and exist as they do, because this is for the (metaphysical) best.

[…]

But why should it be that optimalism obtains? What sort of plausible argument can be given on this position's behalf? Why should what is for the best exist? The answer to these questions lies in the very nature of the principle itself. It is self-substantiating, seeing it is automatically for the best that the best alternative should exist rather than an inferior rival.

[…]

Yet what is to be the status of a Law of Optimality to the effect that 'whatever possibility is for the best is *ipso facto* the possibility that is actualized'? It is certainly not a logico-conceptually *necessary* truth; from the angle of theoretical logic it has to be seen as a contingent fact.[…] But if it is contingent then surely it must itself rest on some further explanation? Granted. It itself presumably has an explanation, seeing that one can and should maintain the Leibnizian Principle of Sufficient Reason to the effect that for every contingent fact there is a reason why it is so rather than otherwise. But there is no decisive reason why that explanation has to be deeper and different – that is, no decisive reason why the prospect of *self-explanation* has to be excluded at this fundamental level.[2]

The reasoning at issue proceeds as follows:

- The prevailing world order is the best that *can* be actualized – i.e. the best that it is possible to realize.
- The best possible order exists because that is for the best.

Therefore: The prevailing world order exists.

[…]

[…] The impetus to realization inherent in authentic value lies in the very nature of value itself. A rational person would not favour the inferior alternative; and a rational reality cannot do so either.

[…]

Ontological optimalism is closely related to optimism. The optimist holds that 'Whatever exists is for the best,' the optimalist maintains the converse, that 'Whatever is for the best exists'. But at least when we are dealing with exclusive and exhaustive alternatives the two theses come to the same thing. For if one of the alternatives A, $A_1,...A_n$ must be the case, then if what is realized is for the best it follows automatically that the best is realized.

Optimalism has many theoretical advantages. Here is just one of them. It is conceivable, one might contend, that the *existence* of the world (i.e. of *a* world) is a necessary fact while nevertheless its *nature* (i.e. of *which* world) is contingent. And this would mean that separate and potentially different answers would have to be provided for the questions, 'Why is there anything at all?' and 'Why is the character of existence as is – why is it that this particular world exists?' However, an axiogenetic approach enjoys the advantage of rational economy in that it proceeds uniformly here. It provides a single uniform rationale for both answers – namely that 'this is for the best'. It accordingly also enjoys the significant merit of providing for the rational economy of explanatory principles.

But is not optimalism merely a version of wishful thinking? Not necessarily. For even as in personal life what is best for us is all too often not at all what we individuals want, so in metaphysics what is abstractly for the best is very unlikely to bear any close relationship to what we would want to have if we humans could have things our way.
[…]

[…] [W]hat if there is a *plurality* of perfection-contributory features so interrelated that more of the one demands less of the other? Here it would result that nothing is straightforwardly best. This may be so, but matters need not be straightforward. In such cases one can – and should – resort to a function of combination that allows for the interaction of those different value parameters. For example, with two operative value-making factors, say cheapness (that is, inverse acquisition cost) and durability in the case of a 100-watt light bulb, one will use the ratio (cost of purchase) : (hours of usability) or equally cost/hour of service as a measure of merit. This possibilizes the reduction of the multifactor case to the situation of a single compound and complex factor so that optimization is once again possible. And that this is possible is guaranteed by optimalism itself; it is part and parcel of the best possible order of things that optimalism should be operable within it.

But – really! – how can sensible people possibly embrace the conception that the inherently best alternative is thereby automatically the actual (true) one. Does not the world's all too evident imperfection stand decisively in the way here?

The matter is not all that simple, however. For the issue is going to pivot on the question of what 'inherently best' means. If it means best from that angle of your desires, or of my interests, or even of the advantage of *Homo sapiens* in general, then clearly the thesis loses its strong appeal. For such plausibility that 'best' should be construed as looking to the condition of existence-as-a-whole rather than one particular privileged individual or group. Optimality in this context is clearly not going to be a matter of the affective welfare or standard of living of some particular sector of existence; it is going to have to be a metaphysical good of some synoptic and rather abstract sort that looks to the condition of the whole. The optimalist certainly need not simply shut his eyes to the world's all too evident parochially considered imperfections. There is, in fact, a point of view from which optimalism is a position that is not so much optimistic as deeply pessimistic. For it holds that even the best of possible arrangements is bound to exhibit very real imperfections from the angle of any narrowly parochial concerns or interests.

The Problem of How Value can have Explanatory Efficacy: Overcoming Some Objections

[...]

The overall story that must be narrated here runs as follows: Nature – physical reality as we have it – represents the actualization of certain possibilities. But underlying this existential condition of affairs is the operation of a prior sub- or metaphysical principle, operative within the wider domain of logical possibility, and dividing this domain into disjoint sectors of 'real' and 'purely theoretical' possibility. To put it very figuratively, logical possibilities are involved in a virtual struggle for existence in which the axiologically best win out so as to become real possibilities. Specifically, when there are (mutually exclusive) alternatives that are possible in theory, nevertheless none will be a real ontological possibility for realization as actual or as true if some other alternative is superior to it. The availability of a better alternative disqualifies its inferiors from qualifying as ontologically available – as *real*, that is, metaphysical – possibilities. And so whenever there is a uniquely best alternative, then this alternative is *ipso facto* realized as actual or true.

Optimalism is certainly at teleological theory: it holds that nature's *modus operandi* manifests a tropism towards a certain end or *telos*, to wit, optimization. [...] [V]alue is not productive at all, but merely eliminative in so functioning as to block the way to availability of inferior productions.

[...]

[...] Value-explanation just is not causal; values do not function in the order of efficient causality at all. The Law of Optimality yields those results not via the mysterious attractive power of optimal possibilities but because suboptimal possibilities are excluded because their superior rivals simply pre-empt their place in possibility space.

[...] The real point is that while value does not efficiently *cause* existence it nevertheless *explains* it, exactly because causal explanation is not the only sort of explanation there is. [...] [V]alue explanations [...] present perfectly good answers to 'Why is something-or-other so?' questions. It is just that in relation to laws, values play only an explanatory role through possibility elimination and not a causally productive role through actual creation. And this is no defect because a productive process is simply not called for.

[...]

[...] The point is that the regress of explanatory principles must have a stop and that it is here – with axiology – that we reach a natural terminus by way of self-explanation.

[...]

The Value Efficacy Objection and the Theological Aspect

But what of the theological dimension?

[...]

This [...] demands an answer to the question of how values can possibly figure in the realization of things save through the mediation of the purposes of a creatively active being – a finite agent with mundane things and with the universe as a whole, who else but God.

We may characterize this as a theistically based value-efficacy objection. It clearly poses a challenge with which an axiological theory of explanation must come to terms.

[…] That nature manifests and exemplifies such cognitive values as order, harmony, uniformity was thus explained by regarding these as marks of purpose. On this basis, the mainstream of Western thought regarding axiological explanation has taken the line that there is a supernatural agent (God, demiurge, cosmic spirit) and that values obtain their explanatory bearing by influencing the state of mind which governs his creative endeavours. This essentially *purposive* approach characterizes the traditional argument from design. […] The sequential explanatory slide from design to value to purpose to intelligence was historically seen as inexorable. And so the idea of a recourse to an explanatory principle that is geared to values without any such mediation represents a radical departure. The guiding conception of the present deliberations – that value is the natural place to sever this chain – reflects a break with a longstanding tradition.

However, the justification of this break lies in observing the important distinction between values and purposes. Granted, a purpose must be *somebody's* purpose: it must have some intelligent agent as its owner-operator. […]

A value, however, can be altogether impersonal. Being a value does not require that somebody actually values it (any more than being a fact requires that somebody actually realizes it). […] To be of value is to *deserve* to be valued, but that of course need not actually happen: the value of things can be underestimated or overestimated or totally overlooked. Neither the items that have value [nor] the facts of their being of value depend on apprehending minds for their reality. And this holds in particular for ontological values such as economy, simplicity, regularity, uniformity, etc., that figure in the axiological explanation of laws. The being of values does *not* consist in their being perceived, any more than does the being of most other sorts of things.

[…]

While people indeed can value things, something can be of value – can *have* value – without being valued *by* anybody – not even God. (It must be valuable *for* something or other but it need not be valued *by* somebody; in principle clean air can be valuable for mammals without being valued *by* any of them.)

In general, then, we need not embed values in purposes; axiological explanation can stand on its own feet. Axiological existence-explanation can thus proceed entirely outside the purposive order. […] We need not personify nature to account for its features. To say that nature embodies value is a very far cry from saying that the realization of value is one of its purposes. That reality operates in a certain manner – that its *modus operandi* follows certain laws or principles – is in general an entirely impersonal thesis. The values involved in axiological explanation need not be *somebody's* values. […]

In this respect, the present axiological approach differs decisively from that of Leibniz. He answered the question, 'Why is it that the value-optimizing world should be the one that actually exists?' with reference to the will of a God who *chooses* to adopt value optimization as a creative principle. Leibniz was committed to an idea that it is necessary to account for the obtaining of a principle in terms of the operation of an existing entity (specifically the agency of an intelligent being – namely God). Instead, our axiological approach sees the explanatory bearing of a principle of value as direct, without mediation through the agency of a substantial being (however extraordinary) as final and fundamental.

Value Naturalism

[...]
[...] [A]s we have seen the prospect of self-invoking explanations is available here. For example: nature fosters economy (simplicity, harmony, etc.) because that is the most economical
of things for it to do. Or again: why do its laws exist as they do? Because that's for the axiological best in optimizing the systemic operations that obtain. And why does what is for the
best obtain – just exactly because that itself is for the best. [...]

The axiology at issue should thus be seen as naturalistic. The values involved are to
encompass factors like stability, symmetry, continuity, complexity, order, and even a dynamic
impetus to the development of 'higher' forms possessed of more sophisticated capabilities –
perhaps even a sort of Hegelian impetus towards the evolutionary emergence of a creature
possessed of an intelligence able to comprehend and appreciate the universe itself, creating a
conscious reduplication model of the universe in the realm of thought through the artifice
of intelligence. So in any event these values are mundane and non-transcendental, pivoting
on physico-metaphysical factors.
[...]

Sidestepping Theology

And so, confronted with the challenge, 'What if one is sceptical about theism? Would one then
not have to reject optimalism?' The optimalist replies: 'Not at all. Optimalism does not presuppose theism – it perhaps could but certainly need not call upon God to institute optimalism.'

To reach outside the value domain itself to equip value with a purposive explanation
that is theological in nature is unnecessary and counterproductive – it complicates rather
than simplifies the explanatory process. For we then cannot avoid the question: 'Why does
the putative creator adopt this purpose?' The response must take the form that he deems
(and of course, since it is God that is at issue, *rightly* deems) it to be of value. And this at
once carries us back to axiology. Recourse to divine purpose merely adds a complex epi-
cycle once the question of the rational validity of this purpose arises. We now have a two-
factor explanation of creator plus value, where in principle a one-factor explanation in
terms of value as such can accomplish the explanatory task.
[...]

The salient difference between the present axiological approach and the traditional theological argumentation from design thus turns on keeping values apart from divine intentions and
purposes. To say that reality is subject to an evaluative principle is emphatically not to personify
nature or to personalize the productive forces that serve to explain it. [...] [O]rder no more
requires an orderer or value a valuer than temperature demands a heat-sensitively sentient being.

[...] [T]he history of science – where God has been asked to do less and less explanatory
work over the course of time – is such as to make it reasonable to contemplate an account of
design without recourse to a designer. Our axiogenetic theory is thus without theological
demands or implications. And this is all to the good. For David Hume's point holds good: that
nature is the product of the operations of a designing intelligence is not something we can learn
convincingly merely from a study of the workings of nature itself.

Accordingly, axiology need not be tied to religion as this enterprise is usually understood.[3] It may be tempting for us anthropomorphizing humans to ground nature's elegant laws in the mathematicized planning of an Originative Intelligence, but the merit of an axiological approach shows that this temptation can – and should – be resisted. From the days of Laplace and Darwin onwards, it has become increasingly clear that design *in* nature does not entail a designer *of* nature, a purposing intelligence 'behind' nature, a creator God. The axiological explanation of nature and its laws circumvents the cosmological argument rather than engendering some version of it.

To be sure, axiological explanation is not *incompatible* with theism – on the contrary, it is thoroughly congenial to it. (A benign Creator would certainly create a duly optimal world.) But a theory of axiological ontogenesis certainly does not *require* a further recourse to the theological domain.

[...]

[...] Yet is such a theory of axiological ontogenesis not defeated by the objection: If it really were the case that value explains existence, then why isn't the world altogether perfect?

The answer lies in the inherent complexity of value. An object that is of any value at all is subject to a *complex* of values. For it is the fundamental fact of axiology that every evaluation-admitting object has a *plurality* of evaluative features. Take a car – an automobile. Here the relevant parameters of merit clearly include such factors as speed, reliability, repair infrequency, safety, operating economy, aesthetic appearance, road-handling ability. But in actual practice such features are interrelated. It is unavoidable that they trade off against one another: more of *A* means less of *B*. [...] Analogously the world is not absolutely perfect – perfect in *every* respect – because this sort of absolute perfection is in principle impossible of realization. And of course it makes no sense to ask for the impossible. Accordingly, the objection, 'If value is the key to existence, the world would be perfect', collapses. All that will follow on axiogenetic principles is that the world will exemplify an optimal interactive balance of the relevant natural factors. [...]

Leibniz had the right approach here: optimalism does not maintain that the world is absolutely perfect but just that it be the best that is possible – that it outranks the available alternatives.

[...]

And so the objection, 'If value is the key to existence, the world would be perfect', proves to be untenable. All the will follow on axiogenetic principles is that the world will exemplify an optimal balance of the relevant evaluative factors.

The rationale of reality-as-a-whole is clearly not going to be something that is directly observable – it will have to be a theoretical entity – or, rather, a theoretical fact. Like all other such facts it will have links to observation, but they will almost certainly be very long distance links that provide for only a rather loose coupling.

[...]

The key factor here is not ethical motivation but ontological constraint. For the values contemplated in the present, discussion are *ontological* rather than *ethical* values – that is, values within the spectrum of good/bad rather than that of right/wrong!

Notes

1. The prime spokesman for this line of thought within the Western philosophical tradition was G. W. Leibniz. A present-day exponent is John Leslie. [...] See also N. Rescher, *The Riddle of Existence* (Lanham, Md.: University Press of America, 1984).

2. After all, there is no reason of logico-theoretical principle why propositions cannot be self-certifying. Nothing vicious need be involved in self-substantiation. Think of 'Some statements are true,' or 'This statement stakes a particular rather than a universal claim.'

3. To be sure, some idealists envision a religion in which God plays so small a role that even the present theory can count as 'religious'. J. M. E. McTaggart, for example, defined religion as 'an emotion resting on a connection of a harmony between ourselves and the universe at large'. (*Some Dogmas of Religion* (London: E. Arnold, 1906), 3). But, of course, since we humans are ourselves an evolved part of nature, some degree of affective harmony is pretty well inevitable in a way that need not have much of 'religion' about it on any ordinary understanding of the matter.

22

Can Something Have Value in Itself?

Plato, *Euthyphro*

Implicit within Rescher's proposal, from the previous reading, is the idea that it is possible for something to *have value* independently of whether it is ever actually or actively *valued*. Rescher regards the world – its existing at all – in that way. It could have value in itself, so that its having this value would be why God valued the world (rather than God's valuing the world being why it has value). Given how the world is in itself, its existing could (says Rescher) be more valuable than would any alternative world's existing. It would not necessarily be regarded by someone in particular, such as God, as more valuable. It would just be inherently more valuable.

Well, is that possible? This sort of issue was introduced to philosophy by the reasoning in this reading from Plato's dialogue, the *Euthyphro*. What was at stake, as Socrates conversed with Euthyphro, was the nature of a particular kind of value. How are we to understand the idea of something's being holy – its being worthy of being worshiped? This is a significant concept. Yet what would *explain* a thing's being holy? Euthyphro offers a simple answer: Something is holy because the gods love it. But this answer did not satisfy Socrates: Surely (he replied) that is not quite right; surely the gods love something only because it *merits* that sort of approval by them. Which of these alternatives is it to be? Until we answer that question, how can we ever sensibly ascribe a form of value (such as that of being holy)? Until then, we would not understand the nature of that kind of value.

Philosophers regard this exchange between Socrates and Euthyphro as a classic distillation of philosophical thinking. Confronted by a fundamental conceptual choice, two philosophers are trying to explain how something of some particular

Plato, *Euthyphro* 9e–11b, trans. L. Cooper. From *The Collected Dialogues of Plato*, ed. E. Hamilton and H. Cairns (Princeton: Princeton University Press, 1961). © 1961 by Princeton University Press. Reprinted with permission of Princeton University Press.

significance is even possible; and they do this by seeking to analyze a key concept. So we are meeting again the book's initial themes from Part I: inquiring into what is significant and real; proposing guiding philosophical images; analyzing key concepts; seeking to explain underlying possibilities.

EUTHYPHRO: Yes, I would indeed affirm that holiness is what the gods all love, and its opposite is what the gods all hate, unholiness.

SOCRATES: Are we to examine this position also, Euthyphro, to see if it is sound? Or shall we let it through, and thus accept our own and others' statement, and agree to an assertion simply when somebody says that a thing is so? Must we not look into what the speaker says?

EUTHYPHRO: We must. And yet, for my part, I regard the present statement as correct.

SOCRATES: We shall soon know better about that, my friend. Now think of this. Is what is holy holy because the gods approve it, or do they approve it because it is holy?

EUTHYPHRO: I do not get your meaning.

SOCRATES: Well. I will try to make it clearer. We speak of what is carried and the carrier, do we not, of led and leader, of the seen and that which sees? And you understand that in all such cases the things are different, and how they differ?

EUTHYPHRO: Yes, I think I understand.

SOCRATES: In the same way what is loved is one thing, and what loves is another?

EUTHYPHRO: Of course.

SOCRATES: Tell me now, is what is carried 'carried' because something carries it, or is it for some other reason?

EUTHYPHRO: No, but for that reason.

SOCRATES: And what is led, because something leads it? And what is seen, because something sees it?

EUTHYPHO: Yes, certainly.

SOCRATES: Then it is not because a thing is seen that something sees it, but just the opposite – because something sees it, therefore it is seen. Nor because it is led, that something leads it, but because something leads it, therefore it is led. Nor because it is carried, that something carries it; but because something carries it, therefore it is carried. Do you see what I wish to say, Euthyphro? It is this. Whenever an effect occurs, or something is effected, it is not the thing effected that gives rise to the effect; no, there is a cause, and then comes this effect. Nor is it because a thing is acted on that there is this effect; no, there is a cause for what it undergoes, and then comes this effect. Don't you agree?

EUTHYPHRO: I do.

SOCRATES: Well then, when a thing is loved, is it not in process of becoming something, or of undergoing something, by some other thing?

EUTHYPHRO: Yes, certainly.

SOCRATES: Then the same is true here as in the previous cases. It is not because a thing is loved that they who love it love it, but it is loved because they love it.

EUTHYPHRO: Necessarily.

SOCRATES: Then what are we to say about the holy, Euthyphro? According to your argument, is it not loved by all the gods?

EUTHYPHRO: Yes.

SOCRATES: Because it is holy, or for some other reason?

EUTHYPHRO: No, it is for that reason.

SOCRATES: And so it is because it is holy that it is loved; it is not holy because it is loved.

EUTHYPHRO: So it seems.

SOCRATES: On the other hand, it is beloved and pleasing to the gods just because they love it?

EUTHYPHRO: No doubt of that.

SOCRATES: So what is pleasing to the gods is not the same as what is holy, Euthyphro, nor, according to your statement, is the holy the same as what is pleasing to the gods. They are two different things.

EUTHYPHRO: How may that be, Socrates?

SOCRATES: Because we are agreed that the holy is loved because it is holy, and is not holy because it is love. Isn't it so?

EUTHYPHRO: Yes.

SOCRATES: Whereas what is pleasing to the gods is pleasing to them just because they love it, such being its nature and its cause. Its being loved of the gods is not the reason of its being loved.

EUTHYPHRO: You are right.

SOCRATES: But suppose, dear Euthyphro, that what is pleasing to the gods and what is holy were not two separate things. In that case if holiness were loved because it was holy, then also what was pleasing to the gods would be loved because it pleased them. And, on the other hand, if what was pleasing to them pleased because they loved it, then also the holy would be holy because they loved it. But now you see that it is just the opposite, because the two are absolutely different from each other, for the one [what is pleasing to the gods] is of a sort to be loved because it is loved, whereas the other [what is holy] is loved because it is of a sort to be loved. Consequently, Euthyphro, it looks as if you had not given me my answer – as if when you were asked to tell the nature of the holy, you did not wish to explain the essence of it. You merely tell an attribute of it, namely, that it appertains to holiness to be loved by all the gods. What it *is*, as yet you have not said. So, if you please, do not conceal this from me. No, begin again. Say what the holy is, and never mind if gods do love it, nor if it has some other attribute; on that we shall not split. Come, speak out. Explain the nature of the holy and unholy.

EUTHYPHRO: Now, Socrates, I simply don't know how to tell you what I think. Somehow everything that we put forward keeps moving about us in a circle, and nothing will stay where we put it.

How Are Persons Persons?

23

Is Each Person a Union of Mind and Body?

René Descartes, "Meditation VI"

In the previous-but-one reading, Nicholas Rescher argued that there are criteria whereby a world could exist because of its value. In a Leibnizian spirit, that picture was of an *overall* world's having value: this world would exist because of its having more overall value than any alternative possible world has. But what about the world's *elements*? Is there a possibility of some of these having value in themselves, with others lacking value in themselves, perhaps even lowering the overall value of the world? Let us reflect upon one element of this world – namely, *us*. Many – of us – have regarded the existence of persons as adding value to the world. Have we been correct about that? Or does the existence of persons add nothing to a world's overall value?

René Descartes, "Meditation VI" (excerpts), in *Meditations on First Philosophy* [1641]. From *The Philosophical Works of Descartes*, vol. 1, trans. E.S. Haldane and G.R.T. Ross (Cambridge: Cambridge University Press, 1911). Reprinted with permission of Cambridge University Press.

That could depend upon what it is to be a person; and the next few readings investigate aspects of this. We begin here with one of *the* central philosophical images. It is famously associated with the French mathematician and philosopher René Descartes (1596–1650), often credited with being the first major figure in modern philosophy. The image in question is called *mind–body dualism* (or sometimes *Cartesian dualism*, in honor of Descartes' defense of it). This reading comes from Descartes' *Meditations*, among the most influential of all philosophical writings. Later, in Part III, we will return to the first two of those six meditations, because they are explicitly about the nature and possibility of knowing. But in the final meditation, Descartes reached a view – based, he argued, on knowledge – of his nature as a person. He concluded with a sort of image that has become very natural to many people. It is the image of oneself as a union, a blend, of body and of mind. Whenever you feel the urge to describe yourself as being both body *and* mind, you might choose to acknowledge silently the historical influence of Descartes.

His form of dualism is usually interpreted as meaning that a person is composed of two kinds of "stuff." Some of it is material, physical; some is immaterial, yet nonetheless real. Body has mathematically describable dimensionality – this length here, that length there. Hence it is divisible, at least in mathematical principle, into fully physical parts. But an immaterial mind lacks that sort of dimensionality. Hence it is indivisible in that respect. It is essentially whole. Even in mathematical principle, it cannot be broken into parts – this part of a mind *still* being a mind. To appreciate the difference, look at your body. You can easily view it as having parts – physical parts, *complete* physical parts. But then reflect on your mind, even on individual thoughts "within" it. Are they literally *parts* of your mind? Not according to Descartes; for your mind as a whole is still doing the reflecting. Your mind is your consciousness – a *thing*, although a separate *kind* of thing from your body. Your mind is the essential you, even as your body is also part of you.

That is the image painted by Descartes, at any rate. It may well feel familiar. But how might we argue for it? In this extract we meet Descartes' two arguments for this philosophical picture of the underlying nature of a person.

Of the Existence of Material Things, and of the Real Distinction between the Soul and Body of Man

[...]

And first of all, because I know that all things which I apprehend clearly and distinctly can be created by God as I apprehend them, it suffices that I am able to apprehend one thing apart from another clearly and distinctly in order to be certain that the one is different from the other, since they may be made to exist in separation at least by the omnipotence of God;

and it does not signify by what power this separation is made in order to compel me to judge them to be different: and, therefore, just because I know certainly that I exist, and that meanwhile I do not remark that any other thing necessarily pertains to my nature or essence, excepting that I am a thinking thing, I rightly conclude that my essence consists solely in the fact that I am a thinking thing [or a substance whose whole essence or nature is to think]. And although possibly (or rather certainly, as I shall say in a moment) I possess a body with which I am very intimately conjoined, yet because, on the one side, I have a clear and distinct idea of myself inasmuch as I am only a thinking and unextended thing and as, on the other, I possess a distinct idea of body, inasmuch as it is only an extended and unthinking thing, it is certain that this I [that is to say, my soul by which I am what I am], is entirely and absolutely distinct from my body, and can exist without it.

[...]

[...] [T]hen, I here say, in the first place, that there is a great difference between mind and body, inasmuch as body is by nature always divisible, and the mind is entirely indivisible. For, as a matter of fact, when I consider the mind, that is to say, myself inasmuch as I am only a thinking thing, I cannot distinguish in myself any parts, but apprehend myself to be clearly one and entire; and although the whole mind seems to be united to the whole body, yet if a foot, or an arm, or some other part, is separated from my body, I am aware that nothing has been taken away from my mind. And the faculties of willing, feeling, conceiving, etc. cannot be properly speaking said to be its parts, for it is one and the same mind which employs itself in willing and in feeling and understanding. But it is quite otherwise with corporeal or extended objects, for there is not one of these imaginable by me which my mind cannot easily divide into parts, and which consequently I do not recognise as being divisible; this would be sufficient to teach me that the mind or soul of man is entirely different from the body if I had not already learned it from other sources.

24

Is Self-Consciousness what Constitutes a Person?

John Locke, *An Essay Concerning Human Understanding*

We have met Descartes' famous philosophical image of what it is to be the person one is: each of us is a blend of two kinds of *substance*. There is a physical (material) body, combined with a non-physical (immaterial) mind. Essential to the mind is consciousness – active thinking. But the consciousness as such, it seems, is not enough, on Descartes' view. What really matters is that a person is composed of two kinds of substance. However, this underlying image of personhood is questioned in the present reading, from John Locke. Earlier, we read some of his thoughts on physical objects and their qualities. Now we will examine his much-discussed account of persons – specifically, his philosophical image of what it is to be the *same* person from one time to another. This reveals what he thinks it is to be a person at all.

Locke's explanatory emphasis was not upon substances. It was upon the phenomena of consciousness, *irrespective* of whatever substances are housing the instances of thinking and feeling. Imagine your consciousness – your sense of your self – emanating somehow from your little finger. According to Locke, this would not detract at all from that consciousness being what constitutes you as whichever person you are.

Of course, you are that person now *and* over time – now and at other times. Which aspects of consciousness bind you-now with you-then? Locke highlights *memories* as what join together to bind a person-now with the-same-person-then. These link now with then with before-then with before-before-then, etc. This pattern is enough to constitute a single person over time.

John Locke, *An Essay Concerning Human Understanding* (1690), Book II, ch. XXVII, sects. 4–26 (excerpts). Reprinted with permission of Oxford University Press.

Metaphysics and Epistemology: A Guided Anthology, First Edition. Edited by Stephen Hetherington.

We should note that Locke distinguished *Person* from *Man* (i.e., a member of mankind – a man or woman). A continued bodily substance is enough for being the same man or woman. But it is not enough for being the same person. Locke regarded personhood – remember: one's consciousness – as what would ground or reflect a judgment of one's *responsibility* or *accountability* for an action. For this is a matter of one's *conscious involvement* in the action. Contrast that dimension of assessment with one which merely, in effect, counts molecules – pointing to a substance's presence. What matters is whatever the substance does as a *rational* being. That requires consciousness; so too, therefore, does personhood, on this philosophical image from Locke.

Of Identity and Diversity

[...]

§4. We must therefore consider wherein an Oak differs from a Mass of Matter, and that seems to me to be in this; that the one is only the Cohesion of Particles of Matter any how united, the other such a disposition of them as constitutes the parts of an Oak; and such an Organization of those parts, as is fit to receive, and distribute nourishment, so as to continue, and frame the Wood, Bark, and Leaves, *etc.* of an Oak, in which consists the vegetable Life. That being then one Plant, which has such an Organization of Parts in one coherent Body, partaking of one Common Life, it continues to be the same Plant, as long as it partakes of the same Life, though that Life be communicated to new Particles of Matter vitally united to the living Plant, in a like continued Organization, conformable to that sort of Plants. For this Organization being at any one instant in any one Collection of *Matter*, is in that particular concrete distinguished from all other, and is that individual Life, which existing constantly from that moment both forwards and backwards in the same continuity of insensibly succeeding Parts united to the living Body of the Plant, it has that Identity, which makes the same Plant, and all the parts of it, parts of the same Plant, during all the time that they exist united in that continued Organization, which is fit to convey that Common Life to all the Parts so united.

§5. The Case is not so much different in *Brutes*, but that any one may hence see what makes an Animal, and continues it the same. Something we have like this in Machines, and may serve to illustrate it. For Example, what is a Watch? 'Tis plain 'tis nothing but a fit Organization, or Construction of Parts, to a certain end, which, when a sufficient force is added to it, it is capable to attain. If we would suppose this Machine one continued Body, all whose organized Parts were repair'd, increas'd or diminish'd, by a constant Addition or Separation of insensible Parts, with one Common Life, we should have something very much like the Body of an Animal, with this difference, That in an Animal the fitness of the Organization, and the Motion wherein Life consists, begin together, the Motion coming from within; but in Machines the force, coming sensibly from without, is often away, when the Organ is in order, and well fitted to receive it.

§6. This also shews wherein the Identity of the same *Man* consists; *viz.* in nothing but a participation of the same continued Life, by constantly fleeting Particles of Matter, in succes-sioin vitally united to the same organized Body. [...]

§7. 'Tis not therefore Unity of Substance that comprehends all sorts of *Identity*, or will determine it in every Case: But to conceive, and judge of it aright, we must consider what *Idea* the Word it it applied to stands for: It being one thing to be the same *Substance*, another the same *Man*, and a third the same *Person*, if *Person*, *Man*, and *Substance*, are three Names standing for three different Ideas. [...]

§8. An Animal is a living organized Body; and consequently, the same Animal, as we have observed, is the same continued Life communicated to different Particles of Matter, as they happen successively to be united to that organiz'd living Body. And whatever is talked of other definitions, ingenuous observation puts it past doubt, that the *Idea* in our Minds, of which, the Sound *Man* in our Mouths is the Sign, is nothing else but of an Animal of such a certain Form: Since I think I may be confident, that whoever should see a Creature of his own Shape and Make, though it had no more reason all its Life, than a *Cat* or a *Parrot*, would call him still a *Man*; or whoever should hear a *Cat* or a *Parrot* discourse, reason, and philosophize, would call or think it nothing but a *Cat* or a *Parrot*; and say, the one was a dull irrational *Man*, and the other a very intelligent rational *Parrot*.

[...]

§9. This being premised to find wherein *personal Identity* consists, we must consider what *Person* stands for; which, I think, is a thinking intelligent Being, that has reason and reflection, and can consider it self as it self, the same thinking thing in different times and place; which it does only by that consciousness, which is inseparable from thinking, and as it seems to me essential to it: It being impossible for any one to perceive, without perceiving, that he does perceive. When we see, hear, smell, taste, feel, meditate, or will any thing, we know that we do so. Thus it is always as to our present Sensations and Perceptions: And by this every one is to himself, that which he calls *self*: It not being considered in this case, whether the same *self* be continued in the same, or divers Substances. For since consciousness always accompanies thinking and 'tis that, that makes every one to be, what he calls *self*; and thereby distinguishes himself from all other zthinking things, in this alone consists *personal Identity, i.e.* the sameness of a rational Being: And as far as this consciousness can be extended backwards to any past Action or Thought, so far reaches the Identity of that *Person*; it is the same *self* now it was then; and 'tis by the same *self* with this present one that now reflects on its, that that Action was done.

§10. But it is farther enquir'd whether it be the same Identical Substance. This few would think they had reason to doubt of, if these Perceptions, with their consciousness, always remain'd present in the Mind, whereby the same thinking thing woud be always consciously present, and, as would be thought, evidently the same to it self. But that which seems to make the difficulty is this, that this consciousness, being interrupted always by forgetfulness, there being no moment of our Lives wherein we have the whole train of all our past Actions before our Eyes in one view: But even the best Memories losing the sight of one part whilst they are viewing another; and we sometimes, and that the greatest part of our Lives, not reflecting on our past selves, being intent on our present Thoughts, and in sound sleep, having no Thoughts at all, or at least none with that consciousness, which remarks our waking Thoughts. I say, in all these cases, our consciousness being interrupted, and we losing the sight of our past *selves*, doubts are raised whether we are the same thinking thing; *i.e.* the same substance or no. Which however reasonable, or unreasonable, concerns not *personal Identity* at all. The Question being what makes the same *Person*, and not whether it be the same Identical Substance, which always thinks in the same *Person*, which in this case matters not at all. Different Substances, by the same consciousness (where they do partake in it) being united into one Person; as well as different Bodies, by the same Life are united into one Animal, whose *Identity* is preserved, in that change of Substances, by the unity of one continued. Life. For it being the same consciousness that makes a Man be himself to himself, *personal Identity* depends on that only, whether it be annexed only to one individual Substance, or can be continued in a succession of several Substances. For as far as any intelligent Being can repeat the *Idea* of any past Action with the same consciousness it had of it at first, and with the same consciousness it has of any present Action; so far it is the same *personal self*. For it is by the consciousness it has of its present Thoughts and Actions, that it is *self* to it *self* now, and so will be the same *self* as far as the same consciousness can extend to Actions past or to come; and would be by distance of Time, or change of Substance, no more two *Persons* than a Man be two Men, by wearing other Cloaths to Day than he did Yesterday, with a long or short sleep between: The same consciousness uniting those distant Actions into the same *Person*, whatever Substances contributed to their Production.

§11. That this is so, we have some kind of Evidence in our very Bodies, all whose Particles, whilst vitally united to this same thinking conscious self, so that we feel when they are touch'd, and are affected by, and conscious of good or harm that happens to them, are a part of our *selves*: *i.e.* of our thinking conscious *self*. Thus the Limbs of his Body is to every one a part of *himself*: He sympathizes and is concerned for them. Cut off an hand, and thereby separate it from that consciousness, we had of its Heat, Cold, and other Affections; and it is then no longer a part of that which is *himself* any more than the remotest part of Matter. Thus we see the *Substance*, whereof *personal self* consisted at one time, may be varied at another, without the change of personal *Identity*: There being no Question about the same Person, though the Limbs, which but now were a part of it, be cut off.

[…]

§15. […] [S]hould the Soul of a Prince, carrying with it the consciousness of the Prince's past Life, enter and inform the Body of a Cobler as soon as deserted by his own Soul, every one sees, he would be the same Person with the Prince, accountable only for the Prince's Actions: But who would say it was the same Man? The Body too goes to the making the Man, and would, I guess, to every Body determine the Man in this case, wherein the Soul with all its Princely Thoughts about it, would not make another Man: But he would be the same Cobler to every one besides himself. I know that in the ordinary way of speaking, the same Person, and the same Man, stand for one and the same thing. And indeed every one will always have a liberty to speak, as he pleases, and to apply what articulate Sounds to what *Ideas* he thinks fit, and change them as often as he pleases. But yet when we will enquire, what makes the same *Spirit, Man*, or *Person*, we must fix the *Ideas* of *Spirit, Man*, or *Person*, in our Minds; and having resolved with our selves what we mean by them, it will not be hard to determine, in either of them, or the like, when it is the *same*, and when not.

§16. But though the same immaterial Substance, or Soul does not alone, where-ever it be, and in whatsoever State, make the same Man; yet 'tis plain consciousness, as far as ever it can be extended, should it be to Ages past, unites Existences, and Actions, very remote in time, into the same Person, as well as it does the Existence and Actions of the immediately preceding moment: So that whatever has the consciousness of present: and past Actions, is the same

Person to whom they both belong. Had I the same consciousness, that I saw the Ark and *Noah's* Flood, as that I saw an overflowing of the *Thames* last Winter, or as that I write now, I could no more doubt that I, that write this now, that saw the *Thames* overflow'd last Winter, and that view'd the Flood at the general Deluge, was the same *self*, place that *self* in what Substance you please, than that I that write this am the same *my self* now whilst I write (whether I consist of all the same Substance, material or immaterial, or no) that I was Yesterday. For as to this point of being the same *self* it matters not whether this present *self* be made up of the same or other Substances, I being as much concern'd, and as justly accountable for any Action was done a thousand Years since, appropriated to me now by this self-consciousness, as I am, for what I did the last moment.

§17. *Self* is that conscious thinking thing, (whatever Substance, made up of whether Spiritual, or Material, Simple, or Compounded, it matters not) which is sensible, or conscious of Pleasure and Pain, capable of Happiness or Misery, and so is concern'd for it *self* as far as that consciousness extends. Thus every one finds, that whilst comprehended under that consciousness, the little Finger is as much a part of it *self*, as what is most so. Upon separation of this little Finger, should this consciousness go along with the little Finger, and leave the rest of the Body, 'tis evident the little Finger would be the *Person*, the *same Person*; and *self* then would have nothing to do with the rest of the Body. As in this case it is the consciousness that goes along with the Substance, when one part is separated from another, which makes the same *Person*, and constitutes this inseparable *self*: so it is in reference to Substances remote in time. That with which the *consciousness* of this present thinking thing can join it self, makes the same *Person*, and. is one *self* with it, and with nothing else; and so attributes to it *self*, and owns all the Actions of that thing, as its own, as far as that consciousness reaches, and no farther; as every one who reflects will perceive.

§18. In this *personal Identity* is founded all the Right and justice of Reward and Punishment; Happiness and Misery, being that, for which every one is concerned for *himself*, not mattering what becomes of any Substance, not joined to, or affected with that consciousness For as it is evident in the instance I gave but now, if the consciousness went along with the little Finger, when it was cut off, that would be the same *self* which was concerned for the whole Body Yesterday, as making a part of it *self*, whose Actions then it cannot but admit as its own now. Though if the same Body should still live, and immediately from the separation of the little Finger have its own peculiar consciousness, whereof the little Finger knew nothing, it would not at all be concerned for it, as a part of it *self*, or could own any of its Actions, or have any of them imputed to him.

§19. This may shew us wherein *personal Identity* consists, not in the Identity of Substance, but, as I have said, in the Identity of *consciousness*, wherein, if *Socrates* and the present Mayor of *Quinborough* agree, they are the same Person: If the same *Socrates* waking and sleeping do not partake of the same *consciousness*, *Socrates* waking and sleeping is not the same Person. And to punish *Socrates* waking, for what sleeping *Socrates* thought, and waking *Socrates* was never conscious of, would be no more of Right, than to punish one Twin for what his Brother-Twin did, whereof he knew nothing, because their outsides were so like, that they could not be distinguished; for such Twins have been seen.

[...]

§22. But is not a Man Drunk and Sober the same Person, why else is he punish'd for the Fact he commits when Drunk, though he be never afterwards conscious of it? Just as much the same Person, as a Man that walks, and does other things in his sleep, is the same Person, and is answerable for any mischief he shall do in it. Humane Laws punish both with a justice suitable to their way of Knowledge: Because in these cases, they cannot distinguish certainly what is real, what counterfeit; and so the ignorance in Drunkenness or Sleep is not admitted as a plea. For though punishment be annexed to personality, and personality to consciousness, and the Drunkard perhaps be not conscious of what he did; yet Humane Judicatures justly punish him; because the Fact is proved against him, but want of consciousness cannot be proved for him. But in the great Day, wherein the Secrets of all Hearts shall be laid open, it may be reasonable to think, no one shall be made to answer for what he knows nothing of; but shall receive his Doom, his Conscience accusing or excusing him.

§23. Nothing but consciousness can unite remote Existences into the same Person, the Identity of Substance will not do it. For whatever Substance there is, however framed, without consciousness, there is no Person: And a Carcase may be a Person, as well as any sort of Substance be so without consciousness.

[…]

§25. […] Any Substance vitally united to the present thinking Being, is a part of that very *same self* which now is: Any thing united to it by a consciousness of former Actions makes also a part of the *same self*, which is the same both then and now.

§26. *Person*, as I take it, is the name for this *self*. Where-ever a Man finds, what he calls *himself*, there I think another may say is the same *Person*. It is a Forensick Term appropriating Actions and their Merit; and so belongs only to intelligent Agents capable of a Law, and Happiness and Misery. This personality extends it *self* beyond present Existence to what is past, only by consciousness, whereby it becomes concerned and accountable, owns and imputes to it *self* past Actions, just upon the same ground, and for the same reason, that it does the present. All which is founded in a concern for Happiness the unavoidable concomitant of consciousness, that which is conscious of Pleasure and Pain, desiring, that that *self*, that is conscious, should be happy. And therefore whatever past Actions it cannot reconcile or appropriate to that present *self* by consciousness, it can be no more concerned in, than if they had never been done: And to receive Pleasure or Pain; *i.e.* Reward or Punishment, on the account of any such Action, is all one, as to be made happy or miserable in its first being, without any demerit at all. For supposing a Man punish'd now, for what he had done in another Life, whereof he could be made to have no consciousness at all, what difference is there between that Punishment, and being created miserable? And therefore conformable to this, the Apostle tells us, that at the Great Day, when every one shall *receive according to his doings, the secrets of all Hearts shall be laid open.* The Sentence shall be justified by the consciousness all Persons shall have, that they *themselves* in what Bodies soever they appear, or what Substances soever that consciousness adheres to, are the *same*, that committed those Actions, and deserve that Punishment for them.

25

How Strictly Does Self-Consciousness Constitute a Person?

Roderick M. Chisholm, "Identity through Time"

The theme of personal identity has received much continued philosophical attention over the past half-century. Here is a reading from Roderick Chisholm (1916–99), most of whose career was at Brown University. He was known for his intricate writings both on metaphysics and on epistemology. This extract contains two main lines of thought.

The first links with our earlier discussions of *facts* (courtesy of Russell and Searle, particularly). We were thinking generally about facts. But we did ask about *kinds* of facts. Now let us ask whether there are facts as to a person's having a continuing identity – his or her being still the same person – from one moment to another: Is that a genuine fact within the world? Or are our references to that – "You're still alive" – more of a conventionally useful and convenient way of talking or thinking? When a friend says to you, "You're not the same person any more," we can at least wonder whether he or she is speaking literally or instead loosely. Which is it? *Could* you literally no longer be the same person as you were? Again, is there a real fact here (as against merely a useful way of speaking)? In contrast, for example, Chisholm argues that a ship's identity over time need not be strict. As parts of it are replaced by new ones, we simply choose to continue deeming it to be the same ship. That is all there is to its continuing identity. But Chisholm also argues that this is *not* true of persons: your identity over time is not a matter of a choice being made, by you or by others, as to how to regard you. Rather, there is *strictly* a fact involved in your continuing to be the same person.

Roderick M. Chisholm, "Identity through Time" (excerpts), in H.E. Kiefer and M.K. Munitz (eds.), *Language, Belief, and Metaphysics* (Albany: State University of New York Press, 1970). © 1970, State University of New York. All rights reserved.

Chisholm's second key line of thought in this reading concerns the potential way in which that strict sort of fact might be constituted by your self-consciousness, including your memories. Recall how, in the previous reading, John Locke proposed that personal identity over time is constituted by a maintained self-consciousness, particularly linked memories. Chisholm ends his discussion with a thought-experiment – an imagined story – intended to encourage us as readers to discover exactly what it is that we think about these issues. His story asks you to contemplate two possible futures. Each includes an operation. Is it reasonable for you (asks Chisholm) – caring *now*, as you do, about your *future* you – to choose the inexpensive operation? Its vital characteristics are as follows. For a period during it, the patient experiences extreme pain – followed, however, by no memory of the pain, and with no memories being present during the operation (including therefore no memories of your previous experiences). Thus, there would be a life containing some awful pain. Yet there would be no links of self-conscious memory between that period of pain and the rest of a life (including your life right now). Would that still be a *single* life? Would it still be *you*? Is that possible even in the absence of a fully linked and continuing self-consciousness?

According to Bishop Butler, when we say of a physical thing existing at one time that it is identical with or the same as a physical thing existing at some other time ("this is the same ship we traveled on before"), we are likely to be using the expression "same" or "identical" in a "loose and popular sense." But when we say of a person existing at one time that he is identical with or the same as a person existing at some other time ("the ship has the same captain it had before"), we are likely to be using "same" or "identical" in a "strict and philosophical sense.[1] I shall attempt to give an interpretation to these two theses; and I shall suggest that there is at least an element of truth in each.

To illustrate the first of the two theses – that it is likely to be only in a loose and popular sense that we may speak of the identity of a physical thing through time – let us recall the traditional problem of the ship of Theseus, in a somewhat updated version. The ship, when it came to be, was made entirely of wood. One day a wooden plank was replaced by an aluminum one (this is the updating) and the wooden plank was cast off. But we still had the same ship, it was said, since the change was only slight. Somewhat later, another wooden plank was cast off and also replaced by an aluminum one. Still the same ship, of course, since, once again, the change was only slight. The changes continue, but they are always sufficiently slight so that the ship on any given day can be said to be the same as the ship on the day before. Finally, of course, the ship is made entirely of aluminum. Some will feel certain that the aluminum ship is the same ship as the one that was once made entirely of wood. After all, it preserved its identity from one change to the next, and identity is transitive. Consider, however, this possibility, suggested by Thomas Hobbes: "… if some man had kept the old planks as they were taken out, and by putting them afterwards together in the same order, had again made a ship of them, this, without doubt, had also been the same numerical ship with that which was at the beginning; and so there would have been two ships numerically the same, which is absurd." To compound the problem, let us imagine that the captain of the original ship had taken a vow to the effect that if his ship were ever to go down, then he would go down with it. What now, if the two ships collide at sea and he sees them start to sink together? Where does his duty lie – with the aluminum ship or with the reassembled wooden ship?

Putting the problem schematically, we may suppose that on Monday a simple ship, "The U. S. S. South Dakota," came into being, composed of two principle [*sic*] parts, A and B. On Tuesday, part A is replaced by a new part C. (We may imagine that the replacement was accomplished with a minimum of disturbance: as A was eased off, C was pushed on immediately behind and in such a way that one could not say at any time during the process that there was only half a ship in the harbor.) On Wednesday, there was fission, with B going off to the left and annexing itself to F as it departed from C, and with C going off to the right and annexing itself to J as it departed from B. On Thursday, over at the left, B is replaced by L, while, over at the right, C is replaced by H. And now the captain of the original U. S. S. South Dakota sees FL and JH in equal distress.

Mon		AB	
Tue		BC	
Wed		FB	CJ
Thu	FL		JH

One of his advisers tells him: The ship on the left is the one that took the maiden voyage on Monday, and the ship on the right, therefore, is not. But another of his advisers tells him: No, it's just the other way around. The ship on the right is the one that took the maiden voyage on Monday, and the ship on the left, therefore, is not.

[…]

We could put the matter paradoxically […] by saying that counting ships is not the same, merely, as counting objects that happen to *be* ships. But if we speak strictly and philosophically, we may avoid any such appearance of paradox. We may say that ships are "logical constructions." The things that they are constructed upon are things that satisfy Webster's definition of the loose and popular sense of "ship" – they are structures used for transportation in water. We will not say, therefore, that AB, BC, and the other intact structures […] *are* ships. We will say, instead, that each of these things constitutes a ship. Given the concept of "x constitutes the same ship as does y," we could define "x constitutes a ship" by saying "x is a member of a set of things all constituting the same ship." The U. S. S. South Dakota, therefore, would be a logical construction upon one such set of things. If we continue to speak strictly and philosophically, we will not say of the two different things, AB and FL, that each of them *is*, on its particular day, the U. S. S. South Dakota. We will say instead that each of them *constitutes*, on its particular day, the U. S. S. South Dakota. The statements we ordinarily use to describe the ship (e.g., "It weighs more now than it did then") will be reducible to statements about the things that constitute it ("the thing that constitutes it now weighs more than the thing that constituted it then").

We now have an obvious interpretation for the first of the theses I have attributed to Bishop Butler – namely, that it is only in a loose and popular sense and not in a strict and philosophical sense that we may speak of the identity of such things as ships through time. He could be construed as telling us, first, that the expression "x constitutes at [t] the same ship that y constitutes at t'" does *not* imply "x is identical with y"; and analogously for "constituting the same tree," "constituting the same carriage," and so on. Then he could be construed as telling us, secondly, that if we express the fact that x constitutes at one time the same ship that y constitutes at another time by saying "x is identical with y" or "x is the same as y," then we are speaking only in a loose and popular sense and not in a strict and philosophical sense. And perhaps he could be construed as telling us, finally, that our criteria for x constituting the same ship as y are pretty much in our own hands, after all, and that once we have determined that a given x and y do satisfy our criteria for constituting the same ship, or that they do not, then no possible ground for doubt remains.

[...]

Finding an acceptable definition of "x is a ship" is a problem for dictionary makers. Finding an acceptable definition of "x constitutes the same ship as does y" is more likely to be a problem for jurists. It should be noted, that we may be in agreement with respect to the proper interpretation of the other; or we may be rigid with respect to the one and latitudinarian with respect to the other.

Assuming we have agreed upon our interpretation of "x is a ship," consider the latitude that yet remains with respect to the interpretation of "x constitutes the same ship as does y". According to the particular criterion of constituting the same ship that was satisfied by our example of the U.S.S. South Dakota, today's object and tomorrow's object "constitute the same ship" provided, among other things, that every object that evolves out of today's object and tomorrow's is a ship. And for there to be such evolution, each object, we said, must have some part in common with the object from which it directly evolved. We could say, quoting Hume, that with each step it is "in a manner requisite, that the change of parts be not ... entire";[3] but it is very possible that we will find it convenient to relax these criteria. Thus it may be useful to be able to say, on occasion, that a certain object of last year constitutes the same ship as does a certain object of this year even though one of the objects, into which last year's object evolved and out of which this year's object evolved, was itself not a ship. Perhaps the ship was partially dismantled and used for a while as a tool shed or as; a restaurant; yet, when it was reconverted, we found it convenient, and pleasing to count the result as the same ship that we had before.[4] We may even find it convenient to say on occasion that though a certain object of last year constitutes the same ship as does a certain object of this year, there was no evolution as defined – the change of parts at one stage was entire. Switching for the moment from ships to rivers, consider this situation: We swim in the upper Rio Grande in the early spring; the river dries up in the summer; new waters then flow in and we swim there once again in the fall. Surely we will want our criterion of "x constitutes the same river as does y" to allow us to say that we swam in the same river twice.

The expression "x constitutes the same ship as does y," like "x is a ship," allows for borderline cases. We can readily imagine situations in which the only appropriate answer to the question "Is that a ship?" is "Yes and no" – or, better, situations in which "Yes" is no better an answer than "No," and "No" is no better an answer than "Yes." A hydrofoil that is also a hovercraft may serve as an example. We can readily imagine situations in which to the question "Is this the same ship as that?", i.e., "Does this constitute the same ship that that did?", the only answer is "Yes and no."

It may well happen that when we encounter such a borderline case, we must have an answer other than "Yes and no." The captain, as we have seen, may well need a more definite answer, and we may need a definite answer to the question, "Is the combination

hydrofoil and hovercraft a ship?", for it may be necessary to decide whether such things are
to be subject to the regulations that govern ships or to the regulations that govern aircraft.
Similarly, for the question "Does this constitute the same ship that that did?"

When the existence of such a borderline case does thus require us to make a choice between
"Yes" and "No" the decision is entirely a pragmatic one, simply a matter of convenience. Which
ship is to be called "the Ship of Theseus" – the one that evolved step by step from the original
ship, or the one that was assembled from the discarded planks of the original ship? Here we
have such a borderline question. The question calls for a convention with respect to the interpretation of "constituting the same ship" (or of "is the same ship as," in its loose and popular
sense). We can have it pretty much as we wish, provided we agree. Which, ship should the
captain go down with? Here, too, we have a borderline question. Perhaps you and I cannot
decide, but the courts, or the ships' courts, can decide. If the captain has agreed to go down with
the U. S. S. South Dakota, and. if the court decides that the aluminum ship and not the wooden
one is the one that constitutes the U. S. S. South Dakota, then down with the aluminum ship
he ought to go. Or down with it he ought to go unless the authorities decide subsequently (and
in time) to "defeat" the convention they have adopted – for any such convention is defeasible
and may be altered or defeated if unexpected circumstances show that it will turn out to be
inconvenient. The important, thing here is this: The convention of the courts, or of the proper
authorities will settle the matter. You and I may object to their decision on the ground that
some other decision would have been more convenient. But it would make no sense for us to
say: Well, it just might be, you know, that they are mistaken. It just might be that, unknown to
them, the wooden ship and not the aluminum one is the U.S.S. South Dakota.

[...]

What now of Bishop Butler's second thesis – the thesis according to which, when we say of
a *person* existing at one time that he is identical with a person existing at another time, we are
likely to be using "identical" in a strict and philosophical sense and not merely in a loose and
popular sense?

[...]

If it is clear that if x is a person and y is a person, then we cannot answer the question "Is x the
same person as y?" merely by deciding what would be practically convenient. To be sure, if we lack
sufficient evidence for making a decision, it may yet be necessary for the courts to *rule* that x is
the same person as y, or that he is not. Perhaps the ruling will have to be based upon practical
considerations and conceivably such considerations may lead the court later to "defeat" their ruling. But if Bishop Butler, as I have interpreted him, is right, then one may always ask of any such
ruling "But is it *correct*, or *true*?" For a ruling to the effect that x is the same person as y will be
correct, or true, only if x *is* identical with y.

Here, then, we have one possible interpretation, of the thesis that, in one of its important
uses, the expression "x is the same person as y" must be interpreted in a strict and philosophical sense. It seems clear to me that "x is the same person as y" does have this use. Whenever
a person x asks himself, with respect to some person y, "Will I be he?" or "Was that person
I?" then the answer to his question, if put in the form "x is the same person as y" or "x is not
the same person as y" must be taken in the strict and philosophical sense.

[...]

It will be instructive to elaborate upon an example that C. S. Peirce suggests.[5] Let us assume
that you are about to undergo an operation and that you still have a decision to make. The

utilities involved are, first, financial – you wish to avoid any needless expense – and, secondly, the avoidance of pain, the avoidance, however, just of *your* pain, for pain that is other than yours, let us assume, is of no concern whatever to you. The doctor proposes two operating procedures – one a very expensive procedure in which you will be subjected to total anaesthesia and no pain will be felt at all, and the other of a rather different sort. The second operation will be very inexpensive indeed; there will be no anaesthesia at all and therefore there will be excruciating pain. But the doctor will give you two drugs: first, a drug just before the operation which will induce complete amnesia, so that while you are on the table you will have no memory whatever of your present life; and, secondly, just after the agony is over, a drug that will make you completely forget everything that happened on the table. The question is: Given the utilities involved, namely the avoidance of needless expense and the avoidance of pain that *you* will feel, other pains not mattering, is it reasonable for you to opt for the less expensive operation?

My own belief is that it would *not* be reasonable, even if you could be completely certain that both amnesia injections would be successful. I think that *you* are the one who would undergo that pain, even though you, Jones, would not know at the time that it is Jones who is undergoing it, and even though you would never remember it. Consider after all, the hypothesis that it would *not* be you. What would be your status, in such a case, during the time of the operation? Would you be waiting in the wings somewhere for the second injection, and if so, where? Or would you have passed away? That is to say, would you have *ceased to be*, but with the guarantee that you – you, yourself – would come into being once again when the *agony* was over?[6] And what about the person who *would* be feeling the pain? Who would he be?

I can appreciate that these things might not seem obvious to you as you ponder your decision. You may wonder: "I would certainly like to save that money. Will it really be *I* who feels that pain? How can it be if I won't know that it's I?" Perhaps you would have some ground for hesitation. But there is one point, I think, that ought to be obvious.

Suppose that others come to you – friends, relatives, judges, clergymen – and they offer the following advice and assurance. "Have no fear," they will say. "Take the cheaper operation and we will take care of everything. We will lay it down that the man on the table is not you, Jones, but is Smith. We will not allow this occasion to be mentioned in your biography. And during the time that you lie there on the table – excuse us (they will interject), we mean to say, during the time that *Smith* lies there on the table – we will say, 'poor Smith' and we will not say, even in our hearts, 'poor Jones'." What *ought* to be obvious to you, it seems to me, is that the laying down of this convention should have no effect at all upon your decision. For you may still ask, "But won't that person be I?" and, it seems to me, the question has an answer.

Suppose you know that your body, like that of an amoeba, would one day undergo fission and that you would go off, so to speak, in two different directions. Suppose you also know, somehow, that the one who went off to the left would experience the most wretched of lives and that the one who went off to the right would experience a life of great happiness and value. If I am right in saying that one's question "Will that person be I?" or "Will I be he?" always has a definite answer, then, I think, we may draw these conclusions. There is no possibility whatever that *you* would be *both* the person on the right and the person on the left. Moreover, there *is* a possibility that you would be one or the other of those two persons. And, finally, *you* could be one of those persons and yet have no memory at all of your present existence. It follows that it would be reasonable of you, if you are concerned with *your* future pleasures and pains, to hope that you will be the one on the right and not the one on the left – also that it would be reasonable of you, given such self-concern, to have this hope even if you know that the one on the right would have no memory of your present existence. Indeed it would be reasonable of you to have it even if you know that the one on the *left* thought he remembered the facts of your present existence. And it seems to me to be absolutely certain that no fears that you might have, about being the half on the left, could reasonably be allayed by the adoption of a convention, or by the formulation of a criterion, even if our procedure were endorsed by the highest authorities.

Notes

1. "Of Personal Identity," Dissertation I, in *The Whole Works of Joseph Butler, LL. D.* (London: Thomas Tegg, 1839), pp. 263–270. The dissertation is reprinted in Antony Flew, ed., *Body, Mind and Death* (New York: Macmillan, 1964), pp. 166–172.
2. Thomas Hobbes, *Concerning Body*, Chapter XI ("Of Identity and Difference"). Section 7.
3. *Treatise*, Book I, Part IV, Section vi.
4. An Aristotelian who took ships seriously might say that in such a case two "substantial changes" had occurred.
5. "If the power to remember dies with the material body, has the question of any single person's future life after death any particular interest for him?' As you put the question, it is not whether the matter ought rationally to have an interest but whether as a fact it has; and perhaps this is the proper question, trusting as it seems to do rather to instinct than to reason. Now if we had a drug which would abolish memory for a while, and you were going to be cut for the stone, suppose the surgeon were to say. 'You will suffer damnably, but I will administer this drug so that you will during that suffering lose all memory of your previous life. Now you have, of course, no particular interest in your suffering as long as you will not remember your present and past life, you know, have you?'" *Collected Papers* (Cambridge, Harvard University Press, 1935), Vol. V, p. 355.
6. See Locke's *Essay*, Book II, Ch. xxvii, Sec. i: "One thing cannot have two beginnings of existence." Compare Thomas Reid, *Essays on the Intellectual Powers of Man*, Essay III, Chapter 4.

26

Are Persons Constituted with Strict Identity At All?

Derek Parfit, *Reasons and Persons*

If Roderick Chisholm (in the previous reading) is correct, the identity of a person is fundamentally different to that of a ship, say: whereas ship-identity-over-time is conventional and hence somewhat arbitrary, personal identity over time is far from that. The latter would instead be strict and definitive. There would be real facts of you-now being literally the same person as you-earlier. There could be differences in features: you-now might have differently colored hair, for example. But the world over time would have included only one overall you – not two, three, four, or more. Yet even that is questioned in this reading, from the Oxford philosopher Derek Parfit (b. 1942). His eye-catching career has been centered upon issues about personal identity and ethics. Provocative thought-experiments abound in his writing.

They certainly do so in this extract, with Parfit asking whether identity – literal and strict – is really so vital to the terms in which we conceive of persons. Could there be the same sort of psychological continuity (of inner feelings, experiences, and apparent memories) as other philosophers would call a linked pattern of self-consciousness – *without* this requiring that an underlying self is binding it together? What if there is such continued consciousness *without* some independent and unique existence underlying it? Parfit offers us tales (wholly fanciful ones, along with scientifically based ones) that he argues should incline us to a less rigid conception of what is required for our living from one moment to another. There are tales of physical replication – how to travel to Mars by teletransportation. Welcome also to reports of split brains, and then of split brains plus bodily transplantation. In such cases, who would be whom? How many people would there

Derek Parfit, *Reasons and Persons* (Oxford: Clarendon Press, 1984), pp. 199–201, 245–247, 253, 254–257, 258, 261–262 (excerpts). Reprinted with permission of Oxford University Press.

Metaphysics and Epistemology: A Guided Anthology, First Edition. Edited by Stephen Hetherington.

be? In particular, would there be relations of personal *identity* involved? Parfit guides us towards an alternative image – the possibility that, even when strict identity is absent, maybe what is present is all that we *should* ever want when wishing for continued survival. That is, perhaps it is not really *identity* as such that we should care about in continuing to live as we do, even as the persons we are.

What We Believe Ourselves To Be

I enter the Teletransporter. I have been to Mars before, but only by the old method, a space-ship journey taking several weeks. This machine will send me at the speed of light. I merely have to press the green button. Like others, I am nervous. Will it work? I remind myself what I have been told to expect. When I press the button, I shall lose consciousness, and then wake up at what seems a moment later. In fact I shall have been unconscious for about an hour. The Scanner here on Earth will destroy my brain and body, while recording the exact states of all of my cells. It will then transmit this information by radio. Travelling at the speed of light, the message will take three minutes to reach the Replicator on Mars. This will then create, out of new matter, a brain and body exactly like mine. It will be in this body that I shall wake up.

Though I believe that this is what will happen, I still hesitate. But then I remember seeing my wife grin when, at breakfast today, I revealed my nervousness. As she reminded me, she has been often teletransported, and there is nothing wrong with *her*. I press the button. As predicted, I lose and seem at once to regain consciousness, but in a different cubicle. Examining my new body, I find no change at all. Even the cut on my upper lip, from this morning's shave, is still there.

Several years pass, during which I am often Teletransported. I am now back in the cubicle, ready for another trip to Mars. But this time, when I press the green button, I do not lose consciousness. There is a whirring sound, then silence. I leave the cubicle, and say to the attendant: 'It's not working. What did I do wrong?'

'It's working', he replies, handing me a printed card. This reads: 'The New Scanner records your blueprint without destroying your brain and body. We hope that you will welcome the opportunities which this technical advance offers.'

The attendant tells me that I am one of the first people to use the New Scanner. He adds that, if I stay for an hour, I can use the Intercom to see and talk to myself on Mars.

'Wait a minute', I reply, 'If I'm here I can't *also* be on Mars'.

Someone politely coughs, a white-coated man who asks to speak to me in private. We go to his office, 'Where he tells me to sit down, and pauses. Then he says: I'm afraid that we're having problems with the New Scanner. It records your blueprint just as accurately, as you will see when you talk to yourself on Mars. But it seems to be damaging the cardiac systems which it scans. Judging from the results so far, though you will be quite healthy on Mars, here on Earth you must expect cardiac failure within the next few days.'

The attendant later calls me to the Intercom. On the screen I see myself just as I do in the mirror every morning. But there are two differences. On the screen I am not left-right reversed. And, while I stand here speechless, I can see and hear myself, in the studio on Mars, starting to speak.

What can we learn from this imaginary story? Some believe that we can learn little. This would have been Wittgenstein's view. And Quine writes: 'The method of science fiction has its uses in philosophy, but ... I wonder whether the limits of the method are properly heeded. To seek what is 'logically required' for sameness of person under unprecedented circumstances is to suggest that words have some logical force beyond what our past needs have invested them : with'.[1]

This criticism might be justified if, when considering such imagined cases, we had no reactions. But these cases arouse in most of us strong beliefs. And these are beliefs, not about our words, but about ourselves. By considering these cases, we discover what we believe to be involved in our own continued existence, or what it is that makes us now and ourselves next year the same people. We discover our beliefs about the nature of personal identity over time. Though our beliefs are revealed most clearly when we consider imaginary cases, these beliefs also cover actual cases, and our own lives. I shall argue that some of these beliefs are false, then suggest how and why this matters.

Simple Teletransportation and the Branch-Line Case

At the beginning of my story, the Scanner destroys my brain and body. My blueprint is beamed to Mars, where another machine makes an organic *Replica* of me. My Replica thinks that he is me, and he seems to remember living my life up to the moment when I pressed the green button. In every other way, both physically and psychologically, we are exactly similar, if he returned to Earth, everyone would think that he was me.

Simple Teletransportation, as just described, is a common feature in science fiction. And it is believed, by some readers of this fiction, merely to be the fastest way of travelling. They believe that my Replica *would* be *me*. Other science fiction readers, and some of the characters in this fiction, take a different view. They believe that, when I press the green button, I die. My Replica is *someone else*, who has been made to be exactly like me.

This second view seems to be supported by the end of my story. The New Scanner does not destroy my brain and body. Besides gathering the information, it merely damages my heart. While I am in the cubicle, with the green button pressed, nothing seems to happen. I walk out, and learn that in a few days I shall die. I later talk, by two-way television, to my Replica on Mars. Let us continue the story. Since my Replica knows that I am about to die, he tries to console me with the same thoughts with which I recently tried to console a dying friend. It is sad to learn, on the receiving end, how unconsoling these thoughts are. My Replica then assures me that he will take up my life where I leave off. He loves my wife, and together they will care for my children. And he will finish the book that I am writing. Besides having all of my drafts, he has all of my intentions. I must admit that he can finish my book as well as I could. All these facts console me a little. Dying when I know that I shall have a Replica is not quite as bad as, simply, dying. Even so, I shall soon lose consciousness, forever.

In Simple Teletransportation, I am destroyed before I am Replicated. This makes it easier to believe that this *is* a way of travelling – that my Replica *is* me. At the end of my story, my life and that of my Replica overlap. Call this the *Branch-Line Case*. In this case, I cannot hope to travel on the *Main Line*, waking up on Mars with forty years of life ahead. I shall stay on the Branch-Line, here on Earth, which ends a few days later. Since I can talk to my Replica, it seems clear that he is *not* me. Though he is exactly like me, he is one person, and I am another. When I pinch myself, he feels nothing. When I have my heart attack, he will again feel nothing. And when I am dead he will live for another forty years.

If we believe that my Replica is not me, it is natural to assume that my prospect, on the Branch Line, is almost as bad as ordinary death. I shall deny this assumption. As I shall argue later, being destroyed and Replicated is about as good as ordinary survival.

[…]

Why Our Identity Is Not What Matters

Divided Minds

[…] Human beings have a lower brain and two upper hemispheres, which are connected by a bundle of fibres. In treating a few people with severe epilepsy, surgeons have cut these fibres. The aim was to reduce the severity of epileptic fits, by confining their causes to a single hemisphere. This aim was achieved. But the operations had another unintended consequence. The effect, in the words of one surgeon, was the creation of 'two separate spheres of consciousness'.[2]

This effect was revealed by various psychological tests. These made use of two facts. We control our right arms with our left hemispheres, and vice versa. And what is in the right halves of our visual fields we see with our left hemispheres, and vice versa. When someone's hemispheres have been disconnected, psychologists can thus present to this person two different written questions in the two halves of his visual field, and can receive two different answers written by this person's two hands.

Here is a simplified version of the kind of evidence that such tests provide. One of these people is shown a wide screen, whose left half is red and right half is blue. On each half in a darker shade are the words, 'How many colours can you see?' With both hands the person writes, 'Only one'. The words are now changed to read, 'Which is the only colour that you can see?' With one of his hands the person writes 'Red', with the other he writes 'Blue'.

If this is how this person responds, there seems no reason to doubt that he is having visual sensations – that he does, as he claims, see both red and blue. But in seeing red he is not aware of seeing blue, and vice versa. This is why the surgeon writes of 'two separate spheres of consciousness'. In each of his centres of consciousness the person can see only a single colour. In one centre, he sees red, in the other, blue.

The many actual tests, though differing in details from the imagined test that I have just described, show the same two essential features. In seeing what is in the left half of his visual field, such a person is quite unaware of what he is now seeing in the right half of his visual field, and vice versa. And in the centre of consciousness in which he sees the left half of his visual field, and is aware of what he is doing with his left hand, this person is quite unaware of what he is doing with his right hand, and vice versa.

One of the complications in the actual cases is that for most people, in at least the first few weeks after the operation, speech is entirely controlled by the right-handed hemisphere. As a result, 'if the word "hat" is flashed on the left, the left hand will retrieve a hat from a group of concealed objects if the person is told to pick out what he has seen. At the same time he will insist verbally that he saw nothing.'[3] Another complication is that, after a certain time, each hemisphere can sometimes control both hands. Nagel quotes an example of the kind of conflict which can follow:

> A pipe is placed out of sight in the patient's left hand, and he is then asked to write with his left hand what he was holding. Very laboriously and heavily, the left hand writes the letters P and I. Then suddenly the writing speeds up and becomes lighter, the I is converted to an E, and the word is completed as PENCIL. Evidently the left hemisphere has made a guess based on the appearance of the first two letters, and has interfered ... But then the right hemisphere takes over control of the hand again, heavily cresses out the letters ENCIL, and draws a crude picture of a pipe.[4]

Such conflict may take more sinister forms. One of the patients complained that sometimes, when he embraced his wife, his left hand pushed her away.

Much has been made of another complication in the actual cases, hinted at in Nagel's example. The left hemisphere typically supports or 'has' the linguistic and mathematical abilities of an adult, while the right hemisphere 'has' these abilities at the level of a young child. But the right hemisphere, though less advanced in these respects, has greater abilities of other kinds, such as those involved in pattern recognition, or musicality. It is assumed that, after the age of three or four, the two hemispheres follow a 'division of labour', with each developing certain abilities. The lesser linguistic abilities of the right hemisphere are not intrinsic, or permanent. People who have had strokes in their left hemispheres often regress to the linguistic ability of a young child, but with their remaining right hemispheres many can relearn adult speech: It is also believed that, in a minority of people, there may be no difference between the abilities of the two hemispheres.

Suppose that I am one of this minority, with two exactly similar hemispheres. And suppose that I have been equipped with some device that can block communication between my hemispheres. Since this device is connected to my eyebrows, it is under my control. By raising an eyebrow I can divide my mind. In each half of my divided mind I can then, by lowering an eyebrow, reunite my mind.

This ability would have many uses. Consider

> *My Physics Exam.* I am taking an exam, and have only fifteen minutes left in which to answer the last question. It occurs to me that there are two ways of tackling this question. I am unsure which is more likely to succeed. I therefore decide to divide my mind for ten minutes, to work in each half of my mind on one of the two calculations, and then to reunite my mind to write a fair copy of the best result. What shall I experience?
>
> When I disconnect my hemispheres, my stream of consciousness divides. But this division is not something that I experience. Each of my two streams of consciousness seems to have been straightforwardly continuous with my one stream of consciousness up to the moment of division. The only changes in each stream are the disappearance of half my visual field and the loss of sensation in, and control over, one of my arms.
>
> Consider my experiences in my 'right-handed' stream. I remember deciding that I would use my right hand to do the longer calculation. This I now begin. In working at

this calculation I can see, from the movements of my left hand, that I am also working at the other. But I am not aware of working at the other. I might, in my right-handed stream, wonder how, in my left-handed stream, I am getting on. I could look and see. This would be just like looking to see how well my neighbour is doing, at the next desk. In my right-handed stream I would be equally unaware both of what my neighbour is now thinking and of what I am now thinking in my left-handed stream. Similar remarks apply to my experiences in my left-handed stream.

My work is now over. I am about to reunite my mind. What should I, in each stream, expect? Simply that I shall suddenly seem to remember just having worked at two calculations, in working at each of which I was not aware of working at the other. This, I suggest, we can imagine. And, if my mind had been divided, my apparent memories would be correct.

In describing this case, I assumed that there were two separate series of thoughts and sensations. If my two hands visibly wrote out two calculations, and I also claimed later to remember two corresponding series of thoughts, this is what we ought to assume. It would be most implausible to assume that either or both calculations had been done unconsciously.

It might be objected that my description ignores 'the necessary unity of consciousness'. But I have not ignored this alleged necessity. I have denied it. What is a fact must be possible. And it is a fact that people with disconnected hemispheres have two separate streams of consciousness – two series of thoughts and experiences, in having each of which they are unaware of having the other. Each of these two streams separately displays unity of consciousness. This may be a surprising fact. But we can understand it. We can come to believe that a person's mental history need not be like a canal, with only one channel, but could be like a river, occasionally having separate streams. I suggest that we can also imagine what it would be like to divide and reunite our minds. My description of my experiences in my Physics Exam seems both to be coherent and to describe something that we can imagine.

[…]

What Happens When I Divide?

I shall now describe another natural extension of the actual cases of divided minds. Suppose first that I am one of a pair of identical twins, and that both my body and my twin's brain have been fatally injured. Because of advances in neuro-surgery, it is not inevitable that these injuries will cause us both to die. We have between us one healthy brain and one healthy body. Surgeons can put these together.

This could be done even with existing techniques. Just as my brain could be extracted, and kept alive by a connection with an artifical heart-lung machine, it could be kept alive by a connection with the heart and lungs in my twin's body. The drawback, today, is that the nerves from my brain could not be connected with the nerves in my twin's body. My brain could survive if transplanted into his body, but the resulting person would be paralysed.

Even if he is paralysed, the resulting person could be enabled to communicate with others. One crude method would be some device, attached to the nerve that would have controlled this person's right thumb, enabling him to send messages in Morse Code. Another device, attached to some sensory nerve, could enable him to receive messages.

Many people would welcome surviving, even totally paralysed, if they could still communicate with others. The stock example is that of a great scientist whose main aim in life is to continue thinking about certain abstract problems.

Let us suppose, however, that surgeons are able to connect my brain to the nerves in my twin's body. The resulting person would have no paralysis, and would be completely healthy. Who would this person be?

This is not a difficult question . [...]

If all my brain continues both to exist and to be the brain of one living person, who is psychologically continuous with me, I continue to exist. This is true whatever happens to the rest of my body. When I am given someone else's heart, I am the surviving recipient, not the dead donor. When my brain is transplanted into someone else's body, it may seem that I am here the dead donor. But I am really still the recipient, and the survivor. Receiving a new skull and a new body is just the limiting case of receiving a new heart, new lungs, new arms, and so on.

It will of course be important what my new body is like. If my new body was quite unlike my old body, this would affect what I could do, and might thus indirectly lead to changes in my character. But there is no reason to suppose that being transplanted into a very different body would disrupt my psychological continuity.

[...]

I shall now combine these last two claims. I would survive if my brain was successfully transplanted into my twin's body. And I could survive with only half my brain, the other half having been destroyed. Given these two facts, it seems clear that I would survive if half my brain was successfully transplanted into my twin's body, and the other half was destroyed.

What if the other half was *not* destroyed? This is the case in which a person, like an amoeba, divides. To simplify the case, I assume that I am one of three identical triplets. Consider

> *My Division*: My body is fatally injured, as are the brains of my two brothers. My brain is divided, and each half is successfully transplanted into the body of one of my brothers. Each of the resulting people believes that he is me, seems to remember living my life, has my character, and is in every other way psychologically continuous with me. And he has a body that is very like mine.

This case is likely to remain impossible. Though it is claimed that, in certain people, the two hemispheres may have the same full ranges of abilities, this claim might be false. I am here assuming that this claim is true when applied to me. I am also assuming that it would be possible to connect a transplanted half-brain with the nerves in its new body. And I am assuming that we could divide, not just the upper hemispheres, but also the lower brain. My first two assumptions may be able to be made true if there is enough progress in neurophysiology. But it seems likely that it would never be possible to divide the lower brain, is a way that did not impair its functioning.

Does it matter if, for this reason, this imagined case of complete division will always remain impossible? Given the aims of my discussion, this does not matter. This impossibility is merely technical. The one feature of the case that might be held to be *deeply* impossible – the division of a person's consciousness into two separate streams – is the feature that has actually happened.

[...]

It may help to state, in advance, what I believe this case to show. It provides a further argument against the view that we are separately existing entities. But the main conclusion to be drawn is that *personal identity is not what matters.*

It is natural to believe that our identity is what matters. Reconsider the Branch-Line Case, where I have talked to my Replica on Mars, and am about to die. Suppose we believe that I and my Replica are different people. It is then natural to assume that my prospect is almost as bad as ordinary death. In a few days, there will be no one living who will be me. It is natural to assume that *this* is what matters. In discussing My Division, I shall start by making this assumption.

In this case, each half of my brain will be successfully transplanted into the very similar body of one of my two brothers. Both of the resulting people will be fully psychologically continuous with me, as I am now. What happens to me?

There are only four possibilities: (1) I do not survive; (2) I survive as one of the two people; (3) I survive as the other; (4) I survive as both.

The objection to (1) is this. I would survive if my brain was successfully transplanted. And people have in fact survived with half their brains destroyed. Given these facts, it seems clear that 1 would survive if half my brain was successfully transplanted, and the other half was destroyed. So how could I fail to survive if the other half was also successfully transplanted? How could a double success be a failure?

Consider the next two possibilities. Perhaps one success is the maximum score. Perhaps I shall be one of the two resulting people. The objection here is that, in this case, each half of my brain is exactly similar, and so, to start with, is each resulting person. Given these facts, how can I survive as only one of the two people? What can make me one of them rather than the other?

These three possibilities cannot be dismissed as incoherent. We can understand them. But, while we assume that identity is what matters, (1) is not plausible. My Division would not be as bad as death. Nor are (2) and (3) plausible. There remains the fourth possibility: that I survive as both of the resulting people.

This possibility might be described in several ways. I might first claim: 'What we have called "the two resulting people" are not two people. They are one person. I do survive this operation. Its effect is to give me two bodies, and a divided mind.'

This claim cannot be dismissed outright. As I argued, we ought to admit as possible that a person could have a divided mind. If this is possible, each half of my divided mind might control its own body. But though this description of the case cannot be rejected as inconceivable, it involves a great distortion in our concept of a person. In my imagined Physics Exam I claimed that this case involved only one person. There were two features of the case that made this plausible. The divided mind was soon reunited, and there was only one body. If a mind was permanently divided, and its halves developed in different ways, it would become less plausible to claim that the case involves only one person. (Remember the actual patient who complained that, when he embraced his wife, his left hand pushed her away.)

The case of complete division, where there are also two bodies, seems to be a long way over the borderline. After I have had this operation, the two 'products' each have all of the features of a person. They could live at opposite ends of the Earth. Suppose that they have poor memories, and that their appearance changes in different ways. After many years, they might meet again, and fail even to recognise each other. We might have to claim of such a pair, innocently playing tennis: 'What you see out there is a single person, playing tennis with himself. In each half of his mind he mistakenly believes that he is playing tennis with someone else.' [...]

Suppose we admit that the two 'products' are, as they seem to be, two different people. Could we still claim that I survive as both? There is another way in which we could. I might say: 'I survive the operation as two different people. They can be different people, and yet be me, in the way in which the Pope's three crowns together form one crown.'

This claim is also coherent. But it again greatly distorts the concept of a person. We are happy to agree that the Pope's three crowns, when put together, are a fourth crown. But it is hard to think of two people as, together, being a third person. Suppose the resulting people fight a duel. Are there three people fighting, one on each side, and one on both? And suppose one of the bullets kills. Are there two acts, one murder and one suicide? How many people are left alive? One or two? The composite third person has no separate mental life. It is hard to believe that there really would be such a third person. Instead of saying that the resulting people together constitute me – so that the pair is a trio – it is better to treat them as a pair, and describe their relation to me in a simpler way.

Other claims might be made. It might be suggested that the two resulting people are *now* different people, but that, before My Division, they *were* the same person. Before My Division, they were me. This suggestion is ambiguous. The claim may be that, before My Division, they *together* were me. On this account, there were three different people even before My Division. This is even less plausible than the claim I have just rejected. [...]

It may instead be suggested that, before My Division, *each* of the resulting people *was* me. After My Division, neither is me, since I do not now exist. But, if each of these people *was* me, whatever happened to me must have happened to each of these people. If I did not survive My Division, neither of these people survived. Since there *are* two resulting people, the case involves *five* people. This conclusion is absurd. Can we deny the assumption that implies this conclusion? Can we claim that, though each of the resulting people *was* me, what happened to me did not happen to these people? Assume that I have not yet divided. On this suggestion, it is now true that each of the resulting people *is* me. If what happens to me does not happen to X, X cannot be me.

[...]

I have discussed several unusual views about what happens when I divide. On these views, the case involves a single person, a duo, a trio two of whom compose the third, and a quintet. We could doubtless conjure up the missing quartet. But it would be tedious to consider more of these views. All involve too great distortions of the concept of a person. We should therefore reject the fourth suggested possibility: the claim that, in some sense, I survive as both of the two resulting people.

There are three other possibilities: that I shall be *one*, or *the other*, or *neither* of these people. These three claims seemed implausible. Note next that, as before, we could not *find out* what happens even if we could actually perform this operation. Suppose, for example, that I do survive as one of the resulting people. I would believe that I have survived. But I would know that the other resulting person falsely believes that he is me, and that he survived. Since I would know this, I could not trust my own belief. I might be the resulting person with the false belief. And, since we would both claim to be me, other people would have no reason to believe one of us rather than the other. Even if we performed this operation, we would therefore learn nothing. [...]

What Matters When I Divide?

Some people would regard division as being as bad, or nearly as bad, as ordinary death. This reaction is irrational. We ought to regard division as being about as good as ordinary survival. As I have argued, the two 'products' of this operation would be two different people. Consider my relation to each other of these people. Does this relation fail to contain some vital element that is contained in ordinary survival? It seems clear that it does not. It would survive if I stood in this very same relation to only one of the resulting people. It is a fact that someone can survive even if half his brain is destroyed. And on reflection it was clear that I would survive if my whole brain was successfully transplanted into my brother's body. It was therefore clear that I would survive if half my brain was destroyed, and the other half was successfully transplanted into my brother's body. In the case that we are now considering, my relation to each of the resulting people thus contains everything that would be needed for me to survive as that person. It cannot be the *nature* of my relation to each of the resulting people that, in this case, causes it to fail to be survival. Nothing is *missing*. What is wrong can only be the duplication.

Suppose that I accept this, but still regard division as being nearly as bad as death. My reaction is now indefensible. I am like someone who, when told of a drug that could double his years of life, regards the taking of this drug as death. The only difference in the case of division is that the extra years are to run concurrently. This is an interesting difference; but it cannot mean that there are *no* years to run. We might say: 'You will lose your identity. But there are different ways of doing this. Dying is one, dividing is another. To regard these as the same is to confuse two with zero. Double survival is not the same as ordinary survival. But this does not make it death. It is even less like death.'

Notes

1. W.V. Quine, reviewing Milton K. Munitz, ed., *Identity and Individuation*, in *The Journal of Philosophy* (1972), p. 490.
2. R.W. Sperry, in J.C. Eccles, ed., *Brain and Conscious Experience* (Berlin: Springer, 1966), p. 299.
3. T. Nagel, "Brain Bisection and the Unity of Consciousness," *Synthese* 22 (1971); reprinted in T Nagel, *Mortal Questions* (Cambridge: Cambridge University Press, 1979), p. 152.
4. Ibid., p. 153.

27

Are We Animals?

Eric T. Olson, "An Argument for Animalism"

When you wonder what kind of being you are at a given time (such as right now), should you decide first of all on what would make you still you at some later time? That is the question of whether your personal identity *over* time is vital to your being whatever kind of being you are at a *single* time. Derek Parfit urged us (in the previous reading) *not* to feel any need, when reflecting upon the metaphysics of being a person, to establish what would be an individual person's identity conditions over time. Much earlier, Locke had spurred philosophy in that direction (as we saw in the reading from him in this section). Locke also encouraged us to regard psychological characteristics as the key to understanding what makes a person-at-a-time, numerically even if not qualitatively, identical to some person-at-another-time. And the past few readings have been from within that tradition of thinking about personhood in terms of personal identity, and of thinking about personal identity in terms of psychological characteristics.

But must we follow that tradition if we are to understand our being persons? This reading introduces us to a quite different line of thought. The reading is by Eric Olson (b. 1963), from the University of Sheffield, who has written extensively on the metaphysics of persons. He offers an *animalist* conception of our being the people we are.

How does Olson motivate that way of thinking? Not by asking about strict *identity* conditions, nor by seeking within our *psychological* lives for the key to what we are. He rejoins Descartes in a significant respect. Like Descartes (from the earlier reading within this section), Olson places the question of what we *are* at the prow of his metaphysical inquiry — rather than Locke's question of what

Eric T. Olson, "An Argument for Animalism" (excerpts), in R. Martin and J. Barresi (eds.), *Personal Identity* (Malden, MA: Blackwell, 2003). © Eric T. Olson. Reprinted with kind permission of the author.

Metaphysics and Epistemology: A Guided Anthology, First Edition. Edited by Stephen Hetherington.
© 2014 John Wiley & Sons, Inc. Published 2014 by John Wiley & Sons, Inc.

constitutes a person's *persistence* from one moment to another. Unlike Descartes, though, Olson's answer to the former question does not describe each of us as a composite of two independent kinds of substance, such as mind and body. For Olson, what matters most is that we are *organisms*. In fact, for him we are *animals*. Yes, animals. Why not? He regards this as a more natural account of persons than any other account provided by philosophers over the centuries. Olson does not seek to describe a special or fundamental or essential aspect of each of us, let alone of each possible kind of person. His aim is simply to locate each of us within a biological category – a species. Which one? *Homo sapiens*. Olson thus bypasses any reliance upon the idea of each person as fundamentally a *mind*, for example.

Many will find his idea disturbing. How could we be merely animals? Well, if we are animals at all, why need we be *more* than animals? Moreover, Olson's animalism does not imply that we are never impressive animals in various ways. Bear in mind also that, at any time of your life, wherever you are located and no matter what you are thinking, seemingly a human being – an animal – is in that same place thinking those same thoughts. Should we deny animalism by saying that the world contains you and a *distinct* human being in that one location at that time – two individuals right there, simultaneously thinking identical thoughts? The question is one of whether you *are* that animal, or whether you are merely closely related to it. Olson argues for the former alternative.

It is a truism that you and I are human beings. It is also a truism that a human being is a kind of animal: roughly a member of the primate species *Homo sapiens*. It would seem to follow that we are animals. Yet that claim is deeply controversial. Plato, Augustine, Descartes, Spinoza, Leibniz, Locke, Berkeley, Hume, Kant, and Hegel all denied it. With the notable exception of Aristotle and his followers, it is hard to find a major figure in the history of Western philosophy who thought that we are animals. The view is no more popular in non-Western traditions. And probably nine out of ten philosophers writing about personal identity today either deny outright that we are animals, or say things that are clearly incompatible with it.

This is surprising. Isn't it obvious that we are animals? I will try to show that it isn't obvious, and that Plato and the others have their reasons for thinking otherwise. Before doing that I will explain how I understand the claim that we are animals. My main purpose, though, is to make a case for this unpopular view. I won't rely on the brief argument I began with. My strategy is to ask what it would mean if we weren't animals. Denying that we are animals is harder than you might think.

What Animalism Says

When I say that we are animals, I mean that each of us is numerically identical with an animal. There is a certain human organism, and that organism is you. You and it are one and the same. This view has been called "animalism". [...] Many claims that sound like animalism are in fact different.

[…]

[…] [A]nimalism is not the same as *materialism*. Materialism is the view that we are material things; and we might be material things but not animals. Animalism implies materialism (animals are material things), but not vice versa. It may seem perverse for a materialist to reject animalism. If we are material things of any sort, surely we are animals? Perverse or not, though, the view that we are material non-organisms is widely held.

Animalism says that *we* are animals. That is compatible with the existence of non-animal people (or persons, if you prefer). It is often said that to be a person is to have certain mental qualities: to be rational, intelligent, and self-conscious, say. Perhaps a person must also be morally responsible, and have free will. If something like that is right, then gods or angels might be people but not animals.

Nor does our being animals imply that all animals, or even all human animals, are people. Human beings in a persistent vegetative state are biologically alive, but their mental capacities are permanently destroyed. They are certainly human animals. But we might not want to call them people. The same goes for human embryos.

So the view that we are animals does not imply that to be a person is nothing other than to be an animal of a certain sort – that being an animal is part of what it is to be a person. Inconveniently enough, this view has also been called animalism. It isn't the animalism that I want to defend. In fact it looks rather implausible. I don't know whether there could be inorganic people, as for instance traditional theism asserts. But mere reflection on what it is to be a person doesn't seem to rule it out. Of course, if people are animals by definition, it follows that we are animals, since we are obviously people. But the reverse entailment doesn't hold: we might be animals even if something could be a person without being an animal.

If I don't say that all people are animals, which people do I mean? […] I say that you and I and the other people who walk the earth are animals. If you like, all *human* people are animals, where a human person is roughly someone who relates to a human animal in the way that you and I do, whatever way that is. […] Many philosophers deny that *any* people are animals. So there is nothing trivial about this claim.

"Animalism" is sometimes stated as the view that we are *essentially or most fundamentally* animals. We are essentially animals if we couldn't possibly exist without being animals. It is less clear what it is for us to be most fundamentally animals, but this is usually taken to imply at least that our identity conditions derive from our being animals, rather than from our being, say, people or philosophers or material object – even though we *are* people and philosophers and material objects.

Whether our being animals implies that we are essentially or most fundamentally animals depends on whether human animals are essentially or most fundamentally animals. If the animal that you are is essentially an animal, then so are you. If it is only contingently an animal, then you are only contingently an animal. Likewise, you are most fundamentally an animal if and only if the animal that you are is most fundamentally an animal. The claim that each of us is identical with an animal is neutral on these questions. Most philosophers think that every animal is essentially and most fundamentally an animal, and I am inclined to agree. But you could be an animalist in my sense without accepting this.

Is animalism the view that we are identical with our bodies? That depends on what it is for something to be someone's body. […] One's body might include plastic or metal limbs. Someone might even have an entirely robotic body. I take it that no animal could be partly or wholly inorganic. If you cut off an animal's limb and replace it with an inorganic prosthesis, the animal just gets smaller and has something inorganic attached to it. So perhaps after having some or all of your parts replaced by inorganic gadgets of the right sort you would be identical with your body, but would not be an animal. Animalism may imply that you are your body, but you could be your body without being an animal. [...]

Whether these claims about bodies are true depends on what it is for something to be someone's body. What does it *mean* to say that your body is an animal, or that someone might have a robotic body? [...] I will talk about people and animals, and leave bodies out of it.

Finally, does animalism say that we are *merely* animals? That we are nothing more than biological organisms? This is a delicate point. The issue is whether being "more than just" or "not merely" an animal is compatible with being an animal – that is, with being identical with an animal.

[...]

[...] An animal can have properties other than being an animal, and which don't follow from its being an animal. Our being animals does not rule out our being mathematicians, Frenchmen, or Roman Catholics – or our being people, socialists, mountaineers, and many other things. At least there is no evident reason why it should. Animalism does not imply that we have a fixed, "animal" nature, or that we have only biological or naturalistic properties, or that we are no different, in any important way, from other animals. There may be a vast psychological and moral gulf between human animals and organisms of other species. We may be very special animals. But special animals are still animals.

[...]

Why Animalism is Unpopular

Why is animalism so unpopular? Historically, the main reason (though by no means the only one) is hostility to materialism. Philosophers have always found it hard to believe that a material object, no matter how physically complex, could produce thought or experience. And an animal is a material object (I assume that vitalism is false). Since it is plain enough that *we* can think, it is easy to conclude that we couldn't be animals.

But why do modern-day materialists reject animalism, or at least say things that rule it out? The main reason, I believe, is that when they think about personal identity they don't ask what sort of things we are. [...]

The traditional problem of personal identity is not what we are, but what it takes for us to persist. It asks what is necessary, and what is sufficient, for a person existing at one time to be identical with something present at another time: what sorts of adventures we could survive, and what would inevitably bring our existence to an end. [...] Claims about what it takes for us to persist do not by themselves tell us what other fundamental properties we have: whether we are material or immaterial, simple or composite, abstract or concrete, and so on. At any rate, the single-minded focus on our identity over time has tended to put other metaphysical questions about ourselves out of philosophers' minds.

What is more, the most popular solution to this traditional problem rules out our being animals. It is that we persist by virtue of some sort of psychological continuity. You are, necessarily, that future being that in some sense inherits its mental features – personality, beliefs, memories, values, and so on – from you. And you are that past being whose mental features you have inherited. Philosophers disagree about what sort of inheritance this has to be: whether those mental features must be continuously physically realized, for instance. But most accept the general idea. The persistence of a human animal, on the other hand, does not consist in mental continuity.

The fact that each human animal starts out as an unthinking embryo and may end up as an unthinking vegetable shows that no sort of mental continuity is necessary for a human animal to persist. No human animal is mentally continuous with an embryo or a vegetable.

To see that no sort of mental continuity is sufficient for a human animal to persist, imagine that your cerebrum is put into another head. The being who gets that organ, and he alone, will be mentally continuous with you on any account of what mental continuity is. So if mental continuity of any sort suffices for you to persist, you would go along with your transplanted cerebrum. You wouldn't stay behind with an empty head.

[…] The empty-headed thing left behind, by contrast, *is* an animal. It may even remain alive, if the surgeons are careful to leave the lower brain intact. The empty-headed being into which your cerebrum is implanted is also an animal. It looks for all the world like there are two human animals in the story. One of them loses its cerebrum and gets an empty head. The other has its empty head filled with that organ. No animal moves from one head to another. The surgeons merely move an organ from one animal to another. If this is right, then no sort of psychological continuity suffices for the identity of a human animal over time. One human animal could be mentally continuous with another one (supposing that they can have mental properties at all).

If we tell the story in the right way, it is easy enough to get most people, or at any rate most Western-educated philosophy students, to say that *you* would go along with your transplanted cerebrum. After all, the one who got that organ would act like you and think she was you. Why deny that she would be the person she thinks she is? But "your" animal – the one you would be if you were any animal – would stay behind. That means that you and that animal could go your separate ways. And a thing and itself can never go their separate ways.

It follows that you are not that animal, or indeed any other animal. Not only are you not essentially an animal. You are not an animal at all, even contingently. Nothing that is even contingently an animal would move to a different head if its cerebrum were transplanted. The human animals in the story stay where they are and merely lose or gain organs.

[…]

The Thinking-Animal Argument

I turn now to my case for animalism. It seems evident that there *is* a human animal intimately related to you. It is the one located where you are, the one we point to when we point to you, the one sitting in your chair. It seems equally evident that human animals can think. They can act. They can be aware of themselves and the world. Those with mature nervous systems in good working order can, anyway. So there is a thinking, acting human animal sitting where you are now. But you think and act. *You* are the thinking being sitting in your chair.

It follows from these apparently trite observations that you are an animal. In a nutshell, the argument is this: (1) There is a human animal sitting in your chair. (2) The human animal sitting in your chair is thinking. (If you like, every human animal sitting there is thinking.) (3) You are the thinking being sitting in your chair. The one and only thinking being sitting in your chair is none other than you. Hence, you are that animal. That animal is you. And there is nothing special about you: we are all animals.

[…]

[…] [T]he argument has three premises, and so there are three ways of resisting it. One could deny that there is any human animal sitting in your chair. One could deny that any such animal thinks. Or one could deny that you are the thinking being sitting there. Anyone who denies that we are animals is committed to accepting one of these claims. They are not very plausible. But let us consider them.

Alternative One: There Are No Human Animals

Why suppose that there is no human animal sitting in your chair? Presumably because there are no human animals anywhere. If there are any human animals at all, there is one sitting there. (I assume that you aren't a Martian foundling.) And if there are no human animals, it is hard to see how there could be any organisms of other sorts. So denying the argument's first premise amounts to denying that there are, strictly speaking, any organisms. There appear to be, of course. But that is at best a well-founded illusion.

There are venerable philosophical views that rule out the existence of organisms. […] There is the view that nothing can have different parts at different times. Whenever something appears to lose or gain a part, the truth of the matter is that one object, made of the first set of parts, ceases to exist (or becomes scattered) and is instantly replaced by a numerically different object made of the second set of parts. Organisms, if there were such things, would constantly assimilate new particles and expel others. If nothing can survive a change of any of its parts, organisms are metaphysically impossible. What we think of as an organism is in reality only a succession of different "masses of matter" that each take on organic form for a brief moment – until a single particle is gained or lost – and then pass that form on to a numerically different mass.

But few opponents of animalism deny the existence of animals. They have good reason not to, quite apart from the fact that this is more or less incredible. Anything that would rule out the existence of animals would also rule out most of the things we might be if we are not animals. If there are no animals, there are no beings constituted by animals, and no temporal parts of animals. And whatever rules out animals may tell against Humean bundles of perceptions as well. If there are no animals, it is not easy to see what we *could* be.

Alternative Two: Human Animals Can't Think

The second alternative is that there is an animal sitting in your chair, but it isn't thinking. (Let any occurrence of a propositional attitude, such as the belief that it's raining or the hope that it won't, count as "thinking".) *You* think, but the animal doesn't. The reason for this can only be that the animal can't think. If it were able to think, it would be thinking now. And if *that* animal can't think – despite its healthy, mature human brain, lengthy education, surrounding community of thinkers, and appropriate evolutionary history – then no human animal can. And if no human animal can think, no animal of any sort could. (We can't very well say that dogs can think but human animals can't.) Finally, if no animal could ever think – not even a normal adult human animal – it is hard to see how any organism could have any mental property whatever. So if your animal isn't thinking, that is apparently because it is impossible for any organism to have mental properties.

The claim, then, is that animals, including human animals, are no more intelligent or sentient than trees. We could of course say that they are "intelligent" in the sense of being the bodies of intelligent people who are not themselves animals. And we could call organism like dogs "sentient" in the sense of being the bodies of sentient non-animals that stand to those animals as you and I stand to human animals. But that is loose talk. The strict and sober truth would be that only non-organisms could ever think.

This is rather hard to believe. Anyone who denies that animals can think (or that they can think in the way that we think) needs to explain why they can't. What stops a typical human animal from using its brain to think? Isn't that what that organ is *for*?

[…]

Alternative Three: You Are Not Alone

Suppose, then, that there is a human animal sitting in your chair. And suppose that it thinks. Is there any way to resist the conclusion that you are that thinking animal? We can hardly say that the animal thinks but you don't. (If anything thinks, you do.) Nor can we deny that you exist, when there is a rational animal thinking your thoughts. How, then, could you fail to be that thinking animal? Only if you are not the only thinker there. If you are not *the* thinking thing sitting there, you must be one of at least two such thinkers. You exist. You think. There is also a thinking human animal there. Presumably it has the same psychological qualities as you have. But it isn't you. There are two thinking beings wherever we thought there was just one. There are two philosophers, you and an animal, sitting there and reading this. You are never truly alone: wherever you go, a watchful human animal goes with you.

This is not an attractive picture. Its adherents may try to comfort us by proposing linguistic hypotheses. Whenever two beings are as intimately related as you and your animal are, they will say, we "count them as one" for ordinary purposes. When I write on the copyright form that I am the sole author of this essay, I don't mean that every author of this essay is numerically identical with me. I mean only that every author of this essay bears some relation to me that does not imply identity: that every such author is co-located with me, perhaps. My wife is not a bigamist, even though she is, I suppose, married both to me and to the animal. At any rate it would be seriously misleading to describe our relationship as a *ménage à quatre*.

This is supposed to show that the current proposal needn't contradict anything that we say or believe when engaged in the ordinary business of life. Unless we are doing metaphysics, we don't distinguish strict numerical identity from the intimate relation that each of us bears to a certain human animal. Ordinary people have no opinion about how many numerically different thinking beings there are. Why should they? What matters in real life is not how many thinkers there are strictly speaking, but how many *non-overlapping* thinkers.

Perhaps so. Still, it hardly makes the current proposal easy to believe. Is it not strange to suppose that there are two numerically different thinkers wherever we thought there was just one?

In any event, the troubles go beyond mere overcrowding. If there really are two beings, a person and an animal, now thinking your thoughts and performing your actions, you ought to wonder which one you are. You may think you're the person (the one the isn't an animal). But doesn't the animal think that *it* is a person? It has all the same reasons for thinking so as you have. Yet it is mistaken. If you *were* the animal and not the person, you'd still think you were the person. For all you know, *you're* the one making the mistake. Even if you are a person and not an animal, you could never have any reason to believe that you are.

For that matter, if your animal can think, that ought to make *it* a person. It has the same mental features as you have. (Otherwise we should expect an explanation for the difference, just as we should if the animal can't think at all.) It is, in Locke's words, "a thinking intelligent being, that has reason and reflection, and can consider itself as itself, the same thinking thing, in different times and places" [see reading 24, §9]. It satisfies every ordinary definition of 'person'. But it would be mad to suppose that the animal sitting in your chair is a *person* numerically different from you – that each human person shares her location and her thoughts with *another* person. If nothing else, this would contradict the claim that people – all people – have psychological identity conditions, thus sweeping away the main reason for denying that we are animals in the first place.

On the other hand, if rational human animals are not people, familiar accounts of what it is to be a person are all far too permissive. Having the psychological and moral features that you and I have would not be enough to make something a person. There could be rational, intelligent, self-conscious *non*-people. In fact there would be at least one such rational non-person for every genuine person. That would deprive personhood of any psychological or moral significance.

Hard Choices

That concludes my argument for animalism. We could put the same point in another way. There are about six billion human animals walking the earth. Those animals are just like ourselves. They sit in our chairs and sleep in our beds. They work, and talk, and take holidays. Some of them do philosophy. They have just the mental and physical attributes that we take ourselves to have. So it seems, anyway. This makes it hard to deny that *we* are those animals. The apparent existence of rational human animals is an inconvenient fact for he opponents of animalism. We might call it the *problem of the thinking animal*.

But what of the case against animalism? It seems that you would go along with your cerebrum if that organ were transplanted. More generally, some sort of mental continuity appears to suffice for us to persist. And that is not true of any animal. Generations of philosophers have found this argument compelling. How can they have gone so badly wrong?

One reason, as I have said, is that they haven't asked the right questions. They have thought about what it takes for us to persist through time, but not about what we are.

Here is another. If someone is mentally just like you, that is strong evidence for his being you. All the more so if there is continuously physically realized mental continuity between him and you. In fact it is conclusive evidence, given that brain transplants belong to science fiction. Moreover, most of us find mental continuity more interesting and important than brute physical continuity. When we hear a story, we don't much care which person at the end of the tale is the same animal as a given person at the beginning. We care about who is psychologically continuous with that person. If mental and animal continuity often came apart, we might think differently. But they don't.

These facts can easily lead us to suppose that the one who remembers your life in the transplant story is you. Easier still if we don't know how problematic that claim is − if we don't realize that it would rule out our being animals. To those who haven't reflected on the problem of the thinking animal − and that includes most philosophers − if can seem dead obvious that we persist by virtue of mental continuity. But if we are animals, this is a mistake, though an understandable one.

Of course, opponents of animalism can play this game too. They can attempt to explain why it is natural to suppose that there are human animals, or that human animals can think, or that you are the thinking thing sitting in your chair, in a way that does not imply that those claims are true. (That is the point of the linguistic hypotheses I mentioned earlier.) What to do? Well, I invite you to compare the thinking-animal argument with the transplant argument. Which is more likely? That there are no animals? That no animal could ever think? That you are one of at least two intelligent beings sitting in your chair? Or that you would not, after all, go along with your transplanted cerebrum?

What it would Mean if we were Animals

[…] [D]on't we have a strong conviction that we are animals? We all think that we are human beings. And until the philosophers got hold of us, we took human beings to be animals. We *seem* to be animals. It is the opponents of animalism who insist that this appearance is deceptive: that the animal you see in the mirror is not really you. That we are animals ought to be the default position. If anything is hard to believe, it's the alternatives.

How Do People Ever Have Free Will and Moral Responsibility?

28

Is There No Possibility of Acting Differently To How One Will in Fact Act?

Aristotle, *De Interpretatione*

By now, we have met some attempts to understand how we may need to include the concept of a *fact* within our metaphysics. Talk of truth – and surely we *do* lay claim to uttering and thinking truths – could lead us to talk also of facts. For we could well suspect that countenancing facts would help to explain the presence of truth. When a person has a belief that is true, is this because there is a corresponding fact in virtue of which the belief is true? In effect, that traditional metaphysical image construes facts as *helping* us: some part of the world would be cooperating with some of our beliefs – the true ones – by making them true. But is there a

Aristotle, *De Interpretatione*, ch. 9 (excerpts), trans. E.M. Edghill, in *The Basic Works of Aristotle*, ed. R. McKeon (New York: Random House, 1941). From *The Oxford Translation of Aristotle*, ed. W.D. Ross, vol. 1 (Oxford University Press, 1928). Reprinted with permission of Oxford University Press.

Metaphysics and Epistemology: A Guided Anthology, First Edition. Edited by Stephen Hetherington.
© 2014 John Wiley & Sons, Inc. Published 2014 by John Wiley & Sons, Inc.

possibility also of facts *restricting* us in a surprisingly strong way? This reading raises that confronting question. The reading is from Plato's student Aristotle (384–322 BC), another of ancient Greece's astoundingly influential philosophers. Aristotle contemplates a *fatalist* picture of how the world functions. The concern is that there is a way in which each of us is "trapped" by the interlinked natures of truth and facts.

For example, imagine saying that in exactly ten years from this very moment you will be eating your currently favorite breakfast cereal GreatSugaryStuff. If what you say is true, then (according to the argument advanced by Aristotle) it is true right now that you will be eating GreatSugaryStuff exactly ten years in the future. After all, this is what your claim – a future-tense one – says will be happening. And in general (we might well accept) a claim is true only if it is true in virtue of a corresponding fact. Similar reasoning applies if the claim is false: if you will not be eating GreatSugaryStuff at that future time, then (according to this argument) it is false right now that you will be eating GreatSugaryStuff at that moment. But your claim is either true or false now in what it says about the future. So, in one way or the other, does the world *already* include what will happen in the future – a fact already rendering your present claim either true or false? Does this imply that you cannot now act to *change* the world in that future respect?

Aristotle's own sort of response to this argument was to deny that claims or beliefs about the future can be true or false already. That could sound like a sensible denial. Still, philosophy requires us always to be vigilant about potential problems hidden within even what may seem to be a sensible suggestion. Thus, if we seek to evade Aristotle's argument in the proposed way, do we commit ourselves to the following troubling idea about much of what we say or think?

We do make future-tense claims: "Tomorrow he will be at the beach." Indeed, seemingly we can often be as confident of such a claim's truth as we are of a present-tense one's truth: "He is at the beach." Do we want to be committed to the aptness of accompanying all of those future-tense claims with truth-denials? When saying "Tomorrow he will be at the beach," do we or should we always really mean this: "Although tomorrow he will be at the beach, strictly it is not true now that he will be there"? That sounds quite odd.

In the case of that which is or which has taken place, propositions, whether positive or negative, must be true or false. Again, in the case of a pair of contradictories, either when the subject is universal and the propositions are of an universal character, or when it is individual, [...] one of the two must be true and the other false; whereas when the subject is universal, but the propositions are not of a universal character, there is no such necessity. [...]

When the subject, however, is individual, and that which is predicated of it relates to the future, the case is altered. For if all propositions whether positive or negative are either true or false, then any given predicate must either belong to the subject or not, so that if one man affirms that an event of a given character will take place and another denies it, it is plain that the statement of the one will correspond with reality and that of the other will not. For the predicate cannot both belong and not belong to the subject at one and the same time with regard to the future.

[…]

[…] [I]f a thing is white now, it was true before to say that it would be white, so that of anything that has taken place it was always true to say 'it is' or 'it will be'. But if it was always true to say that a thing is or will be, it is not possible that it should not be or not be about to be, and when a thing cannot not come to be, it is impossible that it should not come to be, and when it is impossible that it should not come to be, it must come to be. All, then, that is about to be must of necessity take place. It results from this that nothing is uncertain or fortuitous, for if it were fortuitous it would not be necessary.

[…] [T]o say that neither the affirmation nor the denial is true, maintaining, let us say, that an event neither will take place nor will not take place, is to take up a position impossible to defend. In the first place, though facts should prove the one proposition false, the opposite would still be untrue. Secondly, if it was true to say that a thing was both white and large, both these qualities must necessarily belong to it; and if they will belong to it the next day, they must necessarily belong to it the next day. But if an event is neither to take place nor not to take place the next day, the element of chance will be eliminated. For example, it would be necessary that a sea-fight should neither take place nor fail to take place on the next day.

These awkward results and others of the same kind follow, if it is an irrefragable law that of every pair of contradictory propositions, […] one must be true and the other false, and that there are no real alternatives, but that all that is or takes place is the outcome of necessity. There would be no need to deliberate or to take trouble, on the supposition that if we should adopt a certain course, a certain result would follow, while, if we did not, the result would not follow. For a man may predict an event ten thousand years beforehand, and another may predict the reverse; that which was truly predicted at the moment in the past will of necessity take place in the fullness of time.

Further, it makes no difference whether people have or have not actually made the contradictory statements. For it is manifest that the circumstances are not influenced by the fact of an affirmation or denial on the part of anyone. For events will not take place or fail to take place because it was stated that they would or would not take place, nor is this any more the case if the prediction dates back ten thousand years or any other space of time. Wherefore, if through all time the nature of things was so constituted that a prediction about an event was true, then through all time it was necessary that that prediction should find fulfillment; and with regard to all events, circumstances have always been such that their occurrence is a matter of necessity. For that of which someone has said truly that it will be, cannot fail to take place; and of that which takes place, it was always true to say that it would be.

Yet this view leads to an impossible conclusion; for we see that both deliberation and action are causative with regard to the future, and that, to speak more generally, in those things which are not continuously actual there is a potentiality in either direction. Such thing may either be or not be; events also therefore may either take place or not take place. There are many obvious instances of this. It is possible that this coat may be cut in half, and yet it may not be cut in half, but wear out first. In the same way, it is possible that it should not be cut in half; unless this were so, it would not be possible that it should wear out first. So it is therefore with all other events which possess this kind or potentiality. It is therefore plain that is not of necessity that everything is or takes place; but in some instances there are real alternatives, in which case the affirmation is no more true and no more false than the denial; while some exhibit a predisposition and general tendency in one direction or the other, and yet can issue in the opposite direction by exception.

Now that which is must needs be when it is, and that which is not must needs not be when it is not. Yet it cannot be said without qualification that all existence and non-existence is the outcome of necessity. For there is a difference between saying that that which is, when it is, must needs be, and simple saying that all that is must needs be, and similarly in the case of that which is not. In the case, also, of two contradictory propositions this holds good. Everything must either be or not be, whether in the present or in the future, but it is not always possible to distinguish and state determinately which of these alternatives must necessarily come about.

Let me illustrate. A sea-fight must either take place to-morrow or not, but it is not necessary that it should take place to-morrow, neither is it necessary that it should not take place, yet it is necessary that it either should or should not take place to-morrow. Since propositions correspond with facts, it is evident that when in future events there is a real alternative, and a potentiality in contrary directions, the corresponding affirmation and denial have the same character.

This is the case with regard to that which is not always existent or not always non-existent. One of the two propositions in such instances must be true and the other false, but we cannot say determinately that this or that is false, but must leave the alternative undecided. One may indeed be more likely to be true than the other, but it cannot be either actually true or actually false. It is therefore plain that it is not necessary that of an affirmation and a denial one should be true and the other false. For in the case of that which exists potentially, but not actually, the rule which applies to that which exists actually does not hold good. The case is rather as we have indicated.

29

Could Our Being Entirely Caused Coexist with Our Acting Freely?

David Hume, *An Enquiry Concerning Human Understanding*

Does fatalism – the challenge we encountered in the previous reading – threaten us with the specter of our present actions having no effect upon the future? If the future is already "in place," are we wasting our time when deciding how to act? The reasoning behind that threatening thought depended upon ideas about truth and facts. But ancient philosophers were also aware of how we might be threatened similarly by some simple ideas about *causality*. This has become known as the conceptual problem of *causal determinism*. It is standardly presented as a challenge to our conceiving of ourselves as having *free will* – abilities to act in ways that express or manifest our having an underlying kind of freedom in how we live. Can we genuinely possess this potential freedom if everything that happens or arises within the world does so because something has caused it to do so? Causal determinism is the thesis that causality does pervade and structure the world in that way. And the worry is that causal determinism seems to imply that we can never act freely. Would our actions be mere links in a longer chain of causality stretching ever backwards in time, far beyond our ever being able to comprehend its details?

This reading from David Hume offers a famous answer to that question. It is a *compatibilist* answer. That is, Hume tries to explain how it is possible for us to act freely (with "liberty" – his term) *even if* everything ever done is caused ("necessitated" – Hume's word). In the previous section from his *Enquiry Concerning Human Understanding* (section VII – reading 11 in this book), Hume developed his view of causation, conceiving of it as a pattern of regularity. Now he asks

David Hume, *An Enquiry Concerning Human Understanding* (1748), sect.VIII (excerpts).

Metaphysics and Epistemology: A Guided Anthology, First Edition. Edited by Stephen Hetherington.
© 2014 John Wiley & Sons, Inc. Published 2014 by John Wiley & Sons, Inc.

us to think about whether in fact we are *worried* by the idea of our actions being embedded within such patterns; and he argues that we do not find this worrying. On the contrary, we depend upon the world being like that, as we act within it. Such causality helps us. It gives us the stability and predictability we need when deciding what to do.

Then we *do* act – stably, predictably. Are we doing what we have *chosen* to do? Whenever this is how we act, on those occasions we have indeed acted freely. Hume argues that to act unfreely is to act while trapped, while constrained; and normally that is not how we act. Certainly that is not an appropriate way of describing what a *causally determined* action is like. To reinforce this point, Hume argues that our only other conception of acting (apart from a view of actions as elements within enveloping causal patterns) is a picture of ourselves as acting *randomly*. But that is hardly what we want as agents. Would it even *be* one's acting with real agency?

Of Liberty and Necessity

Part I

[...]

I hope to make it appear that all men have ever agreed in the doctrine both of necessity and of liberty, according to any reasonable sense, [...]; and that the whole controversy has hitherto turned merely upon words. We shall begin with examining the doctrine of necessity.

It is universally allowed that matter, in all its operations, is actuated by a necessary force, and that every natural effect is so precisely determined by the energy of its cause that no other effect, in such particular circumstances, could possibly have resulted from it. The degree and direction of every motion is, by the laws of nature, prescribed with such exactness that a living creature may as soon arise from the shock of two bodies, as motion, in any other degree or direction than what is actually produced by it. Would we, therefore, form a just and precise idea of *necessity*, we must consider whence that idea arises when we apply it to the operation of bodies.

It seems evident that, if all the scenes of nature were continually shifted in such a manner that no two events bore any resemblance to each other, but every object was entirely new, without any similitude to whatever had been seen before, we should never, in that case, have attained the least idea of necessity, or of a connexion among these objects. We might say, upon such a supposition, that one object or event has followed another; not that one was produced by the other. The relation of cause and effect must be utterly unknown to mankind. Inference and reasoning concerning the operations of nature would, from that moment, be at an end; and the memory and senses remain the only canals, by which the knowledge of any real existence could possibly have access to the mind. Our idea, therefore, of necessity and causation arises entirely from the uniformity observable in the operations of nature, where similar objects are constantly conjoined together, and the mind is determined by custom to infer the one from the appearance of the other. These two circumstances form the whole of that necessity, which we ascribe to matter. Beyond the constant *conjunction* of similar objects, and the consequent *inference* from one to the other, we have no notion of any necessity or connexion.

If it appear, therefore, that all mankind have ever allowed, without any doubt or hesitation, that these two circumstances take place in the voluntary actions of men, and in the operations of mind; it must follow, that all mankind have ever agreed in the doctrine of necessity, and that they have hitherto disputed, merely for not understanding each other.

[...] It is universally acknowledged that there is a great uniformity among the action of men, in all nation and ages, and that human nature remains still the same, in its principles and operations. The same motives always produce the same action: The same events follow from the same causes. Ambition, avarice, self-love, vanity, friendship, generosity, public spirit: these passions, mixed in various degrees, and distributed through society, have been, from the beginning of the world, and still are, the source of all the actions and enterprises, which have ever been observed among mankind. [...] Mankind are so much the same, in all times and places, that history informs us of nothing new or strange in this particular. Its chief use is only to discover the constant and universal principles of human nature, by showing men in all varieties of circumstances and situations, and furnishing us with materials from which we may form our observations and become acquainted with the regular springs of human action and behaviour.

[...]

We must not, however, expect that this uniformity of human actions should be carried to such a length as that all men, in the same circumstances, will always act precisely in the same manner, without making any allowance for the diversity of characters, prejudices, and opinions. Such a uniformity in every particular, is found in no part of nature. On the contrary, from observing the variety of conduct in different men, we are enabled to form a greater variety of maxims, which still suppose a degree of uniformity and regularity.

[...] Even the characters, which are peculiar to each individual, have a uniformity in their influence; otherwise our acquaintance with the persons and our observation of their conduct could never teach us their dispositions, or serve to direct our behaviour with regard to them.

I grant it possible to find some actions, which seem to have no regular connexion with any known motives, and are exceptions to all the measures of conduct which have ever been established for the government of men. [...].

The vulgar, who take things according to their first appearance, attribute the uncertainty of events to such an uncertainty in the causes as makes the latter often fail of their usual influence; though they meet with no impediment in their operation. But philosophers, observing that, almost in every part of nature, there is contained a vast variety of springs and principles, which are hid, by reason of their minuteness or remoteness, find, that it is at least possible the contrariety of events may not proceed from any contingency in the cause, but from the secret operation of contrary causes. [...]

Thus, for instance, in the human body, when the usual symptoms of health or sickness disappoint our expectation; when medicines operate not with their wonted powers; when irregular events follow from any particular cause; the philosopher and physician are not surprised at the matter, nor are ever tempted to deny, in general, the necessity and uniformity of those principles by which the animal economy is conducted. They know that a human body is a mighty complicated machine: That many secret powers lurk in it, which are altogether beyond our comprehension. [...]

The philosopher, if he be consistent, must apply the same reasoning to the actions and volitions of intelligent agents. The most irregular and unexpected resolutions of men may frequently be accounted for by those who know every particular circumstance of their character and situation. A person of an obliging disposition gives a peevish answer: But he has the toothache, or has not dined. [...] Or even when an action, as sometimes happens, cannot be particularly accounted for, either by the person himself or by others; we know, in general, that the characters of men are, to a certain degree, inconstant and irregular. This is, in a manner, the constant character of human nature; though it be applicable, in a more particular manner, to some persons who have no fixed rule for their conduct, but proceed in a continued course of caprice and inconstancy. [...]

Thus it appears, not only that the conjunction between motives and voluntary actions is as regular and uniform as that between the cause and effect in any part of nature; but also that this regular conjunction has been universally acknowledged among mankind, and has never been the subject of dispute, either in philosophy or common life. [...]

The mutual dependence of men is so great in all societies that scarce any human action is entirely complete in itself, or is performed without some reference to the actions of others, which are requisite to make it answer fully the intention of the agent. [...] In proportion as men extend their dealings, and render their intercourse with others more complicated, they always comprehend, in their schemes of life, a greater variety of voluntary actions, which they expect, from the proper motives, to co-operate with their own. In all these conclusions they take their measures from past experience, in the same manner as in their reasonings concerning external objects; and firmly believe that men, as well as all the elements, are to continue, in their operations, the same that they have ever found them. [...] Have we not reason therefore, to affirm that all mankind have always agreed in the doctrine of necessity according to the foregoing definition and explication of it?

Nor have philosophers ever entertained a different opinion from the people in this particular. For, not to mention that almost every action of their life supposes that opinion, there are even few of the speculative parts of learning to which it is not essential. What would become of *history*, had we not a dependence on the veracity of the historian according to the experience which we have had of mankind? How could *politics* be a science, if laws and forms of government had not a uniform influence upon society? Where would be the foundation of *morals*, if particular characters had no certain or determinate power to produce particular sentiments, and if these sentiments had no constant operation on actions?

[...]

[...] A man who at noon leaves his purse full of gold on the pavement at Charing-Cross, may as well expect that it will fly away like a feather, as that he will find it untouched an hour after. Above one half of human reasonings contain inferences of a similar nature, attended with more or less degrees of certainty proportioned to our experience of the usual conduct of mankind in such particular situations.

I have frequently considered, what could possibly be the reason why all mankind, though they have ever, without hesitation, acknowledged the doctrine of necessity in their whole practice and reasoning, have yet discovered such a reluctance to acknowledge it in words, and have rather shown a propensity, in all ages, to profess the contrary opinion. The matter, I think, may be accounted for after the following manner. [...]

It would seem, [...] that men begin at the wrong end of this question concerning liberty and necessity, when they enter upon it by examining the faculties of the soul, the influence of the understanding, and the operations of the will. Let them first discuss a more simple question, namely, the operations of body and of brute unintelligent matter; and try whether they can there form any idea of causation and necessity, except that of a constant conjunction of objects, and subsequent inference of the mind from one to another. If these circumstances form, in reality, the whole of that necessity, which we conceive in matter, and if these circumstances be also universally acknowledged to take place in the operations of the mind, the dispute is at an end; at least, must be owned to be thenceforth merely verbal. But as long as we will rashly suppose, that we have some farther idea of necessity and causation in the operations of external objects; at the same time, that we can find nothing farther in the voluntary actions of the mind; there is no possibility of bringing the question to any determinate issue, while we proceed upon so erroneous a supposition. [...] We may, perhaps, find that it is with difficulty we are induced to fix such narrow limits to human understanding: But we can afterwards find no difficulty when we come to apply this doctrine to the actions of the will. For as it is evident that these have a regular conjunction with motives and circumstances and characters, and as we always draw inferences from one to the other, we must be obliged to acknowledge in words that necessity, which we have already avowed, in every deliberation of our lives, and in every step of our conduct and behaviour.

But to proceed In this reconciling project with regard to the question of liberty and necessity; the most contentious question of metaphysics, the most contentious science; it will not require many words to prove, that all mankind have ever agreed in the doctrine of liberty as well as in that of necessity, and that the whole dispute, in this respect also, has been hitherto merely verbal. For what is meant by liberty, when applied to voluntary actions? We cannot surely mean that actions have so little connexion with motives, inclinations, and circumstances, that one does not follow with a certain degree of uniformity from the other, and that one affords no inference by which we can conclude the existence of the other. For these are plain and acknowledged matters of fact. By liberty, then, we can only mean *a power of acting or not acting, according to the determinations of the will*; that is, if we choose to remain at rest, we may; if we choose to move, we also may. Now this hypothetical liberty is universally allowed to belong to every one who is not a prisoner and in chains. Here, then, is no subject of dispute.

[...]

It is universally allowed that nothing exists without a cause of its existence, and that chance, when strictly examined, is a mere negative word, and means not any real power which has anywhere a being in nature. [...] Had not objects a regular conjunction with each other, we should never have entertained any notion of cause and effect; and this regular conjunction produces that inference of the understanding, which is the only connexion, that we can have any comprehension of. [...] [L]iberty, when opposed to necessity, not to constraint, is the same thing with chance; which is universally allowed to have no existence.

Part II

[...]

The only proper object of hatred or vengeance is a person or creature, endowed with thought and consciousness; and when any criminal or injurious actions excite that passion, it is only by their relation to the person, or connexion with him. Actions are, by their very nature, temporary and perishing; and where they proceed not from some *cause* in the character and disposition of the person who performed them, they can neither redound to his honour, if good; nor infamy, if evil. The actions themselves may be blameable; they may be contrary to all the rules of morality and religion: But the person is not answerable for them; and as they proceeded from nothing in him that is durable and constant, and leave nothing of that nature behind them, it is impossible he can, upon their account, become the object of punishment or vengeance. According to the principle, therefore, which denies necessity, and consequently causes, a man is as pure and untainted, after having committed the most horrid crime, as at the first moment of his birth, nor is his character anywise concerned in his actions, since they are not derived from it, and the wickedness of the one can never be used as a proof of the depravity of the other.

[…]

It will be equally easy to prove, and from the same arguments, that *liberty*, according to that definition above mentioned, in which all men agree, is also essential to morality, and that no human actions, where it is wanting, are susceptible of any moral qualities, or can be the objects either of approbation or dislike. For as actions are objects of our moral sentiment, so far only as they are indications of the internal character, passions, and affections; it is impossible that they can give rise either to praise or blame, where they proceed not from these principles, but are derived altogether from external violence.

30

Would Being Entirely Caused Undermine Our Personally Constitutive Emotions?

P.F. Strawson, "Freedom and Resentment"

We have read David Hume, then, assuring us that our actions could proceed freely – on his conception of what it is to act freely – even if everything we do is caused by prior aspects of the world. In this reading, P.F. Strawson (whom we read earlier, in reading 4, on philosophy as the analyzing of key concepts) offers us further possible comfort: there is a literal sense in which we need not care whether we are wholly produced by the world's prior aspects. Even our having that background would not deprive us of the pivotal grounds on which we react *emotionally* to ourselves and to others – those grounds being the ones, moreover, that we may well have thought would be compromised by causal determinism.

After all, consider how we could be exhorted to be worried by the prospect of causal determinism's applying to all we do: "You are a mere plaything of an overarching or swamping causal history. Your actions come … well, not ultimately from you. Remember that you are simply a causal outcome of a distant and forgotten past." Should that encourage us to view you as never being a moral agent? Would you never be morally responsible for your actions (because you would not really be an autonomous person in causal control of your actions)?

Strawson directs us away from that pessimistic thinking. He highlights instead what he calls *reactive emotions* – love, resentment, gratitude, etc. Why are these so important? Well, without them, would we even be real persons in the first place? Imagine what your life would be without such emotions. *Can* you imagine that? So they matter greatly to us. And part of how they do so is their role in our accepting ourselves and others as being moral agents. When we think that someone has

P.F. Strawson, "Freedom and Resentment" [1962] (excerpts), in P.F. Strawson (ed.), *Studies in the Philosophy of Thought and Action* (London: Oxford University Press, 1968). Reprinted with permission of the British Academy.

acted insanely or compulsively, say, this affects our emotional reaction to him or her. But what would *not* affect our emotional reaction in such a way would be our learning that causal determinism is governing our lives. We would continue having feelings of caring, of respect, of moral disapproval, and the like. These are sufficient also for our regarding a person as being morally responsible for an action. We would not try to discover whether actions are causally determined, *before* regarding our- selves as right to have reactive emotions when assessing people's moral responsibil- ity for actions.

For Strawson, there is no fact to moral responsibility *beyond* the aptness of our reactive emotions. Thus, for him, whether causal determinism is true is irrelevant to whether we are morally responsible for our actions. Our being morally respon- sible for actions is nothing beyond our meriting various socially constituted and developed reactive emotions from others.

Some philosophers say they do not know what the thesis of determinism is. Others say, or imply, that they do know what it is. Of these, some – the pessimists perhaps – hold that if the thesis is true, then the concepts of moral obligation and responsibility really have no applica- tion, and the practices of punishing and blaming, of expressing moral condemnation and approval, are really unjustified. Others – the optimists perhaps – hold that these concepts and practices in no way lose their *raison d'être* if the thesis of determinism is true. Some hold even that the justification of these concepts and practices requires the truth of the thesis. There is another opinion which is less frequently voiced: the opinion, it might be said, of the genuine moral sceptic. This is that the notions of moral guilt, of blame, of moral responsibility are inherently confused and that we can see this to be so if we consider the consequences either of the truth of determinism or of its falsity. The holders of this opinion agree with the pes- simists that these notions lack application if determinism is true, and add simply that they also lack it if determinism is false.

  [...]

Let me enlarge very briefly on this, by way of preliminary only. Some optimists about determinism point to the efficacy of the practices of punishment, and of moral condemna- tion and approval, in regulating behaviour in socially desirable ways. In the fact of their efficacy, they suggest, is an adequate basis for these practices; and this fact certainly does not show determinism to be false. To this the pessimists reply, all in a rush, that *just* punishment and *moral* condemnation imply moral guilt and guilt implies moral responsibility and moral responsibility implies freedom and freedom implies the falsity of determinism. And to this the optimists are wont to reply in turn that it is true that these practices require freedom in a sense, and the existence of freedom in this sense is one of the facts as we know them. But what 'freedom' means here is nothing but the absence of certain conditions the presence of which would make moral condemnation or punishment inappropriate. They have in mind conditions like compulsion by another, or innate incapacity, or insanity, or other less extreme forms of psychological disorder, or the existence of circumstances in which the making of any other choice would be morally inadmissible or would be too much to expect of any man. To this list they are constrained to add other factors which, without exactly being limitations of freedom, may also make moral condemnation or punishment inappropriate or mitigate their force: as some forms of ignorance, mistake, or accident.

[...]

But [...] the pessimist may be supposed to ask: But *why* does freedom in this sense justify blame, etc.? You turn towards me first the negative, and then the positive, faces of a freedom which nobody challenges. But the only reason you have given for the practices of moral condemnation and punishment in cases where this freedom is present is the efficacy of these practices in regulating behaviour in socially desirable ways. But this is not a sufficient basis, it is not even the right *sort* of basis, for these practices as we understand them.

Now my optimist, being the sort of man he is, is not likely to invoke an intuition of fittingness at this point. So he really has no more to say. And my pessimist, being the sort of man he is, has only one more thing to say; and that is that the admissibility of these practices, as we understand them, demands another kind of freedom, the kind that in turn demands the falsity of the thesis of determinism. But might we not induce the pessimist to give up saying this by giving the optimist something more to say?

I have mentioned punishing and moral condemnation and approval; and it is in connection with these practices or attitudes that the issue between optimists and pessimists – or, if one is a pessimist, the issue between determinists and libertarians – is felt to be particularly important. But it is not of these practices and attitudes that I propose, at first, to speak. These practices or attitudes permit, where they do not imply, a certain detachment from the actions or agents which are their objects. I want to speak at least at first, of something else: of the non-detached attitudes and reactions of people directly involved in transactions with each other; of the attitudes and reactions of offended parties and beneficiaries; of such things as gratitude, resentment, forgiveness, love, and hurt feelings.

[...]

We should think of the many different kinds of relationship which we can have with other people – as sharers of a common interest; as members of the same family; as colleagues; as friends; as lovers; as chance parties to an enormous range of transactions and encounters. Then we should think, in each of these connections in turn, and in others, of the kind of importance we attach to the attitudes and intentions towards us of those who stand in these relationships to us, and of the kinds of *reactive* attitudes and feelings to which we ourselves are prone.

[...]

Let us consider, then, occasions for resentment: situations in which one person is offended or injured by the action of another and in which – in the absence of special considerations – the offended person might naturally or normally be expected to feel resentment. Then let us consider what sorts of special considerations might be expected to modify or mollify this feeling or remove it altogether. [...] To the first group belong all those which might give occasion for the employment of such expressions as 'He didn't mean to', 'He hadn't realized', 'He didn't know'; and also all those which might give occasion for the use of the phrase 'He couldn't help it', when this is supported by such phrases as 'He was pushed', 'He had to do it', 'It was the only way', 'They left him no alternative', etc. [...] None of them invites us to suspend towards the agent, either at the time of his action or in general, our ordinary reactive attitudes. They do not invite us to view the *agent* as one in respect of whom these attitudes are in any way inappropriate. They invite us to view the *injury* as one in respect of which a particular one of these attitudes is inappropriate. They do not invite us to see the *agent* as other than a fully responsible agent. [...]

The second and more important subgroup of cases allows that the circumstances were normal, but presents the agent as psychologically abnormal – or as morally undeveloped. The agent was himself; but he is warped or deranged, neurotic or just a child. When we see someone in such a light as this, all our reactive attitudes tend to be profoundly modified. [...] What I want to contrast is the attitude (or range of attitudes) of involvement or participation in a human relationship, on the one hand, and what might be called the objective attitude (or range of attitudes) to another human being, on the other. [...] To adopt the objective attitude to another human being is to see him, perhaps, as an object of social policy; as a subject for what, in a wide range of sense, might be called treatment; as something certainly to be taken account, perhaps precautionary account, of; to be managed or handled or cured or trained. [...] The objective attitude [...] may include pity or even love, though not all kinds of love. But it cannot include the range of reactive feelings and attitudes which belong to involvement or participation with others in inter-personal human relationships; it cannot include resentment, gratitude, forgiveness, anger, or the sort of love which two adults can sometimes be said to feel reciprocally, for each other. [...]

Seeing someone, then, as warped or deranged or compulsive in behavior or peculiarly unfortunate in his formative circumstances – seeing someone so tends [...] to set him apart from normal participant reactive attitudes. [...] But what is above all interesting is the tension there is, in us, between the participant attitude and the objective attitude. One is tempted to say: between our humanity and our intelligence. But to say this would be to distort both notions.

What I have called the participant reactive attitudes are essentially natural human reactions to the good or ill will or indifference of others towards us, as displayed in *their* attitudes and actions. The question we have to ask is: What effect would, or should, the acceptance of the truth of a general thesis of determinism have upon these reactive attitudes? More specifically, would, or should, the acceptance of the truth of the thesis lead to the decay or the repudiation of all such attitudes? Would, or should, it mean the end of gratitude, resentment, and forgiveness; of all reciprocated adult loves; of all the essentially *personal* antagonisms ?
[...]

It does not seem to be self-contradictory to suppose that this might happen. So I suppose we must say that it is not absolutely inconceivable that it should happen. But I am strongly inclined to think that it is, for us as we are, practically inconceivable. The human commitment to participation in ordinary inter-personal relationships is, I think, too thoroughgoing and deeply rooted for us to take seriously the thought that a general theoretical conviction might so change our world that, in it, there were no longer any such things as inter-personal relationships as we normally understand them; and being involved in inter-personal relationships as we normally understand them precisely is being exposed to the range of reactive attitudes and feelings that is in question.
[...]

It might be said that all this leaves the real question unanswered. [...] For the real question is not a question about what we actually do, or why we do it. [...] It is a question about what it would be *rational* to do if determinism were true, a question about the rational justification of ordinary inter-personal attitudes in general. To this I shall reply, first, that such a question could seem real only to one who had utterly failed to grasp the purport of the preceding answer, the fact of our natural human commitment to ordinary inter-personal attitudes. This commitment is part of the general framework of human life, not something that can come up for review as particular cases can come up for review within this general framework. And I shall reply, second, that if we could imagine what we cannot have, viz. a choice in this matter, then we could choose rationally only in the light of an assessment of the gains and losses to human life, its enrichment or impoverishment; and the truth or falsity of a general thesis of determinism would not bear on the rationality of *this* choice.[1]

[…]

[…] The personal reactive attitudes rest on, and reflect, an expectation of, and demand for, the manifestation of a certain degree of goodwill or regard on the part of other human beings towards ourselves; or at least on the expectation of, and demand for, an absence of the manifestation of active ill will or indifferent disregard. […] The generalized or vicarious analogues of the personal reactive attitudes rest on, and reflect, exactly the same expectation or demand in a generalized form; they rest on, or reflect, that is, the demand for the manifestation of a reasonable degree of good will or regard, on the part of others, not simply towards oneself, but towards all those on whose behalf moral indignation may be felt, i.e., as we now think towards all men. […] [T]here are [also] self-reactive attitudes associated with demands on oneself for others. And here we have to mention such phenomena as feeling bound or obliged (the 'sense of obligation'); feeling compunction; feeling guilty or remorseful or at least responsible; and the more complicated phenomenon of shame.

All these three types of attitudes are humanly connected. One who manifested the personal reactive attitudes in a high degree but showed no inclination at all to their vicarious analogues would appear as an abnormal case of moral egocentricity, as a kind of moral solipsist.

[…]

[…] What concerns us now is to inquire, as previously in connection with the personal reactive attitudes, what relevance any general thesis of determinism might have to their vicarious analogues. The answers once more are parallel. […] First, […] as before, […] when the suspension of such an attitude or such attitudes occurs in a particular case, it is *never* the consequence of the belief that the piece of behavior in question was determined in a sense such that all behavior *might be*, and, if determinism is true, all behavior *is*, determined in that sense. For it is not a consequence of any general thesis of determinism which might be true that nobody knows what he's doing or that everybody's behavior is unintelligible in terms of conscious purposes or that everybody lives in a world of delusion or that nobody has a moral sense, i.e. is susceptible of self-reactive attitudes, etc. In fact no such sense of 'determined' as would be required for a general thesis of determinism is ever relevant to our actual suspensions of moral reactive attitudes. Second, suppose it granted, as I have already argued, that we cannot take seriously the thought that theoretical conviction of such a general thesis would lead to the total decay of the personal reactive attitudes. Can we then take seriously the thought that such a conviction – a conviction, after all, that may have held or said they held – would nevertheless lead to the total decay or repudiation of the vicarious analogues of these attitudes? I think that the change in our social world which would leave us exposed to the personal reactive attitudes but not at all to their vicarious analogues, the generalization of abnormal egocentricity which this would entail, is perhaps even harder for us to envisage as a real possibility than the decay of both kinds of attitude together. [...] Finally, to the further question whether it would not be *rational*, given a general theoretical conviction of the truth of determinism, so to change our world that in it all these attitudes were wholly suspended, I must answer, as before, that [...] it is *useless* to ask whether it would not be rational for us to do what it is not in our nature to (be able to) do. To this I must add, as before, that if there were, say, for a moment open to us the possibility of such a god-like choice, the rationality of making or refusing it would be determined by quite other considerations than the truth or falsity of the general theoretical doctrine in question. The latter would be simply irrelevant; and this becomes ironically clear when we remember that for those convinced that the truth of determinism nevertheless really would make the one choice rational, there has always been the insuperable difficulty of explaining in intelligible terms how its falsity would make the opposite choice rational.

[...]

And now we can try to fill in the lacuna which the pessimist finds in the optimist's account of the concept of moral responsibility, and of the bases of moral condemnation and punishment. [...]

[...] When [...] the optimist undertakes to show that the truth of determinism would not shake the foundations of the concept of moral responsibility and of the practices of moral condemnation and punishment, he typically refers, in a more or less elaborated way, to the efficacy of these practices in regulating behavior in socially desirable ways. These practices are represented solely as instruments of policy, as methods of individual treatment and social control. The pessimist recoils from this picture; and in his recoil there is, typically, an element of emotional shock. He is apt to say, among much else, that the humanity of the offender himself is offended by *this* picture of his condemnation and punishment.

The reasons for this recoil – the explanation of the sense of an emotional, as well as a conceptual, shock – we have already before us. The picture painted by the optimists is painted in a style appropriate to a situation envisaged as wholly dominated by objectivity of attitude. The only operative notions invoked in this picture are such as those of policy, treatment, control. But a thoroughgoing objectivity of attitude, excluding as it does the moral reactive attitudes, excludes at the same time essential elements in the concepts of *moral* condemnation and *moral* responsibility. This is the reason for the conceptual shock. The deeper emotional shock is a reaction, not simply to an inadequate conceptual analysis, but to the suggestion of a change in our world. I have remarked that it is possible to cultivate an exclusive objectivity of attitude in some cases, and for some reasons, where the object of the attitude is not set aside from developed inter-personal and moral attitudes by immaturity or abnormality. And the suggestion which seems to be contained in the optimist's account is that such an attitude should be universally adopted to all offenders. This is shocking enough in the pessimist's eyes. But, sharpened by shock, his eyes see further. It would be hard to make *this* division in our natures. If to all offenders, then to all mankind.

[...] What is in question is the pessimist's justified sense that to speak in terms of social utility alone is to leave out something vital in our conception of these practices. The vital thing can be restored by attending to that complicated web of attitudes and feelings which form an essential part of the moral life as we know it, and which are quite opposed to objectivity of attitude. Only by attending to this range of attitudes can we recover from the facts as we know them a sense of what we mean, i.e. of *all* we mean, when, speaking the language of morals, we speak of desert, responsibility, guilt, condemnation, and justice. But we *do* recover it from the facts as we know them. We do not have to go beyond them. Because the optimist neglects or misconstrues these attitudes, the pessimist rightly claims to find a lacuna in his account. We can fill the lacuna for him. But in return we must demand of the pessimist a surrender of his metaphysics.

Optimist and pessimist misconstrue the facts in very different styles. But in a profound sense there is something in common to their misunderstandings. Both seek, in different ways, to over-intellectualize the facts. Inside the general structure or web of human attitudes and feelings [...] there is endless room for modification, redirection, criticism, and justification. But questions of justification are internal to the structure or relate to modifications internal to it. The existence of the general framework of attitudes itself is something we are given with the fact of human society. As a whole, it neither calls for, nor permits, an external 'rational' justification. Pessimist and optimist alike show themselves, in different ways, unable to accept this. The optimist's style of over-intellectualizing the facts is that of a characteristically incomplete empiricism, a one-eyed utilitarianism. He seeks to find an adequate basis for certain social practices in calculated consequences, and loses sight (perhaps wishes to lose sight) of the human attitudes of which these practices are, in part, the expression. The pessimist does not lose sight of these attitudes, but is unable to accept the fact that it is just these attitudes themselves which fill the gap in the optimist's account. Because of this, he thinks the gap can be filled only if some general metaphysical proposition is repeatedly verified, verified in all cases where it is appropriate to attribute moral responsibility. [...]

[...] It is a pity that talk of the moral sentiments has fallen out of favour. The phrase would be quite a good name for that network of human attitudes in acknowledging the character and place of which we find, I suggest, the only possibility of reconciling these disputants to each other and the facts.

Note

---

1. The question, then, of the connection between rationality and the adoption of the objective attitude to others is misposed when it is made to seem dependent on the issue of determinism. But there is another question which should be raised, if only to distinguish it from the misposed question. Quite apart from the issue of determinism, might it not be said that we should be nearer to being purely rational creatures in proportion as our relation to others was in fact dominated by the objective attitude? I think this might be said; only it would have to be added, once more, that if such a choice were possible, it would not necessarily be rational to choose to be more purely rational than we are.

31

Is a Person Morally Responsible
Only for Actions Performed
Freely?

Harry G. Frankfurt, "Alternate Possibilities
and Moral Responsibility"

Strawson, we saw in the previous reading, wondered whether causal determinism, even if true, would really restrict our being morally responsible for our actions – our being moral agents within our lives as these take active shape. Strawson argued that we are not so restricted, because being morally responsible is reflective more of our socially attuned emotional lives. But philosophers have continued to worry about the metaphysics of free will, causal determinism, and moral responsibility. Could the underlying fact of whether all of our actions are causally determined be a fact that leaves those actions as ones for which we bear no moral responsibility? If our actions are causally determined, does the world thereby make it inappropriate for us ever to be either blamed or praised for an action? Harry Frankfurt (b. 1929), a philosopher whose later career was at Princeton University, has influenced recent thinking about this issue. This excerpt is from one of his most significant papers.

   Why have people so often felt that causal determinism, if true, would actually leave our actions as outcomes for which we are not morally responsible? Probably the most traditional answer has been that if causal determinism is true, none of our actions are performed freely. We are then told that a person can only ever be morally responsible for a freely performed action. (It is possible to *feel* as if one is morally responsible for an action anyway. Really, though, there is no moral responsibility for an action that is not *actually* freely performed.) What is it for an action to be free? Hume gave us one answer (namely, that the action is the one *chosen* to be performed). Frankfurt discusses a different possible explanation for an action's

Harry G. Frankfurt, "Alternate Possibilities and Moral Responsibility" [1969] (excerpts), in *The Importance of What We Care About* (Cambridge: Cambridge University Press, 1988).

Metaphysics and Epistemology: A Guided Anthology, First Edition. Edited by Stephen Hetherington.

being free. He asks whether there was a possibility, in the circumstances, of the person's *not* doing what in fact she did. Part of your freely hitting your friend, for instance, is the fact that (even given all else about your circumstance until that moment) you might not have thrown that punch. This possibility is also part of your being *morally responsible* for hitting your friend: you did not have to throw that punch, even given whatever had occurred until that unfortunate moment.

But that is also the supposed link being questioned by Frankfurt: does moral responsibility need that possibility of that sort of freedom? Frankfurt created four hypothetical cases involving Jones. This reading includes two of them: about Jones$_3$ and Jones$_4$. Pay particular attention to the case of Jones$_4$ and Black, because it has attracted so much metaphysical discussion. (These days, kindred cases are generally called Frankfurt-style cases.) Frankfurt's aim was to describe a possible kind of situation where someone is morally responsible for an action she performs, even though (in the circumstances) it was not possible for her not to have performed it. In that sense, she had no freedom in acting as she did; still, she would remain morally responsible for her action.

What would this show about causal determinism and our actions? Frankfurt suggests a way in which causal determinism need *not* be conceived of as depriving us of all moral responsibility for them. This would allow us to be moral agents even in a causally determined world.

A dominant role in nearly all recent inquiries into the free-will problem has been played by a principle which I shall call "the principle of alternate possibilities." This principle states that a person is morally responsible for what he has done only if he could have done otherwise. Its exact meaning is a subject of controversy, particularly concerning whether someone who accepts it is thereby committed to believing that moral responsibility and determinism are incompatible. Practically no one, however, seems inclined to deny or even to question that the principle of alternate possibilities (construed in some way or other) is true. [...]

But the principle of alternate possibilities is false. A person may well be morally responsible for what he has done even though he could not have done otherwise. The principle's plausibility is an illusion, which can be made to vanish by bringing the relevant moral phenomena into sharper focus. [...]

Let us suppose that someone is threatened convincingly with a penalty he finds unacceptable and that he then does what is required of him by the issuer of the threat. We can imagine details that would make it reasonable for us to think that the person was coerced to perform the action in question, that he could not have done otherwise, and that he bears no moral responsibility for having done what he did. But just what is it about situations of this kind that warrants the judgment that the threatened person is not morally responsible for his act?

This question may be approached by considering situations of the following kind. Jones decided for reasons of his own to do something, then someone threatens him with a very harsh penalty (so harsh that any reasonable person would submit to the threat) unless he does precisely that, and Jones does it. Will we hold Jones morally responsible for what he has done? I think this will depend on the roles we think were played, in leading him to act, by his original decision and by the threat.

[…]

[...] [C]onsider a [...] possibility. $Jones_3$ was not stampeded by the threat nor indifferent to it. The threat impressed him, as it would impress any reasonable man, and he would have submitted to it wholeheartedly if he had not already made a decision that coincided with the one demanded of him. In fact, however, he performed the action in question on the basis of the decision he had made before the threat was issued. When he acted, he was not actually motivated by the threat but solely by the considerations that had originally commended the action to him. It was not the threat that led him to act, though it would have done so if he had not already provided himself with a sufficient motive for performing the action in question.

[…]

The following objection will doubtless be raised against the suggestion that the case of $Jones_3$ is a counterexample to the principle of alternate possibilities. There is perhaps a sense in which $Jones_3$ cannot do otherwise than perform the action he performs, since he is a reasonable man and the threat he encounters is sufficient to move any reasonable man. But it is not this sense that is germane to the principle of alternate possibilities. His knowledge that he stands to suffer an intolerably harsh penalty does not mean that $Jones_3$, strictly speaking, *cannot* perform any action but the one he does perform. After all it is still open to him, and this is crucial, to defy the threat if he wishes to do so and to accept the penalty his action would bring down upon him. [...] Hence the case of $Jones_3$ does not constitute an instance contrary to the principle.

[...] I believe that whatever force this objection may be thought to have can be deflected by altering the example in the following way. Suppose someone – Black, let us say – wants $Jones_4$ to perform a certain action. Black is prepared to go to considerable lengths to get his way, but he prefers to avoid showing his hand unnecessarily. So he waits until $Jones_4$ is about to make up his mind what to do, and he does nothing unless it is clear to him (Black is an excellent judge of such things) that $Jones_4$ is going to decide to do something *other* than what he wants him to do. If it does become clear that $Jones_4$ is going to decide to do something else, Black takes effective steps to ensure that $Jones_4$ decides to do, and that he does do, what he wants him to do.[1] Whatever $Jones_4$'s initial preferences and inclinations, then, Black will have his way.

What steps will Black take, if he believes he must take steps, in order to ensure that $Jones_4$ decides and acts as he wishes? [...] Let Black give $Jones_4$ a potion, or put him under hypnosis, and in some such way as these generate in $Jones_4$ an irresistible inner compulsion to perform the act Black wants performed and to avoid others. Or let Black manipulate the minute processes of $Jones_4$'s brain and nervous system in some more direct way, so that casual forces running in and out of his synapses and along the poor man's nerves determine that he chooses to act and that he does act in the one way and not in any other. Given any conditions under which it will be maintained that $Jones_4$ cannot do otherwise, in other words, let Black bring it about that those conditions prevail. [...]

Now suppose that Black never has to show his hand because $Jones_4$, for reasons of his own, decides to perform and does perform the very action Black wants him to perform. In that case, it seems clear, $Jones_4$ will bear precisely the same moral responsibility for what he does as he would have borne if Black had not been ready to take steps to ensure that he do it. It would be quite unreasonable to excuse Jones$_4$ for his action, or to withhold the praise to which it would normally entitle him, on the basis of the fact that he could not have done otherwise. This fact played no role at all in leading him to act as he did. He would have acted the same even if it had not been a fact. Indeed, everything happened just as it would have happened without Black's presence in the situation and without his readiness to intrude into it.

[...]

The fact that a person could not have avoided doing something is a sufficient condition of his having done it. But, as some of my examples show, this fact may play no role whatever in the explanation of why he did it. It may not figure at all among the circumstances that actually brought it about that he did what he did, so that his action is to be accounted for on another basis entirely. Even though the person was unable to do otherwise, that is to say, it may not be the case that he acted as he did *because* he could not have done otherwise. [...]

[...] When a fact is in this way irrelevant to the problem of accounting for a person's action it seems quite gratuitous to assign it any weight in the assessment of his moral responsibility. Why should the fact be considered in reaching a moral judgment concerning the person when it does not help in any way to understand either what made him act as he did or what, in other circumstances, he might have done?

This, then, is why the principle of alternate possibilities is mistaken. It asserts that a person bears no moral responsibility – that is, he is to be excused – for having performed an action, if there were circumstances that made it impossible for him to avoid performing it. But there may be circumstances that make it impossible for a person to avoid performing some action without those circumstances in any way bringing it about that he performs that action. It would surely be no good for the person to refer to circumstances of this sort in an effort to absolve himself of moral responsibility for performing the action in question. For those circumstances, by hypothesis, actually had nothing to do with his having done what he did. He would have done precisely the same thing, and he would have been led or made in precisely the same way to do it, even if they had not prevailed.

We often do, to be sure, excuse people for what they have done when they tell us (and we believe them) that they could not have done otherwise. But this is because we assume that what they tell us serves to explain why they did what they did. [...]

What I have said may suggest that the principle of alternate possibilities should be revised so as to assert that a person is not morally responsible for what he has done if he did it because he could not have done otherwise. It may be noted that this revision of the principle does not seriously affect the arguments of those who have relied on the original principle in their efforts to maintain that moral responsibility and determinism are incompatible. For if it was causally determined that a person perform a certain action, then it will be true that the person performed it because of those causal determinants. And if the fact that it was causally determined that a person perform a certain action means that the person could not have done otherwise, as philosophers who argue for the incompatibility thesis characteristically suppose, then the fact that it was causally determined that a person perform a certain action will mean that the person performed it because he could not have done otherwise. The revised principle of alternate possibilities will entail, on this assumption concerning the meaning of "could have done otherwise," that a person is not morally responsible for what he has done if it was causally determined that he do it. I do not believe, however, that this revision of the principle is acceptable.

Suppose a person tells us that he did what he did because he was unable to do otherwise; or suppose he makes the similar statement that he did what he did because he had to do it. We do often accept statements like these (if we believe them) as valid excuses, and such statements may well seem at first glance to invoke the revised principle of alternate possibilities. But I think that when we accept such statements as valid excuses it is because we assume that we are being told more than the statements strictly and literally convey. We understand the person who offers the excuse to mean that he did what he did *only because* he was unable to do otherwise, or *only because* he had to do it. And we understand him to mean, more particularly, that when he did what he did it was not because that was what he really wanted to do. The principle of alternate possibilities should thus be replaced, in my opinion, by the following principle: a person is not morally responsible for what he has done if he did it only because he could not have done otherwise. This principle does not appear to conflict with the view that moral responsibility is compatible with determinism.

The following may all be true: there were circumstances that made it impossible for a person to avoid doing something; these circumstances actually played a role in bringing it about that he did it, so that it is correct to say that he did it because he could not have done otherwise; the person really wanted to do what he did; he did it because it was what he really wanted to do, so that it is not correct to say that he did what he did only because he could not have done otherwise. Under these conditions, the person may well be morally responsible for what he has done. On the other hand, he will not be morally responsible for what he has done if he did it only because he could not have done otherwise, even if what he did was something he really wanted to do.

Note

1. The assumption that Black can predict what Jones$_4$ will decide to do does not beg the question of determinism. We can imagine that Jones$_4$ has often confronted the alternative – A and B – that he now confronts, and that his face has invariably twitched when he was about to decide to do A and never when he was about to decide to do B. Knowing this, and observing the twitch, Black would have a basis for prediction. This does, to be sure, suppose that there is some sort of causal relation between Jones$_4$'s state at the time of the twitch and his subsequent states. But any plausible view of decision or of action will allow that reaching a decision and performing an action both involve earlier and later phases, with causal relations between them, and such that the earlier phases are not themselves part of the decision or of the action. The example does not require that these earlier phases be deterministically related to still earlier events.

32

Is Moral Responsibility for a Good Action Different to Moral Responsibility for a Bad Action?

Susan Wolf, "Asymmetrical Freedom"

A striking feature of metaphysical accounts of free will and moral responsibility is that *reprehensible* actions tend to have received the attention: "He kicked that kitten. How awful! And no one made him do it. Only he is morally responsible for the animal's suffering." Is that why (as the reading from Frankfurt exemplified) so much focus has been directed at the question of when it is possible for an action *not* to have been performed? After all, most of us would prefer that bad actions not be performed; and many of us would say that it is unfair to blame a person for a bad action she could not have avoided doing. (Remember, from Strawson's reading on moral responsibility, how important emotions might be within this debate.) Then we confront the thought that, if causal determinism is true, *no* actions we perform – including the morally bad ones – are actions we could have avoided performing.

But this reading – from Susan Wolf (b. 1952), a prominent philosopher at the University of North Carolina, Chapel Hill – argues for a substantial modification of that metaphysical debate. If she is right, we need to enrich our conceptual repertoire. Picture someone performing an action of marked moral merit. Imagine her performing the action because she *had* to do so. But suppose that this is not because someone forces her, say, to rescue the kitten from the kicker. Rather, the rescuer had no choice, none at all, given her *character* – her desires, beliefs, instincts, etc. These are what "made her" perform the morally excellent action. Would we (asks Wolf, rhetorically) deny that the person is morally responsible for this praiseworthy action, when her character left her with no alternative to acting in this way?

Wolf argues that in this respect acting well is quite different to acting badly. Whenever one is morally responsible for a morally good action, in part this is

Susan Wolf, "Asymmetrical Freedom" (excerpts), *The Journal of Philosophy* 77 (1980), 151–166. Reprinted with permission of the Journal and the author.

because one *has* been made to do it – by morally good reasons and by how one reacts when presented with such reasons. In contrast, whenever one is morally responsible for a morally bad action, in part this is because one has been able *not* to do it – because one was at least able, however, to have been responsive to morally good reasons (even though one's responding to these was not what actually made one perform the action).

So, if Wolf is right then ascertaining a person's moral responsibility for an action is not only about the metaphysics of what possibilities the world left open for the person. Also significant is the *moral* nature of the action. Wolf regards this result as showing that the issue is not as purely metaphysical as it has traditionally been conceived to be. But might Wolf's thinking have an alternative metaphysical use? When conceiving of the relationship between free will and moral responsibility, should we include moral values within our metaphysical image of the world? Should we regard moral values as real, as genuine components of the world? In an earlier section ("How Do Things Ever Have Qualities?", readings 13 and 14), we wondered whether the world is best thought of as including abstract and repeatable universals. Now we are asking whether it encompasses moral values. Unifying all this is the question of what – and how much – to include in our underlying metaphysical images of reality.

In order for a person to be morally responsible, two conditions must be satisfied. First, he must be a free agent – an agent, that is, whose actions are under his own control. For if the actions he performs are not up to him to decide, he deserves no credit or discredit for doing what he does. Second, he must be a moral agent – an agent, that is, to whom moral claims apply. For if the actions he performs can be neither right nor wrong, then there is nothing to credit or discredit him with. I shall call the first condition, *the condition of freedom*, and the second, *the condition of value*. Those who fear that the first condition can never be met worry about the problem of free will. Those who fear that the second condition can never be met worry about the problem of moral skepticism. Many people believe that the condition of value is dependent on the condition of freedom – that moral prescriptions make sense only if the concept of free will is coherent. In what follows, I shall argue that the converse is true – that the condition of freedom depends on the condition of value. Our doubts about the existence of true moral values, however, will have to be left aside.

I shall say that an agent's action is *psychologically determined* if his action is determined by his interests – that is, his values or desires – and his interests are determined by his heredity or environment. If all our actions are so determined, then the thesis of psychological determinism is true. This description is admittedly crude and simplistic. A more plausible description of psychological determination will include among possible determining factors a wider range of psychological states. There are, for example, some beliefs and emotions which cannot be analyzed as values or desires and which clearly play a role in the psychological explanations of why we act as we do. For my purposes, however, it will be easier to leave the description of psychological determinism uncluttered. The context should be sufficient to make the intended application understood.

Many people believe that if psychological determinism is true, the condition of freedom can never be satisfied. For if an agent's interests are determined by heredity and environment, they claim, it is not up to the agent to have the interests he has. And if his actions are determined by his interests as well, then he cannot but perform the actions he performs. In order for an agent to satisfy the condition of freedom, then, his actions must not be psychologically determined. Either his actions must not be determined by his interests, or his interests must not be determined by anything external to himself. They therefore conclude that the condition of freedom requires the absence of psychological determinism. And they think this is what we mean to express when we state the condition of freedom in terms of the requirement that the agent "could have done otherwise".

[...] There is an asymmetry in our intuitions about freedom which has generally been overlooked. As a result, it has seemed that the answer to the problem of free will can lie in only one of two alternatives: Either the fact that an agent's action was determined is always compatible with his being responsible for it, or the fact that the agent's action was determined will always rule his responsibility out. I shall suggest that the solution lies elsewhere – that both compatibilists and incompatibilists are wrong. What we need in order to be responsible beings, I shall argue, is a suitable combination of determination and indetermination.

When we try to call up our intuitions about freedom, a few stock cases come readily to mind. We think of the heroin addict and the kleptomaniac, of the victim of hypnosis, and the victim of a deprived childhood. These cases, I think, provide forceful support for our incompatibilist intuitions. For of the kleptomaniac it may well be true that he would have done otherwise if he had tried. The kleptomaniac is not responsible because he could not have tried. Of the victim of hypnosis it may well be true that he would have done otherwise if he had chosen. The victim of hypnosis is not responsible because he could not have chosen.

The victim of the deprived childhood who, say, embezzles some money, provides the most poignant example of all. For this agent is not coerced nor overcome by an irresistible impulse. He is in complete possession of normal adult faculties of reason and observation. He seems, indeed, to have as much control over his behavior as we have of ours. He acts on the basis of his choice, and he chooses on the basis of his reasons. If there is any explanation of why this agent is not responsible, it would seem that it must consist simply in the fact that his reasons are determined.

These examples are all peculiar, however, in that they are examples of people doing bad things. If the agents in these cases were responsible for their actions, this would justify the claim that they deserve to be blamed. We seldom look, on the other hand, at examples of agents whose actions are morally good. We rarely ask whether an agent is truly responsible if his being responsible would make him worthy of praise.

[...]

When we ask whether an agent's action is deserving of praise, it seems we do not require that he could have done otherwise. If an agent does the right thing for just the right reasons, it seems absurd to ask whether he could have done the wrong. "I cannot tell a lie," "He couldn't hurt a fly" are not exemptions from praiseworthiness but testimonies to it. If a friend presents you with a gift and says "I couldn't resist," this suggests the strength of his friendship and not the weakness of his will. If one feels one "has no choice" but to speak out against injustice, one ought not to be upset about the depth of one's commitment. And it seems I should be grateful for the fact that if I were in trouble, my family "could not help" but come to my aid.

Of course, these phrases must be given an appropriate interpretation if they are to indicate that the agent is deserving of praise. "He couldn't hurt a fly" must allude to someone's gentleness – it would be perverse to say this of someone who was in an iron lung. It is not admirable in George Washington that he cannot tell a lie, if it is because he has a tendency to stutter that inhibits his attempts. 'He could not have done otherwise' as it is used in the context of praise, then, must be taken to imply something like 'because he was too good'. An action is praiseworthy only if it is done for the right reasons. So it must be only in light of and because of these reasons that the praiseworthy agent "could not help" but do the right thing.

But when an agent does the right thing for the right reasons, the fact that, having the right reasons, he *must* do the right should surely not lessen the credit he deserves. For presumably the reason he cannot do otherwise is that his virtue is so sure or his moral commitment so strong.

[…]

So it seems that an agent can be morally praiseworthy even though he is determined to perform the action he performs. But we have already seen that an agent cannot be morally blameworthy if he is determined to perform the action he performs. Determination, then, is compatible with an agent's responsibility for a good action, but incompatible with an agent's responsibility for a bad action. The metaphysical conditions required for an agent's responsibility will vary according to the value of the action he performs.

The condition of freedom, as it is expressed by the requirement that an agent could have done otherwise, thus appears to demand a conditional analysis after all. But the condition must be one that separates the good actions from the bad – the condition, that is, must be essentially value-laden. An analysis of the condition of freedom that might do the trick is:

> He could have done otherwise if there had been good and sufficient reason.

where the 'could have done otherwise' […] is not a conditional at all. For presumably an action is morally praiseworthy only if there are no good and sufficient reasons to do something else. And an action is morally blameworthy only if there are good and sufficient reasons to do something else. Thus, when an agent performs a good action, the condition of freedom is a counterfactual: though it is required that the agent would have been able to do otherwise *had there been* good and sufficient reason to do so, the situation in which the good-acting agent actually found himself is a situation in which there was no such reason. Thus, it is compatible with the satisfaction of the condition of freedom that the agent in this case could not actually have done other than what he actually did. When an agent performs a bad action, however, the condition of freedom is not a counterfactual. The bad-acting agent does what he does in the face of good and sufficient reasons to do otherwise. Thus the condition of freedom requires that the agent in this case could have done otherwise in just the situation in which he was actually placed. An agent, then, can be determined to perform a good action and still be morally praiseworthy. But if an agent is to be blameworthy, he must unconditionally have been able to do something else.

It may be easier to see how this analysis works, and how it differs from conditional analyses that were suggested before, if we turn back to the case in which these previous analyses failed – namely, the case of the victim of a deprived childhood.

We imagined a case, in particular, of a man who embezzled some money, fully aware of what he was doing. He was neither coerced nor overcome by an irresistible impulse, and he was in complete possession of normal adult faculties of reason and observation. Yet it seems he ought not to be blamed for committing his crime, for, from his point of view, one cannot reasonably expect him to see anything wrong with his action. We may suppose that in his childhood he was given no love – he was beaten by his father, neglected by his mother. And that the people to whom he was exposed when he was growing up gave him examples only of evil and selfishness. From his point of view, it is natural to conclude that respecting other people's property would be foolish. For presumably no one had ever respected his. And it is natural for him to feel that he should treat other people as adversaries.

In light of this, it seems that this man shouldn't be blamed for an action we know to be wrong. For if we had had his childhood, we wouldn't have known it either. Yet this agent seems to have as much control over his life as we are apt to have over ours: he would have done otherwise, if he had tried. He would have tried to do otherwise, if he had chosen. And he would have chosen to do otherwise, if he had had reason. It is because he couldn't have had reason that this agent should not be blamed.

[...]

[...] [H]e, unlike us, could not have had reasons even though there were reasons around. The problem is not that his reason was functioning improperly, but that his data were unfortuitously selective. Since the world for him was not suitably cooperating, his reason cannot attain its appropriate goal.

The goal, to put it bluntly, is the True and the Good. The freedom we want is the freedom to find it. But such a freedom requires not only that we, as agents, have the right sorts of abilities – the abilities, that is, to direct and govern our actions by our most fundamental selves. It requires as well that the world cooperate in such a way that our most fundamental selves have the opportunity to develop into the selves they ought to be.

If the freedom necessary for moral responsibility is the freedom to be determined by the True and the Good, then obviously we cannot know whether we have such a freedom unless we know, on the one hand, that there *is* a True and a Good and, on the other, that there *are* capacities for finding them. As a consequence of this, the condition of freedom cannot be stated in purely metaphysical terms. For we cannot know which capacities and circumstances are necessary for freedom unless we know which capacities and circumstances will enable us to form the *right* values and perform the *right* actions. Strictly speaking, I take it, the capacity to reason is not enough – we need a kind of sensibility and perception as well. But these are capacities, I assume, that most of us have. So when the world cooperates, we are morally responsible.

I have already said that the condition of freedom cannot be stated in purely metaphysical terms. More specifically, the condition of freedom cannot be stated in terms that are value-free. Thus, the problem of free will has been misrepresented insofar as it has been thought to be a purely metaphysical problem. And, perhaps, this is why the problem of free will has seemed for so long to be hopeless.

That the problem should have seemed to be a purely metaphysical problem is not, however, unnatural or surprising. For being determined by the True and the Good is very different from being determined by one's garden variety of causes, and I think it not unnatural to feel as if one rules out the other. For to be determined by the Good is not to be determined by the Past.

[...]

[...] We need the freedom *to* have our actions determined by the Good, and the freedom to be or to become the sorts of persons whose actions will continue to be so determined.

How Could a Person Be Harmed by Being Dead?

33

Is It Impossible To Be Harmed by Being Dead?

Epicurus, "Letter to Menoeceus"

Maybe each person's bodily death is the end of her being; maybe not. That metaphysical issue is not discussed directly in this book. (But indirectly it has arisen earlier, in the section "How Are Persons Persons?", readings 23 to 27.) Still, we may discuss directly the question of whether, *if* bodily death is the ending of a person's life, her being dead can literally be harmful for her. Some care is needed in formulating that question. It is not asking whether a painful death can harm the one who dies: *of course* harm can be caused by a death like that, since pain is generally unwelcome. Nor is the question about the effect upon someone still living who cared about the deceased person: again, *of course* such harm might eventuate. No, the question is simply this. If a person dies instantly with no pain and without

Epicurus, "Letter to Menoeceus" (excerpt), in *Hellenistic Philosophy: Introductory Readings*, 2nd edn., trans. B. Inwood and L.P. Gerson (Indianapolis: Hackett, 1997). Reprinted with permission of Hackett Publishing Company Inc.

having had any indication that her death was imminent, can this be harmful for her? Can it be bad for one to *be* dead?

In recent years, there has been much metaphysical discussion of this topic. The present reading contains a succinct piece of pertinent reasoning – in fact, the argument that continues to be regarded as the key argument with which we must engage, particularly if we believe that being dead *can* be bad for one. This reading comes from a letter written by the influential ancient Greek philosopher Epicurus (341–270 BC). His main aim was to allay the *fear* of death – not the fear of dying painfully, say; but the fear of *being* dead. On Epicurus' way of thinking, this is the fear, in effect, of *not existing*. At most (given our coming to this issue as the existing beings we happen presently to be), it is the fear of not existing, given our *having existed*.

Yet the fear is rationally groundless, according to Epicurus. Once a person is dead, she cannot experience anything, because ultimately all experience is sensory. And once a person cannot experience anything, she cannot be harmed, because ultimately all harm is experiential. So, live well; and one element in doing so should be your lacking all fear of your no longer being alive. This is Epicurus' advice, at any rate.

124. [...] Get used to believing that death is nothing to us. For all good and bad consists in sense-experience, and death is the privation of sense-experience. Hence, a correct knowledge of the fact that death is nothing to us makes the mortality of life a matter for contentment, not by adding a limitless time [to life] but by removing the longing for immortality. **125.** For there is nothing fearful in life for one who has grasped that there is nothing fearful in the absence of life. Thus, he is a fool who says that he fears death not because it will be painful when present but because it is painful when it is still to come. For that which while present causes no distress causes unnecessary pain when merely anticipated. So death, the most frightening of bad things, is nothing to us; since when we exist, death is not yet present, and when death is present, then we do not exist. Therefore, it is relevant neither to the living nor to the dead, since it does not affect the former, and the latter do not exist. But the many sometimes flee death as the greatest of bad things and sometimes choose it as a relief from the bad things in life. **126.** But the wise man neither rejects life nor fears death. For living does not offend him, nor does he believe not living to be something bad. And just as he does not unconditionally choose the largest amount of food but the most pleasant food, so he savours not the longest time but the most pleasant. He who advises the young man to live well and the old man to die well is simple-minded, not just because of the pleasing aspects of life but because the same kind of practice produces a good life and a good death.

34

Is It Impossible To Be Harmed by Being Dead at a Particular Time?

Lucretius, *De Rerum Natura*

We have read Epicurus' succinct argument for the impossibility of a person's being harmed by being dead. A few centuries later, that argument was built upon by the Roman philosopher Lucretius (Titus Lucretius Caro: c.100–55 BC). Like many in those years, he was significantly influenced by Epicurus' writings. Lucretius left us a striking and lengthy poem, comprising six books. Its title is generally translated (from Latin) as *On the Nature of Things*, or *On the Nature of the Universe*. Our excerpts in this reading are from Book III ("liber tertius") of those six. Book III begins by addressing Epicurus, calling him nothing less than the "glory of the Grecian race;" and it ends with a potentially powerful supplement to Epicurus' own famous argument (the one in the previous reading) for death's inability to be a harm for the deceased.

That argument from Lucretius – the culmination of this reading – is often called the *symmetry* argument. It highlights a kind of symmetry between two periods of time – before your living and after your living. Could you be harmed by the fact of not having been alive during the vast expanse of time *prior to your birth*? Surely not. Yet the fact – as it will be – of your not being alive during the similarly vast expanse of time *after you will die* is no more harmful than that. Therefore, it cannot be at all harmful for you not to be alive at that later time.

Why would that be so? Lucretius also accepted the Epicurean argument we encountered in the previous reading. Hence, at least part of what generates the

Lucretius, *De Rerum Natura*, Loeb Classical Library vol. 181, trans. W.H.D. Rouse (1924), revised Martin F. Smith (Cambridge, MA: Harvard University Press, 1975), Book III (excerpts). Copyright © 1975 by the President and Fellows of Harvard College. Loeb Classical Library (R) is a registered trademark of the President and Fellows of Harvard College. Reprinted by permission of the publishers and the Trustees of the Loeb Classical Library.

Lucretian argument is the view that in neither of those two periods of time can you *experience* any harm. But perhaps this is not all that underlies Lucretius' symmetry argument. Notice his parting thought – his reaction to the question of whether one's living *longer* could thereby *lessen* the time in which one experiences nothing. If it could, might this be a potential *a*symmetry between the time prior to one's living and the time after one's living? Lucretius dismisses that objection to his argument. One's living longer makes *no* difference (he says) to how long one will not be alive. Is that because an infinitude of time would remain anyway – so that any additional finite stretch of life would still leave an infinitude of time not being lived in by the person? In this sense, is there also no possible harm in being dead from any given *particular* time onwards?

Therefore death is nothing to us, it matters not one jot, since the nature of the mind is understood to be mortal; and as in time past we felt no distress, while from all quarters the Carthaginians were coming to the conflict, when the whole world, shaken by the terrifying tumult of war, shivered and quaked under the lofty and breezy heaven, and was in doubt under which domination all men were destined to fall by land and sea;[1] so, when we shall no longer be, when the parting shall have come about between body and spirit from which we are compacted into one whole, then sure enough nothing at all will be able to happen to us, who will then no longer be, or to make us feel, not if earth be commingled with sea and sea with sky.

And grant for the moment that the nature of mind and power of spirit does feel after it has been torn away from our body, yet that is nothing to us, who by the welding and wedding together of body and spirit exist compacted into one whole. Even if time should gather together our matter after death and bring it back again as it is now placed, and if once more the light of life should be given to us, yet it would not matter one bit to us that even this had been done, when the recollection of ourselves has once been broken asunder. And even now we are not concerned at all about any self which we have been before, nor does any anguish about it now touch us. For when you look back upon all the past expanse of measureless time, and think how various are the motions of matter, you may easily come to believe that these same seeds of which now we consist have been often before placed in the same arrangement they now are in. And yet we cannot call that back by memory; for in between has been cast a stoppage of life, and all the motions have wandered and scattered afar from those sensations.

For, if by chance anyone is to have misery and pain in the future, he must himself also exist then in that time to be miserable. Since death takes away this possibility, and forbids him to exist for whom these inconveniences may be gathered together, we may be sure that there is nothing to be feared after death, that he who is not cannot be miserable, that it makes not one jot of difference whether or not he has ever been born, when death the immortal has taken away his mortal life.

"No longer now will your happy home give you welcome, no longer will your best of wives; no longer will your sweet children race to win the first kisses, and thrill your heart to its depths with sweetness. You will no longer be able to live in prosperity, and to protect your own. Poor man, poor man!" they say, "one fatal day has robbed you of all these prizes of life." But they do not go on to add: "No longer too does any craving possess you for these things." If they could see this clearly in mind and so conform their speech, they would free themselves from great anguish and fear of mind.

"Yes, you, as you now lie in death's quiet sleep, so you will be for all time that is to come, removed from all distressing pains; but we beside you, as you lay burnt to ashes on the horrible pyre, have bewailed you inconsolably, and that everlasting grief no time shall take from our hearts." Of such a speaker then we may well ask, if all ends in sleep and quiet rest, what bitterness there is in it so great that one could pine with everlasting sorrow.

[…]

[…] [T]he old order always passes, thrust out by the new, and one thing has to be made afresh from others; but no one is delivered into the pit of black Tartarus: matter is wanted, that coming generations may grow; and yet they all, when their life is done, will follow you, and so, no less than you, these generations have passed away before now, and will continue to pass away. So one thing will never cease to arise from another, and no man possesses life in freehold – all as tenants. Look back also and see how the ages of everlasting time past before we were born have been to us nothing. This therefore is a mirror which nature holds up to us, showing the time to come after we at length shall die. Is there anything horrible in that? Is there anything gloomy? Is it not more peaceful than any sleep?

[…]

[…] [W]hat is this great and evil lust of life that drives us to be so greatly agitated amidst doubt and peril? There is an end fixed for the life of mortals, and death cannot be avoided, but die we must. Again we move and have our being always amidst the same things, and by living we cannot forge for ourselves any new pleasure; but while we have not what we crave, that seems to surpass all else; afterwards, when we have attained that, we crave something else; one unchanging thirst of life fills us and our mouths are for ever agape. And it is uncertain what fortune the next years may bring, what chance has in store, what end awaits us. And by protracting life we do not deduct one jot from the duration of death, nor are we able to diminish that, so as to leave perhaps a shorter time after our taking off. Therefore you may live to complete as many generations as you will: nevertheless that everlasting death will still be waiting, and no less long a time will he be no more, who has made an end of life with to-day's sun, than he who fell many a month and year before.

Note

1.   The reference is chiefly to the Second Punic War (218–201 B.C.).

35

Would Immortality Be Humanly Possible and Desirable?

Bernard Williams, "The Makropulos Case: Reflections on the Tedium of Immortality"

Epicurus and Lucretius bequeathed to metaphysics this challenge: Tell us *why* a person's being dead could harm her; do not merely assume that it can do so. And in engaging with this, bear in mind its careful focus. *Of course* a painful unwanted death can harm the person who dies. But this need only be because the pain and the anxiety occur while she is alive. A painful or anxious process of dying remains a part of one's *living* whenever it is present. So, our metaphysical question here is that of whether one's death *apart from* such aspects of one's living can harm one.

Many philosophers have sought to evade those arguments from Epicurus and Lucretius. What would follow if one *could* evade those arguments? Would it then be apt to infer that it could be better *never* to die (even painlessly, without warning)? Might immortality be properly preferable to mortality (immortality in a bodily form or some immaterial form)? Is living that much better than being dead?

Not according to Bernard Williams (1929–2003), a highly respected English philosopher associated mainly with the universities of Oxford and Cambridge. He wrote intriguingly on ethics, metaphysics, epistemology, mind, language, and more. In this reading, Williams asks what it would be for a person never to die – and whether this could be an outcome properly preferable for her. Does it even make sense to contemplate favorably the idea of everlasting life?

The key to resolving this (thinks Williams) is the role of a person's categorical desires – her *un*conditional desires. These are distinct from *conditional* desires – ones that wish for something *so long as* one will still be alive. This distinction matters (Lucretius, in the previous reading, noticed a similar one), especially if we claim

Metaphysics and Epistemology: A Guided Anthology, First Edition. Edited by Stephen Hetherington.
© 2014 John Wiley & Sons, Inc. Published 2014 by John Wiley & Sons, Inc.

that one's unconditional desires are what give substance to one's desire to continue living. Do these give a fundamental point to one's living? ("I want to continue living, so that I can do X.") In contrast, a conditional desire would have a point only *if* there is living. ("If I am to continue living, I will want to do X.") Having *conditional* desires would therefore not be enough to render sensible a desire for continued life in the first place.

Yet Williams asks whether having even unconditional desires is enough. Could an unending life be lived meaningfully in the service of such desires? Not at all (argues Williams). Try to imagine what kind of life that would be. Would it be a life of no personal development? How could it escape being taken over by a crippling boredom? Remember that immortality would stretch infinitely onwards. You would be living unendingly, with more than enough time for all that is even possible. How could you not run out of all possible thoughts, conversations, diversions, chores, illnesses (mental and/or non-mental), etc.? (As Woody Allen has been credited with saying, "Eternity is really long, especially near the end.") Could you overcome this limitation only by changing so much as to make all such ways of passing the time amenable to you? But how can you sensibly look forward to *that*? Indeed, how could that still be *you* after so long long long … long a while and so much much much … much change?

[…] Immortality, or a state without death, would be meaningless, I shall suggest; so, in a sense, death gives the meaning to life. That does not mean that we should not fear death (whatever force that injunction might be taken to have, anyway). Indeed, there are several very different ways in which it could be true at once that death gave the meaning to life and that death was, other things being equal, something to be feared. Some existentialists, for instance, seem to have said that death was what gave meaning to life, if anything did, just because it was the fear of death that gave meaning to life; I shall not follow them. I shall rather pursue the idea that from facts about human desire and happiness and what a human life is, it follows both that immortality would be, where conceivable at all, intolerable, and that (other things being equal) death is reasonably regarded as an evil. Considering whether death can reasonably be regarded as an evil is in fact as near as I shall get to considering whether it should be feared: they are not quite the same question.

My title is that, as it is usually translated into English, of a play by Karel Čapek which was made into an opera by Janáček and which tells of a woman called Elina Makropulos, *alias* Emilia Marty, *alias* Ellian Macgregor, alias a number of other things with the initials 'EM', on whom her father, the Court physician to a sixteenth-century Emperor, tried out an elixir of life. At the time of the action she is aged 342. Her unending life has come to a state of boredom, indifference and coldness. Everything is joyless: 'in the end it is the same', she says, 'singing and silence'. She refuses to take the elixir again; she dies; and the formula is deliberately destroyed by a young woman among the protests of some older men.

EM's state suggests at least this, that death is not necessarily an evil, and not just in the sense in which almost everybody would agree to that, where death provides an end to great suffering, but in the more intimate sense that it can be a good thing not to live too long. It suggests more than that, for it suggests that it was not a peculiarity of EM's that an endless life was meaningless.

[...]

[...] [I]f death, other things being equal, is a misfortune; and a longer life is better than a shorter life; and we reject the Lucretian argument that it does not matter when one dies; then it looks as though – other things always being equal – death is at any time an evil, and it is always better to live than die. [...] If Lucretius is wrong, we seem committed to wanting to be immortal.

That would be, as has been repeatedly said, with other things equal. No-one need deny that since, for instance, we grow old and our powers decline, much may happen to increase the reasons for thinking death a good thing. But these are contingencies. We might not age; perhaps, one day, it will be possible for some of us not to age. If that were so, would it not follow then that, more life being *per se* better than less life, we should have reason so far as that went (but not necessarily in terms of other inhabitants) to live for ever? EM indeed bears strong, if fictional, witness against the desirability of that; but perhaps she still laboured under some contingent limitations, social or psychological, which might once more be eliminated to bring it about that really other things were equal. Against this, I am going to suggest that the supposed contingencies are not really contingencies; that an endless life would be a meaningless one; and that we could have no reason for living eternally a human life. There is no desirable or significant property which life would have more of, or have more unquali-fiedly, if we lasted for ever. [...]

If one pictures living for ever as living as an embodied person in the world rather as it is, it will be a question, and not so trivial as may seem, of what age one eternally is. EM was 342; because for 300 years she had been 42. This choice (if it was a choice) I am personally, and at present, well disposed to salute – if one had to spend eternity at any age, that seems an admirable age to spend it at. Nor would it necessarily be a less good age for a woman: that at least was not EM's problem, that she was too old at the age she continued to be at. Her problem lay in having been at it for too long. Her trouble was it seems, boredom: a boredom connected with the fact that everything that could happen and make sense to one particular human being of 42 had already happened to her. Or, rather, all the sorts of things that could make sense to one woman of a certain character; for EM has a certain character, and indeed, except for her accumulating memories of earlier times, and no doubt some changes of style to suit the passing centuries, seems always to have been much the same sort of person.

There are difficult questions, if one presses the issue, about this constancy of character. How is this accumulation of memories related to this character which she eternally has, and to the character of her existence? Are they much the same kind of events repeated? Then it is itself strange that she allows them to be repeated, accepting the same repetitions, the same limitations – indeed, *accepting* is what it later becomes, when earlier it would not, or even could not, have been that. The repeated patterns of personal relations, for instance, must take on a character of being inescapable. Or is the pattern of her experiences not repetitious in this way, but varied? Then the problem shifts, to the relation between these varied experiences, and the fixed character: how can it remain fixed, through an endless series of very various experiences? The experiences must surely happen to her without really affecting her; she must be, as EM is, detached and withdrawn.

EM, of course, is in a world of people who do not share her condition, and that determines certain features of the life she has to lead, as that any personal relationship requires peculiar kinds of concealment. That, at least, is a form of isolation which would disappear if her condition were generalised. But to suppose more generally that boredom and inner death would be eliminated if everyone were similarly becalmed, is an empty hope: it would be a world of Bourbons, learning nothing and forgetting nothing, and it is unclear how much could even happen.

The more one reflects to any realistic degree on the conditions of EM's unending life, the less it seems a mere contingency that it froze up as it did. That it is not a contingency, is suggested also by the fact that the reflections can sustain themselves independently of any question of the particular character that EM had; it is enough, almost, that she has a human character at all. Perhaps not quite. One sort of character for which the difficulties of unending life would have less significance than they proved to have for EM might be one who at the beginning was more like what she is at the end: cold, withdrawn, already frozen. For him, the prospect of unending cold is presumably less bleak in that he is used to it. But with him, the question can shift to a different place, as to why he wants the unending life at all; for, the more he is at the beginning like EM is at the end, the less place there is for categorical desire to keep him going, and to resist the desire for death. In EM's case, her boredom and distance from life both kill desire and consist in the death of it; one who is already enough like that to sustain life in those conditions may well be one who had nothing to make him want to do so. But even if he has, and we conceive of a person who is stonily resolved to sustain for ever an already stony existence, his possibility will be of no comfort to those, one hopes a larger party, who want to live longer because they want to live more.

To meet the basic anti-Lucretian hope for continuing life which is grounded in categorical desire, EM's unending life in this world is inadequate, and necessarily so relative to just those desires and conceptions of character which go into the hope. That is very important, since it is the most direct response, that which should have been adequate if the hope is both coherent and what it initially seemed to be. It also satisfied one of two important conditions which must be satisfied by anything which is to be adequate as a fulfilment of my anti-Lucretian hope, namely that it should clearly be *me* who lives for ever. The second important condition is that the state in which I survive should be one which, to me looking forward, will be adequately related, in the life it presents, to those aims which I now have in wanting to survive at all. That is a vague formula, and necessarily so, for what exactly that relation will be must depend to some extent on what kind of aims and (as one might say) prospects for myself I now have. What we can say is that since I am propelled forward into longer life by categorical desires, what is promised must hold out some hopes for those desires. The limiting case of this might be that the promised life held out some hope just to that desire mentioned before, that future desires of mine will be born and satisfied; but if that were the only categorical desire that carried me forward into it, at least this seems demanded, that any image I have of those future desires should make it comprehensible to me how in terms of my character they could be my desires.

This second condition, the EM kind of survival failed, on reflection, to satisfy; but at least it is clear why, before reflection, it looked as though it might satisfy the condition – it consists, after all, in just going on in ways in which we are quite used to going on.

[...]

[...] [I]n the minds of many who have hoped for immortality [...] it was not in this world that they hoped to live for ever. As one might say, their hope was not so much that they would never die as that they would live after their death, and while that in its turn can be represented as the hope that one would not really die, or, again, that it was not really oneself that would die, the change of formulation could point to an after-life sufficiently unlike this life, perhaps, to earth the current of doubt that flows from EM's frozen boredom.

But in fact this hope has been and could only be modelled on some image of a more familiar untiring or unresting or unflagging activity or satisfaction; and what is essentially EM's problem, one way or another, remains. In general we can ask, what it is about the imaged activities of an eternal life which would stave off the prinicip[al] hazard to which EM succumbed, boredom. The Don Juan in Hell joke, that heaven's prospects are tedious and the devil has the best tunes, though a tired fancy in itself, at least serves to show up a real and (I suspect) a profound difficulty, of providing any model of an unending, supposedly satisfying, state or activity which would not rightly prove boring to anyone who remained conscious of himself and who had acquired a character, interests, tastes and impatiences in the course of living, already, a finite life. The point is not that for such a man boredom would be a tiresome consequence of the supposed states or activities, and that they would be objectionable just on the utilitarian or hedonistic ground that they had this disagreeable feature. If that were all there was to it, we could imagine the feature away, along no doubt with other disagreeable features of human life in its present imperfection. The point is rather that boredom, as sometimes in more ordinary circumstances, would be not just a tiresome effect, but a reaction almost perceptual in character to the poverty of one's relation to the environment. Nothing less will do for eternity than something that makes boredom *unthinkable*. What could that be? Something that could be guaranteed to be at every moment utterly absorbing? But if a man has and retains a character, there is no reason to suppose that there is anything that could be that. If, lacking a conception of the guaranteedly absorbing activity, one tries merely to think away the reaction of boredom, one is no longer supposing an improvement in the circumstances, but merely an impoverishment in his consciousness of them. Just as being bored can be a sign of not noticing, understanding or appreciating enough, so equally not being bored can be a sign of not noticing, or not reflecting, enough. One might make the immortal man content at every moment, by just stripping off from him consciousness which would have brought discontent by reminding him of other times, other interests, other possibilities. Perhaps, indeed, that is what we have already done, in a more tempting way, by picturing him just now as at every moment totally absorbed – but that is something we shall come back to.

Of course there is in actual life such a thing as justified but necessary boredom. Thus – to take a not entirely typical example – someone who was, or who thought himself, devoted to the radical cause might eventually admit to himself that he found a lot of its rhetoric excruciatingly boring. He might think that he ought not to feel that, that the reaction was wrong, and merely represented an unworthiness of his, an unregenerate remnant of intellectual superiority. However, he might rather feel that it would not necessarily be a better world in which no-one was bored by such rhetoric and that boredom was, indeed, a perfectly worthy reaction to this rhetoric after all this time; but for all that, the rhetoric might be necessary. A man at arms can get cramp from standing too long at his post, but sentry-duty can after all be necessary. But the threat of monotony in eternal activities could not be dealt with in that way, by regarding immortal boredom as an unavoidable ache derived from standing ceaselessly at one's post. (This is one reason why I said that boredom in eternity would have to be *unthinkable*.) For the question would be unavoidable, in what campaign one was supposed to be serving, what one's ceaseless sentry-watch was for.

Some philosophers have pictured an eternal existence as occupied in something like intense intellectual enquiry. Why that might seem to solve the problem, at least for them, is obvious. The activity is engrossing, self-justifying, affords, as it may appear, endless new perspectives, and by being engrossing enables one to lose oneself. It is that last feature that supposedly makes boredom unthinkable, by providing something that is, in that earlier phrase, at every moment totally absorbing. But if one is totally and perpetually absorbed in such an activity, and loses oneself in it, then as those words suggest, we come back to the problem of satisfying the conditions that it should be me who lives for ever, and that the eternal life should be in prospect of some interest. Let us leave aside the question of people whose characteristic and most personal interests are remote from such pursuits, and for whom, correspondingly, an immortality promised in terms of intellectual activity is going to make heavy demands on some theory of a 'real self' which will have to emerge at death. More interesting is the content and value of the promise for a person who *is*, in this life, disposed to those activities. For looking at such a person as he now is, it seems quite unreasonable to suppose that those activities would have the fulfilling or liberating character that they do have for him, if they were in fact all he could do or conceive of doing. If they are genuinely fulfilling, and do not operate (as they can) merely as a compulsive diversion, then the ground and shape of the satisfactions that the intellectual enquiry offers him, will relate to *him*, and not just to the enquiry.

[...]

[...] I shall end by returning to a point from which we set out, the sheer desire to go on living, and shall mention a writer on this subject, Unamuno, whose work *The Tragic Sense of Life*[1] gives perhaps more extreme expression than anyone else has done to that most basic form of the desire to be immortal, the desire not to die.

> I do not want to die – no, I neither want to die nor do I want to want to die; I want to live for ever and ever and ever. I want this 'I' to live – this poor 'I' that I am and that I feel myself to be here and now, and therefore the problem of the duration of my soul, of my own soul, tortures me.[2]

[...]
At the same time, his desire to remain alive extends an almost incomprehensible distance beyond any desire to continue agreeable experiences:

> For myself I can say that as a youth and even as a child I remained unmoved when shown the most moving pictures of hell, for even then nothing appeared quite so horrible to me as nothingness itself.[3]

The most that I have claimed earlier against Lucretius is not enough to make that preference intelligible to me. The fear of sheer nothingness is certainly part of what Lucretius rightly, if too lightly, hoped to exorcise; and the *mere* desire to stay alive, which is here stretched to its limit, is not enough (I suggested before) to answer the question, once the question has come up and requires an answer in rational terms. Yet Unamune's affirmation of existence even through limitless suffering[4] brings out something which is implicit in the claim against Lucretius. It is not necessarily the prospect of pleasant times that create the motive against dying, but the existence of categorical desire, and categorical desire can drive through both the existence and the prospect of unpleasant times.

Suppose, then, that categorical desire does sustain the desire to live. So long as it remains so, I shall want not to die. Yet I also know, if what has gone before is right, that an eternal life would be unliveable. In part, as EM's case originally suggested, that is because categorical desire will go away from it: in those versions, such as hers, in which I am recognisably myself, I would eventually have had altogether too much of myself. There are good reasons, surely, for dying before that happens. But equally, at times earlier than that moment, there is reason for not dying. Necessarily, it tends to be either too early or too late. EM reminds us that it can be too late, and many, as against Lucretius, need no reminding that it can be too early. If that is any sort of dilemma, it can, as things still are and if one is exceptionally lucky, be resolved, not by doing anything, but just by dying shortly before the horrors of not doing so become evident. Technical progress may, in more than one direction, make that piece of luck rarer. But as things are, it is possible to be, in contrast to EM, *felix opportunitate mortis* – as it can be appropriately mistranslated, lucky in having the chance to die.

Notes

1. *Del sentimiento trágico de la vida*, translated by J. E. Crawford Flitch (London: 1921). Page references are to the Fontana Library edition, 1962.
2. *Ibid.*, p. 60.
3. *Ibid.*, p. 28.
4. An affirmation which takes on a special dignity retrospectively in the light of his own death shortly after his courageous speech against Millán Astray and the obscene slogan '¡Viva la Muerte!' See Hugh Thomas, *The Spanish Civil War* (Harmondsworth: Pelican, 1961), pp. 442–4.

36

Can a Person be Deprived of Benefits by Being Dead?

Fred Feldman, *Confrontations with the Reaper*

It is usual among those contemporary metaphysicians who write on the metaphysics of death to argue *against* the Epicurean and Lucretian view (in the earlier readings from them) that no one can be harmed by being dead. The aim of those contemporary metaphysicians is thus to establish a *possibility* – the possibility of being harmed by being dead. This reading, from Fred Feldman (b. 1941) of the University of Massachusetts, Amherst, is a leading instance of that approach. He does not try to show that being dead is often or mostly or always bad for the one who has died. He strives only to explain how it is even possible to be harmed by being dead. Not until that possibility has been established may we usefully wonder about how often, if ever in fact, people are harmed by being dead.

Feldman develops an instance of what is called a *deprivation* analysis of the possible harm in being dead. His basic idea is that being dead could deprive one of benefits one would have received if not for being dead. How should that way of talking ("would have … if not for") be understood? It uses a subjunctive conditional ("If *X* were to be so, *Y* would obtain") to comment on a *counterfactual* state of affairs (one that does not actually obtain). We are being asked to consider what a particular person's life *would* have been like if she had still been alive (after in fact she dies). Contemporary philosophers usually analyze the meanings of counterfactual conditionals – their semantics; what constitutes their truth or their falsity – in terms of *possible worlds*. (Recall the earlier reading from Leibniz – his arguing for God's having actualized this world as the best of all possible worlds.) For example, suppose that the news of a friend Arjuna's death prompts you to think this: "Arjuna was a happy person who died young. So, in most other possible

Fred Feldman, *Confrontations With the Reaper: A Philosophical Study of the Nature and Value of Death* (New York: Oxford University Press, 1992), ch. 8 (excerpts). Reprinted with permission of Oxford University Press.

Metaphysics and Epistemology: A Guided Anthology, First Edition. Edited by Stephen Hetherington.
© 2014 John Wiley & Sons, Inc. Published 2014 by John Wiley & Sons, Inc.

worlds very like this one, *except* that those ones include his continuing to be alive, he is happy." In other words (according to Feldman's approach) you would be thinking that Arjuna's being dead is now – even now, after his death – depriving him of happiness he *would* have had if not for being dead.

It is true that we talk easily of what someone's life would have been like if not for her dying when she did. Yet some doubts may remain. How often do we really know what a life *would* have been like if not for the person's death – rather than merely knowing what that life *could* have been like? But the latter – unlike the former – is not very much to know. Imagine deciding to speak only of how a person's life might have continued if not for the death. There will be so many of these possible continuations (rather than the far more definite commitment contained in a view on how the person's life *would* have continued if not for the death). Will we lose, in each such case, any substantive sense of the person's being actually harmed by being dead?

Epicurus's Argument Against the Evil of Death

One version of one of the most famous arguments for this conclusion was presented by Epicurus in his "Letter to Menoeceus."

[…]

[…] It is an interesting and puzzling argument. The general drift of the argument is fairly clear. It is based on the idea that once we are dead, we will feel no pain. From this, together with some subsidiary premises, Epicurus seems to derive the conclusion that death is no misfortune for the one who dies. […]

[…] Epicurus does not attempt to show that there is nothing bad about […] the often painful terminal process that sometimes takes up the final days of life. […]

[…] [T]he Epicureans surely do not mean to say that a person's death cannot be bad *for others*. One's friends may of course suffer as a result of one's death. I might suffer because my old friend is now dead. The Epicureans have nothing remarkable to say about this. The argument under consideration here is designed to show only that however bad it may be for others, being dead cannot be bad for the person who is dead. […]

The Fallacy in the New Version

[…]

[But] suppose a young man is accepted by two colleges. We can call them College A and College B. After some reflection, he decides to attend College A. Suppose he spends four happy years at College A, but never studies any philosophy – because they do not offer any courses in philosophy at College A. Suppose he never learns anything about philosophy. Suppose, however, that he has outstanding aptitude for philosophy and that he would have enjoyed it enormously if he had been given the opportunity. He goes to his grave never realizing how much enjoyment he missed. If he had not gone to College A, he would have gone to College B, which offers many excellent philosphy courses. He would have become a philosophy major, and his life would have been much happier. In such a case, I would want to say that the fact that he went to College A was a misfortune for this young man. It's a pity; too bad for him. He would have been much happier if he had gone to College B.

For present purposes, one fact about this example is of crucial importance. It is this: although attending College A was bad for this young man, it was not in itself a painful experience, and it did not cause him any pain. Thus, [...] some things are extrinsically bad even though they cause no pain.

Let us consider another example to illustrate the same point. Suppose a girl is born in a strange country – call it Country A. In Country A, they do not permit girls to learn to read and write. In this strange country, girls are taught to do laundry and raise children. Suppose this girl goes through life bearing children and washing laundry. Suppose she is reasonably satisfied, thinking that she has lived as a woman ought to live. She goes to her grave never realizing what she has missed. Suppose also that she had very considerable native talent for poetry – that she would have been a marvelously successful and happy poet if only she had been given the chance. I would want to say that it is a great pity that this woman had not been born in another country. I would say that something very bad happened to her, even though she never suffered any pain as a result.

These two examples illustrate the same point. Some things are bad for us even though they are not themselves painful experiences, and they do not lead to any painful experiences. In each case, as I see it, the thing that is bad for the person is bad for him or her because it deprives the person of pleasures he or she otherwise would have experienced. In the first example, going to College A did not cause our young man any pain. It was bad for him because he would have been happier if he had gone to College B. Similarly in the second example: being born in Country A did not cause the woman any pain. Still, it was very bad for her. She would have been much better off if she had been born elsewhere. [...]

How Death Can Be Bad for the One Who Dies

[...]

[Consider] this principle [linking extrinsic value (E) and intrinsic value (I)]:

> EI: Something is extrinsically bad for a person if and only if he or she would have been intrinsically better off if it had not taken place.

It should be obvious that EI generates much more plausible results in the two cases I have mentioned. Going to College A is extrinsically bad for the young man in the first example, according to EI, because his life would have contained more pleasure if he had gone elsewhere. The same holds true in the second example. Being born in Country A did not lead to any pain for the woman in that example. But she would have experienced more pleasure if she had been born elsewhere. So CP [viz., "the causal hypothesis: If something is extrinsically bad for a person, then it is bad for him or her because it leads to later intrinsic bads for him or her"] is false. EI is a more plausible view about the connection between intrinsic and extrinsic evil.

Now let us consider the application of my proposal to the case of death. Suppose a boy is undergoing minor surgery, and as a result of some foul-up with the anesthesia, he dies while unconscious on the table. His death is utterly painless, since it occurs while he is unconscious. Nevertheless, we might think his death is a terrible misfortune for him. My [EP] proposal (unlike CP) permits us to say this. We may imagine that he would have been quite happy on the whole for another fifty years if he had not died when he did. Then this boy's life contains less intrinsic value for him, measured hedonistically, than it would have contained if he had not died when he did. Therefore, according to my view (which is summarized in EI), this person's death is extrinsically bad for him even though it is not itself a painful experience, and it causes him no pain.

Notice what I am *not* saying. I am not saying that the boy's death is bad for him because it is a painful experience. That would be absurd. Death is not a sort of pain. Furthermore, I am not saying that his death is bad for him because it leads to, or causes, something intrinsically bad for the boy. I am assuming that pain is the only thing that is intrinsically bad for a person and that this boy cannot possibly suffer any pain while he is dead. So the evil of death cannot be explained in that way. What I am saying is that his death is extrinsically bad for him because his life is on the whole intrinsically less valuable for him than it would have been if he had not died when he in fact died. The evil of death is a matter of *deprivation*; it is bad for a person when it deprives him or her of intrinsic value; if he or she would have been better off if it had not happened.

[…] In my view, death would be extrinsically bad for him if his life would have contained more intrinsic value if he had not died then.

So my view is that Epicurus went wrong in thinking that all he had to prove was that nothing intrinsically bad happens to us once we are dead. He thought that it would follow that "death is nothing to us." Given the traditional causal conception of the connection between intrinsic and extrinsic evil, he would be right. But the traditional conception is mistaken. Things can be extrinsically bad even though they do not cause any intrinsic evil. Depriving us of intrinsic good can make something extrinsically bad as well. And that is why death is extrinsically bad. It is bad (when it is bad) because it deprives us of the intrinsic value we would have enjoyed if it had not taken place.

[…]

[…] It may appear that I am claiming that death is always bad for the one who dies. This is in fact not my view, and it is not entailed by my view. My view is that the badness of a given death depends on what would have taken place if that death had not taken place. Consider the case of some very old and unhappy person. Suppose that further life for this person will inevitably contain more pain than pleasure. Suppose he dies peacefully in his sleep. Then his death is not extrinsically bad for him. In fact, it is good for him. Such a death is extrinsically good for the one who dies, according to EI, because he would have been worse off if it had not taken place. His life, as a whole, would have contained more pain if he had lived longer. In such a case, as I see it, death is a blessing.

Further Readings for Part II

Here are some suggestions as to more readings you might wish to pursue, regarding the metaphysical topics in Part II. These readings should help you to spread your philosophical wings further still.

How Is the World at all Physical?

Armstrong, D.M. (1968) *A Materialist Theory of Mind*. London: Routledge & Kegan Paul.
Chalmers, D.J. (1996) *The Conscious Mind: In Search of a Fundamental Theory*. New York: Oxford University Press.
Jacovides, M. (2007) Locke's distinctions between primary and secondary qualities. In L. Newman (ed.), *The Cambridge Companion to Locke's "Essay Concerning Human Understanding."* Cambridge: Cambridge University Press, pp. 101–129.
Mackie, J.L. (1976) *Problems From Locke*. Oxford: Clarendon Press, ch. 1.
McGinn, C. (1983) *The Subjective View: Secondary Qualities and Indexical Thoughts*. Oxford: Clarendon Press.
Nagel, T. (1979) What is it like to be a bat? In T. Nagel, *Mortal Questions*. Cambridge: Cambridge University Press, pp. 165–180.
Nagel, T. (1986) *The View From Nowhere*. New York: Oxford University Press, ch. 2.
Pitcher, G. (1977) *Berkeley*. London: Routledge & Kegan Paul.
Richmond, A. (2009) *Berkeley's Principles of Human Knowledge: A Reader's Guide*. London: Continuum.
Stoljar, D. (2010) *Physicalism*. London: Routledge.

How Does the World Function?

Armstrong, D.M. (1983) *What Is a Law of Nature?* Cambridge: Cambridge University Press.
Cartwright, N. (2000) An empiricist defence of singular causes. In R. Teichmann (ed.), *Logic, Cause & Action: Essays in Honour of Elizabeth Anscombe*. Royal Institute of Philosophy Supplement 46. Cambridge: Cambridge University Press, pp. 47–58.
Mackie, J.L. (1980) *The Cement of the Universe: A Study of Causation*. Oxford: Clarendon Press.

Metaphysics and Epistemology: A Guided Anthology, First Edition. Edited by Stephen Hetherington.
© 2014 John Wiley & Sons, Inc. Published 2014 by John Wiley & Sons, Inc.

Makin, S. (2000) Causality and derivativeness. In R. Teichmann (ed.) *Logic, Cause & Action: Essays in Honour of Elizabeth Anscombe*. Royal Institute of Philosophy Supplement 46. Cambridge: Cambridge University Press, pp. 59–71.

Read, R., and Richman, K.A. (eds.) (2007) *The New Hume Debate*, revised edn. London: Routledge.

Sosa, E. (ed.) (1975) *Causation and Conditionals*. London: Oxford University Press.

Teichmann, R. (2008) *The Philosophy of Elizabeth Anscombe*. Oxford: Oxford University Press, pp. 177–186.

Tooley, M. (1987) *Causation: A Realist Approach*. Oxford: Clarendon Press.

How Do Things Ever Have Qualities?

Almeder, R. (1980) *The Philosophy of Charles S. Peirce: A Critical Introduction*. Oxford: Basil Blackwell, ch. 5.

Armstrong, D.M. (1989) *Universals: An Opinionated Introduction*. Boulder, CO: Westview Press.

Bacon, J. (1995) *Universals and Property Instances: The Alphabet of Being*. Oxford: Blackwell.

Blackson, T.A. (1995) *Inquiry, Forms, and Substances: A Study in Plato's Metaphysics and Epistemology*. Dordrecht: Kluwer Academic Publishers.

Campbell, K. (1990) *Abstract Particulars*. Oxford: Basil Blackwell.

Loux, M.J. (ed.) (1970) *Universals and Particulars: Readings in Ontology*. Garden City, NY: Anchor Books.

Rodriguez-Pereyra, G. (2002) *Resemblance Nominalism: A Solution to the Problem of Universals*. Oxford: Clarendon Press.

Russell, B. (1959 [1912]) *The Problems of Philosophy*. London: Oxford University Press, ch. 9.

Sayre, K.M. (2005 [1983]) *Plato's Late Ontology: A Riddle Resolved*, 2nd edn. Las Vegas: Parmenides Publishing, ch. 1, sect. 1.

Williams, D.C. (1966) The elements of being. In D.C. Williams, *Principles of Empirical Realism: Philosophical Essays*. Springfield, IL: Charles C. Thomas, pp. 74–109.

How Are There Any Truths?

Armstrong, D.M. (2004) *Truths and Truthmakers*. Cambridge: Cambridge University Press.

Burgess, A.G., and Burgess, J.P. (2011) *Truth*. Princeton: Princeton University Press.

Campbell, R. (2011) *The Concept of Truth*. Basingstoke: Palgrave Macmillan.

Devitt, M. (1991) *Realism and Truth*, 2nd edn. Oxford: Blackwell.

Kirk, R. (1999) *Relativism and Reality: A Contemporary Introduction*. London: Routledge.

Kirkham, R.L. (1992) *Theories of Truth: A Critical Introduction*. Cambridge, MA: MIT Press.

Lee, M.-K. (2005) *Epistemology After Protagoras: Responses to Relativism in Plato, Aristotle, and Democritus*. Oxford: Clarendon Press.

Lynch, M.P. (1998) *Truth in Context: An Essay on Pluralism and Objectivity*. Cambridge, MA: MIT Press.

Putnam, H. (1987) *The Many Faces of Realism*. La Salle, IL: Open Court, lectures I and II.

Rorty, R., and Engel, P. (2007) *What's the Use of Truth?* New York: Columbia University Press.

Searle, J.R. (1995) *The Construction of Social Reality*. London: Penguin.

How Is There a World At All?

Charlesworth, M.J. (1965) *St Anselm's Proslogion*. Oxford: Clarendon Press.

Davies, B. (2004) Anselm and the ontological argument. In B. Davies and B. Leftow (eds.), *The Cambridge Companion to Anselm*. Cambridge: Cambridge University Press, pp. 157–178.

Leslie, J. (1989) *Universes*. London: Routledge.

Nozick, R. (1981) *Philosophical Explanations*. Cambridge, MA: Harvard University Press, ch. 2.

Parfit, D. (1998) Why anything? Why this? *London Review of Books*, 20/2 (Jan. 22), pp. 24–27; 20/3 (Feb, 5), pp. 22–25.

Plantinga, A. (ed.) (1965) *The Ontological Argument: From St. Anselm to Contemporary Philosophers*. Garden City, NY: Anchor Books.

Plantinga, A. (1974) *The Nature of Necessity*. Oxford: Clarendon Press, ch. 10.

How Are Persons Persons?

Almog, J. (2002) *What Am I? Descartes and the Mind-Body Problem*. Oxford: Oxford University Press.

Glover, J. (1988) *I: The Philosophy and Psychology of Personal Identity*. London: Penguin.

Hume, D. (1739–40) *A Treatise of Human Nature*, Book I, pt. IV, sect. VI.

Merricks, T. (2001) *Objects and Persons*. Oxford: Clarendon Press.

Olson, E.T. (2007) *What Are We? A Study in Personal Ontology*. New York: Oxford University Press.

Rorty, A.O. (ed.) (1976) *The Identities of Persons*. Berkeley, CA: University of California Press.

Shoemaker, S., and Swinburne, R. (1984) *Personal Identity*. Oxford: Basil Blackwell.

Wilson, M.D. (1978) *Descartes*. London; Routledge & Kegan Paul, ch. 6.

Yaffe, G. (2007) Locke on ideas of identity and diversity. In L. Newman (ed.), *The Cambridge Companion to Locke's "Essay Concerning Human Understanding."* Cambridge: Cambridge University Press, pp. 192–230.

How Do People Ever Have Free Will and Moral Responsibility?

Fischer, J.M. (1994) *The Metaphysics of Free Will: An Essay on Control*. Cambridge, MA: Blackwell.

Fischer, J.M., and Ravizza, M. (1998) *Responsibility and Control: A Theory of Moral Responsibility*. Cambridge: Cambridge University Press.

Frede, M. (2011) *A Free Will: Origins of the Notion in Ancient Thought*. Berkeley, CA: University of California Press.

Kane, R. (1996) *The Significance of Free Will*. New York: Oxford University Press.

Sorensen, R. (2003) *A Brief History of the Paradox: Philosophy and the Labyrinths of the Mind*. New York: Oxford University Press, ch. 9.

Taylor, R. (1992) *Metaphysics*, 4th edn. Englewood Cliffs, NJ: Prentice-Hall, chs. 5 and 6.

van Inwagen, P. (1983) *An Essay on Free Will*. Oxford: Clarendon Press.

Watson, G. (ed.) (2003) *Free Will*, 2nd edn. Oxford: Oxford University Press.

Wolf, S. (1990) *Freedom Within Reason*. New York: Oxford University Press.

How Could a Person Be Harmed by Being Dead?

Bradley, B. (2009) *Well-Being and Death*. Oxford: Clarendon Press.

Fischer, J.M. (ed.) (1993) *The Metaphysics of Death*. Stanford, CA: Stanford University Press.

Kagan, S. (2012) *Death*. New Haven, CT: Yale University Press.

Luper, S. (2009) *The Philosophy of Death*. Cambridge: Cambridge University Press.

Warren, J. (2004) *Facing Death: Epicurus and His Critics*. Oxford: Clarendon Press.

More Generally ...

These collections cover many metaphysical topics.

Kim, J., Sosa, E., and Rosenkrantz, G.S. (eds.) (2009) *A Companion to Metaphysics*, 2nd edn. Malden, MA: Wiley-Blackwell.

Le Poidevin, R., Simons, P., McGonigal, A., and Cameron, R.P. (eds.) (2009) *The Routledge Companion to Metaphysics*. London: Routledge.

Loux, M.J., and Zimmerman, D.W. (eds.) (2003) *The Oxford Handbook of Metaphysics*. Oxford: Oxford University Press.

Part III

Epistemology
Philosophical Images of Knowing

Can We Understand What It Is to Know?

37

Is Knowledge a Supported True Belief?

Plato, *Meno*

Western epistemology began with a few of Plato's dialogues. Pivotal within the *Meno*, in particular, is the question of what knowledge is. What is it to know? What does the property of knowing involve? Philosophers standardly cite this reading from the *Meno* as revealing a vital first step needed if we are to understand what it would be to have knowledge.

The epistemological aim here is generic. What is the nature of knowledge in general – *anyone's* knowledge of *any* fact? Can we understand there being such a shared nature even while recognizing slightly more specific kinds of knowledge? When standing in the rain, you have directly experiential knowledge of its raining; a meteorologist in another city may also know, but in a different way, that it is

Plato, *Meno* 97a–99d, trans. W.K.C. Guthrie. From *The Collected Dialogues of Plato*, ed. E. Hamilton and H. Cairns (Princeton: Princeton University Press, 1961). © 1961 by Princeton University Press. Reprinted with permission of Princeton University Press.

Metaphysics and Epistemology: A Guided Anthology, First Edition. Edited by Stephen Hetherington.
© 2014 John Wiley & Sons, Inc. Published 2014 by John Wiley & Sons, Inc.

raining where you are. Yet will those two kinds of knowledge have much in common – so much so as to explain their each *being* knowledge? Are there shared *characteristics* in virtue of which each is knowledge?

In two earlier readings (from Plato, reading 13, and from Armstrong, reading 14), we confronted the question of whether there are real and repeatable qualities or characteristics, such as a property of being a person. We *call* various things "a person." Do these individual things also share a real and repeatable property of being a person? If so, this could be in virtue of everyone's sharing other properties, too – ones that are jointly constitutive of something's being a person. Now we face similar metaphysical questions about knowledge. (Metaphysics and epistemology often overlap.) Is there a real and repeatable quality of being knowledge? If so, do all individual cases of knowledge share that property of being knowledge? If they do, is this because all of them share other properties, too – ones that are jointly constitutive of something's being knowledge?

We may wonder whether the word "knowledge" is merely a convenience, a term used without corresponding to anything real – namely, *actual* knowledge – in the world. Maybe there is no real property of being knowledge. But even if that is so, a version of Socrates' question would remain. Presumably we would still expect there to be repeatable *patterns* in our using the term "knowledge" (just as we believe there are in our uses of the term "person"). Epistemology can continue prompting us to reflect upon how, and in response to what exactly, we apply the term "knowledge."

We return to Plato's *Meno*. There, we find Socrates bequeathing to us a simple image, one that has been philosophically influential. Need knowledge (asks Socrates) be anything more than an accurate opinion? Or is *only* a true belief – a view that is correct in what it says about reality – needed in knowing? Socrates replies that knowing also includes having some sort of account of why one's belief is true. This account thereby supports the belief's being true. Without such support, one has only what epistemologists now call a *mere* true belief. Think of holding a belief confidently on the basis of a mere hunch and no relevant experience – a belief that happens to be correct, even so. Is it knowledge? Not if Socrates is right.

SOCRATES: But that one cannot guide correctly if one does not have knowledge; to this our agreement is likely to be incorrect. – How do you mean?

S: I will tell you. A man who knew the way to Larissa, or anywhere else you like, and went there and guided others would surely lead them well and correctly? – Certainly.

S: What if someone had had a correct opinion as to which was the way but had not gone there nor indeed had knowledge of it, would he not also lead correctly? – Certainly.

S: And as long as he had the right opinion about that of which the other has knowledge, he will not be a worse guide than the one who knows, as he has a true opinion, though not knowledge. – In no way worse.

S: So true opinion is in no way a worse guide to correct action than knowledge. It is this that we omitted in our investigation of the nature of virtue, when we said that only knowledge can lead to correct action, for true opinion can do so also. – So it seems.

S: So correct opinion is no less useful than knowledge?

MENO: Yes, to this extent, Socrates. But the man who has knowledge will always succeed, whereas he who has true opinion will only succeed at times.

S: How do you mean? Will he who has the right opinion not always succeed, as long as his opinion is right?

M: That appears to be so of necessity, and it makes me wonder, Socrates, this being the case, why knowledge is prized far more highly than right opinion, and why they are different.

S: Do you know why you wonder, or shall I tell you? – By all means tell me.

S: It is because you have paid no attention to the statues of Daedalus, but perhaps there are none in Thessaly.

S: What do you have in mind when you say this?

S: That they too run away and escape if one does not tie them down but remain in place if tied down. – So what?

S: To acquire an untied work of Daedalus is not worth much, like acquiring a runaway slave, for it does not remain, but it is worth much if tied down, for his works are very beautiful. What am I thinking of when I say this? True opinions. For true opinions, as long as they remain, are a fine thing and all they do is good, but they are not willing to remain long, and they escape from a man's mind, so that they are not worth much until one ties them down by (giving) an account of the reason why. And that, Meno my friend, is recollection, as we previously agreed. After they are tied down, in the first place they become knowledge, and then they remain in place. That is why knowledge is prized higher than correct opinion, and knowledge differs from correct opinion in being tied down.

M: Yes, by Zeus, Socrates, it seems to be something like that.

S: Indeed, I too speak as one who does not have knowledge but is guessing. However, I certainly do not think I am guessing that right opinion is a different thing than knowledge. If I claim to know anything else – and I would make that claim about few things – I would put this down as one of the things I know. – Rightly so, Socrates.

S: Well then, is it not correct that when true opinion guides the course of every action, it does no worse than knowledge? – I think you are right in this too.

S: Correct opinion is then neither inferior to knowledge nor less useful in directing actions, nor is the man who has it less so than he who has knowledge. – That is so.

S: And we agreed that the good man is beneficent. – Yes.

S: Since then it is not only through knowledge but also through right opinion that men are good, and beneficial to their cities when they are, and neither knowledge nor true opinion come to men by nature but are acquired – or do you think either of these comes by nature? – I do not think so.

S: Then if they do not come by nature, men are not so by nature either. – Surely not.

S: As goodness does not come by nature, we inquired next whether it could be taught. – Yes.

S: We thought it could be taught, if it was knowledge? – Yes.

S: And that it was knowledge if it could be taught? – Quite so.

S: And that if there were teachers of it, it could be taught, but if there were not, it was not teachable? – That is so.

S: And then we agreed that there were no teachers of it? – We did.

S: So we agreed that it was neither teachable nor knowledge? – Quite

S: But we certainly agree that virtue is a good thing? – Yes.

S: And that which guides correctly is both useful and good? – Certainly.

S:　And that only these two things, true belief and knowledge, guide correctly, and that if a man possesses these he gives correct guidance. The things that turn out right by some chance are not due to human guidance, but where there is correct human guidance it is due to two things, true belief or knowledge. – I think that is so.

S:　Now because it cannot be taught, virtue no longer seems to be knowledge? – It seems not.

S:　So one of the two good and useful things has been excluded, and knowledge is not the guide in public affairs. – I do not think so.

S:　So it is not by some kind of wisdom, or by being wise, that such men lead their cities, those such as Themistocles and those mentioned by Anytus just now? That is the reason why they cannot make others be like themselves, because it is not knowledge which makes them what they are.

M:　It is likely to be as you say, Socrates.

S:　Therefore, if it is not through knowledge, the only alternative is that it is through right opinion that statesmen follow the right course for their cities. As regards knowledge, they are no different from soothsayers and prophets. They too say many true things when inspired, but they have no knowledge of what they are saying. – That is probably so.

S:　And so, Meno, is it right to call divine these men who, without any understanding, are right in much that is of importance in what they say and do? – Certainly.

S:　We should be right to call divine also those soothsayers and prophets whom we just mentioned, and all the poets, and we should call no less divine and inspired those public men who are no less under the gods' influence and possession, as their speeches lead to success in many important matters, though they have no knowledge of what they are saying. – Quite so.

38

When Should a Belief be Supported by Evidence?

W.K. Clifford, "The Ethics of Belief"

The idea that a belief is knowledge only when true and supported has prompted several suggestions as to what form that support should take. The most popular philosophical image here has been one of knowledge as involving *good evidence*. Even a true belief, in order to be knowledge, would have to be supported by good evidence. This is because good evidence supports precisely the belief's being true. A belief is not simply an idle thought drifting through one's mind. It is stronger than that. A belief is a kind of *commitment* as to how the world really is in some respect. It is one thing for you to imagine that you are riding a horse; it is quite another thing for you to believe that you are riding one. Part of the difference is that a belief should not even exist unless one has good evidence of its being true. Only then is the commitment *merited* (that is, the commitment inherent in believing).

At any rate, that is what this reading, from the Cambridge University mathematician and philosopher W.K. Clifford (1845–79), would say. Clifford famously argues that a belief *should* not be held so long as one lacks good evidence supporting it. Clifford was not writing directly about knowing. But if believing is part of knowing then his arguments, if successful, tell us indirectly about one aspect of what it is to have an instance of knowledge.

The "should" for which Clifford argues is ethical. His dramatic view is that it is *ethically wrong* – not merely ill-advised or unhelpful – for a person to have a belief for the truth of which she lacks good evidence. Clifford offers several possible reasons for his stark claim. Think about how connected any belief can be with potential *actions*. Think of how one belief leads to *another* belief – how *habits* of

W.K. Clifford, "The Ethics of Belief" (excerpts), in *Lectures and Essays*, vol. 2 (London: Macmillan, 1879).

Metaphysics and Epistemology: A Guided Anthology, First Edition. Edited by Stephen Hetherington.
© 2014 John Wiley & Sons, Inc. Published 2014 by John Wiley & Sons, Inc.

believing more widely are formed. Think of how one person's beliefs can link with other people's beliefs – with those held by peers, friends, children. Think of how believing blends with other ways of thinking. In general, therefore, a lack of care in believing even on a single occasion can spread far and wide throughout further beliefs and associated actions, both one's own and other people's. Danger lurks within and without, if Clifford is correct. Is the difference between a true belief's being knowledge and its not being knowledge thus a matter of one's wanting, seeking, and gaining good evidence in support of the belief's being true?

I. The Duty of Inquiry

A shipowner was about to send to sea an emigrant-ship. He knew that she was old, and not over-well built at the first; that she had seen many seas and climes, and often had needed repairs. Doubts had been suggested to him that possibly she was not seaworthy. These doubts preyed upon his mind and made him unhappy; he thought that perhaps he ought to have her thoroughly overhauled and refitted, even though this should put him to great expense. Before the ship sailed, however, he succeeded in overcoming these melancholy reflections. He said to himself that she had gone safely through so many voyages and weathered so many storms that it was idle to suppose she would not come safely home from this trip also. He would put his trust in Providence, which could hardly fail to protect all these unhappy families that were leaving their fatherland to seek for better times elsewhere. He would dismiss from his mind all ungenerous suspicious about the honesty of builders and contractors. In such ways he acquired a sincere and comfortable conviction that his vessel was thoroughly safe and seaworthy; he watched her departure with a light heart, and benevolent wishes for the success of the exiles in their strange new home that was to be; and he got his insurance-money when she went down in mid-ocean and told no tales.

What shall we say of him? Surely this, that he was verily guilty of the death of those men. It is admitted that he did sincerely believe in the soundness of his ship; but the sincerity of his conviction can in no wise help him, because *he had no right to believe on such evidence as was before him*. He had acquired his belief not by honestly earning it in patient investigation, but by stifling his doubts. And although in the end he may have felt so sure about it that he could not think otherwise, yet inasmuch as he had knowingly and willingly worked himself into that frame of mind, he must be held responsible for it.

Let us alter the case a little, and suppose that the ship was not unsound after all; that she made her voyage safely, and many others after it. Will that diminish the guilt of her owner? Not one jot. When an action is once done, it is right or wrong for ever; no accidental failure of its good or evil fruits can possibly alter that. The man would not have been innocent, he would only have been not found out. The question of right or wrong has to do with the origin of his belief, not the matter of it; not what it was, but how he got it; not whether it turned out to be true or false, but whether he had a right to believe on such evidence as was before him.

There was once an island in which some of the inhabitants professed a religion teaching neither the doctrine of original sin nor that of eternal punishment. A suspicion got abroad that the professors of this religion had made use of unfair means to get their doctrines taught to children. They were accused of wresting the laws of their country in such a way as to remove children from the care of their natural and legal guardians; and even of stealing them away and keeping them concealed from their friends and relations. A certain number of men formed themselves into a society for the purpose of agitating the public about this matter. They published grave accusations against individual citizens of the highest position and character, and did all in their power to injure these citizens in the exercise of their professions. So great was the noise they made, that a Commission was appointed to investigate the facts; but after the Commission had carefully inquired into all the evidence that could be got, it appeared that the accused were innocent. Not only had they been accused on insufficient evidence, but the evidence of their innocence was such as the agitators might easily have obtained, if they had attempted a fair inquiry. After these disclosures the inhabitants of that country looked upon the members of the agitating society, not only as persons whose judgment was to be distrusted, but also as no longer to be counted honourable men. For although they had sincerely and conscientiously believed in the charges they had made, *yet they had no right to believe on such evidence as was before them.* Their sincere convictions, instead of being honestly earned by patient inquiring, were stolen by listening to the voice of prejudice and passion.

Let us vary this case also, and suppose, other things remaining as before, that a still more accurate investigation proved the accused to have been really guilty. Would this make any difference in the guilt of the accusers? Clearly not; the question is not whether their belief was true or false, but whether they entertained it on wrong grounds. They would no doubt say, "Now you see that we were right after all; next time perhaps you will believe us." And they might be believed, but they would not thereby become honourable men. They would not be innocent, they would only be not found out. Every one of them, if he chose to examine himself *in foro conscientiæ* [lit., "in the court of conscience"], would know that he had acquired and nourished a belief, when he had no right to believe on such evidence as was before him; and therein he would know that he had done a wrong thing.

It may be said, however, that in both of these supposed cases it is not the belief which is judged to be wrong, but the action following upon it. The shipowner might say, "I am perfectly certain that my ship is sound, but still I feel it my duty to have her examined, before trusting the lives of so many people to her." And it might be said to the agitator, "However convinced you were of the justice of your cause and the truth of your convictions, you ought not to have made a public attack upon any man's character until you had examined the evidence on both sides with the utmost patience and care."

In the first place, let us admit that, so far as it goes, this view of the case is right and necessary; right, because even when a man's belief is so fixed that he cannot think otherwise, he still has a choice in regard to the action suggested by it, and so cannot escape the duty of investigating on the ground of the strength of his convictions; and necessary, because those who are not yet capable of controlling their feelings and thoughts must have a plain rule dealing with overt acts.

But [...] it is not possible so to sever the belief from the action it suggests as to condemn the one without condemning the other. No man holding a strong belief on one side of a question, or even wishing to hold a belief on one side, can investigate it with such fairness and completeness as if he were really in doubt and unbiassed; so that the existence of a belief not founded on fair inquiry unfits a man for the performance of this necessary duty.

Nor is that truly a belief at all which has not some influence upon the actions of him who holds it. He who truly believes that which prompts him to an action has looked upon the action to lust after it, he has committed it already in his heart. If a belief is not realised immediately in open deeds, it is stored up for the guidance of the future. It goes to make a part of that aggregate of beliefs which is the link between sensation and action at every moment of all our lives, and which is so organised and compacted together that no part of it can be isolated from the rest, but every new addition modifies the structure of the whole. No real belief, however trifling and fragmentary it may seem, is ever truly insignificant; it prepares us to receive more of its like, confirms those which resembled it before, and weakens others; and so gradually it lays a stealthy train in our inmost thoughts, which may some day explode into overt action, and leave its stamp upon our character for ever.

And no one man's belief is in any case a private matter which concerns himself alone. Our lives are guided by that general conception of the course of things which has been created by society for social purposes. Our words, our phrases, our forms and processes and modes of thought, are common property, fashioned and perfected from age to age; an heirloom which every succeeding generation inherits as a precious deposit and a sacred trust to be handed on to the next one, not unchanged but enlarged and purified, with some clear marks of its proper handiwork. Into this, for good or ill, is woven every belief of every man who has speech of his fellows. An awful privilege, and an awful responsibility, that we should help to create the world in which posterity will live.

In the two supposed cases which have been considered, it has been judged wrong to believe on insufficient evidence, or to nourish belief by suppressing doubts and avoiding investigation. The reason of this judgment is not far to seek: it is that in both these cases the belief held by one man was of great importance to other men. But forasmuch as no belief held by one man, however seemingly trivial the belief, and however obscure the believer, is ever actually insignificant or without it effect on the fate of mankind, we have no choice but to extend our judgment to all cases of belief whatever. Belief, that sacred faculty which prompts the decisions of our will, and knits into harmonious working all the compacted energies of our being, is ours not for ourselves, but for humanity. [...]

It is not only the leader of men, statesman, philosopher, or poet, that owes this bounden duty to mankind. Every rustic who delivers in the village alehouse his slow, infrequent sentences, may help to kill or keep alive the fatal superstitions which clog his race. Every hard-worked wife of an artisan may transmit to her children beliefs which shall knit society together, or rend it in pieces. No simplicity of mind, no obscurity of station, can escape the universal duty of questioning all that we believe.

[...]

Every time we let ourselves believe for unworthy reasons, we weaken our powers of self-control, of doubting, of judicially and fairly weighing evidence. We all suffer severely enough from the maintenance and support of false beliefs and the fatally wrong actions which they lead to, and the evil born when one such belief is entertained is great and wide. But a greater and wider evil arises when the credulous character is maintained and supported, when a habit of believing for unworthy reasons is fostered and made permanent. If I steal money from any person, there may be no harm done by the mere transfer of possession; he may not feel the loss, or it may prevent him from using the money badly. But I cannot help doing this great wrong towards Man, that I make myself dishonest. What hurts society is not that it should lose its property, but that it should become a den of thieves; for then it must cease to be society. This is why we ought not to do evil that good may come; for at any rate this great evil has come, that we have done evil and are made wicked thereby. In like manner, if I let myself believe anything on insufficient evidence, there may be no great harm done by the mere belief; it may be true after all, or I may never have occasion to exhibit it in outward acts. But I cannot help doing this great wrong towards Man, that I make myself credulous. The danger to society is not merely that it should believe wrong things, though that is great enough; but that it should become credulous, and lose the habit of testing things and inquiring into them; for then it must sink back into savagery.

The harm which is done by credulity in a man is not confined to the fostering of a credulous character in others, and consequent support of false beliefs. Habitual want of care about what I believe leads to habitual want of care in others about the truth of what is told to me. Men speak the truth to one another when each reveres the truth in his own mind and in the other's mind; but how shall my friend revere the truth in my mind when I myself am careless about it, when I believe things because I want to believe them, and because they are comforting and pleasant?

[...]

To sum up: it is wrong always, everywhere, and for any one, to believe anything upon insufficient evidence.

If a man, holding a belief which he was taught in childhood or persuaded of afterwards, keeps down and pushes away any doubts which arise about it in his mind, purposely avoids the reading of books and the company of men that call in question or discuss it, and regards as impious those questions which cannot easily be asked without disturbing it – the life of that man is one long sin against mankind.

[...]

Inquiry into the evidence of a doctrine is not to be made once for all, and then taken as finally settled. It is never lawful to stifle a doubt; for either it can be honestly answered by means of the inquiry already made, or else it proves that the inquiry was not complete.

"But," says one, "I am a busy man; I have no time for the long course of study which would be necessary to make me in any degree a competent judge of certain questions, or even able to understand the nature of the arguments." Then he should have no time to believe.

39

Is Knowledge a Kind
of Objective Certainty?

A.J. Ayer, *The Problem of Knowledge*

We are trying to uncover the fundamental nature of what it is to know. If the previous reading should be believed, perhaps part of a belief's being knowledge is one's having good evidence supporting the belief. But *how* good must that evidence be? (For example, must it be very very good? Must it even be perfect?) What is it to *have* the evidence? (For example, must one be aware of it, using it consciously *as* evidence?) This well-known reading bears upon those questions. It is from A.J. Ayer (1910–89), a dominant figure in twentieth-century English philosophy, mainly at the University of Oxford. In this extract, he highlights a few complexities involved in assessing whether someone has a piece of knowledge. These complexities cluster around a need for some appropriate *objective* standard to be satisfied by the would-be knower. Will this standard amount to an objective form of *certainty*? Ayer argues so.

His point is not that knowing must involve one's *feeling* certain. Nor is it that feeling certain would be enough for knowing. What matters, in Ayer's view, is that if one is to have knowledge then one must have the *right* to be certain. Imagine feeling wholly certain that a belief of yours is true. Imagine even that you are completely certain of your having good evidence supporting the belief. Even so, all of this confidence in yourself might be mistaken, misplaced. You could be over-estimating the quality of your evidence. You could be overlooking a reason why your belief is actually false. It is not difficult to imagine someone else having such confidence in a belief of her own when, in your view, she should not. Yet what could be true of her in that respect can equally well be true of you with your own

A.J. Ayer, *The Problem of Knowledge* (London: Macmillan, 1956), pp. 28–32. Reprinted with permission of Palgrave Macmillan.

Metaphysics and Epistemology: A Guided Anthology, First Edition. Edited by Stephen Hetherington.
© 2014 John Wiley & Sons, Inc. Published 2014 by John Wiley & Sons, Inc.

beliefs. The point is that we understand the idea of having – as an objective accomplishment – the *right* to be sure. That idea (Ayer would infer) should be included within our concept of knowledge: *knowing* is to be a correspondingly objective accomplishment.

Ayer notices, equally, how a person may be unwittingly helped in that objective way. You may have formed a belief very reliably and carefully (such as by using good eyesight). This could well give you an objective right to be sure of the belief's truth. But you might also be unaware of being so well placed. You simply *are* well placed, without realizing that you are. Could your belief be knowledge anyway? Can a child, for example, satisfy an objectively excellent standard in forming some beliefs, even when he cannot tell you anything about this standard – even if it is therefore not a standard involving self-consciously reflective use of evidence?

Knowing as Having the Right to be Sure

The answers which we have found for the questions we have so far been discussing have not yet put us in a position to give a complete account of what it is to know that something is the case. The first requirement is that what is known should be true, but this is not sufficient; not even if we add to it the further condition that one must be completely sure of what one knows. For it is possible to be completely sure of something which is in fact true, but yet not to know it. The circumstances may be such that one is not entitled to be sure. For instance, a superstitious person who had inadvertently walked under a ladder might be convinced as a result that he was about to suffer some misfortune; and he might in fact be right. But it would not be correct to say that he knew that this was going to be so. He arrived at his belief by a process of reasoning which would not be generally reliable; so, although his prediction came true, it was not a case of knowledge. Again, if someone were fully persuaded of a mathematical proposition by a proof which could be shown to be invalid, he would not, without further evidence, be said to know the proposition, even though it was true. But while it is not hard to find examples of true and fully confident beliefs which in some ways fail to meet the standards required for knowledge, it is not at all easy to determine exactly what these standards are.

One way of trying to discover them would be to consider what would count as satisfactory answers to the question How do you know? Thus people may be credited with knowing truths of mathematics or logic if they are able to give a valid proof of them, or even if, without themselves being able to set out such a proof, they have obtained this information from someone who can. Claims to know empirical statements may be upheld by a reference to perception, or to memory, or to testimony, or to historical records, or to scientific laws. But such backing is not always strong enough for knowledge. Whether it is so or not depends upon the circumstances of the particular case. If I were asked how I knew that a physical object of a certain sort was in such and such a place, it would, in general, be a sufficient answer for me to say that I could see it; but if my eyesight were bad and the light were dim, this answer might not be sufficient. Even though I was right, it might still be said that I did not really know that the object was there. If I have a poor memory and the event which I claim to remember is remote, my memory of it may still not amount to knowledge, even though in this instance it does not fail me. If a witness is unreliable, his unsupported evidence may not enable us to know that what he says is true, even in a case where we completely trust him and he is not in fact deceiving us. In a given instance it is possible to decide whether the backing is strong enough to justify a claim to knowledge. But to say in general how strong it has to be would require our drawing up a list of the conditions under which perception, or memory, or testimony, or other forms of evidence are reliable. And this would be a very complicated matter, if indeed it could be done at all.

Moreover, we cannot assume that, even in particular instances, an answer to the question How do you know? will always be forthcoming. There may very well be cases in which one knows that something is so without its being possible to say how one knows it. I am not so much thinking now of claims to know facts of immediate experience, statements like 'I know that I feel pain', which raise problems of their own [...]. In cases of this sort it may be argued that the question how one knows does not arise. But even when it clearly does arise, it may not find an answer. Suppose that someone were consistently successful in predicting events of a certain kind, events, let us say, which are not ordinarily thought to be predictable, like the results of a lottery. If his run of successes were sufficiently impressive, we might very well come to say that he knew which number would win, even though he did not reach this conclusion by any rational method, or indeed by any method at all. We might say that he knew it by intuition, but this would be to assert no more than that he did know it but that we could not say how. In the same way, if someone were consistently successful in reading the minds of others without having any of the usual sort of evidence, we might say that he knew these things telepathically. But in default of any further explanation this would come down to saying merely that he did know them, but not by any ordinary means. Words like 'intuition' and 'telepathy' are brought in just to disguise the fact that no explanation has been found.

But if we allow this sort of knowledge to be even theoretically possible, what becomes of the distinction between knowledge and true belief? How does our man who knows what the results of the lottery will be differ from one who only makes a series of lucky guesses? The answer is that, so far as the man himself is concerned, there need not be any difference. His procedure and his state of mind, when he is said to know what will happen, may be exactly the same as when it is said that he is only guessing. The difference is that to say that he knows is to concede to him the right to be sure, while to say that he is only guessing is to withhold it. Whether we make this concession will depend upon the view which we take of his performance. Normally we do not say that people know things unless they have fol-lowed one of the accredited routes to knowledge. If someone reaches a true conclusion without appearing to have any adequate basis for it, we are likely to say that he does not really know it. But if he were repeatedly successful in a given domain, we might very well come to say that he knew the facts in question, even though we could not explain how he knew them. We should grant him the right to be sure, simply on the basis of his success. This is, indeed, a point on which people's views might be expected to differ. Not everyone would regard a successful run of predictions, however long sustained, as being by itself a sufficient backing for a claim to knowledge. And here there can be no question of proving that this attitude is mistaken. Where there are recognized criteria for deciding when one has the right to be sure, anyone who insists that their being satisfied is still not enough for knowledge may be accused, for what the charge is worth, of misusing the verb 'to know'. But it is possible to find, or at any rate to devise, examples which are not covered in this respect by any established rule of usage. Whether they are to count as instances of knowledge is then a question which we are left free to decide.

40

Are All Fallibly Supported True Beliefs Instances of Knowledge?

Edmund L. Gettier, "Is Justified True Belief Knowledge?"

In the previous reading, Ayer talked of the right to be sure of the truth of one's belief. Many philosophers would explain such a right in terms of the evidence that is possessed in support of the belief's being true. But most philosophers (unlike Ayer) would not require knowing always to include one's having a right to be *sure*. They would talk of knowledge as being a true belief supported simply by good evidence, say. They may well regard it as more realistic to require within knowledge the presence only of good evidence – rather than evidence so excellent as to make certain the truth of the belief in question. Indeed, it seems, philosophers had long taken for granted an analysis of the concept of knowledge whereby one's knowing *is* precisely one's having a well-supported or justified true belief. Accordingly, for instance, when they were denying that someone had a particular piece of knowledge, philosophers would contest either the truth of the person's belief or her evidence for its truth. Being true and well supported were presumed to be the only two achievements inherent in knowing.

But that epistemological consensus ended in 1963, with this reading from Edmund Gettier (b. 1927), most of whose career was at the University of Massachusetts, Amherst. Gettier's engaging article convinced epistemologists – dramatically, in a philosophical instant – that knowledge is *not* so easily understood. Gone – also in that philosophical instant – was part of that traditional philosophical image of knowledge (an image that became known, in retrospect, as the justified–true–belief analysis of knowledge). An energetic search began. Could a replacement analysis be found for the concept of knowledge?

Edmund L. Gettier, "Is Justified True Belief Knowledge?", *Analysis* 23 (1963), 121–123. Reprinted with permission of Oxford University Press Journals.

Gettier's challenge aimed to disprove only part of the traditional analysis. His target was the claim that being supported (well justified) and true is always *enough* or *sufficient* to make a belief knowledge. His strategy was to imagine possible situations containing a belief that is true and well supported *without* being knowledge. Those possible situations were Gettier's two thought-experiments (i.e., *Gettier cases*, as these and others like them have subsequently been called). Within each, someone forms a true belief that is well-but-not-perfectly supported – a fallibly justified true belief. Yet in each case, too (claimed Gettier), this belief is not knowledge.

Why are those beliefs not knowledge (if in fact they are not)? The cases are described briefly by Gettier, leaving much room for competing diagnoses of what aspect of them chases away knowledge. *Something* is significantly odd or inadequate in how any Gettier case's justified true belief comes to exist. What exactly is that "something," though? Epistemologists took from Gettier this question: What is *also* needed for making a belief knowledge, if being true and well-but-fallibly supported does not guarantee its being knowledge?

Various attempts have been made in recent years to state necessary and sufficient conditions for someone's knowing a given proposition. The attempts have often been such that they can be stated in a form similar to the following:[1]

(a) S knows that P   *IFF*   (i)   P is true,
                        ['if and only if']   (ii) S believes that P, and
                                              (iii) S is justified in believing that P.

For example, Chisholm has held that the following gives the necessary and sufficient conditions for knowledge:[2]

(b) S knows that P   *IFF*   (i)   S accepts P,
                                              (ii) S has adequate evidence for P, and
                                              (iii) P is true.

Ayer has stated the necessary and sufficient conditions for knowledge as follows:[3]

(c) S knows that P   *IFF*   (i)   P is true,
                                              (ii) S is sure that P is true, and
                                              (iii) S has the right to be sure that P is true.

I shall argue that (a) is false in that the conditions stated therein do not constitute a *sufficient* condition for the truth of the proposition that S knows that P. The same argument will show that (b) and (c) fail if 'has adequate evidence for' or 'has the right to be sure that' is substituted for 'is justified in believing that' throughout.

I shall begin by noting two points. First, in that sense of 'justified' in which S's being justified in believing P is a necessary condition of S's knowing that P, it is possible for a person to be justified in believing a proposition that is in fact false. Secondly, for any proposition P, if S is justified in believing P, and P entails Q, and S deduces Q from P and accepts Q as a result of this deduction, then S is justified in believing Q. Keeping these two points in mind, I shall now present two cases in which the conditions stated in (a) are true for some proposition, though it is at the same time false that the person in question knows that proposition.

Case I:

Suppose that Smith and Jones have applied for a certain job. And suppose that Smith has strong evidence for the following conjunctive proposition:

(d)   Jones is the man who will get the job, and Jones has ten coins in his pocket.

Smith's evidence for (d) might be that the president of the company assured him that Jones would in the end be selected, and that he, Smith, had counted the coins in Jones's pocket ten minutes ago. Proposition (d) entails:

(e)   The man who will get the job has ten coins in his pocket.

Let us suppose that Smith sees the entailment from (d) to (e), and accepts (e) on the grounds of (d), for which he has strong evidence. In this case, Smith is clearly justified in believing that (e) is true.

But imagine, further, that unknown to Smith, he himself, not Jones, will get the job. And, also, unknown to Smith, he himself has ten coins in his pocket. Proposition (e) is then true, though proposition (d), from which Smith inferred (e), is false. In our example, then, all of the following are true: (*i*) (e) is true, (*ii*) Smith believes that (e) is true, and (*iii*) Smith is justified in believing that (e) is true. But it is equally clear that Smith does not *know* that (e) is true; for (e) is true in virtue of the number of coins in Smith's pocket, while Smith does not know how many coins are in Smith's pocket, and bases his belief in (e) on a count of the coins in Jones's pocket, whom he falsely believes to be the man who will get the job.

Case II:

Let us suppose that Smith has strong evidence for the following proposition:

(f)   Jones owns a Ford.

Smith's evidence might be that Jones has at all times in the past within Smith's memory owned a car, and always a Ford, and that Jones has just offered Smith a ride while driving a Ford. Let us imagine, now, that Smith has another friend, Brown, of whose whereabouts he is totally ignorant. Smith selects three place-names quite at random, and constructs the following three propositions:

(g)   Either Jones owns a Ford, or Brown is in Boston;
(h)   Either Jones owns a Ford, or Brown is in Barcelona;
(i)   Either Jones owns a Ford, or Brown is in Brest-Litovsk.

Each of these propositions is entailed by (f). Imagine that Smith realizes the entailment of each of these propositions he has constructed by (f), and proceeds to accept (g), (h), and (i) on the basis of (f). Smith has correctly inferred (g), (h), and (i) from a proposition for which he has strong evidence. Smith is therefore completely justified in believing each of these three propositions. Smith, of course, has no idea where Brown is.

But imagine now that two further conditions hold. First, Jones does *not* own a Ford, but is at present driving a rented car. And secondly, by the sheerest coincidence, and entirely unknown to Smith, the place mentioned in proposition (h) happens really to be the place where Brown is. If these two conditions hold then Smith does *not* know that (h) is true, even though (*i*) (h) *is* true, (*ii*) Smith does believe that (h) is true, and (*iii*) Smith is justified in believing that (h) is true.

These two examples show that definition (a) does not state a *sufficient* condition for someone's knowing a given proposition. The same cases, with appropriate changes, will suffice to show that neither definition (b) nor definition (c) do so either.

Notes

1. Plato seems to be considering some such definition at *Theaetutus* 201, and perhaps accepting one at *Meno* 98.
2. Roderick M. Chisholm, *Perceiving: a Philosophical Study*, Cornell University Press (Ithaca, New York, 1957), p. 16.
3. A. J. Ayer, *The Problem of Knowledge*, Macmillan (London, 1956), p. 34.

41

Must a True Belief Arise Aptly, if it is to be Knowledge?

Alvin I. Goldman, "A Causal Theory of Knowing"

Edmund Gettier, in the previous reading, left us with a powerful question about whether philosophers had ever really understood the nature of knowing. He never developed any proposal for how, given his challenge, we *should* understand what it is to know. But many epistemologists did exactly that, with "post-Gettier epistemology" becoming a thriving philosophical industry. Several potentially promising lines of thought appeared. These were investigated, modified, reinvestigated, discarded, resuscitated, investigated anew, and so on. Current epistemology is still partly post-Gettier epistemology, in the sense of being under the influence of Gettier's challenge. So the next few readings introduce some Gettier-sensitive lines of thought. We begin with a suggestion from Alvin Goldman (b. 1938), a highly influential epistemologist, most recently at Rutgers University.

His suggestion appeared just a few years after Gettier's 1963 paper. Goldman highlighted the fact that each Gettier case involves a strikingly odd *causal* sequence. This is a key to understanding knowledge (thought Goldman). Beliefs *arise*, at times and over time: there can be a time when a particular belief is not yet present, and subsequently a time by when it has come into existence. In Gettier's own first case, for example, Smith comes to believe that the person who will get the job has ten coins in their pocket. Somehow, that belief has *arisen* within Smith. But if Goldman is right, that belief of Smith's has not arisen *aptly* – aptly, that is, for being knowledge. In effect, Goldman is advocating a Gettier-inspired change to the pre-Gettier conception of knowledge. We would acknowledge explicitly, within that conception, the importance of a belief's causal ancestry.

Alvin I. Goldman, "A Causal Theory of Knowing" [1967] (excerpts) (revised), in M.D. Roth and L. Galis (eds.), *Knowing: Essays in the Analysis of Knowledge* (New York: Random House, 1970). First published in *Journal of Philosophy* 64/12 (June 22 1967), pp. 357–373. Reprinted with permission.

The new conception would be something like this: A belief is knowledge when and only when it is true and well supported, having arisen aptly.

What are the apt ways for a belief to arise, if it is to be knowledge? Goldman describes a few, taking his cue from *normal* cases of knowing. Most of us most of the time are not aware of the details of whatever causal mechanism or pattern has given us a particular belief. But Goldman is not requiring that such awareness always be part of knowing. Look out of your window. What do you see? "Gosh. *That* is surprising ...." Maybe you now believe that a fox and an eagle are sitting side by side on your lawn. How, exactly, has this belief arisen? "Perceptually: I see the two animals." Indeed so. There is a *causal* perceptual sequence, even a complex one, responsible for your belief. And although the belief has an odd content, this need not preclude its being knowledge. If it has been caused in a perceptually normal way – by applying good eyesight, for a start – then Goldman's proposal would allow it to be knowledge.

Since Edmund L. Gettier pointed out a certain important inadequacy of the traditional analysis of "S knows that p," several attempts have been made to correct that analysis.[1] In this paper I shall offer still another analysis (or sketch of an analysis) of "S knows that p," one which will avert Gettier's problem. My concern will be with knowledge of empirical propositions only. Although certain elements in my theory would be relevant to the analysis of knowledge of nonempirical truths, my theory is not intended to apply to knowledge of nonempirical truths.

Consider [...] Gettier's second counter-example to the traditional analysis.

[...]

Notice that what *makes p* true is the fact that Brown is in Barcelona, but that this fact has nothing to do with Smith's believing p. That is, there is no *causal* connection between the fact that Brown is in Barcelona and Smith's believing p. If Smith had come to believe p by reading a letter from Brown postmarked in Barcelona, then we might say that Smith knew p. Alternatively, if Jones did own a Ford, and his owning the Ford was manifested by his offer of a ride to Smith, and this in turn resulted in Smith's believing p, then we would say that Smith knew p. Thus, one thing that seems to be missing in this example is a causal connection between the fact that makes p true [or simply: the fact that p] and Smith's belief of p. The requirement of such a *causal connection* is what I wish to add to the traditional analysis.

To see that this requirement is satisfied in all cases of (empirical) knowledge, we must examine a variety of such causal connections. Clearly, only a sketch of the important kinds of cases is possible here.

Perhaps the simplest case of a causal chain connecting some fact p with someone's belief of p is that of *perception*. I wish to espouse a version of the causal theory of perception, in essence that defended by H. P. Grice.[2] Suppose that S sees that there is a vase in front of him. How is this to be analyzed? I shall not attempt a complete analysis of this, but a necessary condition of S's seeing that there is a vase in front of him is that there be a certain kind of causal connection between the presence of the vase and S's believing that a vase is present. I shall not attempt to describe this causal process in detail. Indeed, to a large extent, a description of this process must be regarded as a problem for the special sciences, not for philosophy. But a certain causal process – viz., that which standardly takes place when we say that so-and-so *sees* such-and-such – must occur. That our ordinary concept of sight (i.e., knowledge acquired by sight) includes a causal requirement is shown by the fact that if the relevant causal process is absent we would withhold the assertion that so-and-so *saw* such-and-such. Suppose that, although a vase is directly in front of S, a laser photograph[3] is interposed between it and S, thereby blocking it from S's view. The photograph, however, is one of a vase (a different vase), and when it is illuminated by light waves from a laser, it looks to S exactly like a real vase. When the photograph is illuminated, S forms the belief that there is a vase in front of him. Here we would deny that S *sees* that there is a vase in front of him, for his view of the real vase is completely blocked, so that it has no causal role in the formation of his belief. Of course, S might *know* that there was a vase in front of him even if the photograph is blocking his view. Someone else, in position to see the vase, might tell S that there is a vase in front of him. Here the presence of the vase might be a causal ancestor of *S's* belief, but the causal process would not be a (purely) *perceptual* one. S could not be said to *see* that there is a vase in front of him. For this to be true, there must be a causal process, but one of a very special sort, connecting the presence of the vase with S's belief. [...] I turn next to memory, i.e., knowledge that is based, in part, on memory. Remembering, like perceiving, must be regarded as a causal process. S remembers p at time t only if S's believing p at an earlier time is a cause of his believing p at t [...] Suppose S perceives p at t_0, but forgets it at t_1. At t_2 he begins to believe p again because someone tells him p, but at t_2 he has no memory impression of p. At t_3 we artificially stimulate in S a memory impression of p. It does not follow that S remembers p at t_3. The description of the case suggests that his believing p at t_0 has no causal effect whatever on his believing p at t_3; and if we accepted this fact, we would deny that he remembers p at t_3.

Knowledge can be acquired by a combination of perception and memory. At t_0, the fact p causes S to believe p, by perception. S's believing p at t_0 results, via memory, in S's believing p at t_1. Thus, the fact p is a cause of S's believing p at t_1, and S can be said to know p at t_1. But not all knowledge results from perception and memory alone. In particular, much knowledge is based on *inference*.

As I shall use the term 'inference,' to say that S knows p by "inference" does not entail that S went through an explicit, conscious process of reasoning. It is not necessary that he have "talked to himself," saying something like "Since such-and-such is true, p must also be true." My belief that there is a fire in the neighborhood is based on, or inferred from, my belief that I hear a fire engine. But I have not gone through a process of explicit reasoning, saying "There's a fire engine; therefore there must be a fire." Perhaps the word 'inference' is ordinarily used only where explicit reasoning occurs; if so, my use of the term will be somewhat broader than its ordinary use.

Suppose S perceives that there is solidified lava in various parts of the countryside. On the basis of this belief, plus various "background" beliefs about the production of lava, S concludes that a nearby mountain erupted many centuries ago. Let us assume that this is a highly warranted inductive inference, one which gives S adequate evidence for believing that the mountain did erupt many centuries ago. Assuming this proposition is true, does S know it? This depends on the nature of the causal process that induced his belief. If there is a continuous causal chain of the sort he envisages connecting the fact that the mountain erupted with his belief of this fact, then S knows it. If there is no such causal chain, however, S does not know that proposition.

Suppose that the mountain erupts, leaving lava around the countryside. The lava remains there until S perceives it and infers that the mountain erupted. Then S does know that the mountain erupted. But now suppose that, after the mountain has erupted, a man somehow removes all the lava. A century later, a different man (not knowing of the real volcano) decides to make it look as if there had been a volcano, and therefore puts lava in appropriate places. Still later, S comes across this lava and concludes that the mountain erupted centuries ago. In this case, S cannot be said to know the proposition. This is because the fact that the mountain did erupt is not a cause of S's believing that it erupted. A necessary condition of S's knowing p is that his believing p be connected with p by a causal chain.

Notes

1. "Is Justified True Belief Knowledge?", *Analysis*, XXIII.6, ns 96 (June 1963): 121–123. New analyses have been proposed by Michael Clark, "Knowledge and Grounds: A Comment on Mr. Gettier's Paper," *Analysis*, XXIV.2, ns 98 (December 1963): 46–48; Ernest Sosa, "The Analysis of 'Knowledge That P,'" *Analysis*, XXV.1, ns 103 (October 1964): 1–3; and Keith Lehrer, "Knowledge, Truth, and Evidence," *Analysis*, XXV.5, ns 105 (April 1965); 168–175.
2. "The Causal Theory of Perception," *Proceedings of the Aristotelian Society*, Supp. Vol. XXXV (1961).
3. If a laser photograph (hologram) is illuminated by light waves, especially waves from a laser, the effect of the hologram on the viewer is exactly as if the object were being seen. It preserves three-dimensionality completely, and even gives appropriate parallax effects as the viewer moves relative to it. Cf. E. N. Leith and J. Upatnieks, "Photography by Laser," *Scientific American*, CCXII, 6 (June 1965): 24.

42

Must a True Belief Arise Reliably, if it is to be Knowledge?

reliabilist

Alvin I. Goldman, "Discrimination and Perceptual Knowledge"

The previous reading was Alvin Goldman's first contribution to post-Gettier epistemology. But the causal theory of knowledge was not Goldman's final influential idea about the nature of knowledge. Several years later, for instance, he published the paper from which this reading comes. The paper is centered upon a further thought-experiment. It describes a possible situation that most epistemologists have regarded as another form of Gettier case – a situation differing in a significant way from Gettier's own two stories. This one had been thought of by Carl Ginet (b. 1932), a prominent philosopher from Cornell University. This paper by Goldman brought Ginet's form of Gettier case to wider epistemological attention. Not only that; Goldman proposed an early version of a new idea about knowledge's nature. This idea has become known as *reliabilism*. It is a form of analysis with which Goldman, especially, has become associated. In later publications, he has articulated reliabilism more fully. He has even applied it to the task of understanding how knowing occurs throughout social institutions.

This reading's story is about someone, Henry, with the misfortune to form his well-supported true belief – "That's a barn" – when driving through an area where he *could easily* have been misled unwittingly while having a belief with that particular content. *Fake Barn Country* is what epistemologists often name Henry's setting: it includes many barn façades that only look from the road like real barns, deceiving passers-by. This is not a locale where one is likely to be correct when believing, "That's a barn." However, Henry does not know this odd fact about his context. According to most epistemologists, his belief is not knowledge.

Yet his belief has arisen in a causally *apt* way. That is, it satisfies the causal criterion for knowledge – the criterion of Goldman's outlined in the previous reading.

Alvin I. Goldman, "Discrimination and Perceptual Knowledge" (excerpts), *The Journal of Philosophy* 73 (1976), 771–791. Reprinted with permission.

Goldman is thus offering this case as a problem for that causal theory of knowledge (as well as for some other ways of thinking about knowledge), since that theory fails to explain why the belief is not knowledge.

What is Goldman's proposed solution this time? What, if anything, does this new form of Gettier case reveal about how we should conceive of knowing? Goldman's answer is that a knower must be able to be relevantly *discriminating*: one needs to be able to discriminate – discern a difference at the time – between how the world *appears* to one and any relevant competing possible way it could *actually* be at the time. The idea of relevance is vague. But sometimes it is clear: because there *are* fake barns in Henry's neighborhood, the possibility of their presence is one he needs to eliminate discriminatingly. Yet this he cannot do, when using his actual observational evidence.

How is this a reliabilist conception of knowledge? To require that the believer be able to rule out that sort of possibility discriminatingly is (suggests Goldman) a way of requiring that her belief arise <u>reliably</u>. The belief needs to have been formed in a way that was likely to cause a *true* belief to come into existence. So, Henry's belief has arisen *un*reliably. This is why it is not knowledge (in spite of its being true and its being well supported in an apparently normal way).

✳ knowing something means having the ability to discriminate. ✳

What kinds of causal processes or mechanisms must be responsible for a belief if that belief is to count as knowledge? They must be mechanisms that are, in an appropriate sense, "reliable." Roughly, a cognitive mechanism or process is reliable if it not only produces true beliefs in actual situations, but would produce true beliefs, or at least inhibit false beliefs, in relevant counterfactual situations. The theory of knowledge I envisage, then, would contain an important counterfactual component.

To be reliable, a cognitive mechanism must enable a person to *discriminate* or *differentiate* between incompatible states of affairs. It must operate in such a way that incompatible states of the world would generate different cognitive responses. Perceptual mechanisms illustrate this clearly. A perceptual mechanism is reliable to the extent that contrary features of the environment (e.g., an object's being red, versus its being yellow) would produce contrary perceptual states of the organism, which would, in turn, produce suitably different beliefs about the environment. Another belief-governing mechanism is a reasoning mechanism, which, given a set of antecedent beliefs, generates or inhibits various new beliefs. A reasoning mechanism is reliable to the extent that its functional procedures would generate new true beliefs from antecedent true beliefs.

My emphasis on discrimination accords with a sense of the verb 'know' that has been neglected by philosophers. The O.E.D. lists one (early) sense of 'know' as "*to distinguish* (one thing) *from* (another)," as in "I know a hawk from a handsaw" (*Hamlet*) and "We'll teach him to know Turtles from Jayes" (*Merry Wives of Windsor*). Although it no longer has great currency, this sense still survives in such expressions as "I don't know him from Adam," "He doesn't know right from left," and other phrases that readily come to mind. I suspect that this construction is historically important and can be used to shed light on constructions in which 'know' takes propositional objects. I suggest that a person is said to know that *p* just in case he *distinguishes* or *discriminates* the truth of *p* from relevant alternatives.

A knowledge attribution imputes to someone the discrimination of a given state of affairs from possible alternatives, but not necessarily all logically possible alternatives. In forming beliefs about the world, we do not normally consider all logical possibilities. And in deciding whether someone knows that *p* (its truth being assumed), we do not ordinarily require him to discriminate *p* from all logically possible alternatives. [...]

I

Consider the following example.[1] Henry is driving in the country-side with his son. For the boy's edification Henry identifies various objects on the landscape as they come into view. "That's a cow," says Henry, "That's a tractor," "That's a silo," "That's a barn," etc. Henry has no doubt about the identity of these objects; in particular, he has no doubt that the last-mentioned object is a barn, which indeed it is. Each of the identified objects has features characteristic of its type. Moreover, each object is fully in view, Henry has excellent eyesight, and he has enough time to look at them reasonably carefully, since there is little traffic to distract him.

Given this information, would we say that Henry *knows* that the object is a barn? Most of us would have little hesitation in saying this, so long as we were not in a certain philosophical frame of mind. Contrast our inclination here with the inclination we would have if we were given some additional information. Suppose we are told that, unknown to Henry, the district he has just entered is full of papier-mâché facsimiles of barns. These facsimiles look from the road exactly like barns, but are really just façades, without back walls or interiors, quite incapable of being used as barns. They are so cleverly constructed that travelers invariably mistake them for barns. Having just entered the district, Henry has not encountered any facsimiles; the object he sees is a genuine barn. But if the object on that site were a facsimile, Henry would mistake it for a barn. Given this new information, we would be strongly inclined to withdraw the claim that Henry *knows* the object is a barn. How is this change in our assessment to be explained?

Note first that the traditional justified-true-belief account of knowledge is of no help in explaining this change. In both cases Henry truly believes (indeed, is certain) that the object is a barn. Moreover, Henry's "justification" or "evidence" for the proposition that the object is a barn is the same in both cases. Thus, Henry should either know in both cases or not know in both cases. The presence of facsimiles in the district should make no difference to whether or not he knows.

My old causal analysis cannot handle the problem either. Henry's belief that the object is a barn is caused by the presence of the barn; indeed, the causal process is a perceptual one. Nonetheless, we are not prepared to say, in the second version, that Henry knows.

One analysis of propositional knowledge that might handle the problem is Peter Unger's non-accidentality analysis.[2] According to this theory, *S* knows that *p* if and only if it is not at all accidental that *S* is right about its being the case that *p*. In the initial description of the example, this requirement appears to be satisfied; so we say that Henry knows. When informed about the facsimiles, however, we see that it is accidental that Henry is right about its being a barn. So we withdraw our knowledge attribution. The "non-accidentality" analysis is not very satisfying, however, for the notion of "non-accidentality" itself needs explication. Pending explication, it isn't clear whether it correctly handles all cases.

Another approach to knowledge that might handle our problem is the "indefeasibility" approach.[3] On this view, S knows that p only if S's true belief is justified *and* this justification is not defeated. In an unrestricted form, an indefeasibility theory would say that S's justification j for believing that p is defeated if and only if there is some true proposition q such that the conjunction of q and j does not justify S in believing that p. In slightly different terms, S's justification j is defeated just in case p would no longer be evident for S if q were evident for S. This would handle the barn example, presumably, because the true proposition that there are barn facsimiles in the district is such that, if it were evident for Henry, then it would no longer be evident for him that the object he sees is a barn.

The trouble with the indefeasibility approach is that it is too strong, at least in its unrestricted form. On the foregoing account of "defeat," as Gilbert Harman shows,[4] it will (almost) always be possible to find a true proposition that defeats S's justification. Hence, S will never (or seldom) know. What is needed is an appropriate restriction on the notion of "defeat," but I am not aware of an appropriate restriction that has been formulated thus far.

[...]

What, then, is my proposed treatment of the barn example? A person knows that p, I suggest, only if the actual state of affairs in which p is true is *distinguishable* or *discriminable* by him from a relevant possible state of affairs in which p is false. If there is a relevant possible state of affairs in which p is false and which is indistinguishable by him from the actual state of affairs, then he fails to know that p. In the original description of the barn case there is no hint of any relevant possible state of affairs in which the object in question is not a barn but is indistinguishable (by Henry) from the actual state of affairs. Hence, we are initially inclined to say that Henry knows. The information about the facsimiles, however, introduces such a relevant state of affairs. Given that the district Henry has entered is full of barn facsimiles, there is a relevant alternative hypothesis about the object, viz., that it is a facsimile. Since, by assumption, a state of affairs in which such a hypothesis holds is indistinguishable by Henry from the actual state of affairs (from his vantage point on the road), this hypothesis is not "ruled out" or "precluded" by the factors that prompt Henry's belief. So, once apprised of the facsimiles in the district, we are inclined to deny that Henry knows.

Let us be clear about the bearing of the facsimiles on the case. The presence of the facsimiles does not "create" the possibility that the object Henry sees is a facsimile. Even if there were no facsimiles in the district, it would be possible that the object on that site is a facsimile. What the presence of the facsimiles does is make this possibility *relevant*; or it makes us *consider* it relevant.

The qualifier 'relevant' plays an important role in my view. If knowledge required the elimination of all logically possible alternatives, there would be no knowledge (at least of contingent truths). If only *relevant* alternatives need to be precluded, however, the scope of knowledge could be substantial. This depends, of course, on which alternatives are relevant.

Notes

1. The example is due to Carl Ginet.
2. "An Analysis of Factual Knowledge," *The Journal of Philosophy* LXV, 6 (Mar. 21, 1968): 157–170.
3. See, for example, Keith Lehrer and Thomas Paxson, Jr., "Knowledge: Undefeated Justified True Belief," *The Journal of Philosophy* LXVI, 8 (Apr. 24, 1969): 225–237, and Peter D. Klein, "A Proposed Definition of Propositional Knowledge," *ibid.*, LXVIII, 16 (Aug. 19, 1971): 471–482.
4. *Thought* (Princeton, N.J.: University Press, 1973), p. 152.

43

Where is the Value in Knowing?

Catherine Z. Elgin, "The Epistemic Efficacy of Stupidity"

As post-Gettier epistemologists have striven to understand knowledge's nature, Goldman's concept of reliabilism (introduced in the previous reading) has struck many as a promising idea. Does it reveal part of what could be involved in knowing? Is a true belief knowledge only if it has been formed reliably – namely, in a way that was likely to generate a true belief? Still, even if that is part of knowing, most epistemologists would not regard it as *all* there is to a true belief's being knowledge. Perhaps the use of good *evidence* is needed, too. (Remember how W.K. Clifford, in reading 38, stressed the importance of a belief's being supported by good evidence.) Should we therefore combine the use of good evidence with a reliable way of forming a belief? Is *that* how a true belief manages to be knowledge (rather than merely a true belief)?

Some epistemologists have thought of any adequate answer to that Gettier-sensitive question as needing to reflect also whatever *value* there is in knowing. What knowledge *is* could well affect whether and how we do *and should* want it. For some values of "X" in "Knowledge = X", knowing is valuable – worth wanting. For other values, it is not. That issue is raised engagingly in this reading, by Catherine Elgin (b. 1948) from Harvard University. In effect, she considers a few possible values of "X", ones to which epistemologists have been attracted. She asks whether, given the resulting philosophical images of what it is to know, we should value knowing.

Thus, would it be possible for someone to satisfy the sort of conceptual analysis of knowledge provided by the causal theory or by reliabilism – *yet* to be believing

Catherine Z. Elgin, "The Epistemic Efficacy of Stupidity" (excerpts), in N. Goodman and C.Z. Elgin, *Reconceptions in Philosophy and Other Arts and Sciences* (Indianapolis: Hackett, 1988). Reprinted with permission of Hackett Publishing Company Inc. All rights reserved.

Metaphysics and Epistemology: A Guided Anthology, First Edition. Edited by Stephen Hetherington.
© 2014 John Wiley & Sons, Inc. Published 2014 by John Wiley & Sons, Inc.

less-than-impressively? Elgin argues so. Similarly, would it be possible for someone to satisfy conceptual analyses of knowledge emphasizing the quality of one's evidence – *yet* still to be believing less-than-impressively? Again, Elgin argues so. She calls upon Arthur Conan Doyle's famous literary creations – the cognitively brilliant Sherlock Holmes, along with his plodding friend and assistant Dr. Watson. The result (claims Elgin) is that it is *Watson*, not Holmes, of whom these standard epistemological conceptions of knowing approve; it is Watson, not Holmes, whose beliefs more readily satisfy those conceptions. Nevertheless, it is *Holmes*, not Watson, whose thinking we admire and value.

Does this tell us that knowledge is not *worth* having, as epistemologists have conceived of it? That depends on whether (as Elgin contends is implied by these conceptions of knowledge) knowledge is not something that the imaginative and clever Holmes is well suited to attaining. Have epistemologists conceived of knowledge in ways that render it as something which, as it happens, we should not readily value attaining? Holmes seems to exemplify cognitive excellences other than those described in some influential conceptions of knowledge. Is this a reason for not valuing knowledge? Is it a reason for valuing also – or even instead – those further cognitive excellences?

[...]

Knowledge from Outside

Causal theories of knowledge maintain that for a subject to know that *p*, his true belief that *p* must be caused by the fact that *p* or by facts from which it follows that *p*.[1] Sophisticated versions require that the causal connection be lawlike, so that knowledge cannot result from a fortuitous commingling of circumstances. Such theories account for inferential knowledge by claiming that inferential and logical relations may be parts of causal chains.

According to a causal theory then, my true belief that there is a yellow surface before me is caused by a neurophysiological response to the presence of yellow in my visual field. A sequence of optical and neural events linking the surface with a brain state is responsible for the production of my belief. If that sequence instantiates a natural law, I know that the surface is yellow. It is no accident that I believe what I do; for, given the laws of nature and the circumstances in which I find myself, my belief is a necessary consequence of the fact that the surface is yellow.

[...]

[...] Holmes, we may suppose, is an oenophile, while Watson is oblivious to all but the most obvious differences among wines. The two share a bottle of Bordeaux, and because it stimulates the appropriate nerve endings and brings about the proper neurological connections, it causes each to believe that he is drinking Bordeaux. (For vividness we can assume that their reactions do not differ neurologically.) According to causal theories, both

Holmes and Watson know that the wine they are drinking is Bordeaux. The fact that Watson cannot tell a Bordeaux from a muscatel does not prevent him from knowing about this wine, for it does not intrude upon the causal chain leading to his current belief. And unless we are prepared to conclude that Holmes lacks knowledge, we cannot dismiss the chain of neurological events as anomalous. If a causal law is instantiated in the production of Holmes's belief, it is instantiated in the production of Watson's; for their neurological reactions do not differ. If Holmes knows what he's drinking, so does Watson.

It follows from causal theories that subjects can 'luck into' knowledge. Given Watson's insensitivity to distinctions among wines, it is accidental that the lawful causal chain eventuates in a true belief. Despite its impeccable breeding, Watson's belief is unreliable.

The conviction that unreliability precludes knowledge leads some externalists to reliabilism – the view that knowledge depends on a belief's relation to truth in counterfactual as well as in actual circumstances. On a reliabilist account, a properly tethered belief is, roughly, one the subject would harbor if it were true and would not harbor, at least on account of that tether, if it were false.[2] The truth of a properly tethered belief is no accident; for such a belief tracks truth across possible worlds.

Reliabilism concludes – correctly, it seems – that Watson does not know; for he would believe he was drinking Bordeaux even if he were drinking muscatel. The problem is that Holmes apparently fares no better. Although he can tell Bordeaux from muscatel, he cannot infallibly discriminate Bordeaux from all other sources of sensory stimulation. So Holmes, like Watson, fails the subjunctive test; there are non-Bordeaux he would believe to be Bordeaux, and Bordeaux he would believe to be non-Bordeaux.

[…]

[…] Still, Holmes's epistemic situation is better than Watson's in that significantly more austere restrictions are required to constitute Watson's belief as knowledge. In this respect at least, the smarter man has an epistemic advantage.

It is not clear, though, that Holmes can sustain his advantage. Watson, we may suppose, reliably classifies wines as *rotgut, table wine*, and what he calls '*vintage stuff*'; and his beliefs about wine quality result from lawlike causal chains. So according to both reliabilist and causal theories, Watson knows he's drinking rotgut.

Holmes knows nothing of the sort. 'Rotgut' is not part of his conceptual repertoire, so he formulates no beliefs about rotgut. Since belief is required for knowledge, Watson knows something about their shared experience that Holmes does not. Still, Holmes brings to the wine tasting a wealth of refined, delicate distinctions. The first sip convinces him that he's drinking a 1986 Thunderbird, made from a resoundingly inferior grape grown in vacant lots just off the Santa Monica Freeway; a wine aged for a week in a plastic vat previously used to launder sweat socks. Holmes, with his more sensitive perceptual and conceptual categories, seems to be in a position to know a good deal more than Watson. Being able to frame more hypotheses, he has more candidates for knowledge than Watson does.

The problem is this: the more distinctions a system of categories admits, the less difference there is between adjacent categories. As we refine our conceptual schemes, we increase our chances of error. Although Holmes can usually tell the vintage of the wine he's drinking, no more than anyone else is he infallible. The perceptible differences among vintages are often extremely subtle and difficult to discern. Common conditions – the beginnings of a head cold, a poorly rinsed glass, a moment's inattentiveness, a stuffy room – can throw the most sensitive palate off, leading the taster to confuse a Margaux with a St. Julien. So Holmes's true belief that he's drinking a Margaux does not track truth very far. [...] On a reliabilist theory, Holmes does not know; nor does anyone else whose judgments are vulnerable to such contingencies. The more delicate our distinctions, the more easily circumstances conspire to confound judgment. So as we refine our categories, we diminish our prospects for knowledge.

[...]

Respect for evidence may also inhibit knowledge. Suppose there is such a thing as extrasensory perception, and that the absence of evidence for such a faculty is due to the fact that genuine extrasensory perceptions are extremely hard to distinguish from a variety of unreliable sources of intimation.[3] Watson and Holmes are equally extrasensorily perceptive. But Watson is credulous; Holmes is not. So Watson believes the deliverances of ESP, dismissing the evidence out of hand. Holmes respects the evidence and the methods of the sciences that produced it. So he does not credit his extrasensory perceptions. Although he cannot prevent himself from experiencing them, he withholds belief; for he can find no legitimate grounds for the suspicions they produce. Holmes then does not know; his epistemic scruples prevent him from forming the requisite beliefs.

On both causal and reliabilist accounts, Watson does know. Extrasensory perceptions yield true beliefs via lawful, if unrecognized, causal chains. And if ESP is reliable (even though we have no reason to think it is), Watson would believe its deliverances if they were true, and would not believe them via ESP if they were false. So Watson's obliviousness to the evidence serves him well; it enables him to know.

[...]

Knowledge from Inside

Internalism maintains that a claim is justified to the extent that it is reasonable in light of what is already known. Justification thus depends on coherence with a system of already accepted claims.[4]

[...]

What coheres with a narrow system can fail to cohere with a broader one. So Watson, with his limited purview, knows things that Holmes, burdened with a more comprehensive one, does not. Upon sighting a bird, Holmes and Watson form the belief that it is a superb starling. Watson's relevant background beliefs are truths about the characteristic markings of superb starlings. He has no beliefs about the bird's habitat; for, although he studiously attends to the pictures in the bird watcher's manual, he ignores the accompanying text. Given the information in his acceptance system, Watson's belief is completely justified. And since the bird, an escapee from the London Zoo, is in fact a superb starling, Watson knows that it is. Holmes, however, does not. Although he too recognizes that the bird in question has the markings of a superb starling, he realizes that such birds, being indigenous to equatorial Africa, are unlikely to be found on Baker Street. So, relative to Holmes's acceptance system, it is at least as reasonable to suspect that they've sighted a strangely marked local bird. Watson's ignorance thus enables him to know what Holmes cannot. The fact that prevents Holmes from knowing, being external to Watson's acceptance system, cannot undermine Watson's justification.[5]

[...]

Watson comes by his limitations naturally. So his motives as a knowledge seeker cannot be impugned because of his failure to incorporate certain information into his acceptance system. Indeed, he may be incapable of doing so. Suppose Holmes's confounding belief derives from a complex statistical generalization correlating the intensity of a bird's coloration with the mean temperature of its habitat − a generalization from which it follows that a brightly colored bird like the superb starling is unlikely to be found in a temperate climate. Watson does not know the generalization; moreover, he could not understand or appreciate its import, were it imparted to him. So neither it nor its denial can enter into his personal acceptance system. As a result, the generalization cannot defeat any of his completely justified beliefs. For epistemically inaccessible truths are, for the internalist, epistemically inert. It is then his stupidity, not just his ignorance, that enables Watson to know what the more intelligent Holmes cannot.

[...] [W]hen category systems admit of subtle distinctions, knowledge is much harder to achieve. It is fairly easy to tell whether something is a bird; fairly hard to tell whether it is a tree pipit. So since Watson is given to entertaining hypotheses at the level of

x is a bird

he's likely to generate a good deal of (trivial) knowledge. Since Holmes draws finer distinctions, he has a harder time.[...]

If the only discernible difference Holmes recognizes between a tree pipit and a buff meadow pipit is that the former is slightly plumper than the latter, his justification is defeated if he's even slightly wrong about how plump a tree pipit is expected to be. So Watson is likely to come away from a bird-watching expedition with a lot more knowledge than Holmes. For Watson will have formed many completely justified beliefs

x_1 is a bird
x_2 is a bird
$\ldots$
x_n is a bird.

Holmes, having attempted more precise classifications of $x_1, \ldots , x_n$, will have encountered some birds he could not identify, some whose identification he was not personally justified in accepting, some whose identification he was not completely justified in accepting, and some in which the identification he was completely justified in accepting was nonetheless false. Indeed, under the circumstances, Holmes might reasonably refrain from accepting any claims at this level of refinement. Since he desires to disbelieve falsehoods as well as to believe truths, he would be wise to suspend judgment where the prospect of error looms large. Here again, it seems rational to revert to Watson's safer stance. For Watson achieves the goal of believing truths and disbelieving falsehoods far better than Holmes does.

This might be doubted. It might seem that Holmes, having a richer cognitive repertoire, is in a position to form more undefeated justified true beliefs than Watson. If so, he knows more than Watson, even though Watson knows some things he does not. But the premiss is false; for Watson can generate undefeated justified true beliefs at least as quickly as Holmes.

Of course, Watson's will tend to be trivial, banal, and boring, while Holmes's are often original, interesting, and important. But contemporary epistemology does not have the resources to discriminate between significant and insignificant beliefs. So it has no basis for ruling that Holmes's justified true beliefs are epistemically better than Watson's.

[...]

What Holmes's predicament shows, I believe, is that knowledge, as contemporary theories conceive it, is not and ought not be our overriding cognitive objective. For to treat it as such is to devalue cognitive excellences such as conceptual and perceptual sensitivity, logical acumen, breadth and depth of understanding, and the capacity to distinguish important from trivial truths. Even when Watson knows more than Holmes, he does not appear to be cognitively better off.

This suggests that it is unwise to restrict epistemology to the study of what contemporary theories count as knowledge. What is wanted is a wide-ranging study of cognitive excellences of all sorts, and of the ways they contribute to or interfere with one another's realization. The fruits of such a study might enable us to understand how Socrates, knowing nothing, could be the wisest of men.

Notes

1. Alvin Goldman, "A Causal Theory of Knowing", *Journal of Philosophy* 64 (1967) 357–372; and "Discrimination and Perceptual Knowledge", *Journal of Philosophy* 73 (1976) 771–791. [See readings 41 and 42.]

2. Robert Nozick, *Philosophical Explanations* (Cambridge, Mass.: Harvard University Press, 1981), pp. 172–196; and Fred Dretske, "Conclusive Reasons", *Australasian Journal of Philosophy* 49 (1971) 1–22.

3. This example is a variant of one developed by Laurence Bonjour in "Externalist Theories of Empirical Knowledge", in *Midwest Studies in Philosophy V*, ed. Peter A. French, Theodore E. Uehling, Jr., and Howard K. Wettstein (Minneapolis: University of Minnesota Press, 1980), pp. 53–73.

4. Some internalists – such as Chisholm – recognize basic statements that are supposed to be inherently reasonable. But they acknowledge that most statements are not basic, so justification is mostly a matter of coherence. Cf. Roderick Chisholm, *The Foundations of Knowing* (Minneapolis: University of Minnesota Press, 1982). Moreover, their admission of inherently reasonable statements is problematic. For it would not be reasonable on internalist grounds to accept a putatively basic statement that conflicted with the appropriate background system; I ought not accept the claim that I see something red if I am justifiably convinced that I am color blind.

5. Cf. Carl Ginet, "Knowing Less by Knowing More", in French, Uehling, and Wettstein, *Midwest Studies in Philosophy V*, pp. 151–162.

44

Is Knowledge Always a Virtuously Derived True Belief?

Linda Trinkaus Zagzebski, *Virtues of the Mind*

Confronted by Catherine Elgin's arguments in the previous reading, we might infer that knowing is a significantly less valuable cognitive achievement than most philosophers have traditionally assumed it to be. However, that is not the only possible moral we may infer from Elgin's arguments. Is there also a possibility of expanding our conception of knowing, so as to absorb *within* that conception some recognition of those further cognitive excellences? This reading can be viewed as one way of doing that. It comes from Linda Zagzebski (b. 1946), in recent years at the University of Oklahoma.

Zagzebski offers a version of *virtue* epistemology, an approach that is attracting increased attention. It applies within epistemology some ideas long present within moral philosophy. Virtue epistemology takes seriously an image of knowing as one's believing in what is somehow a virtuous way; which could be part of one's being, in some respects, a virtuous person. We have already met Clifford's view that believing is *wrong* when not based on good evidence, and Ayer's conception of knowledge as one's *having the right* to be sure. Epistemologists have often thought of the support needed if a particular belief is to be knowledge as a matter of the believer being *responsible* in her thinking. (After all, the belief is said to be *justified*. The believing is justified, equally; and "justified" is a term wholly at home in moral appraisals of actions.) Virtue epistemology would regard such suggestions as converging upon an underlying image of knowing as a person's being intellectually virtuous in how she gains and retains her beliefs. Some of these intellectual virtues will be among those mentioned by Elgin at the end of the previous reading; some

Linda Trinkaus Zagzebski, *Virtues of the Mind: An Investigation into the Nature of Virtue and the Ethical Foundations of Knowledge* (Cambridge: Cambridge University Press, 1996), pp. 268–271, 273–275, 277–280, 294–298 (excerpts). © Cambridge University Press 1996. Reproduced with permission.

Metaphysics and Epistemology: A Guided Anthology, First Edition. Edited by Stephen Hetherington.

will not. Zagzebski's particular version of virtue epistemology embraces an ancient conception of virtues, stemming from Aristotle: a virtue is said to involve a properly based and motivated reliability or predictability in acting well. Zagzebski argues that a belief could only be knowledge if it reflects a genuine and reliable motivation to believe only what is true. This idea (also argues Zagzebski) can generate a conception of knowledge no longer susceptible to Gettier cases.

Of course, we should be aware that there is no agreement among epistemologists that anyone *has* yet succeeded in showing us how to analyze the concept of knowledge in a Gettier-proof way. We have read suggestions from Goldman and now we read one from Zagzebski – influential ones, although possibly not yet decisive. So some epistemologists continue to pursue that project, undaunted. The *Gettier problem* (as it is known) is the challenge of finding such a conception, in the face of Gettier's challenge. Maybe Zagzebski's conception of knowledge is correct, solving the Gettier problem; maybe not. This is highly contested conceptual terrain.

[…]

We might look at the difference between knowledge and justified belief as analogous to the difference between act and rule utilitarianism. In rule utilitarianism an act is right because it follows a rule the following of which tends to have good consequences. Similarly, a belief may be justified because it follows epistemic rules the following of which tends to lead to the truth or because it is an instance of a reliable belief-forming process (reliabilism) or on my account, because it is a belief that an intellectually virtuous person might have in the circumstances. That is to say, it is a member of the class of beliefs that a person who has virtuous motivations and is reliable in bringing about the end of those motivations might have in like circumstances. In the case of each theory of justified belief, success in reaching the truth is likely, or as likely as one can get in the circumstances, but is not guaranteed. In act utilitarianism, in contrast, an act is right because *that* act leads to good consequences, not because of some accidental, extraneous feature of the situation, but because of the properties of the act itself. Similarly, a state of knowledge is one in which the truth is reached, not accidentally, but because of certain properties of the belief itself. That particular belief must be successful in reaching the truth through those properties of it that make it epistemically valuable. An act of virtue [is] an act that not only is virtuously motivated and reliable but is successful in the particular case in reaching the aim of the virtue through those features of the act. So an act of intellectual virtue not only is motivated by the particular virtue and expresses the agent's possession of the motivational component of the virtue but is successful in reaching both the immediate and the ultimate aim of that virtue, which is to say, it must lead to the truth because of the operation of the virtue.

[…]

The concept of an act of virtue combines all our moral aims in one concept. The agent has a virtuous motivation (disposition to have a virtuous motive), the act is motivated by such a motive, the agent acts in a way that a virtuous person would (probably) act in the same circumstances, the agent is successful in bringing about the state of affairs that a virtuous person desires, and the agent gets credit for bringing about such a state of affairs because it was brought about *through* the operation of her virtuous motive and activities.

[…] *An act of intellectual virtue A* **is an act that arises from the motivational component of *A*, is something a person with virtue *A* would (probably) do in the circumstances, is successful in achieving the end of the *A* motivation, and is such that the agent acquires a true belief (cognitive contact with reality) through these features of the act.**[1] I am interpreting cognitive contact with reality in a broad enough sense to include understanding and certainty.

I now propose that we define knowledge as follows:

Def 1: Knowledge is a state of cognitive contact with reality arising out of acts of intellectual virtue.

Alternatively,

Def 2: Knowledge is a state of true belief arising out of acts of intellectual virtue.

Since the fact that a belief arises out of acts of intellectual virtue entails that it is true, the second definition can be formulated without redundancy as follows:

Def 3: Knowledge is a state of belief arising out of acts of intellectual virtue.

The second definition follows the contemporary convention of defining knowledge as true belief plus something else, but its redundant element makes it misleading. The first definition may be preferable since it is noncommittal on such questions as the object of knowledge, the nature of truth, and the existence of propositions […]. It also permits a broader interpretation of knowledge since knowledge may include cognitive contact with structures of reality other than the propositional.

[…]

High-grade and low-grade knowledge

The definition of knowledge I have given is fairly rigorous. It requires the knower to have an intellectually virtuous motivation in the disposition to desire truth, and this disposition must give rise to conscious and voluntary acts in the process leading up to the acquisition of true belief (or cognitive contact with reality), and the knower must successfully reach the truth through the operation of this motivation and those acts. Such a definition has an advantage on the high end of knowledge, but a disadvantage on the low end. Let us look at both sides of the matter.

[…] [A] number of problems in contemporary epistemology favor a stricter definition of knowledge than that currently in vogue. Because the examples often used as paradigms of knowledge are on the low end of the scale, little effort is made to distinguish between, say, a person who has real understanding of her environment and one who merely knows that the room she is in has four walls. The neglect of the concept of understanding is one of the problems in contemporary epistemology that I believe a virtue approach can remedy. It is likely that understanding is the sort of state that cannot be reached merely through reliable truth-producing processes or properly functioning faculties, or doing one's epistemic duty or following epistemic rules. On the other hand, cultivating and exercising the intellectual virtues are the best we can do voluntarily to obtain understanding and, ultimately, wisdom. No doubt some virtues in particular are more critical than others in leading us to high-level states of knowledge that include understanding or wisdom, and I realize that I have not gone through enough instances of intellectual virtues and their applications to provide a good sense of the process whereby acts of virtue lead to these high-grade epistemic states. But given what we have said, it is reasonable to expect that the virtues of insightfulness and the various "synthetic" virtues – those that enable us to see patterns or simple structures in sets of data or items of experience – are more closely associated with producing understanding and wisdom than are the more commonplace virtues of intellectual attentiveness, carefulness, and perseverance. [...]

The definition of knowledge proposed [here] has another advantage. Earlier in my book I discussed the higher-order virtue of cognitive integration. A person who is cognitively integrated has positive higher-order attitudes toward her own intellectual character and the quality of her epistemic states. Not only does she know, but she is in a position to know that she knows. In addition, her belief structure is coherent, and she is aware of its coherence. Further, she has a sense of the relative value of the different truths or aspects of reality to which she is related. She has, in short, a good intellectual character. My definition of knowledge is closely connected with having a good intellectual character. Although it does not require that to know *p* one knows that one knows *p* (an advantage), it nonetheless defines knowledge in such a way that the knower is in a good position to find out that she has knowledge when she has it, and that also is an advantage. What's more, a knower according to my definition is in a good position to evaluate her own belief structure for coherence, and as long as she has multiple intellectual virtues, including the virtue of *phronesis* [i.e., practical wisdom], she is also in a good position to determine the relative value of her individual items of knowledge, as well as the status of her knowledge taken as a whole. All of these are advantages of a definition of knowledge based on intellectual virtue.

[...]

Knowledge as I have defined it fares well on the high end of the scale. But what should we say about the low end? [...] This category would include perceptual beliefs and simple short-term memory beliefs. Our definition of knowledge may appear to eliminate beliefs in these categories from the category of knowledge, even when they are true and are formed in the usual way without any defects in the believer or glitches in the environment. Such beliefs not only are typically considered cases of knowledge but may even be offered as paradigm cases. Do these beliefs pose a problem for my theory?

We have already seen that the rigorist tradition in epistemology has been the dominant view. This was often attended by the position that there is no sense knowledge. A multitude of philosophers have thought that what we typically fancy to be objects of knowledge are really illusions, and a common object of attack was the objects of sense perception. A good example of this is the following remark by Aquinas, who not only excludes apprehension by the senses from the realm of knowledge but also claims that such apprehension is not governed by virtues:

> Nevertheless, even if there be habits in such powers [the senses], they cannot be called virtues. For virtue is a perfect habit, by which it never happens that anything but good is done; and so virtue

must be in that power which brings the good act to completion. But the knowledge of truth is not consummated in the sensitive powers of apprehension, for such powers prepare the way to the intellectual knowledge. And therefore in these powers there are none of the virtues by which we know truth; these are rather in the intellect or reason. (*ST* I-II, q. 56, a. 5, obj. 3)

[…] [A] long list of philosophers have been unwilling, or at least hesitant, to ascribe knowledge to states that engage the senses without significant contribution from the intellect. This is not to deny that there can be simple beliefs based on perception, such as "This is a white piece of paper," which are good enough to be states of knowing, but the dominant view in philosophical history has been that such states are states of knowledge only if they are based on *more* than sensory data.

[…] [I]f knowledge is associated with rationality and rationality with powers that are not shared with other animals, then the simpler the belief and the closer it is to bare perceptual data, the less likely it is to be a good candidate for knowledge – certainly not as a *paradigm* case of knowledge.[2]

In spite of the reservations arising from historical precedent, it is clear that the vast majority of contemporary philosophers do not hesitate to think of a multitude of perceptual beliefs as cases of knowledge. So even though I think it a mistake to consider such cases paradigms, it would nonetheless be a disadvantage of my theory if it had the consequence that such perceptual beliefs as "That is a white wall" were excluded from the category of knowledge. An obvious feature of these beliefs favoring their inclusion is that they fare well on the criterion of certainty. Compared to the high-grade beliefs in the sciences, philosophy, or the arts, the best perceptual beliefs are generally regarded as high on the scale of certainty, even if low on the scale of cognitive value. So I assume that we want an account of knowledge according to which true beliefs in normal circumstances based on unreflective perception, memory, or introspection qualify as knowledge. Does my definition include these cases?

The answer depends, of course, upon what it takes to perform an act of intellectual virtue. Recall that on my definition of an act of virtue, it is not necessary that the agent actually possess the virtue. But she must be virtuously motivated, she must act the way a virtuous person would characteristically act in the same circumstances, and she must be successful because of these features of her act. What she may lack is the entrenched habit that allows her to be generally reliable in bringing about the virtuous end. This definition permits those persons who do not yet fully possess a virtue but are virtuous-in-training to perform acts of the virtue in question.

How does a person of intellectual virtue act when it comes to forming beliefs based on sense experience or memory? Presumably, she is *sometimes* skeptical of her own senses, and she *sometimes* doubts her own memory, as in the case when it is weak and she has good contrary evidence. She probably does not doubt such introspective beliefs as that she is in pain, although we might expect her to consider from time to time if and why such introspection is trustworthy. But we would assume that most of the time she does not doubt or even reflectively consider her perceptual and memory beliefs. She does not because she maintains a presumption of truth in such cases until she is given reason to think otherwise. Such an attitude is itself an intellectually virtuous one; to act otherwise is to exhibit a form of intellectual paranoia. So this might give us reason to think that even young children can perform acts of intellectual virtue before they are old enough to acquire the intellectual virtues. As long as they are old enough to imitate the behavior of intellectually virtuous persons in their belief-forming processes, young children (and possibly animals) can have knowledge based on perception and memory. Their behavior is no different from that of the intellectually virtuous, and there may not even be any discernible difference in their motives.

[...]

In order to see how Gettier problems can be avoided on the definition of knowledge I have given, let us examine the moral analogue of Gettier cases: instances in which a person acts out of moral virtues and has no operative moral vices but is morally successful only by accident. [...]

Suppose an Italian judge, weighing the evidence against an accused Mafia killer, determines by an impeccable procedure, motivated by justice and using an abundance of practical wisdom, that the man is guilty. The judge exhibits the virtues of justice and practical wisdom, and perhaps courage as well since he is undeterred by fear of Mafia reprisals. Nonetheless, let us suppose that the judge makes a mistake; the accused is the wrong man. The fact that the judge makes a mistake is not due to any defect in the judge, whether moral or intellectual; it is simply bad luck. Obviously, things have gone wrong and that is too bad, and if the judge found out later that he made a mistake, he would greatly regret it. Other persons would not actually blame the judge for the error, but they would not praise him either. That is, they would not give him the praise that would have been due him if he had made no mistake. The judge then suffers from bad moral luck in Nagel's sense [see 'Moral Luck', in Thomas Nagel's *Mortal Questions* (Cambridge University Press, 1979)]. He may have exhibited numerous virtues in his act, including the virtue of justice, but we would not call the act *an act of justice*. Furthermore, it does not help to distinguish between the evaluation of the agent and the evaluation of the act because the act's lack of success leads to withholding a certain sort of moral praise from the agent. [...] [W]e do not call an act an act *of* virtue unless it succeeds in reaching the internal or external aim of the virtue *in the particular case* through the operation of the features of the act that make the agent praiseworthy for doing it. The judge is just; he may even exhibit justice in his decision; we may even say that he acts justly; but the decision itself is not an act of justice.

[...] [T]he procedure for generating Gettier cases involves "double luck": an instance of good luck cancels out an instance of bad luck. We can use the same procedure in the moral case. Suppose that the actual killer is secretly switched with the man the judge thought he was sentencing so that the judge ends up accidentally sentencing the right man. One error cancels out the other; the right man is sentenced, but it is only accidental that the wrong man is not sentenced instead. In this case we may breathe a sigh of relief for the innocent man who barely escaped punishment, but our judgment of the judge is hardly better than in the former case, the one in which the judge makes the mistake. Again, it would be going too far to blame him, and it is possible our judgment would be somewhat less negative than it would be in the case in which the wrong man is punished. Nonetheless, the judge lacks the level of moral honor that would have been due him if he had been judging the right man in the first place. Once he found out what happened, he would not consider this case one of his great achievements, and even if he exhibited an impressive degree of virtue in hearing the case and rendering a verdict, no one would think to praise him for the decision, and I suggest that it would be inappropriate to call the decision an act of justice. If my appraisal of this case is right, it suggests that there are Gettier-style cases in ethics. The full achievement of the good of morality, like the achievement of the good of knowledge, requires that the good be reached by the right process, not just in general, but in the particular case. I venture the guess that the reason the epistemic cases are more noticeable than their ethical counterparts is that we are very demanding about the state of knowledge, requiring that everything work perfectly, both inside the agent's head and in his cognitive hookup with reality. For whatever reason, we are somewhat more forgiving when it comes to morally correct behavior, perhaps because an elaborate system of rewards and punishments is often involved. Nonetheless, [...] even in ethics there are good reasons for wanting to call attention to a category of acts that gets everything right, both in the agent's head and in his hookup with the moral reality he is trying to produce, and I called these acts "acts of virtue."

The distinction between exhibiting virtue and performing an act *of* virtue can help us resolve Gettier-style cases in a virtue theory. An act of virtue is virtuously motivated, is an act that a virtuous person is apt to do in the circumstances, and successfully leads to the ends of the virtue in question through the operation of these features of the act. The production of the goods that the virtuously motivated person aims to produce enhances the moral merit of the agent, and the production of evils that the virtuously motivated person aims to prevent detracts from the agent's merit, in spite of the fact that the level of the agent's virtue may be no different from what it is in the case in which his acts are morally successful. As we have said, this is because the aim of the moral life is not merely to *be* virtuous but to bring about the goods at which virtue aims by way of the sort of actions that usually result from virtue.

Gettier problems in virtue epistemology [...] can be avoided if we utilize the concept of an act of intellectual virtue. Acts of intellectual virtue are strictly analogous to acts of moral virtue. An act of moral virtue is morally right in a very strong sense because it has all of the morally desirable characteristics of an act. It is virtuously motivated, it is what a morally virtuous person might do, *and* the external good of the virtue (if any) is successfully achieved through the operation of this motive and the act to which it gives rise. Similarly, an act of intellectual virtue is justified or epistemically right in a very strong sense. It is virtuously motivated, it leads to a belief that is acquired and sustained the way an intellectually virtuous person might do it, *and* the good of truth or cognitive contact with reality is successfully achieved by this motivation and process. Intellectual virtues, like such moral virtues as justice or compassion, include an aim that is partially external. We are ethically interested in success, as well as in the goodness of the heart, and we are particularly interested in there being a connection between these two aspects of ethical value. So we are interested in just motives and in the successful achievement of a just state of affairs through the operation of those motives, and for the same reason, we are interested in intellectually virtuous motives and in the successful achievement of cognitive contact with reality through these motives. We honor the resulting state by calling it "knowledge." That is to say, **knowledge is a state of cognitive contact with reality arising out of acts of intellectual virtue**. This definition of knowledge is immune to Gettier problems.

Notes

1. We can modify the definition of an act of intellectual virtue as follows: An act of intellectual virtue A is an act that arises from the motivational component of A, is something a person with virtue A would (probably) do in the circumstances, is successful in achieving the end of the A motivation, and is such that the best explanation for the agent's acquisition of true belief (cognitive contact with reality) is the fact that the belief arises out of an act that is motivated by A and is something persons with virtue A would (probably) do.

2. Compare the distinction between animal knowledge and reflective knowledge made by Ernest Sosa: "Animal knowledge requires only that the belief reflect the impact of its subject matter through the operation of a faculty or virtue. For reflective knowledge one not only must believe out of virtue. One must also be aware of doing so." Ernest Sosa, "Reply to Foley and Fumerton." *Philosophical Issues* 5 (1994), 29–50.

Can We Ever Know Just through Observation?

45

Is All Knowledge Ultimately Observational?

David Hume, *An Enquiry Concerning Human Understanding*

We have seen that epistemologists are yet to agree on what, fully and exactly, knowledge is. But we have also seen that, mostly, they do agree on some broadly described aspects of knowing. In particular, epistemologists routinely accept that knowing always includes one's having some sort of good justification, perhaps good evidence. It is routine, also, to think of a person's justification for a belief as at least part of how she *gains* the belief. This brings us to the general topic of what ways there are of knowing. Is *observation*, for example, a basic way in which people gain some or all of their knowledge? This reading, another from David Hume, offers a classic statement of the idea that *all* of our knowledge is founded ultimately upon observation.

David Hume, *An Enquiry Concerning Human Understanding* (1748), sect. II (excerpts).

Metaphysics and Epistemology: A Guided Anthology, First Edition. Edited by Stephen Hetherington.

Hume's position is a prominent exemplar of what is standardly named *empiricism*. Hume, Locke, and Berkeley – we have read writings from each of them – are empiricism's three most historically cited representatives. According to them, we gain knowledge only when we experience even some of what there is in the world to be observed. Sometimes, our beliefs report the world as directly as is possible through observation. Sometimes, our beliefs are only indirectly observational, being derived appropriately from those more directly observational beliefs. When there is not the right kind of observational basis for all of this, there is no knowledge. The basis (says Hume) consists of *impressions*; from which arise our *ideas*; from which come our *beliefs*; some of which are whatever instances of *knowledge* we have.

All of which may well sound encouraging, as we begin scrutinizing our beliefs, assessing their origins. But is it so encouraging? It could require us to revise our estimation of what we believe ourselves to know. Thus, Hume regards his underlying empiricist image as constraining him fundamentally in how receptive he should be to some of humanity's more *abstract* thoughts. Metaphysics, especially, attracts his epistemological attention. Recall the earlier reading from Hume on causation: he denies that causation is to be conceived of as a necessary connection, because (he argues) we have no real and immediate *impression* of such a connection. The general point is that, although it is all very well to create and ponder seemingly intriguing metaphysical stories, these ways of talking need to be grounded in *real experiences* we have of the world. If they are not, they will never give us metaphysical knowledge. Hume is encouraging us not to stray – lost, without realizing it – from what *could* be known. His empiricism is intended to prevent people from being mired in groundless thoughts, beguiled by unwittingly meaningless words.

Of The Origin of Ideas

EVERY one will readily allow, that there is a considerable difference between the perceptions of the mind, when a man feels the pain of excessive heat, or the pleasure of moderate warmth, and when he afterwards recalls to his memory this sensation, or anticipates it by his imagination. These faculties may mimic or copy the perceptions of the senses; but they never can entirely reach the force and vivacity of the original sentiment. The utmost we say of them, even when they operate with greatest vigour, is, that they represent their object in so lively a manner, that we could *almost* say we feel or see it: But, except the mind be disordered by disease or madness, they never can arrive at such a pitch of vivacity, as to render these perceptions altogether undistinguishable. All the colours of poetry, however splendid, can never paint natural objects in such a manner as to make the description be taken for a real landskip [viz., "landscape"]. The most lively thought is still inferior to the dullest sensation.

We may observe a like distinction to run through all the other perceptions of the mind. A man in a fit of anger, is actuated in a very different manner from one who only thinks of that emotion. If you tell me, that any person is in love, I easily understand your meaning, and form a just conception of his situation; but never can mistake that conception for the real disorders and agitations of the passion. When we reflect on our past sentiments and affections, our thought is a faithful mirror, and copies its objects truly; but the colours which it employs are faint and dull, in comparison of those in which our original perceptions were clothed. It requires no nice discernment or metaphysical head to mark the distinction between them.

Here therefore we may divide all the perceptions of the mind into two classes or species, which are distinguished by their different degrees of force and vivacity. The less forcible and lively are commonly denominated. *Thoughts* or *Ideas*. The other species want a name in our language, and in most others; I suppose, because it was not requisite for any, but philosophical purposes, to rank them under a general term or appellation. Let us, therefore, use a little freedom, and call them *Impressions*; employing that word in a sense somewhat different from the usual. By the term *impression*, then, I mean all our more lively perceptions, when we hear, or see, or feel, or love, or hate, or desire, or will. And impressions are distinguished from ideas, which are the less lively perceptions, of which we are conscious, when we reflect on any of those sensations or movements above mentioned.

Nothing, at first view, may seem more unbounded than the thought of man, which not only escapes all human power and authority, but is not even restrained within the limits of nature and reality. To form monsters, and join incongruous shapes and appearances, costs the imagination no more trouble than to conceive the most natural and familiar objects. And while the body is confined to one planet, along which it creeps with pain and difficulty; the thought can in an instant transport us into the most distant regions of the universe; or even beyond the universe, into the unbounded chaos, where nature is supposed to lie in total confusion. What never was seen, or heard of, may yet be conceived; nor is any thing beyond the power of thought, except what implies an absolute contradiction.

But though our thought seems to possess this unbounded liberty, we shall find, upon a nearer examination, that it is really confined within very narrow limits, and that all this creative power of the mind amounts to no more than the faculty of compounding, transposing, augmenting, or diminishing the materials afforded us by the senses and experience. When we think of a golden mountain, we only join two consistent ideas, *gold*, and *mountain*, with which we were formerly acquainted. A virtuous horse we can conceive; because, from our own feeling, we can conceive virtue; and this we may unite to the figure and shape of a horse, which is an animal familiar to us. In short, all the materials of thinking are derived either from our outward or inward sentiment: the mixture and composition of these belongs alone to the mind and will. Or, to express myself in philosophical language, all our ideas or more feeble perceptions are copies of our impressions or more lively ones.

To prove this, the two following arguments will, I hope, be sufficient. First, when we analyze our thoughts or ideas, however compounded or sublime, we always find that they resolve themselves into such simple ideas as were copied from a precedent feeling or sentiment. Even those ideas, which, at first view, seem the most wide of this origin, are found, upon a nearer scrutiny, to be derived from it. The idea of God, as meaning an infinitely intelligent, wise, and good Being, arises from reflecting on the operations of our own mind, and augmenting, without limit, those qualities of goodness and wisdom. We may prosecute this enquiry to what length we please; where we shall always find, that every idea which we examine is copied from a similar impression. Those who would assert that this position is not universally true nor without exception, have only one, and that an easy method of refuting it; by producing that idea, which, in their opinion, is not derived from this source. It will then be incumbent on us, if we would maintain our doctrine, to produce the impression, or lively perception, which corresponds to it.

Secondly. If it happen, from a defect of the organ, that a man is not susceptible of any species of sensation, we always find that he is as little susceptible of the correspondent ideas. A blind man can form no notion of colours; a deaf man of sounds. Restore either of them that sense in which he is deficient; by opening this new inlet for his sensations, you also open an inlet for the ideas; and he finds no difficulty in conceiving these objects. The case is the same, if the object, proper for exciting any sensation, has never been applied to the organ. A Laplander or Negro has no notion of the relish of wine. And though there are few or no instances of a like deficiency in the mind, where a person has never felt or is wholly incapable of a sentiment or passion that belongs to his species; yet we find the same observation to take place in a less degree. A man of mild manners can form no idea of inveterate revenge or cruelty; nor can a selfish heart easily conceive the heights of friendship and generosity. It is readily allowed, that other beings may possess many senses of which we can have no conception; because the ideas of them have never been introduced to us in the only manner by which an idea can have access to the mind, to wit, by the actual feeling and sensation.

There is, however, one contradictory phenomenon, which may prove that it is not absolutely impossible for ideas to arise, independent of their correspondent impressions. I believe it will readily be allowed, that the several distinct ideas of colour, which enter by the eye, or those of sound, which are conveyed by the ear, are really different from each other; though, at the same time, resembling. Now if this be true of different colours, it must be no less so of the different shades of the same colour; and each shade produces a distinct idea, independent of the rest. For if this should be denied, it is possible, by the continual gradation of shades, to run a colour insensibly into what is most remote from it; and if you will not allow any of the means to be different, you cannot, without absurdity, deny the extremes to be the same. Suppose, therefore, a person to have enjoyed his sight for thirty years, and to have become perfectly acquainted with colours of all kinds except one particular shade of blue, for instance, which it never has been his fortune to meet with. Let all the different shades of that colour, except that single one, be placed before him, descending gradually from the deepest to the lightest; it is plain that he will perceive a blank, where that shade is wanting, and will be sensible that there is a greater distance in that place between the contiguous colours than in any other. Now I ask, whether it be possible for him, from his own imagination, to supply this deficiency, and raise up to himself the idea of that particular shade, though it had never been conveyed to him by his senses? I believe there are few but will be of opinion that he can: and this may serve as a proof that the simple ideas are not always, in every instance, derived from the correspondent impressions; though this instance is so singular, that it is scarcely worth our observing, and does not merit that for it alone we should alter our general maxim.

Here, therefore, is a proposition, which not only seems, in itself, simple and intelligible; but, if a proper use were made of it, might render every dispute equally intelligible, and banish all that jargon, which has so long taken possession of metaphysical reasonings, and drawn disgrace upon them. All ideas, especially abstract ones, are naturally faint and obscure: the mind has but a slender hold of them: they are apt to be confounded with other resembling ideas; and when we have often employed any term, though without a distinct meaning, we are apt to imagine it has a determinate idea annexed to it. On the contrary, all impressions, that is, all sensations, either outward or inward, are strong and vivid: the limits between them are more exactly determined: nor is it easy to fall into any error or mistake with regard to them. When we entertain, therefore, any suspicion that a philosophical term is employed without any meaning or idea (as is but too frequent), we need but enquire, *from what impression is that supposed idea derived?* And if it be impossible to assign any, this will serve to confirm our suspicion. By bringing ideas into so clear a light we may reasonably hope to remove all dispute, which may arise, concerning their nature and reality.

46

Is There a Problem of Not Knowing that One Is Not Dreaming?

René Descartes, "Meditation I"

Not everyone will wish to follow an empiricism such as Hume's (in the previous reading) by regarding all knowledge as more or less directly observational. Yet should all of us find it natural anyway to regard observation as a way of gaining *some* of our knowledge? The most likely object of such knowledge would be the physical world around us. You watch, listen, touch, etc. What could be more reasonable than to credit you with thereby knowing that a table is in front of you, for example? Presumably you could not have known of that table's existence merely by *thinking*; observation was needed. Still, was observation also enough? In other words, is observation ever *all* that is needed for knowing, even for knowing nearby aspects of the physical world? This reading raises a potential problem for observation's having that power, that ability to give us such knowledge. Although the reading is very brief, it is a philosophical classic. It is one of the arguments in René Descartes' "Meditation I." It has come to be called the *dreaming* argument, or the dreaming argument for *external world* skepticism. (Descartes was not the first philosopher to see this possible problem. But he described it so memorably, within a more systematic setting. Hence, it is also often called *Cartesian* external world skepticism.)

The term "external world" reflects Descartes' picture of the physical world as something existing, if at all, beyond anyone's experience of themselves as apparently thinking about that world. Contrast your consciousness with what it could be seeking to report or represent in the physical world. In *that* sense, the physical world is being called "external" – external to one's consciousness.

René Descartes, "Meditation I" (excerpt), in *Meditations on First Philosophy* [1641]. From *The Philosophical Works of Descartes*, vol. 1, trans. E.S. Haldane and G.R.T. Ross (Cambridge: Cambridge University Press, 1911). Reprinted with permission of Cambridge University Press.

Metaphysics and Epistemology: A Guided Anthology, First Edition. Edited by Stephen Hetherington.
© 2014 John Wiley & Sons, Inc. Published 2014 by John Wiley & Sons, Inc.

This argument from Descartes is *skeptical*: its conclusion is a surprising denial of there being any instances of a kind of knowledge widely assumed to be readily available. The argument concludes that no one knows anything about the physical world – the world each of us confidently *believes* we experience through our senses. The argument aims to deny that observation is ever a way of knowing the physical world around one.

How does the argument reach its potentially unwelcome denial? It posits a possibility – that of dreaming. It then uses that possibility to formulate a challenge. Right now, you may well feel that you are observing an aspect of your physical circumstances – there being a table in front of you. The skeptical argument challenges you to know that you are not *dreaming* at this moment. You feel as if you are observing in a normal way; could you actually be asleep and dreaming? If that is possible, your having a feeling of observing is not a guarantee of your actually observing. Yet if your experience right now could – for all that you can know to the contrary – be one of dreaming rather than observing, then (continues the skeptical reasoning) this experience is not one about which you should have no doubts. But wherever one cannot eliminate doubt, knowledge is absent. So, *do* you know, by looking and touching, that there is a table in front of you? Not if the Cartesian dreaming argument wins the day.

[...]

All that up to the present time I have accepted as most true and certain I have learned either from the senses or through the senses; but it is sometimes proved to me that these senses are deceptive, and it is wiser not to trust entirely to any thing by which we have once been deceived.

But it may be that although the senses sometimes deceive us concerning things which are hardly perceptible, or very far away, there are yet many others to be met with as to which we cannot reasonably have any doubt, although we recognise them by their means. For example, there is the fact that I am here, seated by the fire, attired in a dressing gown, having this paper in my hands and other similar matters. And how could I deny that these hands and this body are mine, were it not perhaps that I compare myself to certain persons, devoid of sense, whose cerebella are so troubled and clouded by the violent vapours of black bile, that they constantly assure us that they think they are kings when they are really quite poor, or that they are clothed in purple when they are really without covering, or who imagine that they have an earthenware head or are nothing but pumpkins or are made of glass. But they are mad, and I should not be any the less insane were I to follow examples so extravagant.

At the same time I must remember that I am a man, and that consequently I am in the habit of sleeping, and in my dreams representing to myself the same things or sometimes even less probable things, than do those who are insane in their waking moments. How often has it happened to me that in the night I dreamt that I found myself in this particular place, that I was dressed and seated near the fire, whilst in reality I was lying undressed in bed! At this moment it does indeed seem to me that it is with eyes awake that I am looking at this paper; that this head which I move is not asleep, that it is deliberately and of set purpose that I extend my hand and perceive it; what happens in sleep does not appear so clear nor so distinct as does all this. But in thinking over this I remind myself that on many occasions I have in sleep been deceived by similar illusions, and in dwelling carefully on this reflection I see so manifestly that there are no certain indications by which we may clearly distinguish wakefulness from sleep that I am lost in astonishment. And my astonishment is such that it is almost capable of persuading me that I now dream.

[...]

47

What Is It Really to be Seeing Something?

David Lewis, "Veridical Hallucination and Prosthetic Vision"

Part of the idea behind the Cartesian dreaming argument in the previous reading is the presumption that it is possible for a person to be dreaming even when seeming, to herself, to be perceiving the world in a normal way. So, part of thinking about how to react to that argument could be our reflecting upon the nature of observing. What *is* it to be seeing part of the world – an object, another person, a scene? What key elements would we expect to find within our concept of what it is to perceive something, such as by seeing it? In this reading, David Lewis (1941–2001) describes what he takes to be some of those key elements. Most of his outstanding career was at Princeton University, writing particularly on metaphysics. Here, we have his metaphysical analysis of the epistemologically vital concept of seeing.

Lewis begins with what might seem to be a complete conceptual analysis of seeing. (Then he adds one element to it.) Thus, many will think that one's seeing something is a matter merely of having a visual experience that *matches* the scene in front of one, so long as the visual experience has been properly *caused* by that scene. For instance, suppose that you have a visual experience as of a fox in front of you – and that in fact a fox *is* sitting there. Your visual experience thereby *matches* this circumstance; and suppose that your visual experience has been *caused* by the fox's presence. Is all of that enough to make your visual experience one of seeing the fox? Aspects of this story should remind us of some of this book's earlier metaphysical readings. Your visual experience is an *appearance*, hopefully of a further reality. Your visual experience matches the scene in front of you; this is

David Lewis, "Veridical Hallucination and Prosthetic Vision," *Australasian Journal of Philosophy* 58 (1980), 239–249. Reprinted with permission of Taylor & Francis Journals.

Metaphysics and Epistemology: A Guided Anthology, First Edition. Edited by Stephen Hetherington.
© 2014 John Wiley & Sons, Inc. Published 2014 by John Wiley & Sons, Inc.

like a claim's being *made true* by a *fact*. And how is the visual experience *caused*? We have noticed possible disagreements (in the section "How Does the World Function?", readings 11 and 12) as to what it is for one thing to cause another.

What Lewis adds to that possible conceptual analysis is talk of *counterfactual dependence*. Think of the way in which your visual experience has been caused. That way has produced a matching visual experience: the fox's being in front of you matches the content of your visual experience. Would that same way of causing a visual experience have likewise caused matching ones within relevantly alternative possible settings? (These are *counter*factual possible circumstances.) Suppose that, even if you had been looking at a similarly sized dog (not the fox), again you would have had a visual experience as of a fox. It would still seem to you that a fox is present; you would thereby be deceived. This implies that your actual way of apparently seeing the fox matches the fox's presence only *un*reliably: your connection to the fox's reality is not strong enough in this nuanced way. Although that way of producing your visual experience has produced a matching one, it could easily have produced a *mis*matching one (still of a fox, but when a dog instead was present). Lewis would infer that you have not really been seeing the fox: in effect, your experience is too counterfactually unreliable to be a case of seeing.

Hence, Lewis is requiring even whatever *feels* like a real instance of seeing to be sensitive to counterfactual circumstances if it is genuinely to be an instance of seeing. He is not arguing (as a skeptical thinker might) that we never actually see. He is offering an analysis of the concept of seeing – of what is involved if and when we do see.

I

I see. Before my eyes various things are present and various things are going on. The scene before my eyes causes a certain sort of visual experience in me, thanks to a casual process involving light, the retina, the optic nerve, and the brain. The visual experience so caused more or less matches the scene before my eyes. All this goes on in much the same way in my case as in the case of other people who see. And it goes on in much the same way that it would have if the scene before my eyes had been visibly different, though in that case the visual experience produced would have been different.

How much of all this is essential to seeing?

II

It is not far wrong to say simply that someone sees if and only if the scene before his eyes causes matching visual experience. So far as I know, there are no counterexamples to this in our ordinary life. Shortly we shall consider some that arise under extraordinary circumstances.

But first, what do we mean by 'matching visual experience'? What goes on in the brain (or perhaps the soul) is not very much like what goes on before the eyes. They cannot match in the way that a scale model matches its prototype, or anything like that. Rather, visual experience has informational content about the scene before the eyes, and it matches the scene to the extent that its content is correct.

Visual experience is a state characterised by its typical casual role, and its role is to participate in a double casual dependence. Visual experience depends on the scene before the eyes, and the subject's beliefs about that scene depend in turn partly on his visual experience. The content of the experience is, roughly, the content of the belief it tends to produce.

[...]

Not all of the content of visual experience can be characterised in terms of the beliefs it tends to produce. It is part of the content that the duck-rabbit look like a duck or a rabbit, but the belief produced is that there is no duck and no rabbit but only paper and ink. However, aspects of the content that do not show up in the produced belief also are irrelevant to our task of saying what it is for visual experience to match the scene before the eyes. We can therefore ignore them.

III

[...]

[...] My analysandum [i.e. what is being analysed] is seeing in a strong sense that requires a relation to the external scene. Someone whose visual experience is entirely hallucinatory does not see in this strong sense. I take it that he can be said to see in a weaker, phenomenal sense – he sees what isn't there – and this is to say just that he has visual experience. [...]

IV

My first stab is good enough to deal with some familiar counterexamples to causal analyses of seeing: they are not cases of seeing because they are not cases in which the scene before the eyes causes matching visual experience.[1]

Example 1: The Brain. I hallucinate at random; by chance I seem to see a brain floating before my eyes; my own brain happens to look just like the one I seem to see; my brain is causing my visual experience, which matches it. I do not see. No problem: my brain is no part of the scene before my eyes.

Example 2: The Memory. I hallucinate not at random; visual memory influences the process; thus I seem to see again a scene from long ago; this past scene causes visual experience which matches it. I do not see. No problem: the past scene is not part of the scene before my eyes.[2]

However, more difficult cases are possible. They are cases of *veridical hallucination*, in which the scene before the eyes causes matching visual experience, and still one does not see. They show that what I have said so far does not provide a sufficient condition for seeing.

Example 3: The Brain Before the Eyes. As in Example 1, I hallucinate at random, I seem to see a brain before my eyes, my own brain looks just like the one I seem to see, and my brain is causing my visual experience. But this time my brain is before my eyes. It has been carefully removed from my skull. The nerves and blood vessels that connect it to the rest of me have been stretched somehow, not severed. It is still working and still hallucinating.

Example 4: The Wizard. The scene before my eyes consists mostly of a wizard casting a spell. His spell causes me to hallucinate at random, and the hallucination so caused happens to match the scene before my eyes.

Example 5: The Light Meter. I am blind; but electrodes have been implanted in my brain in such a way that when turned on they will cause me to have visual experience of a certain sort of landscape. A light meter is on my head. It is connected to the electrodes in such a way that they are turned on if and only if the average illumination of the scene before my eyes exceeds a certain threshold. By chance, just such a landscape is before my eyes, and its illumination is enough to turn on the electrodes.

V

Ordinarily, when the scene before the eyes causes matching visual experience, it happens as follows. Parts of the scene reflect or emit light in a certain pattern; this light travels to the eye by a more or less straight path, and is focused by the lens to form an image on the retina; the retinal cells are stimulated in proportion to the intensity and spectral distribution of the light that falls on them; these stimulated cells stimulate other cells in turn, and so on, and the stimulations comprise a signal which propagates up the optic nerve into the brain; and finally there is a pattern of stimulation in the brain cells which either is or else causes the subject's visual experience.

That is not at all what goes on in our three examples of veridical hallucination. Rather, the scene before the eyes causes matching visual experience by peculiar, non-standard causal processes. Perhaps, as has been proposed [...], seeing requires the standard causal process. That would explain why Examples 3, 4, and 5 do not qualify as cases of seeing. [...]

Unfortunately, requiring the standard process would disqualify good cases along with the bad. Some cases in which the scene before the eyes causes matching visual experience by a non-standard process seem fairly clearly to be cases of genuine seeing, not veridical hallucination.

Example 6: The Minority. It might be found that a few of us have visual systems that work on different principles from other peoples'. The differences might be as extreme as the difference between AM versus FM transmission of signals; analogue versus digital processing; or point-by-point measurement of light versus edge detection. If so, would we be prepared to say that the minority don't really see? Would those who belong to the minority be prepared to say it? Surely not.

I anticipate the reply that the abnormal process in the minority is not different enough; the boundaries of the standard process should be drawn widely enough to include it. But I think this puts the cart before the horse. We know which processes to include just because somehow we already know which processes are ones by which someone might see.

Example 7: The Prosthetic Eye. A prosthetic eye consists of a miniature television camera mounted in, or on, the front of the head; a computer; and an array of electrodes in the brain. The computer receives input from the camera and sends signals to the electrodes in such a way as to produce visual experience that matches the scene before the eyes. When prosthetic eyes are perfected, the blind will see. The standard process will be absent, unless by 'standard process' we just mean one that permits seeing; but they will see by a non-standard process.

Some prosthetic eyes are more convincing than others as means for genuine seeing. (1) It seems better if the computer is surgically implanted rather than carried in a knapsack, but better if it's carried in a knapsack rather than stationary and linked by radio to the camera and electrodes. (2) It seems better if the prosthetic eye contains no parts which can be regarded as having wills of their own and cooperating because they want to. (3) It seems better if the prosthetic eye works in some uniform way, rather than dealing with different sorts of inputs by significantly different means. [...]

If you insist that 'strictly speaking' prosthetic vision isn't really seeing, then I'm prepared to concede you this much. Often we do leave semantic questions unsettled when we have no practical need to settle them. Perhaps this is such a case, and you are resolving a genuine indeterminacy in the way you prefer. But if you are within your rights, so, I insist, am I. I do not really think my favoured usage is at all idiosyncratic. But it scarcely matters: I would like to understand it whether it is idiosyncratic or not.

VI

The trouble with veridical hallucination is not that it involves a non-standard causal process. Is it perhaps this: that the process involved produces matching visual experience only seldom, perhaps only this once?

No; someone might go on having veridical hallucinations for a long time. Veridical hallucinations are improbable, and a long run of them is still more improbable, but that doesn't make it impossible. No matter how long they go on, the sorts of occurrences I've classified as cases of veridical hallucination still are that and not seeing.

On the other hand, a process that permits genuine seeing might work only seldom, perhaps only this once.

Example 8: The Deathbed Cure. God might cure a blind man on his deathbed, granting him an instant of sight by means of some suitable non-standard process. For an instant he sees exactly as others do. Then he is dead. The scene before his eyes produces matching visual experience by a suitable process, namely the standard one, but only this once.

Example 9: The Loose Wire. A prosthetic eye has a loose wire. Mostly it flops around; and when it does the eye malfunctions and the subject's visual experience consists of splotches unrelated to the scene before the eyes. But sometimes it touches the contact it ought to be bonded to; and as long as it does, the eye functions perfectly and the subject sees. Whether he sees has nothing to do with whether the wire touches the contact often, or seldom, or only this once.

The proposal isn't far wrong. It asks almost the right question: when the scene before the eyes causes matching visual experience this time, is that an isolated case or is it part of a range of such cases? The mistake is in asking for a range of actual cases, spread out in time. Rather, we need a range of counterfactual alternatives to the case under consideration.

VII

What distinguishes our cases of veridical hallucination from genuine seeing – natural or prosthetic, lasting or momentary – is that there is no proper counterfactual dependence of visual experience on the scene before the eyes. If the scene had been different, it would not have caused correspondingly different visual experience to match that different scene. Any match that occurs is a lucky accident. It depends on the scene being just right. In genuine seeing, the fact of match is independent of the scene. Just as the actual scene causes matching visual experience, so likewise would alternative scenes. Different scenes would have produced different visual experience, and thus the subject is in a position to discriminate between the alternatives.

This is my proposal: if the scene before the eyes causes matching visual experience as part of a suitable pattern of counterfactual dependence, then the subject sees; if the scene before the eyes causes matching visual experience without a suitable pattern of counterfactual dependence, then the subject does not see.

An ideal pattern of dependence would be one such that any scene whatever would produce perfectly matching visual experience. But that is too much to require. Certainly one can see even if the match, actual and counterfactual, is close but imperfect and the content of visual experience is mostly, but not entirely, correct. Perhaps indeed this is our common lot.

[...]

[...] Most of our visual experience is rich in content; but some is poor in content and would match a wide range of alternative scenes equally well. Any pitch-dark scene would produce matching visual experience – what content there is would be entirely correct – but it would be the same in every case. Seeing is a capacity to discriminate, so this sort of match over a wide range of alternatives will not suffice.

I conclude that the required pattern of counterfactual dependence may be specified as follows. There is a large class of alternative possible scenes before the subject's eyes, and there are many mutually exclusive and jointly exhaustive subclasses thereof, such that (1) any scene in the large class would cause visual experience closely matching that scene, and (2) any two scenes in different subclasses would cause different visual experience.

The requirement admits of degree in three ways. How large a class? How many subclasses? How close a match? The difference between veridical hallucination and genuine seeing is not sharp, on my analysis. It is fuzzy; when the requirement of suitable counterfactual dependence is met to some degree, but to a degree that falls far short of the standard set by normal seeing, we may expect borderline cases. And indeed it is easy to imagine cases of partial blindness, or of rudimentary prosthetic vision, in which the counterfactual dependence is unsatisfactory and it is therefore doubtful whether the subject may be said to see.

[...]

X

The following case [...] is a hard one. It closely resembles cases of genuine seeing, and we might well be tempted to classify it as such. According to my analysis, however, it is a case of veridical hallucination. The scene before the eyes causes matching visual experience without any pattern of counterfactual dependence whatever, suitable or otherwise.

Example 13: The Censor. My natural or prosthetic eye is in perfect condition and functioning normally, and by means of it the scene before my eyes causes matching visual experience. But if the scene were any different my visual experience would be just the same. For there is a censor standing by, ready to see to it that I have precisely that visual experience and no other, whatever the scene may be. (Perhaps the censor is external, perhaps it is something in my own brain.) So long as the scene is such as to cause the right experience, the censor does nothing. But if the scene were any different, the censor would intervene and cause the same experience by other means. If so, my eye would not function normally and the scene before my eyes would not cause matching visual experience.

The case is one of causal preemption.[3] The scene before my eyes is the actual cause of my visual experience; the censor is an alternative potential cause of the same effect. The actual cause preempts the potential cause, stopping the alternative causal chain that would other-wise have gone to completion.

The argument for classifying the case as seeing is that it is just like a clear case of seeing except for the presence of the censor; and, after all, the censor doesn't actually do anything; and if the scene before the eyes were different and the censor nevertheless stood idly by – as in actuality – then the different scene would indeed cause suitably different visual experience.

My reply is that the case is really not so very much like the clear case of seeing to which it is compared. [...]

The decisive consideration, despite the misleading resemblance of this case to genuine cases of seeing, is that the censor's potential victim has no capacity at all to discriminate by sight. Just as in any other case of veridical hallucination, the match that occurs is a lucky accident.

Notes

1. Example I and an auditory version of Example 2 are due to P. F. Strawson, 'Causation in Perception', in his *Freedom and Resentment and other essays* (London: Methuen, 1974), pp. 77–78.

2. However, it seems that some past things are part of the scene now before my eyes: distant stars as they were long ago, to take an extreme case. It would be circular to say that they, unlike the past scene in Example 2, are visible now. Perhaps the best answer is that the stars, as I now see them, are not straightforwardly past; for lightlike connection has as good a claim as simultaneity-in-my-rest-frame to be the legitimate heir to our defunct concept of absolute simultaneity. (I owe the problem to D. M. Armstrong and the answer to Eric Melum.)

3. See my discussion of preemption in 'Causation', *Journal of Philosophy* LXX (1973), pp. 556–567.

48

Is There a Possibility of Being a Mere and Unknowing Brain in a Vat?

Hilary Putnam, *Reason, Truth and History*

David Lewis was not arguing (in the previous reading) directly against skeptical thinking. But perhaps an aspect of his approach may be used for that end. Lewis sought to understand what *connection* to the world must be part of really seeing the world. This reading from Hilary Putnam (b. 1926) argues from a related picture, of a connection to the world that would be part even of *apparently* seeing an aspect of the world. Putnam's career, mainly at Harvard University, has been very influential. He has formulated many theories and thought-experiments about language, logic, reality, mind, and more. This much-discussed argument of his is anti-skeptical.

It is directed against a contemporary version – a re-imaging – of Descartes' dreaming argument. This newer version is usually called the *brain-in-a-vat* skeptical argument. Like the dreaming argument, this one raises a possibility in which someone has a pattern of experiences that feel, "from within," like normal perceptual interactions with the physical world – even though in fact they are far from normal. But what makes this skeptical argument distinctive is a further detail. This time, the conscious experiences belong to a *disembodied brain*, floating in a vat of sustaining chemicals. The brain is attached electrically to a machine causing it to have those experiences: the "inner" experiences had by the brain in the vat are programmed through the machine. That is the possibility envisaged by this argument. Then the skeptical argument raises this question: Can you know that you are *not* in that predicament? Indeed, can you know that you have not been in it for a long time? Can you know that you are not merely a long-term brain in a vat – hence, that for a long time you have not actually been observing the world, even when feeling like you are observing it?

Hilary Putnam, *Reason, Truth and History* (Cambridge: Cambridge University Press, 1981), ch. 1 (excerpts). © Cambridge University Press 1981. Reproduced with permission.

Metaphysics and Epistemology: A Guided Anthology, First Edition. Edited by Stephen Hetherington. © 2014 John Wiley & Sons, Inc. Published 2014 by John Wiley & Sons, Inc.

Putnam's reply asks whether the supposed skeptical possibility really is possible. Any experience is the experience it is partly because of its *content*. Yet how would those experiences belonging to the hypothesized long-term brain in the vat *have* a particular content? Putnam asks generally about how an apparently subjectively "owned" experience gains its content (e.g. "That's a fox"). For him, this is a question about how a word such as "fox" refers or denotes, how it is *about* something at all. What is needed for real reference (argues Putnam) is an apt *history of causal interaction* between uses of the word and elements of the world: the word "fox" has its meaning partly by having been used in responses to foxes. But no long-term brain in a vat could have been having that interaction. The long-term brain in the vat has not been responding to foxes. It has merely been "fed" apparently sensory experiences by the machine.

Significantly (continues Putnam), in such a circumstance you could not have had the sort of interaction required for your uses even of the phrase "brain in a vat" to contribute meaningfully to your thoughts. If you were a long-term brain in a vat, you would have been so systematically and sustainedly deceived about your surroundings that your uses of words would not mean what they seem to you to mean. You could not even think to yourself – with real content – "I *might* have long been a brain in a vat." So you cannot really entertain the possibility of being a long-term brain in a vat. Putnam thus claims to reveal as *self-refuting* any attempt to posit the skeptical possibility. Much is at stake in whether he is correct about this.

Brains in a Vat

An ant is crawling on a patch of sand. As it crawls, it traces a line in the sand. By pure chance the line that it traces curves and recrosses itself in such a way that it ends up looking like a recognizable caricature of Winston Churchill. Has the ant traced a picture of Winston Churchill, a picture that *depicts* Churchill?

Most people would say, on a little reflection, that it has not. The ant, after all, has never seen Churchill, or even a picture of Churchill, and it had no intention of depicting Churchill. It simply traced a line (and even *that* was unintentional), a line that *we* can 'see as' a picture of Churchill.

We can express this by saying that the line is not 'in itself' a representation[1] of anything rather than anything else. Similarity (of a certain very complicated sort) to the features of Winston Churchill is not sufficient to make something represent or refer to Churchill. Nor is it necessary: in our community the printed shape 'Winston Churchill', the spoken words 'Winston Churchill', and many other things are used to represent Churchill (though not pictorially), while not having the sort of similarity to Churchill that a picture – even a line drawing – has. If *similarity* is not necessary or sufficient to make something represent something else, how can *anything* be necessary or sufficient for this purpose? How on earth can one thing represent (or 'stand for', etc.) a different thing?

The answer may seem easy. Suppose the ant had seen Winston Churchill, and suppose that it had the intelligence and skill to draw a picture of him. Suppose it produced the caricature *intentionally*. Then the line would have represented Churchill.

On the other hand, suppose the line had the shape WINSTON CHURCHILL. And suppose this was just accident (ignoring the improbability involved). Then the 'printed shape' WINSTON CHURCHILL would *not* have represented Churchill, although that printed shape does represent Churchill when it occurs in almost any book today.

So it may seem that what is necessary for representation, or what is mainly necessary for representation, is *intention*.

But to have the intention that *anything*, even private language (even the words 'Winston Churchill' spoken in my mind and not out loud), should *represent* Churchill, I must have been able to *think about* Churchill in the first place. If lines in the sand, noises, etc., cannot 'in themselves' represent anything, then how is it that thought forms can 'in themselves' represent anything? Or can they? How can thought reach out and 'grasp' what is external?

[...]

Magical Theories of Reference

We saw that the ant's 'picture' has no necessary connection with Winston Churchill. The mere fact that the 'picture' bears a 'resemblance' to Churchill does not make it into a real picture, nor does it make it a representation of Churchill. [...]

What is important to realize is that what goes for physical pictures also goes for mental images, and for mental representations in general; mental representations no more have a necessary connection with what they represent than physical representations do. The contrary supposition is a survival of magical thinking.

Perhaps the point is easiest to grasp in the case of mental *images*. (Perhaps the first philosopher to grasp the enormous significance of this point, even if he was not the first to actually make it, was Wittgenstein.) Suppose there is a planet somewhere on which human beings have evolved (or been deposited by alien spacemen, or what have you). Suppose these humans, although otherwise like us, have never seen *trees*. Suppose they have never imagined trees (perhaps vegetable life exists on their planet only in the form of molds). Suppose one day a picture of a tree is accidentally dropped on their planet by a spaceship which passes on without having other contact with them. Imagine them puzzling over the picture. What in the world is this? All sorts of speculations occur to them: a building, a canopy, even an animal of some kind. But suppose they never come close to the truth.

For *us* the picture is a representation of a tree. For these humans the picture only represents a strange object, nature and function unknown. Suppose one of them has a mental image which is exactly like one of my mental images of a tree as a result of having seen the picture. His mental image is not a *representation of a tree*. It is only a representation of the strange object (whatever it is) that the mysterious picture represents.

Still, someone might argue that the mental image is *in fact* a representation of a tree, if only because the picture which caused this mental image was itself a representation of a tree to begin with. There is a causal chain from actual trees to the mental image even if it is a very strange one.

But even this causal chain can be imagined absent. Suppose the 'picture of the tree' that the spaceship dropped was not really a picture of a tree, but the accidental result of some spilled paints. Even if it looked exactly like a picture of a tree, it was, in truth, no more a picture of a tree than the ant's 'caricature' of Churchill was a picture of Churchill. We can even imagine that the spaceship which dropped the 'picture' came from a planet which knew nothing of trees. Then the humans would still have mental images qualitatively identical with my image of a tree, but they would not be images which represented a tree any more than anything else.

The same thing is true of *words*. A discourse on paper might seem to be a perfect description of trees, but if it was produced by monkeys randomly hitting keys on a typewriter for millions of years, then the words do not refer to anything. If there were a person who memorized those words and said them in his mind without understanding them, then they would not refer to anything when thought in the mind, either.

Imagine the person who is saying those words in his mind has been hypnotized. Suppose the words are in Japanese, and the person has been told that he understands Japanese. Suppose that as he thinks those words he has a 'feeling of understanding'. (Although if someone broke into his train of thought and asked him what the words he was thinking *meant*, he would discover he couldn't say.) Perhaps the illusion would be so perfect that the person could even fool a Japanese telepath! But if he couldn't use the words in the right contexts, answer questions about what he 'thought', etc., then he didn't understand them.

By combining these science fiction stories I have been telling, we can contrive a case in which someone thinks words which are in fact a description of trees in some language *and* simultaneously has appropriate mental images, but *neither* understands the words *nor* knows what a tree is. We can even imagine that the mental images were caused by paint-spills (although the person has been hypnotized to think that they are images of something appropriate to his thought – only, if he were asked, he wouldn't be able to say of what). And we can imagine that the language the person is thinking in is one neither the hypnotist nor the person hypnotized has ever heard of – perhaps it is just coincidence that these 'nonsense sentences', as the hypnotist supposes them to be, are a description of trees in Japanese. In short, everything passing before the person's mind might be qualitatively identical with what was passing through the mind of a Japanese speaker who was *really* thinking about trees – but none of it would refer to trees.

[…] [E]ven a large and complex system of representations, both verbal and visual, still does not have an *intrinsic*, built-in, magical connection with what it represents – a connection independent of how it was caused and what the dispositions of the speaker or thinker are. And this is true whether the system of representations (words and images, in the case of the example) is physically realized – the words are written or spoken, and the pictures are physical pictures – or only realized in the mind. Thought words and mental pictures do not *intrinsically* represent what they are about.

The Case of the Brains in a Vat

Here is a science fiction possibility discussed by philosophers: imagine that a human being (you can imagine this to be yourself) has been subjected to an operation by an evil scientist. The person's brain (your brain) has been removed from the body and placed in a vat of nutrients which keeps the brain alive. The nerve endings have been connected to a super-scientific computer which causes the person whose brain it is to have the illusion that everything is perfectly normal. There seem to be people, objects, the sky, etc; but really all the person (you) is experiencing is the result of electronic impulses travelling from the computer to the nerve endings. The computer is so clever that if the person tries to raise his hand, the feedback from the computer will cause him to 'see' and 'feel' the hand being raised. Moreover, by varying the program, the evil scientist can cause the victim to 'experience' (or hallucinate) any situation or environment the evil scientist wishes. He can also obliterate the memory of the brain operation, so that the victim will seem to himself to have always been in this environment. It can even seem to the victim that he is sitting and reading these very words about the amusing but quite absurd supposition that there is an evil scientist who removes people's brains from their bodies and places them in a vat of nutrients which keep the brains alive. The nerve endings are supposed to be connected to a super-scientific computer which causes the person whose brain it is to have the illusion that ...

When this sort of possibility is mentioned in a lecture on the Theory of Knowledge, the purpose, of course, is to raise the classical problem of scepticism with respect to the external world in a modern way. (*How do you know you aren't in this predicament?*) But this predicament is also a useful device for raising issues about the mind/world relationship.

Instead of having just one brain in a vat, we could imagine that all human beings (perhaps all sentient beings) are brains in a vat (or nervous systems in a vat in case some beings with just a minimal nervous system already count as 'sentient'). Of course, the evil scientist would have to be outside – or would he? Perhaps there is no evil scientist, perhaps (though this is absurd) the universe just happens to consist of automatic machinery tending a vat full of brains and nervous systems.

This time let us suppose that the automatic machinery is programmed to give us all a *collective* hallucination, rather than a number of separate unrelated hallucinations. Thus, when I seem to myself to be talking to you, you seem to yourself to be hearing my words. Of course, it is not the case that my words actually reach your ears – for you don't have (real) ears, nor do I have a real mouth and tongue. Rather, when I produce my words, what happens is that the efferent impulses travel from my brain to the computer, which both causes me to 'hear' my own voice uttering those words and 'feel' my tongue moving, etc., and causes you to 'hear' my words, 'see' me speaking, etc. In this case, we are, in a sense, actually in communication. I am not mistaken about your real existence (only about the existence of your body and the 'external world', apart from brains). From a certain point of view, it doesn't even matter that 'the whole world' is a collective hallucination; for you do, after all, really hear my words when I speak to you, even if the mechanism isn't what we suppose it to be. (Of course, if we were two lovers making love, rather than just two people carrying on a conversation, then the suggestion that it was just two brains in a vat might be disturbing.)

I want now to ask a question which will seem very silly and obvious (at least to some people, including some very sophisticated philosophers), but which will take us to real philosophical depths rather quickly. Suppose this whole story were actually true. Could we, if we were brains in a vat in this way, *say* or *think* that we were?

I am going to argue that the answer is 'No, we couldn't.' In fact, I am going to argue that the supposition that we are actually brains in a vat, although it violates no physical law, and is perfectly consistent with everything we have experienced, cannot possibly be true. *It cannot possibly be true*, because it is, in a certain way, self-refuting.

[...]

A 'self-refuting supposition' is one whose truth implies its own falsity. For example, consider the thesis that *all general statements are false*. This is a general statement. So if it is true, then it must be false. Hence, it is false. Sometimes a thesis is called 'self-refuting' if it is *the supposition that the thesis is entertained or enunciated* that implies its falsity. For example, 'I do not exist' is self-refuting if thought by *me* (for any '*me*'). So one can be certain that one oneself exists, if one thinks about it (as Descartes argued).

What I shall show is that the supposition that we are brains in a vat has just this property. If we can consider whether it is true or false, then it is not true (I shall show). Hence it is not true.

Before I give the argument, let us consider why it seems so strange that such an argument can be given (at least to philosophers who subscribe to a 'copy' conception of truth). We conceded that it is compatible with physical law that there should be a world in which all sentient beings are brains in a vat. As philosophers say, there is a 'possible world' in which all sentient beings are brains in a vat. [...] The humans in that possible world have exactly the same experiences that *we* do. They think the same thoughts we do (at least, the same words, images, thought-forms, etc., go through their minds). Yet, I am claiming that there is an argument we can give that shows we are not brains in a vat. How can there be? And why couldn't the people in the possible world who really *are* brains in a vat give it too?

The answer is going to be (basically) this: although the people in that possible world can think and 'say' any words we can think and say, they cannot (I claim) *refer* to what we can refer to. In particular, they cannot think or say that they are brains in a vat (*even by thinking 'we are brains in a vat'*).

[...]

[...] [T]here is the *illusion* that the ant has caricatured Churchill. [...] [T]he ant would have drawn the same curve even if Winston Churchill had never existed. [...]

Brains in a Vat (Again)

[...] The brains in a vat do not have sense organs, but they do have *provision* for sense organs; that is, there are afferent nerve endings, there are inputs from these afferent nerve endings, and these inputs figure in the 'program' of the brains in the vat just as they do in the program of our brains. The brains in a vat are *brains*; moreover, they are *functioning* brains, and they function by the same rules as brains do in the actual world. For these reasons, it would seem absurd to deny consciousness or intelligence to them. But the fact that they are conscious and intelligent does not mean that their words refer to what our words refer. The question we are interested in is this: do their verbalizations containing, say, the word 'tree' actually refer to *trees*? More generally: can they refer to *external* objects at all? [...]

To fix our ideas, let us specify that the automatic machinery is supposed to have come into existence by some kind of cosmic chance or coincidence (or, perhaps, to have always existed). In this hypothetical world, the automatic machinery itself is supposed to have no intelligent creator–designers. [...]

This assumption does not help. For there is no connection between the *word* 'tree' as used by these brains and actual trees. They would still use the word 'tree' just as they do, think just the thoughts they do, have just the images they have, even if there were no actual trees. Their images, words, etc., are qualitatively identical with images, words, etc., which do represent trees in *our* world; but we have already seen (the ant again!) that qualitative similarity to something which represents an object (Winston Churchill or a tree) does not make a thing a representation all by itself. In short, the brains in a vat are not thinking about real trees when they think 'there is a tree in front of me' because there is nothing by virtue of which their thought 'tree' represents actual trees.

[...] [W]e have seen that the words do not necessarily refer to trees even if they are arranged in a sequence which is identical with a discourse which (were it to occur in one of our minds) would unquestionably *be about trees* in the actual world. Nor does the 'program', in the sense of the rules, practices, dispositions of the brains to verbal behavior, necessarily refer to trees or bring about reference to trees through the connections it establishes between words and words, or *linguistic* cues and *linguistic* responses. If these brains think about, refer to, represent trees (real trees, outside the vat), then it must be because of the way the 'program' connects the system of language to *non-verbal* input and outputs. There are indeed such non-verbal inputs and outputs in the Brain-in-a-Vat world (those efferent and afferent nerve endings again!), but we also saw that the 'sense-data' produced by the automatic machinery do not represent trees (or anything external) even when they resemble our tree-images exactly. Just as a splash of paint might resemble a tree picture without *being* a tree picture, so, we saw, a 'sense datum' might be qualitatively identical with an 'image of a tree' without being an image of a tree. How can the fact that, in the case of the brains in a vat, the language is connected by the program with sensory inputs which do not intrinsically or extrinsically represent trees (or anything external) possibly bring it about that the whole system of representations, the language-in-use, *does* refer to or represent trees or anything external?

The answer is that it cannot. The whole system of sense-data, motor signals to the efferent endings, and verbally or conceptually mediated thought connected by 'language entry rules' to the sense-data (or whatever) as inputs and by 'language exit rules' to the motor signals as outputs, has no more connection to *trees* than the ant's curve has to Winston Churchill. Once we see that the *qualitative similarity* (amounting, if you like, to qualitative identity) between the thoughts of the brains in a vat and the thoughts of someone in the actual world by no means implies sameness of reference, it is not hard to see that there is no basis at all for regarding the brain in a vat as referring to external things.

The Premisses of the Argument

I have now given the argument promised to show that the brains in a vat cannot think or say that they are brains in a vat. It remains only to make it explicit and to examine its structure.

By what was just said, when the brain in a vat (in the world where every sentient being is and always was a brain in a vat) thinks 'There is a tree in front of me', his thought does not refer to actual trees. On some theories that we shall discuss it might refer to trees in the image, or to the electronic impulses that cause tree experiences, or to the features of the program that are responsible for those electronic impulses. These theories are not ruled out by what was just said, for there is a close causal connection between the use of the word 'tree' in vat-English and the presence of trees in the image, the presence of electronic impulses of a certain kind, and the presence of certain features in the machine's program. On these theories the brain is *right*, not *wrong* in thinking 'There is a tree in front of me.' Given what 'tree' refers to in vat-English and what 'in front of' refers to, assuming one of these theories is correct, then the truth-conditions for 'There is a tree in front of me' when it occurs in vat-English are simply that a tree in the image be 'in front of' the 'me' in question – in the image – or, perhaps, that the kind of electronic impulse that normally produces this experience be coming from the automatic machinery, or, perhaps, that the feature of the machinery that is supposed to produce the 'tree in front of one' experience be operating. And these truth-conditions are certainly fulfilled.

By the same argument, 'vat' refers to vats in the image in vat-English, or something related (electronic impulses or program features), but certainly not to real vats, since the use of 'vat' in vat-English has no causal connection to real vats (apart from the connection that the brains in a vat wouldn't be able to use the word 'vat', if it were not for the presence of one particular vat – the vat they are in; but this connection obtains between the use of *every* word in vat-English and that one particular vat; it is not a special connection between the use of the *particular* word 'vat' and vats). Similarly, 'nutrient fluid' refers to a liquid in the image in vat-English, or something related (electronic impulses or program features). It follows that if their 'possible world' is really the actual one, and we are really the brains in a vat, then what we now mean by 'we are brains in a vat' is that *we are brains in a vat in the image* or something of that kind (if we mean anything at all). But part of the hypothesis that we are brains in a vat is that we aren't brains in a vat in the image (i.e. what we are 'hallucinating' isn't that we are brains in a vat). So, if we are brains in a vat, then the sentence 'We are brains in a vat' says something false (if it says anything). In short, if we are brains in a vat, then 'We are brains in a vat' is false. So it is (necessarily) false.

[...]

[...] Concepts are signs used in a certain way; the signs may be public or private, mental entities or physical entities, but even when the signs are 'mental' and 'private', the sign itself apart from its use is not the concept. And signs do not themselves intrinsically refer.

We can see this by performing a very simple thought experiment. Suppose you are like me and cannot tell an elm tree from a beech tree. We still say that the reference of 'elm' in my speech is the same as the reference of 'elm' in anyone else's, viz. elm trees, and that the set of all beech trees is the extension of 'beech' (i.e. the set of things the word 'beech' is truly predicated of) both in your speech and my speech. Is it really credible that the difference between what 'elm' refers to and what 'beech' refers to is brought about by a difference in our *concepts*? My concept of an elm tree is exactly the same as my concept of a beech tree (I blush to confess). (This shows that the determination of reference is social and not individual, by the way; you and I both defer to experts who *can* tell elms from beeches.) If someone heroically attempts to maintain that the difference between the reference of 'elm' and the reference of 'beech' in *my* speech is explained by a difference in my psychological state, then let him imagine a Twin Earth where the words are switched. Twin Earth is very much like Earth; in fact, apart from the fact that 'elm' and 'beech' are interchanged, the reader can suppose Twin Earth is exactly like Earth. Suppose I have a *Doppelganger* on Twin Earth who is molecule for molecule identical with me (in the sense in which two neckties can be 'identical'). If you are a dualist, then suppose my *Doppelganger* thinks the same verbalized thoughts I do, has the same sense data, the same dispositions, etc. It is absurd to think his psychological state is one bit different from mine: yet his word 'elm' represents *beeches*, and my word 'elm' represents *elm*. (Similarly, if the 'water' on Twin Earth is a different liquid – say, XYZ and not H_2O – then 'water' represents a different liquid when used on Twin Earth and when used on Earth, etc.) Contrary to a doctrine that has been with us since the seventeenth century, *meanings just aren't in the head.*

Note

1. The terms 'representation' and 'reference' always refer to a relation between a word (or other sort of sign, symbol, or representation) and something that actually exists (i.e. not just an 'object of thought'). There is a sense of 'refer' in which I can 'refer' to what does not exist; this is not the sense in which 'refer' is used here. An older word for what I call 'representation' or 'reference' is *denotation*.

49

Is It Possible to Observe Directly the Objective World?

John McDowell, "The Disjunctive Conception of Experience as Material for a Transcendental Argument"

We have now met two skeptical arguments. Both the brain-in-a-vat argument and the dreaming argument are intended to generate external world skepticism. We saw earlier how this use of the word "external" is to be understood: in practice, external world skeptical arguments are presented as reasons to doubt our knowing anything of a *physical* world. Can someone know what the world includes *objectively* − what it is like in itself (regardless of anyone's ever trying to know about it)? Each such attempt (according to the skeptical arguments) faces a powerful metaphysical image − of our knowing only *indirectly*, if at all, the world around us. Especially since Descartes formulated the dreaming argument, many people say that the difficulty for our knowing the objective physical world around us is our relying upon *subjective* observational experiences to gain that knowledge. Your observations are only yours; mine are only mine; and ne'er do these merge. Each is "inner" and "private." Your seeing a fox is your having a subjective experience. So, how could you know the real fox existing objectively *beyond* that subjective experience?

But this reading disputes whether we *are* committed to working within that metaphysical image of what is happening when a person attempts to know the world perceptually. The reading is from John McDowell (b. 1924). His eminent career has been at the University of Oxford and the University of Pittsburgh,

John McDowell, "The Disjunctive Conception of Experience as Material for a Transcendental Argument" (excerpts), in A. Haddock and F. Macpherson (eds.), *Disjunctivism: Perception, Action, Knowledge* (Oxford: Oxford University Press, 2008). Reprinted with permission of Oxford University Press.

encompassing several areas of philosophy – epistemology, metaphysics, philosophy of language, philosophy of mind, ethics, the history of philosophy.

Here, we find McDowell arguing for the possibility of what philosophers often call *direct realism*. A fox, say, can sometimes be perceived directly: you could see it without relying on a separately existing and privately subjective "inner" experience representing the fox to you in such a way that the experience amounts, even when accurate, to a potential barrier between your mind and the fox's true nature. McDowell is not saying that such direct success would *always* happen when you feel that you are seeing something: you could be hallucinating, even if only some details. His view is called *disjunctivism*: any instance of experience is *either* directly and accurately of the world *or* it only appears to be. Whenever you do see the fox directly, though, it is "right there" for you.

Disjunctivism about the nature of experience is a comparatively new idea (McDowell is not its originator). Part of its motivation is the optimistic thought that it can undermine the external world skeptical arguments, by rendering optional a metaphysical image essential to their apparent power. McDowell is saying that in principle it is possible to observe the world directly – and that whenever we do so we are not in the same experiential state as when hallucinating. Hence, knowing the world does not require us to transcend an inherent limit placed upon us by inescapably "inner" experiences that are the same when hallucinatory as when accurate. Yet the skeptical argument does require this of us. Thus, disjunctivism denies that we are so restricted by the inherent nature of experience: we could know the world, at least sometimes, by knowing it directly. (Note that McDowell mentions "Descartes' demon" and "the demon scenario." These are references to a dramatic skeptical challenge by Descartes that we will meet in reading 62.)

[…]

I want to consider a different approach to one sort of scepticism. […]

The scepticism in question is scepticism about perceptually acquired knowledge of the external world. And the approach in question is diagnostic. The diagnosis is that this scepticism expresses an inability to make sense of the idea of direct perceptual access to objective facts about the environment. What shapes this scepticism is the thought that even in the best possible case, the most that perceptual experience can yield falls short of a subject's having an environmental state of affairs directly available to her. Consider situations in which a subject seems to see that, say, there is a red cube in front of her. The idea is that even if we focus on the best possible case, her experience could be just as it is, in all respects, even if there were no red cube in front of her. This seems to reveal that perceptual experience provides at best inconclusive warrants for claims about the environment. And that seems incompatible with supposing we ever, strictly speaking, *know* anything about our objective surroundings.[1] The familiar sceptical scenarios – Descartes's demon, the scientist with our brains in his vat, the suggestion that all our apparent experience might be a dream – are only ways to make this supposed predicament vivid.

Suppose scepticism about our knowledge of the external world is recommended on these lines. In that case it constitutes a response if we can find a way to insist that we *can* make sense of the idea of direct perceptual access to objective facts about the environment. That contradicts the claim that what perceptual experience yields, even in the best possible case, must be something less than having an environmental fact directly available to one. And without that thought, this scepticism loses its supposed basis and falls to the ground.

It is important that that is the right description of what this response achieves. We need not pretend to have an argument that would prove that we are not, say, at the mercy of Descartes's demon, using premises we can affirm, and inferential steps we can exploit, without begging questions against someone who urges sceptical doubts. As I said, the point of invoking the demon scenario and its like is only to give vivid expression to the predicament supposedly constituted by its not making sense to think we can have environmental facts directly available to us. But if it does make sense to think we can have environmental facts directly available to us, there is no such predicament. And now someone who proposes those scenarios can no longer seem to be simply emphasizing a discouraging fact about our epistemic possibilities. When we reject the scenarios – if we choose to bother with them at all – we need no longer be hamstrung by a conception of argumentative legitimacy controlled by that understanding of their status. An accusation of question-begging need no longer carry any weight. We can invert the order in which scepticism insists we should proceed, and say – as common sense would, if it undertook to consider the sceptical scenarios at all – that our knowledge that those supposed possibilities do not obtain is sustained by the fact that we know a great deal about our environment, which would not be the case if we were not perceptually in touch with the world in just about the way we ordinarily suppose we are.

Similarly, there is no need to establish, without begging questions against scepticism, that in any particular case of perceptual experience we actually are in the favourable epistemic position that scepticism suggests we could never be in. That would similarly be to accept tendentious ground rules for satisfying ourselves in given cases that we have knowledge of the environment. If we can recapture the idea that it is so much as possible to have environmental states of affairs directly presented to us in perceptual experience, we can recognize that such ground rules reflect a misconception of our cognitive predicament. And then our practice of making and assessing claims to environmental knowledge on particular occasions can proceed as it ordinarily does, without contamination by philosophy. There need no longer seem to be any reason to discount the fact that in real life the assessment is often positive.

Perhaps most people will find it obvious that reinstating the sheer possibility of directly taking in objective reality in perception would undermine a scepticism based on claiming that perceptual experience can never amount to that. [...]

[...] The argument aims to establish that the idea of environmental facts making themselves available to us in perception must be intelligible, because that is a necessary condition for it to be intelligible that experience has a characteristic that is, for purposes of this argument, not in doubt.

The relevant characteristic is that experience purports to be of objective reality. When one undergoes perceptual experience, it at least appears to one as if things in one's environment are a certain way.

Consider Wilfrid Sellars's discussion of "looks" statements in *Empiricism and the Philosophy of Mind*. Sellars urges something on the following lines. In order to understand the very idea of the objective purport of visual experience (to single out one sensory modality), we need to appreciate that the concept of experiences in which, say, it looks to one as if there is a red cube in front of one divides into the concept of cases in which one sees that there is a red cube in front of one and the concept of cases in which it merely looks to one as if there is a red cube in front of one (either because there is nothing there at all or because although there is something there it is not a red cube).

At least implicit here is a thought that can be put as follows. In order to find it intelligible that experience has objective purport at all, we must be able to make sense of an epistemically distinguished class of experiences, those in which (staying with the visual case) one sees how things are — those in which how things are makes itself visually available to one. Experiences in which it merely looks to one as if things are thus and so are experiences that misleadingly present themselves as belonging to that epistemically distinguished class. So we need the idea of experiences that belong to the epistemically distinguished class if we are to comprehend the idea that experiences have objective purport. If one acknowledges that experiences have objective purport, one cannot consistently refuse to make sense of the idea of experiences in which objective facts are directly available to perception.

The scepticism I am considering purports to acknowledge that experiences have objective purport, but nevertheless supposes that appearances as such are mere appearances, in the sense that any experience leaves it an open possibility that things are not as they appear. That is to conceive the epistemic significance of experience as a highest common factor of what we have in cases in which, as common sense would put it, we perceive that things are thus and so and what we have in cases in which that merely seems to be so — so never higher than what we have in the second kind of case. The conception I have found in Sellars can be put, in opposition to that, as a disjunctive conception of perceptual appearance: perceptual appearances are either objective states of affairs making themselves manifest to subjects, or situations in which it is as if an objective state of affairs is making itself manifest to a subject, although that is not how things are.[2]

Experiences of the first kind have an epistemic significance that experiences of the second kind do not have. They afford opportunities for knowledge of objective states of affairs. According to the highest common factor conception, appearances can never yield more, in the way of warrant for belief, than do those appearances in which it merely seems that one, say, sees that things are thus and so. [...]

The highest common factor conception is supposedly grounded on a claim that seems unquestionable: the claim that from a subject's point of view, a misleading appearance can be indistinguishable from a case in which things are as they appear. That might be taken as a self-standing claim about the phenomenology of misleading appearance, available to be cited in explaining the fact that subjects can be misled by appearances. [...] But the right way to take it is as simply registering the fact that, on that interpretation, it is supposed to explain: the undeniable fact that our capacity to get to know things through perception is fallible.

The claim of indistinguishability is supposed to warrant the thought that even in the best case in which a subject, say, has it visually appear to her that there is a red cube in front of her, her experience could be just as it is even if there were no red cube in front of her.

But we need a distinction here. When we say her experience could be just as it is even if there were no red cube in front of her, we might just be registering that there could be a misleading experience that from the standpoint of her experience she could not distinguish from her actually veridical experience. In that case what we say is just a way of acknowledging that our capacity to acquire knowledge through perceptual experience is fallible. It does not follow that even in the best case, the epistemic position constituted by undergoing an experience can be no better than the epistemic position constituted by undergoing a misleading experience, even one that would admittedly be indistinguishable. The acknowledgement of fallibility cannot detract from the excellence of an epistemic position, with regard to the obtaining of an objective state of affairs, that consists in having the state of affairs present itself to one in one's perceptual experience. This is where the disjunctive conception does its epistemological work. It blocks the inference from the subjective indistinguishability of experiences to the highest common factor conception, according to which neither of the admittedly indistinguishable experiences could have higher epistemic worth than that of the inferior case. And the transcendental argument shows that the disjunctive conception is required, on pain of our losing our grip on the very idea that in experience we have it appear to us that things are a certain way.

[...]

The argument I have considered does not offer to establish anything about how things are, let alone must be, in the world apart from us. [...] The conclusion is rather one about how we must conceive the epistemic positions that are within our reach, if it is to be possible that our experience is as it is in having objective purport. That frees us to pursue our ordinary ways of finding out how things are in the world apart from us. The specifics of what we go on to find out are not within the scope of what the argument aims to vindicate.

Notes

1. Stroud regularly depicts scepticism about the external world as arising like this. See, for example, his (1996/2000: 131): "[The philosopher] chooses a situation in which any one of us would unproblematically say or think, for example, that we know that there is a fire in the fireplace right before us, and that we know it is there because we see that it is there. But when we ask what this seeing really amounts to, various considerations are introduced to lead us to concede that we would see exactly what we see now even if no fire was there at all, or if we didn't know that there was one there." See also Stroud (1984).

2. On the disjunctive conception, see Hinton (1973), Snowdon (1980–1), and my (1982) and (1986).

References

Hinton, J. M. (1973) *Experiences*, Oxford: Clarendon Press.

McDowell, J. (1982) 'Criteria, Defeasibility, and Knowledge', in his *Meaning, Knowledge, and Reality*, Cambridge, MA: Harvard University Press, 1998.

McDowell, J. (1986) 'Singular Thought and the Extent of Inner Space', in his *Meaning, Knowledge, and Reality*, Cambridge, MA: Harvard University Press, 1998.

Sellars, W. (1997) *Empiricism and the Philosophy of Mind*, with introduction by R. Rorty and Study Guide by R. Brandom, Cambridge, MA: Harvard University Press.

Snowdon, P. (1980–1) 'Perception, Vision, and Causation', *Proceedings of the Aristotelian Society*, 81: 175–92.

Stroud, B. (1984) *The Significance of Philosophical Scepticism*, Oxford: Clarendon Press.

Stroud, B. (1996) 'Epistemological Reflection on Knowledge of the External World', in his *Understanding Human Knowledge*, Oxford: Clarendon Press, 2000.

Can We Ever Know Innately?

50

Is It Possible to Know Innately Some Geometrical or Mathematical Truths?

Plato, *Meno*

In discussing observational knowledge, we have been asking whether people can acquire knowledge through their senses: once beliefs are formed upon sensing, are those beliefs ever knowledge? But not only the senses have been discussed by epistemologists as potential sources of knowledge. For a start, philosophers have wondered whether it is possible to have some knowledge *prior* to ever using one's senses. Is it possible for a person to enter this world *already* possessing some knowledge?

That is the question – an ancient one – of whether people can ever have *innate* knowledge. Observational knowledge would report circumstances arising

Plato, *Meno* 80c–86c (excerpts), trans. W.K.C. Guthrie. From *The Collected Dialogues of Plato*, ed. E. Hamilton and H. Cairns (Princeton: Princeton University Press, 1961). © 1961 by Princeton University Press. Reprinted with permission of Princeton University Press.

within a person's perceptual neighborhood as her life unfolds. Innate knowledge would precede all of that. It would have been present, even if perhaps hidden from one's awareness, at the outset of one's life. Is that possible? In this reading (another from the *Meno*), Plato presents a famous story in support of its being possible to have some knowledge innately. Indeed, he argues for this possibility by claiming to display its actuality – by uncovering someone who *does* have some innate knowledge. Our role as readers of this story of Plato's is to determine whether its description is coherent and believable – and whether Socrates interprets it correctly in regarding it as describing someone who actually has innate knowledge.

The story involves a slave boy, whom Socrates questions about a geometrical puzzle. Socrates is trying to decide whether there is some associated geometrical knowledge within the boy, even though this knowledge would not be present due to the boy's having received an appropriate *education*. (Of course, Socrates also takes care not to be *imparting* the knowledge in question to the boy when formulating his questions.) What is the result? The slave boy, according to Socrates, *is* revealed as having some such knowledge. But from where has it come? It must *already* have been present within the boy. Prompted by Socrates' careful questioning, the boy has now *recollected* the knowledge.

That is Socrates' interpretation, at any rate. He believes it to have metaphysical implications. To recollect knowledge is to recall knowledge possessed previously. Hence (in Socrates' metaphysical image), innate knowledge is knowledge that was possessed by a person's *soul* prior to a present body's accompanying that soul. This metaphysical image suggests such knowledge's being of *timeless* truths – in accord with the knowledge's belonging to the *eternal* soul. For instance, such knowledge would be mathematical or geometrical. More generally, it would be knowledge of Forms (a Platonic notion we met in readings 13 and 14, in the section "How Do Things Ever Have Qualities?"). Correlatively, it would not be observational knowledge of the transient here-and-now, such as of a fox staring balefully at one.

SOCRATES: [...] So with virtue now. I don't know what it is. You may have known before you came into contact with me, but now you look as if you don't. Nevertheless I am ready to carry out, together with you, a joint investigation and inquiry into what it is.

MENO: But how will you look for something when you don't in the least know what it is? How on earth are you going to set up something you don't know as the object of your search? To put it another way, even if you come right up against it, how will you know that what you have found is the thing you didn't know?

SOCRATES: I know what you mean. Do you realize that what you are bringing up is the trick argument that a man cannot try to discover either what he knows or what he does not know? He would not seek what he knows, for since he knows it there is no need of the inquiry, nor what he does not know, for in that case he does not even know what he is to look for.

MENO: Well, do you think it a good argument?

SOCRATES: No.

MENO: Can you explain how it fails?

SOCRATES: I can. I have heard from men and women who understand the truths of religion …

MENO: What did they say?

SOCRATES: Something true, I thought, and fine. […] They say that the soul of man is immortal. At one time it comes to an end – that which is called death – and at another is born again, but is never finally exterminated. […] Thus the soul, since it is immortal and has been born many times, and has seen all things both here and in the other world, has learned everything that is. So we need not be surprised if it can recall the knowledge of virtue or anything else which, as we see, it once possessed. […]

MENO: I see, Socrates. But what do you mean when you say that we don't learn anything, but that what we call learning is recollection? Can you teach me that it is so?

SOCRATES: I have just said that you're a rascal, and now you ask me if I can teach you, when I say there is no such thing as teaching, only recollection. Evidently you want to catch me contradicting myself straightaway.

MENO: No, honestly. Socrates, I wasn't thinking of that. It was just habit. If you can in any way make clear to me that what you say is true, please do.

SOCRATES: It isn't an easy thing, but still I should like to do what I can since you ask me. I see you have a large number of retainers here. Call one of them, anyone you like, and I will use him to demonstrate it to you.

MENO: Certainly [*To a slave boy.*] Come here.

SOCRATES: He is a Greek and speaks our language?

MENO: Indeed yes – born and bred in the house.

SOCRATES: Listen carefully then, and see whether it seems to you that he is learning from me or simply being reminded.

MENO: I will.

SOCRATES: Now boy, you know that a square is a figure like this?

(*Socrates begins to draw figures in the sand at his feet. He points to the square* ABCD)

BOY: Yes.

SOCRATES: It has all these four sides equal?

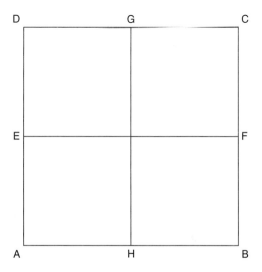

BOY: Yes.

SOCRATES: And these lines which go through the middle of it are also equal? [EF, GH.]

BOY: Yes.

SOCRATES: Such a figure could be either larger or smaller, could it not?

BOY: Yes.

SOCRATES: Now if this side is two feet long, and this side the same, how many feet will the whole
be? Put it this way. If it were two feet in this direction and only one in that, must not the area be
two feet taken once?

BOY: Yes.

SOCRATES: But since it is two feet this way also, does it not become twice two feet?

BOY: Yes.

SOCRATES: And how many feet is twice two? Work it out and tell me.

BOY: Four.

SOCRATES: Now could one draw another figure double the size of this, but similar, that is, with all
its sides equal like this one?

BOY: Yes.

SOCRATES: How many feet will its area be?

BOY: Eight.

SOCRATES: Now then, try to tell me how long each of its sides will be. The present figure has a
side of two feet. What will be the side of the double-sized one?

BOY: It will be double, Socrates, obviously.

SOCRATES: You see, Meno, that I am not teaching him anything, only asking. Now he thinks he
knows the length of the side of the eight-foot square.

MENO: Yes.

SOCRATES: But does he?

MENO: Certainly not.

SOCRATES: He thinks it is twice the length of the other.

MENO: Yes.

SOCRATES: Now watch how he recollects things in order – the proper way to recollect.
You say that the side of double length produces the double-sized figure? Like this I mean, not
long this way and short that. It must be equal on all sides like the first figure, only twice its
size, that is, eight feet. Think a moment whether you still expect to get it from doubling
the side.

BOY: Yes, I do.

SOCRATES: Well now, shall we have a line double the length of this [AB] if we add another the
same length at this end [BJ]?

BOY: Yes.

SOCRATES: It is on this line then, according to you, that we shall make the eight-foot square, by
taking four of the same length?

BOY: Yes.

SOCRATES: Let us draw in four equal lines [*i.e., counting* AJ *and adding* JK, KL, *and* LA *made complete
by drawing in its second half* LD], using the first as a base. Does this not give us what you call the
eight-foot figure?

BOY: Certainly.

SOCRATES: But does it contain these four squares, each equal to the original four-foot one?

(*Socrates has drawn in the lines* CM, CN *to complete the squares that he wishes to point out.*)

BOY: Yes.

SOCRATES: How big is it then? Won't it be four times as big?

BOY: Of course.

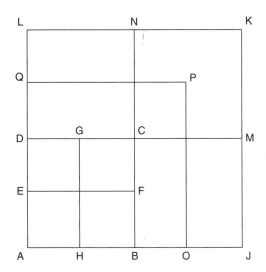

SOCRATES:	And is four times the same as twice?
BOY:	Of course not.
SOCRATES:	So doubling the side has given us not a double but a fourfold figure?
BOY:	True.
SOCRATES:	And four times four are sixteen, are they not?
BOY:	Yes.
SOCRATES:	Then how big is the side of the eight-foot figure? This one has given us four times the original area, hasn't it?
BOY:	Yes.
SOCRATES:	And a side half the length gave us a square of four feet?
BOY:	Yes.
SOCRATES:	Good. And isn't a square of eight feet double this one and half that?
BOY:	Yes.
SOCRATES:	Will it not have a side greater than this one but less than that?
BOY:	I think it will.
SOCRATES:	Right. Always answer what you think. Now tell me. Was not this side two feet long, and this one four?
BOY:	Yes.
SOCRATES:	Then the side of the eight-foot figure must be longer than two feet but shorter than four?
BOY:	It must.
SOCRATES:	Try to say how long you think it is.
BOY:	Three feet.
SOCRATES:	If so, shall we add half of this bit [BO, *half of* BJ] and make it three feet? Here are two, and this is one, and on this side similarly we have two plus one, and here is the figure you want. (*Socrates completes the square* AOPQ.)
BOY:	Yes.
SOCRATES:	If it is three feet this way and three that, will the whole area be three times three feet?
BOY:	It looks like it.
SOCRATES:	And that is how many?
BOY:	Nine.
SOCRATES:	Whereas the square double our first square had to be how many?

BOY: Eight.
SOCRATES: But we haven't yet got the square of eight feet even from a three-foot side?
BOY: No.
SOCRATES: Then what length will give it? Try to tell us exactly. If you don't want to count it up,
just show us on the diagram.
BOY: It's no use, Socrates, I just don't know.
SOCRATES: Observe, Meno, the stage he has reached on the path of recollection. At the beginning he
did not know the side of the square of eight feet. Nor indeed does he know it now, but then he thought
he knew it and answered boldly, as was appropriate – he felt no perplexity. Now however he does feel
perplexed. Not only does he not know the answer; he doesn't even think he knows.
MENO: Quite true.
SOCRATES: Isn't he in a better position now in relation to what he didn't know?
MENO: I admit that too.
SOCRATES: So in perplexing him and numbing him like the sting ray, have we done him any harm?
MENO: I think not.
SOCRATES: In fact we have helped him to some extent toward finding out the right answer, for now
not only is he ignorant of it but he will be quite glad to look for it. Up to now, he thought he could
speak well and fluently, on many occasions and before large audiences, on the subject of a square
double the size of a given square, maintaining that it must have a side of double the length.
MENO: No doubt.
SOCRATES: Do you suppose then that he would have attempted to look for, or learn, what he
thought he knew, though he did not, before he was thrown into perplexity, became aware of his
ignorance, and felt a desire to know?
MENO: No.
SOCRATES: Then the numbing process was good for him?
MENO: I agree.
SOCRATES: Now notice what, starting from this state of perplexity, he will discover by seeking the truth
in company with me, though I simply ask him questions without teaching him. Be ready to catch me
if I give him any instruction or explanation instead of simply interrogating him on his own opinions.
(*Socrates here rubs out the previous figures and starts again.*)
Tell me, boy, is not this our square of four feet? [ABCD.] You understand?

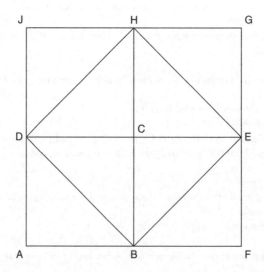

BOY:　　　　Yes.

SOCRATES:　Now we can add another equal to it like this? [BCEF.]

BOY:　　　　Yes.

SOCRATES:　And a third here, equal to each of the others? [CEGH.]

BOY:　　　　Yes.

SOCRATES:　And then we can fill in this one in the corner? [DCHJ.]

BOY:　　　　Yes.

SOCRATES:　Then here we have four equal squares?

BOY:　　　　Yes.

SOCRATES:　And how many times the size of the first square is the whole?

BOY:　　　　Four times.

SOCRATES:　And we want one double the size. You remember?

BOY:　　　　Yes.

SOCRATES:　Now does this line going from corner to corner cut each of these squares in half?

BOY:　　　　Yes.

SOCRATES:　And these are four equal lines enclosing this area? [BEHD.]

BOY:　　　　They are.

SOCRATES:　Now think. How big is this area?

BOY:　　　　I don't understand.

SOCRATES:　Here are four squares. Has not each line cut off the inner half of each of them?

BOY:　　　　Yes.

SOCRATES:　And how many such halves are there in this figure? [BEHD.]

BOY:　　　　Four.

SOCRATES:　And how many in this one? [ABCD.]

BOY:　　　　Two.

SOCRATES:　And what is the relation of four to two?

BOY:　　　　Double.

SOCRATES:　How big is this figure then?

BOY:　　　　Eight feet.

SOCRATES:　On what base?

BOY:　　　　This one.

SOCRATES:　The line which goes from corner to corner of the square of four feet?

BOY:　　　　Yes.

SOCRATES:　The technical name for it is 'diagonal'; so if we use that name, it is your personal opinion that the square on the diagonal of the original square is double its area.

BOY:　　　　That is so, Socrates.

SOCRATES:　What do you think, Meno? Has he answered with any opinions that were not his own?

MENO:　　　No, they were all his.

SOCRATES:　Yet he did not know, as we agreed a few minutes ago.

MENO:　　　True.

SOCRATES:　But these opinions were somewhere in him, were they not?

MENO:　　　Yes.

SOCRATES:　So a man who does not know has in himself true opinions on a subject without having knowledge.

MENO:　　　It would appear so.

SOCRATES:　At present these opinions, being newly aroused, have a dreamlike quality. But if the same questions are put to him on many occasions and in different ways, you can see that in the end he will have a knowledge on the subject as accurate as anybody's.

MENO: Probably.

SOCRATES: This knowledge will not come from teaching but from questioning. He will recover it for himself.

MENO: Yes.

SOCRATES: And the spontaneous recovery of knowledge that is in him is recollection, isn't it?

MENO: Yes.

SOCRATES: Either then he has at some time acquired the knowledge which he now has, or he has always possessed it. If he always possessed it, he must always have known; if on the other hand he acquired it at some previous time, it cannot have been in this life, unless somebody has taught him geometry. He will behave in the same way with all geometric knowledge, and every other subject. Has anyone taught him all these? You ought to know, especially as he has been brought up in your household.

MENO: Yes, I know that no one ever taught him.

SOCRATES: And has he these opinions, or hasn't he?

MENO: It seems we can't deny it.

SOCRATES: Then if he did not acquire them in this life, isn't it immediately clear that he possessed and had learned them during some other period?

MENO: It seems so.

SOCRATES: When he was not in human shape?

MENO: Yes.

SOCRATES: If then there are going to exist in him, both while he is and while he is not a man, true opinions which can be aroused by questioning and turned into knowledge, may we say that his soul has been forever in a state of knowledge? Clearly he always either is or is not a man.

MENO: Clearly.

SOCRATES: And if the truth about reality is always in our soul, the soul must be immortal, and one must take courage and try to discover – that is, to recollect – what one doesn't happen to know, or, more correctly, remember, at the moment.

MENO: Somehow or other I believe you are right.

SOCRATES: I think I am. I shouldn't like to take my oath on the whole story, but one thing I am ready to fight for as long as I can, in word and act – that is, that we shall be better, braver, and more active men if we believe it right to look for what we don't know than if we believe there is no point in looking because what we don't know we can never discover.

MENO: There too I am sure you are right.

SOCRATES: Then since we are agreed that it is right to inquire into something that one does not know, are you ready to face with me the question, 'What is virtue?'

MENO: Quite ready.

51

Is There No Innate Knowledge At All?

John Locke, *An Essay Concerning Human Understanding*

The question of whether people enter the world already knowing some truths is as metaphysical as it is epistemological. It is at once about a possible way of knowing and about what kind of being any person is. Socrates, we saw, even derives an image of people as having eternal souls. In this reading, however, nothing as grand as that is offered.

Instead, we find John Locke presenting an alternative way of interpreting whatever data may otherwise have been thought to support the idea of there being some innate knowledge. There is *no* such knowledge, insists Locke; and he reaches for his *empiricist* model of how people ever gain knowledge. This aims to be a complete account of how we gain knowledge. One part of it is Locke's telling us why there is no need to posit innateness in even some of our knowing. Locke does offer one striking philosophical image here, though: people begin their lives with minds that are, in effect, sheets of blank paper. (Philosophers often refer to this doctrine of Locke's via the Latin phrase – each mind being a *tabula rasa*.) As we live, as we observe the world, slowly that paper within us – initially blank – is written upon by our experiences of the world. *This* is how we acquire knowledge. This is what it is to gain knowledge.

In these extracts from Locke's lengthy discussion of innateness, the emphasis is upon what he calls *principles*. (We may equally well call them theses or propositions.) Locke divides them into *speculative* ones and *practical* ones – respectively, those aiming to be *true* and those advising us how to *act*. These excerpts from Locke's *Essay* focus just upon the speculative principles. For example, are we born already knowing that it is impossible for a single thing at a single time both

John Locke, *An Essay Concerning Human Understanding* (1690), Book I, chs. II–IV (excerpts), Book II, ch. I (excerpts). Reprinted with permission of Oxford University Press.

Metaphysics and Epistemology: A Guided Anthology, First Edition. Edited by Stephen Hetherington.

to exist and not to exist? In the previous reading, Socrates asked whether an uneducated slave boy had some timelessly true geometrical knowledge. Locke is asking whether any of us have some timelessly true metaphysical or logical knowledge.

Again, Locke's answer is that no one does. He describes what he believes would be features of innate knowledge. Then he argues that in fact these are conspicuously lacked by us. For instance, do all of us believe that it is impossible for a single thing both to exist and not to exist? Most likely, *you* do. But not everyone does. If we believe that everyone can *reason* their way to that belief, Locke would reply that even this is not the same as the belief's being knowledge innately. Think of how laboriously a child may develop knowledge even of the simplest mathematical truths. Where (Locke would ask) is the innate knowledge in this?

Locke's argument is not claiming to show that in principle no one *could* ever have innate knowledge. Still, he mounts an extensive case for no one's *actually* having even some innate knowledge. At the very least, then, he may be interpreted as aiming to deprive anyone (such as Socrates in the previous reading) of the inference from "Here is an actual case of innate knowledge" to the conclusion, "Therefore innate knowledge is possible."

No Innate Principles in the Mind

§ 1. IT is an established Opinion amongst some Men, That there are in the Understanding certain *innate Principles*; [...] as it were stamped upon the Mind of Man, which the Soul receives in its very first Being; and brings into the World with it [...]

§ 2. There is nothing more commonly taken for granted, than that there are certain Principles both *Speculative* and *Practical* [...] universally agreed upon by all Mankind: which therefore they argue, must needs be the constant Impressions, which the Souls of Men receive in their first Beings, and which they bring into the World with them, as necessarily and really as they do any of their inherent Faculties.

§ 3. This Argument, drawn from *Universal Consent*, has this Misfortune in it, That if it were true in matter of Fact, that there were certain Truths, wherein all Mankind agreed, it would not prove them innate, if there can be any other way shewn, how Men may come to that Universal Agreement, in the things they do consent in; which I presume may be done.

§ 4. But, which is worse, this Argument of Universal Consent, which is made use of, to prove innate Principles, seems to me a Demonstration that there are none such: Because there are none to which all Mankind give an Universal Assent. I shall begin with the Speculative, and instance in those magnified Principles of Demonstration, *Whatsoever is, is*; and *'Tis impossible for the same thing to be, and not to be*, which of all others I think have the most allow'd Title to innate. These have so setled a Reputation of Maxims universally received, that 'twill, no doubt, be thought strange, if any one should seem to question it. But yet I take liberty to say, That these Propositions are so far from having an universal Assent, that there are a great Part of Mankind, to whom they are not so much as known.

§ 5.   For, first 'tis evident, that all *Children*, and *Ideots*, have not the least Apprehension or Thought of them: and the want of that is enough to destroy that universal Assent, which must needs be the necessary concomitant of all innate Truths: it seeming to me near a Contradiction, to say, that there are Truths imprinted on the Soul, which it perceives or understands not; imprinting, if it signify any thing, being nothing else, but the making certain Truths to be perceived. For to imprint any thing on the Mind without the Mind's perceiving it, seems to me hardly intelligible. If therefore Children and *Ideots* have Souls, have Minds, with those Impressions upon them, they must unavoidably perceive them, and necessarily know and assent to these Truths, which since they do not, it is evident that there are no such Impressions. For if they are not Notions naturally imprinted, How can they be innate? And if they are Notions imprinted, How can they be unknown? To say a Notion is imprinted on the Mind, and yet at the same time to say, that the mind is ignorant of it, and never yet took notice of it, is to make this Impression nothing. No Proposition can be said to be in the Mind, which it never yet knew, which it was never yet conscious of. For if any one may; then, by the same Reason, all Propositions that are true, and the Mind is capable ever of assenting to, may be said to be in the Mind, and to be imprinted: Since if any one can be said to be in the Mind, which it never yet knew, it must be only because it is capable of knowing it; and so the Mind is of all Truths it ever shall know. Nay, thus Truths may be imprinted on the Mind, which it never did, nor ever shall know: for a Man may live long, and die at last in Ignorance of many Truths, which his Mind was capable of knowing, and that with Certainty. So that if the Capacity of knowing be the natural Impression contended for, all the Truths a Man ever comes to know, will, by this Account, be, every one of them, innate; and this great Point will amount to no more, but only to a very improper way of speaking; which whilst it pretends to assert the contrary, says nothing different from those, who deny innate Principles. For no Body, I think, ever denied, that the Mind was capable of knowing several Truths. The Capacity, they say, is innate, the Knowledge acquired. But then to what end such contest for certain innate Maxims? If Truths can be imprinted on the Understanding without being perceived, I can see no difference there can be, between any Truths the Mind is capable of knowing in respect of their Original: They must all be innate, or all adventitious: In vain shall a Man go about to distinguish them. He therefore that talks of innate Notions in the Understanding, cannot (if he intend thereby any distinct sort of Truths) mean such Truths to be in the Understanding, as it never perceived, and is yet wholly ignorant of. For if these Words (*to be in the Understanding*) have any Propriety, they signify to be understood. So that, to be in the Understanding, and, not to be understood; to be in the Mind, and, never to be perceived, is all one, as to say, any thing is, and is not, in the Mind or Understanding. If therefore these two Propositions, *Whatsoever is, is*; and, *It is impossible for the same thing to be, and not to be*, are by Nature imprinted, Children cannot be ignorant of them: Infants, and all that have Souls must necessarily have them in their Understandings, know the Truth of them, and assent to it.

§ 6.   To avoid this, 'tis usually answered, that all Men know and *assent* to them, *when they come to the use of Reason*, and this is enough to prove them innate. I answer,

§ 7. [...] [T]his Answer [...] must signify one of these two things; either, That as soon as Men come to the use of Reason, these supposed native Inscriptions come to be known, and observed by them: Or else, that the Use and Exercise of Men's Reasons assists them in the Discovery of these Principles, and certainly makes them known to them.

§ 8. If they mean that by the *Use of Reason* Men may discover these Principles; and that this is sufficient to prove them innate; their way of arguing will stand thus, (*viz.*) That whatever Truths Reason can certainly discover to us, and make us firmly assent to, those are all naturally imprinted on the Mind; since that universal Assent, which is made the Mark of them, amounts to no more but this; That by the use of Reason, we are capable to come to a certain Knowledge of, and assent to them; and by this Means there will be no difference between the Maxims of the Mathematicians, and Theorems they deduce from them: All must be equally allow'd innate, they being all Discoveries made by the use of Reason, and Truths that a rational Creature may certainly come to know, if he apply his Thoughts rightly that Way.

§ 9. But how can these Men think the *Use of Reason* necessary to discover Principles that are supposed innate, when Reason (if we may believe them) is nothing else, but the Faculty of deducing unknown Truths from Principles or Propositions, that are already known? That certainly can never be thought innate, which we have need of Reason to discover, unless as I have said, we will have all the certain Truths, that Reason ever teaches us, to be innate. We may as well think the use of Reason necessary to make our Eyes discover visible Objects, as that there should be need of Reason, or the Exercise thereof, to make the Understanding see, what is Originally engraven in it, and cannot be in the Understanding, before it be perceived by it. So that to make Reason discover those Truths thus imprinted, is to say, that the use of Reason discovers to a Man, what he knew before; and if Men have these innate, impressed Truths Originally, and before the use of Reason, and yet are always ignorant of them, till they come to the use of Reason, 'tis in effect to say, that Men know, and know them not at the same time.

[...]

§ 15. The Senses at first let in particular *Ideas*, and furnish the yet empty Cabinet: And the Mind by degrees growing familiar with some of them, they are lodged in the Memory, and Names got to them. Afterwards the Mind proceeding farther, abstracts them, and by Degrees learns the use of general Names. In this manner the Mind comes to be furnish'd with *Ideas* and Language, the Materials about which to exercise its discursive Faculty: And the use of Reason becomes daily more visible, as these Materials, that give it Employment, increase. But though the having of general *Ideas*, and the use of general Words and Reason usually grow together: yet, I see not, how this any way proves them innate. The Knowledge of some Truths, I confess, is very early in the Mind; but in a way that shews them not to be innate. For, if we will observe, we shall find it still to be about *Ideas*, not innate, but acquired: It being about those first, which are imprinted by external Things, with which Infants have earliest to do, and which make the most frequent Impressions on their Senses. In *Ideas* thus got, the Mind discovers, That some agree, and others differ, probably as soon as it has any use of Memory; as soon as it is able, to retain and receive distinct *Ideas*. But whether it be then, or no, this is certain, it does so long before it has the use of Words; or comes to that, which we commonly call the *use of Reason*. For a Child knows as certainly, before it can speak, the difference between the *Ideas* of Sweet and Bitter (*i.e.* That Sweet is not Bitter) as it knows afterwards (when it comes to speak) That Worm-wood and Sugar-plumbs, are not the same thing.

§ 16. A Child knows not that Three and Four are equal to Seven, till he comes to be able to count to Seven, and has got the Name and *Idea* of Equality: and then upon the explaining those Words, he presently assents to, or rather perceives the Truth of that Proposition. But neither does he then readily assent, because it is an innate Truth, nor was his Assent wanting, till then, because he wanted the *Use of Reason*; but the Truth of it appears to him, as soon as he has setled in his Mind the clear and distinct *Ideas*, that these Names stand for: And then, he knows the Truth of that Proposition, upon the same Grounds, and by the same means, that he knew before, That a Rod and Cherry are not the same thing; and upon the same Grounds also, that he may come to know afterwards, *That it is impossible for the same thing to be, and not to be*, as shall be more fully shewn hereafter. So that the later it is before any one comes to have those general *Ideas*, about which those Maxims are; or to know the Signification of those general Terms, that stand for them; or to put together in his Mind, the *Ideas* they stand for: the later also will it be, before he comes to assent to those Maxims, whose Terms, with the *Ideas* they stand for, being no more innate, than those of a Cat or a Weesel, he must stay till Time and Observation have acquainted him with them; and then he will be in a Capacity to know the Truth of these Maxims, upon the first Occasion, that shall make him put together those *Ideas* in his Mind, and observe, whether they agree or disagree, according as is expressed in those Propositions. And therefore it is, That a Man knows that Eighteen and Nineteen, are equal to Thirty Seven, by the same self-Evidence, that he knows One and Two to be equal to Three: Yet, a Child knows this, not so soon as the other; not for want of the use of Reason: but because the *Ideas* the Words Eighteen, Nineteen, and Thirty seven stand for, are not so soon got, as those, which are signify'd by One, Two, and Three.

§ 17. This Evasion therefore of general Assent, when Men come to the use of Reason, failing as it does, and leaving no difference between those supposed-innate, and other Truths, that are afterwards acquired and learnt, Men have endeavoured to secure an universal Assent to those they call Maxims, by saying, they are generally *assented to, as soon as proposed*, and the Terms they are propos'd in, understood: Seeing all Men, even Children, as soon as they hear and understand the Terms, assent to these Propositions, they think it is sufficient to prove them innate. For since Men never fail, after they have once understood the Words, to acknowledge them for undoubted Truths, they would inferr, That certainly these Propositions were first lodged in the Understanding, which, without any teaching, the Mind at very first Proposal, immediately closes with, and assents to, and after that never doubts again.

§ 18. In Answer to this, I demand whether ready *assent*, given to a Proposition *upon first hearing*, and understanding the Terms, be a certain mark of an innate Principle? If it be not, such a general assent is in vain urged as a Proof of them: If it be said, that it is a mark of innate, they must then allow all such Propositions to be innate, which are generally assented to as soon as heard, whereby they will find themselves plentifully stored with innate Principles. For upon the same ground (*viz.*) of Assent at first hearing and understanding the Terms, That Men would have those Maxims pass for innate, they must also admit several Propositions about Numbers, to be innate: And thus, *That One and Two are equal to Three, That Two and Two are equal to Four*, and a multitude of other the like Propositions in Numbers, that every Body assents to, at first hearing, and understanding the Terms, must have a place amongst these innate Axioms. Nor is this the Prerogative of Numbers alone, and Propositions made about several of them: But even natural Philosophy, and all the other Sciences afford Propositions, which are sure to meet with Assent, as soon as they are understood. *That two Bodies cannot be in the same place*, is a Truth, that no Body any more sticks at, than at this Maxim, *That it is impossible for the same thing to be, and not to be; That White is not Black, That a Square is not a Circle, That Yellowness is not Sweetness*: These, and a Million of other such Propositions, as many at least, as we have distinct *Ideas*, every Man in his Wits, at first hearing, and knowing what the Names stand for, must necessarily assent to. If then these Men will be true to their own Rule, and have *Assent at first hearing and understanding the Terms*, to be a mark of innate, they must allow, not only as many innate Propositions, as Men have distinct *Ideas*; but as many as Men can make Propositions, wherein different *Ideas* are denied one of another. Since every Proposition, wherein one different *Idea* is denied of another, will as certainly find Assent at first hearing and understanding the Terms, as this general one, *It is impossible for the same to be, and not to be*; or that which is the Foundation of it, and is the easier understood of the two, *The same is not different*: By which Account, they will have Legions of innate Propositions of this one sort, without mentioning any other. But since no Proposition can be innate, unless the *Ideas*, about which it is, be innate, This will be, to suppose all our *Ideas* of Colours, Sounds, Tastes, Figures, *etc.* innate; than which there cannot be any thing more opposite to Reason and Experience.

[...]

§ 21.   But we have not yet done with *assenting to Propositions at first hearing and understanding their Terms*; 'tis fit we first take notice, That this, instead of being a mark, that they are innate, is a proof of the contrary: Since it supposes, that several, who understand and know other things, are ignorant of these Principles, till they are propos'd to them; and that one may be unacquainted with these Truths, till he hears them from others. For if they were innate, What need they be propos'd, in order to gaining assent; when, by being in the Understanding, by a natural and original Impression (if there were any such) they could not but be known before? Or, doth the proposing them, print them clearer in the Mind, than Nature did? If so, then the Consequence will be, That a Man knows them better, after he has been thus taught them, than he did before. Whence it will follow, That these Principles may be made more evident to us by other's teaching, than Nature has made them by Impression: which will ill agree with the Opinion of innate Principles, and give but little Authority to them; but on the contrary, makes them unfit to be the foundations of all our other Knowledge, as they are pretended to be. [...]

§ 22.   If it be said, The Understanding hath an *implicit Knowledge* of these Principles, but not an explicit, before this first hearing, (as they must, who will say, That they are in the Understanding before they are known) it will be hard to conceive what is meant by a Principle imprinted on the Understanding Implicitly; unless it be this, That the Mind is capable of understanding and assenting firmly to such Propositions. And thus all Mathematical Demonstrations, as well as first Principles, must be received as native Impressions on the

Mind: which, I fear they will scarce allow them to be, who find it harder to demonstrate a Proposition, than assent to it, when demonstrated. And few Mathematicians will be forward to believe, That all the Diagrams they have drawn, were but Copies of those innate Characters, which Nature had ingraven upon their Minds.

[...]

§ 24. To conclude this Argument of universal Consent, I agree with these Defenders of innate Principles, That if they are *innate*, they must needs *have universal assent*. For that a Truth should be innate, and yet not assented to, is to me as unintelligible, as for a Man to know a Truth, and be ignorant of it at the same time. But then, by these Men's own Confession, they cannot be innate; since they are not assented to, by those who understand not the Terms, nor by a great part of those who do understand them, but have yet never heard, nor thought of those Propositions; which, I think, is at least one half of Mankind. But were the Number far less, it would be enough to destroy universal assent, and thereby shew these Propositions not to be innate, if Children alone were ignorant of them.

§ 25. But that I may not be accused, to argue from the thoughts of Infants, which are unknown to us, and to conclude, from what passes in their Understandings, before they express it; I say next, That these two general Propositions are not the Truths, that *first possess the Minds* of Children; nor are antecedent to all acquired, and adventitious Notions: which if they were innate, they must needs be. Whether we can determine it or no, it matters not, there is certainly a time, when Children begin to think, and their Words and Actions do assure us, that they do so. [...] The Child certainly knows, that the *Nurse* that feeds it, is neither the *Cat* it plays with, nor the *Blackmoor* it is afraid of; That the *Wormseed* or *Mustard* it refuses, is not the *Apple* or *Sugar* it cries for: this it is certainly and undoubtedly assured of: But will any one say, it is by Virtue of this Principle, *That it is impossible for the same thing to be, and not to be*, that it so firmly assents to these, and other parts of its Knowledge? Or that the Child has any Notion or Apprehension of that Proposition at an Age, wherein yet 'tis plain, it knows a great many other Truths? [...]

§ 26. Though therefore there be several general Propositions, that meet with constant and ready assent, as soon as proposed to Men grown up, who have attained the use of more general and abstract *Ideas*, and Names standing for them: yet they not being to be found in those of tender Years, who nevertheless know other things, they cannot pretend to universal assent of intelligent Persons, and so by no means can be supposed innate: It being impossible, that any Truth which is innate (if there were any such) should be unknown, at least to any one, who knows any thing else. Since, if they are innate Truths, they must be innate thoughts: there being nothing a Truth in the Mind, that it has never thought on. Whereby it is evident, if there be any *innate Truths*, they *must necessarily be the first of any thought on*; the first that appear there.

§ 27. That the general Maxims, we are discoursing of, are not known to Children, *Ideots*, and a great part of Mankind, we have already sufficiently proved: whereby it is evident, they have not an universal assent, nor are general Impressions. But there is this farther Argument in it against their being innate: That these Characters, if they were native and original Impressions, *should appear fairest and clearest in* those Persons, in whom yet we find no Footsteps of them: [...] For *Children, Ideots, Savages*, and *illiterate* People, being of all others the least corrupted by Custom, or borrowed Opinions; Learning, and Education, having not cast their Native thoughts into new Moulds; nor by super-inducing foreign and studied Doctrines, confounded those fair Characters Nature had written there; one might reasonably imagine, that in their Minds these innate Notions should lie open fairly to every one's view, as 'tis certain the thoughts of Children do. [...] A Child knows his Nurse, and his Cradle, and by degrees the Play-things of a little more advanced Age: And a young Savage has, perhaps, his Head fill'd with Love and Hunting, according to the fashion of his Tribe. But he that from a Child untaught, or a wild Inhabitant of the Woods, will expect these abstract Maxims, and reputed Principles of Sciences, will I fear, find himself mistaken. [...]

No Innate Practical Principles

§ 1. If those speculative Maxims, whereof we discoursed in the fore-going Chapter, have not an actual universal assent from all Mankind, as we there proved, it is much more visible concerning *practical Principles*, that they *come short of an universal Reception*: and I think it will be hard to instance any one moral Rule, which can pretend to so general and ready an assent as, *What is, is*, or to be so manifest a Truth as this, *That it is impossible for the same thing to be, and not to be.* Whereby it is evident, That they are farther removed from a title to be innate; and the doubt of their being native Impressions on the Mind, is stronger against these moral Principles than the other. Not that it brings their Truth at all in question. They are equally true, though not equally evident. Those speculative Maxims carry their own Evidence with them: But moral Principles require Reasoning and Discourse, and some Exercise of the Mind, to discover the certainty of their Truth. They lie not open as natural Characters ingraven on the Mind; which if any such were, they must needs be visible by themselves, and by their own light be certain and known to every Body. But this is no Derogation to their Truth and Certainty, no more than it is to the Truth or Certainty, of the Three Angles of a Triangle being equal to two right ones, because it is not so evident, as *The whole is bigger than a part*; nor so apt to be assented to at first hearing.
[...]

§ 3.   Perhaps it will be urged, That the *tacit assent of their Minds agrees to what their Practice contradicts*. I answer, *First*, I have always thought the Actions of Men the best Interpreters of their thoughts. But since it is certain, that most Men's Practice, and some Men's open Professions, have either questioned or denied these Principles, it is impossible to establish an universal consent (though we should look for it only amongst grown Men) without which, it is impossible to conclude them innate. [...] I deny not, that there are natural tendencies imprinted on the Minds of Men; and that, from the very first instances of Sense and Perception, there are some things, that are grateful, and others unwelcome to them; some things that they incline to, and others that they fly: But this makes nothing for innate Characters on the Mind, which are to be the Principles of Knowledge, regulating our Practice. [...]

§ 4.   Another Reason that makes me doubt of any innate practical Principles, is, That I think, *there cannot any one moral Rule be propos'd, whereof a Man may not justly demand a Reason*: which would be perfectly ridiculous and absurd, if they were innate, or so much as self-evident; which every innate Principle must needs be, and not need any Proof to ascertain its Truth, nor want any Reason to gain it Approbation.

[…]

Other Considerations Concerning Innate Principles, Both Speculative and Practical

[…]

§ 3. *It is impossible for the same thing to be, and not to be,* is certainly (if there be any such) an innate Principle. But can any one think, or will any one say, that *Impossibility* and *Identity*, are two innate *Ideas*? Are they such as all Mankind have, and bring into the World with them? And are they those, that are the first in Children, and antecedent to all acquired ones? If they are innate, they must needs be so. Hath a Child an *Idea* of *Impossibility* and *Identity*, before it has of *White* or *Black*; *Sweet* or *Bitter*? And is it from the Knowledge of this Principle, that it concludes, that Wormwood rubb'd on the Nipple, hath not the same Taste, that it used to receive from thence? Is it the actual Knowledge of *impossibile est idem esse, et non esse* [lit., "It is impossible for the same thing to be, and not to be"], that makes a Child distinguish between its Mother and a Stranger; or, that makes it fond of the one, and fly the other? Or does the Mind regulate it self, and its assent by *Ideas*, that it never yet had? Or the Understanding draw Conclusions from Principles, which it never yet knew or understood? The Names *Impossibility* and *Identity*, stand for two *Ideas*, so *far from being innate*, or born with us, that I think it requires great Care and Attention, to form them right in our Understandings. They are so far from being brought into the World with us; so remote from the thoughts of Infancy and Childhood, that, I believe, upon Examination, it will be found, that many grown Men want them.

[…]

Of *Ideas* in General, and their Original

§ 1. EVERY Man being conscious to himself, That he thinks, and that which his Mind is employ'd about whilst thinking, being the *Ideas*, that are there, 'tis past doubt, that Men have in their Minds several *Ideas*, such as are those expressed by the words, *Whiteness, Hardness, Sweetness, Thinking, Motion, Man, Elephant, Army, Drunkenness,* and others: It is in the first place then to be enquired, How he comes by them? I know it is a received Doctrine, That Men have native *Ideas*, and original Characters stamped upon their Minds, in their very first Being. This Opinion I have at large examined already; and, I suppose, what I have said in the fore-going Book, will be much more easily admitted, when I have shewn, whence the Understanding may get all the *Ideas* it has, and by what ways and degrees they may come into the Mind; for which I shall appeal to every one's own Observation and Experience.

§ 2. Let us then suppose the Mind to be, as we say, white Paper, void of all Characters, without any *Ideas*; How comes it to be furnished? Whence comes it by that vast store, which the busy and boundless Fancy of Man has painted on it, with an almost endless variety? Whence has it all the materials of Reason and Knowledge? To this I answer, in one word, From *Experience*: In that, all our Knowledge is founded; and from that it ultimately derives it self. Our Observation employ'd either about *external, sensible Objects; or about the internal Operations of our Minds, perceived and reflected on by our selves*, is that, which supplies our *Understandings with all the materials of thinking*. These two are the Fountains of Knowledge, from whence all the *Ideas* we have, or can naturally have, do spring.

Can We Ever Know Just through Reflection?

52

Is All Knowledge Ultimately Reflective?

René Descartes, *Discourse on Method*

In the previous reading, Locke dismissed the idea of our ever knowing innately – a person's knowing *before* she has had an opportunity to begin observing the world. But what about the idea of our knowing non-observationally *after* having first been able to observe the world? Traditionally, this has been treated as the question of whether we can know some truths purely *reflectively*. Do people in general have a capacity for reason and insight that can provide real knowledge? Are we able to know reflectively-even-when-not-at-all-observationally?

That is the question of whether a kind of *rationalism* is true of at least some of our knowledge. We have read excerpts from Descartes and Leibniz, two of the three

René Descartes, *Discourse on Method* [1637], part II (excerpts). From *The Philosophical Works of Descartes*, vol. 1, trans. E.S. Haldane and G.R.T. Ross (Cambridge: Cambridge University Press, 1911). Reprinted with permission of Cambridge University Press.

most famous "founding" rationalists (Benedict de Spinoza, 1632–77, was the third). Now we will read a famous description by Descartes of how he developed his rationalist method for gaining knowledge (a method with which, he thought, he could unfailingly assess whether a particular belief is knowledge). Is it possible to know a truth – even many truths – by reflection alone? It is (thought Descartes), *if* one follows an appropriate procedure.

That is what he proceeds to explain. His guide is the practice of mathematics. A noted mathematician himself, he viewed it as being *the* home of reasoning that could guarantee to produce knowledge. Again, Descartes sought a method, one he could apply deliberately and consciously in his quest for knowledge. So, he wondered whether a mathematical method could serve for knowing in general. He would be seeking knowledge, even *beyond* mathematics, purely via reason. What were the generalizable elements of mathematical reasoning? Truth and only truth was his primary aim. A method guaranteed to lead to truths and only to truths was his consequent aim.

What were the method's details? Accept only what is clearly and distinctly true (not merely what seems plausible or commonsensical or likely to be true). Analyze – decompose – your questions, concepts, and problems. Then focus first on the simplest challenges, next on the less simple, and so on. Do not overlook any detail. And combine all of this into "chains of reasoning" within a single focused mind. (Do not rely on others. Do the reflecting yourself.)

Part of what has been mind-catching to so many about Descartes' method was his applying it to *all* his beliefs, not only mathematical ones. He was prepared to do so even if this meant his discarding (and never regaining) many of his otherwise most favored beliefs. The story of this intellectual journey is told in his famous *Meditations*. Earlier, we read excerpts from "Meditation I" (where he doubted so much) and "Meditation VI" (where he claimed to regain some key knowledge, including knowledge of his being a blend of mind and body). Later, we will read more from "Meditation I" along with some of "Meditation II" (another pattern of doubting knowledge before claiming knowledge).

[…]

[…] I thought that since we have all been children before being men, and since it has for long fallen to us to be governed by our appetites and by our teachers (who often enough contradicted one another, and none of whom perhaps counselled us always for the best), it is almost impossible that our judgments should be so excellent or solid as they should have been had we had complete use of our reason since our birth, and had we been guided by its means alone.

[…] [A]s regards all the opinions which up to this time I had embraced, I thought I could not do better than endeavour once for all to sweep them completely away, so that they might later on be replaced, either by others which were better, or by the same, when I had made them conform to the uniformity of a rational scheme. And I firmly believed that by this means I should succeed in directing my life much better than if I had only built on old foundations, and relied on principles of which I allowed myself to be in youth persuaded without having inquired into their truth. [...]

[...] Those to whom God has been most beneficent in the bestowal of His graces will perhaps form designs which are more elevated; but I fear much that this particular one will seem too venturesome for many. The simple resolve to strip oneself of all opinions and beliefs formerly received is not to be regarded as an example that each man should follow, and the world may be said to be mainly composed of two classes of minds neither of which could prudently adopt it. There are those who, believing themselves to be cleverer than they are, cannot restrain themselves from being precipitate in judgment and have not sufficient patience to arrange their thoughts in proper order; hence, once a man of this description had taken the liberty of doubting the principles he formerly accepted, and had deviated from the beaten track, he would never be able to maintain the path which must be followed to reach the appointed and more quickly, and he would hence remain wandering astray all through his life. Secondly, there are those who having reason or modesty enough to judge that they are less capable of distinguishing truth from falsehood than some others from whom instruction might be obtained, are right in contenting themselves with following the opinions of these others rather than in searching better ones for themselves.

For myself I should doubtless have been of these last if I had never had more than a single master, or had I never known the diversities which have from all time existed between the opinions of men of the greatest learning. But I had been taught, even in my College days, that there is nothing imaginable so strange or so little credible that it has not been maintained by one philosopher or other, and I further recognised in the course of my travels that all those whose sentiments are very contrary to ours are yet not necessarily barbarians or savages, but may be possessed of reason in as great or even a greater degree than ourselves. I also considered how very different the self-same man, identical in mind and spirit, may become, according as he is brought up from childhood amongst the French or Germans, or has passed his whole life amongst Chinese or cannibals. I likewise noticed how even in the fashions of one's clothing the same thing that pleased us ten years ago, and which will perhaps please us once again before ten years are passed, seems at the present time extravagant and ridiculous. I thus concluded that it is much more custom and example that persuade us than any certain knowledge, and yet in spite of this the voice of the majority does not afford a proof of any value in truths a little difficult to discover, because such truths are much more likely to have been discovered by one man than by a nation. I could not, however, put my finger on a single person whose opinions seemed preferable to those of others, and I found that I was, so to speak, constrained myself to undertake the direction of my procedure.

But like one who walks alone and in the twilight I resolved to go so slowly, and to use so much circumspection in all things, that if my advance was but very small, at least I guarded myself well from falling. I did not wish to set about the final rejection of any single opinion which might formerly have crept into my beliefs without having been introduced there by means of Reason, until I had first of all employed sufficient time in planning out the task which I had undertaken, and in seeking the true Method of arriving at a knowledge of all the things of which my mind was capable.

[...] [I]nstead of the great number of precepts of which Logic is composed, I believed that I should find the four which I shall state quite sufficient, provided that I adhered to a firm and constant resolve never on any single occasion to fail in their observance.

The first of these was to accept nothing as true which I did not clearly recognise to be so: that is to say, carefully to avoid precipitation and prejudice in judgments, and to accept in them nothing more than what was presented to my mind so clearly and distinctly that I could have no occasion to doubt it.

The second was to divide up each of the difficulties which I examined into as many parts as possible, and as seemed requisite in order that it might be resolved in the best manner possible.

The third was to carry on my reflections in due order, commencing with objects that were the most simple and easy to understand, in order to rise little by little, or by degrees, to knowledge of the most complex, assuming an order, even if a fictitious one, among those which do not follow a natural sequence relatively to one another.

The last was in all cases to make enumerations so complete and reviews so general that I should be certain of having omitted nothing.

Those long chains of reasoning, simple and easy as they are, of which geometricians make use in order to arrive at the most difficult demonstrations, had caused me to imagine that all those things which fall under the cognizance of man might very likely be mutually related in the same fashion; and that, provided only that we abstain from receiving anything as true which is not so, and always retain the order which is necessary in order to deduce the one conclusion from the other, there can be nothing so remote that we cannot reach to it, nor so recondite that we cannot discover it. And I had not much trouble in discovering which objects it was necessary to begin with, for I already knew that it was with the most simple and those most easy to apprehend. Considering also that of all those who have hitherto sought for the truth in the Sciences, it has been the mathematicians alone who have been able to succeed in making any demonstrations, that is to say producing reasons which are evident and certain, I did not doubt that it had been by means of a similar kind that they carried on their investigations. I did not at the same time hope for any practical result in so doing, except that my mind would become accustomed to the nourishment of truth and would not content itself with false reasoning.

[...]

[...] [T]he Method which teaches us to follow the true order and enumerate exactly every term in the matter under investigation contains everything which gives certainty to the rules of Arithmetic.

But what pleased me most in this Method was that I was certain by its means of exercising my reason in all things, if not perfectly, at least as well as was in my power. And besides this, I felt in making use of it that my mind gradually accustomed itself to conceive of its objects more accurately and distinctly; and not having restricted this Method to any particular matter, I promised myself to apply it as usefully to the difficulties of other sciences as I had done to those of Algebra. Not that on this account I dared undertake to examine just at once all those that might present themselves; for that would itself have been contrary to the order which the Method prescribes. But having noticed that the knowledge of these difficulties must be dependent on principles derived from Philosophy in which I yet found nothing to be certain, I thought that it was requisite above all to try to establish certainty in it. I considered also that since this endeavour is the most important in all the world, and that in which precipitation and prejudice were most to be feared, I should not try to grapple with it till I had attained to a much riper age than that of three and twenty, which was the age I had reached. I thought, too, that I should first of all employ much time in preparing myself for the work by eradicating from my mind all the wrong opinions which I had up to this time accepted, and accumulating a variety of experiences fitted later on to afford matter for my reasonings, and by ever exercising myself in the Method which I had prescribed, in order more and more to fortify myself in the power of using it.

53

Can Reflective Knowledge Be Substantive and Informative?

Immanuel Kant, *Critique of Pure Reason*

Descartes, we saw, envisaged mathematical reasoning – which can give us mathematical knowledge – as our best model for how we should seek knowledge in general. His advice was that we adapt relevant features of that form of reasoning – the truth-conducive features – so as to help us gain other knowledge. Still, we may wonder whether that model is quite apt for that broader purpose. Is mathematical knowledge significantly *different* to most of our knowledge, so that a good way of gaining it need not be as helpful for other kinds of knowledge? For instance, we could suspect that when pure reason gives us mathematical knowledge the result is only a sophisticated kind of *definitional* knowledge; which seems not to be what most knowledge is like. (You could never know purely by reflecting upon definitions that a fox is approaching your home.)

Accordingly, we have this reading from the German philosopher Immanuel Kant's (1724–1804) *Critique of Pure Reason*. His 1781 book is one of the most widely inspiring, yet also among the most daunting, in all philosophy. Kant sought to ascertain exactly what and how we can know purely by using our powers of reason. This reading sets the scene. Kant does not deny that observation is important to knowing. But he asks whether reason *also* contributes to knowing. When does it help us? When does it hinder us? Does it ever – in systematic ways – lead us astray, tempting us to venture beyond our capacities for gaining knowledge?

In this reading, notice Kant's distinction between *analytic* judgments and *synthetic* ones. He believes that in a sense the former are uninformative: "No bachelor is unmarried" merely expands definitionally upon the concept of being a bachelor. In

Immanuel Kant, *Critique of Pure Reason* [1781], "Introduction" (excerpts), trans. N. Kemp Smith (London: Macmillan, 1929). Reprinted with permission of Palgrave Macmillan.

that same sense, he also believes, synthetic judgments *are* informative. Thus, an observational report like "There is a fox in the room" is synthetic, with various distinct concepts being combined informatively, even if not purely by reason. But (argues Kant) mathematical judgments like "7+5=12" are also synthetic. Part of knowing this mathematical truth is one's synthesizing – informatively combining – the distinct concepts denoted by "7", "5", "+", and "=". This is achieved purely reflectively.

Yet how could a mind do that purely reflectively? This is the question of how synthetic *a priori* knowledge is possible. It was Kant's own question, extending what had already been philosophy's engagement with the following distinction between *a priori* and *a posteriori* knowledge:

> *A priori* knowledge is any knowledge that can be adequately supported by reason without involving any observational support. All other knowledge is *a posteriori* – present only when there is enough observational support for it.

That question of Kant's – How is synthetic *a priori* knowledge possible? – took him far afield. He saw how it bears not only upon mathematics, but even upon some of our most heartfelt metaphysical ideas, such as of God and of free will. How – if at all – is metaphysics itself possible as a means of gaining knowledge? Can pure reason give us metaphysical knowledge?

I.   The Distinction between Pure and Empirical Knowledge

There can be no doubt that all our knowledge begins with experience. For how should our faculty of knowledge be awakened into action did not objects affecting our senses partly of themselves produce representations, partly arouse the activity of our understanding to compare these representations, and, by combining or separating them, work up the raw material of the sensible impressions into that knowledge of objects which is entitled experience? In the order of time, therefore, we have no knowledge antecedent to experience, and with experience all our knowledge begins.

But though all our knowledge begins with experience, it does not follow that it all arises out of experience. For it may well be that even our empirical knowledge is made up of what we receive through impressions and of what our own faculty of knowledge (sensible impressions serving merely as the occasion) supplies from itself. If our faculty of knowledge makes any such addition, it may be that we are not in a position to distinguish it from the raw material, until with long practice of attention we have become skilled in separating it.

This, then, is a question which at least calls for closer examination, and does not allow of any off-hand answer:– whether there is any knowledge that is thus independent of experience and even of all impressions of the senses. Such knowledge is entitled *a priori*, and distinguished from the *empirical*, which has its sources *a posteriori*, that is, in experience.

The expression '*a priori*' does not, however, indicate with sufficient precision the full meaning of our question. For it has been customary to say, even of much knowledge that is derived from empirical sources, that we have it or are capable of having it *a priori*, meaning thereby that we do not derive it immediately from experience, but from a universal rule – a rule which is itself, however, borrowed by us from experience. Thus we would say of a man who undermined the foundations of his house, that he might have known *a priori* that it would fall, that is, that he need not have waited for the experience of its actual falling. But still he could not know this completely *a priori*. For he had first to learn through experience that bodies are heavy, and therefore fall when their supports are withdrawn.

In what follows, therefore, we shall understand by *a priori* knowledge, not knowledge independent of this or that experience, but knowledge absolutely independent of all experience. Opposed to it is empirical knowledge, which is knowledge possible only *a posteriori*, that is, through experience. *A priori* modes of knowledge[1] are entitled pure when there is no admixture of anything empirical. Thus, for instance, the proposition, 'every alteration has its cause', while an *a priori* proposition, is not a pure proposition, because alteration is a concept which can be derived only from experience.

II.   We are in Possession of Certain Modes of *a priori* Knowledge, and even the Common Understanding is never without them

What we here require is a criterion by which to distinguish with certainty between pure and empirical knowledge. Experience teaches us that a thing is so and so, but not that it cannot be otherwise. First, then, if we have a proposition which in being thought is thought as *necessary*, it is an *a priori* judgment; and if, besides, it is not derived from any proposition except one which also has the validity of a necessary judgment, it is an absolutely *a priori* judgment. Secondly, experience never confers on its judgments true or strict, but only assumed and comparative *universality*, through induction. We can properly only say, therefore, that, so far as we have hitherto observed, there is no exception to this or that rule. [...] Necessity and strict universality are thus sure criteria of *a priori* knowledge, and are inseparable from one another. [...]

Now it is easy to show that there actually are in human knowledge judgments which are necessary and in the strictest sense universal, and which are therefore pure *a priori* judgments. If an example from the sciences be desired, we have only to look to any of the propositions of mathematics; if we seek an example from the understanding in its quite ordinary employment, the proposition, 'every alteration must have a cause', will serve our purpose. In the latter case, indeed, the very concept of a cause so manifestly contains the concept of a necessity of connection with an effect and of the strict universality of the rule, that the concept would be altogether lost if we attempted to derive it, as Hume has done, from a repeated association of that which happens with that which precedes, and from a custom of connecting representations, a custom originating in this repeated association, and constituting therefore a merely subjective necessity. Even without appealing to such examples, it is possible to show that pure *a priori* principles are indispensable for the possibility of experience, and so to prove their existence *a priori*. For whence could experience derive its certainty, if all the rules, according to which it proceeds, were always themselves empirical, and therefore contingent? Such rules could hardly be regarded as first principles. At present, however, we may be content to have established the fact that our faculty of knowledge does have a pure employment, and to have shown what are the criteria of such an employment.

Such *a priori* origin is manifest in certain concepts, no less than in judgments. If we remove from our empirical concept of a body, one by one, every feature in it which is [merely] empirical, the colour, the hardness or softness, the weight, even the impenetrability, there still remains the space which the body (now entirely vanished) occupied, and this cannot be removed. Again, if we remove from our empirical concept of any object, corporeal or incorporeal, all properties which experience has taught us, we yet cannot take away that property through which the object is thought as substance or as inhering in a substance (although this concept of substance is more determinate than that of an object in general). Owing, therefore, to the necessity with which this concept of substance forces itself upon us, we have no option save to admit that it has its seat in our faculty of *a priori* knowledge.

III. Philosophy Stands in Need of a Science which shall Determine the Possibility, the Principles, and the Extent of all *a priori* Knowledge

But what is still more extraordinary than all the preceding is this, that certain modes of knowledge leave the field of all possible experiences and have the appearance of extending the scope of our judgments beyond all limits of experience, and this by means of concepts to which no corresponding object can ever be given in experience.

It is precisely by means of the latter modes of knowledge, in a realm beyond the world of the senses, where experience can yield neither guidance nor correction, that our reason carries on those enquiries which owing to their importance we consider to be far more excellent, and in their purpose far more lofty, than all that the understanding can learn in the field of appearances. [...] These unavoidable problems set by pure reason itself are *God, freedom*, and *immortality*. The science which, with all its preparations, is in its final intention directed solely to their solution is metaphysics; and its procedure is at first dogmatic, that is, it confidently sets itself to this task without any previous examination of the capacity or incapacity of reason for so great an undertaking.

Now it does indeed seem natural that, as soon as we have left the ground of experience, we should, through careful enquiries, assure ourselves as to the foundations of any building that we propose to erect, not making use of any knowledge that we possess without first determining whence it has come, and not trusting to principles without knowing their origin. [...] It was thus that Plato left the world of the senses, as setting too narrow limits to the understanding, and ventured out beyond it on the wings of the ideas, in the empty space of the pure understanding. [...] It is, indeed, the common fate of human reason to complete its speculative structures as speedily as may be, and only afterwards to enquire whether the foundations are reliable. […] [W]hat keeps us, during the actual building, free from all apprehension and suspicion, and flatters us with a seeming thoroughness, is this other circumstance, namely, that a great, perhaps the greatest, part of the business of our reason consists in analysis of the concepts which we already have of objects. This analysis supplies us with a considerable body of knowledge, which, while nothing but explanation or elucidation of what has already been thought in our concepts, though in a confused manner, is yet prized as being, at least as regards its form, new insight. But so far as the matter or content is concerned, there has been no extension of our previously possessed concepts, but only an analysis of them. Since this procedure yields real knowledge *a priori*, which progresses in an assured and useful fashion, reason is so far misled as surreptitiously to introduce, without itself being aware of so doing, assertions of an entirely different order, in which it attaches to given concepts others completely foreign to them, and moreover attaches them *a priori*. And yet it is not known how reason can be in position to do this. […] I shall therefore at once proceed to deal with the difference between these two kinds of knowledge.

IV.   The Distinction between Analytic and Synthetic Judgments

In all judgments in which the relation of a subject to the predicate is thought (I take into consideration affirmative judgments only, the subsequent application to negative judgments being easily made), this relation is possible in two different ways. Either the predicate B belongs to the subject A, as something which is (covertly) contained in this concept A; or B lies outside the concept A, although it does indeed stand in connection with it. In the one case I entitle the judgment analytic, in the other synthetic. Analytic judgments (affirmative) are therefore those in which the connection of the predicate with the subject is thought through identity; those in which this connection is thought without identity should be entitled synthetic. The former, as adding nothing through the predicate to the concept of the subject, but merely breaking it up into those constituent concepts that have all along been thought in it, although confusedly, can also be entitled explicative. The latter, on the other hand, add to the concept of the subject a predicate which has not been in any wise thought in it, and which no analysis could possibly extract from it; and they may therefore be entitled ampliative. If I say, for instance, 'All bodies are extended', this is an analytic judgment. For I do not require to go beyond the concept which I connect with 'body' in order to find extension as bound up with it. To meet with this predicate, I have merely to analyse the concept, that is, to become conscious to myself of the manifold which I always think in that concept. The judgment is therefore analytic. But when I say, 'All bodies are heavy', the predicate is something quite different from anything that I think in the mere concept of body in general; and the addition of such a predicate therefore yields a synthetic judgment.

Judgments of experience, as such, are one and all synthetic. For it would be absurd to found an analytic judgment on experience. Since, in framing the judgment, I must not go outside my concept, there is no need to appeal to the testimony of experience in its support. That a body is extended is a proposition that holds *a priori* and is not empirical. For, before appealing to experience, I have already in the concept of body all the conditions required for my judgment. I have only to extract from it, in accordance with the principle of contradiction, the required predicate, and in so doing can at the same time become conscious of the necessity of the judgment – and that is what experience could never have taught me. On the other hand, though I do not include in the concept of a body in general the predicate 'weight', none the less this concept indicates an object of experience through one of its parts, and I can add to that part other parts of this same experience, as in this way belonging together with the concept. From the start I can apprehend the concept of body analytically through the characters of extension, impenetrability, figure, etc., all of which are thought in the concept. Now, however, looking back on the experience from which I have derived this concept of body, and finding weight to be invariably connected with the above characters, I attach it as a predicate to the concept; and in doing so I attach it synthetically, and am therefore extending my knowledge. The possibility of the synthesis of the predicate 'weight' with the concept of 'body' thus rests upon experience. While the one concept is not contained in the other, they yet belong to one another, though only contingently, as parts of a whole, namely, of an experience which is itself a synthetic combination of intuitions.

But in *a priori* synthetic judgments this help is entirely lacking. [I do not here have the advantage of looking around in the field of experience.] Upon what, then, am I to rely, when I seek to go beyond the concept A, and to know that another concept B is connected with it? Through what is the synthesis made possible? Let us take the proposition, 'Everything which happens has its cause. In the concept of 'something which happens', I do indeed think an existence which is preceded by a time, etc., and from this concept analytic judgments may be obtained. But the concept of a 'cause' lies entirely outside the other concept, and signifies something different from 'that which happens', and is not therefore in any way contained in this latter representation. How come I then to predicate of that which happens something quite different, and to apprehend that the concept of cause, though not contained in it, yet belongs, and indeed necessarily belongs, to it? [...] It cannot be experience, because the suggested principle has connected the second representation with the first, not only with greater universality, but also with the character of necessity, and therefore completely *a priori* and on the basis of mere concepts. Upon such synthetic, that is, ampliative principles, all our *a priori* speculative knowledge must ultimately rest; analytic judgments are very important, and indeed necessary, but only for obtaining that clearness in the concepts which is requisite for such a sure and wide synthesis as will lead to a genuinely new addition to all previous knowledge.

V.   In all Theoretical Sciences of Reason Synthetic *a priori* Judgments are contained as Principles

[...]

Mathematical judgments, without exception, are synthetic.

We might [...] at first suppose that the proposition $7+5=12$ is a merely analytic proposition, and follows by the principle of contradiction from the concept of a sum of 7 and 5. But if we look more closely we find that the concept of the sum of 7 and 5 contains nothing save the union of the two numbers into one, and in this no thought is being taken as to what that single number may be which combines both. The concept of 12 is by no means already thought in merely thinking this union of 7 and 5; and I may analyse my concept of such a possible sum as long as I please, still I shall never find the 12 in it. [...] Arithmetical propositions are therefore always synthetic. This is still more evident if we take larger numbers. For it is then obvious that, however we might turn and twist our concepts, we could never, by the mere analysis of them, and without the aid of intuition, discover what [the number is that] is the sum.

Just as little is any fundamental proposition of pure geometry analytic. That the straight line between two points is the shortest, is a synthetic proposition. For my concept of *straight* contains nothing of quantity, but only of quality. The concept of the shortest is wholly an addition, and cannot be derived, through any process of analysis, from the concept of the straight line.

[...]

Metaphysics [...] *ought to contain* a priori *synthetic knowledge*. For its business is not merely to analyse concepts which we make for ourselves a priori of things, and thereby to clarify them analytically, but to extend our *a priori* knowledge. And for this purpose we must employ principles which add to the given concept something that was not contained in it, and through *a priori* synthetic judgments venture out so far that experience is quite unable to follow us, as, for instance, in the proposition, that the world must have a first beginning, and such like. Thus metaphysics consists, at least *in intention*, entirely of *a priori* synthetic propositions.

VI.   The General Problem of Pure Reason

Much is already gained if we can bring a number of investigations under the formula of a single problem. [...] Now the proper problem of pure reason is contained in the question: How are *a priori* synthetic judgments possible?

That metaphysics has hitherto remained in so vacillating a state of uncertainty and contradiction, is entirely due to the fact that this problem, and perhaps even the distinction between analytic and synthetic judgments, has never previously been considered. [...] David Hume came nearest to envisaging this problem, but still was very far from conceiving it with sufficient definiteness and universality. He occupied himself exclusively with the synthetic proposition regarding the connection of an effect with its cause (*principium causalitatis*), and he believed himself to have shown that such an *a priori* proposition is entirely impossible. If we accept his conclusions, then all that we call metaphysics is a mere delusion whereby we fancy ourselves to have rational insight into what, in actual fact, is borrowed solely from experience, and under the influence of custom has taken the illusory semblance of necessity. If he had envisaged our problem in all its universality, [...] he would then have recognised that, according to his own argument, pure mathematics, as certainly containing *a priori* synthetic propositions, would also not be possible; and from such an assertion his good sense would have saved him.

In the solution of the above problem, we are at the same time deciding as to the possibility of the employment of pure reason in establishing and developing all those sciences which contain a theoretical *a priori* knowledge of objects, and have therefore to answer the questions:

How is pure mathematics possible?
How is pure science of nature possible?

Since these sciences actually exist, it is quite proper to ask *how* they are possible; for that they must be possible is proved by the fact that they exist. But the poor progress which has hitherto been made in metaphysics, and the fact that no system yet propounded can, in view of the essential purpose of metaphysics, be said really to exist, leaves everyone sufficient ground for doubting as to its possibility.
[...]
[...][S]ince all attempts which have hitherto been made to answer these natural questions – for instance, whether the world has a beginning or is from eternity – have always met with unavoidable contradictions, we cannot rest satisfied with the mere natural disposition to metaphysics, that is, with the pure faculty of reason itself, from which, indeed, some sort of metaphysics (be it what it may) always arises. It must be possible for reason to attain to certainty whether we know or do not know the objects of metaphysics, that is, to come to a decision either in regard to the objects of its enquiries or in regard to the capacity or incapacity of reason to pass any judgment upon them, so that we may either with confidence extend our pure reason or set to it sure and determinate limits. This last question, which arises out of the previous general problem, may, rightly stated, take the form:

How is metaphysics, as science, possible?

Thus the critique of reason, in the end, necessarily leads to scientific knowledge; while its dogmatic employment, on the other hand, lands us in dogmatic assertions to which other assertions, equally specious, can always be opposed – that is, in *scepticism*.
[...]

VII.   The Idea and Division of a Special Science, under the Title "Critique of Pure Reason"

In view of all these considerations, we arrive at the idea of a special science which can be entitled the Critique of Pure Reason. For reason is the faculty which supplies the principles of *a priori* knowledge. [...] An organon [i.e., a system of principles] of pure reason would be the sum-total of those principles according to which all modes of pure *a priori* knowledge can be acquired and actually brought into being. The exhaustive application of such an organon would give rise to a system of pure reason. But as this would be asking rather much, and as it is still doubtful whether and in what cases, any extension of our knowledge be here possible, we can regard a science of the mere examination of pure reason, of its sources and limits, as the *propaedeutic* [i.e., preparatory instruction] to the system of pure reason. As such, it should be called a critique, not a doctrine, of pure reason. Its utility, in speculation, ought properly to be only negative, not to extend, but only to clarify our reason, and keep it free from errors – which is already a very great gain. I entitle *transcendental* all knowledge which is occupied not so much with objects as with the mode of our knowledge of objects in so far as this mode of knowledge is to be possible *a priori*.

[...]

[...] Transcendental philosophy is therefore a philosophy of pure and merely speculative reason. All that is practical, so far as it contains motives, relates to feelings, and these belong to the empirical sources of knowledge.

If we are to make a systematic division of the science which we are engaged in presenting, it must have first a *doctrine of the elements*, and secondly, a *doctrine of the method of pure reason*. Each of these chief divisions will have its subdivisions, but the grounds of these we are not yet in a position to explain. By way of introduction or anticipation we need only say that there are two stems of human knowledge, namely, *sensibility* and *understanding*, which perhaps spring from a common, but to us unknown, root. Through the former, objects are given to us; through the latter, they are thought. Now in so far as sensibility may be found to contain *a priori* representations constituting the condition under which objects are given to us, it will belong to transcendental philosophy. And since the conditions under which alone the objects of human knowledge are given must precede those under which they are thought, the transcendental doctrine of sensibility will constitute the first part of the science of the elements.

Note

1.   Translator's note: "As the [English] term 'knowledge' [viz., *Erkenntnis*] cannot be used in the plural, I have usually translated *Erkenntnisse* 'modes of knowledge'."

54

Is All Apparently Reflective Knowledge Ultimately Observational?

John Stuart Mill, *A System of Logic*

Traditionally, those philosophers – the rationalists – who believe that some knowledge is genuinely reflective have spoken especially of mathematics and its kin. Are truths of pure mathematics, geometry, and logic, for instance, knowable via reflection? The intended contrast here is with observational knowledge. Do you know *observationally* that $7+5=12$? Of course not (say rationalists). In fact you might well cite no evidence beyond the authority of your first schoolteacher, who introduced you to sums like this one. But you would thereby (according to Descartes and other rationalists) be settling for *lesser* support or justification than is possible – relying just on the implicit empirical evidence of your teacher's having been well trained on simple mathematical matters. Possibly, your teacher has relied similarly on the word of his or her first teacher, too. A rationalist would claim, however, that you, these teachers, and anyone else *could* know purely reflectively that $7+5=12$. Indeed, the rationalist would claim that *only* reflective – not at all observational – knowledge is appropriate for such a truth. Kant insisted, for example, that this knowledge would be of a necessity, a timeless and unalterable truth: you know the timeless truth that $7+5=12$, not merely the passing truth that there are seven foxes in this field and five in the next one and hence twelve in the two fields considered jointly. On the traditional rationalist image, necessary truths are knowable *reflectively*, if at all.

But this reading vigorously disputes that rationalist image. The reading is from John Stuart Mill (1806–73), an English philosopher celebrated particularly for his writings on moral utilitarianism, on liberty, and on women's civil rights. He offers us here an empiricism even about knowledge of mathematics. He does this without

John Stuart Mill, *A System of Logic* [1841], 8th edn. (1882), Book II, chs. V, VI (excerpts).

Metaphysics and Epistemology: A Guided Anthology, First Edition. Edited by Stephen Hetherington.
© 2014 John Wiley & Sons, Inc. Published 2014 by John Wiley & Sons, Inc.

treating mathematical truths as mere conventional manipulations of symbols. For Mill, mathematics can give us quite substantive truths; not timeless necessities, however. Rather, they are generalizations about how the world functions. Yet they are generalizations so non-specific in their descriptions of the world as to *mislead* people into thinking of them as necessary truths, as being timelessly and immutably true. Mill would regard the truth that $7+5=12$ as just a universally true generalization about this observable world. It is a truth that fits with all our experience. This is because implicitly it is *about* only such matters. Maybe we cannot conceive of it possibly being false. Even so, this is no guarantee that it could not be false. Hence, we need not accord it such a metaphysically exalted status as that of being *unable* to be false in this or any other possible world.

Of Demonstration, and Necessary Truths

§ 1. […] Why are mathematical certainty, and the evidence of demonstration, common phrases to express the very highest degree of assurance attainable by reason? Why are mathematics by almost all philosophers, and (by some) even those branches of natural philosophy which, through the medium of mathematics, have been converted into deductive sciences, considered to be independent of the evidence of experience and observation, and characterized as systems of Necessary Truth?

The answer I conceive to be, that this character of necessity, ascribed to the truths of mathematics, and […] the peculiar certainty attributed to them, is an illusion. […]

[…]

§ 4. […] [W]hat is the ground of our belief in axioms – what is the evidence on which they rest? I answer, they are experimental truths; generalizations from observation. The proposition. Two straight lines can not inclose a space – or, in other words, Two straight lines which have once met, do not meet again, but continue to diverge – is an induction from the evidence of our senses. […]

It is not necessary to show that the truths which we call axioms are originally *suggested* by observation, and that we should never have known that two straight lines can not inclose a space if we had never seen a straight line: thus much being admitted by Dr. Whewell [William Whewell, eighteenth-century English philosopher of science], and by all, in recent times, who have taken his view of the subject. But they contend, that it is not experience which *proves* the axiom; but that its truth is perceived a priori, by the constitution of the mind itself, from the first moment when the meaning of the proposition is apprehended; and without any necessity for verifying it by repeated trials, as is requisite in the case of truths really ascertained by observation.

They can not, however, but allow that the truth of the axiom, Two straight lines can not inclose a space, even if evident independently of experience, is also evident from experience. Whether the axiom needs confirmation or not, it receives confirmation in almost every instant of our lives; since we can not look at any two straight lines which intersect one another, without seeing that from that point they continue to diverge more and more. Experimental proof crowds in upon us in such endless profusion, and without one instance in which there can be even a suspicion of an exception to the rule, that we should soon have stronger ground for believing the axiom, even as an experimental truth, than we have for almost any of the general truths which we confessedly learn from the evidence of our senses. Independently of *a priori* evidence, we should certainly believe it with an intensity of conviction far greater than we accord to any ordinary physical truth: and this too at a time of life much earlier than that from which we date almost any part of our acquired knowledge, and much too early to admit of our retaining any recollection of the history of our intellectual operations at that period. Where then is the necessity for assuming that our recognition of these truths has a different origin from the rest of our knowledge, when its existence is perfectly accounted for by supposing its origin to be the same? when the causes which produce belief in all other instances, exist in this instance, and in a degree of strength as much superior to what exists in other cases, as the intensity of the belief itself is superior? The burden of proof lies on the advocates of the contrary opinion: it is for them to point out some fact, inconsistent with the supposition that this part of our knowledge of nature is derived from the same sources as every other part.

[…]

§ 6. […] Axioms (it is asserted) are conceived by us not only as true, but as universally and necessarily true. Now, experience can not possibly give to any proposition this character. I may have seen snow a hundred times, and may have seen that it was white, but this can not give me entire assurance even that all snow is white; much less that snow *must* be white.

[…]

This, therefore, is the principle asserted: that propositions, the negation of which is inconceivable, or in other words, which we can not figure to ourselves as being false, must rest on evidence of a higher and more cogent description than any which experience can afford.

Now I can not but wonder that so much stress should be laid on the circumstance of inconceivableness, when there is such ample experience to show, that our capacity or incapacity of conceiving a thing has very little to do with the possibility of the thing in itself; but is in truth very much an affair of accident, and depends on the past history and habits of our own minds. There is no more generally acknowledged fact in human nature, than the extreme difficulty at first felt in conceiving any thing as possible, which is in contradiction to long established and familiar experience; or even to old familiar habits of thought. And this difficulty is a necessary result of the fundamental laws of the human mind. When we have often seen and thought of two things together, and have never in any one instance either seen or thought of them separately, there is by the primary law of association an increasing difficulty, which may in the end become insuperable, of conceiving the two things apart. […] There are remarkable instances of this in the history of science: instances in which the most instructed men rejected as impossible, because inconceivable, things which their posterity, by earlier practice and longer perseverance in the attempt, found it quite easy to conceive, and which every body now knows to be true. There was a time when men of the most cultivated intellects, and the most emancipated from the dominion of early prejudice, could not credit the existence of antipodes; were unable to conceive, in opposition to old association, the force of gravity acting upward instead of downward. The Cartesians long rejected the Newtonian doctrine of the gravitation of all bodies toward one another, on the faith of a general proposition, the reverse of which seemed to them to be inconceivable – the proposition that a body can not act where it is not. [...]

And they no doubt found it as impossible to conceive that a body should act upon the earth from the distance of the sun or moon, as we find it to conceive an end to space or time, or two straight lines inclosing a space. [...]

If, then, it be so natural to the human mind, even in a high state of culture, to be incapable of conceiving, and on that ground to believe impossible, what is afterward not only found to be conceivable but proved to be true; what wonder if in cases where the association is still older, more confirmed, and more familiar, and in which nothing ever occurs to shake our conviction, or even suggest to us any conception at variance with the association, the acquired incapacity should continue, and be mistaken for a natural incapacity? It is true, our experience of the varieties in nature enables us, within certain limits, to conceive other varieties analogous to them. We can conceive the sun or moon falling; for though we never saw them fall, nor ever, perhaps, imagined them falling, we have seen so many other things fall, that we have innumerable familiar analogies to assist the conception. [...] But when experience affords no model on which to shape the new conception, how is it possible for us to form it? How, for example, can we imagine an end to space or time? We never saw any object without something beyond it, nor experienced any feeling without something following it. When, therefore, we attempt to conceive the last point of space, we have the idea irresistibly raised of other points beyond it. When we try to imagine the last instant of time, we can not help conceiving another instant after it. [...] Now, in the case of a geometrical axiom, such, for example, as that two straight lines can not inclose a space – a truth which is testified to us by our very earliest impressions of the external world – how is it possible (whether those external impressions be or be not the ground of our belief) that the reverse of the proposition *could* be otherwise than inconceivable to us? What analogy have we, what similar order of facts in any other branch of our experience, to facilitate to us the conception of two straight lines inclosing a space?. [...]

The Same Subject Continued

§ 1. [...] [I]t would appear that Deductive or Demonstrative Sciences are all, without exception, Inductive Sciences; that their evidence is that of experience; but that they are also, in virtue of the peculiar character of one indispensable portion of the general formulæ according to which their inductions are made, Hypothetical Sciences. Their conclusions are only true on certain suppositions, which are, or ought to be, approximations to the truth, but are seldom, if ever, exactly true; and to this hypothetical character is to be ascribed the peculiar certainty, which is supposed to be inherent in demonstration.

What we have now asserted, however, cannot be received as universally true of Deductive or Demonstrative Sciences, until verified by being applied to the most remarkable of all those sciences, that of Numbers; the theory of the Calculus; Arithmetic and Algebra. It is harder to believe of the doctrines of this science than of any other, either that they are not truths *a priori*, but experimental truths, or that their peculiar certainty is owing to their being not absolute but only conditional truths. This, therefore, is a case which merits examination apart. [...]

§ 2.   This theory attempts to solve the difficulty apparently inherent in the case, by representing the propositions of the science of numbers as merely verbal, and its processes as simple transformations of language, substitutions of one expression for another. The proposition, Two and one is equal to three, according to these writers, is not a truth, is not the assertion of a really existing fact, but a definition of the word three; a statement that mankind have agreed to use the name three as a sign exactly equivalent to two and one; to call by the former name whatever is called by the other more clumsy phrase. [...]

[...] [But] [t]he doctrine that we can discover facts, detect the hidden processes of nature, by an artful manipulation of language, is so contrary to common sense, that a person must have made some advances in philosophy to believe it. [...]

[...] [T]his apparently so decisive instance is no instance at all. [T]here is in every step of an arithmetical or algebraical calculation a real induction, a real inference of facts from facts; and that what disguises the induction is simply its comprehensive nature, and the consequent extreme generality of the language. All numbers must be numbers of something: there are no such things as numbers in the abstract. *Ten* must mean ten bodies, or ten sounds, or ten beatings of the pulse. But though numbers must be numbers of something, they may be numbers of any thing. Propositions, therefore, concerning numbers, have the remarkable peculiarity that they are propositions concerning all things whatever; all objects, all existences of every kind, known to our experience. [...] The proposition, $2(a+b)=2a+2b$, is a truth co-extensive with all nature. Since then algebraical truths are true of all things whatever, and not, like those of geometry, true of lines only or of angles only, it is no wonder that the symbols should not excite in our minds ideas of any things in particular. [...] The mere written characters, a, b, x, y, z, serve as well for representatives of Things in general, as any more complex and apparently more concrete conception. That we are conscious of them, however, in their character of things, and not of mere signs, is evident from the fact that our whole process of reasoning is carried on by predicating of them the properties of things. In resolving an algebraic equation, by what rules do we proceed? By applying at each step to a, b, and x, the proposition that equals added to equals make equals; that equals taken from equals leave equals; and other propositions founded on these two. These are not properties of language, or of signs as such, but of magnitudes, which is as much as to say, of all things. The inferences, therefore, which are successively drawn, are inferences concerning things, not symbols; though as any Things whatever will serve the turn, there is no necessity for keeping the idea of the Thing at all distinct, and consequently the process of thought may, in this case, be allowed without danger to do what all processes of thought, when they have been performed often, will do if permitted, namely, to become entirely mechanical. Hence the general language of algebra comes to be used familiarly without exciting ideas, as all other general language is prone to do from mere habit, though in no other case than this can it be done with complete safety. But when we look back to see from whence the probative force of the process is derived, we find that at every single step, unless we suppose ourselves to be thinking and talking of the things, and not the mere symbols, the evidence fails.

[...]

The Science of Number is thus no exception to the conclusion we previously arrived at, that the processes even of deductive sciences are altogether inductive, and that their first principles are generalizations from experience. [...]

§ 4. It appears [...] that the method of all Deductive Sciences is hypothetical. They proceed by tracing the consequences of certain assumptions; leaving for separate consideration whether the assumptions are true or not, and if not exactly true, whether they are a sufficiently near approximation to the truth.

55

Is Scientific Reflection Our Best Model for Understanding Reflection?

C.S. Peirce, "Some Consequences of Four Incapacities" and "How To Make Our Ideas Clear"

Mill wrote within the tradition of British empiricism represented most famously by Locke, Berkeley, and Hume. We saw Mill redescribing, in an empiricist way, how people *only seem* to derive reflective knowledge of necessary – inviolable, timeless – truths. (This is not really – said Mill – what they are doing.) We also saw how Descartes had offered a philosophical image of each person as able in principle to pursue such reflection. Descartes' picture is of an inquirer reflecting alone, methodically overcoming hypothetical and motivating doubts, gaining certain knowledge. *Just Think.* That could have been the battle-cry of a rationalist such as Descartes; and can that rationalist call to arms be resisted? Mill tried to do so; as did America's first distinctive contribution to the history of philosophy – namely, *pragmatism.* This reading is from Harvard University's C.S. Peirce (1839–1914), a scientist and logician, as well as one of American pragmatism's three "founding fathers." The other two were William James (1842–1910) and John Dewey (1859–1952). Here, we find Peirce confronting directly Descartes' guiding image of how anyone seeking truth should best inquire.

We meet a few of Peirce's most influential ideas. His key one is that *science* provides our best example of how inquiry will ever lead to knowledge. What implications does that have? For a start, science is collaborative. Knowledge is more readily attained by cooperation than by concentration alone. Descartes'

C.S. Peirce, "Some Consequences of Four Incapacities" [1868] and "How To Make Our Ideas Clear" [1878] (excerpts). In N. Houser and C. Kloesel (eds.), *The Essential Peirce: Selected Philosophical Writings*, vol. 1 (1867–93) (Bloomington and Indianapolis: Indiana University Press, 1992).

image of the solitary hunter after truth is not being endorsed by Peirce. Indeed, science's *arguments* are collaborative: Peirce discards Descartes' image of a single conclusive argument being our goal in inquiry. We should compare and combine arguments. We should seize upon arguments both small and large. Mix them. Meld them. None need be conclusive. But there is strength in their interaction.

Nor need we, if science's arguments are to be our methodological inspiration, focus upon needless and meaninglessly powerful doubts. There is not necessarily truth-seeking power in doubts being applied to all of one's beliefs. Doubts should themselves be motivated by reasons. And what matters, when we *do* engage with doubts while seeking truth, is that we overcome them by forming real beliefs. These are ones with which we will *act*, ones that animate and guide our lives. This is where Peirce becomes clearly a *pragmatist* in how he conceives of beliefs, inquiry, and knowledge.

His pragmatism extends also, it seems, to his conception of truth. Sometimes people wish to contrast what is true with what is practical – even to dismiss the very idea of truth, as empty by not inherently reflecting how we act within the world. Peirce did not share that view. For him, truth *does* inherently reflect how we act; at any rate, how we act as proper inquirers. Truth exists because it *is* whatever real – scientific – collaborative inquiry would ultimately deem true. It is what such reflection moves us towards. (Will we ever *reach* truth? There is no guarantee of this. Peirce, unlike Descartes, is arguing that we must settle for a *fallibilism* about our inquiries. The idea of fallibilism is Peirce's.) Again, though (he would say), this is not to *deny* us truth or knowledge.

Some Consequences of Four Incapacities

Descartes is the father of modern philosophy, and the spirit of Cartesianism – that which principally distinguishes it from the scholasticism which it displaced – may be compendiously stated as follows:

1. It teaches that philosophy must begin with universal doubt; whereas scholasticism had never questioned fundamentals.
2. It teaches that the ultimate test of certainty is to be found in the individual consciousness; whereas scholasticism had rested on the testimony of sages and of the Catholic Church.
3. The multiform argumentation of the middle ages is replaced by a single thread of inference depending often upon inconspicuous premises.

4. Scholasticism had its mysteries of faith, but undertook to explain all created things. But there are many facts which Cartesianism not only does not explain, but renders absolutely inexplicable, unless to say that "God makes them so" is to be regarded as an explanation.

In some, or all of these respects, most modern philosophers have been, in effect, Cartesians. Now without wishing to return to scholasticism, it seems to me that modern science and modern logic require us to stand upon a very different platform from this.

1. We cannot begin with complete doubt. We must begin with all the prejudices which we actually have when we enter upon the study of philosophy. These prejudices are not to be dispelled by a maxim, for they are things which it does not occur to us *can* be questioned. Hence this initial scepticism will be a mere self-deception, and not real doubt; and no one who follows the Cartesian method will ever be satisfied until he has formally recovered all those beliefs which in form he has given up. It is, therefore, as useless a preliminary as going to the North Pole would be in order to get to Constantinople by coming down regularly upon a meridian. A person may, it is true, in the course of his studies, find reason to doubt what he began by believing; but in that case he doubts because he has a positive reason for it, and not on account of the Cartesian maxim. Let us not pretend to doubt in philosophy what we do not doubt in our hearts.
2. The same formalism appears in the Cartesian criterion, which amounts to this: "Whatever I am clearly convinced of, is true." If I were really convinced, I should have done with reasoning, and should require no test of certainty. But thus to make single individuals absolute judges of truth is most pernicious. The result is that metaphysicians will all agree that metaphysics has reached a pitch of certainty far beyond that of the physical sciences; – only they can agree upon nothing else. In sciences in which men come to agreement, when a theory has been broached, it is considered to be on probation until this agreement is reached. After it is reached, the question of certainty becomes an idle one, because there is no one left who doubts it. We individually cannot reasonably hope to attain the ultimate philosophy which we pursue; we can only seek it, therefore, for the *community* of philosophers. Hence, if disciplined and candid minds carefully examine a theory and refuse to accept it, this ought to create doubts in the mind of the author of the theory himself.
3. Philosophy ought to imitate the successful sciences in its methods, so far as to proceed only from tangible premises which can be subjected to careful scrutiny, and to trust rather to the multitude and variety of its arguments than to the conclusiveness of any one. Its reasoning should not form a chain which is no stronger than its weakest link, but a cable whose fibres may be ever so slender, provided they are sufficiently numerous and intimately connected.
4. Every unidealistic philosophy supposes some absolutely inexplicable, unanalyzable ultimate; in short, something resulting from mediation itself not susceptible of mediation. Now that anything *is* thus inexplicable can only be known by reasoning from signs. But the only Justification of an inference from signs is that the conclusion explains the fact. To suppose the fact absolutely inexplicable, is not to explain it, and hence this supposition is never allowable.

[...]

How to Make Our Ideas Clear

I

[...]

When Descartes set about the reconstruction of philosophy, his first step was to (theoretically) permit skepticism and to discard the practice of the schoolmen of looking to authority as the ultimate source of truth. That done, he sought a more natural fountain of true principles, and professed to find it in the human mind; thus passing, in the directest way, from the method of authority to that of apriority [i.e., the use of pure reason] [...]. Self-consciousness was to furnish us with our fundamental truths, and to decide what was agreeable to reason. But since, evidently, not all ideas are true, he was led to note, as the first condition of infallibility, that they must be clear. The distinction between an idea *seeming* clear and really being so, never occurred to him. Trusting to introspection, as he did, even for a knowledge of external things, why should he question its testimony in respect to the contents of our own minds? But then, I suppose, seeing men, who seemed to be quite clear and positive, holding opposite opinions upon fundamental principles, he was further led to say that clearness of ideas is not sufficient, but that they need also to be distinct, i.e., to have nothing unclear about them. What he probably meant by this (for he did not explain himself with precision) was, that they must sustain the test of dialectical examination; that they must not only seem clear at the outset, but that discussion must never be able to bring to light points of obscurity connected with them.

[...]

II

The principles set forth in [an earlier paper] lead, at once, to a method of reaching a clearness of thought of a far higher grade than the "distinctness" of the logicians. We have there found that the action of thought is excited by the irritation of doubt, and ceases when belief is attained; so that the production of belief is the sole function of thought. [...] Doubt and Belief, as the words are commonly employed, relate to religious or other grave discussions. But here I use them to designate the starting of any question, no matter how small or how great, and the resolution of it. If, for instance, in a horse-car, I pull out my purse and find a five-cent nickel and five coppers, I decide, while my hand is going to the purse, in which way I will pay my fare. To call such a question Doubt, and my decision Belief, is certainly to use words very disproportionate to the occasion. To speak of such a doubt as causing an irritation which needs to be appeased, suggests a temper which is uncomfortable to the verge of insanity. Yet, looking at the matter minutely, it must be admitted that, if there is the least hesitation as to whether I shall pay the five coppers or the nickel (as there will be sure to be, unless I act from some previously contracted habit in the matter), though irritation is too strong a word, yet I am excited to such small mental activity as may be necessary to deciding how I shall act. Most frequently doubts arise from some indecision, however momentary, in our action. [...] However the doubt may originate, it stimulates the mind to an activity which may be slight or energetic, calm or turbulent. Images pass rapidly through consciousness, one incessantly melting into another, until at last, when all is over – it may be in a fraction of a second, in an hour, or after long years – we find ourselves decided as to how we should act under such circumstances as those which occasioned our hesitation. In other words, we have attained belief.

[…]

And what, then, is belief? It is the demi-cadence which closes a musical phrase in the symphony of our intellectual life. We have seen that it has just three properties: First, it is something that we are aware of; second, it appeases the irritation of doubt; and, third, it involves the establishment in our nature of a rule of action, or, say for short, a *habit*. As it appeases the irritation of doubt, which is the motive for thinking, thought relaxes, and comes to rest for a moment when belief is reached. But, since belief is a rule for action, the application of which involves further doubt and further thought, at the same time that it is a stopping-place, it is also a new starting-place for thought. That is why I have permitted myself to call it thought at rest, although thought is essentially an action. The *final* upshot of thinking is the exercise of volition, and of this thought no longer forms a part; but belief is only a stadium of mental action, an effect upon our nature due to thought, which will influence future thinking.

The essence of belief is the establishment of a habit, and different beliefs are distinguished by the different modes of action to which they give rise. If beliefs do not differ in this respect, if they appease the same doubt by producing the same rule of action, then no mere differences in the manner of consciousness of them can make them different beliefs, any more than playing a tune in different keys is playing different tunes. Imaginary distinctions are often drawn between beliefs which differ only in their mode of expression.

[…]

[…] [T]he whole function of thought is to produce habits of action; and that whatever there is connected with a thought, but irrelevant to its purpose, is an accretion to it, but no part of it. If there be a unity among our sensations which has no reference to how we shall act on a given occasion, as when we listen to a piece of music, why we do not call that thinking. To develop its meaning, we have, therefore, simply to determine what habits it produces, for what a thing means is simply what habits it involves. Now, the identity of a habit depends on how it might lead us to act, not merely under such circumstances as are likely to arise, but under such as might possibly occur, no matter how improbable they may be. What the habit is depends on *when* and *how* it causes us to act. As for the *when*, every stimulus to action is derived from perception; as for the *how*, every purpose of action is to produce some sensible result. Thus, we come down to what is tangible and practical, as the root of every real distinction of thought, no matter how subtle it may be; and there is no distinction of meaning so fine as to consist in anything but a possible difference of practice.

[…]

It appears, then, that the rule for attaining the third grade of clearness of apprehension is as follows: Consider what effects, which might conceivably have practical bearings, we conceive the object of our conception to have. Then, our conception of these effects is the whole of our conception of the object.

[…]

IV

Let us now approach the subject of logic, and consider a conception which particularly concerns it, that of *reality*. Taking clearness in the sense of familiarity, no idea could be clearer than this. Every child uses it with perfect confidence, never dreaming that he does not understand it. As for clearness in its second grade, however, it would probably puzzle most men, even among those of a reflective turn of mind, to give an abstract definition of the real. Yet such a definition may perhaps be reached by considering the points of difference between reality and its opposite, fiction. A figment is a product of somebody's imagination; it has such characters as his thought impresses upon it. That whose characters are independent of how you or I think is an external reality. There are, however, phenomena within our own minds, dependent upon our thought, which are at the same time real in the sense that we really think them. But though their characters depend on how we think, they do not depend on what we think those characters to be. Thus, a dream has a real existence as a mental phenomenon, if somebody has really dreamt it; that he dreamt so and so, does not depend on what anybody thinks was dreamt, but is completely independent of all opinion on the subject. On the other hand, considering, not the fact of dreaming, but the thing dreamt, it retains its peculiarities by virtue of no other fact than that it was dreamt to possess them. Thus we may define the real as that whose characters are independent of what anybody may think them to be.

But, however satisfactory such a definition may be found, it would be a great mistake to suppose that it makes the idea of reality perfectly clear. Here, then, let us apply our rules. According to them, reality, like every other quality, consists in the peculiar sensible effects which things partaking of it produce. The only effect which real things have is to cause belief, for all the sensations which they excite emerge into consciousness in the form of beliefs. The question therefore is, how is true belief (or belief in the real) distinguished from false belief (or belief in fiction). Now, [...] the ideas of truth and falsehood, in their full development, appertain exclusively to the scientific method of settling opinion. A person who arbitrarily chooses the propositions which he will adopt can use the word truth only to emphasize the expression of his determination to hold on to his choice. [...] When the method of authority prevailed, the truth meant little more than the Catholic faith. All the efforts of the scholastic doctors are directed toward harmonizing their faith in Aristotle and their faith in the Church, and one may search their ponderous folios through without finding an argument which goes any further. It is noticeable that where different faiths flourish side by side, renegades are looked upon with contempt even by the party whose belief they adopt; so completely has the idea of loyalty replaced that of truth-seeking. Since the time of Descartes, the defect in the conception of truth has been less apparent. Still, it will sometimes strike a scientific man that the philosophers have been less intent on finding out what the facts are, than on inquiring what belief is most in harmony with their system. It is hard to convince a follower of the *a priori* method by adducing facts; but show him that an opinion he is defending is inconsistent with what he has laid down elsewhere, and he will be very apt to retract it. These minds do not seem to believe that disputation is ever to cease; they seem to think that the opinion which is natural for one man is not so for another, and that belief will, consequently, never be settled. In contenting themselves with fixing their own opinions by a method which would lead another man to a different result, they betray their feeble hold of the conception of what truth is.

On the other hand, all the followers of science are fully persuaded that the processes of investigation, if only pushed far enough, will give one certain solution to every question to which they can be applied. One man may investigate the velocity of light by studying the transits of Venus and the aberration of the stars; another by the oppositions of Mars and the eclipses of Jupiter's satellites; a third by the method of Fizeau; a fourth by that of Foucault; a fifth by the motions of the curves of Lissajous; a sixth, a seventh, an eighth, and a ninth, may follow the different methods of comparing the measures of statical and dynamical electricity. They may at first obtain different results, but, as each perfects his method and his processes, the results will move steadily together toward a destined centre. So with all scientific research. Different minds may set out with the most antagonistic views, but the progress of investigation carries them by a force outside of themselves to one and the same conclusion. This activity of thought by which we are carried, not where we wish, but to a foreordained goal, is like the operation of destiny. No modification of the point of view taken, no selection of other facts for study, no natural bent of mind even, can enable a man to escape the predestinate opinion. This great law is embodied in the conception of truth and reality. The opinion which is fated[1] to be ultimately agreed to by all who investigate, is what we mean by the truth, and the object represented in this opinion is the real. That is the way I would explain reality.

But it may be said that this view is directly opposed to the abstract definition which we have given of reality, inasmuch as it makes the characters of the real to depend on what is ultimately thought about them. But the answer to this is that, on the one hand, reality is independent, not necessarily of thought in general, but only of what you or I or any finite number of men may think about it; and that, on the other hand, though the object of the final opinion depends on what that opinion is, yet what that opinion is does not depend on what you or I or any man thinks. Our perversity and that of others may indefinitely postpone the settlement of opinion; it might even conceivably cause an arbitrary proposition to be universally accepted as long as the human race should last. Yet even that would not change the nature of the belief, which alone could be the result of investigation carried sufficiently far; and if, after the extinction of our race, another should arise with faculties and disposition for investigation, that true opinion must be the one which they would ultimately come to. "Truth crushed to earth shall rise again," and the opinion which would finally result from investigation does not depend on how anybody may actually think. But the reality of that which is real does depend on the real fact that investigation is destined to lead, at last, if continued long enough, to a belief in it.

But I may be asked what I have to say to all the minute facts of history, forgotten never to be recovered, to the lost books of the ancients, to the buried secrets. [...] Do these things not really exist because they are hopelessly beyond the reach of our knowledge? And then, after the universe is dead (according to the prediction of some scientists), and all life has ceased forever, will not the shock of atoms continue though there will be no mind to know it? To this I reply that, though in no possible state of knowledge can any number be great enough to express the relation between the amount of what rests unknown to the amount of the known, yet it is unphilosophical to suppose that, with regard to any given question (which has any clear meaning), investigation would not bring forth a solution of it, if it were carried far enough. Who would have said, a few years ago, that we could ever know of what substances stars are made whose light may have been longer in reaching us than the human race has existed? Who can be sure of what we shall not know in a few hundred years? Who can guess what would be the result of continuing the pursuit of science for ten thousand years, with the activity of the last hundred? And if it were to go on for a million, or a billion, or any number of years you please, how is it possible to say that there is any question which might not ultimately be solved?

Note

1. Fate means merely that which is sure to come true, and can nohow be avoided. It is a superstition to suppose that a certain sort of events are ever fated, and it is another to suppose that the word fate can never be freed from its superstitious taint. We are all fated to die.

56

Are Some Necessities Known through Observation, Not Reflection?

Saul A. Kripke, *Naming and Necessity*

Kant, we found, accepted the existence of necessary or timeless truths. In asking about knowledge of such truths, he envisaged someone reflecting alone: in principle, you could know reflectively, without assistance from others, that $7+5=12$. But the empiricist Mill and the pragmatist Peirce, we observed, directed us away from there being any such truths and towards the preeminent role of scientific inquiry in gaining knowledge. Might we not know necessary truths at all, then, or at least not reflectively?

That could depend upon ideas in this reading, from the American philosopher Saul Kripke (b. 1940). He gained early – teenage – philosophical fame for his work in logic. The lectures from which this reading comes made a dramatic impact when Kripke (then at Princeton University) was only around 30 years old. Prior to those lectures, philosophers adopted this philosophical image:

> *A priori*, or purely reflective, knowledge could only be of necessary truths; and necessary truths could only be known in that way. (Necessary truths would be true, too, merely because of their meaning. They are what Kant called analytic truths.) *A posteriori*, or at least partly observational, knowledge could therefore only be of contingent truths – ones whose truth is not merely a matter of their meaning. (These are what Kant called synthetic truths.)

Reflective knowledge could only be of necessities: in order to know a necessary truth, *think*. Non-reflective knowledge could only be of contingencies: in order to know a contingent truth, *observe*.

Saul A. Kripke, *Naming and Necessity* (excerpts) (Cambridge, MA: Harvard University Press, 1980), lecture III (excerpts). Reprinted with permission of John Wiley & Sons Ltd.

But these lectures by Kripke questioned that organizational image – convincingly so (thought many philosophers). Here, we meet just one of his lines of thought. Distinguish something's *essential* properties from its *accidental* ones. If Kripke is right, you are essentially the product of a specific egg and sperm. If a different sperm had joined with that egg, *you* would not have been the result. It is therefore *necessarily* true of you that this specific egg and sperm were what combined in creating you. Similarly for gold's having the atomic number 79, say. This is necessary and timeless: in *any* possible world containing some gold, that gold has atomic number 79. (This is so, even as there are also possible worlds containing no gold.)

That is metaphysics; here is the epistemology. Kripke argues that these necessary truths are ones we know *observationally*. It is science – observationally based science – that discovers this necessary truth about gold, for instance. If Kripke is correct, therefore, it *is* possible to know some necessary truths observationally. In which case, the venerable philosophical image mentioned two paragraphs ago – a beguiling blend of metaphysics and epistemology – should be discarded. We noted in an earlier section ("How Is There a World At All?"), with the reading from Leibniz (reading 20), that the metaphysical image of possible worlds is prominent within contemporary philosophy. Kripke is one of those (along perhaps with David Lewis) most responsible for that.

[C]ould the Queen – could this woman herself – have been born of different parents from the parents from whom she actually came? Could she, let's say, have been the daughter instead of Mr. and Mrs. Truman? [...]

[...] [C]an we imagine a situation in which it would have happened that this very woman came out of Mr. and Mrs. Truman? They might have had a child resembling her in many properties. Perhaps in some possible world Mr. and Mrs. Truman even had a child who actually became the Queen of England and was even passed off as the child of other parents. This still would not be a situation in which *this very woman* whom we call 'Elizabeth II' was the child of Mr. and Mrs. Truman, or so it seems to me. It would be a situation in which there was some other woman who had many of the properties that are in fact true of Elizabeth. Now, one question is, in this possible world, was Elizabeth herself ever born? Let's suppose she wasn't ever born. It would then be a situation in which, though Truman and his wife have a child with many of the properties of Elizabeth, Elizabeth herself didn't exist at all. One can only become convinced of this by reflection on how you would describe this situation. [...]

How could a person originating from different parents, from a totally different sperm and egg, be *this very woman*? [...] It seems to me that anything coming from a different origin would not be this object.

In the case of this table,[1] we may not know what block of wood the table came from. Now could *this table* have been made from a completely *different* block of wood, or even of water cleverly hardened into ice – water taken from the Thames River? We could conceivably discover that, contrary to what we now think, this table is indeed made of ice from the river. But let us suppose that it is not. Then, though we can imagine making a table out of another block of wood or even from ice, identical in appearance with this one, and though we could have put it in this very position in the room, it seems to me that this is *not* to imagine *this* table as made of wood or ice, but rather it is to imagine another table, *resembling* this one in all external details, made of another block of wood, or even of ice.

These are only examples of essential properties. I won't dwell on them further because I want to go on to the more general case [...] of some identities between terms for substances, and also the properties of substances and of natural kinds. Philosophers have, as I've said, been very interested in statements expressing theoretical identifications; among them, that light is a stream of photons, that water is H_2O, that lightning is an electrical discharge, that gold is the element with the atomic number 79.

To get clear about the status of these statements we must first maybe have some thoughts about the status of such substances as gold. What's gold? [...] Here is what Immanuel Kant says about gold. [...] Kant is introducing the distinction between analytic and synthetic judgements, and he says: 'All analytic judgements depend wholly on the law of contradiction, and are in their nature *a priori* cognitions, whether the concepts that supply them with matter be empirical or not. For the predicate of an affirmative analytic judgement is already contained in the concept of the subject, of which it cannot be denied without contradiction.... For this very reason all analytic judgements are *a priori* even when the concepts are empirical, as, for example, "Gold is a yellow metal"; for to know this I require no experience beyond my concept of gold as a yellow metal. It is, in fact, the very concept, and I need only analyze it without looking beyond it.'[2] I should have looked at the German. 'It is in fact the very concept' sounds as if Kant is saying here that 'gold' just *means* 'yellow metal'. If he says that, then it's especially strange, so let's suppose that that is not what he's saying. At least Kant thinks it's a *part* of the concept that gold is to be a yellow metal. He thinks we know this *a priori*, and that we could not possibly discover this to be empirically false.

Is Kant right about this? [...]

[...] [L]et's consider something easier – the question of the yellowness of gold. Could we discover that gold was not in fact yellow? Suppose an optical illusion were prevalent, due to peculiar properties of the atmosphere in South Africa and Russia and certain other areas where gold mines are common. Suppose there were an optical illusion which made the substance appear to be yellow; but, in fact, once the peculiar properties of the atmosphere were removed, we would see that it is actually blue. [...] Would there on this basis be an announcement in the newspapers: 'It has turned out that there is no gold. Gold does not exist. What we took to be gold is not in fact gold.'? [...]

It seems to me that there would be no such announcement. On the contrary, what would be announced would be that though it appeared that gold was yellow, in fact gold has turned out not to be yellow, but blue. The reason is, I think, that we use 'gold' as a term for a certain *kind* of thing. Others have discovered this kind of thing and we have heard of it. We thus as part of a community of speakers have a certain connection between ourselves and a certain kind of thing. The kind of thing is *thought* to have certain identifying marks. Some of these marks may not really be true of gold. We might discover that we are wrong about them. Further, there might be a substance which has all the identifying marks we commonly attributed to gold and used to identify it in the first place, but which is not the same kind of thing, which is not the same substance. We would say of such a thing that though it has all the appearances we initially used to identify gold, it is not gold. Such a thing is, for example, as we well know, iron pyrites or fool's gold. This is not another kind of gold. It's a completely different thing which to the uninitiated person looks just like the substance which we discovered and called gold. We can say this not because we have changed the *meaning* of the term gold, and thrown in some other criteria which distinguished gold from pyrites. It seems to me that that's not true. On the contrary, we *discovered* that certain properties were true of gold in addition to the initial identifying marks by which we identified it. These properties, then, being characteristic of gold and not true of iron pyrites, show that the fool's gold is not in fact gold.

We should look at this in another example.

[...]

[...] Suppose we discover an animal which, though having all external appearances of a tiger as [typically] described [...], has an internal structure completely different from that of the tiger. [...] We might find animals in some part of the world which, though they look just like a tiger, on examination were discovered not even to be mammals. Let's say they were in fact very peculiar looking reptiles. Do we then conclude on the basis of this description that some tigers are reptiles? We don't. We would rather conclude that these animals, though they have the external marks by which we originally identified tigers, are not in fact tigers, because they are not of the same species as the species which we called 'the species of tigers'. Now this, I think, is not because, as some people would say, the old concept of tiger has been replaced by a new scientific definition. I think this is true of the concept of tiger *before* the internal structure of tigers has been investigated. Even though we don't *know* the internal structure of tigers, we suppose – and let us suppose that we are right – that tigers form a certain species or natural kind. We then can imagine that there should be a creature which, though having all the external appearance of tigers, differs from them internally enough that we should say that it is not the same kind of thing. We can imagine it without knowing anything about this internal structure – what this internal structure is. We can say in advance that we use the term 'tiger' to designate a species, and that anything not of this species, even though it looks like a tiger, is not in fact a tiger.

Just as something may have all the properties by which we originally identified tigers and yet not be a tiger, so we might also find out tigers had *none* of the properties by which we originally identified them. Perhaps *none* are quadrupedal, none tawny yellow, none carnivorous, and so on; all these properties turn out to be based on optical illusions or other errors, as in the case of gold. So the term 'tiger', like the term 'gold', does *not* mark out a 'cluster concept' in which most, but perhaps not all, of the properties used to identify the kind must be satisfied. On the contrary, possession of most of these properties need not be a necessary condition for membership in the kind, nor need it be a sufficient condition.

Since we have found out that tigers do indeed, as we suspected, form a single kind, then something not of this kind is not a tiger. Of course, we may be mistaken in supposing that there is such a kind. In advance, we suppose that they probably do form a kind. Past experience has shown that usually things like this, living together, looking alike, mating together, do form a kind. If there are two kinds of tigers that have something to do with each other but not as much as we thought, then maybe they form a larger biological family. If they have absolutely nothing to do with each other, then there are really two kinds of tigers. This all depends on the history and on what we actually find out.

[…]

[…] The question remains whether such statements are necessary in the non-epistemological sense. […] So the next thing to investigate is […]: are such statements as 'cats are animals', or such statements as 'gold is a yellow metal', necessary?

So far I've only been talking about what we could find out. I've been saying we could find out that gold was not in fact yellow, contrary to what we thought. […] Gold apparently has the atomic number 79. Is it a necessary or a contingent property of gold that it has the atomic number 79? Certainly we could find out that we were mistaken. The whole theory of protons, of atomic numbers, the whole theory of molecular structure and of atomic structure, on which such views are based, could *all* turn out to be false. Certainly we didn't know it from time immemorial. So in that sense, gold could turn out not to have atomic number 79.

Given that gold *does* have the atomic number 79, could something be gold without having the atomic number 79? Let us suppose the scientists have investigated the nature of gold and have found that it is part of the very nature of this substance, so to speak, that it have the atomic number 79. Suppose we now find some other yellow metal, or some other yellow thing, with all the properties by which we originally identified gold, and many of the additional ones that we have discovered later. An example of one with many of the initial properties is iron pyrites, 'fool's gold.' As I have said, we wouldn't say that this substance is gold. So far we are speaking of the actual world. Now consider a possible world. Consider a counterfactual situation in which, let us say, fool's gold or iron pyrites was actually found in various mountains in the United States, or in areas of South Africa and the Soviet Union. Suppose that all the areas which actually contain gold now, contained pyrites instead, or some other substance which counterfeited the superficial properties of gold but lacked its atomic structure.[3] Would we say, of this counterfactual situation, that in that situation gold would not even have been an element (because pyrites is not an element)? It seems to me that we would not. We would instead describe this as a situation in which a substance, say iron pyrites, which is not gold, would have been found in the very mountains which actually contain gold and would have had the very properties by which we commonly identify gold. But it would not be gold; it would be something else. One should *not* say that it would still be gold in this possible world, though gold would then lack the atomic number 79. It would be some other stuff, some other substance. (Once again, whether people counterfactually would have *called* it 'gold' is irrelevant. *We* do not describe it as gold.) And so, it seems to me, this would not be a case in which possibly gold might not have been an element, nor can there be such a case (except in the epistemic sense of 'possible'). Given that gold *is* this element, any other substance, even though it looks like gold and is found in the very places where we in fact find gold, would not be gold. It would be some other substance which was a counterfeit for gold. In any counterfactual situation where the same geographical areas were filled with such a substance, they would not have been filled with gold. They would have been filled with something else.

So if this consideration is right, it tends to show that such statements representing scientific discoveries about what this stuff *is* are not contingent truths but necessary truths in the strictest possible sense. […] Any world in which we imagine a substance which does not have these properties is a world in which we imagine a substance which is not gold, provided these properties form the basis of what the substance is. In particular, then, present scientific theory is such that it is part of the nature of gold as we have it to be an element with atomic number 79. It will therefore be necessary and not contingent that gold be an element with atomic number 79. (We may also in the same way, then, investigate further how color and metallic properties follow from what we have found the substance gold to be: to the extent that such properties follow from the atomic structure of gold, they are necessary properties of it, even though they unquestionably are not part of the *meaning* of 'gold' and were not known with *a priori* certainty.)

[...]

Let's consider how this applies to the types of identity statements expressing scientific discoveries that I talked about before – say, that water is H_2O. It certainly represents a discovery that water is H_2O. We identified water originally by its characteristic feel, appearance and perhaps taste, (though the taste may usually be due to the impurities). If there were a substance, even actually, which had a completely different atomic structure from that of water, but resembled water in these respects, would we say that some water wasn't H_2O? I think not. We would say instead that just as there is a fool's gold there could be a fool's water; a substance which, though having the properties by which we originally identified water, would not in fact be water. And this, I think, applies not only to the actual world but even when we talk about counterfactual situations. If there had been a substance, which was a fool's water, it would then be fool's water and not water. On the other hand if this substance can take another form – such as the polywater allegedly discovered in the Soviet Union, with very different identifying marks from that of what we now call water – it is a form of water because it is the same substance, even though it doesn't have the appearances by which we originally identified water.

Notes

1. Of course I was pointing to a wooden table in the room.
2. *Prolegomena to Any Future Metaphysics*, Preamble Section 2.b. (Prussian Academy edition, p. 267).
3. Even better pairs of ringers exist; for example, some pairs of elements of a single column in the periodic table which resemble each other closely but nevertheless are different elements.

Can We Know in Other Fundamental Ways?

57

Is Knowing-How a Distinct Way of Knowing?

Gilbert Ryle, "Knowing How and Knowing That"

Observation and reason are the two potential ways of knowing to which epistemologists have devoted the most attention over the centuries. That is why we have the earlier sections, "Can We Ever Know Just through Observation?" (readings 45 to 49) and "Can We Ever Know Just through Reflection?" (readings 52 to 56). One presumption shared by those readings is that knowledge is only ever of what is *true*. Accordingly, we have been discussing *propositional* knowledge, knowledge-*that*. For example, we have asked whether you could know via reason *that* $7+5=12$; or whether you could know via observation *that* there is a fox beside your bed. In each case, the object of your knowledge – namely, "$7+5=12$" or "There is a fox beside the bed" – would be a truth, expressed as a proposition.

Gilbert Ryle, "Knowing How and Knowing That" [1946] (excerpts), in his *Collected Papers*, vol. 2 (London: Hutchinson, 1971). Reprinted with permission of Hertford College.

Metaphysics and Epistemology: A Guided Anthology, First Edition. Edited by Stephen Hetherington.

When philosophers talk of knowledge, almost always they mean to be designating propositional knowledge.

But perhaps there are also some quite different possible ways of knowing – even other *forms* of knowing. This reading argues for the existence and importance of one such form – knowing *how*. The reading is from Gilbert Ryle (1900–76), a very influential Oxford philosopher. His most significant book was *The Concept of Mind* (Hutchison, 1949), one chapter of which extends the ideas from this earlier succinct reading. Here we have Ryle's view of knowing-how – that is, one's knowing *how to do* something – and its fundamental conceptual distinctness from knowing-that. He is telling us that knowing-how and knowing-that are genuinely different ways of knowing. They are directed at different kinds of object – respectively, how to perform an action, and that such-and-such a proposition is true.

Nonetheless, might knowing-how somehow rely upon knowing-that? Does it even *involve* knowing-that in a subtle manner? Ryle argues against what he calls *intellectualism* – the view of knowledge-that as paramount in that way. Intellectualism portrays all actions that manifest knowledge-how (Ryle calls these intelligent actions) as being guided by knowledge-that. Suppose that you know how to ride a bicycle. Then (according to intellectualism) whenever you do actually ride one, your intelligent action of riding the bicycle is being guided by propositional knowledge you have about how bicycles are to be ridden. You would be applying some knowledge-that-this-is-what-to-do *in* performing your action of riding correctly.

Not so, though, if Ryle is right. On his anti-intellectualist account, one can have some knowledge-how that allows one to act intelligently; and this action can occur *without* one's needing to be applying any knowledge-that. You could be riding a bicycle because you know how to do so – without also having to know any *truths about* how to do so. In this sense, it is possible to have a kind of practical knowledge that need not include intellectual or conceptual knowledge.

In this paper, I try to exhibit part of the logical behaviour of the several concepts of intelligence, as these occur when we characterise either practical or theoretical activities as clever, wise, prudent, skilful, etc.

The prevailing doctrine [...] holds: (1) that Intelligence is a special faculty, the exercises of which are those specific internal acts which are called acts of thinking, namely, the operations of considering propositions; (2) that practical activities merit their titles 'intelligent', 'clever', and the rest only because they are accompanied by some such internal acts of considering propositions (and particularly 'regulative' propositions). That is to say, doing things is never itself an exercise of intelligence, but is, at best, a process introduced and somehow steered by some ulterior act of theorising.

[...]

In opposition to this doctrine, I try to show that intelligence is directly exercised as well in some practical performances as in some theoretical performances and that an intelligent performance need incorporate no 'shadow-act' of contemplating regulative propositions.

[...]

[...] I rely largely on variations of one argument. I argue that the prevailing doctrine leads to vicious regresses, and these in two directions. (1) If the intelligence exhibited in any act, practical or theoretical, is to be credited to the occurrence of some ulterior act of intelligently considering regulative propositions, no intelligent act, practical or theoretical, could ever begin. If no one possessed any money, no one could get any money on loan. This is the turn of the argument that I chiefly use. (2) If a deed, to be intelligent, has to be guided by the consideration of a regulative proposition, the gap between that consideration and the practical application of the regulation has to be bridged by some go-between process which cannot by the pre-supposed definition itself be an exercise of intelligence and cannot, by definition, be the resultant deed. This go-between application-process has somehow to marry observance of a contemplated maxim with the enforcement of behaviour. So it has to unite in itself the allegedly incompatible properties of being kith to theory and kin to practice, else it could not be the applying of the one in the other. For, unlike theory, it must be able to influence action, and, unlike impulses, it must be amenable to regulative propositions. Consistency requires, therefore, that this schizophrenic broker must again be subdivided into one bit which contemplates but does not execute, one which executes but does not contemplate and a third which reconciles these irreconcilables. And so on for ever.

[...]

Philosophers have not done justice to the distinction which is quite familiar to all of us between knowing that something is the case and knowing how to do things. In their theories of knowledge they concentrate on the discovery of truths or facts, and they either ignore the discovery of ways and methods of doing things or else they try to reduce it to the discovery of facts. They assume that intelligence equates with the contemplation of propositions and is exhausted in this contemplation.

I want to turn the tables and to prove that knowledge-how cannot be defined in terms of knowledge-that and further, that knowledge-how is a concept logically prior to the concept of knowledge-that. I hope to show that a number of notorious cruces [viz., "riddles"] and paradoxes remain insoluble if knowing-that is taken as the ideal model of all operations of intelligence. They are resolved if we see that a man's intelligence or stupidity is as directly exhibited in some of his doings as it is in some of his thinking.

Consider, first, our use of the various intelligence-predicates, namely, 'wise', 'logical', 'sensible', 'prudent', 'cunning', 'skilful', 'scrupulous', 'tasteful', 'witty', etc., with their converses 'unwise', 'illogical', 'silly', 'stupid', 'dull', 'unscrupulous', 'without taste', 'humourless', etc. What facts or what sorts of facts are known to the sensible which are not known to the silly? For example, what truths does the clever chess-player know which would be news to his stupid opponent? Obviously there is no truth or set of truths of which we could say, 'If only the stupid player had been informed of them, he would be a clever player,' or 'When once he had been apprised of these truths he would play well.' We can imagine a clever player generously imparting to his stupid opponent so many rules, tactical maxims, 'wrinkles', etc. that he could think of no more to tell him; his opponent might accept and memorise all of them, and be able and ready to recite them correctly on demand. Yet he might still play chess stupidly, that is, be unable intelligently to apply the maxims, etc.

The intellectualist (as I shall call him) might defend his case by objecting that the stupid player did not 'really' or 'fully' know these truths. He had them by heart; but this was perhaps just a set of verbal habits, like the schoolboy's rote-knowledge of the multiplication table. If he seriously and attentively considered these truths he would then be or become a clever player. Or, to modify the suggestion to avert an obvious rejoinder, if he seriously and attentively considered these truths not just while in bed or while in church but while playing chess, and especially if he considered the maxim relevant to a tactical predicament at the moment when he was involved in that predicament, then he would make the intelligent move. But, unfortunately, if he was stupid (*a*) he would be unlikely to tell himself the appropriate maxim at the moment when it was needed and (*b*) even if by luck this maxim did occur to him at the moment when it was needed, he might be too stupid to follow it. For he might not see that it was the appropriate maxim or if he did, he might not see how to apply it. In other words it requires intelligence not only to discover truths, but also to apply them, and knowing how to apply truths cannot, without setting up an infinite process, be reduced to knowledge of some extra bridge-truths. The application of maxims, etc., is certainly not any mere contemplation of them. Equally certainly it can be intelligently or stupidly done. [...]

To switch over to a different example. A pupil fails to follow an argument. He understands the premisses and he understands the conclusion. But he fails to see that the conclusion follows from the premisses. The teacher thinks him rather dull but tries to help. So he tells him that there is an ulterior proposition which he has not considered, namely, that *if these premisses are true, the conclusion is true*. The pupil understands this and dutifully recites it alongside the premisses, and still fails to see that the conclusion follows from the premisses even when accompanied by the assertion that these premisses entail this conclusion. So a second hypothetical proposition is added to his store; namely, that the conclusion is true if the premisses are true as well as the first hypothetical proposition that if the premisses are true the conclusion is true. And still the pupil fails to see. And so on for ever. He accepts rules in theory but this does not *force* him to apply them in practice. He considers reasons, but he fails to reason. (This is Lewis Carroll's puzzle in 'What the Tortoise said to Achilles'. I have met no successful attempt to solve it.)

What has gone wrong? Just this, that knowing how to reason was assumed to be analysable into the knowledge or supposal of some propositions, namely, (1) the special premisses, (2) the conclusion, plus (3) some extra propositions about the implication of the conclusion by the premisses, etc., etc., *ad infinitum*.

'Well but surely the intelligent reasoner *is* knowing rules of inference whenever he reasons intelligently.' Yes, of course he is, but knowing such a rule is not a case of knowing an extra fact or truth; it is knowing how to move from acknowledging some facts to acknowledging others. Knowing a rule of inference is not possessing a bit of extra information but being able to perform an intelligent operation. Knowing a rule is knowing how. It is realised in performances which conform to the rule, not in theoretical citations of it.

[...]

There is a not unfashionable shuffle which tries to circumvent these considerations by saying that the intelligent reasoner who has not been taught logic knows the logicians' formulae 'implicitly' but not 'explicitly'; or that the ordinary virtuous person has 'implicit' but not 'explicit' knowledge of the rules of right conduct; the skilful but untheoretical chess-player 'implicitly' acknowledges a lot of strategic and tactical maxims, though he never formulates them and might not recognise them if they were imparted to him by some Clausewitz of the game. This shuffle assumes that knowledge-how must be reducible to knowledge-that, while conceding that no operations of acknowledging-that need be actually found occurring. It fails to explain how, even if such acknowledgements did occur, their maker might still be a fool in his performance.

All this intellectualist legend must be rejected, not merely because it tells psychological myths but because the myths are not of the right type to account for the facts which they are invented to explain. However many strata of knowledge-that are postulated, the same crux always recurs that a fool might have all that knowledge without knowing how to perform, and a sensible or cunning person might know how to perform who had not been introduced to those postulated facts; that is, there still remains the same gulf, as wide as ever, between having the postulated knowledge of those facts and knowing how to use or apply it; between acknowledging principles in thought and intelligently applying them in action.

I must now try to speak more positively about what it is like to know-how. (a) When a person knows how to do things of a certain sort (e.g., make good jokes, conduct battles or behave at funerals), his knowledge is actualised or exercised in what he does. It is not exercised (save *per accidens* [viz., "by chance"]) in the propounding of propositions or in saying 'Yes' to those propounded by others. His intelligence is exhibited by deeds, not by internal or external dicta. A good experimentalist exercises his skill not in reciting maxims of technology but in making experiments. It is a ruinous but popular mistake to suppose that intelligence operates only in the production and manipulation of propositions, i.e., that only in ratiocinating are we rational. (b) When a person knows how to do things of a certain sort (e.g., cook omelettes, design dresses or persuade juries), his performance is in some way governed by principles, rules, canons, standards or criteria. (For most purposes it does not matter which we say.) It is always possible in principle, if not in practice, to explain why he tends to succeed, that is, to state the reasons for his actions. It is tautology to say that there is a method in his cleverness. But his observance of rules, principles, etc. must, if it is there at all, be realised in his performance of his tasks. It need not (though it can) be also advertised in an extra performance of paying some internal or external lip-service to those rules or principles. He *must* work judiciously; he *may* also propound judgments. For propounding judgments is just another special activity, which can itself be judiciously or injudiciously performed. Judging (or propositional thinking) is one (but only one) way of exercising judiciousness or betraying silliness; it has its own rules, principles and criteria, but again the intelligent application of these does not pre-require yet another lower stratum of judgments on how to think correctly.

In short the propositional acknowledgement of rules, reasons or principles is not the parent of the intelligent application of them; it is a step-child of that application.

[...]

There is a point to be expounded here. I have been arguing in effect that ratiocination is not the general condition of rational behaviour but only one species of it. Yet the traditional associations of the word 'rational' are such that it is commonly assumed that behaviour can only be rational if the overt actions taken are escorted by internal operations of considering and acknowledging the reasons for taking them, i.e., if we preach to ourselves before we practise. 'How else [it would be urged] could principles, rules, reasons, criteria, etc. govern performances, unless the agent thought of them while or before acting?' People equate rational behaviour with premeditated or reasoned behaviour, i.e., behaviour in which the agent internally persuades himself by arguments to do what he does. Among the premises of these postulated internal arguments will be the formulae expressing the principles, rules, criteria or reasons which govern the resultant intelligent actions. This whole story now seems to me false in fact and refutable in logic. We do not find in fact that we persuade ourselves by arguments to make or appreciate jokes. What sorts of arguments should we use? Yet it certainly requires intelligence or rationality to make and see jokes. But worse than this, when we do, as often happens, go through the process of persuading ourselves to do things, this process is itself one which can be intelligently or stupidly executed. So, if the assumption were correct, it would be necessary for us to start one stage further back and to persuade ourselves with second-order arguments to employ first-order persuasions of a cogent and not of a silly type. And so on *ad infinitum*. The assumption, that is, credits the rationality of any given performance to the rational execution of some anterior performance, which would in its turn require exactly the same treatment. So no rational performance could ever be begun. Aristotle's Practical Syllogism fails to explain intelligent conduct, since its explanation is circular. For the postulated syllogising would itself need to be intelligently conducted.

What has happened once again is that intellectualists have tried to explain prudence, say, or skill by reference to a piece of acknowledging-that, leaving unexplained the fact that this internal operation would itself have to be cannily executed. They have tried to explain, e.g., practical flair by reference to an intellectual process which, unfortunately for their theory, again requires flair.

[...]

[...] Sometimes we do go through the internal operation of persuading ourselves to do things, just as we often go through the external operation of persuading other people to do things. Let us suppose that the persuasion is cogent, i.e., that the recipient is convinced by it. What happens then? Does he necessarily do what he has been persuaded to do? Does he necessarily practise what he preaches? Notoriously not. I frequently persuade myself to smoke less, filling and lighting my pipe at the very moment when I am saying 'yes' to the conclusion of the argument. Like Medea, I listen and am convinced, but I do not obey. You say, 'Ah, but you weren't "really" or "effectively" convinced. You said "yes" in some theoretical or academic way, but you were not wise enough to say "yes" in the practical way of putting your pipe back in your pocket.' Certainly. This proves that unwisdom in conduct cannot be defined in terms of the omission of any ratiocinations and consequently that wisdom in conduct cannot be defined solely in terms of the performance of any ratiocinations. The intelligent application in practice of principles, reasons, standards, etc. is not a legatee of the consideration of them in theory; it can and normally does occur without any such consideration. Indeed we could not consider principles of method in theory unless we or others already intelligently applied them in practice. Acknowledging the maxims of a practice presupposes knowing how to perform it. Rules, like birds, must live before they can be stuffed.

We certainly can, in respect of many practices, like fishing, cooking and reasoning, extract principles from their applications by people who know how to fish, cook and reason. Hence Izaak Walton, Mrs Beeton and Aristotle. But when we try to express these principles we find that they cannot easily be put in the indicative mood. They fall automatically into the imperative mood. Hence comes the awkwardness for the intellectualist theories of stating what are the truths or facts which we acknowledge when we acknowledge a rule or maxim. We cannot call an imperative a truth or falsehood. The Moral Law refuses to behave like a fact. You cannot affirm or deny Mrs Beeton's recipes. So, in the hope of having it both ways, they tend to speak guardedly of the 'validity' rather than the 'truth' of such regulative propositions, an idiom which itself betrays qualms about the reduction of knowing-how to knowing-that.

What is the use of such formulae if the acknowledgement of them is not a condition of knowing how to act but a derivative product of theorising about the nerves of such knowledge? The answer is simple. They are useful pedagogically, namely, in lessons to those who are still learning how to act. They belong to manuals for novices. They are not quasi-premises in the postulated self-persuasions of those who know how to act; for no such self-persuasions occur. They are imperative because they are disciplinary, because they are in the idiom of the mentor. They are banisters for toddlers, i.e., they belong to the methodology and not to the methods of intelligent practices. What logicians have long half-realised about the *venue* and functions of their rule-formulae has yet to be learned by moral philosophers about their imperatives and ought-statements. When they have learned this they will cease to ask such questions as whether conscience is an intuitive or discursive faculty. For knowing how to behave is not a sort of knowing-that, so it is neither an intuitive nor a discursive sort of knowing-that [...]

One last point. I have, I hope, proved that knowing-how is not reducible to any sandwich of knowing-that, and that our intelligence-predicates are definable in terms of knowing-how. I now want to prove that knowing-that presupposes knowing-how.

(1) To know a truth, I must have discovered or established it. But discovering and establishing are intelligent operations, requiring rules of method, checks, tests, criteria, etc. A scientist or an historian is primarily a man who knows how to decide certain sorts of questions. Only secondarily is he a man who has discovered a lot of facts, i.e., has achieved successes in his application of these rules etc. (though of course he only learns how to discover through exercises in discovery; he does not begin by perfecting his method and only later go on to have successes in applying it). A scientist, that is, is primarily a knower-how and only secondarily a knower-that. He couldn't discover any particular truths unless he knew how to discover. He could know how to discover, without making this or that particular discovery.

[...]

(2) Effective possession of a piece of knowledge that involves knowing how to use that knowledge, when required, for the solution of other theoretical or practical problems. There is a distinction between the museum-possession and the workshop-possession of knowledge. A silly person can be stocked with information, yet never know how to answer particular questions.

The uneducated public erroneously equates education with the imparting of knowing-that. Philosophers have not hitherto made it very clear what its error is. I hope I have provided part of the correction.

58

Is Knowing One's Intention-in-Action a Distinct Way of Knowing?

G.E.M. Anscombe, *Intention*

With the previous reading, we met Gilbert Ryle's much-discussed conception of the nature and epistemological significance of knowing-how. That kind of knowledge has often been called practical knowledge, since it is one's knowing how to *do* something, how to *act* in this way or that. But the concept of practical knowledge could include more besides. Of course, there is the colloquial sense of "practical knowledge" – useful knowledge. However, that is not a different *form* of knowledge. What this reading from Elizabeth Anscombe introduces us to is a kind of practical knowledge that she would claim is different in form.

It is an aspect of knowing an action *as one's own* action. Imagine walking deliberately towards a fox. You know that this is what you are doing. There is something you thereby know which you could not know when knowing that someone *else* is walking towards the same fox. What is that "something" though?

It is knowledge of an aspect of yourself, knowledge you lack of anyone else. But it is not (argues Anscombe) simply knowledge of a *truth* about you that somehow exists already, waiting in place, able to be known once you focus attention upon it. Rather, it is knowledge you create even as you also create that part of reality of which this knowledge is knowledge. It is knowledge you have of an intention of yours *in* action – an intention that is equally part of *what* you are knowing and of *how* you are knowing it. You know that you are intending to walk towards the fox. You know that you are acting on that intention. You thus know something vital about how you are acting. And your acting *is* partly your having this intention and this knowledge of it.

G.E.M. Anscombe, *Intention* [1957], 2nd edn. (Cambridge, MA: Harvard University Press, 2000), pp. 56–57, 82–83, 84–89 (excerpts). Copyright © 1957, 1963 by G.E.M. Anscombe. Reprinted with permission of Harvard University Press.

Indeed (according to Anscombe), you could have that knowledge even if the fox had suddenly left the scene and if you were not yet aware of its departing. There is still a sense in which you know what you are doing – a sense not requiring the world *beyond* your thoughts of it at this moment to be quite as you would describe it. In intending to walk towards the fox, you know that this is what you are doing – even if the fox is no longer there.

Anscombe called this a kind of practical knowledge (even as she was aware of the Rylean tradition of applying the concept of practical knowledge primarily to knowing-how). She thought of such knowledge as fundamentally different in kind to what she termed *contemplative* knowledge. The latter is knowledge-that, being propositional in form. It is often observational in origin. Crucially, it is of facts existing in themselves, apart from whether they are known: it amounts to gazing upon those independently existing facts. But the kind of practical knowledge being highlighted by Anscombe is not like that. It is creative. It is some of the knowledge involved, by being created, in one's acting intentionally. You know that you are walking towards a fox, in part by knowing that you intend to be walking towards it. This knowing is itself part of the intending. It is knowledge of an active reality – the intending – that is being *created* partly by the knowing itself.

32.   Let us consider a man going round a town with a shopping list in his hand. Now it is clear that the relation of this list to the things he actually buys is one and the same whether his wife gave him the list or it is his own list; and that there is a different relation when a list is made by a detective following him about. If he made the list itself, it was an expression of intention; if his wife gave it him, it has the role of an order. What then is the identical relation to what happens, in the order and the intention, which is not shared by the record? It is precisely this: if the list and the things that the man actually buys do not agree, and if this and this alone constitutes a *mistake*, then the mistake is not in the list but in the man's performance (if his wife were to say: 'Look, it says butter and you have bought margarine', he would hardly reply: 'What a mistake! we must put that right' and alter the word on the list to 'margarine'); whereas if the detective's record and what the man actually buys do not agree, then the mistake is in the record.

In the case of a discrepancy between the shopping list and what the man buys, I have to introduce the qualification: If this and this alone constitutes a mistake. For the discrepancy might arise because some of the things were not to be had and if one might have known they were not to be had, we might speak of a mistake (an error of judgment) in constructing the list. If I go out in Oxford with a shopping list including 'tackle for catching sharks', no one will think of it as a mistake in performance that I fail to come back with it. And then again there may be a discrepancy between the list and what the man bought because he changed his mind and decided to buy something else instead.

This last discrepancy of course only arises when the description is of a future action. The case that we now want to consider is that of an agent who says what he is at present doing. Now suppose what he says is not true. It may be untrue because, unknown to the agent, something is not the case which would have to be the case in order for his statement to be true; as when, unknown to the man pumping, there was a hole in the pipe round the corner. But as I said, this relates to his statement that he is replenishing the water-supply as does the fact that the man has no teeth of his own to the order 'Clench your teeth'; that is, we may say that in face of it his statement falls to the ground, as in that case the order falls to the ground, but it is not a direct contradiction. But is there not possible another case in which a man is *simply* not doing what he says? As when I say to myself 'Now I press Button A' – pressing Button B – a thing which can certainly happen. This I will call the *direct* falsification of what I say. And here, to use Theophrastus' expression again, the mistake is not one of judgment but of performance. That is, we do *not* say: What you *said* was a mistake, because it was supposed to describe what you did and did not describe it, but: What you *did* was a mistake, because it was not in accordance with what you said.

It is precisely analogous to obeying an order wrong – and we ought to be struck by the fact that there is such a thing, and that it is not the same as ignoring, disregarding, or disobeying an order. If the order is given 'Left turn!' and the man turns right, there can be clear signs that this was not an act of disobedience. But there is a discrepancy between the language and that of which the language is a description. But the discrepancy does not impute a fault to the language – but to the event.

Can it be that there is something that modern philosophy has blankly misunderstood: namely what ancient and medieval philosophers meant by *practical knowledge*? Certainly in modern philosophy we have an incorrigibly contemplative conception of knowledge. Knowledge must be something that is judged as such by being in accordance with the facts. The facts, reality, are prior, and dictate what is to be said, if it is knowledge. And this is the explanation of the utter darkness in which we found ourselves. For if there are two knowledges – one by observation, the other in intention – then it looks as if there must be two objects of knowledge; but if one says the objects are the same, one looks hopelessly for the different *mode of contemplative knowledge* in acting, as if there were a very queer and special sort of seeing eye in the middle of the acting.

[...]

45. We can now consider 'practical knowledge'. Imagine someone directing a project, like the erection of a building which he cannot see and does not get reports on, purely by giving orders. His imagination (evidently a superhuman one) takes the place of the perception that would ordinarily be employed by the director of such a project. He is not like a man merely considering speculatively how a thing might be done; such a man can leave many points unsettled, but this man must settle everything in *a* right order. *His* knowledge of what is done is practical knowledge.

But what is this 'knowledge of what is done'? First and foremost, he can say what the house is like. But it may be objected that he can only say 'This is what the house is like, if my orders have been obeyed'. But isn't he then like someone saying 'This – namely, what my imagination suggests – is what is the case if what I have imagined is true'?

I wrote 'I am a fool' on the blackboard with my eyes shut. Now when I said what I wrote, ought I to have said: this is what I am writing, if my intention is getting executed; instead of simply: this is what I am writing?

Orders, however, can be disobeyed, and intentions fail to get executed. That intention for example would not have been executed if something had gone wrong with the chalk or the surface, so that the words did not appear. And my knowledge would have been the same even if this had happened. If then my knowledge is independent of what actually happens, how can it be knowledge of what does happen? Someone might say that it was a funny sort of knowledge that was still knowledge even though what it was knowledge of was not the case! On the other hand Theophrastus' remark holds good: 'the mistake is in the performance, not in the judgment'.

Hence we can understand the temptation to make the real object of willing just an idea, like William James [mentioned earlier, at p.355]. For that certainly comes into being; or if it does not, then there was no willing and so no problem. But we can in fact produce a case where someone effects something just by saying it is so, thus fulfilling the ideal for an act of will as perfectly as possible. This happens if someone admires a possession of mine and I say 'It's yours!', thereby giving it him. But of course this is possible only because property is conventional.

[...]

47.   [...] [T]hus there are many descriptions of happenings which are directly dependent on our possessing the *form* of description of intentional actions. It is easy not to notice this, because it is perfectly possible for some of these descriptions to be of what is done unintentionally. For example 'offending someone'; one can do this unintentionally, but there would be no such thing if it were never the description of an intentional action. And 'putting up an advertisement upside down', which would perhaps mostly be unintentional, is a description referring to advertisements, which are essentially intentional; again, the kind of action done in 'putting up' is intentional if not somnambulistic. Or 'going into reverse', which can be intentional or unintentional, is not a concept that would exist apart from the existence of engines, the description of which brings in intentions. If one simply attends to the fact that many actions can be either intentional or unintentional, it can be quite natural to think that events which are characterisable as intentional or unintentional are a certain natural class, 'intentional' being an extra property which a philosopher must try to describe.

In fact the term 'intentional' has reference to a *form* of description of events. What is essential to this form is displayed by the results of our enquiries into the question 'Why?' Events are typically described in this form when 'in order to' or 'because' (in one sense) is attached to their descriptions: 'I slid on the ice because I felt cheerful'. 'Sliding on ice' is not itself a type of description, like 'offending someone', which is directly dependent on our possessing the form of description of intentional actions. Thus we can speak of the form of description 'intentional actions', and of the descriptions which can occur *in* this form, and note that of these some are and some are not dependent on the existence of this form for their own sense.

The class of such descriptions which *are* so dependent is a very large, and the most important, section of those descriptions of things effected by the movements of human beings which go to make up the history of a human being's day or life. A short list of examples of such descriptions should bring this out. I assume a whole body as subject, and divide the list into two columns; the left hand one contains descriptions in which a happening may be intentional or unintentional, the right hand one those which can only be voluntary or intentional (except that the first few members could be somnambulistic).

Intruding	Telephoning
Offending	Calling
Coming to possess	Groping
Kicking (and other descriptions	Crouching
connoting characteristically	Greeting
animal movement)	Signing, signalling
Abandoning, leaving alone	Paying, selling, buying
Dropping (transitive),	Hiring, dismissing
holding, picking up	Sending for
Switching (on, off)	Marrying, contracting
Placing, arranging	

The role of intention in the descriptions in the right hand column will be obvious; 'Crouching' will probably be the only one that occasions any doubt. The left hand column will strike anyone as a very mixed set. Both include things that can, and things that cannot, be done by animals; something involving encounters with artefacts, like switching on or off, can of course be effected by an inanimate object; but the description only exists because we make switches to be switched on and off.

With what right do I include other members in this list? They are all descriptions which go beyond physics: one might call them vital descriptions. A dog's curled tail might have something stuck in it, but that of itself would not make us speak of the dog as holding the object with its tail; but if he has taken between his teeth and kept there some moderate-sized object, he is holding it. To speak of the wind as picking things up and putting them down again is to animalize it in our language, and so also if we speak of a cleft in rocks as holding something; though not if we speak of something as held there by the cleft. Trees, we may say, drop their leaves or their fruit (as cows drop calves); this is because they are living organisms (we should never speak of a tap as dropping its drips of water), but means no more to us than that the leaves or fruit drop off them. These descriptions are all basically at least animal. The 'characteristically animal movements' are movements with a normal role in the sensitive, and therefore appetitive, life of animals. The other descriptions suggest backgrounds in which characteristic things are done – e.g. the reactions to an intruder.

Since I have defined intentional action in terms of language – the special question 'Why?' – it may seem surprising that I should introduce intention-dependent concepts with special reference to their application to animals, which have no language. Still, we certainly ascribe intention to animals. The reason is precisely that we describe what they do in a manner perfectly characteristic of the use of intention concepts: we describe what *further* they are doing *in* doing something (the latter description being *more* immediate, nearer to the merely physical): the cat is stalking a bird *in* crouching and slinking along with its eye fixed on the bird and its whiskers twitching. The enlarged description of what the cat is doing is not all that characterises it as an intention (for enlarged descriptions are possible of any event that has describable effects), but to this is added the cat's perception of the bird, and what it does if it catches it. The two features, knowledge and enlarged description, are quite characteristic of description of intention in acting. Just as we naturally say 'The cat thinks there is a mouse coming', so we also naturally ask: Why is the cat crouching and slinking like that? and give the answer: It's stalking that bird; see, its eye is fixed on it. We do this, though the cat can utter no thoughts, and cannot give expression to any knowledge of its own action, or to any intentions either.

48. We can now see that a great many of our descriptions of events effected by human beings are *formally* descriptions of executed intentions. That this is so for descriptions of the type in the right hand column is evident enough. But this might be explained by saying that intention is required (as an extra feature) by the definitions of the concepts employed. This, it might be said, is no more than a quasi-legal point, or even an actual one in the case of marriage, for example. But even here it might strike someone as curious that in general special proof of intention is not required; it is special proof of lack of it (because one of the parties did not know the nature of the ceremony, for example) that would invalidate a marriage.

Surprising as it may seem, the failure to execute intentions is necessarily the rare exception. This seems surprising because the failure to achieve what one would finally like to achieve is common. [...] It often happens for people to do things for pleasure and perhaps get none or little, or for health without success, or for virtue or freedom with complete failure; and these failures interest us. What is necessarily the rare exception is for a man's performance in its more immediate descriptions not to be what he supposes. Further, it is the agent's knowledge of what he is doing that gives the descriptions under which what is going on is the execution of an intention.

If we put these considerations together, we can say that where (*a*) the description of an event is of a type to be formally the description of an executed intention (*b*) the event is actually the execution of an intention (by our criteria) then the account given by Aquinas[1] of the nature of practical knowledge holds: Practical knowledge is 'the cause of what it understands', unlike 'speculative' knowledge, which 'is derived from the objects known'. This means more than that practical knowledge is observed to be a necessary condition of the production of various results; or that an idea of doing such-and-such in such-and-such ways is such a condition. It means that without it what happens does not come under the description – execution of intentions – whose characteristics we have been investigating. This can seem a mere *extra* feature of events whose description would otherwise be the same, only if we concentrate on small sections of action and slips which can occur in them.

'Practical knowledge' is of course a common term of ordinary language, no doubt by inheritance from the Aristotelian philosophy. For that philosophy has conferred more terms on ordinary language than any other, in senses more, or less, approximating to those of Aristotle himself: 'matter', 'substance', 'principle', 'essence' come readily to mind; and 'practical knowledge' is one of them. A man has practical knowledge who knows how to do things; but that is an insufficient description, for he *might* be said to know how to do things if he could give a lecture on it, though he was helpless when confronted with the task of doing them. When we ordinarily speak of practical knowledge we have in mind a certain sort of general capacity in a particular field; but if we hear of a capacity, it is reasonable to ask what constitutes an exercise of it. E.g., if my knowledge of the alphabet by rote is a capacity, this capacity is exercised when I repeat these noises, starting at any letter. In the case of practical knowledge the exercise of the capacity is nothing but the doing or supervising of the operations of which a man has practical knowledge; but this not *just* the coming about of certain effects, like my recitation of the alphabet or of bits of it, for what he effects is formally characterised as subject to our question 'Why?' whose application displays the A–D order which we discovered.

Naturally my imaginary case, in which a man directs operations which he does not see and of which he gets no information, is a very improbable one. Normally someone doing or directing anything makes use of his senses, or of reports given him, the whole time: he will not go on to the next order, for example, until he knows that the preceding one has been executed, or, if he is the operator, his senses inform him of what is going on. This knowledge is of course always 'speculative' as opposed to 'practical'. Thus in any operation we really can speak of two knowledges – the account that one could give of what one was doing, without adverting to observation; and the account of exactly what is happening at a given moment (say) to the material one is working on. The one is practical, the other speculative.

Although the term 'practical knowledge' is most often used in connexion with specialised skills, there is no reason to think that this notion has application only in such contexts. 'Intentional action' always presupposes what might be called 'knowing one's way about' the matters described in the description under which an action can be called intentional, and this knowledge is exercised in the action and is practical knowledge.

Notes

1.   *Summa Theologica*, Ia IIae, Q3, art. 5, obj. 1.

59

Is Knowing via What Others Say or Write a Distinct Way of Knowing?

Jennifer Lackey, "Knowing from Testimony"

Epistemologists have long sought to describe the *ways* in which people can know. More pressingly, that epistemological aim has been to catalogue and understand our conceptually *basic* ways of knowing. In this book we have considered several candidates: observation, reason, innateness, knowing-how, knowing one's intention in action. Now we consider *testimony*. Manifestly, people live partly by treating other people – those people's words, written or spoken – as a way of gaining knowledge. Friends, teachers, family members, public speakers, journalists, and so on: almost every day of your cognitive life contains reliance on other people for one view after another. Are all of those views giving you knowledge? Probably not. Are some or even many of them doing so? We tend to assume so.

Yet even if we are correct in that assumption, would reliance upon what others say or write be a conceptually *basic* way of gaining knowledge? This is the question of whether testimony *in itself* can impart knowledge. No epistemologist would say that testimony always imparts knowledge. Still, whenever it does do so, is this because it has satisfied a standard apt specifically for testimonial knowledge? Or is there instead a further kind of knowledge underwriting the testimony? For example, do you gain knowledge via testimony only when you have gathered enough *observational* knowledge to support a belief in the trustworthiness of the person talking to you? If so, her testimony as such is not functioning as a conceptually basic source of knowledge for you. If testimony only ever imparts knowledge because of "background" non-testimonial knowledge, then describing

Jennifer Lackey, "Knowing from Testimony" (excerpts), *Philosophy Compass* 1 (2006), 432–448. Cuts made with approval. Reprinted with permission of John Wiley & Sons Ltd.

testimony as a distinct way of knowing would amount merely to a conversation-
ally convenient shorthand for speaking of how observation, reason, and so on can
impart knowledge.

Jennifer Lackey (b. 1972), from Northwestern University, is a prominent
voice within contemporary discussions of this issue. She has helped epistemologists to realize how important such discussions can be. In this reading, she
explains the key epistemological question, mentioned just now, of whether
testimony is a conceptually basic source of knowledge. In practice, testimony
is treated as fundamental: people often do accept, as knowledge, beliefs they
gain simply from hearing or reading other people's words. But again, our question is that of whether testimony is *conceptually* fundamental: is mentioning a
belief's testimonial source ever sufficient for explaining why the belief is
knowledge?

This reading also includes one of Lackey's distinctive discussions of the nature
of testimonial knowledge. Even considered apart from whether it is a conceptually basic form of knowledge, what are testimonial knowledge's important
features? Imagine being told by a friend that a fox is in your garden, awaiting
your return home. If you are thereby to gain knowledge of the fox's presence,
must your friend be imparting knowledge she already has herself? Or might
there be something sufficiently apt about her saying what she says, *irrespective* of
whether she believes it in a way that constitutes her knowing it? Could she give
you knowledge *she* lacks?

Testimony is a vital and ubiquitous source of knowledge. We rely on the reports of others for
our beliefs about the food we eat, the medicine we ingest, the products we buy, the geography of the world, discoveries in science, historical information, and many other areas that
play crucial roles in both our practical and our intellectual lives. Even many of our most
important beliefs about ourselves were learned at an earlier time from our parents and care-
takers, such as the date of our birth, the identity of our parents, our ethnic backgrounds, and
so on. Were we to refrain from accepting the testimony of others, our lives would be impov-
erished in startling and debilitating ways.

Despite the vital role that testimony occupies in our epistemic lives, traditional epistemological theories have focused primarily on other sources, such as sense perception, memory,
and reason, with relatively little attention devoted specifically to testimony. In recent years,
however, the epistemic significance of testimony has been more fully appreciated, and the
current literature has benefited from the publication of a considerable amount of interesting
and innovative work in this area. I shall here focus on two questions that have received the
most attention in recent work in the epistemology of testimony. First, is testimonial knowledge acquired only by being *transmitted* from speaker to hearer? Second, must a hearer have
positive reasons to justifiedly accept a speaker's testimony?

1. Testimony and Testimony-Based Belief

The central concern in contemporary discussions of the epistemology of testimony has not been what testimony is, but, rather, how we successfully acquire justified belief or knowledge on the basis of what other people tell us. As a result, it is typical for those who are interested in the epistemic status of testimonial beliefs to embrace a very broad notion of what it is to testify. So, for instance, Elizabeth Fricker holds that the domain of testimony that is of epistemological interest is that of "tellings generally" with "no restrictions either on subject matter, or on the speaker's epistemic relation to it." Similarly, Robert Audi claims that in accounting for testimonial knowledge and justification, we must understand testimony as "… people's telling us things." And Ernest Sosa embraces "… a broad sense of testimony that counts posthumous publications as examples … [it] requires only that it be a statement of someone's thoughts or beliefs, which they might direct to the world at large and to no one in particular."

But clearly not everything we learn through the testimony of others qualifies as *testimonially based* knowledge. For instance, suppose you hear me say: "ten people have spoken in this room today" and, having counted the previous nine, come to know that ten people have spoken in this room today. Here, although my statement is causally relevant to your forming this belief, the basis of your knowledge is perceptual, not testimonial; it results from your having heard and counted the speakers. […] What is important for distinctively testimonial justification or knowledge is that a hearer form a given belief *on the basis of the content of a speaker's testimony*. So cases […] where a belief is formed entirely on the basis of features *about* the speaker's testimony are precluded from qualifying as instances of *testimonial* justification or knowledge.

There are also intermediate cases in which a hearer has relevant background information and uses it to derive knowledge from the statement of a speaker. Suppose, for example, that you know from past experience that I report that there is no milk in the refrigerator only when there is some. Now when I report to you that there is no milk in the refrigerator, you may supplement my testimony with your background information and thereby derive knowledge that there is milk in the refrigerator. Because the epistemic status of beliefs formed in these types of cases relies so heavily on memory and inference, the resulting justification and knowledge are only partially testimonially based. Hence, such beliefs may fall outside the scope of theories purporting to capture only those beliefs that are entirely based on testimony.

2. Transmission of Epistemic Properties

Most current views in the epistemology of testimony are built around a central thesis, which we may call the *Transmission of Epistemic Properties* (hereafter, TEP). According to TEP, a testimonial exchange involves a speaker's belief, along with the epistemic properties it possesses, being *transmitted* to a hearer. […] Support for this view, […] derives from a purported analogy between testimony and memory. Just as memory is thought to be capable of only *preserving* epistemic properties from one time to another – and cannot therefore *generate* new epistemic properties – testimony is said to be capable of only *transmitting* epistemic properties from one person to another. So, on this view, just as I cannot know that p on the basis of memory unless I non-memorially knew that p at an earlier time, a hearer cannot know that p on the basis of testimony unless the speaker from whom it was acquired herself knows that p. [...]

Recently, however, objections have been raised to [...] TEP, thereby calling into question the widely accepted view that transmission lies at the heart of the epistemology of testimony. [...] The first type involves speakers who fail to believe, and hence know, a proposition to which they are testifying, but nevertheless reliably convey the information in question through their testimony. So, for instance, consider the following:

> Clarissa is a devoutly Christian fourth-grade teacher whose faith includes a firm belief in the truth of creationism and an equally firm belief in the falsity of evolutionary theory. Nevertheless, Clarissa recognizes that there is an overwhelming amount of scientific evidence against both of these beliefs. Indeed, she readily admits that she is not basing her own commitment to creationism on evidence at all but, rather, on the personal faith that she has in an all-powerful Creator. Because of this, Clarissa does not think that she should impose her religious convictions on her fourth-grade students. Instead, she regards her duty as a teacher to include presenting material that is best supported by the available evidence, which clearly includes the truth of evolutionary theory. As a result, while presenting her biology lesson today, she asserts to her students "Modern-day *Homo sapiens* evolved from *Homo erectus*." Although Clarissa neither believes nor knows this proposition, her students form the corresponding true belief on the basis of her reliable testimony.

What [this case] reveals is that an *unreliable believer* may nonetheless be a *reliable testifier*, and so may reliably convey knowledge (justified belief, warranted belief) to a hearer despite the fact that she fails to possess it herself. For although Clarissa herself ignores the relevant scientific evidence concerning evolutionary theory and thus lacks the belief that modern-day *Homo sapiens* evolved from *Homo erectus*, she bases her testimony regarding this topic firmly on such evidence. This enables Clarissa to impart knowledge (justified belief, warranted belief) to her students that she fails to possess herself.

[...]

One of the central conclusions that the above considerations motivate is the replacement of TEP [...] with conditions focusing on the *statements* of speakers rather than on their states of believing or knowing. For instance, [...] when unreliable believers are nonetheless reliable testifiers, speakers can impart knowledge (justified belief, warranted belief) to hearers that they fail to possess themselves. This motivates [...] the following *Reliability of the Statement-Necessity* thesis (RS-N):

> RS-N: For every speaker, A, and hearer, B, B's belief that p is known (justified, warranted) on the basis of A's testimony that p only if A's statement that p is reliable or otherwise truth-conducive.

[...]

3. Non-Reductionism and Reductionism

What precisely is needed in order for a hearer to be justified in accepting the testimony of a speaker? This question lies at the center of the epistemology of testimony and the current philosophical literature contains two main options for answering it: *non-reductionism* and *reductionism*.

According to non-reductionists – whose historical roots are standardly traced back to the work of Thomas Reid – testimony is *just as basic* a source of justification (warrant, knowledge) as sense perception, memory, inference, and the like. Accordingly, so as long as there are no relevant undefeated defeaters, hearers can justifiedly accept the assertions of speakers *merely* on the basis of a speaker's testimony. Otherwise put, so long as there is no available evidence *against* accepting a speaker's report, the hearer has no positive epistemic work to do in order to justifiedly accept the testimony in question.

There are two different kinds of defeaters that are typically taken to be relevant. First, there are what we might call *psychological defeaters*. A psychological defeater is a doubt or belief that is had by S that indicates that S's belief that *p* is either false or unreliably formed or sustained. Defeaters in this sense function by virtue of being *had* by S, regardless of their truth value or justificatory status. Second, there are what we might call *normative defeaters*. A normative defeater is a doubt or belief that S *ought to have* that indicates that S's belief that *p* is either false or unreliably formed or sustained. Defeaters in this sense function by virtue of being doubts or beliefs that S *should have* (whether or not S does have them) given the presence of certain available evidence. The underlying thought here is that certain kinds of doubts and beliefs contribute epistemically unacceptable *irrationality* to doxastic systems and, accordingly, justification and knowledge can be defeated or undermined by their presence.

Moreover, a defeater may itself be either defeated or undefeated. Suppose, for instance, that Holly believes that there is a hawk nesting in her backyard because she saw it there this afternoon, but Dominick tells her, and she thereby comes to believe, that the bird is instead a falcon. Now, the justification Holly had for believing that there is a hawk in her backyard has been defeated by her belief that the bird is a falcon. But since psychological defeaters can themselves be beliefs, they, too, are candidates for defeat. For instance, suppose that Holly consults a bird guidebook to check whether the bird in her backyard is a falcon and she discovers that it is in fact a Cooper's hawk. In this case, the belief that she acquires from the bird book provides her with a psychological defeater for the belief that she acquired via Dominick's testimony, and hence it provides her with a *defeater-defeater* for her original belief that there is a hawk nesting in her backyard. And, as should be suspected, defeater-defeaters can also be defeated by further doubts and beliefs, which, in turn, can be defeated by further doubts and beliefs, and so on. Similar considerations involving reasons, rather than doubts and beliefs, apply in the case of normative defeaters. Now, when one has a defeater *d* for one's belief that *p* that is not itself defeated, one has what is called an *undefeated defeater* for one's belief that *p*. It is the presence of undefeated defeaters, not merely defeaters, that is incompatible with testimonial justification (warrant, knowledge).

In contrast to non-reductionism, reductionists – whose historical roots are typically traced back to the work of David Hume – maintain that in order to justifiedly accept the testimony of speakers, more is needed than the mere absence of undefeated defeaters. In particular, proponents of reductionism argue that hearers must have sufficiently good *positive reasons* for accepting a given report, reasons that are not themselves ineliminably based on the testimony of others. Typically, these reasons are the result of induction: for instance, we observe a general conformity between facts and reports and, with the aid of memory and reason, we inductively infer that certain speakers, contexts, or types of reports are reliable sources of information. In this way, the justification of testimony is *reduced* to the justification we have for sense perception, memory, and inductive inference.

There are, however, at least two different answers given to what *relata* [viz., "the items related by the relation"] are involved in the relevant testimonial reductions. The first answer – a view often called *global reductionism* – is that the justification of *testimony as a source of belief* reduces to the justification of sense perception, memory, and inductive inference. In particular, global reductionists maintain that in order to justifiedly accept a speaker's report, a hearer must have non-testimonially based positive reasons for believing that *testimony is generally reliable*. The second version of reductionism – often called *local reductionism* – is that the justification of *each particular report or instance of testimony* reduces to the justification of instances of sense perception, memory, and inductive inference. Specifically, local reductionists claim that in order to justifiedly accept a speaker's testimony, a hearer must have non-testimonially based positive reasons for accepting *the particular report in question*.

Motivation for preferring non-reductionism over reductionism derives in large part from considering problems that are said to face the latter but not the former. Let us begin with two objections targeting the global version of reductionism. The first is that in order to have non-testimonially based positive reasons that testimony is generally reliable, one would have to be exposed not only to a non-random, wide-ranging sample of reports, but also to a non-random, wide-ranging sample of the corresponding facts. But both are said to be problematic. With respect to the reports, most of us have been exposed only to a very limited range of reports from speakers in our native language in a handful of communities in our native country. This limited sample of reports provides only a fraction of what would be required to legitimately conclude that testimony is *generally* reliable. With respect to the corresponding facts, a similar problem arises: the observational base of ordinary epistemic agents is simply far too small to allow the requisite induction about the reliability of testimony. [...] Moreover, with many reports, such as those involving complex scientific, economic, or mathematical theories, most of us simply lack the conceptual machinery needed to properly check the reports against the facts. Global reductionism, then, is said to ultimately lead to skepticism about testimonial knowledge, at least for most epistemic agents. Obviously, since non-reductionism does not require that a hearer have any positive beliefs about the general reliability of testimony, such a view does not face any problem of this sort.

A second objection raised against global reductionism is that it is questionable whether there even is an epistemically significant *fact of the matter* regarding the general reliability of testimony. To see this, consider, for instance, the following epistemically heterogeneous list of types of reports, all of which are subsumed under "testimony in general": reports about the time of day, what one had for breakfast, the achievements of one's children, whether one's loved one looks attractive in a certain outfit, the character of one's political opponents, one's age and weight, one's criminal record, and so on. Some of these types of reports may be generally highly reliable (e.g. about the time of day and what one had for breakfast), others generally highly unreliable (e.g. about the achievements of one's children, the looks of one's loved ones, and the character of one's political opponents), yet others generally very epistemically mixed, depending on the speaker (e.g. about one's age, weight, and criminal record). Because of this epistemic heterogeneity, it is doubtful, not only whether "testimony" picks out an epistemically interesting or unified *kind*, but also whether it even makes sense to talk about testimony being a *generally reliable source*. [...] Once again, non-reductionism is said to avoid this type of problem since such a view does not require any positive beliefs about the general reliability of testimony.

Let us now turn to two central problems that are said to face the local version of reductionism. The first is that young children clearly acquire a great deal of knowledge from their parents and teachers, and it is doubtful that they possess – or even could possess – positive reasons for accepting much of what they are told. For instance, an 18-month-old baby may come to know that the stove is hot from the testimony of her mother, but it is unclear whether she has the cognitive sophistication to have reasons for believing her mother to be a reliable source of information. Given this, reductionists may be hard-pressed to explain how such young subjects could possess all of the knowledge they appear to have. In contrast, since the only evidential condition non-reductionists require is the absence of undefeated defeaters – a condition that can clearly be satisfied by even the most cognitively immature subjects – such a view can easily account for the testimonial knowledge possessed by young children.

The second problem that is said to face local reductionism is that most of us frequently acquire testimonial knowledge from speakers about whom we know very little. For instance, upon arriving in Chicago for the first time, I may receive accurate directions to Navy Pier from the first passerby I see. Most agree that such a transaction can result in my acquiring testimonial knowledge of Navy Pier's whereabouts, despite the fact that my positive reasons for accepting the directions in question – if indeed I possess any – are scanty at best. Once again, since the only condition required of hearers by non-reductionism is the absence of undefeated defeaters, such a view of testimony is able to accommodate this kind of knowledge with no difficulty.

Support for preferring reductionism over non-reductionism derives primarily from considering the consequences of not requiring any positive epistemic work from recipients of testimony. For notice that non-reductionists commit themselves to saying that testimonial justification (warrant, knowledge) can be acquired in the complete absence of *any* positive reasons on the part of the hearer. So, for instance, consider the following:

> George, an average human being, is taking a walk through the forest one sunny morning and he sees someone in the distance. Although the individual's physical appearance enables George to identify her as an alien from another planet, he does not know anything about either this kind of alien or the planet from which she comes. When George catches up to the alien, she turns to him and immediately says in what sounds like English that tigers have eaten some of the inhabitants of her planet. Without hesitation, George forms the corresponding belief that tigers have eaten some of the inhabitants of the alien's planet. It turns out that the alien does, in fact, communicate in English, tigers have eaten some of the inhabitants of her planet, and she is a reliable testifier, both in general and in this particular instance.

Now, since the testifier in question is an alien about whom George knows nothing, he truly has no epistemically relevant positive reasons: he has no commonsense psychological alien theory, he has no beliefs about the general reliability of aliens as testifiers, he has no beliefs about the reliability of this particular alien, and so on. We can also suppose that there is nothing about the alien that provides George with relevant undefeated defeaters. Now, is George justified in believing that tigers have eaten some of the inhabitants of the planet in question on the basis of the alien's testimony?

Here reductionists argue that the answer should clearly be no. For despite the fact that the alien's report is both true and reliable, it is argued that it is plainly irrational epistemically for George to form the belief in question on the basis of the alien's testimony. For instance, it may very well be accepted practice in alien society to be insincere and deceptive when testifying to others. Or normal alien psychology may be what we Earthlings would consider psychosis. Or the language that the aliens use, although superficially indistinguishable from English, may really be Twenglish, where Twenglish uses the "negation" sign for affirming a proposition. For all George knows when he accepts the alien's testimony, each of these scenarios is just as likely as the possibility that these aliens are reliable testifiers who speak English. But, in the absence of any way to discriminate among these possibilities, reductionists argue that the appropriate epistemic response is to withhold belief. Because non-reductionists do not require any positive epistemic work from recipients of testimony in order to acquire justified belief or knowledge, they are committed to granting George justified belief and ultimately knowledge of the alien's testimony, thereby sanctioning what reductionists regard as gullibility, epistemic irrationality, and intellectual irresponsibility.

Thus, both non-reductionism and reductionism have been subject to various objections, objections that opponents use to motivate their own views. The direction that most recent work in the epistemology of testimony is taking is to avoid these problems by developing qualified or hybrid views of either non-reductionism or reductionism. Whether such views inherit versions of their ancestors' problems has, however, yet to be seen.

60

Is Knowing through Memory a Distinct Way of Knowing?

Bertrand Russell, *The Analysis of Mind*

We must not forget to spend some time on the epistemology of … oh yes, of memory. Earlier, we met a possible way of making *metaphysical* use of the concept of memory: we read John Locke on whether memory is part of what constitutes a person's being the same person from one time to another. Now let us consider what possible role memory ever plays in our *knowing* something. In particular, can the use of memory be a fundamentally *distinct* way of gaining knowledge? Is memory an epistemologically *basic* means of knowing?

The previous reading asked that sort of question about testimony. (If people do learn from others, is this ultimately a *distinct* way of gaining knowledge? Or is it really just knowing via other means, such as perception and reason?) The question is no less pressing – along the same lines – about memory. Behind those questions is this one: In how many ultimately distinct ways can people gain knowledge? Philosophers have often thought of memory as one of those ways. Whenever we seek or happen upon some knowledge, our apparent reliance upon memory is no less real and substantial than our apparent reliance upon testimony. Indeed, memory could well be involved in knowing via a specific piece of testimony. Do you need to remember how the testimony *started*, as it nears its conclusion? Must you remember what its various words *mean*?

Memory might also be involved in knowing something by yourself, unassisted by testimony from other people. Imagine attempting to construct a proof in mathematics or logic. As you proceed through the proof, you have to remember how it began and what its words or symbols mean. Or imagine drawing upon past observations of a phenomenon in order to reach a view about its nature or potential. You have to

Bertrand Russell, *The Analysis of Mind* (London: George Allen & Unwin, 1921), lecture IX (excerpts). Reprinted with kind permission of the Bertrand Russell Peace Foundation.

remember those observations as you reflect upon them. The same sort of reliance upon memory could be present even in knowledge gained from a *single* observation, if the observation takes time to occur or if use of it to gain knowledge involves conceptually classifying whatever one is observing.

For these reasons and more, we should reflect philosophically upon what memory involves. One idea will occur quickly to us: Is memory like *perception*? Is it, in effect, perception of the past? Or does that line of thought fail because perception is only ever of the present? If so, maybe memory is not really a kind of perception, even of the past. This reading, another from Bertrand Russell, develops what has become a classic philosophical account of what it is to remember something. On Russell's picture of memory, there are two elements. There is an *image*, along with a *belief*. The belief is about the image. It claims that the image is of the past. ("This existed." "This happened.")

Once such an account is proposed, we must ask how well it allows us to understand someone's gaining memory-*knowledge* — knowledge acquired distinctively through memory (even if this knowledge might then be absorbed within some larger body of knowledge, not all of which is memory-knowledge). On Russell's picture, for example, is the memory-*belief* the memory-knowledge? Or is the image-*plus*-the-belief the memory-knowledge? (In either case, *how* is it knowledge? Here we might consult our earlier readings on the nature of knowledge.)

Memory

Memory, which we are to consider to-day, introduces us to knowledge in one of its forms. [...]

I do not myself believe that the analysis of knowledge can be effected entirely by means of purely external observation, such as behaviourists employ. [...] In the present lecture I shall attempt the analysis of memory-knowledge, both as an introduction to the problem of knowledge in general, and because memory, in some form, is presupposed in almost all other knowledge. [...]

One reason for treating memory [...] is that it seems to be involved in the fact that images are recognized as "copies" of past sensible experience. [...] Why do we believe that images are, sometimes or always, approximately or exactly, copies of sensations? What sort of evidence is there? And what sort of evidence is logically possible? The difficulty of this question arises through the fact that the sensation which an image is supposed to copy is in the past when the image exists, and can therefore only be known by memory, while, on the other hand, memory of past sensations seems only possible by means of present images. How, then, are we to find any way of comparing the present image and the past sensation? The problem is just as acute if we say that images differ from their prototypes as if we say that they resemble them; it is the very possibility of comparison that is hard to understand. We think we can know that they are alike or different, but we cannot bring them together in one experience and compare them. To deal with this problem, we must have a theory of memory. In this way the whole status of images as "copies" is bound up with the analysis of memory.

In investigating memory-beliefs, there are certain points which must be borne in mind. In the first place, everything constituting a memory-belief is happening *now*, not in that past time to which the belief is said to refer. It is not logically necessary to the existence of a memory-belief that the event remembered should have occurred, or even that the past should have existed at all. There is no logical impossibility in the hypothesis that the world sprang into being five minutes ago, exactly as it then was, with a population that "remembered" a wholly unreal past. There is no logically necessary connection between events at different times; therefore nothing that is happening now or will happen in the future can disprove the hypothesis that the world began five minutes ago. Hence the occurrences which are *called* knowledge of the past are logically independent of the past; they are wholly analysable into present contents, which might, theoretically, be just what they are even if no past had existed.

I am not suggesting that the non-existence of the past should be entertained as a serious hypothesis. Like all sceptical hypotheses, it is logically tenable, but uninteresting. All that I am doing is to use its logical tenability as a help in the analysis of what occurs when we remember.

In the second place, images without beliefs are insufficient to constitute memory; and habits are still more insufficient. The behaviourist, who attempts to make psychology a record of behaviour, has to trust his memory in making the record. "Habit" is a concept involving the occurrence of similar events at different times; if the behaviourist feels confident that there is such a phenomenon as habit, that can only be because he trusts his memory, when it assures him that there have been other times. And the same applies to images. If we are to know – as it is supposed we do – that images are "copies," accurate or inaccurate, of past events, something more than the mere occurrence of images must go to constitute this knowledge. For their mere occurrence, by itself, would not suggest any connection with anything that had happened before.

Can we constitute memory out of images together with suitable beliefs? We may take it that memory-images, when they occur in true memory, are (*a*) known to be copies, (*b*) sometimes known to be imperfect copies. How is it possible to know that a memory-image is an imperfect copy, without having a more accurate copy by which to replace it? This would *seem* to suggest that we have a way of knowing the past which is independent of images, by means of which we can criticize image-memories. But I do not think such an inference is warranted.

What results, formally, from our knowledge of the past through images of which we recognize the inaccuracy, is that such images must have two characteristics by which we can arrange them in two series, of which one corresponds to the more or less remote period in the past to which they refer, and the other to our greater or less confidence in their accuracy. We will take the second of these points first.

Our confidence or lack of confidence in the accuracy of a memory-image must, in fundamental cases, be based upon a characteristic of the image itself, since we cannot evoke the past bodily and compare it with the present image. It might be suggested that vagueness is the required characteristic, but I do not think this is the case. We sometimes have images that are by no means peculiarly vague, which yet we do not trust – for example, under the influence of fatigue we may see a friend's face vividly and clearly, but horribly distorted. In such a case we distrust our image in spite of its being unusually clear. I think the characteristic by which we distinguish the images we trust is the feeling of *familiarity* that accompanies them. Some images, like some sensations, feel very familiar, while others feel strange. Familiarity is a feeling capable of degrees. In an image of a well-known face, for example, some parts may feel more familiar than others; when this happens, we have more belief in the accuracy of the familiar parts than in that of the unfamiliar parts. I think it is by this means that we become critical of images, not by some imageless memory with which we compare them. I shall return to the consideration of familiarity shortly.

I come now to the other characteristic which memory-images must have in order to account for our knowledge of the past. They must have some characteristic which makes us regard them as referring to more or less remote portions of the past. That is to say if we suppose that A is the event remembered, B the remembering, and t the interval of time between A and B, there must be some characteristic of B which is capable of degrees, and which, in accurately dated memories, varies as t varies. It may increase as t increases, or diminish as t increases. The question which of these occurs is not of any importance for the theoretic serviceability of the characteristic in question.

In actual fact, there are doubtless various factors that concur in giving us the feeling of greater or less remoteness in some remembered event. There may be a specific feeling which could be called the feeling of "pastness," especially where immediate memory is concerned. But apart from this, there are other marks. One of these is context. A recent memory has, usually, more context than a more distant one. When a remembered event has a remembered context, this may occur in two ways, either (*a*) by successive images in the same order as their prototypes, or (*b*) by remembering a whole process simultaneously, in the same way in which a present process may be apprehended, through akoluthic [viz., "fading"] sensations which, by fading, acquire the mark of just-pastness in an increasing degree as they fade, and are thus placed in a series while all sensibly present. It will be context in this second sense, more specially, that will give us a sense of the nearness or remoteness of a remembered event.

There is, of course, a difference between knowing the temporal relation of a remembered event to the present, and knowing the time-order of two remembered events. Very often our knowledge of the temporal relation of a remembered event to the present is inferred from its temporal relations to other remembered events. It would seem that only rather recent events can be placed at all accurately by means of feelings giving their temporal relation to the present, but it is clear that such feelings must play an essential part in the process of dating remembered events.

We may say, then, that images are regarded by us as more or less accurate copies of past occurrences because they come to us with two sorts of feelings: (1) Those that may be called feelings of familiarity; (2) those that may be collected together as feelings giving a sense of pastness. The first lead us to trust our memories, the second to assign places to them in the time-order.

We have now to analyse the memory-belief, as opposed to the characteristics of images which lead us to base memory-beliefs upon them.

[...] Remembering has to be a present occurrence in some way resembling, or related to, what is remembered. And it is difficult to find any ground, except a pragmatic one, for supposing that memory is not sheer delusion, if, as seems to be the case, there is not, apart from memory, any way of ascertaining that there really was a past occurrence having the required relation to our present remembering. [...] [T]he "object" in memory, i.e. the past event which we are said to be remembering, is unpleasantly remote from the "content," i.e. the present mental occurrence in remembering. There is an awkward gulf between the two, which raises difficulties for the theory of knowledge. But we must not falsify observation to avoid theoretical difficulties. For the present, therefore, let us forget these problems, and try to discover what actually occurs in memory.

Some points may be taken as fixed, and such as any theory of memory must arrive at. [...]

The first of our vague but indubitable data is that there is knowledge of the past. We do not yet know with any precision what we mean by "knowledge," and we must admit that in any given instance our memory may be at fault. Nevertheless, whatever a sceptic might urge in theory, we cannot practically doubt that we got up this morning, that we did various things yesterday, that a great war has been taking place, and so on. How far our knowledge of the past is due to memory, and how far to other sources, is of course a matter to be investigated, but there can be no doubt that memory forms an indispensable part of our knowledge of the past.

The second datum is that we certainly have more capacity for knowing the past than for knowing the future. We know some things about the future, for example what eclipses there will be; but this knowledge is a matter of elaborate calculation and inference, whereas some of our knowledge of the past comes to us without effort, in the same sort of immediate way in which we acquire knowledge of occurrences in our present environment. We might provisionally, though perhaps not quite correctly, define "memory" as that way of knowing about the past which has no analogue in our knowledge of the future. [...]

A third point, perhaps not quite so certain as our previous two, is that the truth of memory cannot be wholly practical, as pragmatists wish all truth to be. It seems clear that some of the things I remember are trivial and without any visible importance for the future, but that my memory is true (or false) in virtue of a past event, not in virtue of any future consequences of my belief. The definition of truth as the correspondence between beliefs and facts seems peculiarly evident in the case of memory, as against not only the pragmatist definition but also the idealist definition by means of coherence. [...]

It is important not to confuse the two forms of memory which [the philosopher, Henri] Bergson distinguishes in the second chapter of his *Matter and Memory*, namely the sort that consists of habit, and the sort that consists of independent recollection. He gives the instance of learning a lesson by heart: when I know it by heart I am said to "remember" it, but this merely means that I have acquired certain habits; on the other hand, my recollection of (say) the second time I read the lesson while I was learning it is the recollection of a unique event, which occurred only once. The recollection of a unique event cannot, so Bergson contends, be wholly constituted by habit, and is in fact something radically different from the memory which is habit. The recollection alone is true memory. This distinction is vital to the understanding of memory. [...]

[...] The fact that a man can recite a poem does not show that he remembers any previous occasion on which he has recited or read it. Similarly, the performances of animals in getting out of cages or mazes to which they are accustomed do not prove that they remember having been in the same situation before. Arguments in favour of (for example) memory in plants are only arguments in favour of habit-memory, not of knowledge-memory. [...] It is this [knowledge-memory] that is of interest to theory of knowledge. I shall speak of it as "true" memory, to distinguish it from mere habit acquired through past experience.

[...]

True memory, which we must now endeavour to understand, consists of knowledge of past events, but not of all such knowledge. Some knowledge of past events, for example what we learn through reading history, is on a par with the knowledge we can acquire concerning the future: it is obtained by inference, not (so to speak) spontaneously. There is a similar distinction in our knowledge of the present: some of it is obtained through the senses, some in more indirect ways. I know that there are at this moment a number of people in the streets of New York, but I do not know this in the immediate way in which I know of the people whom I see by looking out of my window. It is not easy to state precisely wherein the difference between these two sorts of knowledge consists, but it is easy to feel the difference. For the moment, I shall not stop to analyse it, but shall content myself with saying that, in this respect, memory resembles the knowledge derived from the senses. It is immediate, not inferred, not abstract; it differs from perception mainly by being referred to the past.

In regard to memory, as throughout the analysis of knowledge, there are two very distinct problems, namely: [...]

(1) What is the present occurrence when we remember?
(2) What is the relation of this present occurrence to the past event which is remembered?

[...]

Suppose you ask me what I ate for breakfast this morning. Suppose, further, that I have not thought about my breakfast in the meantime, and that I did not, while I was eating it, put into words what it consisted of. In this case my recollection will be true memory, not habit-memory. The process of remembering will consist of calling up images of my breakfast, which will come to me with a feeling of belief such as distinguishes memory-images from mere imagination-images. Or sometimes words may come without the intermediary of images; but in this case equally the feeling of belief is essential.

[...]

Memory-images and imagination-images do not differ in their intrinsic qualities, so far as we can discover. They differ by the fact that the images that constitute memories, unlike those that constitute imagination, are accompanied by a feeling of belief which may be expressed in the words "this happened." The mere occurrence of images, without this feeling of belief, constitutes imagination; it is the element of belief that is the distinctive thing in memory.

There are, if I am not mistaken, at least three different kinds of belief-feeling, which we may call respectively memory, expectation and bare assent. In what I call bare assent, there is no time-element in the feeling of belief, though there may be in the content of what is believed. If I believe that Cæsar lauded in Britain in B.C. 55, the time-determination lies, not in the feeling of belief, but in what is believed. I do not remember the occurrence, but have the same feeling towards it as towards the announcement of an eclipse next year. But when I have seen a flash of lightning and am waiting for the thunder, I have a belief-feeling analogous to memory, except that it refers to the future: I have an image of thunder, combined with a feeling which may be expressed in the words: "this will happen." So, in memory, the pastness lies, not in the content of what is believed, but in the nature of the belief-feeling. I might have just the same images and expect their realization; I might entertain them without any belief, as in reading a novel; or I might entertain them together with a time-determination, and give bare assent, as in reading history. I shall return to this subject in a later lecture, when we come to the analysis of belief. For the present, I wish to make it clear that a certain special kind of belief is the distinctive characteristic of memory.

[…]

We must now consider somewhat more closely the content of a memory-belief. The memory-belief confers upon the memory-image something which we may call "meaning"; it makes us feel that the image points to an object which existed in the past. In order to deal with this topic we must consider the verbal expression of the memory-belief. We might be tempted to put the memory-belief into the words: "Something like this image occurred." But such words would be very far from an accurate translation of the simplest kind of memory-belief. "Something like this image" is a very complicated conception. In the simplest kind of memory we are not aware of the difference between an image and the sensation which it copies, which may be called its "prototype." When the image is before us, we judge rather "this occurred." The image is not distinguished from the object which existed in the past: the word "this" covers both, and enables us to have a memory-belief which does not introduce the complicated notion "something like this."

[…]

[…] We may then set up the following definitions:

An instrument is "reliable" with respect to a given set of stimuli when to stimuli which are not relevantly different it gives always responses which are not relevantly different.

An instrument is a "measure" of a set of stimuli which are serially ordered when its responses, in all cases where they are relevantly different, are arranged in a series in the same order.

The "degree of accuracy" of an instrument which is a reliable measurer is the ratio of the difference of response to the difference of stimulus in cases where the difference of stimulus is small. That is to say, if a small difference of stimulus produces a great difference of response, the instrument is very accurate; in the contrary case, very inaccurate.

A mental response is called "vague" in proportion to its lack of accuracy, or rather precision.

These definitions will be found useful, not only in the case of memory, but in almost all questions concerned with knowledge.

It should be observed that vague beliefs, so far from being necessarily false, have a better chance of truth than precise ones, though their truth is less valuable than that of precise beliefs, since they do not distinguish between occurrences which may differ in important ways.

The above discussion of vagueness and accuracy was occasioned by the attempt to interpret the word "this" when we judge in verbal memory that "this occurred." The word "this," in such a judgment, is a vague word, equally applicable to the present memory-image and to the past occurrence which is its prototype. […] A word is vague when it is in fact applicable to a number of different objects because, in virtue of some common property, they have not appeared, to the person using the word, to be distinct. I emphatically do not mean that he has judged them to be identical, but merely that he has made the same response to them all and has not judged them to be different. […]

But we have not yet finished our analysis of the memory-belief. The tense in the belief that "this occurred" is provided by the nature of the belief-feeling involved in memory; the word "this," as we have seen, has a vagueness which we have tried to describe. But we must still ask what we mean by "occurred." The image is, in one sense, occurring now; and therefore we must find some other sense in which the past event occurred but the image does not occur.

There are two distinct questions to be asked: (1) What causes us to say that a thing occurs? (2) What are we feeling when we say this? As to the first question, in the crude use of the word, which is what concerns us, memory-images would not be said to occur; they would not be noticed in themselves, but merely used as signs of the past event. Images are "merely imaginary"; they have not, in crude thought, the sort of reality that belongs to outside bodies. Roughly speaking, "real" things would be those that can cause sensations, those that have correlations of the sort that constitute physical objects. A thing is said to be "real" or to "occur" when it fits into a context of such correlations. The prototype of our memory-image did fit into a physical context, while our memory-image does not. This causes us to feel that the prototype was "real," while the image is "imaginary."

But the answer to our second question, namely as to what we are feeling when we say a thing "occurs" or is "real," must be somewhat different. We do not, unless we are unusually reflective, think about the presence or absence of correlations: we merely have different feelings which, intellectualized, may be represented as expectations of the presence or absence of correlations. A thing which "feels real" inspires us with hopes or fears, expectations or curiosities, which are wholly absent when a thing "feels imaginary." The feeling of reality is a feeling akin to respect: it belongs *primarily* to whatever can do things to us without our voluntary co-operation. This feeling of reality, related to the memory-image, and referred to the past by the specific kind of belief-feeling that is characteristic of memory, seems to be what constitutes the act of remembering in its pure form.

We may now summarize our analysis of pure memory.

Memory demands (a) an image, (b) a belief in past existence. The belief may be expressed in the words "this existed."

The belief, like every other, may be analysed into (1) the believing, (2) what is believed. The believing is a specific feeling or sensation or complex of sensations, different from expectation or bare assent in a way that makes the belief refer to the past; the reference to the past lies in the belief-feeling, not in the content believed. There is a relation between the belief-feeling and the content, making the belief-feeling refer to the content, and expressed by saying that the content is what is believed.

The content believed may or may not be expressed in words. Let us take first the case when it is not. In that case, if we are merely remembering that something of which we now have an image occurred, the content consists of (a) the image, (b) the feeling, analogous to respect, which we translate by saying that something is "real" as opposed to "imaginary," (c) a relation between the image and the feeling of reality, of the sort expressed when we say that the feeling refers to the image. This content does not contain in itself any time-determination: the time-determination lies in the nature of the belief-feeling, which is that called "remembering" or (better) "recollecting." It is only subsequent reflection upon this reference to the past that makes us realize the distinction between the image and the event recollected. When we have made this distinction, we can say that the image "means" the past event.

The content expressed in words is best represented by the words "the existence of this," since these words do not involve tense, which belongs to the belief-feeling, not to the content. Here "this" is a vague term, covering the memory-image and anything very like it, including its prototype. "Existence" expresses the feeling of a "reality" aroused primarily by whatever can have effects upon us without our voluntary co-operation. The word "of" in the phrase "the existence of this" represents the relation which subsists between the feeling of reality and the "this."

This analysis of memory is probably extremely faulty, but I do not know how to improve it.

Can We Fundamentally Fail
Ever To Know?

61

Are None of our Beliefs More
Justifiable than Others?

Sextus Empiricus, *Outlines of Pyrrhonism*

The section "Can We Ever Know Just through Observation?" included two versions
of a classic argument for external world skepticism. Descartes' version (reading 46)
talked of the possibility of dreaming; Putnam's version (reading 48) mused upon
possibly being a brain in a vat. Might we fail to know, via observation, the world
around us? Putnam (reading 48) and McDowell (reading 49) then responded
non-skeptically to that question. Most of our epistemological discussions have been
of non-skeptical ideas attempting to understand aspects of how people can know in
this way or that. Still, skeptical impulses linger within epistemology. This reading and
the next two contain further skeptical arguments.

Sextus Empiricus, *Outlines of Pyrrhonism*, Loeb Classical Library vol. 273, trans. R.G. Bury (Cambridge, MA:
Harvard University Press, 1933), Book I (excerpts). Copyright © 1933 by the President and Fellows of Harvard
College. Loeb Classical Library (R) is a registered trademark of the President and Fellows of Harvard College.
Reprinted by permission of the publishers and the Trustees of the Loeb Classical Library.

Metaphysics and Epistemology: A Guided Anthology, First Edition. Edited by Stephen Hetherington.
© 2014 John Wiley & Sons, Inc. Published 2014 by John Wiley & Sons, Inc.

This time we begin where skepticism itself began, with ancient Greek philosophy's most enduring skeptical challenge. It is Pyrrhonian skepticism or, more simply, Pyrrhonism. It is named for Pyrrho (from Elis: c.360–c.270 BC). This reading is from our best surviving record of Pyrrhonism, by Sextus Empiricus (AD c.160–c.210) – a doctor, probably Greek.

How do we ever form beliefs about reality? We rely upon what *appears* to be the world's real nature: things can appear to us really to be thus-and-so. This could feel like sufficient reason to believe that the world *is* thus-and-so. But Sextus finds within that comforting image a less reassuring one: he describes an apparently inescapable clash of appearances regarding how the world is. These need not all be sensory; for Pyrrhonism, *any* apparent evidence is an appearance. Nor need the clashes always be noticed. It seems to Sextus that whenever one has apparent evidence of how the world is in some respect, apparently equally good but conflicting evidence is available. So, if all appearances – all available apparent evidence regarding reality – were somehow to be combined, one's evidence would no longer favor a specific belief as to how the world is. Each appearance would be cancelled out by a conflicting one.

Sextus gives us a taxonomy – a structured list – of ways in which that sort of clash between pieces of evidence can unfold. How the world appears to you in some respect may conflict with how it appears to someone else, or to a dog, or to you at another time, or to you in another circumstance, or to people from another culture, and so on. Even those are not the only sources of conflict highlighted by Sextus.

What would happen if one was to become aware of such a conflict (as could happen after reading Sextus)? One would, it seems, *suspend* one's beliefs as to how the world is, beyond the competing appearances. No longer would one feel the manifest rightness of whatever evidence – the appearances – one had been using for ascertaining the world's nature. Beliefs about how the world *appears* could survive; not so for beliefs about the world *beyond* these appearances. Is that a worry? To Sextus, it does not appear so; for a kind of calmness will envelop one. "Is that *really* how the world is?" No longer must one strive to answer that question. No longer will one feel the stress of such striving. Appearances will be a sufficient guide for living. Pyrrhonist skepticism is thus presented as an aid to living, even if it challenges our conception of ourselves as living with beliefs amounting to knowledge of how the world really is.

What Scepticism Is

Seepticism is an ability, or mental attitude, which opposes appearances to judgements in any way whatsoever, with the result that, owing to the equipollence of the objects and reasons thus opposed, we are brought firstly to a state of mental suspense and next to a state of "unperturbedness" or quietude. [...] By "appearances" we now mean the objects of sense-perception, whence we contrast them with the objects of thought or "judgements." [...] [W]e oppose these in a variety of ways – appearances to appearances, or judgements to judgements, or *alternando* [viz., "crosswise"] appearances to judgements, – in order to ensure the inclusion of all these antitheses we employ the phrase "in any way whatsoever." [...] The phrase "opposed judgements" we do not employ in the sense of negations and affirmations only but simply as equivalent to "conflicting judgements."[a] "Equipollence" we use of equality in respect of probability and improbability, to indicate that no one of the conflicting judgements takes precedence of any other as being more probable. "Suspense" is a state of mental rest owing to which we neither deny nor affirm anything. "Quietude" is an untroubled and tranquil condition of soul. [...]

Of the Sceptic

In the definition of the Sceptic system there is also implicitly included that of the Pyrrhonean philosopher: he is the man who participates in this "ability."

Of the Principles of Scepticism

The originating cause of Scepticism is, we say, the hope of attaining quietude. Men of talent, who were perturbed by the contradictions in things and in doubt as to which of the alternatives they ought to accept, were led on to inquire what is true in things and what false, hoping by the settlement of this question to attain quietude. The main basic principle of the Sceptic system is that of opposing to every proposition an equal proposition; for we believe that as a consequence of this we end by ceasing to dogmatize.

Does the Sceptic dogmatize?

When we say that the Sceptic refrains from dogmatizing we do not use the term "dogma," as some do, in the broader sense of "approval of a thing" (for the Sceptic gives assent to the feelings which are the necessary results of sense-impressions, and he would not, for example, say when feeling hot or cold "I believe that I am not hot or cold"); but we say that "he does not dogmatize" using "dogma" in the sense, which some give it, of "assent to one of the non-evident objects of scientific inquiry"; for the Pyrrhonean philosopher assents to nothing that is non-evident. Moreover, even in the act of enunciating the Sceptic formulae concerning things non-evident – such as the formula "No more (one thing than another)," or the formula "I determine nothing," or any of the others which we shall presently mention, – he does not dogmatize. [...] If then, while the dogmatizer posits the matter of his dogma as substantial truth, the Sceptic enunciates his formulae so that they are virtually cancelled by themselves, he should not be said to dogmatize in his enunciation of them. And, most important of all, in his enunciation of these formulae he states what appears to himself and announces his own impression in an undogmatic way, without making any positive assertion regarding the external realities.

Do the Sceptics abolish Appearances?

Those who say that "the Sceptics abolish appearances," or phenomena, seem to me to be unaequainted with the statements of our School. For, as we said above, we do not overthrow the affective sense-impressions which induce our assent involuntarily; and these impressions are "the appearances." And when we question whether the underlying object is such as it appears, we grant the fact that it appears, and our doubt does not concern the appearance itself but the account given of that appearance, – and that is a different thing from questioning the appearance itself. For example, honey appears to us to be sweet (and this we grant, for we perceive sweetness through the senses), but whether it is also sweet in its essence is for us a matter of doubt, since this is not an appearance but a judgement regarding the appearance.

Of the Criterion of Scepticism

[...]

Adhering, then, to appearances we live in accordance with the normal rules of life, undogmatically, seeing that we cannot remain wholly inactive. And it would seem that this regulation of life is fourfold, and that one part of it lies in the guidance of Nature, another in the constraint of the passions, another in the tradition of laws and customs, another in the instruction of the arts. Nature's guidance is that by which we are naturally capable of sensation and thought; constraint of the passions is that whereby hunger drives us to food and thirst to drink; tradition of customs and laws, that whereby we regard piety in the conduct of life as good, but impiety as evil; instruction of the arts, that whereby we are not inactive in such arts as we adopt. But we make all these statements undogmatically.

What is the End of Scepticism?

Our next subject will be the End of the Sceptic system. Now an "End" is "that for which all actions or reasonings are undertaken, while it exists for the sake of none". [...] We assert still that the Sceptic's End is quietude in respect of matters of opinion and moderate feeling in respect of things unavoidable. For the Sceptic, having set out to philosophize with the object of passing judgement on the sense-impressions and ascertaining which of them are true and which false, so as to attain quietude thereby, found himself involved in contradictions of equal weight, and being unable to decide between them suspended judgement; and as he was thus in suspense there followed, as it happened, the state of quietude in respect of matters of opinion. For the man who opines that anything is by nature good or bad is for ever being disquieted: when he is without the things which he deems good he believes himself to be tormented by things naturally bad and he pursues after the things which are, as he thinks, good; which when he has obtained he keeps falling into still more perturbations because of his irrational and immoderate elation, and in his dread of a change of fortune he uses every endeavour to avoid losing the things which he deems good. On the other hand, the man who determines nothing as to what is naturally good or bad neither shuns nor pursues anything eagerly; and, in consequence, he is unperturbed.

The Sceptic, in fact, had the same experience which is said to have befallen the painter Apelles [court painter to Alexander the Great (*circa* 350–300 B.C.)]. Once, they say, when he was painting a horse and wished to represent in the painting the horse's foam, he was so unsuccessful that he gave up the attempt and flung at the picture the sponge on which he used to wipe the paints off his brush, and the mark of the sponge produced the effect of a horse's foam. So, too, the Sceptics were in hopes of gaining quietude by means of a decision regarding the disparity of the objects of sense and of thought, and being unable to effect this they suspended judgement; and they found that quietude, as if by chance, followed upon their suspense, even as a shadow follows its substance. We do not, however, suppose that the Sceptic is wholly untroubled; but we say that he is troubled by things unavoidable; for we grant that he is cold at times and thirsty, and suffers various affections of that kind. But even in these cases, whereas ordinary people are afflicted by two circumstances, – namely, by the affections themselves and, in no less a degree, by the belief that these conditions are evil by nature, – the Sceptic, by his rejection of the added belief in the natural badness of all these conditions, escapes here too with less discomfort. Hence we say that, while in regard to matters of opinion the Sceptic's End is quietude, in regard to things unavoidable it is "moderate affection." [...]

Of the general Modes leading to Suspension of Judgement

Now that we have been saying that tranquillity follows on suspension of judgement, it will be our next task to explain how we arrive at this suspension. Speaking generally, one may say that it is the result of setting things in opposition. We oppose either appearances to appearances or objects of thought to objects of thought or *alternando*. For instance, we oppose appearances to appearances when we say "The same tower appears round from a distance, but square from close at hand"; and thoughts to thoughts, when in answer to him who argues the existence of Providence from the order of the heavenly bodies we oppose the fact that often the good fare ill and the bad fare well, and draw from this the inference that Providence does not exist. And thoughts we oppose to appearances, as when Anaxagoras [philosopher, circa 500–428 B.C.] countered the notion that snow is white with the argument, "Snow is frozen water, and water is black; therefore snow also is black." With a different idea we oppose things present sometimes to things present, as in the foregoing examples, and sometimes to things past or future, as, for instance, when someone propounds to us a theory which we are unable to refute, we say to him in reply, "Just as, before the birth of the founder of the School to which you belong, the theory it holds was not as yet apparent as a sound theory, although it was really in existence, so likewise it is possible that the opposite theory to that which you now propound is already really existent, though not yet apparent to us, so that we ought not as yet to yield assent to this theory which at the moment seems to be valid."

But in order that we may have a more exact understanding of these antitheses I will describe the Modes by which suspension of judgement is brought about, but without making any positive assertion regarding either their number or their validity; for it is possible that they may be unsound or there may be more of them than I shall enumerate.

Concerning the Ten Modes

The usual tradition amongst the older Sceptics is that the "modes" by which "suspension" is supposed to be brought about are ten in number; and they also give them the synonymous names of "arguments" and "positions." They are these: the first, based on the variety in animals; the second, on the differences in human beings; the third, on the different structures of the organs of sense; the fourth, on the circumstantial conditions; the fifth, on positions and intervals and locations; the sixth, on intermixtures; the seventh, on the quantities and formations of the underlying objects; the eighth, on the fact of relativity; the ninth, on the frequency or rarity of occurrence; the tenth, on the disciplines and customs and laws, the legendary beliefs and the dogmatic convictions.

[...]

The *First* argument (or *Trope*), as we said, is that which shows that the same impressions are not produced by the same objects owing to the differences in animals. This we infer both from the differences in their origins and from the variety of their bodily structures.

[...]

But if the same things appear different owing to the variety in animals, we shall, indeed, be able to state our own impressions of the real object, but as to its essential nature we shall suspend judgement. For we cannot ourselves judge between our own impressions and those of the other animals, since we ourselves are involved in the dispute and are, therefore, rather in need of a judge than competent to pass judgement ourselves.

[...]

[...] The *Second Mode* is, that based on the differences in men; for even if we grant for the sake of argument that men are more worthy of credence than irrational animals, we shall find that even our own differences of themselves lead to suspense. For man, you know, is said to be compounded of two things, soul and body, and in both these we differ one from another.

[...]

This *Third Mode* is based on differences in the senses. That the senses differ from one another is obvious. Thus, to the eye paintings seem to have recesses and projections, but not so to the touch. Honey, too, seems to some pleasant to the tongue but unpleasant to the eyes; so that it is impossible to say whether it is absolutely pleasant or unpleasant. The same is true of sweet oil, for it pleases the sense of smell but displeases the taste. [...] Rain-water, too, is beneficial to the eyes but roughens the wind-pipe and the lungs; as also does olive-oil, though it mollifies the epidermis. The cramp-fish, also, when applied to the extremities produces cramp, but it can be applied to the rest of the body without hurt. Consequently we are unable to say what is the real nature of each of these things, although it is possible to say what each thing at the moment appears to be.

[...][W]e further adopt the *Fourth Mode* of suspension. This is the Mode based, as we say, on the "circumstances," meaning by "circumstances" conditions or dispositions. And this Mode, we say, deals with states that are natural or unnatural, with waking or sleeping, with conditions due to age, motion or rest, hatred or love, emptiness or fulness, drunkenness or soberness, predispositions, confidence or fear, grief or joy. [...]

The *Fifth Argument* (or *Trope*) is that based on positions, distances, and locations; for owing to each of these the same objects appear different; for example, the same porch when viewed from one of its corners appears curtailed, but viewed from the middle symmetrical on all sides; and the same ship seems at a distance to be small and stationary, but from close at hand large and in motion; and the same tower from a distance appears round but from a near point quadrangular.

[...]

The *Sixth Mode* is that based on admixtures, by which we conclude that, because none of the real objects affects our senses by itself but always in conjunction with something else, though we may possibly be able to state the nature of the resultant mixture formed by the external object and that along with which it is perceived, we shall not be able to say what is the exact nature of the external reality in itself. That none of the external objects affects our senses by itself but always in conjunction with something else, and that, in consequence, it assumes a different appearance, is, I imagine, quite obvious. Thus, our own complexion is of one hue in warm air, of another in cold, and we should not be able to say what our complexion really is, but only what it looks like in conjunction with each of these conditions. And the same sound appears of one sort in conjunction with rare air and of another sort with dense air; and odours are more pungent in a hot bath-room or in the sun than in chilly air: and a body is light when immersed in water but heavy when surrounded by air.

[...]

The *Seventh Mode* is that based, on the quantity and constitution of the underlying objects, meaning generally by "constitution" the manner of composition. And it is evident that by this Mode also we are compelled to suspend judgement concerning the real nature of the objects. Thus, for example, the filings of a goat's horn appear white when viewed simply by themselves and without combination, but when combined in the substance of the horn they look black. [...]

As a general rule, it seems that wholesome things become harmful when used in immoderate quantities, and things that seem hurtful when taken to excess cause no harm when in minute quantities. [...]

The *Eighth Mode* is that based on relativity; and by it we conclude that, since all things are relative, we shall suspend judgement as to what things are absolutely and really existent. But this point we must notice – that here as elsewhere we use the term "are" for the term "appear," and what we virtually mean is "all things appear relative." And this statement is twofold, implying, firstly, relation to the thing which judges (for the external object which is judged appears in relation to that thing), and, in a second sense, relation to the accompanying percepts, for instance the right side in relation to the left. Indeed, we have already argued that all things are relative – for example, with respect to the thing which judges, it is in relation to some one particular animal or man or sense that each object appears, and in relation to such and such a circumstance: and with respect to the concomitant percepts, each object appears in relation to some one particular admixture or mode or combination or quantity or position.

[...]

The *Mode* which, comes *Ninth* in order is based on constancy or rarity of occurrence, and we shall explain it as follows. The sun is, of course, much more amazing than a comet; yet because we see the sun constantly but the comet rarely we are so amazed by the comet that we even regard it as a divine portent, while the sun causes no amazement at all.

[...]

There is a *Tenth Mode*, which is mainly concerned with Ethics, being based on rules of conduct, habits, laws, legendary beliefs, and dogmatic conceptions. A rule of conduct is a choice of a way of life, or of a particular action, adopted by one person or many. [...] A law is a written contract amongst the members of a State, the transgressor of which is punished. A habit or custom (the terms are equivalent) is the joint adoption of a certain kind of action by a number of men, the transgressor of which is not actually punished. [...] Legendary belief is the acceptance of unhistorical and fictitious events, such as, amongst others, the legends about Cronos; for these stories win credence with many. Dogmatic conception is the acceptance of a fact which seems to be established by analogy or some form of demonstration, as, for example, that atoms are the elements of existing things. [...]

And each of these we oppose now to itself, and now to each of the others. For example, we oppose habit to habit in this way: some of the Ethiopians tattoo their children, but we do not; and while the Persians think it seemly to wear a brightly dyed dress reaching to the feet, we think it unseemly. [...] And law we oppose to law in this way: among the Romans the man who renounces his father's property does not pay his father's debts, but among the Rhodians he always pays them [...]. And we oppose rule of conduct to rule of conduct, as when we oppose the rule of Diogenes [of Sinope, circa 400–325 B.C.] to that of Aristippus [4th century B.C.] or that of the Laconians to that of the Italians. And we oppose legendary belief to legendary belief when we say that whereas in one story the father of men and gods is alleged to be Zeus, in another he is Oceanos. [...] And we oppose dogmatic conceptions to one another when we say that some declare that there is one element only, others an infinite number; some that the soul is mortal, others that it is immortal; and some that human affairs are controlled by divine Providence, others without Providence.

[...]

We might indeed have taken many other examples in connexion with each of the antitheses above mentioned; but in a concise account like ours, these will be sufficient. [...] So because of this Mode also we are compelled to suspend judgement regarding the real nature of external objects. And thus by means of all the Ten Modes we are finally led to suspension of judgement.

62

Are None of Our Beliefs Immune from Doubt?

René Descartes, "Meditation I"

Pyrrhonism aimed to relieve people of a kind of anxiety. This was the anxiety of struggling to reach beliefs about how the world really is, potentially distinct from how it appears to be. Such beliefs (explained Pyrrhonism) are about what is *non*-evident; what appears to a person to be so is thereby evident to her. Whatever is non-evident is what, seemingly, we need not continue seeking to ascertain. Let those beliefs – any claims to be describing the world beyond how it appears – fade away.

So said Sextus Empiricus, on behalf of Pyrrhonism; so too, with different reasoning, said René Descartes. We met his dreaming argument earlier (in the section "Can We Ever Know Just through Observation?", reading 46). It was intended to undermine all claims to observational knowledge, all knowledge of the physical world. That argument is one of two key ideas in his "Meditation I." The other is this reading's, the conclusion of "Meditation I."

This is a skeptical argument, too – the *evil genius* argument, the *evil demon* argument. Descartes this time portrays himself as suspending all beliefs (not only those supposedly about an external world). Far from being driven by a desire to avoid anxiety, though, this argument is often regarded as a paradigm of how skeptical thinking can reflect or cause a form of anxiety. The evil genius ["*genium malignum*"] argument is a mnemonic, a snappy way for Descartes not to forget the moral of the confronting argument he presents immediately beforehand, also for a universally skeptical conclusion.

René Descartes, "Meditation I" (excerpt), in *Meditations on First Philosophy* [1641]. From *The Philosophical Works of Descartes*, vol. 1, trans. E.S. Haldane and G.R.T. Ross (Cambridge: Cambridge University Press, 1911). Reprinted with permission of Cambridge University Press.

Metaphysics and Epistemology: A Guided Anthology, First Edition. Edited by Stephen Hetherington.
© 2014 John Wiley & Sons, Inc. Published 2014 by John Wiley & Sons, Inc.

In that first argument, Descartes ponders his own ultimate origins and how these could affect him when forming beliefs. Is he clearly created by, and under the control of, a wholly good and powerful God? If so, why would he ever make *mistakes* in his beliefs? Yet he does, contrary to what – it seems natural to surmise – such a God would allow. Maybe therefore he does not form beliefs under the control and care of God after all. But then, insofar as his functioning as a believer is due to something *less* good and powerful than God, correlatively *even more* likely is his making mistakes in his beliefs. In either case, Descartes cannot wholly trust his beliefs to be true.

However, that disturbing conclusion could be difficult to retain in one's mind. Hence, Descartes formulates his evil genius argument. Its structure is similar to his dreaming argument. Descartes asks himself how he could know that his beliefs are not present due to intervention and control by a spirit or demon intent on allowing him only *false* beliefs. (Imagine the demon having God's power to do this, without God's goodness.) If that possibility cannot ever be eliminated, a doubt attaches to all beliefs; and this (thinks Descartes) is a concern. Far from giving him any Pyrrhonist relief, it prompts Descartes to try to *overcome* such doubts.

Other epistemologists have sought that same sort of victory. How can we protect our beliefs – those we hope are knowledge – from a universally applicable doubt, such as this one by Descartes? *Can* you know that no evil demon is deceiving you both through and throughout your beliefs?

[…] I have long had fixed in my mind the belief that an all-powerful God existed by whom I have been created such as I am. But how do I know that He has not brought it to pass that there is no earth, no heaven, no extended body, no magnitude, no place, and that nevertheless [I possess the perceptions of all these things and that] they seem to me to exist just exactly as I now see them? And, besides, as I sometimes imagine that others deceive themselves in the things which they think they know best, how do I know that I am not deceived every time that I add two and three, or count the sides of a square, or judge of things yet simpler, if anything simpler can be imagined? But possibly God has not desired that I should be thus deceived, for He is said to be supremely good. If, however, it is contrary to His goodness to have made me such that I constantly deceive myself, it would also appear to be contrary to His goodness to permit me to be sometimes deceived, and nevertheless I cannot doubt that He does permit this.

There may indeed be those who would prefer to deny the existence of a God so powerful, rather than believe that all other things are uncertain. But let us not oppose them for the present, and grant that all that is here said of a God is a fable; nevertheless in whatever way they suppose that I have arrived at the state of being that I have reached – whether they attribute it to fate or to accident, or make out that it is by a continual succession of antecedents, or by some other method – since to err and deceive oneself is a defect, it is clear that the greater will be the probability of my being so imperfect as to deceive myself ever, as is the Author to whom they assign my origin the less powerful. To these reasons I have certainly nothing to reply, but at the end I feel constrained to confess that there is nothing in all that I formerly believed to be true, of which I cannot in some measure doubt, and that not merely through want of thought or through levity, but for reasons which are very powerful and maturely considered; so that henceforth I ought not the less carefully to refrain from giving credence to these opinions than to that which is manifestly false, if I desire to arrive at any certainty [in the sciences].

But it is not sufficient to have made these remarks, we must also be careful to keep them in mind. For these ancient and commonly held opinions still revert frequently to my mind, long and familiar custom having given them the right to occupy my mind against my inclination and rendered them almost masters of my belief; nor will I ever lose the habit of deferring to them or of placing my confidence in them, so long as I consider them as they really are, i.e. opinions in some measure doubtful, as I have just shown, and at the same time highly probable, so that there is much more reason to believe in than to deny them. That is why I consider that I shall not be acting amiss, if, taking of set purpose [viz., specific intention] a contrary belief, I allow myself to be deceived, and for a certain time pretend that all these opinions are entirely false and imaginary, until at last, having thus balanced my former prejudices with my latter [so that they cannot divert my opinions more to one side than to the other], my judgment will no longer be dominated by bad usage or turned away from the right knowledge of the truth. For I am assured that there can be neither peril nor error in this course, and that I cannot at present yield too much to distrust, since I am not considering the question of action, but only of knowledge.

I shall then suppose, not that God who is supremely good and the fountain of truth, but some evil genius not less powerful than deceitful, has employed his whole energies in deceiving me; I shall consider that the heavens, the earth, colours, figures, sound, and all other external things are nought but the illusions and dreams of which this genius has availed himself in order to lay traps for my credulity; I shall consider myself as having no hands, no eyes, no flesh, no blood, nor any senses, yet falsely believing myself to possess all these things; I shall remain obstinately attached to this idea, and if by this means it is not in my power to arrive at the knowledge of any truth, I may at least do what is in my power [i.e. suspend my judgment], and with firm purpose avoid giving credence to any false thing, or being imposed upon by this arch deceiver, however powerful and deceptive he may be. But this task is a laborious one, and insensibly a certain lassitude leads me into the course of my ordinary life. And just as a captive who in sleep enjoys an imaginary liberty, when he begins to suspect that his liberty is but a dream, fears to awaken, and conspires with these agreeable illusions that the deception may be prolonged, so insensibly of my own accord I fall back into my former opinions, and I dread awakening from this slumber, lest the laborious wakefulness which would follow the tranquillity of this repose should have to be spent not in daylight, but in the excessive darkness of the difficulties which have just been discussed.

63

Are We Unable Ever To Extrapolate Justifiedly Beyond Our Observations?

David Hume, *An Enquiry Concerning Human Understanding*

The reading after this one will be Descartes' reply to his evil genius argument. His reply will focus upon knowledge of what one is *thinking* at a particular time. But that reply, even if successful in what it tries to show, will leave untouched this reading's argument from David Hume. This argument is usually called Humean *inductive* skepticism. Understood as a skeptical argument, it denies that beliefs can ever be inductively justified, let alone inductive knowledge.

Inductive justification is present when a belief whose content *extrapolates* beyond what some observations report is nonetheless justified by those observations. Beliefs extrapolating beyond some observations can include predictions, as well as retrodictions ("Way back in time, a velociraptor lived here") and many generalizations ("All swans are white," "Most swans are white," etc.). Imagine reflecting on your history of eating shrimp, while gazing at an enticing shrimp on a plate before you. "Am I about to experience the same taste as I have previously enjoyed when eating shrimp?" That is what you ask yourself. You answer optimistically: "I believe so." This is a prediction about a future subjective experience. Other predictions might concern the physical world: "This shrimp will be digested within my body." (So, inductive *reasoning* takes one from a description of observations to some sort of extrapolation beyond them.)

Hume's argument applies to all inductive extrapolations, outside *and* within the domain of experiences or subjective appearances. Your prediction that you will have a familiar experience of tasting shrimp concerns how something will appear to you. In the previous-but-one reading, Sextus did not develop a Pyrrhonist

David Hume, *An Enquiry Concerning Human Understanding* (1748), sect. IV (excerpts).

Metaphysics and Epistemology: A Guided Anthology, First Edition. Edited by Stephen Hetherington.
© 2014 John Wiley & Sons, Inc. Published 2014 by John Wiley & Sons, Inc.

skepticism about appearances: *these* he accepted. But Hume's argument is about appearances and non-appearances equally. It concerns any belief moving beyond, even while reflecting, some actual observations or experiences. The argument asks whether any such belief (even when about possible observations or experiences) can be supported at all by those actual observations or experiences beyond which its content goes.

Not all philosophers regard Hume's argument as skeptical. Some see it as motivating an image of people forming inductive beliefs in response to observations as an exercise of knowledge-*how*. But the argument's usual interpretation renders it as skeptical, concluding that no belief could be justified inductively *at all*. And if there is no inductive justification, presumably there is no inductive knowledge. You would not know what this shrimp will taste like, no matter how often you have previously eaten shrimp. You would not know that the sun will rise tomorrow, no matter how many sunrises you have observed (*and* no matter how much scientific evidence you are given; for that evidence itself must be supported inductively, by observations). The surprising and substantial skeptical implication is not merely that the observational experiences do not *prove* the truth of the inductive extrapolation. It is that they provide *no* real justification for its being true.

The Humean argument, interpreted in this skeptical way, has had a powerful historical impact. For instance, philosophers of science have long regarded it as potentially significant, needing to be either accommodated or defused. Does Hume's argument reveal science to be less rational – less a home for justified beliefs or hypotheses – than we might wish it to be?

Sceptical Doubts Concerning the Operations of the Understanding

Part I

[...]

It may [...] be a subject worthy of curiosity, to enquire what is the nature of that evidence which assures us of any real existence and matter of fact, beyond the present testimony of our senses, or the records of our memory. [...]

All reasonings concerning matter of fact seem to be founded on the relation of *Cause and Effect*. By means of that relation alone we can go beyond the evidence of our memory and senses. If you were to ask a man, why he believes any matter of fact, which is absent; for instance, that his friend is in the country, or in France; he would give you a reason; and this reason would be some other fact; as a letter received from him, or the knowledge of his former resolutions and promises. A man finding a watch or any other machine in a desert island, would conclude that there had once been men in that island. All our reasonings concerning fact are of the same nature. And here it is constantly supposed that there is a connexion between the present fact and that which is inferred from it. Were there nothing to bind them together, the inference would be entirely precarious. The hearing of an articulate voice and rational discourse in the dark assures us of the presence of some person: Why? because these are the effects of the human make and fabric, and closely connected with it. If we anatomize all the other reasonings of this nature, we shall find that they are founded on the relation of cause and effect, and that this relation is either near or remote, direct or collateral. Heat and light are collateral effects of fire, and the one effect may justly be inferred from the other.

If we would satisfy ourselves, therefore, concerning the nature of that evidence, which assures us of matters of fact, we must enquire how we arrive at the knowledge of cause and effect.

I shall venture to affirm, as a general proposition, which admits of no exception, that the knowledge of this relation is not, in any instance, attained by reasonings *a priori*; but arises entirely from experience, when we find that any particular objects are constantly conjoined with each other. Let an object be presented to a man of ever so strong natural reason and abilities; if that object be entirely new to him, he will not be able, by the most accurate examination of its sensible qualities, to discover any of its causes or effects. Adam, though his rational faculties be supposed, at the very first, entirely perfect, could not have inferred from the fluidity and transparency of water that it would suffocate him, or from the light and warmth of fire that it would consume him. No object ever discovers, by the qualities which appear to the senses, either the causes which produced it, or the effects which will arise from it; nor can our reason, unassisted by experience, ever draw any inference concerning real existence and matter of fact.

[...] We are apt to imagine that we could discover these effects by the mere operation of our reason, without experience. We fancy, that were we brought on a sudden into this world, we could at first have inferred that one Billiard-ball would communicate motion to another upon impulse; and that we needed not to have waited for the event, in order to pronounce with certainty concerning it. Such is the influence of custom, that, where it is strongest, it not only covers our natural ignorance, but even conceals itself, and seems not to take place, merely because it is found in the highest degree.

But to convince us that all the laws of nature, and all the operations of bodies without exception, are known only by experience, the following reflections may, perhaps, suffice. Were any object presented to us, and were we required to pronounce concerning the effect, which will result from it, without consulting past observation; after what manner, I beseech you, must the mind proceed in this operation? It must invent or imagine some event, which it ascribes to the object as its effect; and it is plain that this invention must be entirely arbitrary. The mind can never possibly find the effect in the supposed cause, by the most accurate scrutiny and examination. For the effect is totally different from the cause, and consequently can never be discovered in it. Motion in the second Billiard-ball is a quite distinct event from motion in the first; nor is there anything in the one to suggest the smallest hint of the other. A stone or piece of metal raised into the air, and left without any support, immediately falls: but to consider the matter *a priori*, is there anything we discover in this situation which can beget the idea of a downward, rather than an upward, or any other motion, in the stone or metal?

And as the first imagination or invention of a particular effect, in all natural operations, is arbitrary, where we consult not experience; so must we also esteem the supposed tie or connexion between the cause and effect, which binds them together, and renders it impossible that any other effect could result from the operation of that cause. When I see, for instance, a Billiard-ball moving in a straight line towards another; even suppose motion in the second ball should by accident be suggested to me, as the result of their contact or impulse; may I not conceive, that a hundred different events might as well follow from that cause? May not both these balls remain at absolute rest? May not the first ball return in a straight line, or leap off from the second in any line or direction? All these suppositions are consistent and conceivable. Why then should we give the preference to one, which is no more consistent or conceivable than the rest? All our reasonings *a priori* will never be able to show us any foundation for this preference.

In a word, then, every effect is a distinct event from its cause. It could not, therefore, be discovered in the cause, and the first invention or conception of it, *a priori*, must be entirely arbitrary. And even after it is suggested, the conjunction of it with the cause must appear equally arbitrary; since there are always many other effects, which, to reason, must seem fully as consistent and natural. In vain, therefore, should we pretend to determine any single event, or infer any cause or effect, without the assistance of observation and experience.

[…]

Part II

But we have not yet attained any tolerable satisfaction with regard to the question first proposed. Each solution still gives rise to a new question as difficult as the foregoing, and leads us on to farther enquiries. When it is asked, *What is the nature of all our reasonings concerning matter of fact?* the proper answer seems to be, that they are founded on the relation of cause and effect. When again it is asked, *What is the foundation of all our reasonings and conclusions concerning that relation?* it may be replied in one word, Experience. But if we still carry on our sifting humour, and ask, *What is the foundation of all conclusions from experience?* this implies a new question, which may be of more difficult solution and explication. […]

I shall content myself, in this section, with an easy task, and shall pretend only to give a negative answer to the question here proposed. I say then, that, even after we have experience of the operations of cause and effect, our conclusions from that experience are *not* founded on reasoning, or any process of the understanding. This answer we must endeavour both to explain and to defend.

It must certainly be allowed, that nature has kept us at a great distance from all her secrets, and has afforded us only the knowledge of a few superficial qualities of objects; while she conceals from us those powers and principles on which the influence of these objects entirely depends. Our senses inform us of the colour, weight, and consistence of bread; but neither sense nor reason can ever inform us of those qualities which fit it for the nourishment and support of a human body. Sight or feeling conveys an idea of the actual motion of bodies; but as to that wonderful force or power, which would carry on a moving body for ever in a continued change of place, and which bodies never lose but by communicating it to others; of this we cannot form the most distant conception. But notwithstanding this ignorance of natural powers and principles, we always presume, when we see like sensible qualities, that they have like secret powers, and expect that effects, similar to those which we have experienced, will follow from them. If a body of like colour and consistence with that bread, which we have formerly eat, be presented to us, we make no scruple of repeating the experiment, and foresee, with certainty, like nourishment and support. Now this is a process of the mind or thought, of which I would willingly know the foundation. It is allowed on all hands that there is no known connexion between the sensible qualities and the secret powers; and consequently, that the mind is not led to form such a conclusion concerning their constant and regular conjunction, by anything which it knows of their nature. As to past *Experience*, it can be allowed to give *direct* and *certain* information of those precise objects only, and that precise period of time, which fell under its cognizance: but why this experience should be extended to future times, and to other objects, which for aught we know, may be only in appearance similar; this is the main question on which I would insist. The bread, which I formerly eat, nourished me; that is, a body of such sensible qualities was, at that time, endued with such secret powers: but does it follow, that other bread must also nourish me at another time, and that like sensible qualities must always be attended with like secret powers? The consequence seems nowise necessary. At least, it must be acknowledged that there is here a consequence drawn by the mind; that there is a certain step taken; a process of thought, and an inference, which wants to be explained. These two propositions are far from being the same, *I have found that such an object has always been attended with such an effect*, and *I foresee, that other objects, which are, in appearance, similar, will be attended with similar effects*. I shall allow, if you please, that the one proposition may justly be inferred from the other: I know, in fact, that it always is inferred. But if you insist that the inference is made by a chain of reasoning, I desire you to produce that reasoning. The connexion between these propositions is not intuitive. There is required a medium, which may enable the mind to draw such an inference, if indeed it be drawn by reasoning and argument.

[...]

All reasonings may be divided into two kinds, namely, demonstrative reasoning, or that concerning relations of ideas, and moral reasoning, or that concerning matter of fact and existence. That there are no demonstrative arguments in the case seems evident; since it implies no contradiction that the course of nature may change, and that an object, seemingly like those which we have experienced, may be attended with different or contrary effects. May I not clearly and distinctly conceive that a body, falling from the clouds, and which, in all other respects, resembles snow, has yet the taste of salt or feeling of fire? Is there any more intelligible proposition than to affirm, that all the trees will flourish in December and January, and decay in May and June? Now whatever is intelligible, and can be distinctly conceived, implies no contradiction, and can never be proved false by any demonstrative argument or abstract reasoning *a priori*.

If we be, therefore, engaged by arguments to put trust in past experience, and make it the standard of our future judgement, these arguments must be probable only, or such as regard matter of fact and real existence, according to the division above mentioned. But that there is no argument of this kind, must appear, if our explication of that species of reasoning be admitted as solid and satisfactory. We have said that all arguments concerning existence are founded on the relation of cause and effect; that our knowledge of that relation is derived entirely from experience; and that all our experimental conclusions proceed upon the supposition that the future will be conformable to the past. To endeavour, therefore, the proof of this last supposition by probable arguments, or arguments regarding existence, must be evidently going in a circle, and taking that for granted, which is the very point in question.

[...]

Should it be said that, from a number of uniform experiments, we *infer* a connexion between the sensible qualities and the secret powers; this, I must confess, seems the same difficulty, couched in different terms. The question still recurs, on what process of argument this *inference* is founded? Where is the medium, the interposing ideas, which join propositions so very wide of each other? It is confessed that the colour, consistence, and other sensible qualities of bread appear not, of themselves, to have any connexion with the secret powers of nourishment and support. For otherwise we could infer these secret powers from the first appearance of these sensible qualities, without the aid of experience; contrary to the sentiment of all philosophers, and contrary to plain matter of fact. Here, then, is our natural state of ignorance with regard to the powers and influence of all objects. How is this remedied by experience? It only shows us a number of uniform effects, resulting from certain objects, and teaches us that those particular objects, at that particular time, were endowed with such powers and forces. When a new object, endowed with similar sensible qualities, is produced, we expect similar powers and forces, and look for a like effect. From a body of like colour and consistence with bread we expect like nourishment and support. But this surely is a step or progress of the mind, which wants to be explained. When a man says, *I have found, in all past instances, such sensible qualities conjoined with such secret powers*: And when he says, *Similar sensible qualities will always be conjoined with similar secret powers*, he is not guilty of a tautology, nor are these propositions in any respect the same. You say that the one proposition is an inference from the other. But you must confess that the inference is not intuitive; neither is it demonstrative: Of what nature is it, then? To say it is experimental, is begging the question. For all inferences from experience suppose, as their foundation, that the future will resemble the past, and that similar powers will be conjoined with similar sensible qualities. If there be any suspicion that the course of nature may change, and that the past may be no rule for the future, all experience becomes useless, and can give rise to no inference or conclusion. It is impossible, therefore, that any arguments from experience can prove this resemblance of the past to the future; since all these arguments are founded on the supposition of that resemblance. Let the course of things be allowed hitherto ever so regular; that alone, without some new argument or inference, proves not that, for the future, it will continue so. In vain do you pretend to have learned the nature of bodies from your past experience. Their secret nature, and consequently all their effects and influence, may change, without any change in their sensible qualities. This happens sometimes, and with regard to some objects: Why may it not happen always, and with regard to all objects? What logic, what process of argument secures you against this supposition? My practice, you say, refutes my doubts. But you mistake the purport of my question. As an agent, I am quite satisfied in the point; but as a philosopher, who has some share of curiosity, I will not say scepticism, I want to learn the foundation of this inference. No reading, no enquiry has yet been able to remove my difficulty, or give me satisfaction in a matter of such importance. Can I do better than propose the difficulty to the public, even though, perhaps, I have small hopes of obtaining a solution? We shall at least, by this means, be sensible of our ignorance, if we do not augment our knowledge.

Can Skeptical Arguments Be Escaped?

64

Can We Know at Least Our Conscious Mental Lives?

René Descartes, "Meditation II"

One of epistemology's recurring challenges is that of finding answers to skeptical questions. *Can* we know? *Can* we at least have true beliefs that are justified by good evidence, or are reliably formed, or are formed from a genuine desire for truth, say? Earlier (in the section "Can We Ever Know Just through Observation?"), we read attempts by Putnam (reading 48) and McDowell (reading 49) to squash or evade a skeptical argument. There, the focus was on external world skepticism; in this section we consider reactions to some other forms of skepticism.

This reading displays one of philosophy's most famous images. It is Descartes' response in his "Meditation II" to his own evil genius argument from "Meditation I." That argument's central image envisaged a striking possibility – of an evil demon

René Descartes, "Meditation II" (excerpt), in *Meditations on First Philosophy* [1641]. From *The Philosophical Works of Descartes*, vol. 1, trans. E.S. Haldane and G.R.T. Ross (Cambridge: Cambridge University Press, 1911). Reprinted with permission of Cambridge University Press.

Metaphysics and Epistemology: A Guided Anthology, First Edition. Edited by Stephen Hetherington.
© 2014 John Wiley & Sons, Inc. Published 2014 by John Wiley & Sons, Inc.

manipulating your thinking, with *any* belief of yours being present merely because of the demon's meddling. How can you ever know that this is not happening within you?

In reply to which, Descartes offered what is generally called the *Cogito*. This name is from the Latin version of Descartes' idea: *Cogito, ergo sum* ("I think, therefore I am"). That version is in his *Discourse on Method* (part of which we met at reading 52 in the section "Can We Ever Know Just through Reflection?"). The version in "Meditation II" is slightly different, although the same anti-skeptical move persists. It is Descartes' attempt to prove that he has *some* knowledge even given his encounter with his evil genius argument. Is there any kind of idea or belief that could not be false *even* if an evil demon had created it? There is (said Descartes): no one can think falsely that he is thinking. More carefully: no thinking that no thinking is occurring can be false. And no such thinking (presumes Descartes) can be ownerless. His anti-skeptical conclusion is that he knows there to be thinking occurring – namely, thinking he knows as his own.

He does not claim to know that it is thereby thinking belonging to someone – himself – with features *other* than this thinking; for it is *only* the thinking (no further features) of which this argument provides knowledge. But that is enough for Descartes' immediate purpose. He is supremely confident at this special moment of reflection – certain that he is reflecting, therefore that he exists as that thinker.

Then he expands upon that insight, as he ponders the *ways* in which he is thinking. His conclusion remains: he knows his conscious mental life whenever it is present; and he does this without inferring at this stage of his thinking that there is anything more to him than his conscious mental life. In reading 23, in the section "How Are Persons Persons?" we saw Descartes ending his "Meditation VI" by believing that he does know of his physical reality. Not *yet*, though, does he claim to have that knowledge; not in "Meditation II." His anti-skeptical claim at this early stage of his *Meditations* is just that he knows of his own conscious *mental* reality.

Of the Nature of the Human Mind; and that it is more easily known than the Body

The Meditation of yesterday filled my mind with so many doubts that it is no longer in my power to forget them. And yet I do not see in what manner I can resolve them; and, just as if I had all of a sudden fallen into very deep water, I am so disconcerted that I can neither make certain of setting my feet on the bottom, nor can I swim and so support myself on the surface. I shall nevertheless make an effort and follow anew the same path as that on which I yesterday entered, i.e. I shall proceed by setting aside all that in which the least doubt could be supposed to exist, just as if I had discovered that it was absolutely false; and I shall ever follow in this road until I have met with something which is certain, or at least, if I can do nothing else, until I have learned for certain that there is nothing in the world that is certain. [The mathematician] Archimedes, in order that he might draw the terrestrial globe out of its place, and transport it elsewhere, demanded only that one point should be fixed and immoveable; in the same way I shall have the right to conceive high hopes if I am happy enough to discover one thing only which is certain and indubitable.

I suppose, then, that all the things that I see are false; I persuade myself that nothing has ever existed of all that my fallacious memory represents to me. I consider that I possess no senses; I imagine that body, figure, extension, movement and place are but the fictions of my mind. What, then, can be esteemed as true? Perhaps nothing at all, unless that there is nothing in the world that is certain.

But how can I know there is not something different from those things that I have just considered, of which one cannot have the slightest doubt? Is there not some God, or some other being by whatever name we call it, who puts these reflections into my mind? That is not necessary, for is it not possible that I am capable of producing them myself? I myself, am I not at least something? But I have already denied that I had senses and body. Yet I hesitate, for what follows from that? Am I so dependent on body and senses that I cannot exist without these? But I was persuaded that there was nothing in all the world, that there was no heaven, no earth, that there were no minds, nor any bodies: was I not then likewise persuaded that I did not exist? Not at all; of a surety I myself did exist since I persuaded myself of something [or merely because I thought of something]. But there is some deceiver or other, very powerful and very cunning, who ever employs his ingenuity in deceiving me. Then without doubt I exist also if he deceives me, and let him deceive me as much as he will, he can never cause me to be nothing so long as I think that I am something. So that after having reflected well and carefully examined all things, we must come to the definite conclusion that this proposition: I am, I exist, is necessarily true each time that I pronounce it, or that I mentally conceive it.

But I do not yet know clearly enough what I am, I who am certain that I am; and hence I must be careful to see that I do not imprudently take some other object in place of myself, and thus that I do not go astray in respect of this knowledge that I hold to be the most certain and most evident of all that I have formerly learned. That is why I shall now consider anew what I believed myself to be before I embarked upon these last reflections; and of my former opinions I shall withdraw all that might even in a small degree be invalidated by the reasons which I have just brought forward, in order that there may be nothing at all left beyond what is absolutely certain and indubitable.

What then did I formerly believe myself to be? Undoubtedly I believed myself to be a man. But what is a man? Shall I say a reasonable animal? Certainly not; for then I should have to inquire what an animal is, and what is reasonable; and thus from a single question I should insensibly fall into an infinitude of others more difficult; and I should not wish to waste the little time and leisure remaining to me in trying to unravel subtleties like these. But I shall rather stop here to consider the thoughts which of themselves spring up in my mind, and which were not inspired by anything beyond my own nature alone when I applied myself to the consideration of my being. In the first place, then, I considered myself as having a face, hands, arms, and all that system of members composed of bones and flesh as seen in a corpse which I designated by the name of body. In addition to this I considered that I was nourished, that I walked, that I felt, and that I thought, and I referred all these actions to the soul: but I did not stop to consider what the soul was, or if I did stop, I imagined that it was something extremely rare and subtle like a wind, a flame, or an ether, which was spread throughout my grosser parts. As to body I had no manner of doubt about its nature, but thought I had a very clear knowledge of it; and if I had desired to explain it according to the notions that I had then formed of it, I should have described it thus: By the body I understand all that which can be defined by a certain figure: something which can be confined in a certain place, and which can fill a given space in such a way that every other body will be excluded from it; which can be perceived either by touch, or by sight, or by hearing, or by taste, or by smell: which can be moved in many ways not, in truth, by itself, but by something which is foreign to it, by which it is touched [and from which it receives impressions]: for to have the power of self-movement, as also of feeling or of thinking, I did not consider to appertain to the nature of body: on the contrary, I was rather astonished to find that faculties similar to them existed in some bodies.

But what am I, now that I suppose that there is a certain genius which is extremely power-ful, and, if I may say so, malicious, who employs all his powers in deceiving me? Can I affirm that I possess the least of all those things which I have just said pertain to the nature of body? I pause to consider, I revolve all these things in my mind, and I find none of which I can say that it pertains to me. It would be tedious to stop to enumerate them. Let us pass to the attributes of soul and see if there is any one which is in me? What of nutrition or walking [the first mentioned]? But if it is so that I have no body it is also true that I can neither walk nor take nourishment. Another attribute is sensation. But one cannot feel without body, and besides I have thought I perceived many things during sleep that I recognised in my waking moments as not having been experienced at all. What of thinking? I find here that thought is an attribute that belongs to me; it alone cannot be separated from me. I am, I exist, that is certain. But how often? Just when I think; for it might possibly be the case if I ceased entirely to think, that I should likewise cease altogether to exist. I do not now admit anything which is not necessarily true: to speak accurately I am not more than a thing which thinks, that is to say a mind or a soul, or an understanding, or a reason, which are terms whose significance was formerly unknown to me. I am, however, a real thing and really exist; but what thing? I have answered: a thing which thinks.

And what more? I shall exercise my imagination [in order to see if I am not something more]. I am not a collection of members which we call the human body: I am not a subtle air distributed through these members, I am not a wind, a fire, a vapour, a breath, nor any-thing at all which I can imagine or conceive; because I have assumed that all these were nothing. Without changing that supposition I find that I only leave myself certain of the fact that I am somewhat. But perhaps it is true that these same things which I supposed were non-existent because they are unknown to me, are really not different from the self which I know. I am not sure about this, I shall not dispute about it now; I can only give judgment on things that are known to me. I know that I exist, and I inquire what I am, I whom I know to exist. But it is very certain that the knowledge of my existence taken in its precise signifi-cance does not depend on things whose existence is not yet known to me; consequently it does not depend on those which I can feign in imagination. And indeed the very term *feign* in imagination proves to me my error, for I really do this if I image myself a something, since to imagine is nothing else than to contemplate the figure or image of a corporeal thing.

But I already know for certain that I am, and that it may be that all these images, and, speaking generally, all things that relate to the nature of body are nothing but dreams [and chimeras]. For this reason I see clearly that I have as little reason to say, 'I shall stimulate my imagination in order to know more distinctly what I am,' than if I were to say, 'I am now awake, and I perceive somewhat that is real and true: but because I do not yet perceive it distinctly enough, I shall go to sleep of express purpose, so that my dreams may represent the perception with greatest truth and evidence.' And, thus, I know for certain that nothing of all that I can understand by means of my imagination belongs to this knowledge which I have of myself, and that it is necessary to recall the mind from this mode of thought with the utmost diligence in order that it may be able to know its own nature with perfect distinctness.

But what then am I? A thing which thinks. What is a thing which thinks? It is a thing which doubts, understands, [conceives], affirms, denies, wills, refuses, which also imagines and feels.

Certainly it is no small matter if all these things pertain to my nature. But why should they not so pertain? Am I not that being who now doubts nearly everything, who nevertheless understands certain things, who affirms that one only is true, who denies all the others, who desires to know more, is averse from being deceived, who imagines many things, sometimes indeed despite his will, and who perceives many likewise, as by the intervention of the bodily organs? Is there nothing in all this which is as true as it is certain that I exist, even though I should always sleep and though he who has given me being employed all his ingenuity in deceiving me? Is there likewise any one of these attributes which can be distinguished from my thought, or which might be said to be separated from myself? For it is so evident of itself that it is I who doubts, who understands, and who desires, that there is no reason here to add anything to explain it. And I have certainly the power of imagining likewise; for although it may happen (as I formerly supposed) that none of the things which I imagine are true, nevertheless this power of imagining does not cease to be really in use, and it forms part of my thought. Finally, I am the same who feels, that is to say, who perceives certain things, as by the organs of sense, since in truth I see light, I hear noise, I feel heat. But it will be said that these phenomena are false and that I am dreaming. Let it be so; still it is at least quite certain that it seems to me that I see light, that I hear noise and that I feel heat. That cannot be false; properly speaking it is what is in me called feeling; and used in this precise sense that is no other thing than thinking.

65

Can We Know Some Fundamental Principles by Common Sense?

Thomas Reid, *Essays on the Intellectual Powers of Man*

Descartes' reply (in the previous reading) to his evil genius argument amounts to a claim that the argument is self-refuting. So does Putnam's response (reading 48 in the section "Can We Ever Know Just through Observation?") to the brain-in-a-vat argument. We can find within each of their arguments a view of the skeptical reasoning as developing so dramatically that somehow it applies even to attempts to present the reasoning. Maybe we fail when trying to *formulate* such reasoning (e.g. with the brain-in-a-vat possibility, according to Putnam). Or perhaps we find something significant that *escapes* the skeptical reasoning's grip (e.g. Descartes' evil genius argument's attempt to doubt everything). In either case, no successful skeptical reasoning succeeds in showing there to be no possible instances of the kind of knowledge being questioned.

This reading presents a variation on that theme – along with a potentially tempting way to understand how, once skepticism is no threat, much knowledge could be ours. Thomas Reid (1710–96) is one of Scotland's most famous philosophers. He is the best-known advocate of what is usually called *common sense philosophy*; and we may well feel that if ever there have been forms of philosophy needing to be countered with a strongly administered dose of common sense, skeptical reasoning is one of these. A refusal to become enmeshed in such reasoning's snares: that is what we need; or so we may be reassured by common sense philosophy. Many philosophers would agree that if anything could undermine skeptical arguments, common sense should be able to do so.

Thomas Reid, *Essays on the Intellectual Powers of Man* [1785], Essay I, ch. II, and Essay VI, chs. 2, 4, 5 (excerpts), ed. D.R. Brookes (University Park, PA: Pennsylvania State University Press, 2002).

Metaphysics and Epistemology: A Guided Anthology, First Edition. Edited by Stephen Hetherington.
© 2014 John Wiley & Sons, Inc. Published 2014 by John Wiley & Sons, Inc.

But *can* it do that? Reid argues so. He refines a practical version of the idea of self-refutation. The result is the idea of no one's ever actually *living* a skeptical argument. That amounts to the idea of no one's really *being* a skeptic: no one presenting a skeptical argument actually believes – and therefore no one *lives* even partly on the basis of – the argument's conclusion. Skeptical arguments cannot be applied as far as they are being claimed to apply.

The point is not that most people live without reflecting philosophically upon their lives. The point is more that living a life at all embodies various principles of common sense, and that these clash with skeptical ideas. Reid's strategy includes his sharpening the concept of common sense. He links it to the concept of our most fundamental principles for believing – *first* principles (as he calls them). In this way, common sense becomes *systematic*, not a merely random gathering of everyday opinions. So much so that (given the content of some of those first principles) Reid views skeptical ways of thinking as being contrary to reason.

And so we can know; *how*, though? We build houses of knowledge, based upon *foundations*. These are foundations of self-evident knowledge. This sort of building we *can* accomplish; for skeptical reasoning – Reid has already argued – has no power to weaken those foundations. Descartes the rationalist shared this foundationalist metaphor with Reid the common sense philosopher. Many since have found it an appealing philosophical image.

Principles Taken for Granted

As there are words common to Philosophers and to the vulgar, which need no explication; so there are principles common to both, which need no proof, and which do not admit of direct proof.

One who applies to any branch of science must be come to years of understanding, and consequently must have exercised his reason, and the other powers of his mind, in various ways. He must have formed various opinions and principles by which he conducts himself in the affairs of life. Of those principles, some are common to all men, being evident in themselves, and so necessary in the conduct of life, that a man cannot live and act according to the rules of common prudence without them.

All men that have common understanding agree in such principles, and consider a man as lunatic or destitute of common sense, who denies, or calls them in question. Thus, if any man were found of so strange a turn as not to believe his own eyes; to put no trust in his senses, nor have the least regard to their testimony; would any man think it worth while to reason gravely with such a person, and, by argument, to convince him of his error? Surely no wise man would. For before men can reason together, they must agree in first principles; and it is impossible to reason with a man who has no principles in common with you.

There are, therefore, common principles, which are the foundation of all reasoning, and of all science. Such common principles seldom admit of direct proof, nor do they need it. Men need not to be taught them; for they are such as all men of common understanding know; or such, at least, as they give a ready assent to, as soon as they are proposed and understood.

[...]

In all other sciences, as well as in mathematics, [...] there are a few common principles, upon which all the reasonings in that science are grounded, and into which they may be resolved. If these were pointed out and considered, we should be better able to judge what stress may be laid upon the conclusions in that science. If the principles be certain, the conclusions justly drawn from them must be certain. If the principles be only probable, the conclusions can only be probable. If the principles be false, dubious, or obscure, the superstructure that is built upon them must partake of the weakness of the foundation.

[...]

It is so irksome to reason with those who deny first principles, that wise men commonly decline it. Yet it is not impossible, that what is only a vulgar prejudice may be mistaken for a first principle. Nor is it impossible, that what is really a first principle may, by the enchantment of words, have such a mist thrown about it, as to hide its evidence, and to make a man of candour doubt of it. Such cases happen more frequently perhaps in this science than in any other; but they are not altogether without remedy. There are ways by which the evidence of first principles may be made more apparent when they are brought into dispute; but they require to be handled in a way peculiar to themselves. Their evidence is not demonstrative, but intuitive. They require not proof, but to be placed in a proper point of view. This will be shown more fully in its proper place, and applied to those very principles which we now assume. In the mean time, when they are proposed as first principles, the reader is put on his guard, and warned to consider whether they have a just claim to that character.

[...]

I need hardly say, that I shall also take for granted such facts as are attested to the conviction of all sober and reasonable men, either by our senses, by memory, or by human testimony. Although some writers on this subject have disputed the authority of the senses, of memory, and of every human faculty; yet we find, that such persons, in the conduct of life, in pursuing their ends, or in avoiding dangers, pay the same regard to the authority of their senses, and other faculties, as the rest of mankind. By this they give us just ground to doubt of their candour in their professions of scepticism.

This, indeed, has always been the fate of the few that have professed scepticism, that, when they have done what they can to discredit their senses, they find themselves, after all, under a necessity of trusting to them. Mr HUME has been so candid as to acknowledge this; and it is no less true of those who have not shown the same candour: For I never heard that any sceptic run his head against a post, or stept into a kennel [viz., a gutter or drain beside the street], because he did not believe his eyes.

[...]

Of Common Sense

The word *sense*, in common language, seems to have a different meaning from that which it has in the writings of Philosophers; and those different meanings are apt to be confounded, and to occasion embarrassment and error.

[…][M]odern Philosophers consider sense as a power that has nothing to do with judgment. Sense they consider as the power by which we receive certain ideas or impressions from objects; and judgment as the power by which we compare those ideas, and perceive their necessary agreements and disagreements.

The external senses give us the idea of colour, figure, sound, and other qualities of body, primary or secondary. Mr LOCKE gave the name of an internal sense to consciousness, because by it we have the ideas of thought, memory, reasoning, and other operations of our own minds. […]

[…] [A]ll these senses, whether external or internal, have been represented by Philosophers, as the means of furnishing our minds with ideas, without including any kind of judgment. Dr HUTCHESON defines a sense to be a determination of the mind to receive any idea from the presence of an object independent on our will.

[…]

On the contrary, in common language, sense always implies judgment. A man of sense is a man of judgment. Good sense is good judgment. Nonsense is what is evidently contrary to right judgment. Common sense is that degree of judgment which is common to men with whom we can converse and transact business.

Seeing and hearing by Philosophers are called senses, because we have ideas by them; by the vulgar they are called senses, because we judge by them. We judge of colours by the eye: of sounds by the ear; of beauty and deformity by taste; of right and wrong in conduct by our moral sense or conscience.

[…]

I cannot pretend to assign the reason why a word, which is no term of art, which is familiar in common conversation, should have so different a meaning in philosophical writings. I shall only observe, that the philosophical meaning corresponds perfectly with the account which Mr LOCKE and other modern Philosophers give of judgment. For if the sole province of the senses, external and internal, be to furnish the mind with the ideas about which we judge and reason, it seems to be a natural consequence, that the sole province of judgment should be to compare those ideas, and to perceive their necessary relations.

These two opinions seem to be so connected, that one may have been the cause of the other. I apprehend, however, that if both be true, there is no room left for any knowledge or judgment, either of the real existence of contingent things, or of their contingent relations.

[…]

[…][An] inward light or sense is given by Heaven to different persons in different degrees. There is a certain degree of it which is necessary to our being subjects of law and government, capable of managing our own affairs, and answerable for our conduct towards others: This is called common sense, because it is common to all men with whom we can transact business, or call to account for their conduct.

[…]

All knowledge, and all science, must be built upon principles that are self-evident; and of such principles, every man who has common sense is a competent judge, when he conceives them distinctly. Hence it is, that disputes very often terminate in an appeal to common sense.

While the parties agree in the first principles on which their arguments are grounded, there is room for reasoning; but when one denies what to the other appears too evident to need, or to admit of proof, reasoning seems to be at an end; an appeal is made to common sense, and each party is left to enjoy his own opinion.

There seems to be no remedy for this, nor any way left to discuss such appeals, unless the decisions of common sense can be brought into a code, in which all reasonable men shall acquiesce. This indeed, if it be possible, would be very desirable, and would supply a desideratum [lit., "something to be desired"] in logic; and why should it be thought impossible that reasonable men should agree in things that are self-evident?

All that is intended in this chapter, is to explain the meaning of common sense, that it may not be treated, as it has been by some, as a new principle, or as a word without any meaning. I have endeavoured to shew, that sense, in its most common, and therefore its most proper meaning, signifies judgment, though Philosophers often use it in another meaning. From this it is natural to think, that common sense should mean common judgment; and so it really does.

What the precise limits are which divide common judgment from what is beyond it on the one hand, and from what falls short of it on the other, may be difficult to determine; and men may agree in the meaning of the word who have different opinions about those limits, or who even never thought of fixing them. This is as intelligible as, that all Englishmen should mean the same thing by the county of York, though perhaps not a hundredth part of them can point out its precise limits.

Indeed, it seems to me, that common sense is as unambiguous a word, and as well understood as the county of York. We find it in innumerable places in good writers; we hear it on innumerable occasions in conversation; and, as far as I am able to judge, always in the same meaning. And this is probably the reason why it is so seldom defined or explained.

[...]

It is absurd to conceive that there can be any opposition between reason and common sense. It is indeed the first-born of reason, and as they are commonly joined together in speech and in writing, they are inseparable in their nature.

We ascribe to reason two offices, or two degrees. The first is to judge of things self-evident; the second to draw conclusions that are not self-evident from those that are. The first of these is the province, and the sole province of common sense; and therefore it coincides with reason in its whole extent, and is only another name for one branch or one degree of reason. Perhaps it may be said, Why then should you give it a particular name, since it is acknowledged to be only a degree of reason? [...]

But there is an obvious reason why this degree of reason should have a name appropriated to it; and that is, that in the greatest part of mankind no other degree of reason is to be found. It is this degree that entitles them to the denomination of reasonable creatures. It is this degree of reason, and this only, that makes a man capable of managing his own affairs, and answerable for his conduct towards others. There is therefore the best reason why it should have a name appropriated to it.

[...]

I have only this farther to observe, that the province of common sense is more extensive in refutation than in confirmation. A conclusion drawn by a train of just reasoning from true principles cannot possibly contradict any decision of common sense, because truth will always be consistent with itself. Neither can such a conclusion receive any confirmation from common sense, because it is not within its jurisdiction.

But it is possible, that, by setting out from false principles, or by an error in reasoning, a man may be led to a conclusion that contradicts the decisions of common sense. In this case, the conclusion is within the jurisdiction of common sense, though the reasoning on which it was grounded be not; and a man of common sense may fairly reject the conclusion, without being able to shew the error of the reasoning that led to it.

Thus, if a Mathematician, by a process of intricate demonstration, in which some false step was made, should be brought to this conclusion, that two quantities, which are both equal to a third, are not equal to each other, a man of common sense, without pretending to be a judge of the demonstration, is well entitled to reject the conclusion, and to pronounce it absurd.

[…]

Of first Principles in General

One of the most important distinctions of our judgments is, that some of them are intuitive, others grounded on argument.

It is not in our power to judge as we will. The judgment is carried along necessarily by the evidence, real or seeming, which appears to us at the time. But in propositions that are submitted to our judgment, there is this great difference; some are of such a nature that a man of ripe understanding may apprehend them distinctly, and perfectly understand their meaning without finding himself under any necessity of believing them to be true or false, probable or improbable. The judgment remains in suspense, until it is inclined to one side or another by reasons or arguments.

But there are other propositions which are no sooner understood than they are believed. The judgment follows the apprehension of them necessarily, and both are equally the work of nature, and the result of our original powers. There is no searching for evidence, no weighing of arguments; the proposition is not deduced or inferred from another; it has the light of truth in itself, and has no occasion to borrow it from another.

Propositions of the last kind, when they are used in matters of science, have commonly been called *axioms*; and on whatever occasion they are used, are called *first principles, principles of common sense, common notions, self-evident truths.* […]

What has been said, I think, is sufficient to distinguish first principles, or intuitive judgments, from those which may be ascribed to the power of reasoning; nor is it a just objection against this distinction, that there may be some judgments concerning which we may be dubious to which class they ought to be referred. There is a real distinction between persons within the house, and those that are without; yet it may be dubious to which the man belongs that stands upon the threshold.

The power of reasoning, that is of drawing a conclusion from a chain of premises, may with some propriety be called an art. "All reasoning," says Mr LOCKE, "is search and casting about, and requires pains and application."[1] It resembles the power of walking, which is acquired by use and exercise. Nature prompts to it, and has given the power of acquiring it; but must be aided by frequent exercise before we are able to walk. After repeated efforts, much stumbling, and many falls, we learn to walk; and it is in a similar manner that we learn to reason.

But the power of judging in self-evident propositions, which are clearly understood, may be compared to the power of swallowing our food. It is purely natural, and therefore common to the learned, and the unlearned; to the trained, and the untrained: It requires ripeness of understanding, and freedom from prejudice, but nothing else.

I take it for granted, that there are self-evident principles. Nobody, I think, denies it. And if any man were so sceptical as to deny that there is any proposition that is self-evident, I see not how it would be possible to convince him by reasoning.

But yet there seems to be great difference of opinions among Philosophers about first principles. What one takes to be self-evident, another labours to prove by arguments, and a third denies altogether.

Thus, before the time of DES CARTES, it was taken for a first principle, that there is a sun and a moon, an earth and sea, which really exist, whether we think of them or not. DES CARTES thought that the existence of those things ought to be proved by argument; and in this he has been followed by MALEBRANCHE, ARNAULD, and LOCKE. They have all laboured to prove, by very weak reasoning, the existence of external objects of sense; and BERKELEY and HUME, sensible of the weakness of their arguments, have been led to deny their existence altogether.

[...]

DES CARTES thought one principle, expressed in one word *cogito*, a sufficient foundation for his whole system, and asked no more.

Mr LOCKE seems to think first principles of very small use. Knowledge consisting, according to him, in the perception of the agreement or disagreement of our ideas; when we have clear ideas, and are able to compare them together, we may always fabricate first principles as often as we have occasion for them. Such differences we find among Philosophers about first principles.

It is likewise a question of some moment, whether the differences among men about first principles can be brought to any issue? When, in disputes, one man maintains that to be a first principle, which another denies, commonly both parties appeal to common sense, and so the matter rests. Now, is there no way of discussing this appeal? Is there no mark or criterion, whereby first principles that are truly such, may be distinguished from those that assume the character without a just title? I shall humbly offer in the following propositions what appears to me to be agreeable to truth in these matters, always ready to change my opinion upon conviction.

1. *First*, I hold it to be certain, and even demonstrable, That all knowledge got by reasoning must be built upon first principles.

This is as certain as that every house must have a foundation. The power of reasoning, in this respect, resembles the mechanical powers or engines; it must have a fixed point to rest upon, otherwise it spends its force in the air, and produces no effect.

When we examine, in the way of analysis, the evidence of any proposition, either we find it self-evident, or it rests upon one or more propositions that support it. The same thing may be said of the propositions that support it; and of those that support them, as far back as we can go. But we cannot go back in this track to infinity. Where then must this analysis stop? It is evident that it must stop only when we come to propositions, which support all that are built upon them, but are themselves supported by none, that is, to self-evident propositions.

[...]

2. A *second* proposition is, That some first principles yield conclusions that are certain, others such as are probable, in various degrees, from the highest probability to the lowest.

In just reasoning, the strength or weakness of the conclusion will always correspond to that of the principles on which it is grounded.

[…]

3. A *third* proposition is, that it would contribute greatly to the stability of human knowledge, and consequently to the improvement of it, if the first principles upon which the various parts of it are grounded were pointed out and ascertained.

[…]

4. A *fourth* proposition is, that Nature hath not left us destitute of means whereby the candid and honest part of mankind may be brought to unanimity when they happen to differ about first principles.

When men differ about things that are taken to be first principles or self-evident truths, reasoning seems to be at an end. Each party appeals to common sense. When one man's common sense gives one determination, another man's a contrary determination, there seems to be no remedy but to leave every man to enjoy his own opinion. This is a common observation, and I believe a just one, if it be rightly understood.

It is in vain to reason with a man who denies the first principles on which the reasoning is grounded. Thus, it would be in vain to attempt the proof of a proposition in EUCLID to a man who denies the axioms. Indeed, we ought never to reason with men who deny first principles from obstinacy and unwillingness to yield to reason.

But is it not possible, that men who really love truth, and are open to conviction, may differ about first principles?

I think it is possible, and that it cannot, without great want of charity, be denied to be possible.

When this happens, every man who believes that there is a real distinction between truth and error, and that the faculties which God has given us are not in their nature fallacious, must be convinced that there is a defect, or a perversion of judgment on the one side or the other.

A man of candour and humility will, in such a case, very naturally suspect his own judgment, so far as to be desirous to enter into a serious examination, even of what he has long held as a first principle. He will think it not impossible, that although his heart be upright, his judgment may have been perverted, by education, by authority, by party zeal, or by some other of the common causes of error, from the influence of which neither parts nor integrity exempt the human understanding.

In such a state of mind, so amiable, and so becoming every good man, has Nature left him destitute of any rational means by which he may be enabled, either to correct his judgment if it be wrong, or to confirm it if it be right?

I hope it is not so. I hope that, by the means which Nature has furnished, controversies about first principles may be brought to an issue, and that the real lovers of truth may come to unanimity with regard to them.

It is true, that, in other controversies, the process by which the truth of a proposition is discovered, or its falsehood detected, is, by shewing its necessary connection with first principles, or its repugnancy to them. It is true, likewise, that when the controversy is, whether a proposition be itself a first principle, this process cannot be applied. The truth, therefore, in controversies of this kind, labours under a peculiar disadvantage. But it has advantages of another kind to compensate this.

For, in the *first* place, in such controversies, every man is a competent judge; and therefore it is difficult to impose upon mankind.

To judge of first principles, requires no more than a sound mind free from prejudice, and a distinct conception of the question. The learned and the unlearned, the Philosopher and the day-labourer, are upon a level, and will pass the same judgment, when they are not misled by some bias, or taught to renounce their understanding from some mistaken religious principle.

In matters beyond the reach of common understanding, the many are led by the few, and willingly yield to their authority. But, in matters of common sense, the few must yield to the many, when local and temporary prejudices are removed. No man is now moved by the subtile arguments of ZENO against motion, though perhaps he knows not how to answer them.

The ancient sceptical system furnishes a remarkable instance of this truth. That system, of which PYRRHO was reputed the father, was carried down, through a succession of ages, by very able and acute Philosophers, who taught men to believe nothing at all, and esteemed it the highest pitch of human wisdom to with-hold assent from every proposition whatsoever. It was supported with very great subtilty and learning, as we see from the writings of SEXTUS EMPIRICUS, the only author of that sect whose writings have come down to our age. The assault of the Sceptics against all science seems to have been managed with more art and address than the defence of the Dogmatists.

Yet, as this system was an insult upon the common sense of mankind, it died away of itself; and it would be in vain to attempt to revive it. The modern scepticism is very different from the ancient, otherwise it would not have been allowed a hearing; and, when it has lost the grace of novelty, it will die away also, though it should never be refuted.

The modern scepticism, I mean that of Mr HUME, is built upon principles which were very generally maintained by Philosophers, though they did not see that they led to scepticism. Mr HUME, by tracing, with great acuteness and ingenuity, the consequences of principles commonly received, has shewn that they overturn all knowledge, and at last overturn themselves, and leave the mind in perfect suspense.

[…]

Thus I conceive, that first principles, which are really the dictates of common sense, and directly opposed to absurdities in opinion, will always, from the constitution of human nature, support themselves, and gain rather than lose ground among mankind.

[…]

Thirdly, I conceive, that the consent of ages and nations, of the learned and unlearned, ought to have great authority with regard to first principles, where every man is a competent judge.

Our ordinary conduct in life is built upon first principles, as well as our speculations in philosophy; and every motive to action supposes some belief. When we find a general agreement among men, in principles that concern human life, this must have great authority with every sober mind that loves truth.

It is pleasant to observe the fruitless pains which Bishop BERKELEY takes to shew, that his system of the non-existence of a material world did not contradict the sentiments of the vulgar, but those only of the Philosophers.

With good reason he dreaded more to oppose the authority of vulgar opinion in a matter of this kind, than all the schools of Philosophers.

Here perhaps it will be said, What has authority to do in matters of opinion? Is truth to be determined by most votes? Or is authority to be again raised out of its grave to tyrannise over mankind?

I am aware that, in this age, an advocate for authority has a very unfavourable plea; but I wish to give no more to authority than is its due.

[…]

In a matter of common sense, every man is no less a competent judge than a Mathematician is in a mathematical demonstration; and there must be a great presumption that the judgment of mankind, in such a matter, is the natural issue of those faculties which God hath given them. Such a judgment can be erroneous only when there is some cause of the error, as general as the error is: When this can be shewn to be the case, I acknowledge it ought to have its due weight. But to suppose a general deviation from truth among mankind in things self-evident, of which no cause can be assigned, is highly unreasonable.

Perhaps it may be thought impossible to collect the general opinion of men upon any point whatsoever; and therefore, that this authority can serve us in no stead in examining first principles. But I apprehend, that in many cases this is neither impossible nor difficult.

Who can doubt whether men have universally believed the existence of a material world? Who can doubt whether men have universally believed, that every change that happens in nature must have a cause? Who can doubt whether men have universally believed, that there is a right and a wrong in human conduct; some things that merit blame, and others that are entitled to approbation?

The universality of these opinions, and of many such that might be named, is sufficiently evident, from the whole tenor of human conduct, as far as our acquaintance reaches, and from the history of all ages and nations of which we have any records.

[…]

The first Principles of contingent Truths

"Surely, says Bishop BERKELEY, it is a work well deserving our pains, to make a strict enquiry concerning the first principles of knowledge; to sift and examine them on all sides."[2] What was said in the preceding section is intended both to shew the importance of this enquiry, and to make it more easy.

But, in order that such an enquiry may be actually made, it is necessary that the first principles of knowledge be distinguished from other truths, and presented to view, that they may be sifted and examined on all sides. In order to this end, I shall attempt a detail of those I take to be such, and of the reasons why I think them entitled to that character.

[…]

As the minds of men are occupied much more about truths that are contingent than about those that are necessary, I shall first endeavour to point out the principles of the former kind.

[…]

[One] first principle is, That the natural faculties, by which we distinguish truth from error, are not fallacious. If any man should demand a proof of this, it is impossible to satisfy him. For suppose it should be mathematically demonstrated, this would signify nothing in this case; because, to judge of a demonstration, a man must trust his faculties, and take for granted the very thing in question.

If a man's honesty were called in question, it would be ridiculous to refer it to the man's own word, whether he be honest or not. The same absurdity there is in attempting to prove, by any kind of reasoning, probable or demonstrative, that our reason is not fallacious, since the very point in question is, whether reasoning may be trusted.

If a Sceptic should build his scepticism upon this foundation, that all our reasoning and judging powers are fallacious in their nature, or should resolve at least to with-hold assent until it be proved that they are not; it would be impossible by argument to beat him out of this strong hold, and he must even be left to enjoy his scepticism.

DES CARTES certainly made a false step in this matter; for having suggested this doubt among others, that whatever evidence he might have from his consciousness, his senses, his memory, or his reason; yet possibly some malignant being had given him those faculties on purpose to impose upon him; and therefore, that they are not to be trusted without a proper voucher: To remove this doubt, he endeavours to prove the being of a Deity who is no deceiver; whence he concludes, that the faculties he had given him are true and worthy to be trusted.

It is strange that so acute a reasoner did not perceive, that in this reasoning there is evidently a begging of the question.

For if our faculties be fallacious; why may they not deceive us in this reasoning as well as in others? And if they are to be trusted in this instance without a voucher, why not in others?

Every kind of reasoning for the veracity of our faculties, amounts to no more than taking their own testimony for their veracity; and this we must do implicitly, until God give us new faculties to sit in judgment upon the old; and the reason why DES CARTES satisfied himself with so weak an argument for the truth of his faculties, most probably was, that he never seriously doubted of it.

If any truth can be said to be prior to all others in the order of nature, this seems to have the best claim; because in every instance of assent, whether upon intuitive, demonstrative, or probable evidence, the truth of our faculties is taken for granted, and is, as it were, one of the premises on which our assent is grounded.

How then come we to be assured of this fundamental truth on which all others rest? Perhaps evidence, as in many other respects it resembles light, so in this also, that as light, which is the discoverer of all visible objects, discovers itself at the same time; so evidence, which is the voucher for all truth, vouches for itself at the same time.

This, however, is certain, that such is the constitution of the human mind, that evidence discerned by us, forces a corresponding degree of assent. And a man who perfectly understood a just syllogism, without believing that the conclusion follows from the premises, would be a greater monster than a man born without hands or feet.

We are born under a necessity of trusting to our reasoning and judging powers; and a real belief of their being fallacious cannot be maintained for any considerable time by the greatest Sceptic, because it is doing violence to our constitution. It is like a man's walking upon his hands, a feat which some men upon occasion can exhibit; but no man ever made a long journey in this manner. Cease to admire his dexterity, and he will, like other men, betake himself to his legs.

We may here take notice of a property of the principle under consideration, that seems to be common to it with many other first principles, and which can hardly be found in any principle that is built solely upon reasoning; and that is, that in most men it produces its effect without ever being attended to, or made an object of thought. No man ever thinks of this principle, unless when he considers the grounds of scepticism; yet it invariably governs his opinions. When a man in the common course of life gives credit to the testimony of his senses, his memory, or his reason, he does not put the question to himself, whether these faculties may deceive him; yet the trust he reposes in them supposes an inward conviction, that, in that instance at least, they do not deceive him.

It is another property of this and of many first principles, that they force assent in particular instances, more powerfully than when they are turned into a general proposition. Many Sceptics have denied every general principle of science, excepting perhaps the existence of our present thoughts; yet these men reason, and refute, and prove, they assent and dissent in particular cases. They use reasoning to overturn all reasoning, and judge that they ought to have no judgment, and see clearly that they are blind. Many have in general maintained that the senses are fallacious, yet there never was found a man so sceptical as not to trust his senses in particular instances when his safety required it; and it may be observed of those who have professed scepticism, that their scepticism lies in generals, while in particulars they are no less dogmatical than others.

[…]

Another first principle appears to me to be, That there is a certain regard due to human testimony in matters of fact, and even to human authority in matters of opinion.

Before we are capable of reasoning about testimony or authority, there are many things which it concerns us to know, for which we can have no other evidence. The wise Author of nature hath planted in the human mind a propensity to rely upon this evidence before we can give a reason for doing so. This, indeed, puts our judgment almost entirely in the power of those who are about us, in the first period of life; but this is necessary both to our preservation and to our improvement. If children were so framed, as to pay no regard to testimony or to authority, they must, in the literal sense, perish for lack of knowledge. It is not more necessary that they should be fed before they can feed themselves, than that they should be instructed in many things, before they can discover them by their own judgment.

But when our faculties ripen, we find reason to check that propensity to yield to testimony and to authority, which was so necessary and so natural in the first period of life. We learn to reason about the regard due to them, and see it to be a childish weakness to lay more stress upon them than reason justifies. Yet, I believe, to the end of life, most men are more apt to go into this extreme than into the contrary; and the natural propensity still retains some force.

The natural principles, by which our judgments and opinions are regulated before we come to the use of reason, seem to be no less necessary to such a being as man, than those natural instincts which the Author of nature hath given us to regulate our actions during that period.

Notes

1. Locke, *Essay*, I.ii. 10, p. 52.
2. George Berkeley, *A Treatise Concerning the Principles of Human Knowledge*, Introduction, §4.

66

Do We Know a Lot, but Always Fallibly?

Karl R. Popper, "On the Sources of Knowledge and of Ignorance"

We have seen examples of how philosophers might accuse skeptical reasoning of being self-refuting. Now we may consider a different strategy – a *compatibilist* one – for responding to skepticism. Philosophers most often use the term "compatibilism" when trying to reconcile the concepts of free will and causal determinism. Can a person freely choose to do something, even if everything that ever happens is caused strictly by a previous aspect of the world? Compatibilists are those who seek possible ways of coherently combining these two states of affairs. But compatibilist strategies are also possible elsewhere within philosophy. This reading offers a broadly described example. It aims to describe a conceptual option for evading the supposed power of skeptical arguments.

The reading is from Karl Popper (1902–94), a highly influential Austrian-British philosopher probably most famous for his principle of falsifiability. This was proposed in 1934 as a contribution to the debate, feverish at the time, about how to demarcate science from non-science. Popper's idea was that scientific claims are *falsifiable*: for instance, if a theory as formulated precludes its even possibly being shown to be false, it is not scientific.

What we have in this reading is Popper's sketch of epistemology's history, built around his distinguishing between epistemological optimism and epistemological pessimism. The latter is skepticism in its various guises. Should we dismiss it swiftly? Actually, Popper deems *both* sides of that kind of clash to have limitations. What we should do, he suggests, is to blend together what is worth retaining from each of those two approaches. And what will that mixture be? From epistemological

Karl R. Popper, "On the Sources of Knowledge and of Ignorance" (excerpts), in his *Conjectures and Refutations: The Growth of Scientific Knowledge* (London: Routledge & Kegan Paul, 1963). Reprinted with permission of the Karl Popper Library.

optimism, Popper agrees that there is knowledge. From epistemological pessimism, he concedes that there is no certainty. How does he reconcile those two?

He is not perturbed by the prospect of inescapable uncertainty. Part of why we rationally fall short of certainty is that there is objective truth. (For more on this, see "How Are There Any Truths?", readings 15 to 17) But our attempts to know such truths are forever fallible – a feature that could be seen as a generalization of Popper's idea of falsifiability. Fallibility would thus be a criterion of what a claim to knowledge – any kind of knowledge; not only scientific knowledge – should be. In the section "Can We Ever Know Just through Reflection?", we met Peirce's pragmatism (in reading 55). In this reading (even if possibly not in everything related that he wrote) Popper's view is similar. Here, he tells us that whenever we know – and we *do* at times have knowledge; science is testament to this – we do it fallibly. All knowledge is fallible knowledge. Even as skeptical arguments deny us certainty, they need not be interpreted as depriving us of knowledge. (And recall Bertrand Russell on the value in philosophy, in reading 2 of this book. He thought that a lack of certainty is itself a consequence of what is valuable within philosophy – namely, the sustained questioning. Could something like that be true of knowing in general?)

III

The great movement of liberation which started in the Renaissance and led through the many vicissitudes of the reformation and the religious and revolutionary wars to the free societies in which the English-speaking peoples are privileged to live, this movement was inspired throughout by an unparalleled epistemological optimism: by a most optimistic view of man's power to discern truth and to acquire knowledge.

At the heart of this new optimistic view of the possibility of knowledge lies the doctrine that *truth is manifest*. Truth may perhaps be veiled. But it may reveal itself. And if it does not reveal itself, it may be revealed by us. Removing the veil may not be easy. But once the naked truth stands revealed before our eyes, we have the power to see it, to distinguish it from falsehood, and to know that it *is* truth.

The birth of modern science and modern technology was inspired by this optimistic epistemology whose main spokesmen were Bacon and Descartes. They taught that there was no need for any man to appeal to authority in matters of truth because each man carried the sources of knowledge in himself; either in his power of sense-perception which he may use for the careful observation of nature, or in his power of intellectual intuition which he may use to distinguish truth from falsehood by refusing to accept any idea which is not clearly and distinctly perceived by the intellect.

Man can know: thus he can be free. This is the formula which explains the link between epistemological optimism and the ideas of liberalism.

This link is paralleled by the opposite link. Disbelief in the power of human reason, in man's power to discern the truth, is almost invariably linked with distrust of man. Thus epistemological pessimism is linked, historically, with a doctrine of human depravity, and it tends to lead to the demand for the establishment of powerful traditions and the entrenchment of a powerful authority which would save man from his folly and his wickedness. [...]

The contrast between epistemological pessimism and optimism may be said to be fundamentally the same as that between epistemological traditionalism and rationalism. (I am using the latter term in its wider sense in which it is opposed to irrationalism, and in which it covers not only Cartesian intellectualism but empiricism also.) For we can interpret traditionalism as the belief that, in the absence of an objective and discernible truth, we are faced with the choice between accepting the authority of tradition, and chaos; while rationalism has, of course, always claimed the right of reason and of empirical science to criticize, and to reject, any tradition, and any authority, as being based on sheer unreason or prejudice or accident.

[...]

V

In examining the optimistic epistemology inherent in certain ideas of liberalism, I found a cluster of doctrines which, although often accepted implicitly, have not, to my knowledge, been explicitly discussed or even noticed by philosophers or historians. The most fundamental of them is one which I have already mentioned – the doctrine that truth is manifest. The strangest of them is the conspiracy theory of ignorance, which is a curious outgrowth from the doctrine of manifest truth.

By the doctrine that truth is manifest I mean, you will recall, the optimistic view that truth, if put before us naked, is always recognizable as truth. Thus truth, if it does not reveal itself, has only to be unveiled, or dis-covered. Once this is done, there is no need for further argument. We have been given eyes to see the truth, and the 'natural light' of reason to see it by.

This doctrine is at the heart of the teaching of both Descartes and Bacon. Descartes based his optimistic epistemology on the important theory of the *veracitas dei* [viz., "the truthfulness of God"]. What we clearly and distinctly see to be true must indeed be true; for otherwise God would be deceiving us. Thus the truthfulness of God must make truth manifest.

In Bacon we have a similar doctrine. It might be described as the doctrine of the *veracitas naturae*, the truthfulness of Nature. Nature is an open book. He who reads it with a pure mind cannot misread it. Only if his mind is poisoned by prejudice can he fall into error.

[...]

But [...] the theory of manifest truth [...] was a myth.

For the simple truth is that truth is often hard to come by, and that once found it may easily be lost again. Erroneous beliefs may have an astonishing power to survive, for thousands of years, in defiance of experience, with or without the aid of any conspiracy. The history of science, and especially of medicine, could furnish us with a number of good examples. One example is, indeed, the general conspiracy theory itself. I mean the erroneous view that whenever something evil happens it must be due to the evil will of an evil power. Various forms of this view have survived down to our own day.

Thus the optimistic epistemology of Bacon and of Descartes cannot be true. Yet perhaps the strangest thing in this story is that this false epistemology was the major inspiration of an intellectual and moral revolution without parallel in history. It encouraged men to think for themselves. It gave them hope that through knowledge they might free themselves and others from servitude and misery. It made modern science possible. It became the basis of the fight against censorship and the suppression of free thought. It became the basis of the non-conformist conscience, of individualism, and of a new sense of man's dignity; of a demand for universal education, and of a new dream of a free society. It made men feel responsible for themselves and for others, and eager to improve not only their own condition but also that of their fellow men. It is a case of a bad idea inspiring many good ones.

VI

This false epistemology, however, has also led to disastrous consequences. The theory that truth is manifest – that it is there for everyone to see, if only he wants to see it – this theory is the basis of almost every kind of fanaticism. For only the most depraved wickedness can refuse to see the manifest truth; only those who have reason to fear truth conspire to suppress it.

Yet the theory that truth is manifest not only breeds fanatics – men possessed by the conviction that all those who do not see the manifest truth must be possessed by the devil – but it may also lead, though perhaps less directly than does a pessimistic epistemology, to authoritarianism. This is so, simply, because truth is not manifest, as a rule. The allegedly manifest truth is therefore in constant need, not only of interpretation and affirmation, but also of re-interpretation and re-affirmation. An authority is required to pronounce upon, and lay down, almost from day to day, what is to be the manifest truth, and it may learn to do so arbitrarily and cynically. And many disappointed epistemologists will turn away from their own former optimism and erect a resplendent authoritarian theory on the basis of a pessimistic epistemology. It seems to me that the greatest epistemologist of all, Plato, exemplifies this tragic development.

VII

Plato plays a decisive part in the pre-history of Descartes' doctrine of the *veracitas dei* – the doctrine that our intellectual intuition does not deceive us because God is truthful and will not deceive us; or in other words, the doctrine that our intellect is a source of knowledge because God is a source of knowledge. This doctrine has a long history which can easily be traced back at least to Homer and Hesiod.

[...]

[...] [T]he doctrine of the divine source of our knowledge plays a decisive part in Plato's famous theory of *anamnēsis* which in some measure grants to each man the possession of divine sources of knowledge. (The knowledge considered in this theory is knowledge of the *essence or nature* of a thing rather than of a particular historical fact.) According to Plato's *Meno* (81b–d) there is nothing which our immortal soul does not know, prior to our birth. [...] In being born we forget; but we may recover our memory and our knowledge, though only partially: only if we see the truth again shall we recognize it. All knowledge is therefore re-cognition – recalling or remembering the essence or true nature that we once knew. [...]

[...]

It is clear that there is a close link between this theory of *anamnēsis* and the doctrine of the divine origin or source of our knowledge. At the same time, there is also a close link between the theory of *anamnēsis* and the doctrine of manifest truth: if, even in our depraved state of forgetfulness, we see the truth, we cannot but recognize it as the truth. So, as the result of *anamnēsis*, truth is restored to the status of that which is not forgotten and not concealed (*alēthēs*): it is that which is manifest.

Socrates demonstrates this in a beautiful passage of the *Meno* by helping an uneducated young slave to 'recall' the proof of a special case of the theorem of Pythagoras. Here indeed is an optimistic epistemology, and the root of Cartesianism. It seems that, in the *Meno*, Plato was conscious of the highly optimistic character of his theory, for he describes it as a doctrine which makes men eager to learn, to search, and to discover.

Yet disappointment must have come to Plato; for in the *Republic* (and also in the *Phaedrus*) we find the beginnings of a pessimistic epistemology. In the famous story of the prisoners in the cave [see reading 1] he shows that the world of our experience is only a shadow, a reflection, of the real world. And he shows that even if one of the prisoners should escape from the cave and face the real world, he would have almost insuperable difficulties in seeing and understanding it – to say nothing of his difficulties in trying to make those understand who stayed behind. The difficulties in the way of an understanding of the real world are all but super-human, and only the very few, if anybody at all, can attain to the divine state of understanding the real world – the divine state of true knowledge, of *epistēmē*.

This is a pessimistic theory with regard to almost all men, though not with regard to all. (For it teaches that truth may be attained by a few – the elect. With regard to these it is, one might say, more wildly optimistic than even the doctrine that truth is manifest.) [...]

Thus we find in Plato the first transition from an optimistic to a pessimistic epistemology. Each of these forms a basis for one of two diametrically opposed philosophies of the state and of society: on the one hand an anti-traditionalist, anti-authoritarian, revolutionary and Utopian rationalism of the Cartesian kind, and on the other hand an authoritarian traditionalism.

[...]

VIII

[...] [W]hat interests us here is Plato's optimistic epistemology, the theory of *anamnēsis* in the *Meno*. It contains, I believe, not only the germs of Descartes' intellectualism, but also the germs of Aristotle's and especially of Bacon's theories of induction.

For Meno's slave is helped by Socrates' judicious questions to remember or recapture the forgotten knowledge which his soul possessed in its pre-natal state of omniscience. It is, I believe, this famous Socratic method, called in the *Theaetetus* the art of midwifery or *maieutic*. [...]

[...] The *maieutic* art of Socrates consists, essentially, in asking questions designed to destroy prejudices; false beliefs which are often traditional or fashionable beliefs; false answers, given in the spirit of ignorant cocksureness. Socrates himself does not pretend to know. His attitude is described by Aristotle in the words, 'Socrates raised questions but gave no answers; for he confessed that he did not know.' (*Sophist. El.*, 183b7; cf. *Theaetetus*, 150c–d, 157c, 161b.) Thus Socrates' *maieutic* is not an art that aims at teaching any belief, but one that aims at purging or cleansing (cf. the allusion to the *Amphidromia* in *Theaetetus* 160e) the soul of its false beliefs, its seeming knowledge, its prejudices. It achieves this by teaching us to doubt our own convictions.

Fundamentally the same procedure is part of Bacon's induction.

IX

The framework of Bacon's theory of induction is this. He distinguishes in the *Novum Organum* between a true method and a false method. His name for the true method, '*interpretatio naturae*', is ordinarily translated by the phrase 'interpretation of nature', and his name for the false method, '*anticipatio mentis*', by 'anticipation of the mind'. [...] What Bacon means by '*interpretatio naturae*' is, I suggest, the reading of, or better still, *the spelling out of, the book of Nature*. [...]
[...]
Thus the translation 'the interpretation of nature' is misleading; it should be replaced by something like 'the (true) reading of nature'; analogous to 'the (true) reading of the law'. And I suggest that 'reading the book of Nature as it is' or better still 'spelling out the book of Nature' is what Bacon meant. The point is that the phrase should suggest the avoidance of all interpretation in the modern sense, and that it should *not* contain, more especially, any suggestion of an attempt to interpret what is manifest in nature in the light of non-manifest causes or of hypotheses; for all this would be an *anticipatio mentis*, in Bacon's sense. [...]

As to the meaning of '*anticipatio mentis*' we have only to quote Locke: 'men give themselves up to the first anticipations of their minds' (*Of the Conduct of the Understanding* [1706], 26). This is, practically, a translation from Bacon; and it makes it amply clear that '*anticipatio*' means 'prejudice' or even 'superstition'. We can also refer to the phrase '*anticipatio deorum*' which means harbouring naïve or primitive or superstitious views about the gods. But to make matters still more obvious: 'prejudice' (cp. Descartes, *Principles of Philosophy* [1644], I, 50) derives from a legal term, and according to the *Oxford English Dictionary* it was Bacon who introduced the verb 'to prejudge' into the English language, in the sense of 'to judge adversely in advance' – that is, in violation of the judge's duty.

Thus the two methods are (1) 'the spelling out of the open book of Nature', leading to knowledge or *epistēmē*, and (2) 'the prejudice of the mind that wrongly prejudges, and perhaps misjudges, Nature', leading to *doxa*, or mere guesswork, and to the misreading of the book of Nature. This latter method, rejected by Bacon, is in fact a method of interpretation, in the modern sense of the word. It is the *method of conjecture or hypothesis* (a method of which, incidentally, I happen to be a convinced advocate).

How can we prepare ourselves to read the book of Nature properly or truly? Bacon's answer is: by purging our minds of all anticipations or conjectures or guesses or prejudices (*Novum Organum* [1620], i, 68, 69 end). There are various things to be done in order so to purge our minds. We have to get rid of all sorts of 'idols', or generally held false beliefs; for these distort our observations (*Nov. Org.* i, 97). But we have also, like Socrates, to look out for all sorts of counter-instances by which to destroy our prejudices concerning the kind of thing whose true essence or nature we wish to ascertain. Like Socrates, we must, by purifying our intellects, prepare our souls to face the eternal light of essences or natures (cf. St Augustine, *De Civitate Dei*, viii. 3 [5th century CE; trans., *The City of God*].): our impure prejudices must be exorcised by the invocation of counter-instances (*Nov. Org.* ii, 16 ff).

Only after our souls have been cleansed in this way may we begin the work of spelling out diligently the open book of Nature, the manifest truth.

In view of all this I suggest that Baconian (and also Aristotelian) induction is the same, fundamentally, as Socratic *maieutic*; that is to say, the preparation of the mind by cleansing it of prejudices, in order to enable it to recognize the manifest truth, or to read the open book of Nature.

Descartes' method of systematic doubt is also fundamentally the same: it is a method of destroying all false prejudices of the mind, in order to arrive at the unshakable basis of self-evident truth.

[...]

X

[...] Bacon's and Descartes' attacks upon prejudice, and upon traditional beliefs which we carelessly or recklessly harbour, are clearly anti-authoritarian and anti-traditionalist. For they require us to shed all beliefs except those whose truth we have perceived ourselves. And their attacks were certainly intended to be attacks upon authority and tradition. They were part of the war against authority which it was the fashion of the time to wage, the war against the authority of Aristotle and the tradition of the schools. Men do not need such authorities if they can perceive the truth themselves.

But I do not think that Bacon and Descartes succeeded in freeing their epistemologies from authority; not so much because they appealed to religious authority – to Nature or to God – but for an even deeper reason.

In spite of their individualistic tendencies, they did not dare to appeal to our critical judgment – to your judgment, or to mine; perhaps because they felt that this might lead to subjectivism and to arbitrariness. Yet whatever the reason may have been, they certainly were unable to give up thinking in terms of authority, much as they wanted to do so. They could only replace one authority – that of Aristotle and the Bible – by another. Each of them appealed to a new authority; the one to *the authority of the senses*, and the other to *the authority of the intellect*.

This means that they failed to solve the great problem: How can we admit that our knowledge is a human – an all too human – affair, without at the same time implying that it is all individual whim and arbitrariness?

Yet this problem had been seen and solved long ago; first, it appears, by Xenophanes, and then by Democritus, and by Socrates (the Socrates of the *Apology* rather than of the *Meno*). The solution lies in the realization that all of us may and often do err, singly and collectively, but that this very idea of error and human fallibility involves another one – the idea of *objective truth*: the standard which we may fall short of. Thus the doctrine of fallibility should not be regarded as part of a pessimistic epistemology. This doctrine implies that we may seek for truth, for objective truth, though more often than not we may miss it by a wide margin. And it implies that if we respect truth, we must search for it by persistently searching for our errors: by indefatigable rational criticism, and self-criticism.

Erasmus of Rotterdam attempted to revive this Socratic doctrine – the important though unobtrusive doctrine, 'Know thyself, and thus admit to thyself how little thou knowest!' Yet this doctrine was swept away by the belief that truth is manifest, and by the new self-assurance exemplified and taught in different ways by Luther and Calvin, by Bacon and Descartes.

It is important to realize, in this connection, the difference between Cartesian doubt and the doubt of Socrates, or Erasmus, or Montaigne. While Socrates doubts human knowledge or wisdom, and remains firm in his rejection of any pretension to knowledge or wisdom, Descartes doubts everything – but only to end up with the possession of *absolutely certain* knowledge; for he finds that his universal doubt would lead him to doubt the truthfulness of God, which is absurd. Having proved that universal doubt is absurd, he concludes that we *can* know securely, that we *can* be wise – by distinguishing, in the natural light of reason, between clear and distinct ideas whose source is God, and all other ideas whose source is our own impure imagination. Cartesian doubt, we see, is merely a *maieutic* instrument for establishing a criterion of truth and, with it, a way to secure knowledge and wisdom. Yet for the Socrates of the *Apology*, wisdom consisted in the awareness of our limitations; in knowing how little we know, every one of us.

It was this doctrine of an essential human fallibility which Nicolas of Cusa and Erasmus of Rotterdam (who refers to Socrates) revived; and it was this 'humanist' doctrine (in contradistinction to the optimistic doctrine on which Milton relied, the doctrine that truth will prevail) which Nicolas and Erasmus, Montaigne and Locke and Voltaire, followed by John Stuart Mill and Bertrand Russell, made the basis of the doctrine of tolerance. 'What is tolerance?' asks Voltaire in his *Philosophical Dictionary*; and he answers: 'It is a necessary consequence of our humanity. We are all fallible, and prone to error; let us then pardon each other's folly. This is the first principle of natural right.' (More recently the doctrine of fallibility has been made the basis of a theory of political freedom; that is, freedom from coercion. See F. A. Hayek, *The Constitution of Liberty*, especially pp. 22 and 29.)

[...]

XVI

It is high time now, I think, to formulate the epistemological results of this discussion. I will put them in the form of ten theses.

1. There are no ultimate sources of knowledge. Every source, every suggestion, is welcome; and every source, every suggestion, is open to critical examination. Except in history, we usually examine the facts themselves rather than the sources of our information.

2. The proper epistemological question is not one about sources; rather, we ask whether the assertion made is true – that is to say, whether it agrees with the facts. [...] And we try to find this out, as well as we can, by examining or testing the assertion itself; either in a direct way, or by examining or testing its consequences.

3. In connection with this examination, all kinds of arguments may be relevant. A typical procedure is to examine whether our theories are consistent with our observations. But we may also examine, for example, whether our historical sources are mutually and internally consistent.

4. Quantitatively and qualitatively by far the most important source of our knowledge – apart from inborn knowledge – is tradition. Most things we know we have learned by example, by being told, by reading books, by learning how to criticize, how to take and to accept criticism, how to respect truth.

5. The fact that most of the sources of our knowledge are traditional condemns anti-traditionalism as futile. But this fact must not be held to support a traditionalist attitude: every bit of our traditional knowledge (and even our inborn knowledge) is open to critical examination and may be overthrown. Nevertheless, without tradition, knowledge would be impossible.

6. Knowledge cannot start from nothing – from a *tabula rasa* – nor yet from observation. The advance of knowledge consists, mainly, in the modification of earlier knowledge. Although we may sometimes, for example in archaeology, advance through a chance observation, the significance of the discovery will usually depend upon its power to modify our earlier theories.

7. Pessimistic and optimistic epistemologies are about equally mistaken. The pessimistic cave story of Plato is the true one, and not his optimistic story of *anamnēsis* (even though we should admit that all men, like all other animals, and even all plants, possess inborn knowledge). But although the world of appearances is indeed a world of mere shadows on the walls of our cave, we all constantly reach out beyond it; and although, as Democritus said, the truth is hidden in the deep, we can probe into the deep. There is no criterion of truth at our disposal, and this fact supports pessimism. But we do possess criteria which, *if we are lucky*, may allow us to recognize error and falsity. Clarity and distinctness are not criteria of truth, but such things as obscurity or confusion *may* indicate error. Similarly coherence cannot establish truth, but incoherence and inconsistency do establish falsehood. And, when they are recognized, our own errors provide the dim red lights which help us in groping our way out of the darkness of our cave.

8. Neither observation nor reason are authorities. Intellectual intuition and imagination are most important, but they are not reliable: they may show us things very clearly, and yet they may mislead us. They are indispensable as the main sources of our theories; but most of our theories are false anyway. The most important function of observation and reasoning, and even of intuition and imagination, is to help us in the critical examination of those bold conjectures which are the means by which we probe into the unknown.

9. Although clarity is valuable in itself, exactness or precision is not: there can be no point in trying to be more precise than our problem demands. Linguistic precision is a phantom, and problems connected with the meaning or definition of words are unimportant. [...] Words are significant only as instruments for the formulation of theories, and verbal problems should be avoided at all cost.

10. Every solution of a problem raises new unsolved problems; the more so the deeper the original problem and the bolder its solution. The more we learn about the world, and the deeper our learning, the more conscious, specific, and articulate will be our knowledge of what we do not know, our knowledge of our ignorance. For this, indeed, is the main source of our ignorance – the fact that our knowledge can be only finite, while our ignorance must necessarily be infinite.

We may get a glimpse of the vastness of our ignorance when we contemplate the vastness of the heavens: though the mere size of the universe is not the deepest cause of our ignorance, it is one of its causes. 'Where I seem to differ from some of my friends', F. P. Ramsey wrote in a charming passage of his *Foundations of Mathematics* (p. 291), 'is in attaching little importance to physical size. I don't feel in the least humble before the vastness of the heavens. The stars may be large but they cannot think or love; and these are qualities which impress me far more than size does. I take no credit for weighing nearly seventeen stone.' I suspect that Ramsey's friends would have agreed with him about the insignificance of sheer physical size; and I suspect that if they felt humble before the vastness of the heavens, this was because they saw in it a symbol of their ignorance.

I believe that it would be worth trying to learn something about the world even if in trying to do so we should merely learn that we do not know much. This state of learned ignorance might be a help in many of our troubles. It might be well for all of us to remember that, while differing widely in the various little bits we know, in our infinite ignorance we are all equal.

67

Is It Possible to have Knowledge even when Not Knowing that One Is Not a Brain in a Vat?

Robert Nozick, *Philosophical Explanations*

Karl Popper's response to skeptical ideas (in the previous reading) was a broadly described form of compatibilism. Robert Nozick's response (in this reading) is more specifically compatibilist. He concedes something substantive and specific to skeptical reasoning – but far less than such reasoning would most likely claim we must concede. In reading 5, we met Nozick's view of philosophy as able to prosper by seeking explanations of important possibilities (rather than as needing always to prove how the world is or must be). We are ending the book with an example of how Nozick put that view into practice.

His aim is to explain how it is possible to have quite normal knowledge (such as of being at home, reading in a chair) *even* if skeptical arguments are correct to deny that anyone ever knows that she is not dreaming, or that she is not a brain in a vat, or that she is not being deceived by an evil demon, say. Some earlier readings have discussed these classic skeptical possibilities. Such possibilities arise in skeptical arguments precisely because of the thought that we *do* need to know of their not applying to us if we are to have normal knowledge. The arguments reflect a way in which many a person would be perturbed at the idea of not knowing that she is not a brain in a vat: "If I do not know *that*, then I do not know even where and what I am right now!" So this kind of inference is what Nozick questions. He aims to explain why even a concession of not knowing that one is not a brain in a vat would leave open the possibility of having "normal" knowledge of being at home, reading in a chair.

How does Nozick hope to reveal that possibility? First he develops an account of knowledge. (His account – partly motivated as a response to Gettier's challenge – has

Robert Nozick, *Philosophical Explanations* (Cambridge, MA: The Belknap Press of Harvard University Press, 1981), ch. 3, "Knowledge and Skepticism" (excerpts). Copyright © 1981 by Robert Nozick. Reprinted with permission of Harvard University Press.

Metaphysics and Epistemology: A Guided Anthology, First Edition. Edited by Stephen Hetherington.
© 2014 John Wiley & Sons, Inc. Published 2014 by John Wiley & Sons, Inc.

attracted much philosophical discussion. It could have been included in our section "Can We Understand What It Is to Know?") Next he applies his account to instances of skeptical reasoning. Doing so leads him to this result: No one *can* know that a skeptical possibility, such as that of being a brain in a vat, is not true of her. But then Nozick explains how, *even so,* normal knowledge is possible. His strategy is thereby to deny a principle (the closure of knowledge under known entailment, to be explained below) which he deems to be pivotal within skeptical reasoning.

This anti-skeptical strategy of Nozick's is indirect. Its goal is to reveal a weakness in the skeptical reasoning, not to deny directly the skeptical reasoning's conclusion that we have no knowledge. (A similarly indirect anti-skeptical strategy was used in reading 49, from John McDowell, in the section "Can We Know Just through Observation?") Still, *do* we know? Nozick's conclusion is that it is at least possible; and that it is possible even if the skeptical reasoning is right to deny us some knowledge – such as, for each of us, the knowledge that one is not a brain in a vat. Nozick strives to weaken the skeptical reasoning's impact even while respecting something within it. His conclusion is that even if we do know, maybe we know *less* than we would have assumed we do.

Conditions for Knowledge

Our task is to formulate further conditions to go alongside

(1) *p* is true
(2) S believes that *p*.

[…]

The causal condition on knowledge [see reading 41] provides an inhospitable environment for mathematical and ethical knowledge; also there are well-known difficulties in specifying the type of causal connection. If someone floating in a tank oblivious to everything around him is given (by direct electrical and chemical stimulation of the brain) the belief that he is floating in a tank with his brain being stimulated, then even though that fact is part of the cause of his belief, still he does not know that it is true.

Let us consider a different third condition:

(3) If *p* weren't true, S wouldn't believe that *p*.

Throughout this work, let us write the subjunctive 'if-then' by an arrow, and the negation of a sentence by prefacing "not-" to it. The above condition thus is rewritten as:

(3) not-*p* $\rightarrow$ not-(S believes that *p*).

[…]

The subjunctive condition 3 […] tells us only half the story about how his belief is sensitive to the truth-value of p. It tells us how his belief state is sensitive to p's falsity, but not how it is sensitive to p's truth; it tells us what his belief state would be if p were false, but not what it would be if p were true.

To be sure, conditions 1 and 2 tell us that p is true and he does believe it, but it does not follow that his believing p is sensitive to p's being true. This additional sensitivity is given to us by a further subjunctive: if p were true, he would believe it.

(4) $p \rightarrow S$ believes that p.

[…] 4 holds true if not only does he actually truly believe p, but in the "close" worlds where p is true, he also believes it. He believes that p for some distance out in the p neighborhood of the actual world; similarly, condition 3 speaks not of the whole not-p neighborhood of the actual world, but only of the first portion of it. (If, as is likely, these explanations do not help, please use your own intuitive understanding of the subjunctives 3 and 4.)

[…]

Skepticism

The skeptic about knowledge argues that we know very little or nothing of what we think we know, or at any rate that this position is no less reasonable than the belief in knowledge. The history of philosophy exhibits a number of different attempts to refute the skeptic: to prove him wrong or show that in arguing against knowledge he presupposes there is some and so refutes himself. Others attempt to show that accepting skepticism is unreasonable, since it is more likely that the skeptic's extreme conclusion is false than that all of his premisses are true, or simply because reasonableness of belief just means proceeding in an anti-skeptical way. Even when these counterarguments satisfy their inventors, they fail to satisfy others, as is shown by the persistent attempts against skepticism. The continuing felt need to refute skepticism, and the difficulty in doing so, attests to the power of the skeptic's position, the depth of his worries.

An account of knowledge should illuminate skeptical arguments and show wherein lies their force. If the account leads us to reject these arguments, this had better not happen too easily or too glibly. To think the skeptic overlooks something obvious, to attribute to him a simple mistake or confusion or fallacy, is to refuse to acknowledge the power of his position and the grip it can have upon us. We thereby cheat ourselves of the opportunity to reap his insights and to gain self-knowledge in understanding why his arguments lure us so. Moreover, in fact, we cannot lay the specter of skepticism to rest without first hearing what it shall unfold.

Our goal is not, however, to refute skepticism, to prove it is wrong or even to argue that it is wrong. In the Introduction we distinguished between philosophy that attempts to prove, and philosophy that attempts to explain how something is possible. Our task here is to explain how knowledge is possible, given what the skeptic says that we do accept (for example, that it is logically possible that we are dreaming or are floating in the tank). In doing this, we need not convince the skeptic, and we may introduce explanatory hypotheses that he would reject. What is important for our task of explanation and understanding is that *we* find those hypotheses acceptable or plausible, and that they show us how the existence of knowledge fits together with the logical possibilities the skeptic points to, so that these are reconciled within our own belief system. These hypotheses are to explain to ourselves how knowledge is possible, not to prove to someone else that knowledge *is* possible.[1]

[...]

Skeptical Results

According to our account of knowledge, S knows that the skeptic's situation SK doesn't hold if and only if

(1)   SK doesn't hold
(2)   S believes that SK doesn't hold
(3)   If SK were to hold, S would not believe that SK doesn't hold
(4)   If SK were not to hold, S would believe it does not.

Let us focus on the third of these conditions. The skeptic has carefully chosen his situations SK so that if they held we (still) would believe they did not. We would believe we weren't dreaming, weren't being deceived, and so on, even if we were. He has chosen situations SK such that if SK were to hold, S would (still) believe that SK doesn't hold – and this is incompatible with the truth of 3.

Since condition 3 is a necessary condition for knowledge, it follows that we do not know that SK doesn't hold. If it were true that an evil demon was deceiving us, if we were having a particular dream, if we were floating in a tank with our brains stimulated in a specified way, we would still believe we were not. So, we do not know we're not being deceived by an evil demon, we do not know we're not in that tank, and we do not know we're not having that dream. So says the skeptic, and so says our account. And also so we say – don't we? For how could we know we are not being deceived that way, dreaming that dream? If those things *were* happening to us, everything would seem the same to us. There is no way we can know it is not happening for there is no way we could tell if it were happening; and if it were happening we would believe exactly what we do now – in particular, we still would believe that it was not. For this reason, we feel, and correctly, that we don't know – how could we? – that it is not happening to us. It is a virtue of our account that it yields, and explains, this result.

The skeptic asserts we do not know his possibilities don't obtain, and he is right. Attempts to avoid skepticism by claiming we do know these things are bound to fail. The skeptic's possibilities make us uneasy because, as we deeply realize, we do not know they don't obtain; it is not surprising that attempts to show we do know these things leave us suspicious, strike us even as bad faith. Nor has the skeptic merely pointed out something obvious and trivial. It comes as a surprise to realize that we do not know his possibilities don't obtain. It is startling, shocking. For we would have thought, before the skeptic got us to focus on it, that we did know those things, that we did know we were not being deceived by a demon, or dreaming that dream, or stimulated that way in that tank. The skeptic has pointed out that we do not know things we would have confidently said we knew. And if we don't know these things, what can we know? So much for the supposed obviousness of what the skeptic tells us.

[...]
What more could the skeptic ask for or hope to show? Even readers who sympathized with my desire not to dismiss the skeptic too quickly may feel this has gone too far, that we have not merely acknowledged the force of the skeptic's position but have succumbed to it.

The skeptic maintains that we know almost none of what we think we know. He has shown, much to our initial surprise, that we do not know his (nontrivial) possibility SK doesn't obtain. Thus, he has shown of one thing we thought we knew, that we didn't and don't. To the conclusion that we know almost nothing, it appears but a short step. For if we do not know we are not dreaming or being deceived by a demon or floating in a tank, then how can I know, for example, that I am sitting before a page writing with a pen, and how can you know that you are reading a page of a book?

However, although our account of knowledge agrees with the skeptic in saying that we do not know that not-SK, it places no formidable barriers before my knowing that I am writing on a page with a pen. It is true that I am, I believe I am, if I weren't I wouldn't believe I was, and if I were, I would believe it. (I leave out the reference to method.) Also, it is true that you are reading a page (please, don't stop now!), you believe you are, if you weren't reading a page you wouldn't believe you were, and if you were reading a page you would believe you were. So according to the account, I do know that I am writing on a page with a pen, and you do know that you are reading a page. The account does not lead to any general skepticism.

Yet we must grant that it appears that if the skeptic is right that we don't know we are not dreaming or being deceived or floating in the tank, then it cannot be that I know I am writing with a pen or that you know you are reading a page. So we must scrutinize with special care the skeptic's "short step" to the conclusion that we don't know these things, for either this step cannot be taken or our account of knowledge is incoherent.

Nonclosure

In taking the "short step", the skeptic assumes that if S knows that p and he knows that 'p entails q' then he also knows that q. In the terminology of the logicians, the skeptic assumes that knowledge is closed under known logical implication; that the operation of moving from something known to something else known to be entailed by it does not take us outside of the (closed) area of knowledge. He intends, of course, to work things backwards, arguing that since the person does not know that q, assuming (at least for the purposes of argument) that he does know that p entails q, it follows that he does not know that p. For if he did know that p, he would also know that q, which he doesn't.

[...]
You know that your being in a tank on Alpha Centauri entails your not being in place X where you are. (I assume here a limited readership.) And you know also the contrapositive, that your being at place X entails that you are not then in a tank on Alpha Centauri. If you knew you were at X you would know you're not in a tank (of a specified sort) at Alpha Centauri. But you do not know this last fact (the skeptic has argued and we have agreed) and so (he argues) you don't know the first. Another intuitive way of putting the skeptic's argument is as follows. If you know that two statements are incompatible and you know the first is true then you

know the denial of the second. You know that, your being at X and your being in a tank on Alpha Centauri are incompatible; so if you knew you were at X you would know you were not in the (specified) tank on Alpha Centauri. Since you do not know the second, you don't know the first.

[...]

[...] [H]owever, [...] knowledge is not closed under known logical implication. S knows that p when S has a true belief that p, and S wouldn't have a false belief that p (condition 3) and S would have a true belief that p (condition 4). Neither of these latter two conditions is closed under known logical implication.

Let us begin with condition

(3) if p were false, S wouldn't believe that p.

When S knows that p, his belief that p is contingent on the truth of p, contingent in the way the subjunctive condition 3 describes. Now it might be that p entails q (and S knows this), that S's belief that p is subjunctively contingent on the truth of p, that S believes q, yet his belief that q is not subjunctively dependent on the truth of q, in that it (or he) does not satisfy:

(3′) if q were false, S wouldn't believe that q.

For 3′ talks of what S would believe if q were false, and this may be a very different situation than the one that would hold if p were false, even though p entails q. That you were born in a certain city entails that you were born on earth.[2] Yet contemplating what (actually) would be the situation if you were not born in that city is very different from contemplating what situation would hold if you weren't born on earth. Just as those possibilities are very different, so what is believed in them may be very different.

[...]

Consider now the two statements:

p = I am awake and sitting on a chair in Jerusalem;
q = I am not floating in a tank on Alpha Centauri being stimulated by electrochemical means to believe that p.

The first one entails the second: p entails q. Also, I know that p entails q; and I know that p. If p were false, I would be standing or lying down in the same city, or perhaps sleeping there, or perhaps in a neighboring city or town. If q were false, I would be floating in a tank on Alpha Centauri. Clearly these are very different situations, leading to great differences in what I then would believe. If p were false, if I weren't awake and sitting on a chair in Jerusalem, I would not believe that p. Yet if q were false, if I was floating in a tank on Alpha Centauri, I would believe that q, that I was not in the tank, and indeed, in that case, I would still believe that p. According to our account of knowledge, I know that p yet I do not know that q, even though (I know) p entails q.

This failure of knowledge to be closed under known logical implication stems from the fact that condition 3 is not closed under known logical implication; condition 3 can hold of one statement believed while not of another known to be entailed by the first. It is clear that any account that includes as a necessary condition for knowledge the subjunctive condition 3, not-$p \rightarrow$ not-(S believes that p), will have the consequence that knowledge is not closed under known logical implication.

[...]

Knowledge is a real factual relation, subjunctively specifiable, whose structure admits our standing in this relation, tracking, to p without standing in it to some q which we know p to entail. Any relation embodying some variation of belief with the fact, with the truth (value), will exhibit this structural feature. The skeptic is right that we don't track some particular truths – the ones stating that his skeptical possibilities SK don't hold – but wrong that we don't stand in the real knowledge-relation of tracking to many other truths, including ones that entail these first mentioned truths we believe but don't know.

The literature on skepticism contains writers who endorse these skeptical arguments (or similar narrower ones), but confess their inability to maintain their skeptical beliefs at times when they are not focusing explicitly on the reasoning that led them to skeptical conclusions. The most notable example of this is Hume:

> I am ready to reject all belief and reasoning, and can look upon no opinion even as more probable or likely than another ... Most fortunately it happens that since reason is incapable of dispelling these clouds, nature herself suffices to that purpose, and cures me of this philosophical melancholy and delirium, either by relaxing this bent of mind, or by some avocation, and lively impression of my senses, which obliterate all these chimeras. I dine, I play a game of backgammon, I converse, and am merry with my friends; and when after three or four hours' amusement, I would return to these speculations, they appear so cold, and strained, and ridiculous, that I cannot find in my heart to enter into them any farther. (*A Treatise of Human Nature*, Book I, Part IV, section VII)

> The great subverter of Pyrrhonism or the excessive principles of skepticism is action, and employment, and the occupations of common life. These principles may flourish and triumph in the schools; where it is, indeed, difficult, if not impossible, to refute them. But as soon as they leave the shade, and by the presence of the real objects, which actuate our passions and sentiments, are put in opposition to the more powerful principles of our nature, they vanish like smoke, and leave the most determined skeptic in the same condition as other mortals ... And though a Pyrrhonian may throw himself or others into a momentary amazement and confusion by his profound reasonings; the first and most trivial event in life will put to flight all his doubts and scruples, and leave him the same, in every point of action and speculation, with the philosophers of every other sect, or with those who never concerned themselves in any philosophical researches. When he awakes from his dream, he will be the first to join in the laugh against himself, and to confess that all his objections are mere amusement. (*An Enquiry Concerning Human Understanding*, Section XII, Part II)

The theory of knowledge we have presented explains why skeptics of various sorts have had such difficulties in sticking to their far-reaching skeptical conclusions "outside the study", or even inside it when they are not thinking specifically about skeptical arguments and possibilities SK.

The skeptic's arguments do show (but show only) that we don't know the skeptic's possibilities SK do not hold; and he is right that we don't track the fact that SK does not hold. (If it were to hold, we would still think it didn't.) However, the skeptic's arguments don't show we do not know other facts (including facts that entail not-SK) for we do track these other facts (and knowledge is not closed under known logical entailment.) Since we do track these other facts – you, for example, the fact that you are reading a book; I, the fact that I am writing on a page – and the skeptic tracks such facts too, it is not surprising that when he focuses on them, on his relationship to such facts, the skeptic finds it hard to remember or maintain his view that he does not know those facts. Only by shifting his attention back to his relationship to the (different) fact that not-SK, which relationship is not tracking, can he revive his skeptical belief and make it salient. However, this skeptical triumph is evanescent, it vanishes when his attention turns to other facts. Only by fixating on the skeptical possibilities SK can he maintain his skeptical virtue; otherwise, unsurprisingly, he is forced to confess to sins of credulity.

Notes

1. From the perspective of explanation rather than proof, the extensive philosophical discussion, deriving from Charles S. Peirce, of whether the skeptic's doubts are real is beside the point. The problem of explaining how knowledge is possible would remain the same, even if no one ever claimed to doubt that there was knowledge.
2. Here again I assume a limited readership, and ignore possibilities such as those described in James Blish, *Cities in Flight*.

Further Readings for Part III

Like metaphysics, epistemology is a vast area of philosophy. Here I mention just some of the many possible further readings for Part III's epistemological topics. Intellectual stimulation aplenty awaits you in these extra readings.

Can We Understand What It Is To Know?

Conee, E., and Feldman, R. (2004) *Evidentialism: Essays in Epistemology*. Oxford: Clarendon Press.

Craig, E. (1990) *Knowledge and the State of Nature: An Essay in Conceptual Synthesis*. Oxford: Clarendon Press.

Goldman, A.I. (1986) *Epistemology and Cognition*. Cambridge, MA: Harvard University Press.

Goldman, A.I. (1999) *Knowledge in a Social World*. Oxford: Clarendon Press.

Greco, J. (2010) *Achieving Knowledge: A Virtue-Theoretic Account of Epistemic Normativity*. Cambridge: Cambridge University Press.

Hetherington, S. (2011) The Gettier problem. In S. Bernecker and D. Pritchard (eds.), *The Routledge Companion to Epistemology*. New York: Routledge, pp. 119–130.

Kvanvig, J.L. (2003) *The Value of Knowledge and the Pursuit of Understanding*. Cambridge: Cambridge University Press.

Pappas, G.S., and Swain, M. (eds.) (1978) *Essays on Knowledge and Justification*. Ithaca, NY: Cornell University Press.

Roberts, R.C., and Wood, W.J. (2007) *Intellectual Virtues: An Essay in Regulative Epistemology*. Oxford: Clarendon Press.

Shope, R.K. (1983) *The Analysis of Knowing: A Decade of Research*. Princeton: Princeton University Press.

Sosa, E. (2011) *Knowing Full Well*. Princeton: Princeton University Press.

Williamson, T. (2000) *Knowledge and Its Limits*. Oxford: Clarendon Press, ch. 1.

Can We Ever Know Just through Observation?

Armstrong, D.M. (1961) *Perception and the Physical World*. New York: The Humanities Press.

Ayer, A.J. (1956) *The Problem of Knowledge*. London: Macmillan, ch. 2, sects. ix and x, and ch. 3.

Buckle, S. (2001) *Hume's Enlightenment Tract: The Unity and Purpose of* An Enquiry Concerning Human Understanding. Oxford: Clarendon Press, pt. 2, sect. II.

Dancy, J. (ed.) (1988) *Perceptual Knowledge.* Oxford: Oxford University Press.

DeRose, K., and Warfield, T.A. (eds.) (1999) *Skepticism: A Contemporary Reader.* New York: Oxford University Press.

Jackson, F. (1977) *Perception: A Representative Theory.* Cambridge: Cambridge University Press.

McDowell, J. (2011) *Perception as a Capacity for Knowledge.* Milwaukee: Marquette University Press.

Moore, G.E. (1959) Proof of an external world. In G.E. Moore, *Philosophical Papers.* London: George Allen & Unwin, pp. 127–150.

Nozick, R. (1980) Fiction. *Ploughshares* 6, 74–78.

Sosa, E. (2007) *A Virtue Epistemology: Apt Belief and Reflective Knowledge*, vol. 1. Oxford: Clarendon Press, ch. 1.

Stroud, B. (1984) *The Significance of Philosophical Scepticism.* Oxford: Clarendon Press, ch. 1.

Swartz, R.J. (ed.) (1965) *Perceiving, Sensing, and Knowing: A Book of Readings from Twentieth-Century Sources in the Philosophy of Perception.* Garden City, NY: Anchor Books.

Williams, B. (1978) *Descartes: The Project of Pure Inquiry.* Harmondsworth: Penguin, appendix 3.

Can We Ever Know Innately?

Jolley, N. (1984) *Leibniz and Locke: A Study of the* New Essays on Human Understanding. Oxford: Clarendon Press.

Leibniz, G.W. (1981 [1765]) *New Essays on Human Understanding*, ed. and trans. P. Remnant and J. Bennett. Cambridge: Cambridge University Press, Book I.

Mares, E. (2011) *A Priori.* Durham: Acumen, ch. 4.

Sayre, K.M. (2005 [1983]) *Plato's Late Ontology: A Riddle Resolved*, 2nd edn. Las Vegas: Parmenides Publishing, pp. 188–193.

Stich, S.P. (ed.) (1975) *Innate Ideas.* Berkeley, CA: University of California Press.

Tipton, I.C. (ed.) (1977) *Locke on Human Understanding: Selected Essays.* Oxford: Oxford University Press, chs. 1 and 2.

Can We Ever Know Just through Reflection?

Almeder, R. (1980) *The Philosophy of Charles S. Peirce: A Critical Introduction.* Oxford: Basil Blackwell, ch. 1.

BonJour, L. (1998) *In Defense of Pure Reason: A Rationalist Account of* A Priori Justification. Cambridge: Cambridge University Press.

Forster, M.N. (2008) *Kant and Skepticism.* Princeton: Princeton University Press.

Hookway, C. (2012) American pragmatism: Fallibilism and cognitive progress. In S. Hetherington (ed.), *Epistemology: The Key Thinkers.* London: Continuum, pp. 153–171.

Kitcher, P. (1983) *The Nature of Mathematical Knowledge.* New York: Oxford University Press.

Kitcher, P. (1998) Mill, mathematics, and the naturalist tradition. In J. Skorupski (ed.), *The Cambridge Companion to Mill.* Cambridge: Cambridge University Press, pp. 57–111.

Kornblith, H. (2002) *Knowledge and Its Place in Nature.* Oxford: Clarendon Press, ch. 4.

Mares, E. (2011) *A Priori.* Durham: Acumen.

Moser, P.K. (ed.) (1987) *A Priori Knowledge.* Oxford: Oxford University Press.

Ryan, A. (1987) *The Philosophy of John Stuart Mill*, 2nd edn. Basingstoke: Macmillan, ch. 5.

Savile, A. (2005) *Kant's* Critique of Pure Reason: *An Orientation to the Central Theme.* Malden, MA: Blackwell.

Skorupski, J. (1989) *John Stuart Mill*. London: Routledge, ch. 5.
Soames, S. (2003) *Philosophical Analysis in the Twentieth Century*, vol. 2: *The Age of Meaning*. Princeton: Princeton University Press, ch. 15.
Williams, B. (1978) *Descartes: The Project of Pure Inquiry*. Harmondsworth: Penguin, ch. 2.

Can We Know in Other Fundamental Ways?

Ayer, A.J. (1956) *The Problem of Knowledge*. London: Macmillan, ch. 4.
Bernecker, S. (2010) *Memory: A Philosophical Study*. Oxford: Oxford University Press.
Coady, C.A.J. (1992) *Testimony: A Philosophical Study*. Oxford: Clarendon Press.
Fantl, J., and McGrath, M. (2009) *Knowledge in an Uncertain World*. Oxford: Oxford University Press.
Ford, A., Hornsby, J., and Stoutland, F. (eds.) (2011) *Essays on Anscombe's* Intention. Cambridge, MA: Harvard University Press.
Hetherington, S. (2011) *How To Know: A Practicalist Conception of Knowledge*. Malden, MA: Wiley-Blackwell.
Lackey, J. (2008) *Learning From Words: Testimony as a Source of Knowledge*. Oxford: Oxford University Press.
Ryle, G. (1949) *The Concept of Mind*. London: Hutchinson, ch. 2.

Can We Fundamentally Fail Ever To Know?

Ayer, A.J. (1956) *The Problem of Knowledge*. London: Macmillan, ch. 2, sects. ix and x.
Fogelin, R.J. (1994) *Pyrrhonian Reflections on Knowledge and Justification*. New York: Oxford University Press.
Frances, B. (2005) *Scepticism Comes Alive*. Oxford: Clarendon Press.
Nozick, R. (1980) Fiction. *Ploughshares* 6, 74–78.
Perin, C. (2010) *The Demands of Reason: An Essay on Pyrrhonian Scepticism*. Oxford: Oxford University Press.
Stroud, B. (1984) *The Significance of Philosophical Scepticism*. Oxford: Clarendon Press, ch. 7.
Stroud, B. (2000) *Understanding Human Knowledge: Philosophical Essays*. Oxford: Oxford University Press.
Swinburne, R. (ed.) (1974) *The Justification of Induction*. London: Oxford University Press.
Unger, P. (1975) *Ignorance: A Case for Scepticism*. Oxford: Clarendon Press.

Can Skeptical Arguments Be Escaped?

Cooke, E.F. (2006) *Peirce's Pragmatic Theory of Inquiry: Fallibilism and Indeterminacy*. London: Continuum.
DeRose, K., and Warfield, T.A. (eds.) (1999) *Skepticism: A Contemporary Reader*. New York: Oxford University Press.
Hetherington, S. (2001) *Good Knowledge, Bad Knowledge: On Two Dogmas of Epistemology*. Oxford: Clarendon Press, chs. 1 and 2.
Huemer, M. (2001) *Skepticism and the Veil of Perception*. Lanham, MD: Rowman & Littlefield.
Lemos, N. (2004) *Common Sense: A Contemporary Defense*. Cambridge: Cambridge University Press.
Luper-Foy, S. (ed.) (1987) *The Possibility of Knowledge: Nozick and His Critics*. Totowa, NJ: Rowman & Littlefield.

Miller, D. (1994) *Critical Rationalism: A Restatement and Defence*. Chicago: Open Court.

Strawson, P.F. (1985) *Skepticism and Naturalism: Some Varieties*. New York: Columbia University Press, ch. 1.

Williams, B. (1978) *Descartes: The Project of Pure Inquiry*. Harmondsworth: Penguin, ch. 3.

Williams, M. (1991) *Unnatural Doubts: Epistemological Realism and the Basis of Scepticism*. Oxford: Blackwell.

Wolterstorff, N. (2001) *Thomas Reid and the Story of Epistemology*. Cambridge: Cambridge University Press, chs. 8 and 9.

More Generally …

These collections span a large number of epistemological topics.

Bernecker, S., and Pritchard, D. (eds.) (2011) *The Routledge Companion to Epistemology*. New York: Routledge.

Dancy, J., Sosa, E., and Steup, M. (eds.) (2010) *A Companion to Epistemology*, 2nd edn. Malden, MA: Wiley-Blackwell.

Greco, J. (ed.) (2008) *The Oxford Handbook of Skepticism*. New York: Oxford University Press.

Moser, P.K. (ed.) (2002) *The Oxford Handbook of Epistemology*. New York: Oxford University Press.